About This Book

Why is this topic important?

Blended learning environments combine traditional face-to-face instruction with computer-mediated or online instruction. The term *blended learning* has become a corporate buzzword during the past few years (Lamb, 2001). Recently, the American Society for Training and Development identified blended learning as one of the top ten trends to emerge in the knowledge delivery industry in 2003 (cited by Rooney, 2003). As noted by Barbian (2002), Marc Rosenberg, author of *E-Learning: Strategies for Delivering Knowledge in the Digital Age* (2001), has argued that "the question is not if we should blend . . . rather the question is what are the ingredients." Based on our travels the past few years to Asia, Europe, the Middle East, and Australia, this perspective seems to be universal. In fact, surveys published in the United Kingdom in *Training News* (2003, 2004) not only indicate that most companies in the United Kingdom and North America already find blended learning effective; they predict significant increases in the use of blended learning for delivering training as well as associated changes of blended learning evaluation. The reasons for this sudden increase in blended learning include improvements in the rate of learning, as well as the efficiency of training, maximizing corporate investments in reusable training materials, and, of course, attempts to save on training time.

In higher education, the term *blended learning* is being used with increasing frequency in academic conferences and publications. Issues related to the design and implementation of blended learning environments are surfacing as technological advances continue to blur the lines between distributed learning and traditional campus-based learning. Many universities are beginning to recognize the advantages of blending online and residential instruction. In 2002 the *Chronicle of Higher Education* quoted the president of Pennsylvania State University as saying that the convergence between online and residential instruction was "the single-greatest unrecognized trend in higher education today" (Young, 2002, p. A33). Along the same lines, the editor of the *Journal of Asynchronous Learning Networks* has predicted a dramatic increase in the number of hybrid (blended) courses to include as many as 80 to 90 percent of the range of courses (Young, 2002).

What can you achieve with this book?

This book documents global perspectives related to blended learning, including models at the institutional level for designing blended learning environments. Such documentation will help to raise awareness of the issues associated with adopting a blended approach from an institutional perspective. The chapter authors hail from countries around the planet, in particular, countries that have become dependent on online learning environments such as Australia, Korea, Malaysia, the United Kingdom, Canada, and South Africa, thereby adding to the global perspective of this book. At the same time, this book presents cases related to local implementations of blended learning environments. These case studies provide a unique perspective on the strengths and weaknesses inherent in the implementation of certain approaches to blending. Both the contributions to the global perspectives and the local designs raise research issues that will prompt future studies related to the design and use of blended learning environments.

How is this book organized?

This book begins with forewords from Jay Cross and Michael Moore, two respected leaders in the corporate and academic worlds. The body of the book is then organized into eight parts that share a wide variety of cases and perspectives on blended learning.

Part One: Introduction to Blended Learning. The four chapters in this part introduce the concept of blended learning.

Part Two: Corporate Blended Learning Models and Perspectives. The six chapters in this part describe institutional models of blended learning that large global corporations use.

Part Three: Higher Education Blended Learning Models and Perspectives. The five chapters in this part describe models of blended learning for higher educational institutions.

Part Four: For-Profit and Online University Perspectives. The three chapters in this part share the perspectives on blended learning from three high-profile for-profit universities.

Part Five: Cases of Blended Learning in Higher Education from Around the World. The eleven chapters in this part share cases of blended learning in higher education contexts from countries around the world.

Part Six: Multinational Blended Learning Perspectives. The three chapters in this part provide insights into blended learning from individuals with a multinational perspective.

Part Seven: Workplace, On-Demand, and Authentic Learning. The four chapters in this part highlight cases of blended learning that focus on workplace and authentic learning environments.

Part Eight: Future Trends in Blended Learning. The three chapters in this part provide a glimpse into mixed-reality learning environments and the future directions of blended learning systems.

References

Barbian, J. (2002, Summer). Blended works: Here's proof! *Online Learning Magazine, 6*(6) 26–30.

Lamb, J. (2001, June 4). "Blended learning" is the new buzz phrase. *FT.com.*

Rooney, J. E. (2003). Blending learning opportunities to enhance educational programming and meetings. *Association Management, 55*(5), 26–32.

Rosenberg, M. J. (2001). *E-learning: Strategies for delivering knowledge in the digital age.* New York: McGraw-Hill.

Training News. (2003). *New survey provides insight into blended learning in the UK.* Retrieved March 1, 2005, from http://www.trainingreference.co.uk/news/bl031111.htm.

Training News. (2004). *Survey predicts transatlantic increase in blended learning.* Retrieved March 1, 2005, from http://www.trainingreference.co.uk/news/bl041118.htm.

Young, J. R. (2002, March 22). "Hybrid" teaching seeks to end the divide between traditional and online instruction. *Chronicle of Higher Education,* p. A33.

About Pfeiffer

Pfeiffer serves the professional development and hands-on resource needs of training and human resource practitioners and gives them products to do their jobs better. We deliver proven ideas and solutions from experts in HR development and HR management, and we offer effective and customizable tools to improve workplace performance. From novice to seasoned professional, Pfeiffer is the source you can trust to make yourself and your organization more successful.

Essential Knowledge Pfeiffer produces insightful, practical, and comprehensive materials on topics that matter the most to training and HR professionals. Our Essential Knowledge resources translate the expertise of seasoned professionals into practical, how-to guidance on critical workplace issues and problems. These resources are supported by case studies, worksheets, and job aids and are frequently supplemented with CD-ROMs, websites, and other means of making the content easier to read, understand, and use.

Essential Tools Pfeiffer's Essential Tools resources save time and expense by offering proven, ready-to-use materials—including exercises, activities, games, instruments, and assessments—for use during a training or team-learning event. These resources are frequently offered in looseleaf or CD-ROM format to facilitate copying and customization of the material.

Pfeiffer also recognizes the remarkable power of new technologies in expanding the reach and effectiveness of training. While e-hype has often created whizbang solutions in search of a problem, we are dedicated to bringing convenience and enhancements to proven training solutions. All our e-tools comply with rigorous functionality standards. The most appropriate technology wrapped around essential content yields the perfect solution for today's on-the-go trainers and human resource professionals.

www.pfeiffer.com

Essential resources for training and HR professionals

THE HANDBOOK OF BLENDED LEARNING

THE HANDBOOK OF BLENDED LEARNING

Global Perspectives, Local Designs

Curtis J. Bonk, Charles R. Graham

Forewords by Jay Cross, Michael G. Moore

Pfeiffer
A Wiley Imprint
www.pfeiffer.com

Library of Congress Cataloging-in-Publication Data

Handbook of blended learning : global perspectives, local designs / editors, Curtis J. Bonk and Charles R. Graham.
    p. cm.
  ISBN-13: 978-0-7879-7758-0 (alk. paper)
  ISBN-10: 0-7879-7758-6 (alk. paper)
  1. Education, Higher--Computer-assisted instruction. 2. Education, Higher--Effect of technological innovations on. 3. Internet in higher education. 4. Blended learning. I. Bonk, Curtis Jay. II. Graham, Charles Ray, 1942-
    LB2395.7.H22 2006
    378.1'734--dc22   2005014650

Acquiring Editor: Lisa Shannon
Director of Development: Kathleen Dolan Davies
Editor: Bev Miller
Production Editor: Susan Geraghty
Manufacturing Supervisor: Becky Carreño
Editorial Assistant: Jesse Wiley

Printed in the United States of America
FIRST EDITION
HB Printing   10 9 8 7 6 5 4 3 2

CONTENTS

Contents

PART SIX: MULTINATIONAL BLENDED LEARNING PERSPECTIVES 417

FOREWORDS

One unique feature of this handbook is that it contains two forewords. The foreword by Jay Cross, a thought leader in learning technology, performance improvement, and organizational culture, who coined the terms *e-learning* and *work flow learning*, reflects the corporate training aspects of this handbook. The second foreword, by Michael G. Moore, a pioneer in distance education and founder and editor of the *American Journal of Distance Education* among other accomplishments, is written from a higher education perspective.

Foreword

Jay Cross

When Curt Bonk asked me to contribute a chapter to this book, I flat out refused. As you might guess from the quantity of top-notch authors who appear here, Curt is persistent. He asked me again, and again I turned him down, this time with an explanation.

I told him I considered *blended learning* a useless concept. To my way of thinking, *blending* is new only to people who were foolish enough to think that delegating the entire training role to the computer was going to work. I could not imagine *unblended* learning. My first-grade teacher used a blend of storytelling, song, recitation, reading aloud, flash cards, puppetry, and corporal punishment.

Is it not nutty for a learning strategist to ask, "Why blend?" The more appropriate question is, "Why not blend?" Imagine an episode of *This Old House* asking, "Why should we use power tools? Hand tools can get the job done." For both carpenters and learning professionals, the default behavior is using the right tools for the job.

My perspective is corporate, not academic. My bottom line is organizational performance, not individual enlightenment. Not that I am dismissive of research. In nearly thirty years in what we used to call the training business, I have read my share of Dewey, Kolb, Bransford, Gagné, Schank, and John Seely Brown, but as a businessman, I also pay allegiance to Peter Drucker, Stan Davis, and the *Harvard Business Review*. And I hobnob with least a dozen of the authors whose work you are about to read.

Here are a few issues for you to consider as you ponder this fine collection of observations and advice from learning pioneers around the globe.

What's a Blend?

First of all, these are not useful blends:

40 percent online, 60 percent classroom

80 percent online, 20 percent face-to-face

80 percent workshop, 20 percent online reinforcement

After reading a few chapters of this book, you will see these for what they are: over-simplifications.

Four or five years ago, it was commonplace to hear, "We've tried e-learning. People didn't like it. It didn't work very well." This is akin to saying, "I once read a book. It was difficult to understand. I'm not going to do that again." The book in your hands describes rich variations and applications of e-learning. After reading it, you'll find that you can no more generalize about e-learning than you can generalize about books. Consider this description of a blend from Macromedia's Ellen Wagner (see Chapter Four, this volume):

Evolving blended learning models provide the essential methodological scaffolding needed to effectively combine face-to-face instruction, online instruction, and arrays of content objects and assets of all form factors. For example, in such a blended learning scenario, a student may find him or herself participating in a face-to-face class discussion; he or she may then log in and complete an online mastery exercise or two, then copy some practice exercises to a PDA to take advantage of what David Metcalf calls "stolen moments for learning"—those times between classes or meetings, while on the train, or waiting for an appointment. Think about sending a text message with results of your practice sessions to someone in your virtual study group using your mobile phone—and getting a voice mail with feedback on your results when you arrive at the end of your flight.

People do not know what they like; they like what they know. For example, many assume that face-to-face instruction is the one best way to teach and that on-line learning is inherently inferior. They seek ways for online initiatives to support the high-grade face-to-face experience. Capella University turns this view on its head, asking what face-to-face support is required to supplement online learning. Having found online learning universally effective, Capella uses face-to-face only to further social goals such as building a support network or creating informal affinity groups. From its perspective, a blend may contain no face-to-face element at all.

Blended learning can take place while waiting in line at the grocery store or taking the bus home. Its ingredients may be courses, content chunks, instant messaging pings, blog feedback, or many other things. Interaction is the glue that holds all these pieces together. Interaction comes in many forms, not just learner and instructor, but also learner-to-content, learner-to-learner, and learner-to-infra-structure. Interaction can create an experience so compelling that it makes workers hungry to learn and drives otherwise sane people to pay four dollars for a cup of coffee at Starbucks.

What Goes into the Blend?

Great recipes are the product of generations of experimentation, tasting, and refinement. E-learning is at the same embryonic stage as American cuisine when home chefs rarely started a sauce without a can of condensed mushroom soup, and garlic was reserved for scaring away vampires.

First-generation e-learning initiated, delivered, and completed online; its consumers lost their appetites. Today's tastier recipes include organizational skills assessments, books, content objects, workshops, clinics, seminars, simulations, collaboration, technical references, learning games, and links to communities of practice.

At the University of Phoenix, I developed a classroom-based business curriculum in 1976. A dozen years later, an online program debuted. More recently, the university introduced blended programs that combine some classroom and some online. Add more classroom, and the result is the "local model" blend; add more online and the result is the "distance model." Some blends are like "vibration cooking": a pinch of this, a handful of that, and however much wine is left in the bottle. *C'est bricolage.*

IBM's four-tier model shows how the ingredients of the blend must be matched to the nature of the outcomes sought. Web pages work fine for performance support. Simulations are good for developing understanding. Groups learn from community interaction and live virtual programs. Higher-order skills require coaching, role play, and perhaps face-to-face sessions. Each dish requires its own recipe.

Blends are more than a learning stew, for as the authors here amply demonstrate, blends fall along many dimensions (Figure F.1).

A Blend of Blends

The ideal blend is a blend of blends. Take the last dimension in Figure F.1: formal to informal learning. Studies find that most corporate learning is informal. It's unscheduled. It's learning on the job. It's trial-and-error. It's asking someone who knows.

FIGURE F.1.   DIMENSIONS OF THE BLENDED LEARNING STEW.

Fleeting know-how	|--+--+--+-+--|	Lasting knowledge
Individual	|--+--+--+-+--|	Community
Generic	|--+--+--+-+--|	Proprietary
Training	|--+--+--+-+--|	Knowledge sharing
Text	|--+--+--+-+--|	Visual
Self-directed	|--+--+--+-+--|	Guided navigation
Content focus	|--+--+--+-+--|	Experience focus
Exploring	|--+--+--+-+--|	Participating
Push	|--+--+--+-+--|	Pull
Personalized	|--+--+--+-+--|	One-size-fits-all
Skills	|--+--+--+-+--|	Values
Information	|--+--+--+-+--|	Transformation
Formal	|--+--+--+-+--|	Informal

If informal learning is so important, dare we leave it to chance? If we seek an optimal result, we cannot. Instead of a single blend that calls for x percent of this and y percent of that, I propose we take the blends of many of the authors here into account. We must replace one-dimensional thinking with simultaneous consideration of dozens of pie charts.

The many cooks of *The Handbook of Blended Learning* do not spoil the broth. On the contrary, their diversity of opinion and method enriches the book. Editors Curt Bonk and Charles Graham are to be congratulated for preserving the unique flavor contributed by each author.

Mike Wenger and Chuck Ferguson of Sun Microsystems make a strong argument for thinking in terms of a learning ecology instead of a blend of classroom and e-learning. "Classroom" deprives the concept of the rich, multifaceted experiences that take place there (see Chapter Six, this volume). Similarly, "e-learning" covers over the multiple possibilities born of the marriage of the learner and the Internet. There's simply a lot more to it than that.

School's Out

Corporations seek self-reliant workers they can trust to do the right thing without supervision. Every manager wants self-starters on her team. Yet when it comes to learning, many workers wait for others to tell them what to do. Why don't they take matters into their own hands? I think it's a vestige of schooling.

Several hundred years ago, compulsory schools were set up as a separate reality. Students were seedlings, while schools were the greenhouses to protect them from outside elements. The mission of schools was transmitting values and teaching a body of knowledge. The noise of the real world might taint the righteousness and clarity of the lessons.

Many of us equate learning with schooling. That is why we think of learning as something a person does in isolation and that its ideal delivery takes place in the classroom or the library, cloistered from the outside. Group work is by and large discouraged (it's called "cheating"). Authorities choose the curriculum. Self-direction is viewed as rebellion.

People credit me with coining the term *e-learning*. I would never use the word in the executive suite. Why? Because senior managers too equate learning and schooling; they remember school as an inefficient way to learn. They are not willing to pay for it.

What Is Wrong with This Picture?

How many times have you seen a diagram of the learner-centric model that's supposed to crowd out the instructor-centric model? It usually shows various learning modalities (for example, content, the Web, discussion groups, videoconferencing, live help) arrayed around the worker.

The image is misleading. It implies that the learner is of paramount importance. In the corporation, the work of the group comes before the work of any individual. The learner-centric model retains vestiges of the classroom and its one-to-many oversimplification of how things really work.

There's an even larger problem: work is not part of the picture at all. Imagine a situation where a worker must respond in real time. Say there's an important customer asking about an order or something has gone haywire in the automated warehouse. Learning must be filtered through what is happening in the work environment. Otherwise the worker may accept the customer's order even though there's nothing in the warehouse to ship.

Blending Work Flow Learning

In the knowledge era, learning *is* the work. Harvey Singh's prescient chapter proposes the most important blend of all: the marriage of learning and work (see Chapter Thirty-Four, this volume). He describes self-perpetuating systems of continuous improvement. Smart software applies its awareness of conditions and context to take a hand in concocting the ever-changing blend. Cycle times shrink to the point that all business becomes a real-time activity.

The components of Harvey's work flow learning blend are:

- Portals and Web parts
- Internet and mobility
- Granular knowledge nuggets
- Collaboration
- Work flow automation and knowledge linking
- Human and automated virtual mentoring
- Presence awareness
- Simulations
- Business process and performance monitoring
- Continuous knowledge capture and feedback
- Real-time notification, aggregation, and decision support
- Integrated learning and enterprise applications
- Interoperable, reusable content framework

The End of Blend

So, given the breadth of choices, is it worthwhile to read a book about blended learning? Yes. As Elliott Masie says, "The magic is in the mix."

Blended is a transitory term. In time it will join *programmed instruction* and *transactional analysis* in the dustbin of has-beens. In the meantime, *blended* is a stepping-stone on the way to the future. It reminds us to look at learning challenges from many directions. It makes computer-only training look ridiculous. It drives us to pick the right tools to get the job done.

Enjoy the book. Don't just read it. Make it a *blended* learning experience. Discuss its cases with colleagues. Incorporate it into your plans. Reflect on how to apply its wisdom. Blending will help you learn.

Foreword

Michael G. Moore

Writing in 1886, William Rainey Harper (1886), the first president of the University of Chicago, declared: "The correspondence system would not, if it could, supplant oral instruction, or be regarded as its substitute. There is a field for each which the other cannot fill. Let each do its proper work." Always effusive in his enthusiasm for using printed text as a teaching medium, Harper went on to assert that "the student who has prepared a certain number of lessons in the correspondence school knows more of the subject treated in those lessons, and knows it better, than the student who has covered the same ground in the classroom" (Harper, 1971, p. 12).

The truth of this second of Harper's insights, that the quality of learning in a well-designed distance education program is often superior to that of the classroom, is now becoming more widely appreciated by a growing proportion of the population. What of the other assertion? Could correspondence, in its modern, online version, "supplant oral instruction"? Harper would not dare say so, but given the numerous research studies that show the effectiveness of distance learning, in an age when we have become accustomed to book our travel, mortgage our homes, and obtain our medicines online, it does not seem so unreasonable to consider the proposition that some educational programs, or at least components of such programs, might be accessed that way and be removed from the classroom in the interest of both the quality of learning as well as cost-effectiveness of teaching.

At last, it seems that the assumed superiority of classroom teaching, above all alternatives, a dogma that has been so pervasive for so long throughout academia, is beginning to give way to a more nuanced understanding of the suitability of non-classroom environments for formal study and the desirability of adding new forms of communications to enhance, and yes, sometimes to supplant, the professorial lecture. The emerging view is of a mutually respectful relationship between teaching at a distance and teaching in the classroom, and the idea that "each can do its proper work" is now encapsulated in the concept of blended learning. Like distance education itself, under whatever name one prefers to call it, blended learning is a long-neglected idea whose time has arrived. Importantly, growing numbers of educators and influential policymakers are discovering not only the advantages but also the lack of threat in combining the advantages of teaching and learning in the two different environments: classroom and home or workplace.

It is by no means a new idea, however. You may be intrigued, as I was, to discover that blending classroom and mediated delivery of instruction at the high school level can be traced as far back as the 1920s, when it was known as "supervised correspondence study." Started by an innovative school principal in Benton Harbour, Michigan, it was promoted by educators at the University of Nebraska to the extent that by 1930, it was a method used in more than a hundred public high schools across the nation and in 1932 was the subject of a national conference held in Cleveland Ohio.

In more recent history, as noted by authors in this handbook, blended learning was introduced in 1969 as a basic component of the teaching system of the world's principal distance teaching institution, the United Kingdom's Open University. When I was a tutor at the OU, I had the dual responsibility of providing instruction by correspondence to a cadre of distance learners based on their study of prescribed texts and video programs. At the same time, I had the responsibility of traveling to study centers and summer schools to meet these students in classrooms, to advise, discuss, and in other ways supplement the teaching materials designed by colleagues at the Open University's central campus.

There is often misunderstanding among academics who have not had this kind of experience, voiced in their expression of concern that it might be demeaning or diminishing of one's expertise to be a mere "facilitator" of learning content that has been chosen and organized by another person—or in the case of the Open University, by a team of other persons. In reality, in my experience and that of most others with whom I have discussed this, there is an enormous sense of freedom provided by the relief of not having to "cover" basic information or design the course structure, but instead being able to concentrate on interaction with individual students and engage in a creative interpretation with each individual or group, of the issues and subtleties lying within and beyond the previously determined content and instructional design. Essentially, blending the expertise of content and instructional design specialists with the facilitator's skill at inducing knowledge creation is simply an application of the sensible principle of division of labor that is common to all professions. Perhaps more important, for the purposes of this book, it is one of the explanations why teaching and learning is so good in high-quality distance education institutions like the Open University and its analogues around the world.

At this point, I would like to insert a plea that readers, being interested in blended learning, should be sure to consolidate their understanding of its manifestation in the distance education context. Certainly one can, and should, study the concept from the point of view of the classroom teacher and the pedagogical theories underlying classroom practice. However, blending face-to-face teaching with those forms of teaching in which the principal delivery technology is *not* the classroom, but is a mechanical or electronic technology, that is, distance education, is so important that blended learning will not be fully understood if one's perspective is only that of the classroom teacher and does not include knowledge of research and practice in the distance education field. From my perspective, we have to rise above the limitations of American experience since in the United States, distance education has rarely included face-to-face tutorials. That is not universally the case however, as a single reading about study centers in, for example, the Indira Ghandi National Open University, would soon prove.

When I reflect on my own Open University tutoring experience and try to explain such views of distance education to American students or when I am a consultant and try to explain to a client the advantages of letting go of certain teaching responsibilities and outsourcing them to external specialists, the following is one of the ways I explain it. Begin by recognizing that each form of every communication medium and technology has distinctive qualities and also that students respond to these in different ways. It follows that a composite of two or more applications of these media or technologies is therefore likely to disseminate a message better than is possible by any one alone. In addition, it is important to provide more than one opportunity of satisfying each student's style of learning. (A medium is the form in which a message is communicated, for example, a still image; the technology is the vehicle that transports the medium, as, for example, a television, computer screen, or photo album.) Furthermore, recognize that technologies vary in cost of installation and maintenance, and media vary in cost of production and dissemination. It follows that responsible educational administrators and program designers have to face the difficult decision about which are the most cost-effective combinations of these media and technologies for their particular teaching purposes, and the decision taken in one case cannot be assumed to apply with equal validity in others.

In this argument, together with the technologies that deliver teaching materials by recorded and interactive audio, video, and text media, the teacher in a face-to-face classroom can be regarded as a communications technology, albeit an expensive one. The administrator's and designer's challenge is to know when to use this costly classroom technology and when to substitute an equally effective and less costly alternative. In higher education, this is a challenge that has more often than not been avoided, with administrators and faculty frequently failing to select media and technology for good pedagogical reasons. In turn, correspondence, broadcasting, teleconferencing, and the Internet all have been employed for reasons other than because they had proven to be the most suitable form of communication for particular content, teaching process, or student characteristics. And so has the teacher-in-the-classroom.

The classroom is an ideal technology for achieving some learning outcomes, but for others it can be disastrously unsuitable. With the potential offered by alternative technologies to provide control of pace, redundancy in practice, multiple testing, access to alternative media, and a vast virtual library, I venture to suggest that there are many ways to provide a superior environment for all learning objectives that do not require spontaneous, person-to-person interaction. However, even readers who consider that view to be overly enthusiastic will concede that getting the right mixture of media and technologies that includes the right use of the classroom teacher in a well-designed integrated multimedia program is the most promising approach to obtaining both a high-quality learning experience, and, at the same time, the best return for dollars invested in the educational enterprise.

This *Handbook of Blended Learning* is strong evidence of the growing acceptance of this simple concept and strategy that advocates mixing the technologies of distance education and the classroom. It is also a unique source of information, stimulation, and encouragement for those who have not yet fully understood or accepted the importance of this concept.

It is not for me to introduce the authors and their themes. This has been ably done by the editors. However, I will venture to make just two short, general comments. First, with regard to the themes represented by the chapters in this book, I suggest that whereas the approach taken by many authors is to describe the effects and potential benefits of blending newer forms of computer-based technology with classroom teaching, beyond these immediate and local benefits are major policy issues—indeed, political issues—of great significance, whether considered at the institutional, national, or indeed global level.

In this brief foreword, I am not able to expand on, among other vital elements, the component movement toward creation and application of learning objects, but I want to at least underscore its importance. If one accepts the rationale for these developments and the underlying movement toward blended learning, one is, in fact, aligning with what I believe is an inexorable trend toward fundamental change not only in ancient concepts about teaching, learning, and the place of the academy in society, but in how society allocates the resources it invests in education—particularly, the relative apportionment of resources between people and hardware. Far more than the mere application of new hardware in the classroom, the ideas and practices represented by authors in this book lead, at the minimum, to questions about what roles of teachers are worth paying for in the information age, what should be their relationship to students in an increasingly consumerist culture, what their rights and responsibility for ownership of content are, and what training, monitoring, and control will become the norm when teaching takes place in a blended system as compared with the privacy and monopoly of control that characterized the classroom of the past.

Beyond such changes in thinking about teaching, what is represented by this handbook is the expansion of a slowly growing political movement that anticipates strategic changes in how national and institutional resources are allocated for the educational enterprise and how they are managed. Questions are raised about public and private ownership of educational institutions and the changing responsibility and power of local administrators and managers in emerging large-scale systems. One of the core issues can be summarized as follows: given that certain teaching functions can be equally effective when provided through technologies outside the classroom, as the pressure for more cost-effective undergraduate education and also for adult lifelong learning continues to have an impact on the demand for the services of colleges and universities to be delivered in blended forms, institutional survival will depend on moving financial resources from a large labor pool of full-time faculty resident on campus to a greater proportion of the teaching load carried by communications technologies supported by part-time instructors.

In a competitive market, dominance will be achieved by those institutions that offer superior-quality products and services, and this requires higher dollar investment in a wide range of mediated programs as well as superior student support services. Within emerging, blended delivery systems, both campus-based (and extramural) faculty will find employment and satisfaction, not as the Jacks-and-Jills-of-all-trades, but in a variety of new specializations. Both the financial and technical resources as well as these changing human resources must be orchestrated by managers responding to pressures and opportunities that are quite different from those of the undergraduate residential subject-oriented university of the past. Increasingly specialization will characterize higher education institutions also, as each finds its comparative advantage, that is, what it can do better than others, and then offers its more narrowly chosen curriculum to a global constituency in an effort to recapture high investment costs.

I am tempted to refer for illustration to institutions and interinstitutional arrangements represented in this book, as well as to suprainstitutional arrangements (which I believe is the strategy that will press particularly hard on established institutions). However, resisting that temptation, I ask only that readers reflect on my suggestion that the contents of these chapters reflect a gathering movement with enormous policy implications as they go forward.

Finally, it has given me great personal satisfaction to discover so many old friends and distinguished colleagues among the chapter authors of this handbook, including Ellen Wagner, Alan Chute, Insung Jung, Randy Garrison, and Bob Wisher, to mention those who (as well as editor Curt Bonk) contributed to my own *Handbook of Distance Education* (Moore & Anderson, 2003). Perhaps even more pleasing when I first read the *Handbook of Blended Learning* was being introduced to a rich constellation of emerging leaders, new voices who are coming to address some of the same issues that have occupied distance educators, but from a fresh and powerful new perspective. That the editors have obtained contributions from such authors in so many different countries is especially impressive.

It may be argued that the United States retains its leading place in inventing and developing many of the computer-based communications technologies that underpin most of the developments talked about in this book. Still, there should be little doubt that it is to nations such as South Africa, South Korea, Mexico, and Malaysia, to mention only some of those that I have some personal knowledge of, that we should look to for ideas about resource allocation and examples of related national policies that could be of value to the United States as well as other nations. One need look no further than the use of study centers in the world's open universities referred to earlier, where millions of students have learned to study in a blended mode. I assume, of course, that policymakers and leaders of educational institutions will, before too many more years go by, be willing to hear and understand what is being reported, both domestically and internationally.

The *Handbook of Blended Learning* should prove to be a splendid contribution to this improved understanding. I commend it to readers, and I compliment the editors on their initiative in conceiving it as well as their fortitude in producing it.

References

Harper, W. R. (1886). The system of correspondence. In J. H. Vincent (Ed.), *Chautauqua movement* (pp. 183–193). Boston: Chautauqua Press.

Harper, W. R. (1971). The system of correspondence. In O. Mackenzie (Ed.), The *changing world of correspondence stud*. University Park: Pennsylvania State University Press.

Moore, M. G. (2002). The Benton Harbour plan. *American Journal of Distance Education, 16*(4), 201–204

Moore, M. G., & Anderson, W. (2003). *Handbook of distance education*. Mahwah, NJ: Erlbaum.

Jay Cross is CEO of Internet Time Group and founder of the Workflow Institute. A thought leader in learning technology, performance improvement, and organizational culture, he coined the terms *e-learning* and *work flow learning.* He is CEO of the eighteen-hundred-member Emergent Learning Forum. He is the author of *Implementing eLearning,* writes the "Effectiveness" column for *Chief Learning Officer* magazine, and is writing a book on informal learning.

Michael G. Moore published the first statement of theory about distance education in 1972 and has achieved a number of other "firsts" in this field. While teaching the first course about distance education at University of Wisconsin-Madison, he helped plan the annual Wisconsin Distance Teaching and Learning Conference there. Moving to Penn State in 1986, where he is now professor of education, he founded the American Center for Study of Distance.

I thank all the wonderful people I have met in
blended learning environments and positions around
the world who have opened my eyes to many
exciting and significant global perspectives
with their local designs.
Curt Bonk

To family and friends and particularly to my wife, Dawn.
Charles Graham

PREFACE AND ACKNOWLEDGMENTS

Curtis J. Bonk, Charles R. Graham

Institutions of higher education as well as corporate and nonprofit training settings are increasingly embracing online education, especially blended learning (Allen & Seaman, 2003; Bonk, 2004). It is clear from the chapters in this handbook that the number of learners enrolled in distance programs are rapidly rising not only in colleges and universities within the United States (National Center for Education Statistics, 2003), but in higher education and corporate training settings around the globe. Given this enrollment explosion, many states, countries, organizations, and institutions are working on strategic plans for implementing online education (see, for example, NGA Center for Best Practices, 2001).

Purpose

This book highlights issues and trends within blended learning from a global point of view and then provides more specific information on individual blended learning situations. Basically, this is a book about adult learning in the twenty-first century, illustrating dozens of learning options that combine aspects of face-to-face (FTF) instruction with online learning in formal academic settings and the workplace. Roughly half of the chapters focus on blended learning in higher education settings, and most of the rest address workplace learning. Consequently, the chapter authors include professors, provosts, presidents of for-profit universities, distance learning center directors, learning and strategy evangelists, general managers of learning, chief executive officers, chancellors, deans, and directors of global talent and organizational development. These individuals are in key leadership roles in higher education, corporate training, military training, government, and nonprofit settings.

This book clarifies where blended learning may find significant and effective application given the vastly different opinions about the current status of online education in higher education and corporate as well as military training. It ranges from excitement to disappointment, as noted in a recent issue of the *Chronicle of Higher Education* (Detweiler, 2004; Zemsky & Massy, 2004). Accordingly, questions arise about where blended learning is headed. For instance, what will the blended learning scenarios and events look like in the next five or ten years? Clearly, a better understanding of the current state and the future direction of blended learning is warranted.

There are many other goals for this handbook. For instance, it is the first book to cover blended learning situations and scenarios around the globe. Second, it is likely that it is the first blended learning book to provide a broad picture of the applications of blended learning in both higher education and workplace settings. Our goal is to get those involved in the adult learning arena, across a range of settings, to grasp their respective commonalities and differences, as well as the potential for innovative partnerships. Too often, instead of focusing on similarities, connections, and relationships, the emphasis is on the differences in the learning goals and associated delivery mechanisms within higher education and corporate training. This book therefore is meant to provide a connection between the providers of adult learning by using blended learning commonalities as the bridging mechanism. Third, the book is meant to start a conversation about what blended learning is. As is apparent throughout the book, there are a plethora of definitions related to blended learning. Typically, however, blended learning environments combine traditional face-to-face instruction with computer-mediated instruction. Fourth, we hope that this book will inspire others to create innovative and wildly successful blended learning courses, programs, and training events, as well as graduate seminars, conference symposia, presentations, institutes, and panels that discuss and debate findings and ideas reflected in this book and extend beyond them.

The stories, models, and examples found here should provide a means to reflect on learning options and help foster intelligent decisions regarding blended learning. We hope that the many personal stories and reflections included in this book can serve as guideposts to others making similar journeys into blended learning environments. At the same time, we hope that those reading this book will reach out to the chapter contributors for advice, ideas, and feedback. We truly hope you enjoy the book. In addition, we welcome your suggestions regarding follow-up volumes or themes.

Audience

This book can provide valuable information to corporate executives, higher education administrators, educators, researchers, trainers, instructional designers, and anyone else interested in how to blend traditional face-to-face and online learning environments. In particular, this handbook will be valuable to corporate executives seeking examples of how to blend their training as well as insights into where such blending might be financially attractive, efficient, and strategically beneficial. Training managers might take advantage of examples from the book to help justify e-learning initiatives and strategic plans. This book should appeal to higher education administrators struggling with issues of where to place valued resources. Clarification of the range of blended learning models can help administrators and staff from learning and teaching centers on college campuses to train faculty members for a wealth of online teaching possibilities. Teaching in a blended fashion is a new experience for most college faculty, so having a range of examples is vital. Readers will see that in some instances, it may involve the creation of an elaborate online mentoring program; in other cases, it might simply be establishing online office hours or embedding online exams or review materials in one's course. Along these same lines, in order for instructional designers to be effective, they will also need information about blended learning options. Those conducting research in blended learning environments will benefit from reading chapters on the state of blended learning in both corporate and higher education settings. Finally, and perhaps most important, politicians reading or accessing this book will discover that online learning is not an either-or decision. Instead, most of the time, online learning is blended or mixed. Hence, governmental spending for online learning needs to reflect this fact, as should policies that governments establish related to student financial aid, institutional accreditation, and university budgets. We live in an age of university budget crises that are often resolved with part-time and clinical instructors. Corporate training budgets are also among the first to be slashed in tough economic times. Increasingly, blended learning is playing a significant role in such situations.

Handbook Overview

The chapter authors were selected because of their leadership roles within blended learning as well as the unique stories that they had to tell. With the mix of corporate and military training, nonprofit organizations, and higher education institutions, a wide range of perspectives is covered in this book. The chapters are not necessarily organized by industry type. Instead, they are divided into eight key sections or themes: introductory and overview information as well as sections on for-profit universities, blended learning models (in both higher education and corporate training), case examples of blended learning from around the world, workplace and authentic learning, and future trends in blended learning. The chapters discuss topics such as access, flexibility, e-learning partnerships, enrollment demands, return on investment, online interaction, and strategic planning for blended learning. At the start of each part, we provide a brief introduction of the theme for that section, along with chapter synopses.

The chapter authors share specifics about what is happening in blended learning in their respective organization, institution, state, province, region, or country. They provide interesting data regarding trends in enrollments, new programs, technologies, and pedagogies. Some chapters discuss the unique or powerful aspects of a particular blended learning approach, including specific information on what is being blended and how successful that blend is. Others put forth models of blended learning that might be compared, adopted, and critiqued. And still others summarize the benefits, success stories, and return on investment from the blended strategies that they adopted, as well as the problems, challenges, and dilemmas still faced. In the end, this book contains a wide range of ideas, examples, guidelines, success stories, models, and solutions.

Acknowledgments

We thank the people at Pfeiffer Publishing for their help and support on this project, including Lisa Shannon, Laura Reizman, and Kathleen Dolan Davies. They were truly fantastic to work with. We thank the book reviewers for their insightful and informative suggestions. In addition, we deeply thank Mary, Alex, and Nicki Bonk and Dawn, Bobbe, Julie, William, Bethany, and Daniel Graham for their love, understanding, and encouragement during this project. As is usual with a project like this, there were countless late nights and several missed events. The first author would especially like to thank Robert Clasen, who, twenty years ago, roused his interest in distance learning as his teacher in two correspondence courses that qualified him for graduate school at the University of Wisconsin. Serendipity occurred when Bob and his wonderful wife, Donna Rae Clasen, later employed him in the production of a television-based correspondence course, *Teachers Tackle Thinking*, during his first couple of years in graduate school. Given the trends of the past two decades in distance learning, the mentoring and modeling that Bob provided within this field were extremely timely and fortuitous. You are the best, Bob! Finally, we thank all the chapter authors who each shed some light on the world of blended learning and show us opportunities that we may not have previously been aware of. It was truly a joy to work with each of you.

References

Allen, E. I., & Seaman, J. (2003). *Sizing the opportunity: The quality and extent of online education in the United States, 2002 and 2003.* Needham and Wellesley, MA: Sloan Consortium. Retrieved August 21, 2005, from http://www.sloan-c.org/resources/sizing_opportunity.pdf

Bonk, C. J. (2004). *The perfect e-storm: Emerging technologies, enhanced pedagogy, enormous learner demand, and erased budgets.* London: Observatory on Borderless Higher Education.

Detweiler, R. (2004, July 9). At last, we can replace the lecture. *Chronicle of Higher Education, 50*(44), B8.

National Center for Education Statistics. (2003). *Distance education at degree-granting postsecondary institutions: 2000–2001.* Washington, DC: Department of Education.

NGA Center for Best Practices. (2001). *The state of e-learning in the states.* Washington, DC: National Governor's Association.

Zemsky, R., & Massy, W. F. (2004, July 9). Why the e-learning boom went bust. *Chronicle of Higher Education, 50*(44), B6.

Bloomington, Indiana

Provo, Utah

Curtis J. Bonk

Charles R. Graham

October 2005

THE HANDBOOK OF BLENDED LEARNING

PART ONE

INTRODUCTION TO BLENDED LEARNING

As blended learning emerges as perhaps the most prominent delivery mechanism in higher education, business, government, and military settings, it is vital to define it, as well as explain where it is useful and why it is important. This part, with chapters by Charles R. Graham, Elliott Masie, Jennifer Hofmann, and Ellen D. Wagner, does just that. These authors discuss the elements that are important to consider in blended learning while also touching on some of the emerging trends and issues.

In Chapter One, Charles R. Graham describes the historical emergence of blended learning as the convergence between traditional face-to-face learning environments and computer-mediated (or distributed) learning environments. He discusses four critical dimensions to interactions that occur in both of these environments (space, time, fidelity, and humanness) and presents a working definition for blended learning systems. This chapter also addresses current trends seen in both corporate and higher education, including blends that focus on enabling access and flexibility, enhancing current teaching and learning practices, and transforming the way individuals learn. The chapter ends with six important issues relevant to the design of blended learning systems, followed by some directions for the future.

In Chapter Two, Elliott Masie presents a brief and provocative perspective on blended learning. The central theme of his chapter is that all great learning is blended. In the predigital age, combinations of different learning contexts were used. Similarly, learning environments increasingly will incorporate "e elements" into varied instructional contexts. Masie outlines compelling reasons for why blending has been popular and will continue to be so.

In Chapter Three, Jennifer Hofmann addresses several of the typical challenges facing those who are attempting to implement blended solutions. She notes some of the common mistakes designers make: assuming that it will take less time to redesign an existing program than it would to design a blended program from scratch, putting too much emphasis on the "live" components of a training situation, and assuming that traditional facilitators are the best choices for managing a blended version of the training. An emphasis is placed on the importance of training the design team as well as the trainers. In addition, she outlines an example of a blended train-the-trainer course.

In Chapter Four, Ellen D. Wagner shares a vision for the next generation of blended learning. She addresses the impact that personal and mobile devices are likely to have on emerging models of blended learning and suggests that interaction strategies offer a useful means for enhancing individualization, personalization, and relevancy. She discusses current models of interaction and shares eleven ways that interaction can be used to focus on performance outcomes.

CHAPTER ONE

BLENDED LEARNING SYSTEMS

Definition, Current Trends, and Future Directions

Charles R. Graham

The term *blended learning* is being used with increased frequency in both academic and corporate circles. In 2003, the American Society for Training and Development identified blended learning as one of the top ten trends to emerge in the knowledge delivery industry (Rooney, 2003). In 2002, the *Chronicle of Higher Education* quoted the president of Pennsylvania State University as saying that the convergence between online and residential instruction was "the single-greatest unrecognized trend in higher education today" (Young, 2002, p. A33). Also quoted in that article was the editor of the *Journal of Asynchronous Learning Networks*, who predicted a dramatic increase in the number of hybrid (that is, blended) courses in higher education, possibly to include as many as 80 to 90 percent of all courses (Young, 2002).

So what is this blended learning that everyone is talking about? This chapter provides a basic introduction to blended learning systems and shares some trends and issues that are highly relevant to those who are implementing such systems. To accomplish these goals, the chapter addresses five important questions related to blended learning systems:

- What is blended learning?
- Why blend?
- What current blended learning models exist?
- What issues and challenges are faced when blending?
- What are the future directions of blended learning systems?

Background and Definitions

The first question asked by most people when hearing about blended learning is, "What is blended learning?" Although *blended learning* has become somewhat of a buzzword in corporate and higher education settings, there is still quite a bit of ambiguity about what it means (see Jones, Chapter Thirteen, this volume). How is blended learning different from other terms in our vernacular, such as *distributed learning, e-learning, open and flexible learning,* and *hybrid courses?* Some define the term so broadly that one would be hard pressed to find any learning system that was not blended (Masie, Chapter Two, this volume; Ross and Gage, Chapter Eleven, this volume). Others challenge the very assumptions behind blending as holding on to relics of an old paradigm of learning (Offerman and Tassava, Chapter Seventeen, this volume). In the first section of this chapter, I articulate a practical working definition for the term *blended learning* and provide a historical context for its emergence.

What Is Being Blended?

One frequent question asked when one hears about blended learning (BL) is, "What is being blended?" Although there is a wide variety of responses to this question (Driscoll, 2002), most of the definitions are just variations of a few common themes. The three most commonly mentioned definitions, documented by Graham, Allen, and Ure (2003), are:

- Combining instructional modalities (or delivery media) (Bersin & Associates, 2003; Orey, 2002a, 2002b; Singh & Reed, 2001; Thomson, 2002)
- Combining instructional methods (Driscoll, 2002; House, 2002; Rossett, 2002)
- Combining online and face-to-face instruction (Reay, 2001; Rooney, 2003; Sands, 2002; Ward & LaBranche, 2003; Young, 2002)

The first two positions reflect the debate on the influences of media versus method on learning (Clark, 1983, 1994a, 1994b; Kozma, 1991, 1994). Both of these positions suffer from the problem that they define BL so broadly that they encompass virtually all learning systems. One would be hard-pressed to find any learning system that did not involve multiple instructional methods and multiple delivery media. So defining BL in either of these two ways waters down the definition and does not get at the essence of what blended learning is and why it is exciting to so many people. The third position more accurately reflects the historical emergence of blended learning systems and is the foundation of the author's working definition (see Figure 1.1).

FIGURE 1.1.   DEFINITION OF BLENDED LEARNING SYSTEMS.

Definition:
Blended learning systems combine face-to-face instruction
with computer-mediated instruction.

The working definition in Figure 1.1 reflects the idea that BL is the combination of instruction from two historically separate models of teaching and learning: traditional face-to-face learning systems and distributed learning systems. It also emphasizes the central role of computer-based technologies in blended learning.

Past, Present, and Future

BL is part of the ongoing convergence of two archetypal learning environments. On the one hand, we have the traditional face-to-face learning environment that has been around for centuries. On the other hand, we have distributed learning environments that have begun to grow and expand in exponential ways as new technologies have expanded the possibilities for distributed communication and interaction.

In the past, these two learning environments have remained largely separate because they have used different media and method combinations and have addressed the needs of different audiences (see Figure 1.2). For example, traditional face-to-face learning typically occurred in a teacher-directed environment with person-to-person interaction in a live synchronous, high-fidelity environment. On the other hand, distance learning systems emphasized self-paced learning and learning materials interactions that typically occurred in an asynchronous, low-fidelity (text only) environment.

Figure 1.3 shows the continuum for four critical dimensions of interactions that occur in both of these environments. Historically, face-to-face learning has operated at the left-hand side of each of these dimensions, and distributed learning has operated at the right of each of these dimensions. To a large degree, the media available placed constraints on the nature of the instructional methods that could be used in each environment. For example, it was not possible to have synchronous or high-fidelity interactions in the distributed environment. Because of these constraints, distributed learning environments placed emphasis on learner-material interactions, while face-to-face learning environments tended to place priority on the human-human interaction.

FIGURE 1.2.   PROGRESSIVE CONVERGENCE OF TRADITIONAL
FACE-TO-FACE AND DISTRIBUTED ENVIRONMENTS ALLOWING
DEVELOPMENT OF BLENDED LEARNING SYSTEMS.

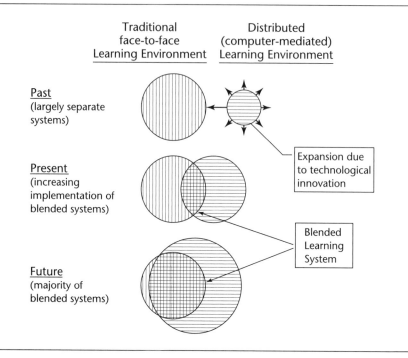

The rapid emergence of technological innovations over the past half-century (particularly digital technologies) has had a huge impact on the possibilities for learning in the distributed environment. In fact, if you look at the four dimensions, distributed learning environments are increasingly encroaching on instructional territory that was once possible only in face-to-face environments. For example, in the time and fidelity dimensions, communication technologies now allow us to have synchronous distributed interactions that occur in real time with close to the same levels of fidelity as in the face-to-face environment. In the humanness dimension, there is an increasing focus on facilitating human interaction in the form of computer-supported collaboration, virtual communities, instant messaging, and blogging. In addition, there is ongoing research investigating how to make machines and computer interfaces more social and human (the work with automated agents and virtual worlds, for example). Even in the space dimension, there are some interesting things happening with mixed reality environments (see Kirkley and Kirkley, Chapter Thirty-Eight, this volume) and environments that

FIGURE 1.3.   FOUR DIMENSIONS OF INTERACTION IN FACE-TO-FACE AND DISTRIBUTED LEARNING ENVIRONMENTS.

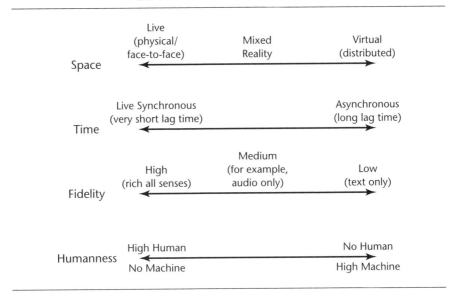

simultaneously facilitate both distributed and face-to-face interactions (see Wisher, Chapter Thirty-Seven, this volume).

The widespread adoption and availability of digital learning technologies has led to increased levels of integration of computer-mediated instructional elements into the traditional face-to-face learning experience. From the distributed learning perspective, we see evidence of the convergence in face-to-face residency requirements (Offerman and Tassava, Chapter Seventeen, this volume; Pease, Chapter Eighteen, this volume) and limited face-to-face events, such as orientations and final presentations (Lindquist, Chapter Sixteen, this volume). In addition, there is greater emphasis on person-to-person interaction, and increasing use of synchronous and high-fidelity technologies to mediate those interactions. Figure 1.2 depicts the rapid growth of distributed learning environments and its convergence with face-to-face learning environments. The intersection of the two archetypes depicts where blended learning systems are emerging.

Although it is impossible to see entirely what the future holds, we can be pretty certain that the trend toward blended learning systems will increase. It may even become so ubiquitous that we will eventually drop the word *blended* and just call it learning, as both Masie (see Chapter Two, this volume) and Massy (see Chapter Thirty, this volume) predict. But regardless of what we decide to call blended learning in the future, it is clear that it is here to stay. Therefore, it is imperative that we understand how to create effective blended learning experiences that incorporate both face-to-face and computer-mediated (CM) elements.

Current Trends and Issues

Here we look at current trends and issues that are relevant to blended learning systems.

Why Blend?

There are many reasons that an instructor, trainer, or learner might pick blended learning over other learning options. Osguthorpe and Graham (2003) identified six reasons that one might choose to design or use a blended learning system: (1) pedagogical richness, (2) access to knowledge, (3) social interaction, (4) personal agency, (5) cost-effectiveness, and (6) ease of revision. In the BL literature, the most common reason provided is that BL combines the best of both worlds. Although there is some truth to this, it is rarely acknowledged that a blended learning environment can also mix the least effective elements of both worlds if it is not designed well. Beyond this general statement, Graham, Allen, and Ure (2003, 2005) found that, overwhelmingly, people chose BL for three reasons: (1) improved pedagogy, (2) increased access and flexibility, and (3) increased cost-effectiveness.

Improved Pedagogy. One of the most commonly cited reasons for blending is more effective pedagogical practices. It is no secret that most current teaching and learning practice in both higher education and corporate training settings is still focused on transmissive rather than interactive strategies. In higher education, 83 percent of instructors use the lecture as the predominant teaching strategy (U.S. Department of Education, 2001). Similarly, distance education often suffers from making large amounts of information available for students to absorb independently (Waddoups & Howell, 2002). Some have seen blended learning approaches increase the level of active learning strategies, peer-to-peer learning strategies, and learner-centered strategies used (Collis, Bruijstens, & van der Veen, 2003; Hartman, Dziuban, & Moskal, 1999; Morgan, 2002; Smelser, 2002). There are many examples of this in this handbook, including the model used by IBM (Lewis and Orton, Chapter Five, this volume) where learners go through three phases: (1) online self-paced learning to acquire background information, (2) face-to-face learning lab focused on active learning and application experiences instead of lecture, and (3) online learning and support for transferring the learning to the workplace environment. Using a similar strategy, a Brigham Young University accounting professor uses online modules to help students acquire the tool-related skills and technical information and then uses precious face-to-face class time to focus on application, case studies, and develop decision-making skills (Cottrell & Robison, 2003). It is interesting to note such overlaps in blended learning models between the corporate training world and higher education.

A few other ideas for using BL to improve pedagogy included in this handbook are provided by Oliver, Herrington, and Reeves (Chapter Thirty-Six, this volume), who provide insights into how computer-mediated environments can bring a level of authenticity to the traditional classroom experience. Collis (see Chapter Thirty-Three, this volume) shares a model for how BL can be used to integrate formal classroom learning and informal workplace learning. Wisher (Chapter Thirty-Seven this volume) and Kirkley and Kirkley (see Chapter Thirty-Eight, this volume) share ideas for collaborative learning and problem solving in environments that mix live face-to-face elements with virtual reality.

Increased Access and Flexibility. Access to learning is one of the key factors influencing the growth of distributed learning environments (Bonk, Olson, Wisher, & Orvis, 2002). Many chapters in this book emphasize programs that would not be possible if students were not able to have a majority of their learning experiences at a distance from instructors and/or other students (for examples, see Kaur and Ahmed, Chapter Twenty-Two; Lee and Im, Chapter Twenty; Reynolds and Greiner, Chapter Fifteen, this volume). Learner flexibility and convenience are also of growing importance as more mature learners with outside commitments such as work and family seek additional education. Many learners want the convenience offered by a distributed environment yet do not want to sacrifice the social interaction and human touch they are used to in a face-to-face classroom. There are numerous examples in this handbook of how blending is used to provide a balance between flexible learning options and the high-touch human interactive experience. WebCT executives Barbara Ross and Karen Gage (Chapter Eleven, this volume), for example, have seen an expansion of reduced seat-time courses that allow increased flexibility but retain some traditional face-to-face contact. The University of Central Florida's M (i.e., mixed mode) courses (Dziuban, Hartman, Juge, Moskal, and Sorg, Chapter Fourteen, this volume) are also good examples. As a third example, the University of Phoenix model allows face-to-face socializing in orientations as well as presentation experiences at the beginning and ending of a course, with online learning experiences in between (see Chapter Sixteen, this volume).

Increased Cost-Effectiveness. Cost-effectiveness is a third major goal for BL systems in both higher education and corporate institutions. Blended learning systems provide an opportunity for reaching a large, globally dispersed audience in a short period of time with consistent, semipersonal content delivery. Bersin and Associates (2003) have done an exemplary job of documenting corporate cases that have effectively used blended learning to provide a large return on investment (ROI). Similarly, in this handbook, the IBM chapter by Lewis and Orton reports ROI figures as high as 47 to 1 for their implementation of BL. In adding to these results, the Avaya chapter (Chute, Williams, and Hancock, Chapter Eight, this volume) and Microsoft chapter (Ziob and Mosher, Chapter Seven, this volume) provide cases in which BL solutions have resulted in a significant ROI.

In higher education, there is also interest in finding solutions that are cost-effective. The Center for Academic Transformation with support from the Pew Charitable Trust recently completed a three-year grant program designed to help universities explore ways of using technology to achieve quality enhancements and cost savings simultaneously. More detailed information for each of the thirty grant redesign projects that Pew funded can be found at the grant Web site (Pew, 2003). A summary of the significant role blended learning played in the various Pew projects can be found in Graham and Allen (Graham, Allen, & Ure, 2003, 2005).

Part Two of this handbook on for-profit universities has several chapters that address this issue (Pease, Chapter Eighteen, this volume). The University of Central Florida, for example, has predicted cost savings due to cost reductions in physical infrastructure and improved scheduling efficiencies, which have yet to materialize (Dziuban, Hartman, Juge, Moskal, and Sorg, Chapter Fourteen, this volume).

What Models of Blending Exist?

One of the goals of this handbook is to look broadly across many sectors to see what the current state of blended learning is and what we can learn from innovative people and organizations in this arena. This book provides a wide range of perspectives and flavors of blended learning to learn from. Although there is a wide variance in the blended learning practices that are occurring, there are also some strategic similarities that will be articulated in following section.

Blending at Many Different Levels

All of the BL examples in this handbook occur at one of the following four levels: activity level, course level, program level, or institutional level. Several chapters

(Ross and Gage, Chapter Eleven, this volume; Wright, Dewstow, Topping, and Tappenden, Chapter Twelve, this volume) specifically address different levels of blending that are occurring. Across all four levels, the nature of the blends is determined by the learner or the designer or instructor. Blending at the institutional and program levels is often left to the discretion of the learner, while designers and instructors are more likely to take a role in prescribing the blend at the course and activity levels.

Activity-Level Blending. Blending at the activity level occurs when a learning activity contains both face-to-face and CM elements. For example, Wisher (Chapter Thirty-Seven, this volume) outlines large-scale military training events that incorporate both face-to-face and virtual elements. Kirkley and Kirkley (Chapter Thirty-Eight, this volume) also discuss how mixed reality technologies blend the virtual and the real together during learning activities. In higher education, Oliver, Herrington, and Reeves (Chapter Thirty-Six, this volume) talk about strategies for using technological tools to make learning activities more authentic, while examples like those of Jung and Suzuki (Chapter Nineteen, this volume) share how technology is used to bring experts at a distance into the classroom, creating a simultaneous face-to-face and CM experience.

Course-Level Blending. Course-level blending is one of the most common ways to blend. It entails a combination of distinct face-to-face and CM activities used as part of a course. Some blended approaches engage learners in different but supportive face-to-face and CM activities that overlap in time, while other approaches separate the time blocks so that they are sequenced chronologically but not overlapping (see the examples in Huang and Zhou, Chapter Twenty-One, this volume, and Jagannathan, Chapter Thirty-Two, this volume). Owston, Garrison, and Cook (Chapter Twenty-Four, this volume) describe eight cases of blending at the course level across universities in Canada. Collis (Chapter Thirty-Three, this volume) describes an approach to course-level blending for a suite of courses used by Shell EP.

Program-Level Blending. Ross and Gage (Chapter Eleven, this volume) observe that blends in higher education are often occurring at the degree program level. Blending at a program level often entails one of two models: a model in which the participants choose a mix between face-to-face courses and online courses or one in which the combination between the two is prescribed by the program. Jung and Suzuki (Chapter Nineteen, this volume) discuss a program-level blend in the Japan context in which there are certain face-to-face courses that are required for a program and the rest can be taken at a distance. Salmon and Lawless (Chapter Twenty-Eight, this volume) describe a business management certificate program that allows students the choice of completing the program completely online or online with face-to-face tutoring session or participation in an extended on-campus management challenge. The New Zealand Law Diploma program is conducted mostly online, with about 15 percent of the learning time in a face-to-face setting. Reynolds and Greiner (Chapter Fifteen, this volume) and Wright, Dewstow, Topping, and Tappenden (Chapter Twelve, this volume) describe teacher education programs that blend face-to-face and CM experiences at the program level.

In the corporate arena, BL is often applied to a particular training program, as was the case with Oracle's Leader Track training (Hanson and Clem, Chapter Ten, this volume), Avaya's Executive Solutions Selling Business Acumen program (Chute, Williams, and Hancock, Chapter Eight, this volume), and cases of three training programs provided by Microsoft (Ziob and Mosher, Chapter Seven, this volume).

Institutional-Level Blending. Some institutions have made an organizational commitment to blending face-to-face and CM instruction. Many corporations as well as institutions of higher education are creating models for blending at an institutional level. IBM (Lewis and Orton, Chapter Five, this volume) and Sun Microsystems (Wenger and Ferguson, Chapter Six, this volume) are corporate examples of organizations with institutional models of blended learning. The University of Phoenix (Lindquist, Chapter Sixteen, this volume) also has an institutional model for blending, where students have face-to-face classes at the beginning and end of the course, with online activities in between. At a university level, the University of Central Florida (Dziuban, Hartman, Juge, Moskal, and Sorg, Chapter Fourteen, this volume) has created the "M course" designation for blended courses that have some reduction in face-to-face seat-time. Other institutions, such as Brigham Young University (BYU) Idaho, have a general education requirement that students must have one online learning course experience to graduate (BYU-Idaho, 2004). Brigham Young University (Provo campus) has experimented with "semester online" courses where on-campus students can enroll for a distributed course along with other campus-based courses (Waddoups & Howell, 2002). Similarly, at the University of Illinois, traditional on-campus economics students have been allowed to take a required course online while they were off-campus for the summer (Wang, Kanfer, Hinn, & Arvan, 2001).

It is important to note that dual-mode institutions (Rumble, 1992) that support both face-to-face and CM instruction are not necessarily in the business of blending learning. For the institution to be engaged in blended learning, there must be a concerted effort to enable the learner to take advantage of both ends of the spectrum. It is not sufficient for the institution to have a distance learning division that is largely separate from the on-campus operations.

General Categories of Blends

One of the reasons that we are interested in models of blended learning is that we are interested in the practical question, "How to blend?" Each model provides ideas about how to blend with examples implemented in specific contexts and with real constraints. Table 1.1 provides three categories for blended learning systems found in this handbook based on the primary purpose of the blend. Some blends in this handbook fit into multiple categories; however, usually a blend most closely matches the focus of one category. It is also important to note that none of these blends is necessarily bad; they just have different foci.

We see the greatest focus on enabling blends in programs that come out of a distance learning tradition. A good example is the University of Phoenix (Lindquist, Chapter Sixteen, this volume), which attempts to provide an "equivalent" learning experience through its face-to-face residential programs, entirely online programs, and blended learning programs. In this system, learners pick the option that best meets their cost and time constraints.

There is an enormous focus on enhancing blends in traditional university settings. With the widespread adoption of learning management systems (LMS) and

TABLE 1.1. CATEGORIES OF BLENDED LEARNING SYSTEMS.

Enabling blends	Primarily focus on addressing issues of access and convenience—for example, blends that are intended to provide additional flexibility to the learners or blends that attempt to provide the same opportunities or learning experience but through a different modality.
Enhancing blends	Allow incremental changes to the pedagogy but do not radically change the way teaching and learning occurs. This can occur at both ends of the spectrum. For example, in a traditional face-to-face learning environment, additional resources and perhaps some supplementary materials may be included online.
Transforming blends	Blends that allow a radical transformation of the pedagogy—for example, a change from a model where learners are just receivers of information to a model where learners actively construct knowledge through dynamic interactions. These types of blends enable intellectual activity that was not practically possible without the technology.

technology-equipped classrooms, it is becoming increasingly commonplace for instructors to use some level of technology. Both Jones (Chapter Thirteen, this volume) and Wright, Dewstow, Topping, and Tappenden (Chapter Twelve, this volume) provide models that span the spectrum from a minimum level of integration to a high level of integration. The hope of some is that enhancing blends are the first steps toward more transformative blends.

There seems to be a greater abundance of examples of transforming blends in the corporate environment than in the university environment. Examples like the Live-Virtual-Constructive simulations (Wisher, Chapter Thirty-Seven, this volume) and mixed-reality and problem-based embedded training (Kirkley and Kirkley, Chapter Thirty-Eight, this volume) show how high-end technologies can transform the learning experience. Other examples include the increased use of knowledge management, electronic performance support systems, and mobile devices to situate learning in the context of work flow (see Chute, Williams, and Hancock, Chapter Eight; Collis, Chapter Thirty-Three; DeViney and Lewis, Chapter Thirty-Five; and Singh, Chapter Four, this volume). In higher education environments, constraints such as class duration, size, location, and availability of technology can provide a formidable barrier to making transformative changes. Oliver, Herrington, and Reeves (Chapter Thirty-Six, this volume), for instance, point to several ways that technology can support the development of authentic learning environments. A growing number of faculty are experimenting with innovative technology-mediated approaches to teaching (such as the use of tools for simulations, visualization, communication, and feedback) that are transforming the ways that their students learn (West & Graham, 2005).

What Issues or Challenges Are Faced When Blending?

Six major issues are relevant to designing blended learning systems: (1) the role of live interaction, (2) the role of learner choice and self-regulation, (3) models for support and training, (4) finding balance between innovation and production, (5) cultural adaptation, and (6) dealing with the digital divide.

The Role of Live Interaction. Under what conditions is human interaction important to the learning process and to learner satisfaction with the process? Hanson and Clem, Chapter Ten; Hofmann, Chapter Three; and Owston, Garrison, and Cook, Chapter Twenty-Four, among others (this volume) observed a preference among many learners for the live (or face-to-face) components of a blended experience. When CM and face-to-face elements were combined, learners often placed a greater value or emphasis on the face-to-face aspects of the experience. Juxtaposed to this, Offerman and Tassava (Chapter Seventeen, this volume) make the claim that the face-to-face components are unnecessary and primarily used for socialization reasons. Similarly, the University of Phoenix (Lindquist, Chapter Sixteen, this volume) takes the position that the live, completely online, and blended options to its courses are "equivalent" experiences to be selected based on learner preference. When and why should we be considering human interaction such as collaboration and learning communities? How does live interaction versus low-fidelity, asynchronous interaction affect the learning experience?

Role of Learner Choice and Self-Regulation. How are learners making choices about the kinds of blends that they participate in? Many of the chapters in this book as well as other blended learning publications make it seem that learners are primarily selecting blended learning based on convenience and access. But this begs questions about the type and amount of guidance that should be provided to learners in making their choices about how different blends might affect their learning experience. Online learning components often require a large amount of self-discipline on the part of the learners (Collis, Bruijstens, & van der Veen, 2003). Huang and Zhou (Chapter Twenty-One, this volume) mention the challenge that many of their Chinese students have in regulating their own learning without the close guidance of an instructor. How can blended learning environments be designed to support increasing learner maturity and capabilities for self-regulation?

Models for Support and Training. There are many issues related to support and training in blended environments, including (1) increased demand on instructor time (Hartman et al., 1999; Lee and Im, Chapter Twenty, this volume), (2) providing learners with technological skills to succeed in both face-to-face and CM environments (Levine & Wake, 2000; Morgan, 2002), and (3) changing organizational culture to accept blended approaches (Hartman et al., 1999). There is also a need to provide professional development for instructors who will be teaching online and face-to-face (Lee and Im, Chapter Twenty, this volume; Lindquist, Chapter Sixteen, this volume). It is important to see more successful models of how to support a blended approach to learning from the technological infrastructure perspective as well as from the organizational (human) perspective.

Digital Divide. The divide between the information and communication technologies available to individuals and societies at different ends of the socioeconomic spectrum can be great (see chapters by Massy, Chapter Thirty; Jagannathan, Chapter Thirty-Two; and Kaur and Ahmed, Chapter Twenty-Two, this volume). Massy raises the issue that e-learning is often perceived as being an approach that favors the advantaged. Yet e-learning is a strategy that might be considered for educating the masses because of its low cost and ability to be distributed widely. But the jury is still out on whether blended learning models can be developed that are affordable and still address the needs of different populations with different socioeconomic conditions around the world.

Cultural Adaptation. What role can and should blended approaches play in adapting materials to local audiences? One strength of e-learning is the ability to distribute uniform learning materials rapidly. Yet there is often a need for customizing the materials to the local audience to make them culturally relevant. Jagannathan (Chapter Thirty-Two, this volume) and Selinger (Chapter Thirty-One, this volume) both address the need to find balance between global and local interests. Selinger suggests that a face-to-face instructor plays an important role in helping to make globally distributed materials culturally relevant and meaningful.

Balance Between Innovation and Production. In design, there is a constant tension between innovation and production. On the one hand, there is a need to look to the possibilities that new technological innovations provide, and, on the other hand, there is a need to be able to produce cost-effective solutions. However, due to the constantly changing nature of technology, finding an appropriate balance between innovation and production will be a constant challenge for those designing blended learning systems.

Directions for the Future

We live in a world in which technological innovation is occurring at breakneck speed and digital technologies are increasingly becoming an integral part of our lives. Technological innovation is also expanding the range of possible solutions that can be brought to bear on teaching and learning. Whether we are primarily interested in creating more effective learning experiences, increasing access and flexibility, or reducing the cost of learning, it is likely that our learning systems will provide a blend of both face-to-face and CM experiences.

Ross and Gage (Chapter Eleven, this volume) state that future learning systems will be differentiated not based on *whether* they blend but rather by *how* they blend. This question of how to blend face-to-face and CM instruction effectively is one of the most important we can consider. Like any other design problem, this challenge is highly context dependent, with a practically infinite number of possible solutions. So in this handbook we do not present any one solution as *the solution;* rather, we share examples of successful blends across many contexts. We hope that the wide range of global perspectives and specific local examples

FIGURE 1.4.   THE CHALLENGE OF FINDING BLENDS THAT TAKE ADVANTAGE OF THE STRENGTHS OF EACH ENVIRONMENT AND AVOID THE WEAKNESSES.

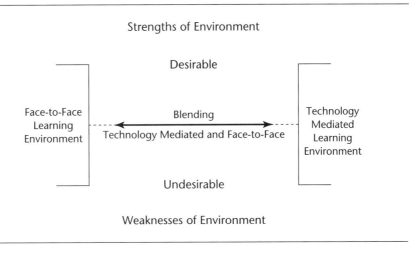

available in this handbook will help readers gain a better understanding of options for meeting instructional design challenges in varied contexts. Our charge is to try and understand the strengths and weaknesses of both face-to-face and CM environments so that when we are faced with trade-offs, we can make appropriate decisions. Figure 1.4 is a simplified representation of this complex challenge. From a pedagogical standpoint, the designers of blending learning systems should be seeking best practices for how to combine instructional strategies in face-to-face and CM environments that take advantages of the strengths of each environment and avoid their weaknesses (Osguthorpe & Graham, 2003; Martyn, 2003).

To illustrate the importance of understanding the strengths and weaknesses afforded by a face-to-face or CM learning environment, consider the following example of an activity-level blend. Class discussions are one of the most common instructional methods used in education. Unlike the lecture, the instructional method of class discussion focuses on learner interaction rather than knowledge transmission. Typically, the goal of class discussion is to have the learners negotiate and co-construct an understanding of the discussion topic. The face-to-face and CM environments have many complementary strengths and weaknesses that impact class discussion. Table 1.2 lists some of the strengths and weaknesses of conducting discussions in each of these environments.

TABLE 1.2. STRENGTHS AND WEAKNESSES OF CONDUCTING DISCUSSIONS IN FACE-TO-FACE AND COMPUTER-MEDIATED LEARNING ENVIRONMENTS.

	Computer-Mediated Environment (Asynchronous Text-Based Discussion)	Face-to-Face Environment (In-Class Discussion)
Strengths	*Flexibility:* Students can contribute to the discussion at the time and place that is most convenient to them. *Participation:* All students can participate because time and place constraints are removed. *Depth of reflection:* Learners have time to more carefully consider and provide evidence for their claims and provide deeper, more thoughtful reflections (Mikulecky, 1998; Benbunan-Fich & Hiltz, 1999).	*Human connection:* It is easier to bond and develop a social presence in a face-to-face environment. This makes it easier to develop trust. *Spontaneity:* Allows the generation of rapid chains of associated ideas and serendipitous discoveries (Mikulecky, 1998).
Weaknesses	*Spontaneity:* Does not encourage the generation of rapid chains of associated ideas and serendipitous discoveries (Mikulecky, 1998). *Procrastination:* There may be a tendency toward procrastination (Benbunan-Fich & Hiltz, 1999). *Human connection:* The medium is considered to be impersonal by many (Benbunan-Fich & Hiltz, 1999), which may cause a lower satisfaction level with the process (Haytko, 2001).	*Participation:* Cannot always have everyone participate, especially if there are dominating personalities. *Flexibility:* Limited time, which means that you may not be able to reach the discussion depth that you would like.

Although Table 1.2 certainly does not contain all of the possible strengths and weaknesses of conducting discussions in the face-to-face and CM environments, instructors might use this understanding to make decisions about whether to use one or the other or both learning environments to meet instructional goals. For example, by understanding the affordances of face-to-face and CM environments, an instructor of a large-enrollment class might choose to use the CM environment so that everyone in the class can contribute to the discussion. Another instructor concerned about unmotivated students and procrastination might choose to use a face-to-face discussion where social presence and excitement for the topic can be communicated through voice as well as gesture. A third instructor might choose to blend the two learning environments, starting with a brief exploratory face-to-face discussion to generate excitement for the topic and set the stage for a more in-depth follow-up discussion online in a CM environment.

As we move into the future it is important that we continue to identify successful models of blended learning at the institutional, program, course, and activity levels that can be adapted to work in contexts. This effort will involve understanding and capitalizing on the unique affordances available in both face-to-face and computer-mediated or distributed learning environments.

References

Benbunan-Fich, R., & Hiltz, S. R. (1999). Educational applications of CMCS: Solving case studies through asynchronous learning networks. *Journal of Computer-Mediated Communication, 4*(3). Retrieved July 12, 2005, from http://jcmc.indiana.edu/vol4/issue3/benbunan-fich.html.

Bersin & Associates. (2003). *Blended learning: What works? An industry study of the strategy, implementation, and impact of blended learning.* Oakland, CA: Bersin & Associates.

Bonk, C. J., Olson, T., Wisher, R. A., & Orvis, K. L. (2002). Learning from focus groups: An examination of blended learning. *Journal of Distance Education, 17*(3), 97–118.

BYU-Idaho. *General education requirement.* BYU Idaho. Retrieved October 30, 2004, from http://www.byui.edu/catalog/2001–2002/GeneralEd.htm.

Clark, R. E. (1983). Reconsidering research on learning from media. *Review of Educational Research, 53*(4), 445–459.

Clark, R. E. (1994a). Media and method. *Educational Technology Research and Development, 42*(3), 7–10.

Clark, R. E. (1994b). Media will never influence learning. *Educational Technology Research and Development, 42*(2), 21–29.

Collis, B., Bruijstens, H., & van der Veen, J. K. (2003). Course redesign for blended learning: Modern optics for technical professionals. *International Journal of Continuing Engineering Education and Lifelong Learning, 13*(1/2), 22–38.

Cottrell, D., & Robison, R. (2003). Blended learning in an accounting course. *Quarterly Review of Distance Education, 4*(3), 261–269.

Driscoll, M. (2002, March 1). Blended learning: Let's get beyond the hype. *e-learning.* http://www.ltimagazine.com/ltimagazine/article/articleDetail.jsp?id=11755.Graham, C. R., & Allen, S. (2005). Blended learning: An emerging trend in education. In C. Howard, J. V. Boettecher, L. Justice, K. D. Schenk, P. L. Rogers, & G. A. Berg (Eds.), *Encyclopedia of distance learning* (pp. 172–179). Hershey, PA: Idea Group.

Graham, C. R., Allen, S., & Ure, D. (2003). *Blended learning environments: A review of the research literature.* Unpublished manuscript, Provo, UT.

Graham, C. R., Allen, S., & Ure, D. (2005). Benefits and challenges of blended learning environments. In M. Khosrow-Pour (Ed.), *Encyclopedia of information science and technology* (pp. 253–259). Hershey, PA: Idea Group.

Hartman, J. L., Dziuban, C., & Moskal, P. (1999, August 16–18). *Faculty satisfaction in ALNs: A dependent or independent variable?* Paper presented at the Sloan Summer ALN Workshops, Learning Effectiveness and Faculty Satisfaction, Urbana, IL.

Haytko, D. L. (2001). Traditional versus hybrid course delivery systems: A case study of undergraduate marketing planning courses. *Marketing Education Review, 11*(3), 27–39.

House, R. (2002, January 8). Clocking in column. *Spokesman-Review.*

Kozma, R. B. (1991). Learning with media. *Review of Educational Research, 61*(2), 179–211.

Kozma, R. B. (1994). Will media influence learning? Reframing the debate. *Educational Technology Research and Development, 42*(2), 7–19.

Levine, S. L., & Wake, W. K. (2000, October 20). *Hybrid teaching: Design studios in virtual space.* Paper presented at the National Conference on Liberal Arts and the Education of Artists, School of Visual Arts, New York.

Martyn, M. (2003). The hybrid online model: Good practice. *Educause Quarterly, 26*(1), 18–23.

Mikulecky, L. (1998). Diversity, discussion, and participation: Comparing Web-based and campus-based adolescent literature classes. *Journal of Adolescent and Adult Literacy, 42*(2), 84–97.

Morgan, K. R. (2002). *Blended learning: A strategic action plan for a new campus.* Seminole: University of Central Florida.

Orey, M. (2002a). *Definition of blended learning.* University of Georgia. Retrieved February 21, 2003, from http://www.arches.uga.edu/~mikeorey/blendedLearning.

Orey, M. (2002b). *One year of online blended learning: Lessons learned.* Paper presented at the Annual Meeting of the Eastern Educational Research Association, Sarasota, FL.

Osguthorpe, R. T., & Graham, C. R. (2003). Blended learning systems: Definitions and directions. *Quarterly Review of Distance Education, 4*(3), 227–234.

Pew. (2003). *Program in course redesign.* Center for Academic Transformation. Retrieved August, 20, 2003, from http://www.center.rpi.edu/PewGrant.html.

Reay, J. (2001). Blended learning—a fusion for the future. *Knowledge Management Review, 4*(3), 6.

Rooney, J. E. (2003). Blending learning opportunities to enhance educational programming and meetings. *Association Management, 55*(5), 26–32.

Rossett, A. (2002). *The ASTD e-learning handbook.* New York: McGraw-Hill.

Rumble, G. (1992). Open learning. *Open Learning, 7*(2), 31–45.

Sands, P. (2002). Inside outside, upside downside: Strategies for connecting online and face-to-face instruction in hybrid courses. *Teaching with Technology Today, 8*(6). Retrieved July 12, 2005, from http://www.uwsa.edu/ttt/articles/sands2.htm. .

Singh, H., & Reed, C. (2001). *A white paper: Achieving success with blended learning.* Centra Software. Retrieved July 12, 2005, from http://www.centra.com/download/whitepapers/blendedlearning.pdf.

Smelser, L. M. (2002, March 20–23). *Making connections in our classrooms: Online and off.* Paper presented at the Annual Meeting of the Conference on College Composition and Communication, Chicago.

Thomson, I. (2002). *Thomson job impact study: The next generation of corporate learning.* Retrieved July 7, 2003, from http://www.netg.com/DemosAndDownloads/Downloads/JobImpact.pdf.

U.S. Department of Education. (2001). *The condition of education 2001.* Washington, DC: National Center for Educational Statistics.

Waddoups, G., & Howell, S. (2002). Bringing online learning to campus: The hybridization of teaching and learning at Brigham Young University. *International Review of Research in Open and Distance Learning, 2*(2). Retrieved July 12, 2005, from http://www.irrodl.org/content/v2.2/waddoups.html.

Wang, X. C., Kanfer, A., Hinn, D. M., & Arvan, L. (2001). Stretching the boundaries: Using ALN to reach on-campus students during an off-campus summer session. *Journal of Asynchronous Learning Networks, 5*(1), 1–20.

Ward, J., & LaBranche, G. A. (2003). Blended learning: The convergence of e-learning and meetings. *Franchising World, 35*(4), 22–23.

West, R. E., & Graham, C. R. (2005). Five powerful ways technology can enhance teaching and learning in higher education. *Educational Technology, 45*(3), 20–27.

Young, J. R. (2002, March 22). "Hybrid" teaching seeks to end the divide between traditional and online instruction. *Chronicle of Higher Education*, p. A33.

Charles R. Graham is an assistant professor of instructional psychology and technology at Brigham Young University with a focus on technology-mediated teaching and learning. He earned his doctorate in instructional systems technology at Indiana University, where he worked for the Center for Research on Learning and Technology and helped to develop an online professional development environment for K-12 teachers. He has an M.S. in electrical and computer engineering from the University of Illinois, where he helped to develop an asynchronous learning environment used in many undergraduate engineering courses. His research interests include the study of online collaborative learning environments and the use of technology to enhance teaching and learning.

CHAPTER TWO

THE BLENDED LEARNING IMPERATIVE

Elliott Masie

All learning is blended learning! That is a bold statement and reflects our view of the definition of blended learning: the use of two or more styles of content or context delivery or discovery.

In 1998, the training field popularized the term *blended learning* to refer to the mixture of e-learning and classroom learning. Many people started to use it as a way of addressing what they perceived to be the structural weaknesses of e-learning at that time, mainly in its limited ability to foster interaction, context, and remediation.

However, blended learning has always been a major part of the landscape of training, learning, and instruction. Think back to your best class in college. The faculty member often used a pedagogical approach that might have included:

- Formal lectures
- Classroom discussion
- Homework or reading assignments
- Development of papers
- Group projects
- Assessments or exams
- One-to-one coaching during office hours

In addition, the learners made the blend even richer with the following strategies:

- Conversations between peers
- Sharing notes
- Study sessions
- Library research
- Checking with former students about exams or grading models

Why all of these elements? Because as complex beings, we don't learn in a simple or uniform fashion. Even when all learning seems to be confined to a single delivery system, such as a classroom or an online class, learners often break out of those confines and independently enrich the material.

Reasons for Creating Blended Learning

Learners and their teachers and trainers have always created overt or covert blended learning for many compelling reasons. We look at seven of them.

Multiple Perspectives on Content

Learners are a varied group of individuals and have a varied set of learning styles. They seem to achieve higher mastery of content when they can take multiple passes through the material and deal with it through different learning processes.

Cognitive Rehearsal

David and Roger Johnson, pioneers of collaborative education in the K-12 space, termed the phrase *cognitive rehearsal* to refer to the process by which learners master newly presented material by talking about the content (Johnson & Johnson, 1985). For example, a colleague comes back from a management class and talks to her spouse or cubicle mate about the newly acquired content. Ironically, the value of this conversation is often richer for the speaker than the listener. Johnson and Johnson have often referred to this as "hearing the content for the second time from your own lips." We see this often in the e-learning world as learners push back from their terminals and start to discuss the screen-based material with a neighbor.

Context Is Often More Important Than Content

I am a strong proponent of the vital need to raise the status of and recognition for context. It is easy to author and deliver content. Most e-learning is filled with organizationally approved content. Yet learners have an incredible thirst and instructional need for context, the unofficial and peer-validated view of the authored content. The classroom instructor delivers the content as reflected in the Power-Point slides or courseware. Then she takes a few steps to the right or left of the podium and tells the story about how the content is really being implemented, and that is what people remember. One of the key values that face-to-face or other interactions have in the blended learning model is the ability to add context.

Value Sorting Is Core to Blended Learning

One of the behaviors that the learner is always struggling through is their need to sort the content by value. There are three general sorting categories:

High-value stuff: The content and context that I need to remember, even memorize. It is what I take away from this learning activity.

Medium-value stuff: The content and context that I might need to use at some future date. I will become familiar with it but won't memorize it. I know how to get to it when and if I need it.

No-value stuff: The content that I don't need and won't bother to learn or think about.

Blended learning provides a richer environment for learners to make these decisions. In fact, instructional designers often are in denial about this core sorting process and naively believe that all content is equally important. One of the prime drivers from the learner point of view toward blended learning is the need to reduce and target learning objectives and activities. Multiple processes and models increase the learner's ability to sort.

Learning Is Longitudinal

Much of the dialogue about e-learning has been about the acceleration and compression of learning time. A clear benefit of e-learning can be to accelerate the access of a learner to knowledge. Yet sometimes we have to accept that learning is accomplished over time. The blended learning model fits nicely into this longitudinal view of knowledge acquisition. A learner will learn computer security techniques over a period of weeks or months, mixing formal and informal bursts of training. What we have to work on is to make our assessment and evaluation processes more aligned to longitudinal learning. Let's move beyond testing for competency at the end of a short module. Why not shift the assessment to a more object-based and over-time paradigm?

Learning Is Social

As humans, we thrive on social experiences, and learning is one of those very primal social experiences. Yet the role of a student is often structured to be quite unsocial. We often see the student as a passive viewer of slides, listener of lectures, screen and mouse clicker, or quiet taker of evaluations. Blended learning recognizes and aligns with the social dimensions of learning.

Learning Is Often Tacit and Unstructured

Some of the most powerful training experiences are often unconventional and not in the common tool kit of an instructional designer. Consider a lunch conversation. A new manager will probably get more value and learning from a targeted invitation to have lunch with a senior mentor than from several hours in a class or several modules in an e-learning course. When we expand our thinking about blended learning, we recognize that these experiences are a big piece of the mix. We can take a great online course and add invitations to lunch, tours of the factory, open structured online searches, and other nontraditional elements to supercharge the learning.

Conclusion

I started to use the phrase "magic is in the mix" when *blended learning* became popular as a term in the 1990s. The magic is the power of adding two or more learning elements. Learners have always known this. They have been blended learning for thousands of years. They add what is missing, they mix it with what they need, and they subtract what is not valuable. They socialize it. They find context. And they transform training and instruction into learning.

Our imperative is to accept and embrace blended learning. We can even stop using the word *blended* just as we can stop using the letter *e* in *e-learning*. Great learning is blended. And learning in the 2000s will always have an element of *e*.

We have to change much to move toward accepting and leveraging blended learning. The imperative must be embraced by:

- Instructional designers, who must expand their models and templates to include blended learning.
- Learning and training organizations, which must encourage blended learning through their marketing and charge-back models.

- Technology and system suppliers, who must develop authoring tools, learning systems, and content collections to allow blended learning in a rapid development era.
- Learners, who must continue to see blended learning as a natural aspect of what they do and not an extender of training time.

Blended learning is an imperative. It reflects the blended nature of our world, our workforce, and the natural process of how people really learn.

Reference

Johnson, D. W., & Johnson, R. T. (1985). Classroom conflict: Controversy versus debate in learning groups. *American Educational Research Journal, 22*(2), 237–256.

Elliott Masie is an internationally recognized futurist, analyst, researcher, and humorist on the critical topics of technology, business, learning, and workplace productivity. He is the editor of *TRENDS by Elliott Masie,* an Internet newsletter, and a regular columnist in professional publications. He recently authored a free digital book, *701 E-Learning Tips.* Masie serves as an adviser to a wide range of government, education, and nonprofit groups.

CHAPTER THREE

WHY BLENDED LEARNING HASN'T (YET) FULFILLED ITS PROMISES

Answers to Those Questions That Keep You Up at Night

Jennifer Hofmann

I am a product of Public Television. As a child, my hours of daytime television were limited to the line-up on local channel 13. *Mr. Rogers' Neighborhood* taught me about how to interact and "play nice." *Sesame Street* introduced counting, the alphabet, and how to identify commonality among objects. ("One of these things is not like the other . . .")

The Electric Company opened up the world of multiplication tables and grammar. Whenever I think of the silent letter *E*, I recall that words are indeed more powerful than a locomotive.

On Saturday mornings I was fixated not on the cartoons depicting superheroes and talking animals but on the enchanting series *Schoolhouse Rock!*. Those wonderful five-minute videos explained the U.S. Constitution, the line-up of the planets in the solar system, and the difference between verbs and adjectives.

I could read just about anything by the age of five. What was missing was reading comprehension. The meaning of the words eluded me. To master that advanced skill, I needed to be exposed to those more expert than I: parents, teachers, and older children. Aha! My first (successful) blended learning experience.

Is it any wonder that I embrace the concept of alternative learning technologies? I instinctively knew the value before I was even a teenager. As an adult, however, the results have been far less satisfying.

Why Is Blended Learning the Current Trend?

Those of us who have been in the training profession for any length of time know that there are always trends and fads. We've been introduced to learning organizations, life-long learning, matrixed teams, learning communities, and a myriad other concepts. Although these practices all have true merit, it takes quite a bit of effort to implement the requisite changes. Worse still, such ideas are often just introduced at the conceptual level and forgotten about at the next reorganization or management change.

So why is blended learning a true shift in our profession instead of a passing fad? In part, it makes significant economic sense that even the bean counters can see immediately. Blended learning also makes sense due to the emergence of geographically dispersed work environments in which staffing levels are constantly being changed. While one part of an organization is being downsized, requiring fewer people to accomplish more work, another part of the organization is growing and hiring.

Gone are the days when we could start all new employees at the same time and conduct two-day orientation programs. Flying instructors and participants around to attend training classes is not economical and is often disruptive to business and personal relationships. Unlike old training models and expectations, we need our training now! Not a month ago, when we didn't have the need for it; not in two weeks, after we have been struggling and making up ways of getting our work done. Now! There is a true need for just-in-time training.

Traditional classroom approaches are not very flexible, and they are expensive. We often wait until we can fill a class before we teach it and hope that the need for the classroom coincides with one being available. The blended learning experience, incorporating synchronous (or live and online) classrooms, makes it cost-effective to train small groups or even provide one-on-one coaching. And these blended classes can be offered more frequently without incurring a lot of extra costs, so a participant who cannot attend a training session on Tuesday or is called away because of an emergency can simply enroll in the next offering.

Since blended learning can have a positive effect the bottom line and can theoretically increase the skills and knowledge of the entire organization, management tends to support and, more important, persist in supporting this shift to nontraditional delivery methods.

A Chronology of Learning Delivery Technologies

For decades, training professionals have had a wide menu of learning technologies from which to choose. Historically, the opportunity to pick and choose from different delivery technologies has been around since at least the 1800s. In addition to the traditional Socratic and Didactic classroom models, educators have had access to a wide variety of tools that were cutting edge when they were introduced:

1450—Johannes Gutenberg introduces the first Western printing press

1840—First correspondence study (a secretarial program focused on teaching shorthand)

1900s—Audio recordings

1920s—Radio stations

1930s—Television

1960s—Satellite

1960s—Pre–World Wide Web Internet (text-based databases and discussion boards)

1980s—Fiber optic, audiovisual tech/CD-ROM

1990s to the present—World Wide Web

There was great excitement with the introduction of each of these technologies. We educators and trainers kept thinking that the nut was finally cracked and had discovered the best and most efficient way for people to learn.

Edison, with his invention of the moving picture, predicted that we would eventually never need to attend a class again; we would just need to attend recorded lectures of experts in order to become educated. Sound familiar? We (the training profession) have jumped on similar bandwagons with the introduction of every delivery technology since. Somehow we are still using traditional methods as much as ever before.

Imaginative educators, with the assistance of technical experts, have found ways to exploit and combine (or blend) these technologies to meet their learning objectives.

Where We Are Today?

New conventional wisdom and years of academic research tell us that the best programs are a blend of learning technologies. Blending technologies that take advantage of learning styles, learner convenience, and the best practices of instructional design enable course developers to create programs that engage the learner and maximize learning retention. For this reason, mixing the best blend of learning technologies is a critical success factor in creating effective learning of any kind. And the new online learning technologies are so varied, widely available, and relatively inexpensive that creating this type of effective learning experience is something that almost any content development team can do.

And that's great—except (and this probably won't surprise many of you) it hasn't been working. Of course, this is a generalization. You can turn to many chapters in this book to find examples of successfully blended initiatives that met or exceeded expectations, and we can learn from every one of them. Still, most organizations have yet to break the code and create a successful truly blended experience.

So What's the Problem, Really?

We have identified the need for a blended solution; we have technology that can support a wide variety of designs and delivery methods; we have experts who can create the content; and organizations have budgets supporting the design and development of such programs. So what's the problem with this underwhelming return on investment and expectations on a seemingly-can't-lose scenario?

Actually, there are issues that have historically created roadblocks for blended learning initiatives. These are at the heart of why blended learning has not yet fulfilled its promise of being the best way to deliver information since Gutenberg invented the printing press:

Designing Blended Learning Experiences

- Creating programs without using a formal design process
- Assuming that redesigning an existing program is easier than starting from scratch
- Stringing together stand-alone components into a learning path instead of truly weaving learning experiences together

Facilitating Blended Learning Experiences

- Overemphasizing the live components and undervaluing the self-directed components of the blend
- Lack of experience on the part of the training team in facilitating the blend
- No formal training for the implementation team

Supporting Blended Learning Experiences

- Lack of organizational understanding, and therefore support for blended programs
- Inexperienced learners who have not been taught how to learn online

In the rest of this chapter, I address these issues and others, and provide answers to those burning questions that are keeping you up at night.

Designing Blended Learning Experiences

During my early days as a training professional, I employed, I admit, techniques that were less than structured. I worked in financial services and delivered custom software training to medical professionals. Back then I designed programs by talking with the subject matter expert (SME) and "designing" on my best instinct, generally with a positive result. Then my team was told we would be trained to be instructional designers, and we rebelled. How dare they tell us we need to be trained on a function we had been performing well until then?

Twelve years, multiple workshops, and a master's degree in instructional technology later, and now I am not only a convert but an evangelist. So as a card-carrying, blue-blooded instructional designer, I'll tell you that any type of program, from a one-hour "lunch and learn" to a five-day "boot camp," should be formally designed. I'll tell you that, but realistically I know that doesn't happen.

Experienced designers (cum trainers) often know their audiences and content so thoroughly that they can create effective presentations and training interventions with minimal design actually written down on paper. That is not to say that programs are not designed, just that the experienced team always needs to identify subordinate skill objectives and domains of learning formally. Pilots are informal, if they occur at all. Programs can be rapidly created and deployed. When a skilled trainer identifies design gaps by looking at confused or bored faces or interpreting negative body language, the design is modified on the fly, and can often go unnoticed by the audience.

We simply cannot get away with this practice when creating a blended learning experience. Lack of a formal instructional design process is much more obvious in a nontraditional environment. Even worse, the participants are most often aware of the issues before the blended learning facilitator. Without the immediate opportunity for eye contact, body language, or (in self-directed formats) verbal feedback, we cannot easily ascertain if a participant understands instructions or content. As a result, participants often leave these programs confused, unsatisfied, and, worst of all, without the training they need. And we may never know it.

I follow the same instructional systems design (ISD) process I was taught over a decade ago. That happens to be the Dick and Carey model (Dick, Carey, & Carey, 2004). (There are others that are just as legitimate.) This ISD process suggests the following process for the creation of any training intervention.

Stages of Instructional Systems Design

1. Identification of instructional goals
2. Subordinate skill analysis
3. Learner and context analysis
4. Construction of performance objectives
5. Identification of assessment techniques
6. Identification of instructional strategies
7. Determination of appropriate delivery media
8. Course development
9. Evaluation

The key here is Step 7: determination of appropriate delivery media. Most of us find this to be quite unusual. We are accustomed to starting a project already knowing what the delivery medium will be. ISD tells us that just about everything is done before you determine what tools will be used to deliver the content.

In a world where our clients/managers/sponsors come to us and say that they need a four-hour Web-based course on how to package cheese effectively, this process seems unrealistic. We talk to our experts, we look at our resources, and we build our courses based on the client's stated specifications. With the time lines and budgets available to us, this seems to be the most expeditious solution.

If we had the time for a formal ISD process, we might often discover that the delivery method requested by the client was not at all appropriate for the audience, content, technology, or budget. This is perhaps the most important argument in favor of formal design. Going down the wrong delivery path results in less-than-optimal learning results and can eventually lead to an undertrained workforce, a drained development budget, and a lack of confidence in the training team.

How Do We Design the Blend?

The most common instructional design question I am asked when discussing blending learning technologies is, "What can be taught online?" Of course, there are some subjects that just don't seem to lend themselves to an online approach. But you don't know what these subjects are until you go though the instructional design process.

Do not restrict your options by looking at an entire subject (or goal). Look at each individual objective. Understanding your objectives gives you the flexibility to determine the best way to deliver each component.

Here are a few things to keep in mind when considering your blend:

• Some objectives may be best taught in a traditional classroom, like completing technical lab work. Think of those kinesthetic task-based objectives that can result in disastrous outcomes when not performed well. (I still want my future brain surgeon to practice on real people with a seasoned doctor nearby.)

• Maybe you need an expert available in a live format but don't need true face-to-face interaction. For instance, if there is a need for application demonstrations and instructions, a live, online classroom (synchronous) would work well for the demonstration. In addition, participants might be able to toggle to their desktops to practice the techniques. With such an approach, immediate access to experts is still available, and participants leave this component of the curriculum having already applied their new knowledge.

• Objectives requiring memorization and knowledge absorption might lend themselves best to self-directed approaches. These objectives tend to be verbal and are often easy to identify. In a traditional environment, these verbal objectives are often taught in a lecture format. Note that when the verbal content is more advanced and clarifications need to made throughout, self-directed may not be the appropriate choice. A good gauge may be to ask yourself how many questions or clarifications are needed when the information is delivered in a traditional format. If it is minimal, self-directed might be a valid alternative.

By carefully determining the most appropriate ways to deliver the content at the objective level, you craft the most effective blend of technologies and can weave together a true curriculum. Be careful not to create individual stand-alone modules, string them together, and call it a blend. The modules need to be tied together and built on one another. Only then is the learning experience complete.

There is no specific recipe for mixing up the ingredients of the blend. The amount of traditional classroom, synchronous classroom, and self-directed work is prescribed by the identified learning objectives and resulting design. And the self-directed work does not need to be expensive multimedia. Workbooks, reading assignments, discussion boards, and e-mail are all easy to use, inexpensive to implement, and extremely effective when designed and facilitated well.

Don't assume it's going to take less time to redesign an existing traditional program than it would to design a blended program from scratch. Always approach these initiatives from a fresh perspective, and you won't be worried about slaying the sacred cows of successful traditional programs.

What Is the Role of Community in Designing Blended Learning Experiences

One of the most exciting opportunities afforded by blended learning experiences is the opportunity to create learning communities. All of us have participated in traditional learning programs, but how often do we interact with other students after the program is complete? Often we cannot even recall the names of people sitting adjacent to us.

One of the benefits of a blended learning curriculum that includes asynchronous collaboration between participants is that they tend to form more long-lasting relationships and rely on each other after the formal experience is over. E-mail, instant messaging, and community discussion boards facilitate the participants' seeing each other as resources, especially since communication is only a click away. Earlier, I spoke of learning communities as a potential trendy fad. With the right design, blended learning can turn the jargon of learning communities into a reality.

How Do We Know if the Blend Works?

The last, and ever continuous, step in the ISD model is evaluation, and a critical component of evaluation is piloting. For most of us, creating truly blended experiences that are not grounded in the traditional classroom is new. Because of this, a pilot test or sample becomes even more crucial to success.

In such a pilot, you should implement your program including all participant materials, leader materials, and technologies. Use a representative audience as well as facilitators trained in the use of the various delivery technologies. Keep your design team close at hand so it can evaluate the design. Pay special attention to instructions. This is where many blended programs fall apart. Can participants follow the instructions easily with minimal to no questions? If not, serious consequences will surely ensue. Participants will either stop moving forward with the program or will struggle to try to complete the experience and find it less than satisfying.

Assessment and continuous improvement should continue even once the program is out of the pilot phase. When problems are identified, they should be fixed and communicated immediately.

Facilitating Blended Learning Experiences

Concurrent with the design process, the training team should be considering another critical success factor: how to facilitate the blended learning experience.

Do not make the assumption that traditional facilitators for a particular subject are the best choices for managing the blended version of the same content. Effective classroom facilitators rely heavily on the ability to manage the room by interpreting eye contact and body language. They may also have a physically animated personality that is visually engaging to their audiences. These individuals have invested quite a bit of their professional credibility in their physical presence.

Online instruction takes the physical language of the classroom away and replaces it with many nonverbal and nonphysical cues that may (in the case of a synchronous classroom) or may not (during self-directed activities) be available in real time. Add to this the need to manage the technical aspects and associated problems that accompany blended learning experiences, and we have truly created a new job description, not simply added to the existing definition of *trainer.*

Remember that the entire blended learning experience, including the self-directed components, is instructor led. There is a different level of commitment for the blended learning facilitators, who are forced to pay attention to the participants' welfare before, during, and after all live events. Well-designed participant materials certainly help to manage the process, but the program is not over once the participants leave the building.

A blended solution can contain many components. Asynchronous components may include technologies ranging from self-directed tutorials to facilitated discussion boards. Synchronous technologies range from traditional classrooms to virtual online classrooms. We need to be careful not to overemphasize the live (synchronous) and undervalue the asynchronous components of the blend. All aspects, including assessment, required communication, participation, and exercise completion, need to be considered as important as attending any live (live meaning face-to-face or synchronous online) events. We need to remember to reinforce the blend, so that participants understand the importance as well. Otherwise participants will wait for the live events to obtain the "important stuff," and the blend will not be successful. The technology, not the implementation, will be seen as ineffective, and future blended learning projects will not be as warmly embraced.

How Do We Get It All Done?

During synchronous interactions, many trainers opt not to take advantage of all of the tools available to increase interaction. They can't see themselves being able to multitask to the extent required, so they limit participant use of chat, whiteboard tools, and other interactive features of the synchronous classroom. The trainer's role in the synchronous classroom is then reduced to pushing content and lecturing instead of facilitating interactions and knowledge sharing.

The self-directed components of the blend pose different problems. It is difficult to keep up with all discussion board postings, required e-mails, off-line technical and instructional support, and the amount of communication needed to keep the participants on track. The solution to this dilemma lies in the idea of team teaching. An assistant trainer (I call this person a *producer*) can help transform blended programs into trouble-free, interesting, interactive events that keep learners involved and the trainer on track. In short, the trainer can stay focused on content while the producer takes care of everything else. This person does not need to be an expensive resource. I have used training assistants and interns to great result, and at the same time created a job path for these individuals in the training department.

How Do We Teach Our Team?

Because many of the technologies included in a blend are so new and the ways these technologies can be arranged are so varied, a serious concern is the lack of facilitator experience in managing the blend. Without experience as a participant and formal training, facilitators have little choice but to approach the initiative in the same ways as they would a traditional learning experience. They then are left to learn from their mistakes. This can be frustrating for the facilitator and can have a negative impact on results.

To prepare to manage a blended program, new facilitators should:

• Participate in as many blended learning experiences as possible. Enroll in programs that allow them to participate as a learner and experience the same types of problems. This will help them to understand participant questions and frustrations and deal with them appropriately.

• Learn how to use all of the technologies ("point-and-click" training) that may be included in the blend. The desired level of mastery is the ability of the facilitator to answer participants' technical questions without being able to see their screens. ("Look for the letter *A* in your whiteboard toolbar, which is located in the upper left corner of the screen. The letter *A* is located directly under the Help pull-down menu . . . ")

• Learn how to facilitate the individual technologies. There are nuances that need to be learned and practiced in order to achieve mastery. Facilitating each type of technology is different, and those differences need to be appreciated.

• Practice managing the blend. After facilitators have mastered the technology, they should review the participant guides and leader materials and make sure they understand the exercises and can articulate the connections between the different components. When recorded synchronous sessions are available, they should be viewed. The designer should be available to answer questions and the producer available to help prepare.

Train the Trainer Using Blended Learning

I recently created a curriculum for a client that exposes the training team to all of the preparation components mentioned above. Most sessions listed in Table 3.1 are delivered using a synchronous classroom. Sessions 3 and 4 are delivered in a traditional format. All programs are followed by independent work in discussion areas and distributed group work in which small groups create and deliver a blended solution. Virtual office hours are formally scheduled to support the initiative, and all live events are recorded for those who must miss a class. A seventy-five-page participant guide, two textbooks, and a list of online readings support the content. By participating in this program, learners are exposed to (and immersed in) a true blended learning curriculum. The "collaboratory" (session 4) exposes participants to developing these nontraditional programs and provides resources for achieving mastery.

You will notice that modules on designing blended learning are included. It is always a good idea to train the design and facilitation teams together so these individuals mutually understand the strategy for the design and the unique experience of the blended learning facilitator.

Supporting Blended Learning Experiences

Having a robust design and a well-prepared facilitation team are truly critical to the success of the program. In addition, the organization needs to be ready to support all aspects of the blend. Often, implementing blended learning is considered a technology initiative. An organization would be much better served looking at it as a change initiative. Let's face it: someone will be able to make the technology work (if not, it will be replaced). Let information technology worry about technology issues.

We are asking people to teach and learn in very different ways, without properly preparing the organization for this change. The most challenging part of changing the learning culture is impressing on participants that prework and intersession work is not optional. We seem to have become a culture that believes that if a particular concept is important, the facilitator will discuss it during the

TABLE 3.1. BLENDED LEARNING TRAIN-THE-TRAINER DETAILED AGENDA.

Session 1	Session 2	Session 3	Session 4	Session 5
Learn How to Learn Online Focuses on learning in the online environment; demystifies the technology for the participants so they have a positive learning	*e-Learning 101* Addresses definitions and terminology, demonstrates various delivery technologies, and introduces the changing roles of instructional designers, facilitators, and learners	*The Basics of Blending* Introduces blending asynchronous, synchronous, and traditional learning technologies	*Collaboratory!* Hands-on, experiential interaction with various delivery technologies	*Ready, Willing, and Able* Addresses preparing the learners for online learning

Session 6	Session 7	Session 8	Final Project	Session 9
More on Blended Learning Design After introducing a media selection matrix, participants work in breakout rooms to create blended solutions based on case study examples	*Facilitating Online Learning* Focuses on online interactions and the nuances of facilitating synchronous, asynchronous deliveries, and blended; teaches the critical steps to prepare to train online.	*Creating Materials for the Blended Classroom* Provides design strategies for creating learner-centered materials that tie together synchronous and asynchronous components of blended online programs.	*Practicum* In this individualized project, participants design, assemble, and deliver a blended program.	*Implementing E-Learning Within the Organization* Discusses partnering with IT, vendors, consultants, and management and the marketing of the e-learning initiative to ensure its acceptance and success.

live event. While blended experiences are very learner centered and participants need to make decisions regarding their priorities, they need to realize that the drastically reduced live time does not allow us to reteach content that was supposed to be reviewed prior to the live event. All components of the blend are equally important, and we should not overemphasize the live events.

How Do We Prepare the Organization?

In order for a blended solution to be successful, we need to prepare organizations to support the change. For organizations introducing these concepts, we are changing the learning culture, and even individuals open to and supporting the change will experience frustrations and doubts.

To create your change plan, I suggest the following conceptual framework:

1. Being *ready* means having the requisite skills and training needed to be successful.

    Provide technology training to facilitators, participants, and technical support staff.

    Ensure that participant desktops have necessary hardware, software, and bandwidth.

    Train facilitators to manage the blend effectively.

    Provide a learner orientation to teach participants how to be successful online learners in your organization.

2. Being *willing* means believing that the blended solutions can work and the time invested is worthwhile.

    Publish success stories to motivate participants to enroll.

    Create early successes for participants by starting with less intensive blends.

    Have facilitators work closely with designers so the strategy behind the blend is understood.

3. Being *able* means having an organization that actively supports the new learning culture.

    Participants need to be able to feel as if they can be successful at desktop learning and will not be interrupted by coworkers or managers.

    Participants need to be recognized for successful completion by the learning being recognized in performance reviews.

    Facilitators need the time to prepare to teach and manage the self-directed components of the blend.

    Designers need time to pilot and continuously revise designs to ensure the program meets its stated objectives.

Conclusion

Blended learning is more than the delivery technologies; it is certainly not a plug-and-play proposition. Instead, it is a shift in our profession. It takes time and effort to be successful at blended learning. We need to embrace new ideas about the way we design content, the way we facilitate programs, and the way participants learn. We also need to enable organizational success by providing tools, training, and support to all of the key stakeholders. We will all experience some less-than-successful programs. It will be frustrating, and sometimes we will doubt it was worth the effort. But if the required time and effort are expended, we will soon start to see the promises of blended learning come to fruition. We will have programs that are effective, memorable, and maybe even fun. Maybe even as memorable and fun as my Saturday morning *Schoolhouse Rock!*

Reference

Dick, W. O., Carey, L., & Carey, J. O. (2004). *The systematic design of instruction* (6th ed.). Needham Heights, MA: Allyn & Bacon.

Jennifer Hofmann is the principal eLearning consultant at InSync Training, a consulting firm that specializes in the design and delivery of synchronous eLearning. In the field since 1997, she has experience using all of the major synchronous delivery platforms. She is the author of *The Synchronous Trainer's Survival Guide: Facilitating Successful Live and Online Courses, Meetings and Events* (2003), and *Live and Online! Tips, Techniques, and Ready-To-Use Activities for the Virtual Classroom* (2004). She also moderates InSync Center, an online community for synchronous training professionals.

CHAPTER FOUR

ON DESIGNING INTERACTION EXPERIENCES FOR THE NEXT GENERATION OF BLENDED LEARNING

Ellen D. Wagner

We live in a world where we send e-mail from our personal digital assistants (PDAs) and can shoot a digital movie with our mobile phone and then post it to a personal Web site while waiting at a stoplight. We have real-time online chats with colleagues, as well as with family and friends, in the middle of meetings. Global positioning services (GPS) make sure we will never be lost again. Text messaging and mobile instant messaging services raise expectations for new varieties of telephone and Web services alike. Presence-sensing technologies and peer-to-peer networks take the notion of the "next best thing to being there" to new levels. Connected, converged media surround us in everyday life. The vision of a world where ubiquitous, pervasive, and fully interactive access to information is available for all citizens becomes more real every day.

No vision for the future of learning is complete until we can imagine the power of converged digital and mobile technologies for education, training, and performance support. The potential reach of the mobile and personal device market alone makes it worth considering the size and range of the opportunities. Malik (2004) recently noted that the 620 million cell phones sold annually are creating insatiable demand for applications and content. When also considering the more than 500 million personal computers estimated to be in use on a global basis (International Data Corporation, 2004), more than 1 billion devices have the potential to create, store, display, and distribute digital content.

Significant opportunities currently exist for creators, publishers, distributors, and managers of digital content for industries such as news, media business publishing, and education and training. With the promise of digital device ubiquity, high-quality multimedia content must also be available for mobile phones and PDAs, upping the ante on digital skills competencies in industries beyond art and design. Anecdotal evidence that only 10 percent of the world's population is currently "online" (W. Hodgins, personal communication, August 30, 2004) suggests that we are standing at the front edge of a significant adoption curve.

The broad extension of wireless networks continues to raise expectations for what a well-connected world should look like and what should be expected from one's personal—and business—personal communication and computing tools. Civic initiatives, such as OneCleveland (http://ramble.case.edu/its/news/archives/000103.html), an initiative launched by Case Western Reserve University in 2003 to provide public access to broadband wireless computer networks, are now being met by responses from other cities. For example, in June 2004, Mayor John Street of Philadelphia announced plans to make wireless access available for the entire city of Philadelphia (http://www.imakenews.com/innovationphiladelphia/e_article000300850.cfm?x=b3vn5LM,b1NyrLJC).

Clearly, with capabilities for Web conferencing and digital television, streaming audio and video, voice-over-IP or digital telephony emerging at the time when the world of cellular communications stands on the early curve of product ubiquity, it seems likely that anytime, anywhere access to information is about to become the norm. And when considered in the context of continually expanding use of wireless computer networks and the emergence of personal digital devices and handheld computers that provide the necessary power for successful mobile computing, the promise for fully integrated technology in the service of true lifelong learning seems within reach.

What kind of demand will there be for digital content for learning? Will flexible digital content make it possible to truly personalize blended learning experiences? Will blended learning give universities and colleges the means of participating in the upcoming digital content revolution?

Digital content currently available for mobile and personal devices tends to feature online services such as news, sports, entertainment, and weather. Downloads for tones, songs, and digital images are popular with consumers. Two very successful digital content offerings are aimed at personal entertainment, featuring music services and gaming. Mobile device users increasingly demand rich user experiences from the mobile telephone and network services providers.

So where can one find digital educational content? Federated repositories, including but certainly not limited to such initiatives as MERLOT (the Multimedia Educational Resource for Learning and Online Teaching; www.merlot.org), the ARIADNE European Knowledge Pool (http://www.ariadne-eu.org/), and EdNA, the Education Network Australia (http://www.edna.edu.au) continue to grow. Repositories formed around a shared interest encourage discipline-specific content. These repositories feature many file and form types and are created by subject matter experts for peers and students to be available by and for relevant communities of interest and practice. Publishers have created extensive collections of digital learning content to accompany textbooks and are now finding that demand is growing for content that works as a component inside a learning management system. Digital marketplaces such as Macromedia Central (http://www.macromedia.com/software/central/) also look to promote and enable the exchange of files, applets, and applications for a range of devices including computers, PDAs, communicators, and mobile phones. And while all this activity occurs, connected communication networks continue to extend their reach and capacity, spurring future growth.

The Next Wave of Blended Learning: Education Unplugged

Welcome to a world of occasionally connected, fully interactive digital learning experiences. Rich Internet applications for learning take advantage of distribution media such as WiFi and cellular, ethernet and cable, and radio and television and provide rich learning content for the deployment on a variety of digital devices. Whether integrated into face-to-face, formal classes on campus or connected to online, self-paced learning (or some combination of both), education unplugged represents an evolution of blended learning that leverages the portability and utility of notebook and tablet computers, Palms and pocket PCs, telephones, communicators, and IPods, enabling rich multimedia experiences in a variety of forms.

What instructional paradigm could be better suited for exploiting the potential of education unplugged than blended learning? As *education unplugged* comes to stand for the body of practice that takes full advantage of digital content for learning, those ever-expanding converged networks will enable rich new opportunities for personalizing learning to emerge. Portable personal digital devices and flexible learning content represent opportunities for individualizing learning experiences by extending the blended learning paradigm. Now it includes courses and modular content, including both face-to-face and online learning experiences, in whatever combination makes the most sense given the audience, the context, and the criticality. Next-generation blended learning experiences, marked by the integration of mobile and personal devices, will evolve from face-to-face and online instructional blends toward a blend that also features modular content objects for personalizing, customizing, and enriching learning at times, and increasingly on terms, defined by the learner.

Evolving blended learning models provide the essential methodological scaffolding needed to effectively combine face-to-face instruction, online instruction, and arrays of content objects and assets of all form factors. For example, in such a blended learning scenario, a student may find himself participating in a face-to-face class discussion; he may then log in and complete an online mastery exercise or two, then copy some practice exercises to a PDA to take advantage of what David Metcalf (2002) calls "stolen moments for learning"—those times between classes or meetings while on the train or waiting for an appointment. Think about sending a text message with results of your practice sessions to someone in your virtual study group using your mobile phone—and getting a voice mail with feedback on your results when you arrive at the end of your flight.

The picture gets a little more complicated as wireless Web surfing becomes the norm rather than the exception. The always-accessible information access enabled by wireless devices literally burst open the walls of the classroom and rocks the locus of classroom control. Being able to check on facts and figures in the middle of a professor-led discussion democratizes classroom dynamics in previously unimaginable ways. It means richer and more productive online tools such as auto-generating messages in your course Web site's online calendar, reminding you to post your report on the course Web site before launching your browser for class. It also means being turbo-connected, where nobody is surprised when you receive a text message from a colleague in another state, warning you that you are being blogged—while you are in the midst of delivering that very presentation on which you are being blogged.

Why Interaction Matters

The ability to interact—with instructors, students, content interfaces, features, code, channels, and environments—is analogous to being connected. For technology-mediated learning, interaction is a key value proposition. Interaction has been and continues to be one of the most hotly debated constructs in the realms of distance learning, instructional design, and academic transformation, to name three. Interaction continues to be perceived as the defining attribute for quality and value in online learning experience. And while interactivity (equated with interaction) is no longer as expensive, unusual, or technologically challenging as it has been even in the recent past, interaction continues to be an essential component of a technology-mediated learning design success. As more and more distributed models of learning and collaboration emerge, interaction increasingly serves as the so-called glue that holds together all of those variables being blended. As noted by Moore and Kearsley

(1996), the more distributed the teaching and learning paradigm, the more critical the need for interaction.

Schools of Thought on Interaction

For the purposes of this discussion, interactions are defined as reciprocal events that require at least two objects and two actions. Interactions occur when the objects and events mutually influence one another (Wagner, 1994). A number of schools of thought have emerged in the past two decades that explore interaction in the context of technology-mediated learning. The rationale for doing so revolves around two commonly held beliefs:

- The perceived quality of a learning experience is directly proportional to and positively correlated with the degree to which that experience is seen as interactive.
- If technology-mediated learning designs are to have any significant impact on current and future pedagogical practices, then learning design and development decisions need to maximize the benefit of interaction.

The following section reviews several perspectives on interaction to compare and contrast aspects of each point of view. Although they are not presented in any particular chronological order, it is telling that a number of these views on interaction predate the current wave of connected personal digital tools and communication devices. Given the following discussion, a case can certainly be made for proposing a new dimension of the interaction that focuses on the interaction experience, technology mediated or otherwise.

Interactions as Transactions

For those subscribing to Michael G. Moore's views on the subject, interactions are transactions between teacher and learner, learner and learner, and learner and content (Moore, 1989). The addition of learner-interface interactions as proposed by Hillman, Willis, and Gunawardena (1994) was a nod in the direction of increasingly responsive computer systems and networks emerging in the early 1990s.

Quests to define interaction as an expression of the relationships between and among Moore's three interaction categories have shaped much of the current understanding of interaction in distance and online learning settings. In describing Moore's theory of transactional distance, Moore and Kearsley (1996) noted that transactional distance explores the relationship between structure (specifically a course design) and dialogue (referring to the communication between instructors and learners during implementation). It focuses on shifts in understanding and perception created by the separation of teachers and learners. Moore's model considered the relationships between teachers and students (as well as learners with learners and learners with content) by examining the effect that (transactional) distance has on instruction and learning. This interaction schema aimed to indicate who or what was to be involved in an interaction or transaction. The agents and directions of these transactions were as important as the perceived and real distance between and among them. However, the explicit description of an interaction's purposes, intents, and outcomes was open.

While Saba and Shearer (1994) validated the relationship between dialogue and structure, later explorations by Jung (2001) added a number of dimensions to Moore's theory that responded to the evolving sophistication of content creation tools, content distribution networks, and collaboration technologies. These new dimensions include considerations related to:

> *Infrastructure*—aimed at such issues as content expandability, content availability, and visual layout
>
> *Dialogue*—aimed at such issues as academic interaction, collaborative interaction, and interpersonal interaction
>
> *Learner collaboration*—aimed at issues such as the degree and quality of engagement with others
>
> *Learner autonomy*—aimed at issues related to the degree and quality of learner independence

Interactions as Outcomes

I got involved (Wagner, 1994, 1997, 1999) in the interaction debate a number of years ago, originally from the perspective of an academic researcher, but later from the perspective of a working instructional designer. At that time, creating compelling interactive experiences was frequently the most expensive attribute of a technology-mediated learning design. Under these conditions, I found myself viewing interaction less as a theoretical construct and more as a variable that needed to be exploited, accommodated, leveraged, or managed when crafting digital learning designs. From this perspective, interaction became a strategy for achieving specific learning or performance outcomes.

Between 1992 and 1999, my colleagues and I observed that the learning interventions, solutions, and programs we were designing for clients tended to exhibit a range of interactions that appeared as targeted outcomes. By describing these interaction categories to one another, we were better able to demonstrate how we were providing value from our technology-mediated learning designs:

- *Interaction for participation* provided learners with a means of engaging with one another. Participative interaction ranges from using names of participants in discussions to articulating one's interest in assuming leadership responsibilities in a learning cohort.
- *Interaction for communication* offered the ability to share information and opinions or to influence intentionally the opinions or beliefs of others.
- *Interaction for feedback* referred to any information that allows learners to judge the quality of their performance. From a behaviorist perspective, feedback provides reinforcement, which is intended to correct and direct performance. Cognitivists suggest that feedback provides learners with information about the correctness of a response so that they can determine if a response is right or wrong or a correct or an incorrect response, so that long-term retention of correct information is enabled.
- *Interaction for elaboration* meant coming up with alternative examples to explain a new idea or developing alternative explanations for why an idea may be framed in a particular way. It makes new information more meaningful for learners. By expanding or even manipulating a bit of information associated with a given idea, it is easier to recognize all of the conceptual hooks, or points of conceptual similarity, that may be associated with that information.
- *Interaction for learner control and self-regulation* provided learners with the information needed to manage the depth of study, range of content covered, type of alternative media needed for information presentations, and time spent on a specific learning task.
- *Interaction for motivation* suggested that curiosity, creativity, and higher-order thinking are stimulated by relevant, authentic learning tasks of optimal difficulty and novelty for each student.
- *Interaction for negotiation* involved the willingness of another individual to engage in a dialogue, come to consensus, or agree to conform to terms of an agreement.
- *Interaction for team building* was necessary to ensure that individual members of a team actively support the goals of the group. Interactions facilitate such desirable behaviors as recognition and acceptance of individual differences, expression of respect for the team as well as for its members, effective listening, a shared sense of responsibility, and confirmation of expectations within the group.
- *Interaction for discovery* referred to the cross-fertilization of ideas that occurs when people share their ideas and perspectives with one another in the pursuit of defining new constructs, concepts, and procedures.

- *Interaction for exploration* provided a vehicle for defining the scope, depth, and breadth of a new idea. Just as it is important to recognize a new idea, it is important to distinguish a new idea from extant ideas and determine parameters within which a new idea will retain its unique identity.

- *Interaction for clarification* related to the navigation of one's way through a sea of performance expectations that may or may not be clearly articulated (Wagner, 1999).

Interactions and Social Presence

As the numbers of World Wide Web users continues to climb (International Data Corporation, 2004) and as technology becomes the means of providing "next best thing to being there" experiences, the more users seek to leverage technology to establish, extend, and maintain bonds of interpersonal connectedness. Whether establishing a framework for supporting distributed teams or establishing a link that provides deeper insight into the personological attributes of learners (Soles & Moller, 2001), the desire to transcend psychological distances and establish interpersonal connections has helped focus attention on the notion of social presence, where interaction is the means of realizing that connectedness.

Social presence represents a context for evaluating interaction that focuses on taking advantage of the social and democratic features of technology (Gunawardena, 1995). It refers to the degree to which an individual feels real or is seen as real by colleagues working in an online context (Moller, 1998). Current interest in social presence reflects the current interest with real-time connectedness, particularly when working with peer-to-peer and real-time collaborative technologies. A learner who possesses a high degree of social presence is more likely to feel connected to the group, which leads to greater satisfaction and reduces the likelihood that the learner will leave the environment.

This view was reiterated by Garrison, Anderson, and Archer (2003) when describing social presence as the ability of learners to project themselves (their personal characteristics, socially and emotionally) as real people in a community of inquiry. Garrison and his colleagues' work had previously suggested that educational experiences intended to promote and encourage higher-order thinking skills were most effective when embedded in a community of inquiry. Jelfs and Whitelock (2000) also explored the importance of perceptions of presence, making a variety of observations, including that audio feedback engenders a sense of presence. They noted that the ease of navigation within a virtual environment has a positive impact on perceptions of presence. In all cases, interaction as social presence contributed to a stronger sense of identity with community, virtual or otherwise.

One of the best places to see social presence in action is with peer-to-peer applications such as Groove, with next-generation Web conferencing systems such as Macromedia Breeze Live, and with instant messaging programs such as Yahoo Instant Messenger, MSN Messenger, and AOL Instant Messenger. All include presence-sensing features in their client applications. Consider instant messaging as an interactive social environment: members of an individual's group or "buddy list" are announced on logging in with a sound such as knocking, a ringing telephone, or a doorbell. Chat programs routinely provide visual indicators that a respondent is keyboarding a response. As each person logs off, the exit is marked by the sound of a closing or slamming door. When accompanied by emoticoms, .wav file recordings, photographs, and avatars, real-time chat can take on many of the same attributes of a real-time, face-to-face conversation.

Interaction as Experience

A promising new perspective on interaction considers interaction as a dimension of experience. Gilmour (2003) described the phenomenon of experience in the context of what he called the "experience economy." He suggested that consumers increasingly desire sensation-filled experiences that engage them in a personal and memorable way. In making his case, he suggested that someone who charges for the time people spend with him or her is in the experience business. Gilmour noted that consumers seek to spend less time and money on goods and services, but they do want to spend more time and money on compelling experiences that engage and inspire in personal and memorable ways.

A common example of a business focused on experience is Starbucks. Starbucks has capitalized on something as simple as a cup of coffee and turned the concept of a coffee experience into a multiple-million-dollar international business success. Convincing consumers to spend $3.25 or more on a double latte may seem like a challenge, but the Starbucks experience is about much more than a simple cup of coffee. Knowing how to navigate the menu of coffee choices gives customers a sense of affiliation. Combined with comfortable chairs and tables, a (real or imagined) community gathering place, and the current addition of a reliable wireless access point for surfing the Web, and that $3.25 seems a small price to pay for the experience.

Extending better sensory-filled experiences, particularly richly immersive online experiences, is the driving obsession of the software and Web services industries. The demand for applications of increasing complexity has continued to outpace the ability of traditional Web applications to represent that complexity in online settings. The result that comes from pushing most flat-file Web sites beyond their ability to manage their own complexities is often a frustrating, confusing, or disengaging user experience, resulting in dropped users, low click-through rates, lost connections, and increased costs.

The promises of enterprise-wide system integrations that marry back office infrastructure with rich presentation layers continue to push consumers toward enterprise information portals with very high expectations of good online experiences are hugely compelling goals. As each successive wave of client and Web server technology ups the ante on the previous generation, improvements regarding capability, integration, and responsiveness continue to come forward. Web applications have come a long way from the first hard-coded unchanging Web pages and CGI Web server scripts (Duhl, 2003). Taking a technological view of what it takes to enable a high-quality, interactive online experience, some of the attributes includes the following:

- It must use a ubiquitous client to maximize the audience reach.
- It must run unchanged across the Internet on multiple platforms.
- It must execute well across low- or high-bandwidth connections.
- It needs to restore processing power (not just rendering capabilities) to the client.
- It must deliver engaging user interfaces with high degrees of interactivity.
- It needs to represent processes, data configuration, sale, and feedback complexity.
- It must use audio, video images, and text in a seamless manner.
- It must support the mobile work flow by allowing users to work on and offline.
- It must allow the client to determine for itself what content or data to access and when.
- It must access multiple middle-tier services (both .NET or Java) and back-end data stores.
- It must provide a dynamic and powerful front end for the evolving Web services–based network using emerging standards such as XML and SOAP.
- It must integrate with legacy applications and systems.
- It must allow the incremental addition of new functions to existing Web applications and environments to get the most out of existing Web application investments.

The model resulting from an analysis of these experience-enabling attributes was developed by Macromedia in 2003 to describe what the company then referred to as "the experience layer" of rich Internet applications (see Figure 4.1). From Macromedia's perspective, the experience layer was based on the ubiquitous rich client framework (in this case, Macromedia Flash Player) through which the user received a rich visible experience. It also depended on a rich server

FIGURE 4.1.   THE EXPERIENCE LAYER FOR CREATING RICH INTERNET EXPERIENCES.

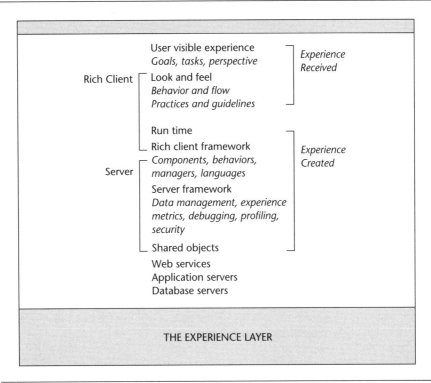

Source: Courtesy Macromedia, 2003.

environment that ensured maximum flexibility, security, efficiency, and control, linking users to enterprise resources in innovative ways to get the most value from existing IT investments.

The "Experience Received–Experience Created" dimension of this model was vaguely reminiscent of the notion of the field of experience introduced in Shannon and Schramm's communication model (Heinich, Molenda, Russell, & Smaldino, 1996) (see Figure 4.2). In the late 1940s, Claude Shannon developed a theory of communication as a mathematical model that communication scholars immediately applied the theory to human interaction.

In 1954 Wilbur Schramm adapted the model to deal with the concern of what he called "communication, reception, and interpretation of meaningful symbols— processes at the heart of instruction." Schramm emphasized that communication cannot occur unless the field of experiences of the sender and receiver overlap, in

FIGURE 4.2.   SHANNON SCHRAMM MODEL
OF COMMUNICATION, 1954.

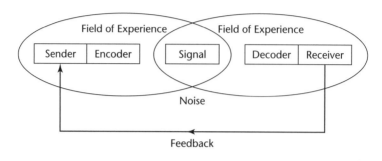

Source: Heinich, Molenda, Russell, and Smaldino (1996).

order to challenge and extend the knowledge of the receiver. In this case, the notion of experience referred specifically to the background knowledge likely to influence the interpretation direction or influence of a particular communication dynamic, rather than to that which a participant in a communication dynamic might posit or feel as a result of the communication. Still, the notion of improving the quality of experience as the goal of an interaction offers some intriguing and compelling design possibilities.

In Support of Interaction Strategies for the Future of Blended Learning

Each of these four schools of thought about interaction provides very different views on the value that interaction brings to a learning experience. Each also shares a number of similarities:

• Each perspective is shaped by some degree of technology mediation and is looking for a way to transcend distance.
• Each perspective assumes some degree of self-regulation and independence on the part of the learner.
• Each perspective acknowledges the value of facilitation by an instructor, agent, or guide.

The introduction of unplugged educational experiences may have shifted the dynamics of learning design possibilities where the blended learning paradigm may be uniquely suited for success and where interaction strategies of all kinds will be highly relevant. Interaction strategies will be the conceptual glue that will hold distributed, distant, e-learning experiences together. Interaction strategies will help monitor patterns of communication dynamics between and among agents of instructional transactions. Being able to determine the kinds of outcomes that an interaction should foster guide instructional designs, concept specifications, functional specifications, and technical specifications. They will also provide metrics for evaluation. Interactions that promote and enable a strong sense of social presence help keep learners engaged and motivated. Keeping an eye on interaction-as-experience acknowledges the significant role played by technology mediation and the value that rich, engaging content creation, distribution, and management tools contribute to the experience of blended learning.

Summary Thoughts

This chapter considered the impact that personal and mobile digital devices are likely to have on emerging models of blended learning. It then suggested that interaction strategies, regardless of their theoretical bases, can help improve individualization, personalization, and relevancy of blended learning experiences. Finally, various models of instructional interaction were reviewed and discussed.

References

Duhl, J. (2003). *Rich Internet applications.* San Francisco: Macromedia.

Garrison, D. R., Anderson, T., & Archer, W. (2003). A theory of critical inquiry in online distance education. In M. G. Moore & W. Anderson (Eds.), *Handbook of distance education.* Mahwah, NJ: Erlbaum.

Gilmour, J. H. (2003, Autumn). Frontiers of the experience economy. In *Batten briefings: From the Darden Graduate School of Business Administration* (pp. 1, 6–7). Charlottesville, VA: Darden Graduate School of Business Administration.

Gunawardena, C. (1995). Social presence theory and implications for interaction and collaborative learning in computer conferencing. *International Journal of Educational Telecommunications, 1*(2–3), 147–166.

Heinich, R., Molenda, M., Russell, J., & Smaldino, S. (1996). *Instructional media and technologies for learning.* Upper Saddle River, NJ: Prentice Hall.

Hillman, D. C., Willis, D. J., & Gunawardena, C. N. (1994). Learner-interface interaction in distance education: An extension of contemporary models and strategies for practitioners. *American Journal of Distance Education, 8*(2), 30–42.

International Data Corporation. (2004). *Online user forecast.* Retrieved July 20, 2005, from http://www.macromedia.com/software/player_census/flashplayer/penetration.html.

Jelfs, A., & Whitelock, D. (2000). The notion of presence in virtual learning environments: What makes the environment "real." *British Journal of Educational Technology, 31*(2), 145–152.

Jung, I. (2001, July). Issues and challenges of providing online inservice teacher training: Korea's experience. *International Review of Research in Open and Distance Learning, 2*(1). Retrieved July 20, 2005, from http://www.irrodl.org/content/v2.1/jung.html.

Malik, O. (2004). The new road to riches. *Business 2.0, 5*(5), 86.

Metcalf, D. (2002, March). Stolen moments for learning. *eLearning Developers' Journal.* Retrieved July 15, 2005, from http://www.elearningguild.com/articles/abstracts/index.cfm?action=viewonly2&id=52&referer=http%3A%2F%2Fwww% 2Eelearning guild%2Ecom%2Farticles%2Fabstracts%2Findex%2Ecfm%3Faction%3 Dview%26frompage%3D1%26StartRow%3D81%26maxrows%3D40.

Moller, L. (1998). Designing communities of learners for asynchronous distance education. *Educational Technology Research and Development, 46*(4), 116–117.

Moore, M. (1989). Editorial: Three types of interaction. *American Journal of Distance Education, 3*(2), 1–7.

Moore, M. G., & Anderson, W. (Eds.). (2003). *Handbook of distance learning.* Mahwah, NJ: Erlbaum. NPD. 2003.

Moore, M. G., & Kearsley, G. (1996). *Distance education: A systems view.* Belmont, CA: Wadsworth.

NPD Research. (2003). *Results of an online survey conducted by NPR Research on Worldwide Flash Player penetration.* Retrieved July 20, 2005, from http://www.macromedia.com/software/player_census/npd/.

Saba, F., & Shearer, R. L. (1994). Verifying key theoretical concepts in a dynamic model of distance education. *American Journal of Distance Education, 8*(1), 36–59.

Soles, C., & Moller, L. (2001, January). Myers Briggs type preferences in distance education. *International Journal of Educational Technology, 2*(2). Retrieved July 20, 2005, from http://www.ao.uiuc.edu/ijet/v2n2/soles/index.html.

Wagner, E. D. (1994). In support of a functional definition of interaction. *American Journal of Distance Education, 8*(2), 6–29.

Wagner, E. D. (1997). Interactivity: From agents to outcomes. In T. E. Cyrs (Ed.), *Teaching and learning at a distance: What it takes to effectively design, deliver and evaluate programs.* San Francisco: Jossey-Bass.

Wagner, E. D. (1999). Beyond distance education: Distributed learning systems. In H. Stolovich & E. Keeps (Eds.), *Handbook of human performance technology* (2nd ed.). San Francisco: Jossey-Bass.

Ellen D. Wagner is director of global education solutions, Macromedia, where she shapes the strategic directions of Macromedia's postsecondary education business. Before joining Macromedia, she was chief learning officer of Viviance New Education and vice president, consulting services, for Informania. Wagner's prior career as a tenured professor and administrator included positions as chair of educational technology, academic affairs coordinator of instructional and research technologies, and director of the Western Institute for Distance Education at the University of Northern Colorado. She has designed and managed enterprise performance improvement and training programs for organizations including the New York Stock Exchange, Dell Computer, Hewlett Packard, Sun Microsystems, Volkswagen, US WEST, Nortel, and AT&T. Her Ph.D. in educational psychology is from the University of Colorado, Boulder.

PART TWO

CORPORATE BLENDED LEARNING MODELS AND PERSPECTIVES

The chapters in Part Two showcase blended learning models and frameworks of six major corporations: IBM, Sun Microsystems, Microsoft, Avaya, Cisco, and Oracle. Several of these models have some commonalities, such as the front-end assessment of learners, the choices between independent study and facilitated learning paths, the development of communities of interest or communities of learning, and the alternation and variation of delivery mechanisms. In addition, each model offers insight into online course structuring, cost savings, and learning delivery efficiency, while also lending support to organizational efforts in knowledge management. These are comprehensive models that move beyond one dimension or focus to the consideration of a learning ecology, as noted in Chapter Six. Finally, embedded in some of these chapters are unique partnerships and growth opportunities for blended learning.

In Chapter Five, Nancy J. Lewis and Peter Z. Orton share IBM's blended four-tier learning model, consisting of (1) information and just-in-time performance support, (2) interactive online learning, (3) online collaboration, and (4) classroom learning labs. Each tier in the model meets a unique learning or performance need. The chapter then describes how the model is implemented in the year-long Basic Blue for Managers program. In the first phase of this program, new managers take part in forty-eight hours of self-paced learning for the first twenty-six weeks of training. During this time, they also receive online coaching and support for the selection of their learning paths and completion of workplace activities.

Phase II of the program consists of a five-day in-class learning lab that focuses on experiential, higher-order learning. In the third and final phase of the program, managers create an individualized development plan for the concluding twenty-five weeks of online learning. The third phase also emphasizes peer coaching and transfer of knowledge to the workplace setting. After describing IBM's model and a program where the model was implemented, the authors share their strategy for evaluating the effectiveness of the program, which projected a return on investment of forty-seven to one.

In Chapter Six, Mike S. Wenger and Chuck Ferguson promote an ecology framework for guiding blended learning solutions developed at Sun Microsystems. This model was designed to overcome some of the inherent limitations in classifying instruction based on modalities (for example, classroom training versus e-learning). Their ecology framework focuses on four means or ways of experiencing different instructional elements: (1) studying, (2) practicing, (3) teaching, and (4) coaching. These four categories make up the quadrants of a matrix with two dimensions: the first dimension (x-axis) ranging from a focus on content delivery to experience and practice, and the second dimension (y-axis) ranging from self-navigation to guided navigation. Specific instructional elements for each category are shared. A second evolution of the learning ecology matrix is also articulated, which incorporates the concept of knowledge management into the matrix. This knowledge ecology matrix changes the dimensions ranging along the x-axis to collecting content (explicit knowledge) on the one end to connecting people (tacit knowledge) on the other.

Chapter Seven, by Lutz Ziob and Bob Mosher, outlines a strategy and several case histories of Microsoft Learning's approach to blended learning. The authors emphasize that one of the drivers for blended learning is the ability to provide solutions to customers' problems rather than just training, and this requires a highly flexible approach. Three major forms of learning to be blended are outlined: (1) live, (2) instructor-led training, and (3) self-paced learning, as well as the tools for supporting learning communities, such as peer-to-peer learning. Three diverse cases are described involving finding learning solutions for the State of Wisconsin, a Philippine apparel supply chain, and Microsoft de Argentina. In all cases, blended solutions were introduced and resulted in time and cost savings to the customers.

Chapter Eight, by Alan G. Chute, J. O. David Williams, and Burton W. Hancock, highlights two cases of blended learning implemented at Avaya. In the first case, Avaya enhanced the value and use of the knowledge assets available through the company knowledge management system by beginning a weekly live audio and Internet teleconference seminar series. In this program, live knowledge sharing was emphasized as authors highlighted knowledge assets in the system and interacted with the audience about the assets. In the second case, Avaya developed Executive Solutions Selling Business Acumen training that spanned a two-and-a-half-month period and resulted in $36.3 million in incremental revenue in the first six months following the program. The training involved early teleconferences and online training modules followed by two week-long face-to-face seminars and mentoring as the participants attempted to incorporate what they learned into their business practices.

Chapter Nine, by Alan Dennis, Barbara Bichelmeyer, and their colleagues at Indiana University is about blended learning at Cisco Systems. This research team outlines the blended approach used by the Cisco Networking Academy (CNA), a global program in all 50 states and more than 150 countries across the globe. The CNA program is designed to provide technical knowledge and training for the information technology industry. The authors point to several critical dimensions in which to compare online and face-to-face instruction, including synchronicity versus asynchronicity, consistency versus variability of content, and standardization versus individualization of course activities. The blended approach used by the CNA courses is based on (1) a centralized curriculum development, (2) online content delivery, (3) on-site implementation (and individualization) of instruction, and (4) standardized assessment of learners.

Chapter Ten by Kirsten S. Hanson and Frances A. Clem introduces Oracle's experimentation with a blended approach in leadership training. Managers were given the opportunity to participate in a leadership track that was completely instructor-led training or a track that took a blended learning approach by adding virtual synchronous and asynchronous activities before and after the face-to-face sessions. Exploratory research conducted with the participants found similar degrees of content retention between the instructor-led training and blended learning groups but uncovered higher degrees of perceived benefits and an enhanced sense of community among the blended learning participants. Additional issues of interest related to community development are raised for further investigation, such as the predominant learner use of the community for task-oriented rather than social reasons and learners' placing greater levels of importance on the "high-touch" elements of the training.

CHAPTER FIVE

BLENDING LEARNING FOR BUSINESS IMPACT

IBM's Case for Learning Success

Nancy J. Lewis, Peter Z. Orton

From its inception, IBM Management Development (MD) has taught leadership and management in nearly every business and economic cycle. IBM MD's knowledge base derives from its experts in business and its own experience in managing one of the most dynamic companies in the world. Its programs are designed and taught by successful managers with firsthand, first-rate knowledge of their field, and an ability to impart their insights in meaningful and compelling ways. This chapter describes a blended learning model for training at IBM, as well as a strategy used to evaluate the effectiveness of this model.

To promote effective training and development, IBM MD uses designs that link active learning with the business environment. One such design, which became fully developed and deployed throughout IBM, is its industry-acclaimed blended four-tier learning model (Figure 5.1). IBM MD took the lead within IBM to develop a model of leadership development that incorporates four distinct instructional approaches (tiers) to provide an array of technology-enhanced learning to support the standard classroom intervention. IBM managers now use this four-tier learning approach to master skills and behaviors that develop them as outstanding managers and leaders.

Tier 1 provides information and just-in-time online performance support. These online resources primarily address an ongoing, immediate management concern. The manager with an existing problem accesses the relevant topic using an index or the keyword search engine and brings the material directly to the desktop for online reading, printing to hard copy, or mailing to an e-mail account. Best thinking on over fifty

FIGURE 5.1.   IBM FOUR-TIER LEARNING MODEL.

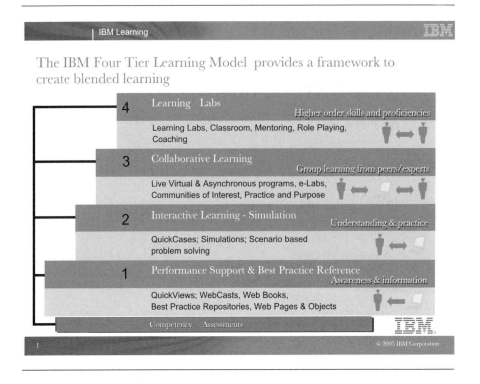

leadership and people management topics of concern to managers are available, including ManageMentor provided by Harvard Business School Publishing. Tools—printable worksheets and checklists—are also available for specific action issues. Links to important external Web sites are highlighted. Because IBM teams are global, managers need to have access to policies and practices in different countries. Tier 1 offerings allow managers quick and easy access to all global management material.

Tier 2 is interactive online learning. Managers enhance their knowledge and personal development beyond the awareness level by engaging in immersive simulations of the issues presented in tier 1. The online Coaching Simulator comprises eight different scenarios, with over five thousand screens of actions, decision points, and branching results. Twenty-six other simulations cover other management topics, such as business conduct guidelines, multicultural issues, work-life issues, retention, and personal business commitments. Going Global, IBM MD's Web site on multicultural business, features over three hundred interactive culture clashes.

Online collaboration, tier 3, brings e-learners together through technology. Through IBM products such as TeamRoom, CustomerRoom, and Lotus

LearningSpace, managers team with other managers in virtual groupware spaces. Here they learn collaboration skills and create and build real-life learning networks to enhance the company's intellectual capital. Collaborative spaces using same-place, different-time communication enable a global learning environment, eliminating the problems of time zones and travel. This part of the learning process introduces the give-and-take of human dynamics and uses the benefits of technology to transcend time and space. Management Development supports virtual teams with materials and consulting to maximize business results and learning at the same time.

For developing people skills, face-to-face human interaction is arguably the most powerful of learning interventions. In tier 4, classroom activities provide immediate responses, are flexible to human needs, and can adapt to different learners' styles. For leadership development, nothing quite duplicates face-to-face learning. In addition, a classroom of peer learners can provide motivation, inspiration, and a community environment, which further stimulates interest and involvement. Management Development continues to offer interactive classroom experiences. The in-class experiences require the learner to master the material contained in tiers 1, 2, and 3 so that the time spent in classroom Learning Labs in tier 4 can target deeper and richer skills development.

Basic Blue for Managers: IBM's New Manager Program

Basic Blue for Managers equips all new IBM managers with the fundamental knowledge and skills they need as leaders and people managers (Figure 5.2). Aligned with IBM's strategic focus on e-business, the program combines e-learning with in-class activities. Basic Blue's founding principle is that learning is an extended process, not a one-time event. It immerses managers in a collaborative Lotus Notes LearningSpace with online self-study, online simulators, individual competency assessments, an online tutor, second-line management coaching, and classroom experiences. The ten-month process focuses on developing skilled managers and leaders with the competencies required to lead high-performance teams.

Phase I: Twenty-Six Weeks of Self-Paced, Online Learning

New first-line managers engage in forty-eight hours of self-paced instructional activities within a Lotus LearningSpace, available twenty-four hours a day on the company intranet via each manager's desktop or laptop computer. Each LearningSpace cohort numbers twenty-four new managers, who engage with each other in a virtual, asynchronous workroom. However, each manager

FIGURE 5.2. BASIC BLUE: NEW FIRST-LINE MANAGER PROGRAM.

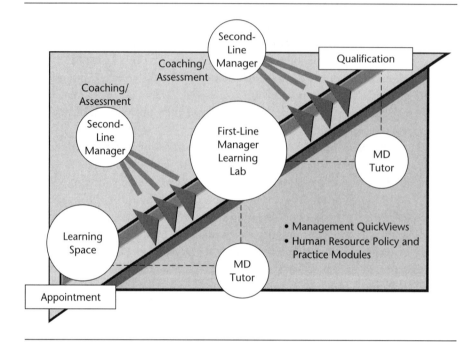

progresses individually at his or her own pace, at an average of two hours per week, working through five online units of modular content: in all, eighteen mandatory and elective managerial topics, custom-developed for IBM's culture and business environment, with additional content from the online Harvard ManageMentor (Harvard Business School Publishing).

Phase I has these features:

• Each mandatory topic requires the manager to display knowledge mastery by achieving a minimum score on an online test, which can be repeated until mastery is attained.

• Fourteen interactive online simulation modules immerse the user in typical, real-life business scenarios—situations in Human Resource Policies and Programs issues. The manager makes decisions by consulting the company intranet's HR policy database and learns from his or her mistakes how to search effectively within this huge and critical online information resource.

• A LearningSpace tutor (an experienced company manager or trainer skilled in facilitating in a collaborative online workspace) guides managers via online and telephone support.

• Each new manager's second-line manager works closely with him or her to support four in-field activities (meeting management, goal setting, and retention, for example) with direct reports.

Phase II: The Learning Lab

The in-class five-day Learning Lab is held at company learning centers world-wide. Because information transfer has occurred in phase I, the Learning Lab focuses on experiential, higher-order learning. For example, the coaching model based on Sir John Whitmore's (1996) *Coaching for Performance* was introduced in the phase I online activities. Managers practiced applying this new knowledge in the eight interactive scenarios within the online Coaching Simulator, which contained five thousand screens of possible actions, decision points, and branching results. In the Learning Lab, students move directly into action learning, as all managers bring a real-life situation from their jobs and are coached by a student colleague to define and address the issue. Participants are thus able to jump into higher-order application because both the basic information transfer and skills practice first occurred through e-learning. Other leadership and management topics are addressed similarly.

The focus of the Learning Lab is for the manager to gain self-knowledge as an individual and understand the role as a team or group leader and as a member of the organization. Validated 360-degree instruments, case studies, and experiential exercises are used to address each perspective. These include the Leadership Competencies Survey, Hermann Brain Dominance Instrument, the Hay/McBer Climate and Managerial Style Assessment, and a validated feedback tool created by IBM's research division. Case studies include cases customized from *Harvard Business Review* and several developed by in-house subject matter experts. Experiential exercises were created from work done at the U.S. Military Academy at West Point and the Fuqua School of Business at Duke University. Teaming is important at IBM, and students are assigned to learning teams. This creates small learning communities as teams remain together through all three phases. This recursive approach creates an environment where students learn from each other as much as they learn from experts. Within the five-day Learning Lab, less than one hour is used for lecture.

Phase III: Online Learning

Phase III consists of twenty-five weeks of online learning, similar to phase I. However, the content is more complex and focused on application of skills and knowledge. On conclusion of the Learning Lab, each manager creates an individual development plan and an organizational action plan. During phase III, these plans are reviewed with the first-line's manager. When satisfied that the student has demonstrated competency in the workplace, the second-line manager signs off. This final step in the learning process ensures that learnings are applied in the workplace. In addition to such application activities, students also complete more e-learning modules. Unlike phase I, where most modules are mandatory, the student chooses topics of personal relevance in phase III. This design encourages managers to take an active role in the planning and execution of their own development. Phase III completes the new manager process.

Evaluation Strategy

Using the Kirkpatrick (1979, 1998) model on training impact evaluation, we evaluated the overall effectiveness along two dimensions, leadership and e-learning, that correspond to our primary objectives. Outcomes were also evaluated along a continuum comprising a chain of impact leading from direct training effects to higher-order business outcomes. When investigating business outcomes, we distinguished between cost avoidance and business result enhancements. Because this program represents a full year of investment in the development in each manager, we considered it important to measure success throughout the different phases of the program, not just at the end, and also eight months after the intervention. Furthermore, because our ultimate interest is in documenting long-term organizational changes, results from the previous year were also used as comparisons. We strive for two goals with our new evaluation framework: (1) to spread training effectiveness information throughout the internal staff in order to drive continuous improvement and (2) to measure with sufficient research rigor to illuminate true training effects.

Level I: Reaction

Two separate and independent studies of representative cohorts of students ($N = 520$ managers) were done in August 1999 and August 2000 using confidential questionnaires and in-depth telephone interviews by a Harvard Business School professor to assess student satisfaction with content and delivery modality. Also, at the end of every Learning Lab, a company-administered student perception survey assesses content and delivery of every participant. Results are analyzed formally each quarter, and modules are changed or supplemented to respond to student needs. In phase III, student feedback is posted in LearningSpace, and Learning Lab facilitators receive individual feedback.

Level II: Learning

In phase I, fifteen mastery tests (220 items on basic leadership and people-management principles and theory, legal and policy understanding, and other areas) are taken; all students must achieve 90 percent passing grades in order to move to phase II. Mastery is also demonstrated in phase II through collaborative role playing, feedback, and case studies. In phase III, mastery tests measure advanced content areas that are dependent on knowledge mastered in phases I and II. Individual assessment is done using 360-degree feedback from managers, peers, and direct reports of students on competencies, managerial styles, and climate.

Level III: Transfer

An alumni assessment is conducted eight to nine months after completion (the time lag between course completion and measurement is intended to capture ingrained behavior change versus immediate posttraining effect) to measure two behavior change dimensions: (1) actual observed behavior changes and (2) changes in factors that social science research has indicated are strong predictors of behavior. These behavioral precursors include gains in self-efficacy and reduction of perceived barriers. For new managers, perceptions of barriers to effective leadership can be powerful in influencing behavior. Hence, a large part of the training is spent on building skill in overcoming leadership barriers, as well as building intention to increase positive change activity. The assessment is one of two online, anonymous surveys administered to all graduates (we believe this follow-up intervention reinforces the importance of desired behavior transfer). The 40 percent response rate from the first wave of alumni (637 students who completed course work in 1999) was satisfying, and the data were examined for response pattern match to other assessments to confirm the representativeness of the respondent group.

Level IV: Business Impact

Business impact attributable to training was measured in the same survey used for level III measurement. These include the extent to which students have become better leaders, the extent to which their teams have been positively affected, and types of impact on business results (such as impacts on people, teamwork, and morale; productivity and effectiveness; and customer and financial indicators). Large-scale leadership effectiveness was measured as well.

The Employee Research group conducts a global opinion survey each year in which many items critical to the corporation are measured. Recently a detailed analysis investigated the connection between leadership and the key corporate measurement of customer satisfaction. This piece of research was examined for high-level leadership trends and linkage to important business outcomes. These results are widely distributed and strategically used across the corporation, so our quest to isolate training effects is confounded. For evaluation purposes, the research is important nonetheless because we believe that using multiple measures representing a variety of depth and specificity of impact can help to triangulate global training effects.

Level V: Return on Investment

Most easily measured was the cost efficiency achieved using an e-learning approach over classroom-only delivery. Cost of development returns and learner efficiencies have been quantified and tracked since the inception of the program. More difficult is the measurement of the ultimate success of training: the extent to which it has a noticeable impact on business success. The bottom-line impact of leadership training on business operations is notoriously hard to measure, but we endeavored using a chains of impact approach, following the trail of training effects down two paths: (1) cost avoidance and savings and (2) results enhancement. For example, tangible cost savings from cost of discrimination and harassment lawsuit avoidance are estimated by comparing internal legal action rates with other top-tier corporation rates. In addition to savings, we measured return on investment (ROI) by results enhancements, such as manager estimation of business impact due to leadership improvements.

The Results

The Basic Blue for Managers intervention achieved positive effects at each Kirkpatrick level.

Level I: Reaction

All three satisfaction instruments yielded high participant satisfaction with both content and modes of delivery. The Harvard Business School professor's findings ($N = 520$) indicated:

> The company made significant strides in selecting learning modalities that are most appropriate to the learning situation, and implementing those modalities in an effective fashion. . . . The student interview results revealed *unequivocal enthusiasm for [the company's] implementation of both the online and classroom components of the program* . . . [and that the company] has appeared to recognize that when implemented appropriately, learning modalities can be synergistic, rather than competing.

The internally conducted student survey showed that certain modules, such as coaching and climate, consistently receive the most positive scores. Summary ratings (a five-point scale, with 1 the highest score) for overall satisfaction had a mean of 1.16; "lessons learned were useful" had a mean of 1.06; the "overall experience was valuable" had 100 percent yes; and "recommend program to others" was 100 percent yes.

Level II: Learning

The program's second goal was that attainment of level II (knowledge gain) would be greater than the previous classroom-only new-manager intervention. On the fifteen knowledge mastery tests, slightly over 96 percent of the sixty-six hundred participants to date have achieved mastery in all fifteen subject areas, and these students attained an average of 92 percent mastery on the 220 online-delivered knowledge items. Moreover, five times as much content is covered in the new year-long process than in the previous five-day new managers' classroom program. Use of the e-learning architecture is regularly monitored. Based on a student population of three thousand students per year, nearly 500,000 intranet Web page requests per year signifies an average of approximately 150 page requests per year per student. Since the program's inception, there have been 2.3 million page requests.

Level III: Transfer

Based on the alumni survey, significant behavior change occurred as a direct result of training, with the largest behavior changes in the content areas most heavily emphasized in training: coaching, competencies, styles, and climate. Samples of the most powerful findings on a five-point scale of degree of change, with 1 representing the greatest degree of change, are straight talk (mean $=1.82$), coaching as a competency (1.9), teamwork (1.92), active listening (1.94), using the intranet to increase leadership knowledge (1.96), team leadership (1.97), and coaching as a managerial style (1.97). These results match facilitator observations of degree of behavior change throughout the course. Furthermore, they demonstrate that the overall goals for themes of behavior change are being met.

Self-efficacy items also showed outstanding results: the graduates believe they can make a difference and they are still enthusiastic eight to nine months after completion of the course; the impact has staying power. The most powerful results are "confidence in ability to be an effective leader" (1.75), representing the biggest change found in the survey; belief that "positive changes in team are within my control" (1.87); "increased knowledge of leadership capabilities and needs" (1.93); and belief that I can make a positive impact on climate" (1.95). The greatest barrier reduction was found for lack of understanding of how to resolve "people" issues (2.31) and difficulty in leading remote employees (2.62).

Level IV: Business Impact

Self-reports on observable changes in leadership behavior and impact on the business were also uniformly positive. Regarding "overall effect of the training on their leadership," 8 percent of managers reported "extraordinary improvement"; 50 percent reported "large amount of improvement"; and 41 percent reported "some improvement." Most frequently selected types of impact on subordinate teams that resulted directly from leadership improvement were development of the group as a team (71 percent), increased focus on strategy and goals (68 percent), morale improvement and empowerment of staff (both 65 percent), stronger relationships among teams (53 percent), and increased productivity (50 percent).

To further establish the relationship between behavior change and business impact, eleven indexes were created from the key behavior topics and then correlated with the measures of business impact. The strongest correlation (or "prediction" of impact) was found between behaviors regarding changing organizational climate and impact (correlation $= .41$, indicating a high degree of relationship, statistically significant at the $p < .0001$ level), and leadership competency behavior and impact (correlation $= .35$, $p < .0001$). A factor analysis on eleven index variables yielded a three-factor solution, consisting of Impact on Business Measures, Impact on Strategic Outcomes, and Impact on Relationships. Impact on Business Measures correlates with many of the behavior change indexes, most notably self-efficacy (correlation $= .35$, $p = 0.0001$) and managerial styles (correlation $= .33$, $p = 0.0003$).

We conclude that alumni perceive leadership improvements that relate to improvements in their business as a result of training. This finding is supported by results from the internal research study, which showed proof of linkage between leadership and customer satisfaction that were particularly compelling. A company-specific linkage model was created using structural equation modeling to demonstrate that leadership quality influences teamwork and, ultimately, customer satisfaction.

Level V: Return on Investment

Total financial cost including room and board, travel and infrastructure cost, not typically included in standard education industry accounting templates, is calculated by estimating per student cost for 128 hours of learning. Given the $8,708 cost per student for program completion, our estimated delivery ROI is 17 to 1. (The ROI is based on the total cost of creating and deploying a module

TABLE 5.1. IMPROVED BEHAVIOR EFFECT ON THE BUSINESS.

Attribute Emphasized in Training	Correlation with Financial Indicators
Increase in leadership competencies	.34***
Improvement in managerial style behaviors	.31***
Increase emphasis on aspects surrounding organizational climate	.27**
Increase in coaching behaviors	.32***
Improvement in managing telling behaviors	.29**
Better diagnosing and managing resistance to change	.24*
Gains from case study approach adopted in program	.35***
Increase in knowledge about leadership	.22*
Improved efficacy (confidence in managerial ability)	.26**
Reduction in perceived barriers to behavior change	.19^

$^\wedge p < .1. ^*p < .05. ^{**}p < .01; ^{***}p < .0.$

and the tangible cost benefits based on the use over the past eighteen months.) Reuse of the e-learning methodology, using content object templates or simulation templates, is another source of savings.

In the survey, we asked graduates to assess the first-year annual impact, in dollars, that the leadership change due to training has had on their departments. The average direct impact value that managers placed on department improvement was $415,000. This leads to an ROI of 47 to 1.

Correlates of impact on revenues were based on responses from graduates ($N = 121$), and impact on financial indicators was predicted by key behavior change indexes. Improvement in the areas in Table 5.1 predicted impact on financial indicators.

Together these analyses led to the conclusion that students perceive real and lasting leadership improvements directly linked to the training, which drive observable and financial value for their business.

Impact of This Learning Practice on the Organization

In making the content available to all managers worldwide over the company Internet, we have contributed to establishing a greater consistency of language, knowledge, and company culture across the globe than previously when different geographies developed and deployed their own separate programs for new managers.

The early success of this practice has sparked interest and enthusiasm across other parts of the company to use a similar blended approach for other company professions. Not only do all business units plan their development based on the blended four-tiered learning approach, but because the templates are reusable, they are being adapted for content beyond management development. The customization of Lotus LearningSpace to students' needs—for example, to provide a progress view for each student and an aggregate progress tracking map for administrators—and the successful deployment for such a huge number of students has helped inform and improve subsequent LearningSpace endeavors within the company.

There are other selected impacts of the new process as well:

• *Adaptation of common nomenclature and conceptual models.* Prior to the practice, different organizational functions and geographies used different terms and concepts to describe the work of managers. For example, seven dissimilar change models were used within the company. That has now been replaced with one commonly agreed-on model. Common approaches and ideas have subsequently fostered more cross-functional understanding and teamwork.

• *Online workplace behavior evaluations.* Online 360-degree survey instruments with input from direct reports and peers on managerial styles, leadership competencies, and organizational climate are now used over the intranet to measure the behaviors exhibited by participants.

• *Participants now develop an organizational action plan aimed at measurable improvements in the business.* Completion of the program is dependent on the new manager's sign-off that real workplace behaviors have changed, as evidenced by completion of plan objectives. This new approach has been well received.

• *Rip and read requests.* Participants can use the print version of online learning modules to retain the content in hard copy for later use. Nearly 50 percent of 896,000 annual site hits are print requests. This suggests that managers are using the material while traveling and in places where online access is unavailable.

All of these impacts are believed to be long term, as this e-learning approach has been increasingly accepted throughout our company.

Lessons Learned

IBM learning developers gained insight into effective e-learning design from third-party evaluations of Basic Blue for Managers. Most notably IBM learned:

- *Learning preferences are poor predictors of e-learning acceptance.* Harvard Business School professor Youngme Moon's studies (1999, 2000) reveal it is difficult for preintervention students to express accurately their preference for a particular learning modality (e-learning) because their range of classroom experiences far exceeds that of online learning. E-learning should thus be viewed as an innovation with attributes unclear to its users. With this approach, we used the findings of nearly fifty years of "diffusion of innovations" research (Rogers, 1995) to inform our design and deployment.

- *The relative advantage of e-learning must be salient and promoted.* The degree to which the innovation is perceived as better than existing alternatives is the primary driver of its use. With our students, online learning is anytime, anyplace access, and it has the advantage of being able to focus learners on a specific skill or information module desired instead of having to sit through an entire class program covering a broader set of skills or wade through a larger body of information.

- *The compatibility of e-learning with existing tools, navigation, and usability is important to students.* Any learning design features inducing students to regard the innovation as familiar increases satisfaction and speeds its adoption. For instance, if online applications are consistent with familiar interfaces and navigation, such as their e-mail, learners feel more comfortable adopting the new learning technology (Moon, 2000).

- *The simplicity of an e-learning application, as perceived by its potential adopters, will speed its rate of adoption.* Conversely, perceived complexity of installing "plug-ins," commonly required for various online learning programs, is one example of how complexity slows adoption of online learning. Thus, we designed and built everything with a simple "point-and-click" mentality.

- *Trialability, or the degree to which e-learning can be experimented with on a limited basis, helps dispel uncertainty and drives its adoption.* Deploying e-learning features with "no risk to try" helped speed adoption. All simulators, online cases, and Web pages are neither tracked nor password required, so users could try them—and make mistakes—without feeling they were being watched. Trialability appears to be especially critical for earlier adopters, who have no precedent to follow when they adopt, unlike later adopters, who may be surrounded by peers whom they can observe and experience via "vicarious trialability."

- *"Observability," or the degree to which the innovation's results are visible to others, speeds the innovation's adoption.* Some effects of e-learning are more immediate and easier to see, and these help drive future usage. For example, we learned that building and implementing observable and practical management skills content that can be used immediately by the student helps whet appetites for more e-learning. So we made these available first. Such immediate-skill gains are more quickly observed than other leadership skills, which typically have long-term accrued effects. These immediately perceived benefits help promote continued adoption of the e-learning approach.

Moon (1999, 2000) assessed IBM managers' responses to the Basic Blue experiences and found that users universally extolled both learning modalities—classroom and online—without reservation and with equal enthusiasm. All respondents reported in interviews that they preferred learning the informational material (phase I, cognitive-based development) online from their own home or office rather than in a classroom setting. Representative comments from interviewees include:

> "Because the information was the type of stuff I could learn on my own, there was really no reason for it to be communicated in a classroom. I think I would have been resentful if it had been dumped on me in a classroom. We're no dummies . . . we can learn this kind of stuff on our own."

> "The key thing was the hybrid model. Rather than adopting a totally online training program or a totally in-classroom training program, they decided to take a best-of-both-worlds approach, and it really worked."

> "Neither phase could have worked without the other. Phase I set up phase II really nicely, and phase II would have been impossible to pull off if we hadn't done the prep work in phase I."

> "It's too much information to be taught in a classroom format. You need to be able to sift through this stuff from the comfort of your own home, at your own pace."

> "There's no question that the ability to work at home or in my office made some material easier. . . . This was a huge advantage."

It is clear that technologies and frameworks for learning have delivered much more value to IBM as an organization than just cost savings. These innovations and productivity that have come about as a result of the blended learning programs have enabled IBM to be more responsive to changing business demands, develop deeper relationships within and across the extended enterprise, and deliver financial results. We have no doubt that in the future, learning will become a competitive differentiator separating those organizations that are merely surviving from those that are leaders in the knowledge economy.

References

Kirkpatrick, D. L. (1979). Techniques for evaluating training programs. *Training and Development Journal, 33*(6), 78–92.

Kirkpatrick, D. L (1998). *Evaluating training programs: The four levels* (2nd ed.). San Francisco: Berrett-Koehler.

Lewis, N. J., & Orton, P. Z. (2000, June). The five attributes of innovative e-learning. *Training and Development, 54*(6), 47–51.

Moon, Y. (1999). *An evaluation of IBM manager preferences for "Basic Blue for Managers" online learning approach.* Unpublished study, Harvard Business School, Boston.

Moon, Y. (2000). *An evaluation of innovation characteristics of the "Basic Blue for Managers" online learning approach.* Unpublished study, Harvard Business School, Boston.

Rogers, E. M. (1995). *Diffusion of innovations* (4th ed.). New York: Free Press.

Whitmore, J. (1996). *Coaching for performance: The new edition of the practical guide.* London: Nicholas Brealey Publishing.

Nancy J. Lewis is vice president, IBM On Demand Learning, with responsibility for IBM's leadership in learning design and development, learning systems, collaborative learning, and expertise. Her organization is focused on learning innovation and the effectiveness of IBM's top strategic learning initiatives. In 1998, she launched the four-tier learning model and developed an award-winning global program. A regular speaker at industry conferences on learning best practices, Lewis has been selected to serve on the ASTD Certification Institute board of directors; is a member of the Conference Board's Council on Learning, Development and Organizational Performance; and serves on *Training Magazine*'s editorial advisory board.

Peter Z. Orton designs technology-enhanced learning for IBM. His contributions have been honored by ASTD, ISPI, and international training and development organizations. Orton received his B.A. from Princeton University, M.Ed. from Harvard University Graduate School of Education, and Ph.D. from Stanford University, where he studied how adults learn from media. He spent seventeen years designing adult programs for the California State University system and coauthored twelve textbooks. Orton's videos, audiotapes, and CD-ROMs for corporate clients have won many awards, including a Grammy nomination (Spoken Word/Educational Cassettes). Before joining IBM, Orton produced New Media at Harvard Business School Publishing.

CHAPTER SIX

A LEARNING ECOLOGY MODEL FOR BLENDED LEARNING FROM SUN MICROSYSTEMS

Mike S. Wenger, Chuck Ferguson

Sun Microsystems is a worldwide provider of information technology (IT) infrastructure solutions and services. To support worldwide customer needs, Sun offers several hundred training solutions in a wide variety of delivery options. More than 250,000 students per year participate in Sun's Web-based courses or in classroom instruction at over 250 authorized training centers in more than 60 countries. A large portion of Sun's instructional content is localized into nine languages.

Why a Learning Ecology?

Since 2000, Sun has used an ecology framework to guide the design and deployment of blended learning solutions in the global corporate IT training market. We find John Seely Brown's (2000) description useful: "An ecology is basically an open, complex, adaptive system comprising elements that are dynamic and interdependent. One of the things that makes an ecology so powerful and adaptable to new contexts is its diversity" (p. 19). It is this ability to bring coherence and simplicity to an ever changing diversity of new possibilities for technology application that is so valuable.

From the start, we found the classroom and e-learning conception of blended learning severely lacking. For us, such a conception diverted attention from the observable fact that a well-designed physical classroom already is a rich blend of many different learning modalities. Furthermore, perpetuating the catch-all label *e-learning* tends to gloss over all the exciting potential that the Internet offers. In our work, we needed to articulate exactly what brings the full richness to a classroom experience, understand what the emerging technologies could add to the equation, and describe how we could bring everything together in a way that supported what we knew about adult learning theory. In short, we needed a model that would help us express coherence in the multimode whole yet not be overwhelmed by the endless stream of apparently disconnected parts. This was the genesis of our learning ecology framework.

To set the stage properly for a discussion of the learning ecology, two of our original concerns require further detail. First, the gross label *e-learning* shortchanged the rich potential diversity of online learning modalities. The Internet enables modes ranging from simple content delivery to global communities of practice; from simulations to real-time work flow performance support; from instructor-mediated experience to learner-initiated research activities. It did not require great foresight to realize that the industry would outgrow page-turning HTML presentations fairly quickly. It seemed to us that lumping all online learning into one conceptual bucket is as wrong as treating every learning experience in a classroom-based course as the same. Second, it was also clear to us that such a restricted definition of blended learning underestimated the extent to which the Internet would become a part of traditional classroom training.

In those early days, many people saw classroom and e-learning as distinct and often competing ways to approach education. However, this seemed to us to be a temporary conception reflecting several factors at the time, including the relatively limited familiarity with the Internet, generally bad previous experiences with computer-based training, and few good tools and content available for online options. As more people came to understand the Internet as a communications medium as well as a presentation medium, we believed that its use would pervade traditional classrooms. Certainly this has come to pass. While it is possible to conceive of purely online training experiences, it is increasingly difficult to envision a purely classroom experience. Instructors use network technologies to enhance their face-to-face classes in myriad ways: the use of online course registration, posted syllabi, online chats, e-mail connections with students, and reference materials online are increasingly the norm. Although face-to-face classes remain a mainstay in the corporate world, it is difficult to find companies (even very small ones) that do not use the Internet in some way to support employee learning and knowledge needs. If all learning experiences are in this sense blended, then the term loses distinction. What is *not* blended learning?

Ultimately we needed to be able to design, create, deploy, and sell IT training offerings to our worldwide customer set. We needed to examine all the emerging potential components of a training offer and understand how they might fit together in a coherent whole. We needed to create a vocabulary so the multiple actors in our corporate production chain could effectively communicate. And we needed to help our customers navigate an increasingly complicated set of only partially understood possibilities. In short, we needed more finely grained detail than classroom or e-learning provided.

For these reasons, we rapidly embraced the more textured notion of a learning ecology. That is, we developed a simple framework onto which we could map then current possibilities as well as new possibilities emerging from new technologies or learning designs. The biggest advantage in an ecology model is that it enables a stable view of the totality but also accommodates a constantly changing set of components. This approach solves a practical business problem. Individual products have increasingly short life cycles, but big powerful new ideas require consistent expression over years before they take root. An ecology model allows us to capture the subtlety and sophistication of adult learning theory yet express ourselves in simple, practical terms that communicate effectively with our constituents in the corporation.

We believe that our learning ecology framework could apply in university or K-12 settings as well as the corporate world. However, our specific intent and our experience have remained completely in the realm of workplace learning, and that colors our presentation. In the workplace, employees participate in learning to assume a new role in the organization or to maintain their competency in an existing role. Role specifications define the knowledge, skills, and performance that employees must accomplish to demonstrate proficiency in a new role. Content or experience that supports the role acquisition populates the overall learning ecology. Thus, we presuppose an overarching value set, workplace performance, that provides both design and navigation choices for all who participate in the ecology.

Our model must not merely cope with a sophisticated set of learning theory issues; it must also cope with a sophisticated set of business issues. The business requirement is easily stated (though notoriously difficult to measure) as return on investment (ROI). There is a constant pressure for lower costs and more effectiveness. In other words, any training or knowledge project must be effective, and it must operate within a budget. The components that constitute the learning ecology must be justifiable relative to specific learning outcomes and development costs. So the learning ecology must also provide a framework for business analysis and decision making, as well as learning effectiveness analysis.

Background to the Learning Ecology Framework

Here, we list a few of the more important background ideas that have guided our thinking.

Quality of Learning Experience

Quality of both components and the whole learning experience is critical, and there are many aspects of quality that are not directly articulated in the learning ecology. Much training is badly designed, poorly timed, disconnected from business needs, or presented to the wrong audience. And even in courses that are excellent overall, some parts may be weak. These are significant issues of design, and although the learning ecology provides sufficient granularity to match learning modalities with specific design outcomes, it does not address these issues. Designing the blend of components is not the same as creating high-quality standardized components or ensuring that the blend is presented in a favorable workplace context.

Control over Learning Experience

In classroom training, designers tend to overestimate their control over the learning experience. Instructional designers, content creators, and subject matter experts often fall into the trap that the course they design is the course that is delivered and the course that is experienced. The reality is that traditional classroom training is a craft where the instructor takes the building blocks (only some of which are supplied by the course designers) and brings together a whole learning experience. The instructor provides a field of possibilities; the learner engages that potential. The learner and the instructor collaborate, implicitly or explicitly, to bring all the building blocks together for a (more or less) effective learning experience. Both partners are presumed to be expert in traditional classroom training (we recognize that this is not always true, even if it is frequently presumed), so minimal explicit discussion about the teacher's role and the student's role in constructing the overall learning experience is expressed. But with new and unfamiliar learning modalities, the roles of the participants must be part of the design discussion. A learning ecology model must invite an ongoing discussion about learning to learn (and teach) in new ways.

Formal versus Informal Learning

Formal learning is a small percentage of workplace learning. The reality is that most learning in the workplace (perhaps in all life) derives from informal experiences and self-engagement. Although we talk mostly about things like ROI, courses and catalogues, training budgets, explicit projects, and trade-offs between classroom and work time, these investments are only the tip of the learning iceberg. Adults on the job enhance their performance through an entire spectrum of self-study, informal mentoring, asking friends, listening to their boss, and now and again sitting through some formal training. An ecology model must potentially connect to the total system of learning, formal and informal, in a company.

Social Nature of Learning

Learning is a social process (Brown & Duguid, 2000). In 1999, many people thought of e-learning primarily in terms of asynchronous content delivery and consequently assumed that a traditional classroom experience was required for any social aspects of learning. This is not true. The reality is that the Internet opens up new vistas for social interaction. In many industries (ours especially), the Internet is a primary mode of social intercourse that can take advantage of global social networks. Furthermore, we have experienced face-to-face classrooms that had essentially no social dimension. The learning ecology recognizes that, depending on the desired outcome, social connection is often needed for effective learning. However, we do not assume that the only (or even best) way to achieve social connection is in face-to-face classrooms.

Cost-Effectiveness

Cost is a significant issue in any corporate training discussion. Cost is also a complex issue, particularly in emerging technologies. Initial infrastructure investment is high, yet once the investment is made, the additional variable cost for new users tends to be lower. Cost of content remains high, but with new tools and techniques and more extensive content repositories, multipurpose use can be increased, thereby lowering costs for additional applications. Conditions such as these mean that detailed cost analysis must usually be done on a project-by-project basis. We can simplify this concept by saying that in general, when applying the learning ecology, we try to combine parts to achieve the overall learning outcome from the whole at a minimum total cost.

Learning Ecology Framework

A learning ecology requires a unifying model of instructional theory that drives the architecture of such a learning environment. The matrix presented in Figure 6.1 forms the foundation of a design model we have developed to enable our holistic learning ecology environment.

FIGURE 6.1.   LEARNING ECOLOGY MATRIX.

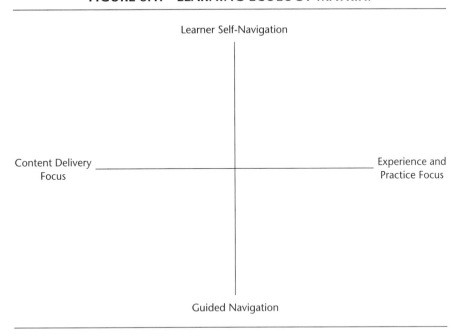

In this matrix, the *x*-axis illustrates a focus on the delivery of instruction. The left end of the *x*-axis targets delivery of instructional content. Content includes factual information delivered in a variety of methods. Some delivery methods are documentation, a lecture, demonstration of a procedure, a job aid, or a guided discussion. The right end of the *x*-axis targets delivery of instructional experiences through activities such as hands-on lab exercises, case studies, collaborative team activities, and coached problem-solving activities.

The *y*-axis in the matrix illustrates who controls the navigation of the learning process. At the bottom of the *y*-axis, navigation of the learning process is controlled by a guide, traditionally a teacher or facilitator. The guide makes decisions on the selection and delivery of information and learning events to the student. As new technologies mature, varieties of machine-based agents or intelligent tutoring systems will begin to fulfill this guiding role. At the top of the *y*-axis, navigation of the learning process is controlled by the learner. Self-directed learners own the responsibility for identifying their learning needs and implementing their unique learning paths. In this environment, students actively locate, select, and initiate their learning from various information sources and activities.

Taking this matrix a step further, we arrive at the four general families of learning modalities that comprise potential parts of a learning ecology:

FIGURE 6.2.   GENERAL LEARNING MODALITIES.

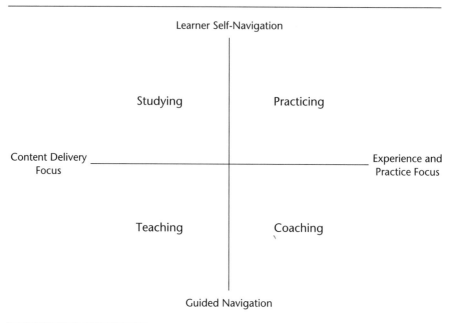

teaching, coaching, studying, and practicing (Figure 6.2). Each of these learning modalities can be accomplished with classroom learning or e-learning. These modalities open up the possibilities for creating a much more granular, and ultimately effective, blended learning approach.

The teaching quadrant offers a presentation of content to students. Examples of teaching include an instructor presenting a lecture to a group of students using a whiteboard and digitally projected slides, a videotaped presentation made available to employees, and a teacher demonstrating how a software application works.

In the coaching quadrant, students are given the opportunity to practice skills through structured lab exercises that are supported and facilitated by an expert. Examples of exercises include students working with an instructor on simple drill-and-practice activities, an instructor mentoring students in authentic problem-solving lab scenarios, and a group of learners participating in a collaborative problem-based learning exercise that is facilitated by a subject matter expert.

In the studying quadrant, a student spends time working with and learning from information. The information may or may not be designed as instructional content. Examples of studying include a student reading a white paper or book and students working through a specific technology-based training module.

In the practicing quadrant, students learn by working on problems or project requirements they may encounter in their job role. Examples of projects include students working through case studies and authentic scenario-based activities and students encountering and working on actual job-centered projects with their peers.

Figure 6.3 illustrates examples of specific learning elements that may come into play as we design instruction within the learning ecology. In a sense, this is a menu of learning options that could be developed and delivered to support a learning requirement. The learning ecology enables us (and our customers) to make choices about which options we will bring to a learning offering to meet the specified learning and cost objectives.

Each of the high-level categories on the matrix contains a number of distinct instructional, learning, and knowledge elements. These elements can be assembled into models of best practice aggregation strategies that produce different types of learning events. Koper (2001) refers to these aggregations of instructional and learning strategies as "units of study, the smallest unit providing learning events for learners, satisfying one or more interrelated objectives."

To illustrate an ecology aggregation, we can use the example of a collaborative group activity that has been identified as a best practice strategy for teaching

FIGURE 6.3.   SPECIFIC LEARNING ELEMENTS.

Studying	Learner Self-Navigation	Practicing
	• Books, articles, guides • References • White papers • Asynchronous content • Job aids • Glossaries • FAQs	• Authentic tasks • Role play • Projects • Case studies • Peer discussion • Discussion forums
Content Delivery Focus		Experience and Practice Focus
	• Classroom lectures • Synchronous content • Demonstrations • Reviews/discussions • Video • Videoconferencing	• Exercises • Diagnostic labs • Practice labs • Mentoring/tutoring • Experiments
Teaching	Guided Navigation	Coaching

a problem-solving skill. The design criteria for creating this best practice unit of study are:

- It is a collaborative group activity.
- The activity uses an authentic problem scenario.
- The activity is mentored by an expert.
- Correct performance is demonstrated by an expert.
- Learners will work in self-managed project teams.
- The activity will be supported with:
    Reference manuals
    Procedure guides
    Asynchronous Web-based instructional content

In this example, the instructional strategy uses elements aggregated from all quadrants of the learning ecology to form a unit of study to address the specific instructional strategy.

A partial list of our current learning elements is shown in Table 6.1. The variety of these elements provides a rich palette for developing units of learning. Applying the model is a relatively straightforward activity of deciding overall strategies and then aggregating elements.

We have found that coupling a blend of online modalities with traditional classroom treatment has allowed more efficient use of classroom time (through prework) as well as extending the overall learning time (through postclass

TABLE 6.1.   LEARNING ELEMENTS.

- Classroom (instructional) content
- Self-paced Web content
- Self-study guides
- Certification
- Practice tests
- Remote labs
- E-mentoring
- Asynchronous discussion forums
- Documentation
- Procedural job aids
- Guided lab activities
- Learning management system
- Transfer of information (recorded audio and slide presentations)
- Webcasts
- Video
- Performance support

e-mentoring and online discussion). We have also found that individual instructors and students come to use the palette of learning elements in individualized ways that we had not anticipated. For example, nonnative English speakers sometimes prefer English content, which they then translate themselves. Clearly this can be time-consuming. In some cases, they use online English content to supplement their native language classroom because it affords the additional time to translate.

It is noteworthy that much of our application of the learning ecology model has a feel of experimentation. This is not unexpected given that new technologies, designs, business pressures, and possibilities keep shifting the field. At the outset, we decided not to attempt to create a model for *the* learning design but rather a framework where emerging models could grow and experimentation could thrive.

In this sense of evolution, we find an emerging modality particularly interesting: remote laboratories. Here the initial problem is quite simple. As the cost of equipment for high-end IT courses increases (into the millions of dollars), it becomes impractical to locate training equipment in each training center. Consequently, like most other IT trainers, we have concentrated costly equipment in a few locations, which are then remotely accessed by learners. Lab activities have always been an important part of practical, hands-on IT training classes. Now, however, the lab equipment may be in another state or country. Originally this was simply a practical exercise in cost management as a way to fill classroom needs. Given our learning ecology, the next logical step is to move "remote labs" beyond the classroom as "online labs." From this perspective, the guidance, monitoring, feedback, and support for the student's lab experience are provided by an online instructor rather than a classroom instructor. The learning ecology focuses on the learning outcomes (within technical limitations), not whether the experience is classroom or online.

Another interesting, and unexpected, business possibility has begun to emerge from the learning ecology model: personalization of the online experience. From a technical point of view, automated personalization of an online experience (beyond simple display variations) can be very complex and is always costly. Such personalization systems require not only many different potential components, but also (at least) rich, dynamically updated user data; interaction and data capture between systems distributed across many electronic domains; meta data appended to all the "objects" in each of the potential elements; and secure identity management. These types of requirements drive system costs in significant ways. Consequently, the decision to support automated personalization is always a difficult trade-off between demonstrable improvement in effectiveness and cost. The learning ecology model has reminded us that individual learners play a very important role in personalizing their own experience. They make choices. This invites exploring learner choice–based personalization modes that may be effective and yet of lesser cost and system complexity. Perhaps developing feedback modes, improved navigation cues, and other "meta modalities" for the ecological mix provides an avenue for important developments. Along this line, we find the potential role of learning management systems (LMS) intriguing.

Regardless of what other advantages LMS may or may not offer, we believe that they are critical in the evolution of the learning ecology. Specifically, an LMS is conceivably where the whole learning ecology can be made explicit. By moving away from the notion of courses and toward a notion of learning paths and resources, the individual (and his or her manager or training administrator or mentor) can examine the total range of possibilities and discuss the totality of a person's learning needs. The LMS can also anchor the conversation in a discussion of assessment and effectiveness at various levels. At the highest level, the conversation can be about the individual's career and life learning requirements, whereas at more component level, there is a need to engage a specific component of the total learning ecology. This allows the individual to make informed and personally advantageous choices.

LMS implementations are still quite immature in most cases. They are only now emerging from the implementation phase and entering the mainstream of culture. As the ecology expands and LMSs become more embedded in the culture of corporations, we anticipate a virtuous cycle of self-directed learner engagement.

From Learning Ecology to Knowledge Ecology

The managed e-learning environment combined with a common learning ecology has the potential to bring together communities of geographically dislocated employees in an enterprise to work toward common performance goals. By providing enterprise work groups open access to information, collaborative or problem-based learning activities, and discussion and chat tools, there is increased opportunity for the groups to use their learning experiences to formulate best practice processes and procedures that improve their overall organizational performance. As these best practice methods are developed, they can be added to the learning ecology, thus extending the knowledge base of the ecology and the enterprise.

Our conception of the learning ecology originally focused on the question of engaging new networked-enabled technology in the world of workplace learning for Sun Microsystems. Over the past year, our worldview has expanded to address knowledge management issues. Like many others in industry, we are seeing the convergence of learning, libraries, and knowledge management efforts, all increasingly enabled by digitization, technical compatibility, and a vision for content and data interoperability. In our case, this trend has been punctuated by our organizational and business changes. We have merged our education and training business with our knowledge management initiatives. Thus, we are expanding the learning ecology into a knowledge ecology.

One important area of focus is internal employee support, providing critical up-to-date access to new product information, software and hardware updates, performance-support procedures and diagnostics, localized content, and rule-based content and systems. An even more important area is a focus on the needs of our external customers, providing role-based and role-driven content, supporting content for new products and technologies, solutions-oriented content, software and hardware updates, and performance-support tools for solutions.

We have discovered that by modifying our original learning ecology framework, we can conceptualize the creation and delivery of diverse knowledge or learning options that support knowledge services. The resulting knowledge ecosystem creates an environment in which people are provided opportunities to gain knowledge or learning through methods and models that best support their needs, interests, personal situations, and individual learning styles.

Returning to our learning ecology matrix, we have modified the *x*-axis to reflect the ways a person accesses content (Figure 6.4). The left end of the *x*-axis focuses on a

FIGURE 6.4. KNOWLEDGE ECOLOGY MATRIX.

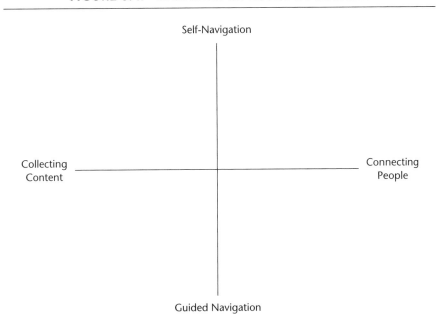

person locating explicit knowledge resources by using methods designed for "collecting content." Knowledge resources are explicit, codified content such as facts, concepts, principles, procedures, or processes. These resources are domain neutral; they are generalized, serve a broad audience, and are applicable in a variety of situations because they are valid regardless of the context in which they are applied.

The right end of the *x*-axis focuses on people who are sharing tacit knowledge resources while participating in activities designed for exposing distributed, collective intelligence by means of connecting people. Tacit knowledge resources are exposed through dialogue, social interactions, and collaboration as people interact within a realistic, situated environment. These exposed resources are unique to specific situations or problem domains, serve a specific community of practice, and apply only to the dynamic context in which the problem occurs.

By modifying the *x*-axis, we can reconceptualize the quadrants of the matrix to arrive at four general families of knowledge modalities for a knowledge ecology: exploring, informing, guiding, and participating (Figure 6.5). People *explore* resources for ideas and practical insights in a neutral environment. Experts *inform* people in common theories and practice in a neutral environment. In addition, experts *guide* people as they apply both knowledge and skills to new situations in a realistic environment. People *participate* in a community to create understanding

FIGURE 6.5.   GENERAL KNOWLEDGE MODALITIES.

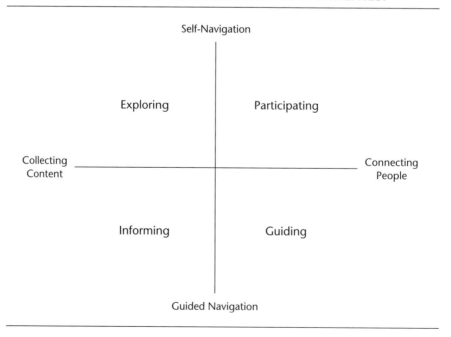

FIGURE 6.6. SPECIFIC KNOWLEDGE SERVICES.

Exploring	Self-Navigation	Participating
• Content repositories • Learning content management • Performance support • Resource centers • Learning portals • E-books	• Online communities of practice • Discussion forums and chats • Talent directories • Learning communities • Instant messaging	

Collecting Content

Connecting People

• Continuous learning • Skills assessment • Pretests • Online learning • Virtual classrooms • Blended learning • Online certification • Learning management	• Collaboration • E-mentoring or remote coaching • Web conferencing • Simulations • Skills management • Interaction with experts • Online labs

Informing	Guided Navigation	Guiding

in a realistic environment. Figure 6.6 illustrates examples of specific knowledge services that may be implemented within this ecology.

Conclusion

As we gain design experience with the ecology framework of network-enabled modalities (and as employees, managers, designers, and instructors also gain more experience), exciting and interesting possibilities are continually emerging. The list of new questions and need for further study is constantly growing. What are the global textures? In cultures where collectivist learning styles predominate (for example, much of Asia), are there tendencies toward different preferred combinations of ecology components (that is, components supporting collaborative learning and mentoring versus personalized content delivery)? What about presentation technologies that enable a seamless online experience as a learner navigates from one component to another? Is such seamlessness even necessary? (Is the experience of going from self-study in a library to a classroom and then to a dorm study group seamless?) As digital natives (Prensky, 2001) become increasingly the typical learner (as they inexorably will), what new modes of self-navigation will emerge? What will be the impact in the coming years of digital native instructors or managers? At what level is assessment properly done? Do we assess the learning effectiveness of individual components or aggregations? As content objects, industry standards, and legal protocols mature, will new businesses emerge, or will the current ones change? How will the convergence of learning and knowledge management activities progress?

As we continue to engage in designing and deploying new learning and knowledge systems under the ecology framework, we believe these kinds of questions are critical to both our technical and business issues.

References

Brown, J. S. (2000, March–April). Growing up digital: How the Web changes work, education, and the ways people learn. *Change Magazine*, pp. 11–20.

Brown, J. S., & Duguid, P. (2000). *The social life of information*. Boston: Harvard Business School Press.

Koper, R. (2001). *Modeling units of study from a pedagogical perspective: the pedagogical meta-model behind EML*. Open University of the Netherlands. Retrieved August 8, 2004, from http://eml.ou.nl/introduction/articles.htm.

Prensky, M. (2001, October). Digital natives, digital immigrants. *On the Horizon, 9*(5), 1–6.

Mike S. Wenger has served in a variety of leadership roles in Sun Microsystems centered on how human learning and collaboration can be enhanced through the application of network technologies. Currently, he is senior director of strategy and innovation for Sun Knowledge Services, leading a team of learning technologists, instructional designers, and visionaries focused explicitly on the learning and knowledge industry. They work to evangelize open standards, interoperability, design coherence, and effectiveness across all of Sun's learning services. Wenger received a B.S. degree from the U.S. Air Force Academy, an M.B.A. from UCLA, and the D.Phil. in organization communication and control from the University of Oxford. He is a frequent speaker on emerging trends in technology-enhanced learning.

Chuck Ferguson has served in a variety of strategic roles at Sun Microsystems, with an emphasis on learning technologies, e-learning, knowledge management, and innovation management. His areas of interest include integrating emerging learning theory, technologies, and standards into practice; defining and creating holistic knowledge ecosystems; and creating frameworks for innovation management. Ferguson has more than twenty years of industry experience that includes teaching classes for Fortune 1000 corporations, delivering conference presentations, developing technical training and education programs, and creating multimedia and Web-based instruction. Prior to joining Sun Microsystems, he participated in projects sponsored by the National Science Foundation and the Defense Advanced Research Projects Agency. Ferguson holds a master's in education from the University of Colorado–Denver with an emphasis in instructional and learning technologies.

CHAPTER SEVEN

PUTTING CUSTOMERS FIRST AT MICROSOFT

Blending Learning Capabilities with Customer Needs

Lutz Ziob, Bob Mosher

Organizations today operate under intense global competition. Wherever these organizations are located, they have access to essentially the same equipment and technology. The difference is in how that technology is applied and operated by personnel. Even with the mandate for workforce development, training budgets have fallen. Customers are confused about the options in training today. The hype around the cost and time benefits of the first e-learning solutions soured many when the promise was not fulfilled. The training industry, however, is rebounding and applying solutions in new ways and with exceptional results. This chapter shares three case histories of how Microsoft Learning is putting the customer first and blending learning capabilities with customer needs.

Microsoft Learning, one of the largest providers of learning products in the world, helps customers realize their full potential by unleashing creativity and productivity through skills development. Microsoft Learning products are delivered to customers through more than two thousand academic and commercial training organizations across the globe. It provides these partner organizations with a diverse portfolio of print and electronic products that includes individual and organizational skills assessments, books, courses, workshops, clinics, seminars, training kits, technical references, and certifications. Microsoft Learning's value to customers is based on three core pillars: (1) learning expertise, (2) product innovation, and (3) partner ecosystem (see Table 7.1).

TABLE 7.1.   CORE PILLARS OF MICROSOFT LEARNING.

Learning expertise
- Maintain deep technical product expertise and world-class instructional design methodologies
- Ensure a rich understanding of job roles and skills development
- Provide customizable skill paths, job task analyses, and job role definitions
- Define curricula and manage a portfolio of leading-edge products

Product innovation
- Design and deliver a flexible product offering and product family
- Provide guidance on blended learning solutions
- Deliver industry-leading learning products on Microsoft technologies
- Ensure fast time-to-market

Partner ecosystem
- Offer innovative business models
- Develop and ignite a partner ecosystem that meets emerging customer needs in terms of custom solutions and consultation
- Create deep and meaningful customer relationships

Global Perspective on Technology Training

Like nearly every other sector of the world economy, the market for corporate technology training was negatively affected by the post-2000 global recession. Corporations implemented deep budget cuts, causing a shakeout among content and training providers. The global corporate technology training market—primarily representing instructor-led classroom-based training (ILT), asynchronous e-learning (self-paced), and synchronous e-learning (live)—peaked at $20 billion in 2000. By 2003, the market had contracted by 13 percent to $17 billion (Gelfuso et al., 2005).

The market for corporate IT training is forecast to reach $18.2 billion in 2005, a 2.3 percent compound annual growth rate (CAGR) for the years 2002 to 2005 (see Figure 7.1). ILT is expected to lose 2.5 percent market share to self-paced and live e-learning training methods, which are projected to grow 8 percent and 22 percent CAGR, respectively, for 2002 to 2005 (Gelfuso et al., 2005).

The following key factors are driving growth in demand for e-learning:

- Improved technology and content, with greater interoperability among learning technologies and integration with other business applications and richer, more engaging content
- Integration of e-learning with learner work flows and the need to have ever more competent and trained employees

FIGURE 7.1.   WORLDWIDE CORPORATE TECHNOLOGY TRAINING MARKET.

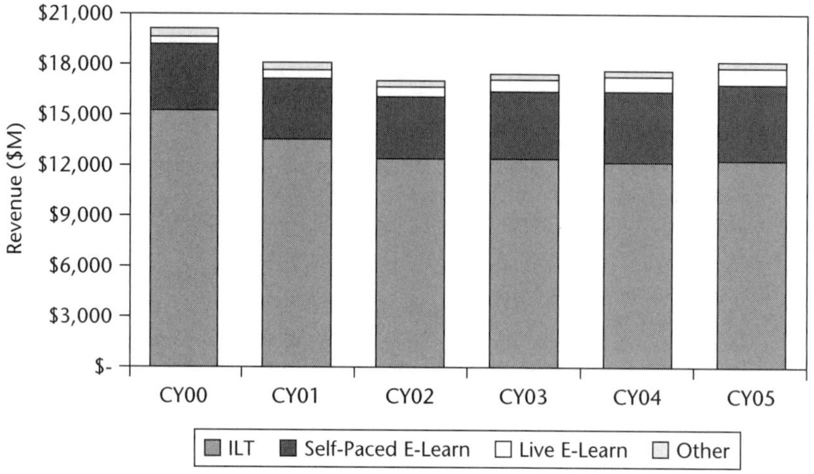

Source: Gelfuso et al. (2004).

- Increasing presence and use of collaborative technologies that have a direct impact on the demand for synchronous (live) content and training
- A mobile workforce that increasingly demands flexible, modular, anytime, and anywhere access to training
- Emphasis by corporations to cut costs by reducing travel and training expenses and the need to prove return on investment (ROI)

Customer Needs

The trends described, however, do not tell the whole story of the technology market. Fundamentally, technology training is changing focus from "help my organization understand and master the features of these products and systems" to "help my organization acquire the skills and knowledge to apply these products and systems to improve productivity, competitiveness, and customer and supplier loyalty." In this regard, customers today feel that the word *development*, rather than *training*, more closely describes their needs. Customers say they want training (development) to be tied as closely as possible to specific projects. ROI will be calculated not on training per se but on performance measured against key project requirements. Customers want customized training that tailors instruction to the needs of individuals on the project team and to the project itself. They do not want one-size-fits-all training.

In this landscape, ILT, e-learning, books, CD-ROM, instant messaging, and more can be seen as powerful tools, but not solutions. The shift in emphasis to solutions is causing a fundamental realignment in the relationship of product suppliers, training channel partners, and customers. The shift is also affecting the formulation of training content and delivery. The most sought-after technology training providers of the future will be those who become consultants first and trainers second. Only through the consultative process can development needs be accurately assessed, skill gaps identified, blended solutions prepared, and value ultimately measured.

There are a number of key technology training developments and trends to watch for:

- Growing demand for customized, blended training within organizations and just-in-time, individually tailored learning plans for employees
- Increasing need for simulations, virtual lab environments, and case study exercises to make training more relevant to job roles
- Greater access to training and technology experts through synchronous learning driven by growth of collaborative technologies
- Emerging opportunity for training organizations to delve deeper into consultative engagements with corporations and be directly involved as solutions providers
- Communities of practice, that is, peer-to-peer interaction, which will increasingly be accepted as an effective means of maintaining and updating professional skill levels

A New Framework for Empowering Partners and Creating More Successful Customers

These trends demand a new framework for approaching organizational development through training. Microsoft Learning believes that this new framework begins with assessment, moves to training, and progresses to validation and post-training assessment (see Figure 7.2).

Assess

In May 2004, Microsoft Learning unveiled Microsoft Skills Assessment for Organizations, a powerful Web-based tool for assessing organizational and individual skills. Microsoft Skills Assessment for Organizations measures individual

FIGURE 7.2   ASSESS, LEARN, AND APPLY.

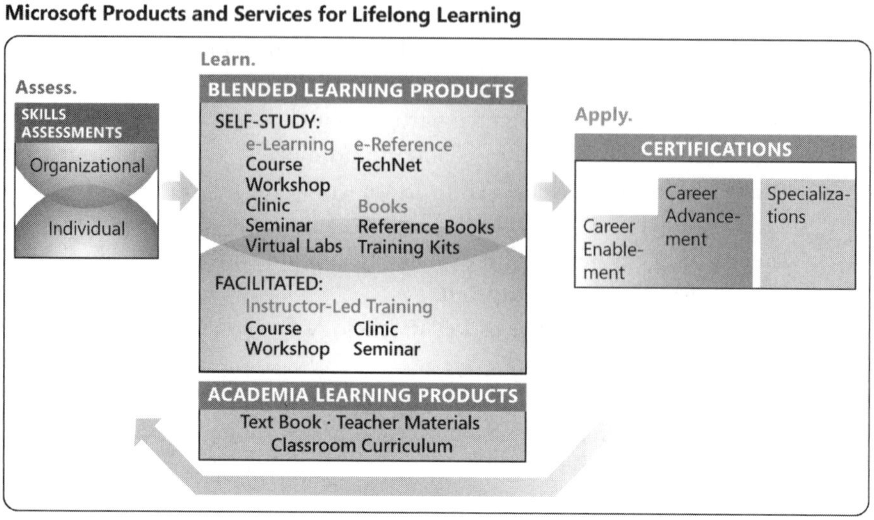

Microsoft Products and Services for Lifelong Learning

baseline skill levels, compares those skills to the required proficiency for a team project to identify skill gaps, and then reports an organizational view of this information. Armed with reliable and credible assessment data for both individuals and the organization, Microsoft training partners—Certified Partner for Learning Solutions (CPLS)—consult with customers to create a customized development plan based on blended learning and aimed at helping the customer organization meet its specific project and business needs. This approach offers maximum flexibility. Through skill gap analysis, learning plans can be tailored to the needs of the individual, the team, and the organizational development project. Microsoft Skills Assessment for Organizations provides CPLS partners with a skills consultancy process that serves customers well through the power of blended learning.

Figure 7.3 shows a screen shot from the assessment tool. The project being assessed is designed to enhance information system security within a Windows Server 2003 environment. Appropriate blended learning is identified for the five project team members who will be trained based on where they are currently in terms of skills and knowledge and where they need to be.

Microsoft Learning's emphasis on individual and organizational assessment helps to move CPLS partners from purveyors of standardized courses to true solution providers. These partners will have the tools necessary to help solve important development issues in the application, operation, and support of advanced information technology.

FIGURE 7.3.   MICROSOFT SKILLS ASSESSMENT TOOL FOR ORGANIZATIONS.

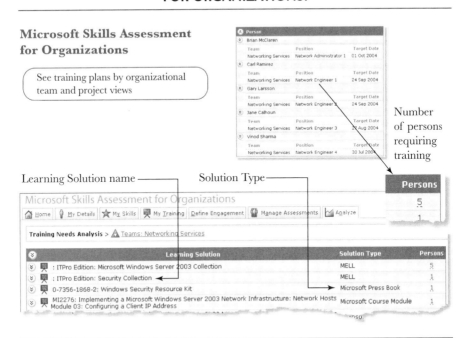

Learn

Blended learning is any combination of self-paced, instructor-led, distance, and classroom delivery with various digital and print form factors to achieve a positive business outcome. This training is designed to reach the widest audience not only geographically but also in terms of learning preferences and lifestyles. Blended learning combines e-learning tools (everything from video streaming over the Web to e-mail) with facilitated training to ensure maximum effectiveness. Microsoft Learning delivers blended learning to customers through its CPLS partners.

A blended learning approach can offer the following benefits:

- Social benefits of classroom training focused on subjects that gain the most from face-to-face interaction
- Individualized benefits of self-paced, online learning for content that requires minimum interaction
- Improved retention and reinforcement through follow-up mechanisms on the Web
- Greater flexibility to meet the different learning styles and levels of individuals and customization

TABLE 7.2.   BLENDED LEARNING FORM FACTORS.

Live Instructor Led	Self-Paced Learning	Tools for Learning Communities
• Traditional classroom • On-site engagement • Virtual online class-room • Live video via satellite or videoconferencing • Online coaching and mentoring	• Instructor-led classroom via e-mail • Online or computer-based training • Self-study guides, manuals, texts • Online resources and databases	• Chat • Instant messaging • Newsgroups and forums • Collaboration

- Cost savings through minimizing time away from the job and travel, classroom, and instructor expenses
- The ability to create extended communities of practice where peer-to-peer interactions provide a vital learning environment

Table 7.2 presents examples of blended learning form factors, tools, and delivery methods.

In the learning stage, individuals will have the correct materials and learning environments to assist in moving them from where they are to where they need to be. Microsoft Learning moved to a blended strategy by creating a new product family of clinics, workshops, and courses. Each is designed for blended delivery, including multiple form factors (both print and electronic) and a detailed blended delivery guide. CPLS partners deliver these products in a variety of settings—in the classroom, on site at customer locations, and online. The Official Microsoft Learning Products family also comprises learning units in digital format, such as Adobe Acrobat PDF and Word documents, PowerPoint slides, and HTML/XML files. Learning units enable CPLS partners to assemble and sequence the learning units in a customized format appropriate for the customer project. The portfolio of products can be applied as is or customized for the application.

Table 7.3 shows how a CPLS partner can transform a traditional five-day classroom experience into a blended learning solution through the application of official learning products. In this scenario, only two days of in-class work are required. The impetus for a scenario such as this one can be a need to minimize the time employees are off the job, while ensuring maximum learning. Pretraining assessment is used to determine the optimum mix of learning strategies for the blended solution.

TABLE 7.3.   BLENDED LEARNING SCENARIO.

Preclass	Self-study prep
Day 1	In classroom
Day 2	Virtual class
Day 3	e-learning
Day 4	Virtual class
Day 5	In classroom
Postclass	Community newsgroups

Apply

CPLS partners conduct a postproject assessment to determine the value of the learning experience and ensure the organization will be successful in achieving the goals outlined during the assessment stage of the project. This analysis compares the organization's progress as measured against goals. The assessment may include validation of skills mastery through certification, as well as quantitative measures of improvements to productivity, competitiveness, and customer and supplier relationships. The results of the posttraining assessment are fed back into the next development project for continuous improvement.

Case Histories

The following three case histories illustrate the power of blended learning within the framework of assess, learn, and apply. The first is from the United States, the second from the Philippines, and the third from Argentina. They present a truly global picture of the impact that blended learning can have.

State of Wisconsin

The State of Wisconsin Technology Leadership Council, an organization of the chief information officers and IT directors from various state agencies, and the Department of Administration, Division of Enterprise Technology, mandated that all state agencies consolidate server and e-mail services. The goals of this multiyear project were to have a single source or state agency that would house or control all of the state's thousands of servers and to perform upgrades using a host of products from numerous suppliers in order to standardize on Windows Server 2003 and Exchange Server 2003 by the first quarter of 2005. Furthermore, a significant number of personnel had to be trained and ready to fill vacancies left by the growing number of retiring senior employees.

Microsoft training partner Inacom Information Systems played an instrumental role in this project. Inacom specializes in technology consulting, education, and procurement.

Assess

Inacom first analyzed knowledge gaps for key groups and prepared a customized foundational training solution to mitigate those gaps. This was an extensive and much needed process because there was a wide range of skill and knowledge levels among personnel.

Learn

The solution required training of two thousand State of Wisconsin employees and consultants on the latest Microsoft technologies. The training solution embodied all major training vehicles, including ILT, e-learning, mentoring, ongoing technical telephone support, and architecture design role playing. The training solution not only spanned many training mechanisms but also included important pillars of IT: application development, office productivity, and enterprise information technologies. Drawing from a host of Microsoft official products, Inacom presented a range of both standardized and customized courses.

In addition, Inacom worked with other well-known providers to deliver the e-learning portion of the solution. Nearly four hundred e-learning courses were hosted on a Web-based learning portal made available to personnel. Courses were offered not only in English but also in a host of languages to support those for whom English was not their first language. The selection of languages beyond English included German, French, Spanish, Dutch, Italian, Brazilian, Portuguese, Hungarian, Turkish, Polish, Korean, Chinese, Japanese, Russian, and Arabic. Accommodations were made for hearing- and sight-impaired learners.

Apply

More than seventeen hundred individuals were trained in a twelve-month period. The cost of the IT Core Training Program to Wisconsin was close to $900,000. The e-learning portion was close to $250,000. The state estimated it saved more than $1.2 million compared to purchasing standardized training. Content from the courses continues to provide employee and organizational value through an ongoing offering from Wisconsin Employees' Virtual University.

Mary Chandler, enterprise IT training director for the State of Wisconsin, says: "We have trained thousands of information technology professionals, and as a result of continued state-of-the-art training, we have increased job satisfaction and employee retention and built one of the best IT organizations in the country. Inacom has adapted this program to offer each type of learner the optimum experience for learning. We have traditional classroom, private events with intense custom material, e-learning, and side-by-side consulting. This solution has allowed the State of Wisconsin to deploy technology with speed and predictable outcomes."

Integrated Solutions Technology, Philippines

Integrated Solutions Technology (IST), headquartered in Hong Kong with operations in the Philippines, is an industry leader in collaborative apparel supply chain solutions. Its ability to provide knowledge-based services to customers is founded on the recruitment, skills enhancement, and empowerment of a world-class development and service support team. IST required a training solution that would enable software developers to improve productivity when creating and launching cutting-edge Web services and applications.

Data Base Wizards (dB Wizards), located in the Philippines, led the development of a flexible, highly customized. NET-based learning solution that combines instructor-led training and e-learning for IST. The company's main lines of business are training, consulting, and Microsoft solutions sales.

Assess

Assessment focused on determining IST's needs and job competencies. Skill gaps for the ninety developers in the program were identified and mapped to IST's business project needs. dB Wizards identified appropriate Microsoft courseware and developed a learning plan. The plan used a combination of classroom, e-learning, self-paced learning, and supplemental materials. dB Wizards' instructors were involved in the assessment from the beginning, working hand-in-hand with sales representatives to understand client needs. This early involvement and understanding helped to produce a customized plan dB Wizards believed would be optimum for IST.

Learn

dB Wizards was able to offer a degree of blended learning never before available through the expanded range of official Microsoft products in both print and electronic formats. Overall, dB Wizards used twenty Microsoft courses for developers. In addition, it developed two customized courses and assembled a host of reference materials in print and electronic formats. Blending was key to the success of the project.

For example, a course designed to build developer skills for Microsoft .NET was offered in a blended format of instructor-led classes and e-learning with supplemental content available in print and electronic formats. The training was designed to be relevant to personnel possessing a range of skill levels. The instructor-led version of this course typically requires twenty-eight days in the classroom. IST personnel obtained equivalent training in just twenty days through blending. IST employees trained at their own pace and spent less time away from their jobs while acquiring cutting-edge skills. Blended learning helped IST meet its aggressive time frame for implementing new technology.

Apply

After completing their training, IST developers, using new Microsoft software, were able to build and launch new applications more quickly, improving time to market by 20 percent. The blended solution helped to lower the cost of training, sometimes as much as 30 percent per course.

Floyd B. Castro, IST program manager, notes, "dB Wizards has gained IST's confidence as our training provider. This confidence is based on their capability to deliver quality training to our staff that helped us achieve a high level of technical maturity."

Microsoft de Argentina

Due to slow economic growth in Argentina, IT professionals there have typically lacked access to the latest technology. Microsoft de Argentina wanted to update the skills of IT professionals throughout Argentina prior to the launch of Windows Server 2003 so that the adoption of this new software would be seamless for organizations. At that time, Microsoft Spanish-language training content was not yet available. To respond to customer needs, Microsoft de Argentina turned to one of its principal training partners, Buffa Sistemas, Srl. (BS Training), for a solution.

Assess

To be effective, Microsoft de Argentina estimated that more than five thousand IT professionals needed to be skilled in Windows 2003 quickly. Given the extent of the project, short deadline, and limited budget, BS Training identified a blended solution as the optimum one. It developed a free Web-based course, "Windows Server 2003, Step by Step." Content was customized from the range of Microsoft training materials, and the course was mapped to Microsoft certification. Because it was Web based, it could reach professionals throughout Argentina.

Learn

A two-server system was set up that could accommodate twenty thousand users and handle three thousand new registrations per minute. Learners were encouraged to progress through the online course at their own pace. When they paused in their studies, they could begin again later at the same spot in the course for a seamless experience. Exercises and practice exams were threaded throughout the course, and links to additional information were embedded. Commonly asked questions were handled on a Frequently Asked Questions page. Microsoft certified systems engineers were available via e-mail to answer learners' individual questions. A final exam evaluated knowledge at the conclusion of the course. The final exam was promoted as the first step for those wishing to continue professional development through Microsoft Certified Professional exams.

Apply

Microsoft de Argentina judged that training five thousand individuals would constitute a success. As it turned out, more than ten thousand were trained. The cost of the blended solution was a fraction of what it would have been for the equivalent classroom experience. Thanks to the success of this program, this initiative was ultimately expanded throughout Latin America.

Iván Labra, manager of Audiencias, Microsoft Chile, says, "The work on the Spanish content for 'Windows Server 2003, Step by Step' was completed on time and provided an outstanding learning experience. The fact that the course was subsequently made available throughout Latin America is a testament to its effectiveness."

Conclusion

The combined effect of cost cutting and customer confusion has resulted in low training investments overall and a slowed adoption of new learning methods. Discussions about e-learning can seem too focused on technology and standards and miss the point. Training is not an either-or decision between e-learning or ILT. Instead, training must be focused on developing combinations of methods of learning: typically blended, flexible offerings. In addition, more attention must be placed on understanding where the learner is in terms of skills at the start of process. At the same time, efforts to identify the overall project goals have to be ascertained. Assessment therefore becomes a greater focus of the process. New tools such as Microsoft Skills Assessment for Organizations will help automate and simplify this process.

Training organizations must continue the transformation into learning consultancies. This is essential if the solutions offered are going to transcend the mentality of providing off-the-shelf products. Local training organizations must develop their own personnel into experts in assessment as well as the development of blended learning solutions. Trust between training provider and customer is essential for these programs to move forward. Training providers must put the customer first in order to succeed.

Reference

Gelfuso, J., Truax, D., O'Brien, D., Dennis, L., Rosi, I., Weisbeek, M., Caylor, L., Kothari, K., & Church, R. (2005, March). *Microsoft learning: e-learning business plan—fiscal year 05–fiscal year 08.* Redmond, WA: Microsoft Corporation.

Lutz Ziob joined Microsoft in July 2002 as general manager of Microsoft Learning. He oversees the development, distribution, and worldwide marketing of a comprehensive line of products that include books, e-learning, reference materials, courses, workshops, skills assessments, and certifications. Prior to joining Microsoft, he was vice president of certification at CompTIA and director of Worldwide Education Sales Programs at Novell. He holds a master's degree in education and history from the University of Bochum, Germany.

Bob Mosher joined Microsoft in December 2003 as director of learning and strategic evangelism for Microsoft Learning. He joined Microsoft with over twenty years of experience in the IT training industry as a computer trainer, instructor development specialist, instructional consultant, and public school teacher. Most recently, he was the executive director of education for Element K, where he helped direct and influence its learning model and products. He has acted as an influential voice in the IT training industry by speaking at conferences and by being an active participant within industry associations such as CompTIA and ASTD.

CHAPTER EIGHT

TRANSFORMATION OF SALES SKILLS THROUGH KNOWLEDGE MANAGEMENT AND BLENDED LEARNING

Alan G. Chute, J. O. David Williams, Burton W. Hancock

In the past two decades, technology companies have had to face incredible challenges just to survive. An unpredictable marketplace characterized by the staggering pace of technological innovations, ever increasing global competitiveness, and acts of terrorism have forced many companies to rethink their business models and their strategies for building long-term trusted relationships with their customers. Companies that have learned how to leverage knowledge management practices and create blended learning programs for employee skills development are the survivors. This chapter addresses how knowledge management and blended learning can enable the transformation of selling skills and sales strategies in technology companies.

In the past, companies could be successful by providing quality products and services at a reasonable price and delivering them on schedule to their customers. Quality products or services at a reasonable price continue to be important to customers, but companies that focus solely on this strategy find themselves in a commodity relationship with their customer. When companies are seen as a supplier of a commodity, their products and services do not have any differentiating qualities or value. It is easy to get positioned at this level, but there is no leverage for establishing a long-term trusted relationship with customers. Moreover, companies that are perceived as a provider of a commodity product or service have little control in managing the relationship with their customer. Their only bargaining position is availability and a low bid.

Today, many companies are finding it difficult to make the transformation from a product- and services-focused business model to a customer relationship–centric business model. One of the biggest challenges they face is how to upgrade the business acumen and the consultative selling skills of the sales representatives of the company. Sophisticated customers expect their supplier companies to go the extra mile for them. Going the extra mile means the supplier becomes a trusted business partner who understands business drivers and forms lasting, trusted relationships with their customers. Customers are seeking suppliers that are business partners that take an interest in helping them run a successful business. Suppliers that understand their customer's business challenges and objectives become an important part of their customer's success. When suppliers provide their customers with products and services that address their customers' concerns, improve their customers' operational efficiency, and help them with their bottom line, they find themselves in a strategic business partnership with those customers. Such partnerships help maintain the financial viability of a company. In fact, often when suppliers establish themselves as business partners committed to the success of their customers, they find that even if their products and services cost more than those of their competitors, customers prefer doing business with them.

An example of a company that made the transition from a product-centric company to a customer relationship–focused company is Avaya. Avaya was operating as a supplier of high-tech telecommunications equipment in a highly competitive business environment where technology was changing rapidly. Avaya was well known for its quality products and services that supported the rapidly growing call center environment. However, this business was moving to a global marketplace that had many new competitors. The Avaya sales force traditionally sold to customers by focusing on their products' features, benefits, reliability, and price. With the increase in global competition in the call center environment, the sales force often found itself in a position of offering what were perceived to be commodity products and services without a distinctive value proposition for its customers.

Realizing that operating as a provider of commodity products and services was resulting in lost business opportunities, Avaya embarked on a new approach for training its sales force to sell business value in the dynamic global market environment. It employed a blended learning model to accelerate the adoption of a new customer-centric consultative sales approach. The Avaya leadership team realized that effectively disseminating and managing knowledge about customer relationship management (CRM) strategies could differentiate Avaya in the global call center marketplace because the sales force could offer more value to their customers.

At Avaya there were many sources of call center–related information; however, accessing the right information, anytime, anywhere, and in a way meaningful to the sales force proved to be a major challenge. The Avaya leadership team commissioned the Avaya Customer Relationship Management Institute to create a knowledge repository that could be used as a stand-alone knowledge resource or used in conjunction with continuing education seminars or formal training programs. The CRM Institute team believed that the key to cultural transformation was an appropriate blending of knowledge, skills and experience; in other words, knowledge is necessary but not sufficient to bring about sales culture transformation: Knowledge + skills + experiences = Transformation.

The CRM Institute team started the transformation journey by creating a comprehensive CRM knowledge management (KM) program. After the program was established, the team created an innovative CRM blended learning sales curriculum that provided for authentic CRM sales experiences in order to transform the sales culture.

Knowledge Management

Avaya implemented a number of KM initiatives, including the Knowledge NET project and the CRM Portal. The purpose of these projects was to enhance the impact of the KM discipline on instructional effectiveness, business results, customer relationships, and the quality of work life for associates. The projects were internally focused and sought to apply CRM theoretical principles to real-world settings. Although associates reported that the resources developed from these projects were essential, they could not easily point to precise quantifiable business (that is, return on investment) impacts. However, it became clear that KM and blended learning were rapidly converging as both appeared to be geared toward providing highly relevant, just-in-time knowledge.

Avaya expanded its KM with additional initiatives and was ranked among the top companies practicing KM. One of these projects, the Knowledge Net, was implemented by the Professional Services Organization, an externally focused consultancy in the call center marketplace. The Knowledge Net project tested assumptions about the use of communities of practice and communities of interest as a means of focusing consultants on the use of core knowledge that they needed to do their jobs smarter, better, and faster. The Knowledge Net communities had specific roles and responsibilities such as mentor, subject matter expert (SME), and community leader. Researchers tested the value of those roles and found them useful in dividing the labor of a knowledge community.

CRM Portal

In the year 2000, based on promise in the potential of Knowledge Net and other KM initiatives, the CRM Institute created the CRM Portal to address the KM needs of Avaya's CRM business unit. The CRM Institute was responsible for changing the focus of the call center business from one of hardware, software, and services to one that focused on bringing value to the customer. The CRM Institute developed a vertical portal with hundreds of knowledge assets that were rich with contextual metadata that enabled users to perform powerful searches and to associate the knowledge assets with the needs of specific classes or users with unique job tasks.

Any sales or marketing employee at Avaya could nominate a knowledge asset to the CRM Portal. A knowledge asset could be a white paper, case study, research report, competitive assessment, or PowerPoint presentation, for example. If the knowledge asset was approved by the CRM Portal managing editor, it was added to the knowledge repository. Once the asset was in the repository, its frequency of use could be tracked. This capability gave the CRM Institute team the ability to identify people who were key contributors to the company's body of CRM knowledge and to identify frequent users of CRM knowledge assets. The CRM Institute used these data to determine natural affinities between authors and users of specific classes of CRM knowledge assets similar to the way that Amazon.com establishes affinities between book authors and potential readers of those books.

The research of affinity associations, moreover, provided the CRM Institute a basis for drawing peer attention and rewarding people who contributed assets to the CRM Portal that were frequently used and highly valued by other employees. For example, the institute would conduct focus groups with employees who regularly used the CRM Portal if the use of a specific author's assets had a positive impact on their business results. These evaluations enabled the institute to begin to assign a value derived for specific knowledge assets on the portal. If a positive result was noted, the CRM Institute team would then determine to what extent the asset or class of assets grew or protected revenue, reduced expenses, or improved customer or employee satisfaction. This asset of value-derived monitoring enabled the CRM Institute to reward authors and drive awareness that knowledge assets should be considered intellectual capital.

The CRM Institute managing editor was the key individual for ensuring the quality of CRM assets and consistency of the metadata tagging of assets in the knowledge repository. In addition to the managing editor, domain editor roles were assigned to subject matter experts in each strategic solution group. An indexing tool was employed to help all of the editors make consistent contextual metadata decisions.

The editors conducted periodic training sessions to promote the use of the CRM Portal and elevate the visibility of certain classes of high-value CRM assets like white papers and current research reports. The managing editor also established a monthly audio plus Internet teleconference seminar series, "First Friday's" program, which featured CRM Portal authors. These programs frequently had over one hundred participants on a two-hour teleconference. During the program, the authors directed the audience to knowledge assets on the CRM Portal such as PowerPoint presentations or Word documents and then engaged in live voice interactions with the audience using audio conference calls. The interactions were also facilitated through e-mail questions and instant messages with the presenters. This blended learning approach that leveraged high-value knowledge assets on the portal with live knowledge-sharing sessions dramatically improved the impact of the CRM Portal assets on business results.

Avaya Solutions Knowledge Center

In 2001 Avaya created the Avaya Institute, a new KM organization responsible for the Knowledge Net project, the CRM Portal, and the CRM Institute. The Avaya Institute created the building blocks of a new comprehensive KM portal, the Avaya Solutions Knowledge (ASK) Center. The expanded knowledge base and the information-sharing capabilities of the ASK Center created a new level of complexity for the KM schema, necessitating the development of a conceptual model to help describe the way knowledge was segmented and differentiated. The Avaya Institute adopted a cube model perspective to organize the domains related to knowledge at Avaya. One axis was the strategic solutions disciplines, another was the product information, and the last was the market distribution channels. Users could find information by following an information map along a linear axis or employing an extremely powerful search engine, which used the rich contextual metadata that described every knowledge object in the database.

The ASK Center was a powerful and dynamic resource for Avaya sales and marketing knowledge. It provided a wealth of knowledge, ranging from information and news to marketing materials, sales collateral, training, and various support services. And the ASK Center enabled employees to share their knowledge and experience with other employees worldwide. In 2001, thousands of Avaya employees recorded over 660,000 hits on the ASK Center and downloaded over

FIGURE 8.1.   ASK CENTER PORTAL.

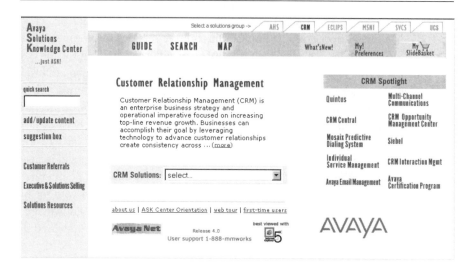

Note: This portal and that for Executive Solutions Selling Business Acumen, discussed later in the chapter, were designed and developed by InfoMedia Designs, located in Easton, Pennsylvania (www.infomediadesigns.com).

100 billion bytes of data, equivalent to over 260,000 pounds of paper. The ASK Center employed some highly innovative tools to enable employees to navigate the information repository (see Figure 8.1).

Accessing Relevant Information

The ASK Center portal gave employees access to all of Avaya's channel marketing knowledge and expertise in a way that made most sense to them. There were several ways to find what they needed. The Map function provided a menu of case studies, presentations, white papers, and competitive information. The Search function focused a search on a solution, author, topic, or date and delimited the results to slides, documents, applications, and video media types. The Guide function helped employees tune into information that would be the most relevant to the tasks that they were working on at the time. The Guide asked questions and then retrieved items that matched what other employees found to be useful in addressing similar questions in the past.

The portal provided shortcuts to get quick access to background information and resources on Avaya solutions, collateral, customer references, and performance support tools. Spotlights were included for each of the Avaya Solutions groups to call attention to unique strategic events, learning, and updates on Avaya alliances. Each selection included a brief abstract that helped users decide whether to dig deeper or continue a search. Some items provided a list of related training courses that had been recommended by education experts at Avaya. There were affinity links that allowed users to check out related content that colleagues were using.

Chunking Content

The ASK Center included powerful tools like the Presentation Chunker, an innovative feature that made it easy to access and share PowerPoint content. At a glance, users could view all the slides from any PowerPoint presentation, add slides to their Slide Basket from different presentations, and download them with a single click. The Presentation Chunker was also regularly employed during live sessions to conduct online meetings and presentations to large groups. The sales force at Avaya referred to the Presentation Chunker as their "killer application" for quickly accessing the information they needed to do their jobs. Thousands of sales and service employees participated in the teleconference that blended live training sessions with online access to knowledge assets hosted on the ASK Center.

The ASK Center supported knowledge sharing and self-nomination of content for the Web site. Users could easily share their own files and Web links with other users by clicking the add/update content. Users received valuable feedback and information on how their content was being accessed, and rated, by other Avaya associates. The ASK Center facilitated collaboration with a number of communities of practice that shared a dynamic library of information, threaded discussions, and downloadable materials, securely, for members only. The ASK Center managing editor updated content, managed who had access, and sent courtesy messages to group members informing them of what was new.

Personalizing the Portal

Users could personalize the ASK Center to fit the way they work. When users identified their organizational function, the interface adjusted to their job context. From here, they set personal preferences to customize their own ASK Center home page. Users who were new to the ASK Center were invited to visit and get acquainted. A quick start for first-time users and an online tour were always available from the home page. The ASK Center was dynamic, growing, and improving all the time, which made Avaya expertise and knowledge accessible and usable to employees worldwide.

Formal and Informal Learning Experiences

In addition to the work to create comprehensive KM portals, the management team created formal and informal learning experiences to bring about the desired cultural transformations in the sales culture. Knowledge hosted in portals alone is necessary but not sufficient to bring about cultural transformation. Sales employees also need time to practice new skills and apply them in authentic learning situations. The Executive Solutions Selling Business Acumen (ESSba) program is an example program.

Executive Solutions Selling Business Acumen

The ESSba curriculum was a 100-hour curriculum delivered over two and one-half months. A total of 208 students participated in sixteen class sessions offered in the ESSba program. The students were senior sales leaders in the CRM business at Avaya, and they were required to keep up with their job-related requirements and immediately apply what they learned as they progressed through the curriculum.

The curriculum used the theme of a mountain expedition to communicate to the students that this was not a traditional corporate training experience and that a great deal of student preparation was required to achieve success in this sales transformation program. The idea behind the theme was that sales representatives needed to be thoroughly prepared to make strategic sales at the top levels in client organizations similar to the way that successful mountain climbers must be thoroughly prepared if they intend to reach the summit of Mt. Everest. For example, an expert mountain climber proceeds from orientation camp to staging camp to base camp before the ascents are attempted to high camp and then the final ascent to the summit.

Similarly, the ESSba curriculum was designed with a series of preparation steps to prepare the students for the top-level executive presentation experience. The curriculum plan had three one-hour teleconferences, various online learning experiences, two week-long face-to-face classroom experiences at a ranch in the Rocky Mountains, and an orientation session for the students with their mountain climber's backpack filled with essential reading materials for the ascent.

The students could track their progress along the twelve steps in the ESSba blended learning curriculum on an ESSba program guide Web site. They needed to complete an actual customer sales experience using the knowledge and skills learned during the program in order to reach the summit and graduate from the ESSba program. The students were selected from various work assignments, countries, and job titles to ensure innovative thinking and cross-fertilization of new ideas in the sales culture of Avaya. The purpose of the program was to reinvent the sales culture, change the perspective on how customer value was created, increase revenues and margins, and expand market share for new products and services.

The ESSba blended learning curriculum employed unique background research activities and outcome objectives. The business acumen assessment content was assembled by interviewing a selected list of customers, interviewing best-in-class sales performers, working with retired corporate executives from Fortune 100 companies, and researching publications from faculty of major business schools. The advanced communications and computer technology content was derived through interviews with faculty from major universities and from interviews with Avaya CRM experts with multiple patents in call center technology. The CRM assessment content was derived from interviewing customers to identify how they viewed their business relationship with Avaya.

The overarching objective of the ESSba curriculum was to transform the selling strategies employed at Avaya from commodity selling to product and services differentiation and then to CRM (see Figure 8.2).

FIGURE 8.2.   ESSba TRANSFORMATIONS IN SELLING STRATEGIES.

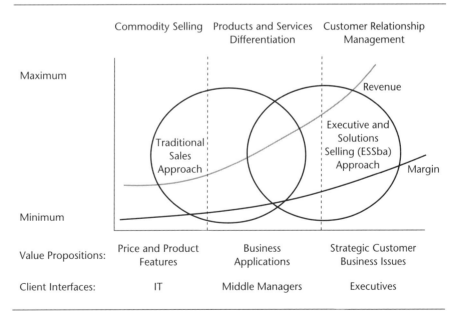

The emphasis was on learning how to offer value propositions that went beyond price and features to address real customer business applications and then build relationships that focused on strategic customer business issues. The intended audience for the sales presentations that the students developed in the ESSba curriculum was the top executive decision maker in the client organization.

The Avaya Institute leadership realized that it needed to employ a new and more innovative approach to design the transformation-focused ESSba curriculum. Therefore, they assembled a design team that consisted of individuals from the ASK Center team, high-performing CRM sales professionals, industry experts, CRM training managers, and contractors including Christensen/Roberts Solutions, Prosci Research, and Kirby-Arnold Associates. The team members were charged with designing a curriculum that provided each student with the knowledge, skills, and confidence-building experiences to achieve the ambitious sales objectives.

ESSba Curriculum Learning Techniques and Delivery Methodologies

The ESSba curriculum was built on a blended learning model that employed a mix of instructor-led training and technology-mediated learning activities. The intent of the design was to emulate the mountain climbing expedition theme and convey a sense of adventure and discovery throughout the experience. A wide variety of innovative learning activities and instruction purposes were designed into the curriculum, as shown in Table 8.1.

ESSba Curriculum Road Map

The ESSba curriculum consisted of five major learning activities. A graphic representation of these activities is provided in Figure 8.3.

Prior to the first teleconference, all students who registered for ESSba session received a carefully designed backpack with all of their essentials: a compass, water bottle, map, cap, and flashlight to symbolize that preparation is required to complete a journey to a lofty goal. The backpack contained the weekly assignments and expectations, homework books, CD-ROMs, and instructions regarding how to access and use their team Web site. They also received an information package outlining the twelve steps to complete their journey (see Figure 8.4).

Staging Camp Teleconference

After the students completed their registration and initial reading assignment and reviewed their materials, they participated in a "staging camp" conference call to set expectations relating to their participation, program purpose, events, and outcomes. The critical topic addressed in the first teleconference was an introduction to the

TABLE 8.1.   EXAMPLES OF LEARNING ACTIVITIES DESIGNED INTO THE ESSba CURRICULUM.

Learning Activity	Instructional Purpose
Assigned reading from textbooks	To provide the theoretical basis for the new customer relationship management model
Assignments on ESSba Web site	To practice applying concepts and monitor learning progress through the curriculum
Audio conference calls	To review prerequisite learning and highlight prior successful CRM sales experiences
Face-to-face role-play experiences	To practice new selling strategies in authentic sales presentation experiences
Mentoring relationships with the instructors	To establish a sounding board and provide constructive feedback in a nonthreatening environment
Online research activity	To search customers' investor relations Web sites and compare financial data with industry trend data
Sales presentation development	To design, develop, and deliver a presentation that would be eventually delivered to customer
Simulation and productivity tools	To estimate benefits of proposed solutions and to incorporate data in the case exercises
Team collaboration	To reinforce the concept that sales professionals are more effective when they team for success
Writing assignments	To ascertain how well students exercised critical thinking skills in their solutions development

FIGURE 8.3.   ESSba CURRICULUM ROAD MAP.

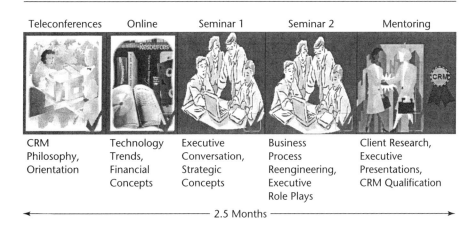

Teleconferences	Online	Seminar 1	Seminar 2	Mentoring
CRM Philosophy, Orientation	Technology Trends, Financial Concepts	Executive Conversation, Strategic Concepts	Business Process Reengineering, Executive Role Plays	Client Research, Executive Presentations, CRM Qualification

◄——————————— 2.5 Months ———————————►

FIGURE 8.4. ESSba PROGRAM GUIDE.

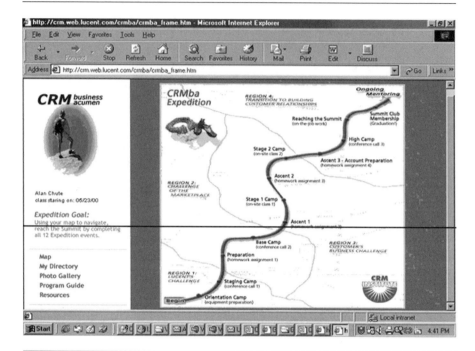

CRM philosophy. The ESSba facilitators led an exercise to draw the group into a discussion of where the company had been, why change was necessary, and how the ESSba program would accelerate the transformation to the new desired state.

The first homework assignment was due two weeks after the base camp teleconference. Students were required to complete a list of required reading and writing assignments as well as access the ESSba Web site. Each person also was required to select an account from his or her sales portfolio to be used as a "living laboratory" for the duration of the curriculum. After the students completed the homework, they e-mailed the two papers to the program leader: one describing their understanding of CRM and one describing their customer's business model as based on their reading and research assignments.

Base Camp Teleconference

The ESSba facilitators then conducted a "base camp" conference call and focused the discussions on understanding targeted customers and the nature of existing relationships. In addition, these discussions attempted to help understand the customer's business culture, decision-making process, and overall business strategy. The objective of this teleconference was to provide the program facilitator an opportunity to assess each participant's business and social skills, as well as to determine potential matches for team assignments. By the end of this teleconference, each student would have acquired a common understanding of CRM concepts and entry-level knowledge of corporate financial metrics.

On-Site Seminars

One month after the base camp conference call, the students were scheduled to arrive at a guest ranch in the Rocky Mountains, west of Denver, Colorado. The site selection was based on a carefully defined need to remove the student from a traditional business environment; minimize access to telephone, Internet, radio, and television; and promote team development of projects. The class was led by an instructor who was a retired executive at the chief executive officer (CXO) level for a Fortune 500 company. During the first week, students learned how they could effectively communicate with a CXO-level client. The class learned advanced business financials and advanced converged technologies and how they affected business processes and work environments. Teams were used to accelerate learning of this content and technology. The evening assignments tied the concepts learned into the development of the students' customer account.

One month later, a second one-week seminar was held at the ranch. During this seminar, each team member made group and individual presentations to share how they could execute the steps of the sales strategy. The role-play experiences with the executive gave the students insights into executive presentation skills and reassured the students that they were able to present effectively to a CXO-level executive. After the seminar, the student needed to schedule a sales call with a CXO-level executive in the client organization and prepare a meeting plan report.

High Camp Teleconference

This teleconference prepared the students to reach the summit and was the last formal training intervention in the curriculum. During the teleconference, the students discussed how they had prepared for their meeting with their CXO-level clients. The students needed to describe the interactions they planned with the customers and discuss the business solution and the new consultative sales concepts they intended to use. If the students needed additional coaching, a mentor was assigned to them.

Return on Investment

Because the CRM sales cycle can take months to close, the ESSba delivery team employed follow-up interviews to determine the impact of the ESSba curriculum on sales results over time. The quantitative sales metrics and revenue results were tracked so that ROI metrics and customer satisfaction indexes could be reported. Over two hundred people, including many senior sales leaders, completed the ESSba curriculum at Avaya. The impact of ESSba was considerable. In the first six months after the curriculum experience, salespeople reported that they were able to increase the close rate on existing sales opportunities, broaden the product mix of each sale, increase the average return on sales, reduce the margin discounting, and trim the sales cycle time by up to ninety days. In the first six months of the program, the financial impact was that the ESSba blended learning curriculum helped generate over $36.3 million in incremental revenue reported with a 46.1 percent program return on investment.

Conclusion

In the past two decades, technology companies have faced incredible challenges. Many technology companies have created comprehensive KM systems and blended learning programs so that sales employees can access existing knowledge and acquire new skills. Successful companies have designed innovative learning programs that enable sales employees to leverage the new knowledge and skills in role-play sessions. Practice in authentic sales experiences with coaching from experienced mentors gives sales employees' confidence that they can perform at world-class levels during executive client engagements. Blended learning models can enable sales employees to transform their sales strategies and achieve significant business results. Knowledge is necessary but not sufficient to bring about sales culture transformation. The recipe for success is: Knowledge + skills + experiences = Transformation.

Alan G. Chute is the strategic marketing vice president for Unisys Corporation. For over twenty-five years, he has been designing and establishing teleconferencing, e-learning, and knowledge management systems for higher education, corporate, and government settings. He has led major learning systems development projects at Unisys, Avaya, Lucent Technologies, AT&T, Indiana University, and the University of South Dakota. He has been elected to the Hall of Fame of the U.S. Distance Learning Association and the International Teleconferencing Association. He received the Outstanding Civilian Service Medal for four years of consulting on the Secretary of the Army's Distance Learning Task Force. He has also published over fifty articles and books on advanced learning systems and telecommunications solutions. Chute has a Ph.D. from the University of Wisconsin-Madison and a Six Sigma Lean Black Belt certification from Juran Institute.

J. O. David Williams is the owner of Business Partner of Colorado, a marketing communications firm focusing on helping other businesses profitably acquire and develop customers. He has worked in the areas of strategic marketing, sales channel strategies, and business development for twenty-five years. He has created original research in customer relationship management business strategies, directed the worldwide sales channel transformation of Lucent Technologies and Avaya Communication, and established sales organizations for AT&T in forty-two countries. He conceived and managed the development of the Executive and Solutions Selling Business Acumen program as a method of changing the sales culture from one of selling product price and feature to a business value–based process that included both academic rigor and

personal transformation of the participants. Williams has a B.A. in business administration from Park University and an M.S. in telecommunications and global business cultures from the University of Denver.

Burton W. Hancock has consulted in building training organizations that focused on improving business performance for Fortune 500 companies. He has been a senior manager with Ernst and Young and now is a senior manager with Deloitte Consulting. He has a successful track record building and turning around training organizations to improve business performance. He introduced blended learning, corporate university, and performance improvement concepts in the organizations that he built for AT&T and Nationwide Insurance. Hancock has also consulted in building training organizations that focused on improving business performance for Fortune 500 companies when he was with Ernst & Young. He has published numerous articles both nationally and internationally in the areas of e-learning, learning strategies, and improving business performance. He also joint-authored *The McGraw-Hill Handbook on Distance Learning.*

CHAPTER NINE

THE CISCO NETWORKING ACADEMY

A Model for the Study of Student Success in a Blended Learning Environment

Alan Dennis, Barbara Bichelmeyer, Dan Henry, Hasan Cakir, Ali Korkmaz, Carol Watson, JoAnne Bunnage

Most of the recent innovation in secondary and higher education has been the result of the integration of digital technologies into the day-to-day work of school administration, teaching, and learning. The economic investments required to provide schools with the hardware, software, and cabling that are necessary for Internet connectivity have created unprecedented school-corporate partnerships in the history of public education. The ability to develop and warehouse large databases has led to the development of national standards for education and computer-based assessment tools that allow the tracking of schools and students in their progress toward meeting those standards. The asynchronous nature of Internet communication has provided a powerful tool for the professional development of teachers, who have historically been restricted in learning opportunities by the constraint of the time they are required to spend in their own classrooms. The development of capabilities for transmitting video and audio through the Internet has led to Internet-based delivery of instructional content that is the basis of virtual schools and degree programs that students can access from anyplace, eliminating the historical emphasis on local control of schools and educational practices. Together, these developments are leading to the blurring of traditional lines of distinction within education sectors and are forever changing the way that schooling and education are administered in the United States and around the world. We are living out an observation made by John Chambers, president and chief executive officer of Cisco Systems, that the Internet is changing the way the world works, lives, plays, and learns (News@Cisco, 2004).

Chambers is responsible for the creation and development of the Cisco Networking Academy, a comprehensive blended learning program that provides students with Internet technology skills that are highly valued in the current global economy. The academy provides Web-based content, online assessment, and tracking of student performance, as well as instructor training and support in order to prepare students for industry standard certification tests and careers in networking and information technology.

Launched in October 1997 with sixty-four educational institutions in seven states, the Cisco Networking Academy is now operating in all states and more than 150 countries around the world. Over 400,000 students have enrolled at more than ten thousand academies located in high schools, technical schools, colleges, universities, and community-based organizations.

The Cisco Networking Academy (CNA) is one example of how blended learning is creating fundamental changes in the nature of public education.

Literature Review

The term *blended learning* is coming into common use in both business and academic environments. The literature base for blended learning has its roots in distance and online education. Theorists and practitioners have somewhat different perspectives regarding the various features of blended learning; however, both groups would likely agree that the essential nature of blended learning is the online delivery of instructional content with on-site implementation of instructional strategies. In corporate settings, blended learning is viewed generally as a combination of any possible instructional solution to a specific business problem (Bernnan, 2004; Thorne, 2003). In academic settings, blended learning has been specifically defined as the combination of the unique and good practices of face-to-face and online learning environments (Osguthorpe & Graham, 2003; Wonacott, 2002) rather than the use of any possible solution for instruction. Ostguthorpe and Graham (2003) also emphasize the use of the term *blended learning* rather than *hybrid learning* because the term *blended* focuses on the harmonic and balanced combination of face-to-face and online learning environments.

Comparing Face-to-Face and Online Learning Environments

Various researchers have attempted to compare the effectiveness of online learning and face-to-face instruction. The research in this area seems inconclusive; there is no strong evidence that one type of learning environment is superior to the other in terms of student learning and satisfaction. Many studies conducted with different subjects and different class sizes have shown no significant differences in student learning outcomes and student satisfaction between online courses and conventional courses (Bolliger & Martindale, 2001; Johnson, Aragon, Shaik, & Palma-Rivas, 1999; Redding & Rotzien, 2001). In some cases, students in online classes demonstrated greater higher-order cognitive skills than students in traditional classes, but these differences were later attributed to student selection. Early research regarding the hypertext delivery format of online instruction found no significant difference in student learning between online and face-to-face learning environments (Dillon & Gabbard, 1998; Neuhauser, 2002; Shapiro & Niederhauser, 2004).

Unique Features of Face-to-Face and Online Learning Environments

When thinking of blended learning as a combination of the unique practices of face-to-face learning and online learning, it is helpful to consider the unique features of both environments.

Synchronicity versus Asynchronycity. One unique instructional feature of a face-to-face learning environment is that it provides direct, place-based, social interaction between the student, the instructor, and other students. This direct, place-based social feature provides a synchronous mode of communication that fosters high motivation and engagement by allowing learners to test their understanding immediately through interactions with instructors and peers.

While face-to-face learning is immediate, online learning is flexible. In online learning environments, course materials and messages between students and instructors are available anywhere and anytime that the student has Internet access, which allows the student to study independently of time and space and to read messages and send messages to the instructor and peers at the student's own convenience. In other words, the online learning environment provides flexibility to students by allowing them to access class materials, resources, and communications at any time and from any location that is convenient (and has an Internet connection).

Fidelity is also an aspect of asynchronicity and synchronicity that has impact on engagement and social presence in learning environments. Fidelity is a measure of richness of communication; generally, synchronous environments such as face-to-face formats have very high fidelity, while asynchronous environments that are primarily audio and text based have very low fidelity.

Consistency versus Variability of Course Content. Every time an instructor presents course content in a face-to-face learning environment, the presentation is in some way unique. For example, time spent on a single point with one class of students is longer than the time spent on the same point with another class; the instructor may forget a key example during a particular presentation; and students ask different questions that require emphasis on different content areas. Therefore, the content presented to students is never exactly the same between one section of a course and another section of the same course. The fact that course content varies easily (and informally) in a face-to-face learning environment means that there is little consistency in the presentation of curriculum content across several iterations of the course.

In the online learning environment, the quality of content is more likely to be consistent throughout all presentations of the material (Boyle, Bradley, Chalk, Jones, & Pickard, 2003) because the content is created and posted to the Web so that all students have access to the same materials throughout the course. Any customization of content is likely a deliberate decision by the instructor to provide different or additional materials for students.

An additional feature related to consistency in online learning environments is that when changes are made to the master resource in an online environment, those changes become immediately available to multiple remote sites.

Standardization versus Individualization of Course Activities. One drawback of face-to-face learning environments is that course activities in these environments generally are one size fits all. In other words, what one student hears or experiences in a classroom presentation is generally what all students hear or experience in the classroom presentation. It is difficult (and perhaps impossible) for an instructor to individualize classroom activities so that the unique needs of twenty-five students are each sufficiently addressed during one class meeting. As a result, individual differences are difficult to address in face-to-face learning environments.

While face-to-face instruction does not adequately allow individualization of course activities, online learning can accommodate students who have different expertise levels, prefer different learning strategies, or are self-directed learners. Individualization of course activities can be achieved using online delivery by providing learners with choices for learning activities that they can complete at their own pace.

Benefits of Blended Learning Environments

By bringing the unique features of online and face-to-face learning environments together, blended learning uses the best of both in order to address the different needs of students.

Osguthorpe and Graham (2003) compiled the results of various case studies of blended learning in order to identify the benefits of blended learning environments; they include (1) pedagogical richness, (2) access to knowledge, (3) social interaction, (4) personal agency, (5) cost-effectiveness, and (6) ease of revision. The first four benefits have to do with possibilities for addressing different needs of learners in order to increase the learning output for all learners. Blended learning creates a flexible environment in which students are engaged in their own learning experiences and in which social interactions between peers and teachers are unrestricted by time and location. Although Osguthorpe and Graham list cost-effectiveness as a benefit of blended learning, it is not necessarily true that online education costs less than face-to-face instruction (Milam, 2000). Nevertheless, one of the great benefits of blended learning in large-scale education initiatives (like the Cisco Networking Academy) is that they provide a centralized curriculum, which makes revisions easy for instructors since changes are required to only one source, while at the same time providing consistent quality for the content of instruction.

In a study examining Australian vocational education programs, researchers found that the combination of flexibility in online learning environments and the interaction between student and instructor in face-to face-learning environments is the most desired combination in blended learning (Cashion & Palmieri, 2002). While flexibility of the online environment allows learners to access and study the material at their convenience, students identify the immediate feedback and corrective action of teachers in face-to-face environments as the most desirable elements of instruction.

One important caveat regarding learning in online environments is that while face-to-face instruction is a familiar and comfortable approach to learning for almost all students and instructors, online learning does not appeal to everyone because it requires some basic level of technology knowledge, as well as the infrastructure to access the Internet and use it. Furthermore, the instructional approaches used for online education are generally more appropriate for individuals who are self-directed learners. The online learning experience can be frustrating, if not impossible, for those who do not have the appropriate prerequisite skills, resources, and attitudes to engage in it (Boyle et al., 2003).

Since blended learning is a new topic of research and practice, there are only a few studies about the effectiveness of these environments. Initial conclusions from research conducted by Burgon and Williams (2003) and Boyle et al. (2003) suggest that student engagement and successful learning outcomes are increased for students in blended learning environments. However, much more work needs to be completed in these areas before any conclusive findings will be reached.

The Cisco Networking Academy as a Blended Learning Environment

In the light of the definitions of blended learning presented earlier in this chapter, the Cisco Networking Academy may be viewed as a blended learning environment based on four key features of the academy: (1) centralized curriculum development, (2) online delivery of content, (3) on-site implementation of instruction, and (4) standardized assessment of learners.

In the remainder of this chapter, we provide an overview of the Cisco Networking Academy, describe in detail the four key features of the academy that characterize it as a blended learning environment, and propose a theoretical framework that may be used to study the effectiveness of the academy, as well as other blended learning environments.

The Cisco Networking Academy was originally developed by Cisco Systems in order to prepare high school and college students to pass the Cisco Networking Certification examination, a certification that provides individuals with opportunities to take good-paying jobs with titles such as network engineer, network administrator, or information technology specialist. These positions are usually with solid, well-performing companies and may well lead the successful student to a career in the information technology sector.

Infrastructure of the Cisco Networking Academy

The programs and courses that are available from the Cisco Networking Academy are all delivered over the Web from Cisco Learning Institute to participating educational institutions, which include high schools, community colleges, technical schools, liberal arts colleges, universities, community organizations, and even a few middle schools. (Since its inception in 1997, the Cisco Learning Institute, a public nonprofit corporation, has evolved from a support organization into a key visionary and contributor to the Cisco Networking Academy Program and a recognized strategic partner to major nonprofits, nongovernmental organizations, governments, and commercial enterprises in advancing the effective use of technology in the process of teaching and learning.)

The courses available through the academy are implemented on-site at the participating educational institution by program instructors. These instructors are generally the regular faculty of the school, who may be teaching courses in information technology, vocational education, computer science, math, English, or any other subject when they are not teaching Cisco Networking Academy courses. In order to teach academy courses, these instructors receive training through an implementation hierarchy that has been developed by Cisco Systems.

Cisco Systems staff have established relationships with approximately twenty educational institutions throughout the United States that serve as Cisco Academy Training Centers (CATCs). Cisco staff provide training to the CATC faculty regarding the curricular content, pedagogical approaches, resources, and materials of the Cisco Networking Academy programs, as well as information about updates to courses on an ongoing basis. In turn, each CATC is responsible for training and support of instructors at between ten and fifty regional training centers (RTCs), which are responsible for training and support of the instructors who teach students at local academies. Each RTC supports between five and fifty local academies, which are generally located near the RTCs that serve them. While the CATCS are the link between Cisco Systems and the participating educational institutions, the RTCs are the link between the CATCs and the local academies. RTC staff make annual visits to academies to ensure the quality of program implementation. In addition, they ensure that each instructor completes sixteen hours of professional development each year. RTCs pass their information up to the CATCs, which are ultimately responsible for collecting data on quality assurance and best practices from the RTCs and local academies under them. (A CATC or RTC may also serve as a local academy, and most CATCs and RTCs offer CNA courses and teach directly to students.) Figure 9.1 is a graphical representation of the CNA hierarchical structure.

The Cisco Networking Academy offers programs and courses on topics such as networking, information technology, Web design, Java, and UNIX. The first and most popular program offered was the Cisco Certified Networking Associate (CCNA) program, which consists of four courses. Students who complete the four courses must pass a final exam at the end of each course; after they complete the program, they may register for and take a certification exam from a third-party assessment company that offers the examination independently of Cisco Systems.

Educational Components of the Cisco Networking Academy

The Cisco Networking Academy provides an interesting example of a blended learning environment that attempts to foster both accountability and meaningful

FIGURE 9.1. CISCO NETWORKING ACADEMY ORGANIZATIONAL HIERARCHY.

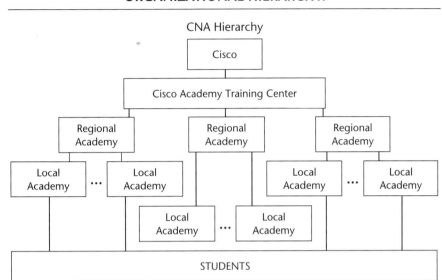

learning in a manner that respects teachers' needs for time and autonomy. The four key elements of the academy are centralized curriculum development; Web-based delivery of curricular content; on-site implementation by instructors who guide, support, and give feedback to students who complete hands-on labs and other learning activities; and standardized online assessment and tracking of student performance in order to prepare students for industry standard certifications.

Centralized Curriculum Development. Centralized development of the academy curriculum provides a cost-effective way to design and revise the content of instruction that has been delivered to approximately 400,000 students in 10,000 academies in 150 countries.

The academy curriculum for students and curriculum guides for instructors are developed by Cisco based on the recommendations of industry experts and program faculty for what students need to know and be able to do in order to be successful in network engineering and network administration positions. Curriculum objectives are set for each course, and course content is developed and tightly organized in order to meet each objective.

The use of a centralized curriculum development strategy allows Cisco to maintain the Standards Alignment Database, which stores and reports the relationships between course objectives for the four CCNA courses and national standards and individual state standards. Each set of standards tracks the curriculum against subject categories such as mathematics, science, and language arts.

The curriculum includes texts, laboratory work, and, increasingly, online simulations. Instructors are invited to join curriculum development teams, offering input on the strengths and weaknesses of all aspects of the curriculum and helping make changes.

One instructor contrasted the CCNA curriculum with the typical situation he faces as a teacher, in which he must decide on a text and build all of the lessons. His opinion is that the CCNA curriculum is thoughtfully assembled by people with greater expertise in the subject area and more time to develop materials than the typical teacher. He noted that the instructional activities in the Cisco program foster conceptual understanding rather than simply practical application of lessons. He also noted that having a centralized, standardized curriculum provides him with more time to think about his students and how to be working with them in class. From his perspective, the CCNA curriculum yields good-quality materials and allows teachers to use more of their time to think about teaching.

Online Content Delivery. All curriculum materials are delivered over the Internet. When students register for a CCNA course, they are provided a log-in identification and password that allow them to access the course content at any time and from anywhere they have an Internet connection.

The primary benefit of online content delivery for students is that it provides consistent content that is updated and improved on a regular basis, and these materials are made available to students in a cost-effective manner.

Online content delivery provides the same benefits for instructors as for students. For the instructor, the online content becomes the background or prework that students complete leading up to a classroom activity or a hands-on lab. Teachers' primary concerns regarding online content generally have to do with issues of accessibility in case hardware breaks or Internet connections go down. Yet these concerns are not apparently too great because although books are available to supplement the online materials, few academies choose to purchase them or recommend them to their students.

On-Site Implementation of Instruction. For students, on-site implementation provides opportunities for the social interaction of face-to-face learning environments, including time to receive guidance, feedback, and support from instructors and to work with peers while solving practical problems in hands-on lab activities.

For instructors, online implementation means that although the curriculum is provided by Cisco, instructors can rearrange, deemphasize some content sections, and enhance the curriculum as they deem appropriate. They can choose any of a variety of instructional strategies to support students' achievement of curricular objectives, customize lessons by providing remediation or enrichment experiences, check on students' readiness for assessment before students take online tests, and provide specific contextual guidance for how a general concept or procedure might work in their particular networking environment. Because instructors are responsible for the on-site implementation of the curriculum, all the resources provided by Cisco serve as support for, rather than an imposition on, instructors.

Standardized Assessment of Learners. The Cisco Networking Academy assessment strategy comprises a variety of interactive online exams and hands-on performance assessments. Assessments, like the curriculum, are developed by Cisco and administered at the academies. The assessments are closely matched with the objectives, curriculum materials, and instructional activities for each course in order to facilitate students' mastery of course objectives effectively and efficiently. The online assessments are administered directly to students through a Web-based interface, and the hands-on performance assessments are administered by instructors in labs based on resource materials provided by Cisco. In both cases, assessments are designed to inform students about their performance in order to improve learning, as well as to hold students and teachers accountable for results.

The online tests are scored by computer programs, and results are warehoused in large databases by Cisco's staff in assessment, research, and evaluation. Students, instructors, and CCNA program administrators receive test results. Testing provided to students also provides immediate personalized feedback to students. Because they are designed using advanced statistical techniques most commonly found in statewide or national exams, each test also allows normative comparisons between students, academies, RTCs, and CATCs. Over thirty thousand online assessments are taken each day in the academy program around the world.

Instructors have freedom in how they use tests and test results. Test scores may be a primary or a minimal factor in the student's final grade; therefore, testing is not necessarily a high-stakes experience for the student. One instructor noted that on occasion, the class will collaborate in taking the test as a learning exercise.

Instructors may provide input about the tests just as they do with the curriculum, having the opportunity to join test development teams and work on revising tests with Cisco staff. The result is that the test development process involves a good mixture of expertise in testing, the content domain, and instructional strategies.

Although teachers have flexibility in test administration, it is also true that low test scores at an academy will trigger an administrative flag in the program hierarchy. CATC or RTC staff will visit the academy, observe teaching practices, and review instructional activities to ensure that they are sound. If it appears that teaching practices are not engaging to the students or teachers are not setting appropriate expectations for learning, professional development support will be provided. Finally, data from assessments are also used by staff at Cisco to adapt curriculum content in order to improve instructional activities and resulting student achievement.

An important distinction exists between the standardized assessments that are used as part of CCNA course work and the standardized assessment known as the CCNA certification examination, which students take from an independent test administrator after they have completed all four courses of the CCNA program. An analogy that may help to distinguish between the standardized assessments that are part of CCNA course work and the certification examination would be to think of the certification examination as equivalent to the Scholastic Aptitude Test and the standardized assessments as equivalent to unit tests that classroom teachers administer to students. This analogy should also help readers understand the revolutionary difference between traditional classroom tests and CCNA's standardized assessments: CCNA assessments serve to determine students' course grades, but they are based on item analysis, norm referencing, and database warehousing that are the hallmark of national examinations that measure student achievement.

Approaches to Blended Learning in the Cisco Networking Academy

Research is underway in order to understand the impact of the Cisco Networking Academy model on student achievement. Part of this research initiative includes developing an understanding of the approaches to blended learning that are used in various academy programs and courses. Although curriculum and assessments are standardized and delivered over the Web, instructors are free to implement curriculum and tests in whatever ways they deem appropriate to support student learning and achievement.

Four general approaches to blended learning may be used by instructors in the CNA environment. One approach, drawn from traditional classroom practice, is to structure the course following the lecture method, using the online curriculum to prepare learners for lecture and the online tests for postlecture student assessment. A second approach in this blended learning environment is for students to read online curriculum in advance of class meetings, complete online tests, and receive feedback at the beginning of class; then the majority of class time is spent with the instructor and students working together through discussion and activities to address knowledge gaps identified in the testing. A third approach follows a format in which students read online materials prior to class and then attend class sessions, which are primarily discussions or question-and-answer sessions, after which students complete online tests. A fourth approach to blended learning in the CNA environment is similar to self-regulated learning approaches: students read online materials, complete instructional activities, and take online tests, using the instructor as a resource when needed.

The blended learning approaches demonstrate a range of formats that may be used to support student achievement, which brings us back to the core issue regarding blended learning. The real test of the value of blended learning as a model for education is and always will be its impact on student achievement.

Conclusion

Student achievement is a result of the interaction of complex, multidimensional, and interrelated factors (Rowe & Hill, 1998; Walberg, 1984). Most educational effectiveness studies consider three types of variables: student individual characteristics, instructional elements, and environmental factors (Lee, 2000). It is likely that many of the multiple factors that affect student achievement in face-to-face learning environments will also affect student achievement in blended learning environments. Therefore, we propose that an appropriate starting point for understanding the CCNA program in particular, and blended learning environments in general, would be to focus on the same variables studied by previous educational productivity researchers. The interaction among these variables in a proposed theoretical framework is depicted in Figure 9.2.

Understanding the factors that affect student success will help designers of blended learning environments to improve the instruction and effectiveness of their

FIGURE 9.2. PROPOSED THEORETICAL FRAMEWORK FOR UNDER-STANDING THE VARIABLES THAT BEAR ON STUDENT SUCCESS.

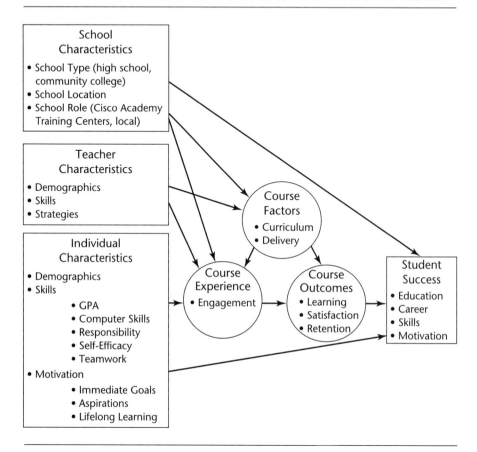

particular programs. The current and ongoing evaluation of the Cisco Networking Academy will provide data to answer this question in a particular blended learning context. We encourage educational researchers to study blended learning in other contexts in the hopes that our shared efforts will shed light on a topic that is becoming of increasing importance as educators everywhere continue to rely more heavily on the Internet and the World Wide Web to support learning and instruction.

More information about the Networking Academy program is available on the Web at cisco.netacad.net.

References

Bernnan, M. (2004). Blended learning and business change. *Chief Learning Officer, 3*(1), 58–60.

Bolliger, D., & Martindale, T. (2001, November 8–12). *Student satisfaction in an online master's degree program in instructional technology.* Paper presented at the 24th National Convention of the Association for Educational Communications and Technology, Atlanta, GA.

Boyle, T., Bradley, C., Chalk, P., Jones, R., & Pickard, P. (2003). Using blended learning to improve student success rates in learning to program. *Journal of Educational Media, 28*(2/3), 165–178.

Burgon, H., & Williams, D. D. (2003). CASE 3: Bringing off-campus students on campus: An evaluation of a blended course. *Quarterly Review of Distance Education, 4*(3), 253–260.

Cashion, J., & Palmieri, P. (2002). *"The secret is the teacher": The learners' view of online learning.* Adelaide, South Australia: National Centre for Vocational Education Research.

Dillon, A., & Gabbard, R. (1998). Hypermedia as an educational technology: A review of the quantitative research literature on learner comprehension, control, and style. *Review of Educational Research, 68*(3), 322.

Johnson, S. D., Aragon, S. R., Shaik, N., & Palma-Rivas, N. (1999). *Comparative analysis of online vs. face-to-face instruction.* Paper presented at the WebNet99 World Conference on the WWW and Internet, Honolulu, HI.

Lee, V. E. (2000). Using hierarchical linear modeling to study social contexts: The case of school effects. *Educational Psychologist, 35*(2), 125–141.

Milam, J. H., Jr. (2000, May 21–23). *Cost analysis of online courses. AIR 2000 annual forum paper.* Paper presented at the 40th Annual Forum of the Association for Institutional Research, Cincinnati, OH.

Neuhauser, C. (2002). Learning style and effectiveness of online and face-to-face instruction. *American Journal of Distance Education, 16*(2), 99.

News@Cisco. (2004). *Celebrating 20 years of changing the way we live, work, play and learn.* Retrieved June 30, 2004, from http://newsroom.cisco.com/dlls/2004/hd_052504f.html.

Osguthorpe, R. T., & Graham, C. R. (2003). Blended learning environments. *Quarterly Review of Distance Education, 4*(3), 227–233.

Redding, T. R., & Rotzien, J. (2001). Comparative analysis of online learning versus classroom learning. *Journal of Interactive Instruction Development, 13*(4), 3–12.

Rowe, K.K.J., & Hill, P.P.W. (1998). Modeling educational effectiveness in classrooms: The use of multi-level structural equations to model students' progress. *Educational Research and Evaluation, 4*(4), 233.

Shapiro, A., & Niederhauser, D. (2004). Learning from hypertext: Research issues and findings. In D. H. Jonassen (Ed.), *Handbook of research for educational communications and technology: A project of the Association for Educational Communications and Technology* (2nd ed.). Mahwah, NJ: Erlbaum.

Thorne, K. (2003). *Blended learning: How to integrate online and traditional learning.* Sterling, VA: Kogan Page.

Walberg, H. J. (1984). Improving the productivity of America's schools. *Educational Leadership, 41*(8), 19.

Wonacott, M. E. (2002). *Blending face-to-face and distance learning methods in adult and career-technical education.* (ERIC Document Reproduction Service No. ED470783)

Alan Dennis is professor of information systems and holds the John T. Chambers Chair of Internet Systems in the Kelley School of Business at Indiana University. He received his Ph.D. in management information systems from the University of Arizona, his M.B.A. from Queen's University, and his bachelor of computer science from Acadia University. His research focuses on team collaboration, knowledge management, and the use of the Internet. He has written four books and more than one hundred journal articles and conference papers and has won numerous awards for teaching and research. He is currently the publisher of *MIS Quarterly Executive* and serves on the editorial boards of *Journal of Management Information Systems, Journal of the Association for Information Systems, Journal of Computer Mediated Communication,* and *Journal of e-Collaboration.*

Barbara Bichelmeyer is associate professor of instructional systems technology in the School of Education at Indiana University. She received her Ph.D.

in curriculum and instruction and her master's in history and philosophy of education from the University of Kansas. She serves as a senior research associate on the Cisco Networking Academy Evaluation project. Her research explores the uses of instructional design and technology to foster intentionality toward learning among students. She has written articles that have been published in refereed journals such as *Educational Technology Research and Development, Performance Improvement Quarterly, College Teaching,* and *Distance Education* and has won numerous awards for teaching and research.

Dan Henry is assistant professor of teacher education at Central Michigan University. He teaches classes in educational psychology and program evaluation. His undergraduate degree (in secondary education) and Ph.D. (in educational psychology) are from Indiana University Bloomington. Henry taught at the secondary level for eleven years and has taught students from elementary to doctoral levels. He has authored articles on inclusion of students in special needs classrooms and has served as principal investigator in several national-level program evaluations, including the Michigan Small Class Size Initiative study. His dissertation and current research focus on application of theories from ecological psychology to online learning environments. His publications include articles in *Teaching Exceptional Children* and *Exceptional Children* and poetry in *Yankee Magazine.*

Hasan Cakir is a doctoral candidate in instructional systems technology at Indiana University. He serves as a research assistant for the Cisco Network Academy Evaluation project. His dissertation focuses on the relationships of instructional practices, student engagement, and student achievement in various learning environments.

Ali Korkmaz is a doctoral candidate in instructional systems technology at Indiana University. He earned his M.S. in science education and B.S. in mathematics education from Bogazici University, Istanbul, Turkey. He is a research assistant for the Cisco Network Academy Evaluation. His research focuses on teaching and learning strategies.

Carol Watson is the associate director for the High School Survey of Student Engagement at Indiana University and faculty at Walden University. She received her Ph.D. in instructional systems technology from Indiana University. Her research explores online courses in undergraduate education and methods for fostering engagement in distance education.

JoAnne Bunnage is project manager for the Cisco Network Academy Evaluation project. Previously, she was project associate with the National Survey of Student Engagement and held administrative positions at the University of Notre Dame, Oregon State University, and the University of Washington. Bunnage consults with GEAR UP, Upward Bound, and Indiana's Twenty-first Century Scholars Program. She has coauthored articles on focus group research and student-athlete achievement. In addition, she has provided technical assistance for a monograph on college choice and women's involvement with the College Board. She is currently researching factors influencing postsecondary participation. Bunnage earned her Ph.D. from Indiana University, master's of administration from the University of Notre Dame, and master's and bachelor's degrees from Oregon State University.

CHAPTER TEN

TO BLEND OR NOT TO BLEND

A Look at Community Development via Blended Learning Strategies

Kirsten S. Hanson, Frances A. Clem

Most large organizations today, and many small ones, are evaluating blended learning approaches as a substitute for either instructor-led training (ILT) or wholly online learning. Blended learning is often seen as being more complete or better supported than ILT, while offering improved student interaction opportunities compared to learning that takes place solely online. Yet few studies have been conducted on the actual outcomes of blended initiatives and experiences.

At Oracle Corporation, the Leader Track courses were designed and developed in a blended format for the foregoing reasons, with the objective of improving student results and cost-effectiveness. Certain domains require students to practice and integrate knowledge and skills if they are to apply them effectively in their real work. Leadership is one such subject area. In addition, Oracle found that the challenges inherent in communicating consistent messages and building its organization and its people across global and cultural boundaries were difficult to manage in purely online or classroom-based environments. As a result, it was hoped that a blended approach would yield improved results.

Like all other competitive corporations, Oracle is eager to remain at the forefront of investing in and retaining its top employee talent. Nevertheless, designing and implementing a blended format for leadership development was deemed reasonable only if it would result in improved learning outcomes and benefits. At the same time, we hoped it would encourage employees to develop stronger professional interconnections and an enhanced sense of being a part of the Oracle community. To evaluate this, we conducted a series of exploratory studies during the first-year implementation of blended courses at Oracle, which had interesting results.

The Background on Blended Learning

Many corporate training departments offer classroom learning or online learning as separate training options. In the past, participants could choose to enroll in their preferred delivery method. More recently, blended learning, usually considered to be the combination of technological solutions and traditional classroom instruction, has attracted increasing interest from corporate trainers and others engaged in education.

It is challenging to find a widely accepted definition of *blended learning*, and even more difficult to find a core set of literature on blended learning methodologies. In general, training approaches can be located on a continuum that runs from traditional, face-to-face class meetings to totally online courses that have no direct interpersonal contact (Schwartzman & Tuttle, 2002). Blended learning, a phenomenon of the last decade, is generally acknowledged as falling somewhere between these two extremes, incorporating elements of each.

It is important to review the theoretical foundations that already exist for blending learning. Instructional designers have a variety of theories to guide them in developing instructional materials for instructor-led training (Gagne, 1965). Increasingly, they are also finding what works in asynchronous, online environments.

It is compelling and relevant to recognize two of the important basic elements in the natural learning process: learning by reflection and experience. As Schank (1995) explains with various teaching architectures or approaches in his book, *Engines for Education,* he reminds us that cognitive scientists agree that learning by reflection is essential for mental processing and understanding. This reflection occurs only when the learner has time to mull something over and contemplate questions or new ways of thinking about a situation. Reflection deepens a learner's understanding of a domain, allowing him or her to become more facile with the subject matter, and it is central for knowledge transfer to the workplace. A major opportunity for it occurs in the reinforcement activities afforded by blended learning. According to Bean (2002), "Reinforcement is where the knowledge transfer takes place. It is the ability to deploy a number of value-added products and services to surround your employees and maximize the transfer of learning to the workplace" (p. 25).

A second important element in a human's natural learning process goes back to John Dewey (1938). Dewey argued that all genuine education comes through experience. Yet he further explained that it "does not mean that all experiences are genuinely or equally educative" (p. 25). Dewey held that poor experiences, not the absence of experiences, are the problem, and what makes them defective is their lack of connection to further experiences. Recent work by Sticht (1994) and others on situated learning and functional context education tends to amplify Dewey's concept that all learning proceeds from prior learning. The concepts of reflection, genuine learning, situated learning, and building on previous experience are particularly important to designers of blended learning because the student's learning outcomes are dependent on a series of experiences created throughout the blended learning process. Although Dewey wrote over sixty years ago, his ideas still have relevance in today's corporate training, because it is the educator's (or trainer's) responsibility to create genuine, meaningful experiences to ensure the learner continues on the blended learning path rather than becoming bored or disinterested.

The challenge for distance education researchers, as Saba (2000) explains, is the theoretical complexity of the field and the lack of corresponding methods of data collection and analysis. Even with novel technologies, improved student outcomes are more likely to be attributed to improved pedagogy and the strong implementation of a supporting infrastructure rather than to the technology that was used to deliver the content. Also, Clark (1983) asserted that the medium does not influence learning. Clark explains that the choice of the delivery method can influence the cost or extent of distributing instruction, but only the content of the chosen method can influence learner achievement. Decades later, instructional designers are well served to remember the lessons learned from Clark, Schank, Dewey, and Saba. Yet student outcomes have not traditionally considered community.

Community Building in Blended Contexts

It is worth exploring how an enhanced sense of corporate community can have an impact on learner achievement. While it is not usually considered a direct learning outcome of training, the creation of a learning community can be the result of pedagogical design.

Although there is descriptive and prescriptive literature regarding fully online learning communities (for example, Bonk & Dennen, 2000; Palloff & Pratt, 1999), it is difficult to find applicable research about the dynamics of learning communities in blended learning (mixed media) environments. One study that compared an entirely classroom experience to an entirely online experience did indicate a statistically significant difference in the amount of confidence and social connection that students felt in each environment (Johnson, Aragon, Shaik, & Palma-Rivas, 1999). There was no difference shown in the learning outcomes with students from both course formats, but student perceptions of confidence and social connection were lower in the online experience than the classroom experience. Interestingly, a recent study by Rovai and Jordan (2004) found that blended courses produced a stronger sense of community among students than either traditional or fully online courses. Given these contrasting findings, we wondered what kind of results we would see at Oracle.

Oracle's Leader Track

Oracle does not believe in training for the sake of training. For example, it does not mandate specific training for its managers (except for required governmental compliance topics). Unlike some other large private sector companies, Oracle uses an organic approach to development, expecting and encouraging employees and managers to take responsibility for their own careers and personal development.

It was this perspective that guided Oracle to move several years ago from a training mind-set to a human development mind-set, acknowledging the need to invest in methodologies (that is, training) that provide meaningful experiences that employees can learn from and apply to their real work responsibilities. Furthermore, Oracle's culture does not require attendance in training courses (unless a specific executive nominates employees to participate). As a result, Oracle employees tend to have limited patience for poor-quality instruction. Given this freedom to select one's own learning and the fact that Oracle employees tend to be facile users of technology, blended learning designs provide learners with a path, that is, a systematic approach to development, of relevant experiences and concepts that can be reinforced through an integrated classroom and online approach over time. Consequently, blended learning is becoming a more complete development solution for the optimal growth of employees, especially those in leadership roles, and often it is more successful than what we had anticipated.

Since quality leadership has the potential to have a great impact on the building of high-performance teams, Oracle decided to focus its initial blended learning development efforts on managers. Oracle's Leader Track is a leadership program that consists of four modules, each containing a two-day, face-to-face workshop and virtual learning opportunities to enhance and practice key skills and concepts. In one module, the face-to-face workshop takes place in the first week, two modules have the workshop in the second week, and the fourth module has the workshop in the fourth week. In each module, three or four synchronous online classes take place before and after the face-to-face experience. (These can also be replayed online and watched if participants miss the live delivery with facilitator, slides, and voice communications.) Online 360-degree assessments and telephone sessions with virtual, personal coaches are also part of each module design. Participants are asked to post reflections to the discussion board on iLearning (Oracle's Learning Management System) and complete an actual work assignment for each of the four modules. Executive involvement also plays an important role, with Oracle executives participating as mentors, guest speakers, or workshop panelists in each module. The blended design philosophy is to scaffold manager learning on real, relevant work activities and help them integrate knowledge and skills on the job over time.

The time commitment for each module is approximately thirty-five to forty hours spread across a five-week period, including the two-day workshop. Although designed to be taken in sequence, each module can be taken based on a manager's current needs.

Studying Blended Outcomes at Oracle

We performed two separate exploratory studies on Oracle's Leader Track. In the larger of the two studies, in which we looked at the benefits of the blended format (we referred to this as the benefits study), we had the unique opportunity to compare two training courses in the management curriculum that teach the same domain. One of the blended learning modules, which focused on helping managers lead with their values, also existed as a classroom-only course. At the time of this study of blended learning benefits, Oracle managers had the option of taking the two-day classroom experience or the blended learning experience, which included the same two-day classroom event as well as four supporting weeks of virtual learning activities. By comparing outcomes of the two versions of the same course, we hoped to understand better the effect of blended learning as compared to the classroom-only version of the course.

Six ILT participants and thirteen blended participants were interviewed for this study. Subjects in each group were of comparable employment levels as department managers and directors and had personally elected to take one of these courses to develop their leadership skills. In this study, participants were interviewed by a non-Oracle researcher using a protocol; each interview was recorded and transcribed. An outside coder, who had been trained for this analysis, read and coded the transcriptions, removing identifying information. The non-Oracle researcher then reviewed all coded responses with the coder to resolve questions and ambiguities.

In the smaller study, we considered the overall Leader Track (not just the values-based leadership module) to explore the learning community aspect of the blending learning design. This learning community study began with a review of three focus group transcripts from the blended modules. These groups were undertaken by Oracle to assess learners' summative opinions about the training after having completed one or more modules. These transcripts helped inform the creation of our interview protocol. We then interviewed five past participants who varied in years of experience at Oracle, types of positions, and gender. Both researchers evaluated the transcribed interviews to discern and analyze participants' comments, categorizing opinions to find unifying themes.

Although both studies were exploratory and limited in subjects, blended learning appeared to introduce several new and exciting dynamics.

Building Community Through Learning

We were gratified that most participants interviewed, regardless of which group they were part of, were positive about their learning experience in the values-based leadership course. Furthermore, when we compared content retention with an online evaluation after three months, there was no significant difference between the blended and ILT based groups, as researchers such as Clark may have predicted.

There was one conspicuous difference between the blended and the ILT groups, however. In the benefits study, blended and ILT participants were asked a series of open-ended questions about their experiences in their respective environments. Blended participants frequently commented on collaboration with peers and support from the program. The ILT participants did not reference interactions with their peers or a sense of community; instead, they focused almost solely on the classroom instructor.

Sample comments from participants in the blended groups included:

"The biggest influence was to give me contacts and a bigger picture and sort of a navigational device, a way to articulate what I felt about strong leadership."

"Basically when you're a supervisor, manager, leader, you have a lot of the same problems, and so the sharing was a really good experience. And I heard a lot of others say the same thing."

"I think this has humanized Oracle a little more for me. Because of my own earlier background, I always had a perception of Oracle as a very aggressive organization, . . . but when I met with other people during the course, I did see that many people have pretty similar issues."

We were struck by the range and types of benefits all the study participants noted for the training; we wondered if there were any trends evident in terms of which group felt it had benefited more from their respective training strategy. We categorized the responses to see patterns, according to whether the perceived benefit was primarily internal (attitudinal or cognitive changes) or external (explicit, observable behavior change), or whether it was simply a reinforcement of what the individual was already thinking, feeling, or doing. We further defined our categories by coupling them with either "self" or "company" labels. This labeling was used to indicate who was the primary beneficiary of the internal or external changes. Reinforcement was not associated with a "self" or "company" label because participants explained it as a general application. Table 10.1 shows examples of each type of benefit:

TABLE 10.1.   TYPES OF BENEFITS IDENTIFIED IN ORACLE'S LEADERSHIP TRAINING.

"The course made me realize that the individual is much more empowered in today's environment than ever before." (Blended)	Self/internal benefit
"I think the leadership training classes have applications . . . probably throughout my life. So I've sort of taken that approach . . . in my dealings with my personal relationships as well." (ILT)	Self/internal benefit
"I think I look at my employees a little differently. . . . I see them as capable of delivering much more and that the only way they can deliver that is for me to motivate them." (Blended)	Company/internal benefit
"I guess the most tangible thing I can point to . . . is maybe I've kept two or three of my people motivated to the point where they haven't resigned." (Blended)	Company/external benefit
"I think it just encouraged me to communicate more with my employees. . . . This is a reinforcement of the benefits of sharing your feelings." (Blended)	Reinforcement

TABLE 10.2. PARTICIPANT BENEFITS FROM ILT AND BLENDED METHODOLOGIES.

	Self/ Internal	Self/ External	Company/ Internal	Company/ External	Reinforcement
Instructor-led training ($N = 6$)	1.33	1.17	0.50	0.67	0.17
Blended participants ($N = 13$)	1.46	0.08	1.00	1.69	0.31

We counted and averaged the benefits for blended and ILT learners according to these labels. In every category except the "self/external" benefits, the blended participants reported more benefits than the ILT participants (Table 10.2).

Although we were looking for trends rather than statistical significance, the data on benefits between ILT and blended learners had a significance of over 90 percent (independent samples test), indicating a fairly strong likelihood of a relationship between total number of benefits (dependent variable) and type of instructional strategy (independent variable).

As blended learners appeared to benefit more and comment more frequently on the sense of community, we turned to the learning community study to focus on the dynamics of community building, particularly how the mix of face-to-face and online interaction might affect the learners.

Dynamics of Blending

According to the literature, learning communities require a level of interpersonal trust (Bonk, Wisher, & Nigrelli, 2004). In fact, we found the development of trust in the blended learning modules to be related to the type of content being taught and the timing of the face-to-face event (that is, which week in the five-week program). It appeared that when people know there is a classroom experience planned later in the program, they might withhold trust until they meet each other face-to-face. This finding surprised us, as many sources (for example, Palloff & Pratt, 1999) comment on the quick development of trust in a solely online environment. Such results raise a question that deserves further investigation: Is trust more closely linked to course content or the expectation of meeting? A lesson we drew from these findings is that trust may not automatically develop online when a follow-up face-to-face event is planned; instead, it is likely affected by other factors. A blended design may ultimately deepen trust in a community because online activities have the potential to extend relationships after face-to-face sessions; however, this too requires additional study.

Comments about trust from a few participants include the following:

"It's hard to build a good, solid, working relationship without some kind of face-to-face."

"I felt more of a connection [to colleagues] in class, but I didn't feel much of a connection online—it was more difficult to form a connection online. It also appeared to me that other people in the course weren't having as much difficulty in doing that; some of the other people in the course seemed like they were more involved than I was."

"I thought the best way of going through the modules was to have everyone in the classroom setting, the sooner the better. . . . For me, I prefer the first week. . . . I think it really brought people together and formed a real sense of community; people got to know each other, they bonded, and then they were more inclined to participate in the online events going forward. . . . You can put a face with a name . . . and you didn't want to let that person down. It definitely builds commitment."

We saw considerable evidence that our learners strongly valued the community in the blended environment. They appeared to realize that this was an aspect of the experience that would be missing if they took only the classroom segment. Our learners were inclined to look at the blended experience instrumentally; the amount of learner investment depended on the amount of value received from the community.

Comments about value from a few participants in these interviews included:

"Being less inclined toward groups by nature, I saw a lot of people in the course where I could see a lot of value in creating a tighter network with a lot of people."

"One of the things I got out of it was meeting people from the rest of the company and understanding that they deal with the same kinds of challenges as I do."

"Trust is important to the learning community . . . the bond . . . one of the things people experienced that they didn't expect to experience . . . this is true in both online and classroom . . . is that they discovered they weren't so isolated. . . . They're so focused on their own little division and they don't realize others are experiencing the same problems or dilemmas."

Content and goal congruence affected learners' involvement in the community and the course. For example, if the content involved more self-discovery than specific task orientation, learners were often more engaged in the course. Interestingly, we also realized that learners seemed to use the community for instrumental (task-oriented) reasons rather than experiential (social) reasons. This led us to suspect that job-oriented training environments may stimulate different motivational factors than academic learning environments would, an issue that instructional designers should consider in organizational training environments as well as those in higher education who are creating workplace learning courses and activities.

Other Blended Outcomes

We saw evidence in this learning community study of other effects of a blended environment that are worth noting. First, blended participants tended to place the most importance on the delivery method with the highest-touch element. For example, the face-to-face classroom experience was often seen as the actual or primary instructional event, while the online and virtual activities were viewed as support elements to the classroom experience. If further research and evaluation continue to support this hypothesis, it could have significant implications for the placement of content within delivery media in blended environments.

Second, it was clear that organizational culture and environment have a strong effect on the formation and building of a learning community. For example, a culture like the one at Oracle Corporation tends to be very action oriented and allows minimal time for reflection and deeper collaboration with classmates, which is a primary factor in learning. Hence, the cultural norms can have an impact on the level of commitment to a learning community in a blended learning design. These factors act as constraints on the formation and functioning of learning communities in corporate environments and change the dynamics of learners' expected benefits in exchange for their investment of time in the community. It is likely that any shift in the training mind-set toward valuing a more integrated and on-the-job learning environment would involve many company cultures and norms.

Finally, the interviews reinforced the fact that different personality types have different needs and require different instructional methods. Similar to the impact of environment, this has implications on how participants tend to view the relevance and value of the learning community, and thus the time and effort they are willing to invest in it. As instructional designers, we must remind ourselves that learners' personality characteristics will affect how they view not only training content, but also the delivery media and interpersonal outcomes of the training as well.

Is Community Worth It?

We saw much in our studies that gratified us and convinced us that a blended approach was advantageous in Oracle's existing training environment, including a higher level of perceived benefits for learners as well as an enhanced sense of community both during and after the training. These are subtle but important effects. In the benefits study, it also seemed that blended participants were more favorable toward Oracle as a result of their learning experience; blended learners were 30.4 percent more positive when asked how strongly they would recommend Oracle to a potential employee. Further study is needed to evaluate this phenomenon adequately, but we found it encouraging.

Despite these positive results, given the additional cost associated with implementing the blended approach, we must ask whether it was worth it. There is much information available now on evaluating the return on investment (ROI) related to corporate training (for example, Goldwasser, 2001; Phillips, 2003; Purcell, 2000), but it is challenging and potentially error prone to evaluate the ROI for results such as community building, perception of benefits, or an improved attitude toward the company.

Calculating the marginal costs associated with a blended module is relatively easy. By adding operating costs for the blended format to the opportunity cost of the extra time blended learners had to devote to a module, then amortizing total blended module development costs across the first year of operation, we found that the additional cost per learner was $3,157. Oracle estimated that 140 employees would participate in a module in the first year, at a total cost of about $440,000. In the years beyond that, assuming all other figures stay constant and the amortized development costs are eliminated, the cost for Oracle to involve another 140 participants would be reduced to approximately $320,000. These figures for the first and second years of implementation turned out to be approximately .0055 percent and .0039 percent of Oracle's overall revenue, respectively.

Clearly, from a financial standpoint, the estimated cost to the company may be unnoticeable when it comes to Oracle's overall finances. From a learning outcomes point of view, since these studies seem to indicate that learners' sense of community, perceived benefits, and employee attitude all improve when enrolled in a blended learning course, Oracle's return on the training investment seems strong. With a relatively small marginal investment from the corporation, it seems that greater employee commitment and increased benefits to the company can be enjoyed.

If a company like Oracle desires to have a positive impact on its employees such that increased contributions to the company may also occur, a blended learning approach may be a step in the right direction. With blended learning, employees feel the company has invested more in them and supported them better in their learning. In response, employees appear to have a more positive attitude about the company. These simple outcomes can go a long way when it comes to developing company loyalty, strong ethical standards, and high productivity, but the extent to which these are valued will vary from company to company.

The Future of Blended Learning at Oracle

Oracle intends to continue its approach of blended learning development. As with any other service, training, or product, 100 percent of the people will never be pleased 100 percent of the time. However, blended approaches seem to generate intangible benefits, such as community formation, that are nearly impossible to measure, although they are ultimately essential to an organization's success.

Community (or human networks) seems to be a key element in extending and sustaining employee learning and contributions over a period of time. Our exploratory studies lead us to believe that blended learning designs help to facilitate such peer interactions and networks better than online or ILT alone. In addition, our studies indicate that learning communities in blended environments were used not for social reasons primarily but for more task-oriented needs. Although the integration of blended learning activities requires a behavioral shift in most organizations, the benefits could prove to be significant for an organization over the long term.

References

Bean, M. (2002, September). Training and technology: Methods that work in global enterprise. *Chief Learning Officer, 1*(1), 22–25.

Bonk, C. J., & Dennen, V. (2000, August). *More advances in Web pedagogy: Fostering interaction and the online learning community.* Paper presented at the Distance Learning Sixteenth Annual Conference on Distance Teaching and Learning, Madison, Wisconsin. (ERIC No. ED456235)

Bonk, C. J., Wisher, R. A., & Nigrelli, M. L. (2004). Learning communities, communities of practice: Principles, technologies, and examples. In K. Littleton, D. Faulkner, & D. Miell (Eds.), *Learning to collaborate, collaborating to learn* (pp. 199–219). Hauppauge, NY: NOVA Science Publishers.

Clark, R. E. (1983). Reconsidering research on learning from media. *Review of Educational Research, 53*(4), 445–459.

Dewey, J. (1938). *Experience and education.* New York: Macmillan.

Gagne, R. M (1965). *The conditions of learning.* New York: Holt.

Goldwasser, D. (2001). Beyond ROI. *Training and Development, 38*(1), 82–90.

Johnson, S., Aragon, S., Shaik, N., & Palma-Rivas, N. (1999). *Comparative analysis of online vs. face-to-face instruction.* Paper presented at WebNet 99 World Conference on the WWW and Internet Proceedings, Honolulu. (ERIC No. ED448722)

Palloff, R. M., & Pratt, K. (1999). *Building learning communities in cyberspace: Effective strategies for the online classroom.* San Francisco: Jossey-Bass.

Phillips, J. (2003). *Ten guiding principles for ROI.* ASTD. Retrieved February 14, 2003, from http://66.89.55.104/synergy/emailmgmt/moreinfo/moreinfo.cfm?member_id=327033 &sponsor_id=377&content_id=3430&b1=221&b2=222&b3=222.

Purcell, A. (2000). 20/20 ROI. *Training and Development, 54*(7), 28–32.

Rovai, A. P., & Jordan, H. M. (2004). Blended learning and sense of community: A comparative analysis with traditional and fully online graduate courses. *International Review of Research in Open and Distance Learning.* Retrieved October 4, 2004, from http:// www.irrodl.org/content/v5.2/rovai-jordan.html.

Saba, F. (2000). Research in distance education: A status report. *International Review of Research in Open and Distance Learning, 1*(1), 1–9.

Schank, R. (1995). *Engines for education.* Mahwah, NJ: Erlbaum.

Schwartzman, R., & Tuttle, H. V. (2002). What can online course components teach about improving instruction and learning? *Journal of Instructional Psychology, 29*(3), 179–189.

Sticht, T. G. (1994). *Functional context education.* El Cajon, CA: Applied Behavioral and Cognitive Science.

Kirsten S. Hanson is the director of global organization and talent development at Oracle Corporation. This team provides targeted learning opportunities to help Oracle employees build leadership and professional skills that contribute to improved business performance. She is also pursuing her doctorate in educational technology, combined with a focus on leadership development and complexity theory, at the joint doctoral program at the University of San Diego and San Diego State University. Kirsten received her M.A. from the Institute of Learning Sciences at Northwestern University and her B.A. from Indiana University. She is an advocate for using technology in creative, constructivist learning designs and is passionate about helping people develop strong leadership skills to navigate ambiguous, complex environments.

Frances A. Clem has over twenty-five years of experience in high-tech training, marketing, and project management in the United States and abroad. She is self-employed as a corporate consultant specializing in the design and implementation of strategic training projects and has worked with a wide variety of high-tech firms. She is an experienced trainer, courseware designer, and training program implementer in a variety of environments and formats and holds a doctorate in educational technology from the University of San Diego and San Diego State University, where her research interests include issues of cultural effects, motivation, and persistence in e-learning. With a master's degree in business, she focuses on achieving a positive cost-benefit profile for all training and performance improvement measures she recommends and designs.

PART THREE

HIGHER EDUCATION BLENDED LEARNING MODELS AND PERSPECTIVES

Blended learning models, stories, and examples are just as rich and important in higher education as they are in corporate models. Part Three contains higher education models for blended learning from universities in New Zealand and Wales, as well as two in the United States. In addition, officers of a popular course management system, WebCT, provide examples of how some of their customers are blending their online learning environments. These five perspectives or models should offer assistance on strategic planning, training, grant writing, and evaluation related to blended learning. Perhaps most important, colleges and universities might attempt to compare their in-house blended designs to one or more of the models presented here.

In Chapter Eleven, Barbara Ross and Karen Gage delineate three types, or "flavors," of blending that they have extrapolated from trends seen among the broad range of WebCT users. The first is technology-enhanced courses where technology is used as a supplement to traditional course practices. The second is reduced face-time courses, which replace some of the traditional face-to-face lecture time with computer-mediated activities. The third is blended programs, in which students can choose to take a mix of both traditional face-to-face and completely online courses. Example vignettes from each of these cases are presented. Some benefits to blending are presented, such as expanding access, improving quality, serving diverse student populations, reducing time to graduation, addressing student desire for technology in education, and greater insight and tracking of student progress. Finally, several institutional strategies for implementing blended learning are shared along with case vignettes of institution wide adoption of technology as well as multi-institutional collaborations in blending. Ross and Gage feel that the trend toward blending is so prevalent that eventually we will not be asking whether institutions are blending but how they are blending.

Chapter Twelve, by Noeline Wright, Ross Dewstow, Sue Tappenden, and Mark Topping, highlights three categories of blending seen at the University of Waikato in New Zealand. It details the history of blended learning at an institutional level and then discusses blends at both course and program levels. Four categories of blends are outlined: fully, mostly, somewhat, and supported online. These four are outlined, and three case studies are provided. The first blend relates to Waikato's Law Diploma program, which is mostly online. In fact, only about 15 percent of learning time in this program involves face-to-face contact, with the remaining time entailing interaction with both materials and people through asynchronous discussion forums. The second case study, also classified as mostly online, is of a program for licensing teachers. In this case, teachers teach one day a week at their rural schools and participate at a distance in the more theoretical aspects of their learning. They were required to attend three weeks of residential campus face-to-face learning annually. The last case is a graduate program for secondary teaching that was classified as somewhat online. This one-year program was conducted mostly face-to-face with some online components related to instructor-led training and online contact with peers during their practicum experience. Finally, the chapter sets out some basic strategies for supporting blended learning.

In Chapter Thirteen, Norah Jones reviews the research literature indicating that blending can improve learning and also shows how widely blended solutions are being adopted and discussed. She acknowledges that we may be behind the curve in terms of the amount of research performed thus far on blended learning environments. She follows that with a cautionary note that people are using all kinds of definitions of *blended learning*, which makes it difficult to understand what is really being researched and promoted. She then shares the technology integration continuum that is used at the University of Glamorgan in Wales. This continuum includes basic information and communication technology usage stage (PowerPoint, Word), e-enhanced stage (use of virtual learning environments, or course management systems for productivity and communication), e-focused stage (use of discussion boards, interactive materials, online assessments), and e-intensive stage (predominantly online courses with minimal face-to-face time for inductions, briefings). She shares a case study in which a curriculum was developed and delivered at a distance and the learners requested more blended experiences. In response, the University of Glamorgan went through the process of incorporating more face-to-face contact for the student socialization.

In Chapter Fourteen, Chuck Dziuban and his colleagues at the University of Central Florida (UCF), an institution known for thoughtful training in the area of online learning and innovation in blended learning, describe the dramatic increase in demand for blended courses that they have witnessed and encouraged. Blended courses at UCF have grown from 8 courses with 125 students in 1997 to 508 courses with 13,600 students in 2003–2004. The UCF approach to blending replaces some face-to-face class time with online activities. Potential benefits outlined in this chapter range from improved learning effectiveness and satisfaction to cost reductions for physical infrastructure. At UCF, the cost reduction due to scheduling efficiencies has not materialized as of yet. Measurements of success rates over three years (as measured by the number of A-C passing grades and withdrawal rates) have shown that the blended approach on the whole is slightly better than the face-to-face-only and online-only modalities. The chapter also provides data on student satisfaction with blended courses as well as information on the quantity and quality of student interactions in UCF courses.

In Chapter Fifteen, Thomas Reynolds and Cathleen Greiner describe National University's online programs with an emphasis on the fast-growing online teacher education program. This program has no on-site meeting requirements with program faculty. Instead, faculty and peer interactions are carried out through the use of asynchronous discussions and other tools in a computer-mediated environment, though the experience is generally less collaborative than a traditional face-to-face experience. To become a certified teacher in California, National University students must have several in-school field experiences. The blending in this entirely online program occurs as the preservice teachers participate in face-to-face field experiences in schools within their respective geographical locations. These field experiences are coordinated by a state coordinator as well as local field experience coordinators of National University.

CHAPTER ELEVEN

GLOBAL PERSPECTIVES ON BLENDING LEARNING

Insight from WebCT and Our Customers in Higher Education

Barbara Ross, Karen Gage

Blended learning has become a highly effective means of addressing diverse student needs, expanding access to flexible learning opportunities, and improving the quality of education. As an e-learning solutions provider, WebCT has insight into how thousands of colleges and universities around the world are leveraging learning technologies to achieve their unique goals and objectives. This chapter presents examples from WebCT's customer base of blended learning strategies for individual courses, degree programs, and enterprisewide deployment.

Blended Learning—In the Beginning

The founding of WebCT as a company was the result of a research project conducted by Murray Goldberg at the University of British Columbia (UBC) to evaluate the impact of the Web on his students' learning experiences. In 1995, Goldberg was experimenting with what we now call blended learning by taking two sections of the same course and teaching one using a traditional face-to-face method and the other with the addition of online components and a reduction in the number of class meetings. Based on the outcomes of his research, Goldberg was convinced of the potential for blended learning to improve student learning outcomes; he founded WebCT to make it easier for instructors to incorporate online components in their teaching.

Today in higher education, *blended learning* has a broad range of meanings. To convey more specific flavors of blended learning, we often hear terms like *Web enhanced, technology enhanced, hybrid,* or *fully online.* Blended learning encompasses a spectrum of learning modes that range from the traditional face-to-face classroom to fully online degree programs. Across this broad range, WebCT has observed three major flavors of blended learning among our customer base in higher education:

• Web-supplemented or technology-enhanced courses, which add supplementary online components to a traditional course without changing the amount of time that students spend face-to-face with instructors. These courses may leverage technology to enable more convenient and efficient handling of administrative aspects of the course or add more instructional activities online.

• Hybrid or reduced face-time courses. Hybrid courses reduce the amount of face-to-face and in-class time and replace it with online learning activities. This can range from a course where labs are conducted online to a course where one or more days of class time are eliminated and replaced with online course work.

• Blended programs or degrees. A hybrid or blended degree program means that a student is not a "traditional student" or an "online student" but has the freedom to choose from all types of courses to earn a degree: some are blended, some face-to-face, and some fully online.

Of the three blended learning flavors, the hybrid or reduced-face-time course is in many ways the most innovative path, the most difficult to achieve, and where the greatest reward may lie in the long run. Hybrid courses do not fit easily into the organizational structure of higher education administration, and they require faculty to rethink the ways they teach. However, we believe that offering hybrid courses is potentially the best way to improve student learning outcomes.

Expanding Access to Education Through Blended Learning

Blended learning, and e-learning in general, have gained popularity in higher education because learning technologies help to address many of the key challenges that colleges and universities face. One of the most important challenges is expanding access to education. The demand for increased access to education comes from a number of different pressures: an increasing percentage of the population participating in higher education, workforce retraining for a dispersed population, population growth in a specific geography, and global demand and opportunities for specialized programs.

As more students enter colleges and universities, there is a clear need to expand access. However, this presents a challenge in that institutions may not have enough buildings and classrooms to support the increasing numbers of learners. Blended learning has become a strategic means of reaching students who otherwise would not have access to face-to-face educational opportunities in a mode or location that is convenient for them and accommodating expanding enrollment without making major facilities investments. Institutional infrastructure can be built virtually rather than physically, often at lower cost.

Typically when people think of widening access with e-learning, they think of distance learning. However, the online degree program is only one model by which access to education can be expanded. There are a number of other blended models (such as technology-supported courses, alternating face-to-face and online class meetings, videoconferencing to multiple class sites, or the use of Webcams), which, combined with course or curriculum redesign, can have a significant impact on a university's enrollment capacity. Institutions that fail to expand educational options for students run the risk of lengthening time to graduation or reducing student retention, particularly as enrollments rise.

Meeting Students' Expectations of Technology in Education

Students who enter colleges and universities today embrace and welcome technology as an expected part of their learning experience. They have grown up with technology and often have experienced it as an integrated part of their secondary education. As a result, colleges and universities face increased demand for providing a high-quality, 24/7 learning environment. Blended learning has become a predominant model for achieving this goal, particularly to serve the needs of traditional, full-time undergraduate students.

A study of more than twelve thousand students across Europe by the SEUSISS (Survey of European Universities Skills in ICT of Students and Staff) Project found that more than 62 percent of new students enter the university using information and communication technology (ICT) in their studies at least two to three times per week (SEUSISS Project, 2003). In the National Survey of Student Engagement's study of undergraduates at four-year colleges and universities in North America, 72 percent of respondents reported spending more than five hours per week online, with almost 39 percent spending more than five hours per week online doing academic work (National Survey of Student Engagement, 2003).

With the global demand for technology in education comes a need for organizational change: the old way of doing things will no longer work. Students want a consistent experience so that no matter what course they take, they receive the same quality experience. Many colleges and universities have responded to this need for consistency and quality of experience by standardizing on a single e-learning system and integrating the e-learning system with other technologies on campus. With an institution-wide blended learning strategy, colleges and universities have been able to provide students, faculty, and staff with a seamless experience where technology is transparent to them.

Improving Quality with Blended Learning

At the end of the day, we want students to learn successfully. How can blended learning play a role in improving quality and educational outcomes, particularly in boosting student retention and graduation rates?

Serve Diverse Student Populations. Students arrive on campus or in classrooms with disparate skills and ways of learning. Blended learning offers new ways to personalize the learning experience and engage students. With e-learning, instructors are able to deliver remedial or advanced content to the right students at the right time based on their individual needs. Blended learning is attractive to more kinds of learners because it incorporates varied instructional modes and supports multiple means of expression, making it possible to appeal to different learning styles.

Reduce Time to Graduation. Today's students face more and more pressures from work and family obligations; the percentage of students working twenty hours per week or more in addition to being a full-time student continues to increase. Often institutions offer required courses at times that may be inconvenient for students, creating bottlenecks for students in completing their degree programs, especially in large-enrollment courses. Blended learning allows institutions to provide more scheduling options for enrolled students to complete their required courses. For example, by offering blended courses that require only one day per week on campus rather than the traditional three, institutions can reduce potential scheduling conflicts that would preclude students from taking the required courses for graduation.

Gain Greater Insight into Student Progress. E-learning systems collect detailed data about student activity and learning behavior in the online environment. The availability of these data presents two key opportunities to higher education to improve quality and enhance student outcomes. First, instructors can track students' learning activities to see which students are falling behind or not keeping up with their reading material and can intervene; this can help prevent at-risk students from failing or dropping out. Second, institutions have the opportunity to assess the learning quality across the curriculum by aggregating learning activity data for analysis by assessment and institutional researchers. Once there is a critical mass of learning activity taking place online, institutions will be able to analyze outcomes and learning activity patterns to better determine what leads to student success and use those insights to improve the overall quality of the institution's educational offerings.

The Blended Learning Spectrum: From a Single Course to a Degree Program

Blended learning takes place at many levels—from individual courses, to degree programs, to institution-wide approaches. This section presents examples from WebCT's customer base of approaches to delivering three main categories of blended learning: technology enhanced, hybrid or reduced seat-time, and blended degree programs.

Web-Supplemented or Technology-Enhanced Courses

Web-supplemented or technology-enhanced courses add supplementary on-line components to a traditional course without changing the amount of time that students spend face-to-face with instructors. Often technology-enhanced courses can help transform communication and participation dynamics. While it may be difficult to get students to raise their hands and participate in a face-to-face classroom, students are often more willing to participate in discussions online. Examples of technology-enhanced courses are those that add online communication and collaboration tools; use online labs, simulations, or streaming media; incorporate additional online resources and study tools for students; and support students who are collaborating virtually on projects and submitting or presenting them online. A technology-enhanced course may also serve to simplify administration by enabling faculty to more efficiently manage enrollment, grades, or other administrative aspects of their courses in the e-learning system.

Virginia Michelich, a professor of biology at Georgia Perimeter College, has infused streaming media content into her online courses and traditional undergraduate biology courses with the goal of increasing student comprehension and success. She found that many processes that her students studied in biology lab took too much time for one lab period yet could not wait until the following week's lab for completion. Streaming media technology helped solve this problem.

Using a video microscope, Michelich created a video file to show egg fertilization and development in sea urchins, thereby allowing her students to view the entire process, accompanied by her audio explanation, in just twenty-three minutes. As Michelich observed, "Online students have remarked that the streaming media files captured from the classroom help them to understand the more difficult concepts that they encounter in this course. . . . Further, I have noticed a significant increase in class participation since these streaming media files have been available for the students. They have been less concerned about taking copious notes and more focused on understanding the concepts during class because the class material will exist online for review" (WebCT, 2002a).

Hybrid or Reduced Face-Time Courses

Hybrid courses reduce the amount of face-to-face in-class time and replace that time with online learning activities. This can range from a course where labs are conducted entirely online to a course where one or more days of class time are eliminated and replaced with online course work. One of the key elements in designing effective hybrid courses is that educators must choose the most effective mode (online asynchronous, online synchronous, or face-to-face) for specific learning activities rather than assuming that a single mode will work for all types of learning activities across a course.

Southern Maine Technical College has an effective, replicable approach to hybrid course design. In the light of the success that Julia Child had in teaching the fine art of cooking using television, Lance Crocker, department chair of the Hotel, Motel, Restaurant Program at Southern Maine Technical College, took a keen interest in translating the success of this approach to the Web. He began by asking himself, "How can I adapt Internet technology to accomplish my goals in such hands-on industries as food and beverage and lodging management?"

Crocker found that all of his courses naturally broke down into two categories: conceptual information (such as the guest cycle, accounting practices, night audit procedures, and case studies) and functional skill (such as guest services, customer service skills, and telephone skills). While the functional skills necessitated a hands-on internship, Crocker's goal was to replace his face-to-face lectures with a comprehensive online course in WebCT as a new method of exposing students to the conceptual subject matter.

Crocker found that the new online format encouraged students to become more active learners and consequently facilitated the comprehension and retention of conceptual information. Crocker received feedback from restaurant owners and managers asking "what he had done to these students" because they knew more about the industry than students ever had in the past. Since students were already well versed in the vocabulary and key concepts of the hospitality industry, owners and managers could spend more time with hands-on training and less time explaining concepts.

The success of Crocker's courses has generated interest throughout the Maine Technical College System (MTCS), consisting of seven colleges located across the state. "The simple exercise of applying hospitality standards to offsite internships and combining that hands-on experience with the online conceptual learning has expanded horizons in the whole Maine Technical College System," states Crocker. The MTCS has begun to use this hybrid course approach across a variety of other hands-on disciplines, including business, dietetic technology, behavioral health, culinary arts, fire science technology, and pharmacology (WebCT, 2002b).

Blended Degree Programs

A hybrid or blended degree program means that a student is not a "traditional student" or an "online student" but has the freedom to choose from all types of courses to earn a degree: some blended, some face-to-face, and some fully online.

Villanova University has provided undergraduate, graduate, and workforce students with a consistent, flexible learning experience through a combination of WebCT and other technologies. Its College of Engineering has developed strategies to accommodate both on-campus and distance learners in a single course using a combination of integrated technology tools that include WebCT and videoconferencing technologies.

In 2001, Villanova began to use videoconferencing technology to deliver distance learning courses for graduate courses. Although this approach helped to expand access to students who were unable to come to campus, a level of interactivity was still missing. Students could watch the lecture but did not have the ability to interact with their instructor or fellow students in real time. In 2002, Villanova began using WebCT to enhance the communication among students and faculty. WebCT has since become the foundation and gateway for all College of Engineering graduate distance education courses, whether they are Web enhanced or delivered entirely online. It is also used by many traditional in-class courses.

The College of Engineering extended this successful approach to an existing degree program: it introduced a master of science in water resources and environmental engineering degree program that offers real-time distance learning for graduate-level courses. Because the courses are held in conjunction with classes at the university, distance students can participate in class discussions with on-campus students, and the lecture is delivered live over the Internet and made available for review.

Having on-campus students and distance learners in the same WebCT courses makes it possible for traditional and distance students to communicate and collaborate with one another and for all students to have the same quality experience, whether they are on campus, at home, or at work.

Institutional Strategies for Blended Learning

Since its introduction in the 1990s, e-learning has been growing rapidly at postsecondary institutions around the world. At leading colleges and universities, a majority of courses are blended, and nearly all students take at least one course with a technology-supported component. As e-learning enters its second decade, many institutions find themselves at a critical juncture. With course management system use continuing to expand, and course, program, and institution-level activities dependent on technology for success, many institutions have outgrown their current approach to e-learning.

For most institutions, linear expansion of blended learning—adding a program, a person, or a larger server to an existing model—will not scale to meet today's needs and tomorrow's demands. Moving blended learning to an enterprise level requires institutions to rethink the way they are currently supporting technology-enhanced instruction. Adopting an enterprise approach to blended learning results in systems and processes that are powerful, reliable, and flexible enough to support all stakeholders and provide benefits across the institution.

The transition from having many different learning systems toward a total enterprise or "all-of-university" approach has become a trend at higher education institutions around the world. Institutions generally consider adopting an enterprise approach to blended learning to respond to the fact that online learning is affecting every instructor and every student across the college or university. Having worked with many diverse institutions as they have moved toward an enterprise approach, WebCT has identified three critical components in successfully deploying blended learning at the enterprise level:

• Institution-wide strategy and participation. First, it is important to secure a commitment from senior administrators to use blended learning as a means of achieving the university's strategic goals. However, commitment from senior administrators alone is not enough. Institutions also need to expand the circle of influence to achieve much greater cross-functional participation. Balancing the autonomy and collaboration between diverse academic and administrative constituents is critical in successfully implementing an enterprisewide e-learning strategy.

• Mission-critical service level. Student and faculty demands and expectations of technology heighten and change as technology becomes an increasingly vital part of their daily activities. In a model where it is expected that every student and every instructor will be served by e-learning technology, the standards for reliability, uptime, and user support will skyrocket. Institutions must seriously evaluate what level of service is required at their institution and design their technology solutions and processes in order to meet these higher standards.

• Proactive measurement of learning effectiveness. With increasing amounts of e-learning activity come detailed quantitative data about student activity during the learning process. Enterprise approaches capitalize on this new asset by developing institutional processes for a regular cycle of measurement, analysis, and change that are designed to continuously improve educational quality.

An Enterprise Approach to Blended Learning

Following are two examples from WebCT's customer base of institutions that have successfully taken an enterprise approach to blended learning.

Deakin University's Institution-Wide E-Learning Strategy. Deakin University in Australia has become known for the distinctiveness of its courses and the large number of programs offered to students through distance learning and on-campus education. Deakin aims to be Australia's most progressive university: internationally recognized for the relevance, innovation, and responsiveness of its teaching and learning, research, partnerships, and international activities. Deakin University is a veteran in the e-learning space and has been able to leverage its expertise in online learning to fuel the success of both its distance education and traditional learning programs.

In conducting a student survey about learning management systems, Deakin found that students wanted consistency. For example, they wanted a single e-learning system that they would have access to no matter which course they took at Deakin. A key aim at Deakin is to ensure that regardless of whether students choose to study online or on campus, all students receive the same high-quality learning experience.

After an extensive evaluation process, Deakin selected WebCT Vista as its central academic enterprise system to support e-learning across the university. The selection of WebCT Vista (a learning management system designed for enterprisewide deployment) was an extremely collaborative process that involved more than twelve hundred students and four hundred faculty. Gaining support from constituents across the university was a critical component in formulating and implementing an enterprise approach to e-learning.

Online learning has become a key component in Deakin University's strategic and operational plans. The university also made substantial organizational changes to support its online teaching and learning objectives, including the establishment of Learning Services, a central academic support unit focused on "ensuring that the online learning environment is a seamless mix of all services and resources required by students for a successful education" (McKnight, 2003, p. 13).

City University, London: Extending Blended Learning Across the Enterprise.

Based in the heart of London, City University serves nearly 11,500 students from 153 countries. Its graduate employment record is one of the best in the country, and the university has close contacts with the leading professional institutions and with business and industry. One of the university's chief aims with e-learning is to develop flexible online degree programs that allow students who otherwise would not be able to participate in the learning process to earn degrees on a flexible schedule.

City University has experienced rapid growth in blended learning. The university selected WebCT Vista as its academic enterprise system in the summer of 2003, and in just one year has over 150 course modules being taught online within WebCT through a mixture of blended and fully online learning. Today, 2,500 students and 250 staff regularly use the system.

City University implemented WebCT Vista as the central e-learning environment and has integrated its e-learning system with other mission-critical technologies and processes, taking a holistic approach to blended learning. Management of WebCT Vista is undertaken by the E-Learning Unit, which sits in the Information Services Portfolio as part of Library Information Services, to ensure collaboration among different service departments and systems. The university has leveraged WebCT Vista as a new mode of delivery to reach out to groups of nontraditional learners and support existing students. With the availability of new online degree programs, City University has attracted students from new markets around the world. This has contributed to an overall increase in enrollment at the university.

The university also has a number of partner institutions and has used WebCT Vista to facilitate closer collaboration, particularly in the field of health care and nursing. One course in renal nursing uses a solution-focused approach to online learning where students are provided with real-life scenarios that require them to apply a variety of skills to realistic situations. WebCT Vista encourages students from different backgrounds to learn from each other and to share expertise as part of a collaborative, flexible learning experience.

Multi-Institutional Collaborations

Taking an enterprisewide approach to blended learning holds particular value for educational systems and consortia. The advent of the academic enterprise system has made it possible for multiple institutions to reap the benefits of a central e-learning system, while allowing each entity to operate autonomously and retain local control of the system. When forming a blended learning strategy across multiple institutions, the advantages of a centralized implementation increase tenfold. Each of the members can:

- Expand access and educational opportunities for learners, making it possible for students at different schools, in different states, or in different parts of the world to access flexible, high-quality learning opportunities.
- Share hardware, IT, training, and human resources, helping to eliminate redundancies and optimize existing investments.
- Reduce duplication of programs and courses across multiple institutions.
- Improve retention rates and student outcomes systemwide.

Here are two examples of WebCT's customers that have taken a multi-institutional, collaborative approach to blended learning.

University System of Georgia: Blended Learning Across Thirty-Four Institutions. In April 2002, the University System of Georgia (USG) signed a comprehensive, statewide license to make WebCT Vista available to all thirty-four institutions under the board of regents. The goals of its statewide e-learning strategy and implementation include:

- Expanding systemwide access and program offerings for every student in the state regardless of their location
- Building a resource network for faculty to share content, courses, curriculum, and best practices across the network
- Building a model to track and monitor student performance across the network to provide personalized learning experiences and develop improved academic programs

One example of the impact of USG's collaborative, enterprise approach to blended learning is the establishment of the eCore program. eCore consists of specific required courses that are delivered online, ultimately making it possible for nontraditional students to pursue the first two years of a university system undergraduate degree anytime and anywhere. USG has taken initial steps toward evaluating the quality of the eCore curriculum by analyzing patterns of student activity based on data gathered from discussion postings and correlating those data with quality measurements and student outcomes.

The USG has also been able to efficiently share the high-quality course content developed for eCore courses with faculty across the member institutions of the Georgia Board of Regents. In February 2003, Advanced Learning Technologies (ALT), a unit within the board of regents, began a pilot project to deconstruct the eCore courses and reassemble them into learning objects (smaller, more modular components that can be used for instruction). Marie Lasseter, project coordinator for instructional development of the board of regents of the University System of Georgia, comments:

> Today, through our FacultyVIEW portal, faculty across the System who use WebCT Vista have a variety of options for developing new online courses or supplementing face-to-face courses. When they attempt to reuse content, they're not locked into a course/unit/lesson format. Faculty have the freedom to develop their courses as they like without having to start from scratch, and they can also participate in online discussions with other educators to share best practices in the use of online content. We believe our learning objects project will produce better courses more quickly and efficiently, especially as the learning object exchange model scales to encompass higher education on national and global scales [Vallone, 2004].

Hawaii Department of Education: Collaborating to Expand Access to Education. Hawaii's Department of Education (DoE) is one of WebCT's K-12 customers that has implemented a collaborative, multischool approach to online learning. Hawaii's DoE launched E-School, a supplementary virtual learning program delivered through WebCT that typically enrolls three hundred to four hundred students per semester in fully accredited Web-based courses. Students from secondary schools across the Hawaiian islands can access both required courses and electives through E-School's Web-based curriculum, enabling the DoE to deliver to students in rural schools the same courses and resources available in urban Honolulu.

From its inception in 1996, E-School expanded from ninety-six students in twelve schools to five hundred students in forty-five schools in 2002–2003. Notably, 47 percent of participating students and 62 percent of participating schools come from the smaller island schools and communities outside the city of Honolulu. In this regard, virtual learning has achieved success in meeting the academic equity and access aspirations of the Hawaiian DoE officials (Newman, Stein, & Trask 2003).

When Blended Learning Becomes "Learning"

Having worked with institutions around the world in planning and implementing their e-learning strategies over time, WebCT has witnessed the evolution of blended learning from an experimental technology to a mission-critical learning solution. As blended learning has become more prevalent, educators have discovered new ways to foster communication with and among students, gain insight into students' learning activities, appeal to diverse learning styles, and ultimately improve learning outcomes. At the enterprise level, blended learning has made it possible for colleges and universities to achieve key institutional goals, such as expanding access to educational opportunities, serving new markets, and improving student satisfaction and retention.

Institutions have made tremendous strides to strategically leverage blended learning as a means of achieving their core mission and goals, and that movement will continue. In the long run, almost all courses offered in higher education will be blended. Given today's growth trends in the use of course management systems, it is almost a certainty that blended learning will become the new traditional model of course delivery in ten years. Moving forward, what will differentiate institutions from one another will not be whether they have blended learning, but rather how they do the blending and where they fall on the blended learning spectrum.

References

McKnight, S. (2003, September). *Changing the mindset—From traditional on-campus and distance education to online teaching and learning.* Paper presented at the Fourth Annual WebCT Asia Pacific User Conference, Queensland, Australia.

National Survey of Student Engagement. (2003). *National Survey of Student Engagement 2003 overview.* Bloomington: Center for Postsecondary Research, Policy and Planning, Indiana University.

Newman, A., Stein, M., & Trask, E. (2003, September). *What can virtual learning do for your school?* Boston: Eduventures.

Surveys of European Universities Skills in Information and Communication Technology for Staff and Students. (2003, April). *SUESISS Project final report.* Edinburgh: Department of Higher and Further Education, University of Edinburgh.

Vallone, C. (2004, July). *Online learning's impact on global education.* Presentation at the Sixth Annual WebCT User Conference, Orlando, FL.

WebCT. (2002a, February). Bringing content to life: Multimedia in WebCT. *WebCT Newsletter.*

WebCT. (2002b, July). Cooking with WebCT—An interesting mix of conceptual and functional learning. *WebCT Newsletter.*

 Barbara Ross launched Universal Learning Technology, which later became WebCT, with founder and CEO Carol Vallone in 1995. Her responsibilities include developing strategy and providing operational management for marketing, support, services, and partnerships. Ross has worked for over twenty years at the nexus of information, technology, and learning. She is recognized as a global leader in the application of e-learning technology to education and is a frequent speaker on the topic.

 Karen Gage is responsible for overseeing all marketing communications, product marketing, market development activities, and user community relations at WebCT. Gage joined WebCT in 1999 from Inso Corporation, where she was director of product marketing. Prior to her career in high-tech marketing, Gage was an equity analyst. She received her B.A. from Duke University and her M.B.A. from Columbia Business School. In early 2002, Gage was named to the advisory board of the Boston e-Learning Association.

CHAPTER TWELVE

NEW ZEALAND EXAMPLES OF BLENDED LEARNING

Noeline Wright, Ross Dewstow, Mark Topping, Sue Tappenden

Blended learning has been a feature of both the tertiary education scene and the compulsory schooling sectors in New Zealand for many years. For instance, traditional distance-based education through Massey University and the Open Polytechnic has existed since the 1960s. The Correspondence School, New Zealand's largest, with over twenty thousand students, serves primary (elementary) and secondary school students from around the country. For most of its sixty years in existence, traditional paper-based distance learning was its core method of delivery.

During the 1980s, universities, polytechnics, and some schools explored PC-based learning, educational television, video, and CD-ROMs. The University of Waikato (UOW) pioneered New Zealand's Internet use with a dial-up connection, which later became an "always-on" connection. The Waikato Institute of Technology, also an early pioneer, developed mobile "classrooms" plus videoconferencing to service remote teaching locations.

In 1995, the Open Polytechnic blended traditional paper-based distance education with computer technology by using emerging Internet-based bulletin boards. It established mixed-mode Web-based teaching in 1996 and graduated the first New Zealand cohort of fully Web-taught students at the end of 1999. The UOW's School of Education mixed media program (MMP) Bachelor of Teaching (Btchg) degree began in 1997. This combination of on-campus residential blocks of time with fully online learning is discussed as a case study. In the compulsory school sector, the Correspondence School has recently developed a range of educational technologies to support its students' learning, including video as well as computer-based or online learning components.

Since about 2000, the Ministry of Education has developed IT-related strategies for the compulsory schooling sector and more recently commissioned a study of tertiary (higher education) sector e-learning. *Highways and Pathways* (Ministry of Education, 2002) contained several key recommendations:

- That government provide leadership and policy to encourage collaboration and adoption of e-learning by tertiary providers
- That issues relating to the development of e-learning for Maori be examined
- That an e-learning leadership center be established
- That a central portal be developed and a collaborative funding pool be established
- That quality assurance standards for e-learning meet the same standards as conventional education
- That tertiary funding be at the same level whatever the mode of learning
- That infrastructure for e-learning be addressed
- That the New Zealand Copyright Act be examined to remove particular barriers to e-learning
- That intellectual property issues be addressed within the tertiary sector

Over the following two years, most of these recommendations were addressed, including a tertiary information strategy setting overall direction for the sector, the initiation of a Web portal development project for the tertiary sector, and the allocation of funding to develop a new-generation high-speed Internet. A significant collaborative funding scheme, the eCDF, has also been established.

The University of Waikato: A Tertiary Institution Case Study of Blended Learning

The UOW, located in Hamilton, a North Island provincial city with a geographically spread-out rural population, offers a number of qualifications described as fully, mostly, somewhat, or supported online. *Fully online* means that students can complete qualifications without coming to the campus. *Mostly online* means that there is a mix of online and some on-campus work in the qualification, and *somewhat online* means there is an online component for on-campus students. Finally, hundreds of individual courses are taught in the traditional lecture-tutorial mode, supported by material provided through the online learning or relevant university schools' document management systems. Such courses are referred to as *supported online*.

Fully and mostly online qualifications encompass a wide spectrum of courses from most faculties. Fully online options include the Arts and Social Sciences faculty's graduate diploma in applied ethics, while the School of Education's fully online options include bachelor's and master's degrees in sport and leisure studies, postgraduate certificates in counseling supervision, school principalship, and e-education, plus postgraduate diplomas in education and sports and leisure studies. The Schools of Management and Maori and Pacific Development also have fully online postgraduate diplomas.

Mostly online options feature in the Arts and Social Sciences faculty, the School of Education, and Law. They include undergraduate and postgraduate diplomas plus master's degrees, allowing students to study wherever they live. Case studies of these are discussed.

Blended learning at Waikato means a mix of online and face-to-face plus traditional distance learning. The mix varies from course to course, depending to a large extent on the subject and the skills of the lecturer in pedagogical knowledge related to using blended forms of learning as well as technological skills. This particular aspect can be significant for students in terms of their access to and familiarity with learning through a technological medium. It is important to foster a lecturer's increasing knowledge of effective pedagogical practices for successful online learning because it supports students. This is therefore an important aspect of the university's online learning strategy.

Fully online courses assess participation and contributions in online discussions as well as more traditional assessment forms like essays. Most of these are submitted online, and many lecturers mark the work online, posting the results to individuals using the facility of the online private learning space. This mirrors on-campus situations where lecturers can shut their office doors for consultations with students.

Online interactions and discussions are mostly asynchronous. On some occasions, lecturers use synchronous chat rooms for "office hours" and tutorial sessions. Time zones are a complicating factor for chatrooms with students living in different countries. Course materials (readings and administrative information) are provided as online HTML Web pages or attached documents, as CD-ROMs (containing videoed lectures, readings, or PowerPoint presentations, although no central unit develops them), or as printed and bound collections of readings that can also be provided by mail.

Although students may not physically visit the university, most staff are keen to form positive relationships with students, as they would in traditional classroom environments. The online environment developed by UOW (ClassForum) specifically supports community and relationship building as a pedagogical tool. By linking to the student records database, students upload their identification photograph (taken at enrollment) so that every time they post an online message, their photograph appears. Lecturers include their photographs too. This relationship-building tool is important, especially for fully or mostly online courses. Communicating with people and responding to faces and voices (or their substitute, the written word) is important. Building trust, for instance, is much easier when students feel that they correspond with a real person.

Secondary school students, for instance, frequently comment on how they develop commitment to a subject. Such commitment is initially based on believing in their teachers and trusting them to provide effective learning environments (Smyth & Hattam, 2004). This sense of trust and commitment partly occurs through connecting with teachers visually and through their actions and speech. Online photographs support this connection while informal and friendly postings by lecturers encourage relationship building. Students who do not display their photograph are represented by a silhouetted blank image. Sometimes this leads to "flaming" when other students become distrustful when they cannot "see" their classmates.

Another strategy that helps students develop a sense of community and trust is beginning an online course with an introductory discussion to meet each other, just as we do when we meet socially. Through this initial activity, students and lecturers share family information, hobbies, something of their learning history, and what they are looking forward to in the program. This ice-breaking helps new online learners get used to posting messages and finding their way around the site before anything challenging is asked of them and encourages a supportive, collegial environment.

ClassForum is also used for mostly online course components. The complementary, compulsory on-campus components often include an orientation program, midcourse tutorials, or end-of-course presentations or exams. Initial orientation sessions include an introduction to ClassForum, logging on, setting up computer accounts, practicing using the software, becoming familiar with the system and how individual courses work, and knowing what to do after leaving the campus. At the same time, students meet each other. Such orientations for new online students reflect Salmon's model (2000) in which students successfully negotiate stage 1, access and motivation, and become more than ready for stage 2, online socialization. Introductory sessions such as these at UOW effectively prepare students to become independent online learners.

UOW has satellite campuses in more rural areas supported by videoconferencing lectures. Students view these lectures from a local videoconferencing campus. They are then supported by their classroom tutor, with ClassForum as an adjunct, since it can be used for discussions about the lecture after the event with the lecturer.

For courses that fit within the somewhat online category, an online assessed component complements the bulk of the course, taught through traditional lectures and tutorials. Lecturers whose courses fit the somewhat online category are often starting out as online educators, and so they experiment in a small way. This helps them develop their skills in a safe and confined way. Lecturers are encouraged to experiment with this sort of approach before committing themselves to more elaborate forms of online teaching. It is during this time that lecturers often seek the most support in terms of technological and pedagogical knowledge. Support for online technologies at UOW encompasses:

- Course documents (such as articles for discussion, or summaries of lectures or other materials) in files such as Word, pdf, and PowerPoint, which can be uploaded within ClassForum.
- Asynchronous discussions. These help students to communicate with each other and their lecturers. They are used to investigate readings or lectures through prompts or questions designed to provoke discussion. Such discussions may be assessed in terms of the quality and frequency of students' contributions and their ability to foster and maintain effective community-building cues (such as supporting and encouraging each other, being critical in a positive way, or suggesting alternatives to ideas).
- Other areas. These are usually nonassessed and noncompulsory. Such areas include online cafés for students, question-and-answer areas so that students can ask questions of the lecturer or tutors about course-related material that do not belong in the discussion areas, or a place where students and lecturers can add resources that could benefit each other.

Examples of Blended Learning at UOW

Pedagogical support systems are described later when Waikato Innovation Centre for e-Education (WICeD) is discussed. What follows now are three examples of blended learning at UOW. The first two are qualifications programs; the third is a course module within a program.

Diploma of Legal Executive Studies (DipLExSt): Mostly Online

The Diploma of Legal Executive Studies (DipLExSt) teaches law to the same standard as the LL.B. (bachelor of law), which is taught to people employed in law offices who have no previous university-level learning. The diploma raises their academic profile and professional standing as legal executives. Maintaining the academic rigor of the program is critical so that it compares favorably with on campus LL.B. courses.

Because of the learning background of most legal executive diploma students, academic rigor was a top consideration for those designing the diploma. A blended learning program satisfies the needs of learners to function independently, studying when and where they please at their own pace, and enables teaching staff and learners to interact in various ways.

The diploma combines online learning with face-to-face contact, plus paper and CD-ROM materials. Face-to-face contact concentrates on ensuring that various electronic media are used effectively and gives learners opportunities to cooperate within group settings that reflect the organization of the online environment. Face-to-face interaction constitutes approximately 15 percent of diploma students' total learning time. A key goal of the program is to create engaged, independent learners who participate fully. To that end, the paper and CD-ROM materials are presented in conjunction with group discussion activities, promoting these learning outcomes:

- Demonstrating an ability to identify relevant facts and legal issues
- Distinguishing relevant laws and their application to specific issues
- Demonstrating an ability to critically analyze outcomes of problems in their social contexts

Lecturers support learners through individual feedback on their written work, online comments, and group discussions where issues may be dealt with without the teacher's intervention. Also, students interact with the supplied materials in a guided manner by lecturers' providing indications of important emphases and explanations of more difficult concepts or topics. Interactions with materials comprise approximately 40 percent of the total learning time; group discussion and other online activity constitute the remaining 45 percent.

In this particular model of blended learning, the proportions of time spent face-to-face, reading and using material presented using CD-ROM, or working online reflect several decisions about the diploma. The legal academic community in New Zealand traditionally favors courses based on written materials and face-to-face teaching, where the main support for students occurs through tutorial sessions and individual critique of students' assessed work. So that the diploma is seen as a serious academic program, its roots are in this model. However, by using UOW's technology, it was possible to create learning environments that improved on the on-campus model. Asynchronous tutorials through the online component allow learners to input ideas or responses at any time. They can therefore take time to absorb and think about concepts, composing thoughtful responses. This facility has resulted in high-quality asynchronous discussions. And by having lectures and presentations using CD-ROM, learners access them whenever they need to, repeating lectures as often as necessary, adding to their course content understanding, and improving their note-taking skills. These diploma students gain a tertiary qualification by studying anywhere they can plug into the Internet.

An added benefit of this blended learning diploma is the cooperation and support for students generated by online group work, increasing their understanding of the subject matter in a safe learning environment. This is often not possible in large face-to-face classes. In ClassForum, every student's input is valued. If it appears, for example, that a few students dominate discussions, various strategies can be used to circumvent this. For example, they may be asked to pose discussion questions related to particular readings or presentations and take on the role of chair rather than participant. Learners' self-esteem and confidence is therefore promoted as they are encouraged to participate in discussions, adding to the class's thinking about various topics and issues.

In the midst of these online teaching innovations, there are several difficulties. For instance, a few diploma students, believing that "real" teaching and learning happen only during face-to-face sessions, are reluctant to commit fully to ClassForum. Awarding grades for online contributions is therefore a necessary incentive. Another difficulty is staff commitment to online teaching because it can be highly intensive and specific as a result of the closer relationship between the teacher and learner. This often means considerable one-to-one feedback and support, particularly in the initial stages of students' using ClassForum, when generous feedback to individuals and groups indicates the extent to which they are on the right path. As students gain security in using ClassForum, the frequency of this kind of feedback decreases. Pedagogical knowledge about such learning activities and needs is necessary for staff to work comfortably online.

Mixed Media Programme (MMP): Primary: Mostly Online

The MMP program began in 1997. Its first bachelor of teaching graduates were capped in 1999, and so this degree program can claim to be the first blended learning bachelor of teaching degree in the country, and possibly elsewhere too. As Barr (2000) notes, it was "initially designed to meet the needs of pre service [primary] education students in the more distant areas of the University's region particularly Gisborne, East Coast, Wairoa, Taumarunui and Thames-Coromandel [and in] 1998 . . . was extended to . . . Taranaki, Northland, Auckland, South Auckland and the Bay of Plenty" (p. 3). In other words, MMP supports students from almost the entire North Island of New Zealand.

MMP is shaped so that during school term times, students work one day per week in their base school (a local primary school that agrees to mentor them; this agreement is a program entry prerequisite). The rest of their week centers on working online to meet course requirements related to the more theoretical aspects. Students attend three compulsory on-campus week-long courses annually: in February, June, and August. The February on-campus section introduces students to the program plus specific courses within it, their lecturers, the technology, and each other. The face-to-face segments build relationships between students and with lecturers and increase learners' self-confidence.

This program has had a number of benefits: more remote areas are better able to staff their schools as they mentor learner-teachers, the new teachers enjoy two support networks (their local schools and their online lecturers), and these new teachers become, simultaneously, effective computer users. The program also broadens the teacher base. Traditionally many MMP students would not have enrolled in teacher education because of their physical distance from a university or their family commitments. Many of these students, who are mainly over age twenty-five, have children. For instance, during the period of research into this program, forty-one of seventy-five children of students across all three year levels of the degree were under age fifteen, with the largest number of children between five and nine years old (Donahy, McGee, Ussher, & Yates, 2003). The levels of support students get by being able to stay at home is crucial. As one participant in the study said, "This opportunity has changed my family, my husband is very proud of me and my children egg me on. I have support coming out of my ears and without that I would be lost" (Donahy et al., 2003, p. 5).

There are also unexpectedly positive benefits for the staff in base schools. For instance, teachers mentoring UOW students have found that their self-reflection has been enhanced as they began theorizing their own practices more explicitly. Many staff subsequently upgrade their qualifications by enrolling in UOW online papers, strengthening the university's relationship with schools, and increasing the schools' professional leadership and learning capacities. This learning circle has strengthened the credibility of the program in ways not initially envisioned. In the first cohort of fifty-two students, forty-eight graduated. Of those, two-thirds did not know how to turn on a computer when they first began the MMP bachelor of teaching. Within eight weeks, most were comfortable computer users, and by the end of the first semester, many had bought their own computer. Schools too, which may initially have had low levels of ICT, benefited from the learner-teachers' developing skills with Internet and e-mail because they shared their knowledge and skills with other staff. As noted by Donahy, McGee, and Yates (2004), "MMP was focused at local people who were more likely to stay in the area and teach after they graduated. The ICT component of the Mixed Media Programme was viewed as complementary to the school's own development" (p. 19).

There are also some challenges. A key one is to sustain the quality and sense of innovation. Once a program becomes institutionalized, it can lose its edge as it becomes commonplace. Some staff too are reluctant volunteers, preferring and being more comfortable with face-to-face pedagogies and struggling with accepting the validity of online learning even though courses successfully cover a wide range of subject areas and disciplines including art and music education.

Secondary Graduate ICT Module: Somewhat Online

In New Zealand, secondary school teachers follow one of two common patterns in preparing for their careers: full-time university study (either bachelor's or master's degree level), followed by a one-year, full-time intensive graduate diploma in teaching or conjoint undergraduate and teacher education degrees. Within the one-year graduate program, learner-teachers focus on pedagogy centered on both their subject disciplines and on wider issues important to learners, teachers, and schools. Compulsory topics include understanding Maori perspectives and issues on learning, ethics, literacy across the curriculum, plus information and communication technology (ICT) and pedagogy. The ICT module has twenty face-to-face hours in four-hour blocks, coupled with an online component that straddles two practicum periods. Face-to-face sessions in this module center on PowerPoint and classrooms, developing and using truth and validity detectors for checking the quality and validity of online sites, developing Web pages for classroom use, and using digital audio and video tools in the classroom. Students are assessed three times in this module:

• Twice via online postings, using ICT tools during their teaching practicum periods (April to May and August to September; the New Zealand compulsory education sector calendar is from February to December). Their task is to explain what tool they used, how and why they used it, and how they could tell if it enhanced student learning. The aim is to focus on pedagogical purposes for ICT. Students also have to comment on someone else's posting by being supportive, critiquing their work, or offering suggestions. This is designed to develop their reflective skills.
• A group face-to-face presentation. Each group uses ICT tools to demonstrate understandings of challenges, provisos, and opportunities regarding ICT and pedagogy. This assessment is intended to help them synthesize their understandings about pedagogy (incorporating learning from other parts of their graduate program) and ICT, while having some cooperative fun. Their source text, a short story, "And Madly Teach" (Biggles, 1975), raises issues about technology and education.

ClassForum components include opportunities for students to learn more about each other, share ideas about using ICT, and discuss issues that may have no other forum. This openness allows these learner-teachers to voice their personal perspectives and their developing knowledge. An area initiated in this online module, called "Chewing It Over," has become hugely popular as students share experiences and keep in touch while on practicum in different schools across the region. This entirely nonassessed informal function proves to be an important aspect of these learner-teachers' growth, as they divulge emotional and relationship-oriented experiences as well as successes and challenges. One first-practicum contribution amusingly captured this: "Hey guys, I'm completely stuffed! Whew, who knew this teaching thing was going to be so tiring?! Trying to juggle the intricate planning of three units really does inforce [*sic*] reality! Hope everyone is having a swell time and enjoying it as much as I am—the bags under the eyes and sleepless nights are all worth it in the end."

Student feedback is also invited, because they can post questions and offer resources to share online. While there are private areas between each student and the lecturer in charge of this module, the areas where students must share their trials with ICT in classrooms are a rich collegial repository of strategies and suggestions they value.

By the end of the ICT module, all students have had opportunities to experiment with common ICT tools available in New Zealand schools, trying out ideas and learning from each other as their confidence and competence with ICT tools improve while also focusing on pedagogy.

All of these case studies rely on effective technological and pedagogical support. The following section explains how this is provided.

Technological and Pedagogical Support

The Waikato Innovation Centre for e-Education (WICeD) was initiated in 2000 to support the university's existing e-learning strategy. This center continually developed the in-house e-learning system by developing pedagogically sound tools to assist lecturers and providing professional development support for lecturers learning about teaching online. The center consisted of programmers, designers, and learning specialists. The learning specialists work closely with lecturers to assist them in developing their pedagogical understanding about working online, while programmers and designers interpret their needs in terms of the technology. This interrelationship means that the online learning system is under continuous development, as lecturers have helped customize its tools to suit their individual pedagogical needs.

Teaching staff within UOW have therefore been the drivers of ClassForum. WICeD has supported staff in these ways:

- *Training courses.* These introductory and advanced courses were regularly scheduled at the start of each semester. Sometimes they were on demand, according to online lecturers' needs, and always focused more on pedagogy rather than software or technical issues.

- *Seminars.* Staff often requested these (for example, for departmental or faculty staff meetings). There are also regular updates of the e-learning software.
- *Weekly drop-in afternoons.* WICeD staff are available every Wednesday afternoon, in the same place, so that staff can drop in for a coffee and ask questions about their online teaching. This tends to be one-to-one casual support.
- *One-on-one consultancy.* Staff can request individual support where WICeD staff visit their offices, or vice versa.
- *The Online Campus (accessible once logged onto ClassForum).* It provides pedagogical, technical, and administrative resources for staff, including spaces to air online problems.
- *E-mail and phone support for e-learning problems.* Staff send e-mails to individuals within WICeDs or to a group list.

In addition to providing support to instructors through the multiple training opportunities listed above, some specific tools have been developed to support lecturers' needs:

- *Group management tools* to establish and manage groups within classes
- *Workbook Wizard* to establish individual discussion areas between lecturers and students for drop boxes, journal entries, assessments, and private conversations
- *Peer Feedback tool,* so groups of learners give feedback to each other for presentations to the group
- *More sophisticated access rights management,* which emulate effective online pedagogies
- *Online testing,* which develops recall-type summative self-assessment tests to help check students' understanding of concepts

WICeD was commercialized in June 2004, becoming ECTUS, an incubator innovative e-learning company supported by UOW. E-learning educational tools so far include products (distributed free through the New Zealand Transport Authority) such as CD-Drives, a new drivers' hazard detection simulation game, currently being modified for motorcyclists.

Another development is Ectus PLACE, a fourth-generation collaborative learning environment (LMS) based on principles of social constructionism. While including all the usual aspects of an LMS, it focuses on tools that encourage the Five Cs: using Collaboration and Communication to build Community and to Construct Content. PLACE also transcends boundaries between the synchronous world of videoconferencing and the asynchronous world of LMS systems with Ectus MEDIA. MEDIA makes the results of videoconferences or video clips available for later streaming and discussion. Because it tightly binds these results into PLACE's discussion environment, the collaborative value of the initial videoconference is greatly extended.

These two features, coupled with developing collaborations with other organizations to extend the capability of PLACE and related tools, clearly position UOW, staff, and ECTUS as innovators in e-learning.

References

Barr, H. (2000, December). *A study of the University of Waikato Bachelor of Teaching degree taught through mixed media.* Hamilton, NZ: School of Education, University of Waikato.

Biggles, L. (1975). *A galaxy of strangers.* New York: Doubleday.

Donahy, A., McGee, C., Ussher, B., & Yates, R. (2003, April). *Online teaching and learning: A study of teacher education students' experiences.* Hamilton, NZ: Wilf Halcolm Institute for Educational Research, University of Waikato.

Donahy, A., McGee, C., & Yates, R. (2004, March). *The impact of information and communication technology upon schools.* Hamilton, NZ: WMIER, University of Waikato.

Ministry of Education. (2002). *Highways and pathways.* Wellington, NZ: Ministry of Education

Salmon, G. (2000). *E-Moderating: The key to teaching and learning online.* London: Kogan Page.

Smyth, J., & Hattam, R. (2004). *"Dropping out," drifting off, being excluded: Becoming somebody without school.* New York: Peter Lang.

Noeline Wright teaches in a graduate secondary teacher education program in the School of Education, University of Waikato. She teaches courses in instructor-led training, pedagogy, and educational leadership. She is also involved in a three-year secondary literacy research project commissioned by the New Zealand Ministry of Education. Her research interests, using narrative analysis and fictionalized storying, include educational leadership issues (especially related to middle leaders in secondary schools and whole school change), online learning, and pedagogy. A recent example is "A Short Story from the Inside" in B. Doeke, D., Homer, and H. Nixon (Eds.), *English Teachers at Work: Narratives, Counter Narratives and Arguments* (2003). Her background includes twenty years in secondary schools.

Ross Dewstow works as a learning designer for ECTUS in Hamilton, New Zealand. He assists the university staff with their online courses, concentrating on issues of pedagogy first and technology second. Within ECTUS, his expertise is in making the teaching tools educationally sound within the context of education and commerce. His research interests center on e-learning best practice in the tertiary sector and the culture of institutions toward e-learning. An example is "Secondary School Students, Online Learning, and External Support in New Zealand," to be published in *Computers in the Schools.* He has considerable teaching experience in secondary schools, the tertiary sector as well as in industry.

Mark Topping is CEO of Ectus, a New Zealand company specializing in collaborative learning, videoconferencing, and video streaming technologies developed by Waikato

University. He was founding director of the Waikato Innovation Centre for electronic Education and director of e-learning at the University of Waikato, from which Ectus was formed. Prior to this, he had a career in information and communications technology. He studied at the University of Auckland, and his Ph.D. is in micropaleontology.

Sue Tappenden came to the School of Law at the University of Waikato, New Zealand, from the United Kingdom in 2001. She has taught law since 1990, having gained an LL.B. and LL.M. in legal theory and history from University College London. For the past ten years, she has been heavily involved in new course development, implementing innovative teaching methods using technologically assisted learning practices. She is responsible for a diploma program at the School of Law that incorporates eleven papers, all of which are centered in blended learning. She is involved in teaching land law, equity, and jurisprudence at undergraduate and postgraduate levels and is researching how blended learning can assist law students to achieve their full potential.

CHAPTER THIRTEEN

E-COLLEGE WALES, A CASE STUDY OF BLENDED LEARNING

Norah Jones

This chapter explores the impact of blended learning on higher education, using a case study of the experiences of the University of Glamorgan (UoG) in Wales. It locates UoG's experiences of blended learning in the context of both wider developments and appropriate research. It is clear that the practice of blended learning has outpaced the research, due, in part, to the rapid increase in technology. As a result, there is a paucity of research on blended learning from universities in the United Kingdom. This chapter contributes to closing this gap by providing evidence from one case study university.

Trends

The introduction of technology into learning and training programs is gaining momentum; for example, Pittinsky (2003), chairman of Blackboard, claims that 80 percent of the top universities in the United States will be offering e-learning programs by the end of 2004. The e-Europe 2005 action plans, which have been adopted by the Council of Ministers and the European Parliament, identify e-learning as their top priority. The findings from the Chartered Institute of Personnel and Development (CIPD) 2004 Training and Development survey revealed that the most significant growth areas in terms of training practices in the United Kingdom are coaching (51 percent increase) and e-learning (47 percent). Rossett and Douglis (2004) report that "studies have shown that blending can help people to learn more, at greater speed" (p. 36).

Although more research is needed, there are many examples of successful blended learning solutions from the United States. DeLacey and Leonard (2002) found that Harvard Business School students learned more when online classes supplemented traditional face-to-face classes. In addition, they discovered that student interaction and satisfaction also improved. Thomson and NETg (2003) reported that blended learning had a greater impact on work performance than e-learning alone.

U.K. Developments

New developments in e-learning and increasingly sophisticated learning technologies are making an impact on U.K. universities, partly in response to demands for greater efficiency and flexibility. As Inglis, Ling, and Joosten (2002) emphasize, "The key factor now driving change is technology. . . . In both education and training there is a shift to offering greater flexibility in relation to time, place, pace, entry and exit" (p. 33).

A large number of early adopters of e-learning failed to attract and retain sufficient students to sustain their operations. Nonetheless, e-learning has been adopted across a number of U.K. universities. In fact, in 2000, the UK eUniversities Worldwide (UKeU) was formed by the government in order to coordinate higher education's Web-based courses and offer them globally. The government provided a £62 million grant to set up the scheme. However, by 2003, the UKeU had attracted only nine hundred students against a target of five thousand, and in 2004 it was disbanded. Simply stated, the UKeU failed because of its emphasis on the technology at the cost of meeting learner expectations and needs. Sir Howard Newby, chief executive of the Higher Education Funding Council for England (HEFCE) (2004b), concluded, "In hindsight it was clear that online learning on its own was not as popular as predicted and there had been a number of e-learning failures by universities in the US. What students wanted was 'blended' learning where online materials were backed up by conventional teaching." In Scotland a blended learning model has been developed with greater success (Flynn, 2004).

Similarly in the training market in the United Kingdom, there is a move to blended learning solutions. Durbin (2004) emphasized, "Despite the hype, e-learning did not catch on, but now companies are realising they can be efficient by combining classroom training with e-learning" (p. 7). Balance Learning (2003), in conjunction with *Training Magazine,* surveyed training officers responsible for almost 2 million U.K. employees in order to discover best practices in e-learning. This survey revealed that over half of the 173 organizations in the study used blended learning. Balance Learning managing director Chris Horseman noted, "The data suggests that organisations appreciate the value of training and that 2004 will be a very busy year for training departments and training providers. Taking into account the planned increases and decreases, we calculate that training budgets overall will rise by 8.14 per cent. The greatest increases are forecast for the financial services and retail sectors. Of those who are increasing their budgets, 67 per cent plan to spend more on blended learning solutions (the combination of two or more learning methods), 53 per cent will spend more on e-learning, and 47 per cent will increase instructor-led training" (Balance Learning, 2004, p. 3).

In a recent funding call by HEFCE (2004a) inviting universities in England to bid for centers of excellence status in learning and teaching, eleven universities based their bids on blended learning solutions; there were no bids on e-learning alone. Another study by HEFCE (2004b) found that universities and colleges preferred a blended approach.

Initially e-learning was led by the technology rather by learning theories and pedagogies, but over the past two to three years, there has been a significant move to redress the balance by combining the best traditional teaching and e-learning models to create blending learning. It is important to note, however, that there are strategic and operational issues to be considered when developing a blend that includes e-learning. Such key issues include the following:

- There is no doubt that online programs are expensive, especially in the development costs. Although it is argued that these costs diminish as larger numbers of students engage in the programs, this assumes stability in the course content. Nonetheless, the starting costs may be prohibitive.
- Blended learning is gaining in popularity, but as yet there is insufficient research on the most effective blend in course designs.
- Blended learning that includes face-to-face elements is time and place limiting.
- Offering more choice in the blend of the learning experience may pose challenges to the way universities are administered.
- There are challenges to the quality assurance processes. Do the various possible blends of learning all meet the same learning outcomes?
- Technology may be problematic and have an impact on equal opportunities since not all students have access to a computer.
- While blended learning offers an opportunity for face-to-face meetings, not all students want this, and some would prefer the totally online program.

Definitional Complexities

There are definitional complexities and ambiguities surrounding such terms as *e-learning* and *blended learning*. From the outset, it is important to understand that the terms *e-learning* and *blended learning* are used in many different and frequently confusing ways. In the United Kingdom, the Department for Education and Skills (2004) suggests: "If someone is learning in a way that uses information and communication technologies, they are using eLearning" (p. 1). This definition includes any activity from the simple use of e-mail and PowerPoint presentations delivered on campus to sophisticated multimedia simulations for use in stand-alone study at any location in the world.

Initially the term *blended learning* tended to be used to describe the linkage between traditional classroom teaching and e-learning. More recently, blended learning programs represent a more diverse combining of a variety of approaches. For example, Rossett, Douglis, and Frazee (2003) defined *blended learning* as follows: "A blend is an integrated strategy for delivering on promises about learning and performance. Blending involves a planned combination of approaches, such as coaching by a supervisor; participation in an online class; breakfast with colleagues; competency descriptions; reading on the beach; reference to a manual; collegial relationships; and participation in seminars, workshops, and online communities" (p. 1).

There have also been definitional complexities surrounding the idea of combining e-learning and traditional face-to-face learning including mixed model, clicks and mortar, blurred learning, hybrid models, and, more recently, blended learning. There is little wonder that Morrison (2003b) concludes, "I can't help reading 'blended learning' as 'we can't make up our mind learning.' We're not sure which type of learning to use so we'll use lots and hope that the whole is greater than the sum of its parts" (p. 1).

Blending different approaches to learning is not a new idea; in business schools traditionally, a variety of pedagogical approaches have been used, for example, lectures, seminars, tutorials, case studies, role play, residential weekend courses, adventure training, and action learning groups. The difference now is that information technology and the development of virtual learning environments (VLEs) are used to support the learning process. In fact, these technology-rich environments are making a major impact on our thinking about pedagogy and learning theory.

We need to be more aware of the use of the terminology surrounding virtual or online environments. For example, when we use the term *blended learning*, there is a danger of believing everyone shares the same understanding or definition of

FIGURE 13.1.   CONTINUUM OF E-LEARNING AT THE UNIVERSITY
OF GLAMORGAN.

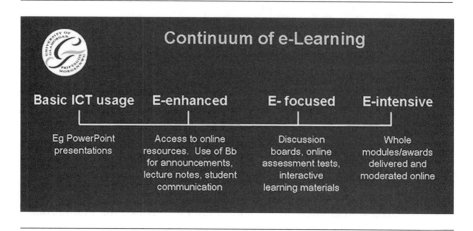

this term. As a result, research findings could be misleading due to confusion arising out of ambiguous terminology.

At the University of Glamorgan, we have adopted a continuum of e-learning that indicates the blend as the use of online medium increases from basic information and communication technology (ICT) use to intensive ICT use (see Figure 13.1).

At the basic ICT use end of the continuum is the blend of current practices plus a basic use of ICT, for example PowerPoint and Word documents. At the e-enhanced stage, current practice is supplemented with access to some online resources provided through the VLE (Blackboard) such as announcements and lecture notes on the Web. The next stage is e-focused, where the instructor might use discussion boards, online assessment tests, and interactive learning materials alongside some face-to-face delivery. The end of the continuum is the e-intensive stage, where modules or complete awards are delivered and moderated online but still may contain some face-to-face elements such as inductions.

The next section offers more specifics about how E-College Wales is using blended learning.

Local Designs

Wales is a country where a quarter of those of working age are not in paid employment. Such high levels of inactivity have led to locally concentrated areas of unskilled people and destructive cycles of low expectations, disaffection, and social exclusion. A large section of Wales has been designated as an Objective One area by the European Union (EU); with this designation, it is eligible for extra funding to stimulate economic growth. Thus, in 2000, the University of Glamorgan, in collaboration with its partnership of further education colleges in Wales, successfully bid to the European Social Fund (ESF) for funding to develop entrepreneurial programs online across the Objective One areas of Wales, resulting in the E-College Wales (ECW) project. ECW is one of Europe's largest and most innovative online learning projects offering an honors degree in enterprise, a master's degree in professional development available in both Welsh and English, a foundation degree in business administration, courses related to finance for nonfinancial managers, and an e-moderation course for developing teaching skills in an online environment. ECW was launched in 2000 and now has over eight hundred learners online. All courses have been popular and attracted many students who would not have enrolled in face-to-face programs at the university. The master's in professional development and the e-moderation courses are growing most rapidly, indicating that professional and training courses attract online learners. On the degree in enterprise, many learners dropped out at the end of the first year, stating that they did not want a degree but rather training in specific business areas (for example, how to write a business plan, marketing, and financial know-how). Our plans are to introduce smaller chunks of learning and training for these small business owners.

The learner target group is diverse; we knew at the outset that many potential online learners would be unlikely to pay for any new opportunity and would have few or no formal educational qualifications. Thus, as a result of EU funding, the courses and programs, mentioned previously, were offered free, and students were loaned personal computers. We knew that motivation and retention would be two of the most crucial issues in delivering successful e-learning programs to these learners. The learner target group is made up of those least likely to participate in open and distance learning without motivation, incentive, and intensive local support. In U.K. universities, in particular those with a widening access policy, retaining students is problematic. Student motivation and satisfaction with the online program are frequently given as reasons that a large number of students drop out (Alexander, 2001; Bonk, 2003).

Although we recognized that motivating, engaging, and retaining individuals would be the key to success in the implementation of e-learning, our retention rate in the first year was low (50 percent). The students provided many reasons why they withdrew including personal issues, such as increased pressure of work, lack of time, illness, and lack of IT skills. There were also a number of course-specific reasons given for withdrawal, and these included technical problems, wrong course selection, and too much course work. Student responses to the e-learning environment ranged from enthusiastic to anxious. Statements were made regarding an initial fear of e-learning, concerns about not having facial and body language in communications, and difficulty in keeping track of the participants. Some students mentioned feelings of isolation and the difficulty of conversing with "strangers"; others disliked not having other students to chat with. Some of the students concluded that e-learning was the wrong mode of learning for them. There was a general feeling that levels of dedication and motivation needed to be higher online than with traditional courses, and some students found it difficult to remain focused online. Overall, the two most significant factors for withdrawal were the course itself (as an entirely online course) and lack of support from course tutors.

At the start of the project, we had been advised to avoid face-to-face meetings, as this would discourage the creation of online communities. However, when we experienced high attrition rates (50 percent during the first cohort), we realized we needed to revise our model. As Rossett and Douglis (2004) noted, the progression from e-learning to blended learning has developed in an organic manner in order to resolve some of the difficulties associated with e-learning, such as high attrition rates. Mullich (2004) noted, "The dirty little secret of e-learning is that a lot of people who try a computer module or online class won't finish it" (p. 1).

According to Forrester Research (Schooley, 2002), 70 percent of those who start an e-learning course never complete it. The Open University's retention statistics for e-learning courses are around 50 percent completion (Tait & Mills, 2003). Such rates are especially noteworthy, given that the Open University is the largest provider of distance education in the U.K. Given the prevailing evidence that attrition rates from online learning programs are high, there is an incorrect impression that e-learning is ineffective. As a result, the development of blended learning is too often seen as a solution to the high attrition rates associated with e-learning, the genesis of which is reactive rather than proactive. In our case, we believe that rather than being reactive, we were proactive in meeting the needs of learners and online teachers. One such example is detailed below. We had developed this course as an online course even though the evolving model was blended learning. We now turn to the rationale for this change.

Induction

The Evaluation Report of ECW (2003) revealed that in the 2001 cohort, the majority of students felt that the one-day induction had not prepared them well for the course. We have addressed this through providing a three-day induction

TABLE 13.1. STUDENTS' PERCEPTIONS OF INDUCTION, 2001–2003.

	Year of Enrollment		
	2001	**2002**	**2003**
Comprehensiveness of the induction	D	B	A
Usefulness of the induction	D	B	A
Induction as preparation for the challenges of your course	E	B	B
Induction as an opportunity to meet students and tutors	B	A	A
Training in the use of the required technology	C	B	A
Accuracy of advice on amount of input required	D	B	B
Induction lecture	C	B	A
Advice on search sources	D	B	A
Training in the use of supporting learning resources/library materials	D	B	A

Source: E-College Wales (2003).

program. The feedback from students has since been highly favorable, as seen in the analysis of students' responses (see Table 13.1) which provides evidence of improvement as a result of expanding the induction from one day to three days. The mean satisfaction ratings were assigned a letter from A (very satisfactory) to E (very unsatisfactory), based on a Likert-type questionnaire.

Mason (2003) emphasizes, "Face-to-face tutoring is less necessary the more advanced the learner, but also . . . the most vulnerable students—least confident or motivated—will benefit from face-to-face provision in terms of increased persistence and higher pass rates" (p. 93).

Our students in both postgraduate and undergraduate e-learning programs unanimously agreed that the face-to-face induction was instrumental in establishing an initial level of socialization and reducing the personal anxieties they had held about their ability to undertake the program. They liked being able to put faces to names when they began the online activities. In addition, it helped to develop rapport and trust between the tutor and the students.

Garrison and Anderson (2003) note the benefit of an initial face-to-face meeting: "This can have an accelerating effect on establishing social presence and can shift the group dynamics more rapidly towards intellectually producing activities"

TABLE 13.2.   STUDENTS' POSITIVE AND NEGATIVE PERCEPTIONS OF ONLINE LEARNING.

Top Five Negative Aspects of Online Learning	Top Five Positive Aspects of Online Learning
Technical problems (29%)	Flexibility (89%)
Isolation (20%)	Opportunities to interact with peers (17%)
Lack of support (16%)	Access to wide resources (11%)
Lack of student interaction (14%)	Effective mode of learning (7%)
Absence of face-to-face opportunities (14%)	Opportunities to interact with tutors (6%)

(p. 54). Moreover, they conclude that "such blended learning approaches have strong advantages that go beyond social presence."

The ECW Evaluation Report (2003) revealed that all online tutors advocated a blended approach of face-to-face sessions combined with e-learning. The timing and frequency of live meetings varied somewhat; 100 percent of the tutors wanted a face-to-face induction program, 36 percent felt that face-to-face sessions were important at the start of the course, and 50 percent felt that regular face-to-face meetings should be built into the programs. The students felt that this blended approach met their needs more successfully and allowed them to learn more effectively. Tutors also noted that students' results improved, as did student satisfaction and retention.

The top five positive and negative features of online learning that we found in our evaluation of the online program between 2001 and 2003 are set out in Table 13.2. We have addressed all the negative aspects of the course identified by the students and now offer a blended model of learning, which we judge is meeting students' needs more comprehensively.

Our Blend

From our perspective, we view blended learning as a Web-based, higher education accredited program, delivered over the Internet using a managed learning environment, mediated by tutor-led synchronous and asynchronous discussion groups and face-to-face meetings. We have adopted a blended learning approach combining online programs, face-to-face induction and tutorials, and tutoring support delivered from a network of geographically dispersed campuses. The blend is complex and includes:

Off-Line

- Face-to-face inductions involving ICT skills training, icebreaker and socialization sessions, tutorials, lectures, and PowerPoint presentations
- Student-led face-to-face meetings
- Videoconferences
- Printed student handbook and relevant journal articles
- CD-ROM with instructions on the VLE (Blackboard)

Online

- Electronic library including access to e-books and e-journals
- Interactive generic content
- Interactive customized content
- Online student support including e-tutors, technical support, customer services, and student services
- Asynchronous online collaborative learning using e-mail, discussion boards, and chat facilities
- Synchronous learning through the virtual classroom

Miller, Jones, Packham, and Thomas (2004), tutors at UoG, report on the positive feedback from the students as a result of the introduction of blended learning: "The students felt it simply met their needs and allowed them to learn more effectively. Comments from students included: 'the initial Blackboard face-to-face training was essential for us to find our way around the system and know what to do.' 'We vote with our feet, if we did not want the face to face sessions we would not attend. We did and we still do'" (p. 4).

Similarly staff members who undertook our e-moderating programs provided similar feedback to the undergraduates' feedback. Additional face-to-face sessions have been very well received, and one of our students, himself a long-serving lecturer, sums up his feelings: "I have no hesitation in placing on record that I have found this to be the most stimulating course I've undertaken in years."

Conclusions

At the start of the ECW project in 2000, we concentrated on developing courses online. Since that time, we have learned that a largely online model of learning does not offer enough choices of engagement or enough social contact—thus our move to blended learning.

Our experiences of blended learning are without exception positive and have resulted in the achievement of higher learning outcomes. All of this evidence, however, could be viewed as post hoc rationalization, opting for a blended approach rather than a major redesign. However, it is important to realize that technology should not be used merely to emulate traditional methods of delivery; the challenge is to identify the gains from applying technology and use these alongside existing best practices in multimodal delivery. It is essential that the technology is not incorporated into programs uncritically. Many students, especially those age eighteen to twenty-five, will probably not want entirely e-learning courses or study at a virtual university. The key features of university life for many young people are the social and recreational activities. In addition, for any age group, sustaining motivation in a virtual environment is problematic. Blended learning offers one solution so that online learning enhances the best of the face-to-face provision.

For many, e-learning is seen as a technical solution to improve teaching. It is commonly viewed as neutral—just another tool in the lecturer's kit bag. This, I believe, is a naive view and hides the extent and complexity of change required at universities (Jones, 2004; Jones & O'Shea, 2004). Technology is not just another way of delivering course content. Blended learning is challenging our education practices and underlying epistemologies and theories. The design of blended learning needs to be grounded in sound education theory. We need to ensure that we blend technological and pedagogical advancements. If we design programs online and ignore education theory, we are in danger of leaving learning to chance. Of course, the disadvantages of a blended learning solution, which includes some face-to-face elements, are obvious: a loss of time and location freedom. Nevertheless, we believe that overall, there are great benefits from adopting a blended approach, and the benefits outweigh the costs.

Laurillard (2002) gives valuable advice emphasizing that the first execution of an e-learning program rarely works well. She recommends that we as academics build a body of knowledge on how we could make best use of technology in learning. There is not enough research evidence on which to base conclusions on the efficacy of blended learning, but this case study goes some way to fill the evidence gaps. There is clear evidence presented in this case study that a blended solution works better than an entirely computer-mediated environment. The variety of blends can be overwhelming and confusing, but the case study illustrates the success of combining elements of traditional and computer-mediated delivery.

References

Alexander, S. (2001). E-learning developments and experiences. *Education and Training, 43*(4), 55–63.

Balance Learning. (2004, March). Budgets set to soar as coaching gains popularity. *Personnel Today,* 1–6.

Bonk, C. J. (2003, February). Navigating the myths and monsoons of online learning strategies and technologies. In *Proceedings of the e-ducation Without Borders Conference,* Abu Dhabi, United Arab Emirates.

Chartered Institute of Personnel and Development. (2004, May). New trends in training and development. *CIPD Impact Report*, no. 7.

DeLacey, B. J., & Leonard, D. A. (2002). Case study on technology and distance in education at the Harvard Business School. *Educational Technology and Society, 5*(2), 13–28.

Department for Education and Skills. (2004). *Unified e-learning strategy.* Retrieved June 27, 2004, from http://www.dfes.gov.uk/elearningstrategy.

Durbin, J. (2004). Current usage of training delivery methods. *ITT Training,* 1–7. Retrieved June 24, 2004, from www.itskillsresearch.co.uk.

E-College Wales. (2003). *Evaluation report.* Glamorgan: University of Glamorgan, Wales.

Flynn, G. (2004, April). How uptake forces re-think for e-university. *People Management.*

Garrison, D., & Anderson, T. (2003). *E-learning in the 21st century.* London: Routledge Falmer.

Higher Education Funding Council England. (2004a). *HEFCE e-learning strategy: Consultation responses and next steps.* Retrieved August 2, 2004, from http://www.hefce.ac.uk/pubs/circlets/2004/cl09_04/.

Higher Education Funding Council England. (2004b). *The Centres for Excellence in Teaching and Learning (CETL).* Retrieved June 27, 2004, from http://www.hefce.ac.uk/learning/tinits/cetl/.

Inglis, A., Ling, P., & Joosten, V. (2002). *Delivering digitally.* London: Kogan Page.

Jones, N. (2004, March). *From here to e-ternity.* Professorial inaugural lecture, University of Glamorgan.

Jones, N. and O'Shea, J. (2004). Challenging hierarchies. *Higher Education, 48*(3), 379–395.

Laurillard, D. (2002). *Rethinking university teaching* (2nd ed.). London: Routledge.

Mason, R. (2003). Online learning and supporting students: New possibilities. In A. Tait and R. Mills (Eds.), *Rethinking learner support in distance education: Change and continuity in an international context.* London: Routledge.

Miller, C., Jones, P., Packham, G., & Thomas, B. (2004, April). Networked learning, A viable solution: The case for blended delivery on an on-line learning programme. Paper presented at the Networked Learning Fourth International Conference, Lancaster University.

Morrison, D. (2003a). *E-learning strategies: How to get implementation and delivery right first time.* New York: Wiley.

Morrison, D. (2003b). *The search for the holy recipe.* Retrieved June 24, 2004, from http://www.morrisonco.com/downloads/blended_learning_holy_recipe.pdf.

Mullich, J. (2004). A recipe for blended learning. *Workforce Management, Training and Development.* Retrieved June 21, 2004, from http://www.workforce.com/section/11/ feature/23/62/89/236291.html.

Newby, H. (2004, June 23). MPs attack e-university bonus payments. *Guardian Newspaper.* p. 2.

Pittinsky, M. (2003, October). *Sharing best practices, innovating together.* European Blackboard Conference, Amsterdam.

Rossett, A., & Douglis, F. (2004, April). The house blend. *People Management,* 36–38.

Rossett, A., Douglis, F., & Frazee, V. (2003). Strategies for building blended learning. *Learning Circuits.* Retrieved June 24, 2004, from http://www.learningcircuits.org/2003/jul2003/rossett.htm.

Schooley, C. (2002). *Ways to encourage completion of e-learning tasks.* Forrester Research. Retrieved June 27, 2004, from http://www.forrester.com/my/1,,1–0,FF.html.

Tait, A., & Mills, R. (2003). *Rethinking learner support in distance education.* London: Routledge Falmer.

Thomson and NETg. (2003). *The next generation of corporate learning: Achieving the right blend.* Retrieved June 24, 2004, from www.netg.com/NewsAndEvents/PressReleases/view.asp?PressID=75#top.

Norah Jones is a professor of education at the University of Glamorgan and head of the Quality and Research Unit, E-College. She has been involved in e-learning since 2000, when she managed the academic team in the Business School that was developing materials online. She has published a number of papers on the way all things "E" are changing universities and colleges and is interested in the change of emphasis from teaching to learning. Previously, she was associate head in the Business School at the University of Glamorgan and has spent most of her career teaching organizational behavior and management. Jones has a doctorate in education management; she is a chartered psychologist and fellow of the Chartered Institute of Personnel and Development.

CHAPTER FOURTEEN

BLENDED LEARNING ENTERS THE MAINSTREAM

Charles Dziuban, Joel Hartman, Frank Juge,
Patsy Moskal, Steven Sorg

The number of colleges and universities engaged in Web-based instruction has increased dramatically over the past decade. Advancements in computer technologies and the Internet, combined with significant research in new learning theories, have helped fuel exploration and research on how to best use these technologies to improve teaching and learning.

There is no doubt that the recent technological advances have, at the very least, fostered much discussion regarding virtual teaching and learning, and in some cases have resulted in transformed practices at many institutions of higher education (Dziuban, Hartman, & Moskal, 2004). The U.S. Department of Education (2003) reported that 56 percent of all two- and four-year Title IV degree-granting institutions are offering distance education courses, with 90 percent of those using asynchronous Internet instruction. *Campus Computing 2003* (Green, 2003) reported that more than half of all college courses are using Internet resources, with nearly half of public university courses using a course Web site. In fact, universities now use the Internet more than any other mode to deliver distance education (Ashby, 2002), and the trend is toward even higher levels of adoption in the future (Allen & Seaman, 2003).

Institutions of higher learning are also seeing changes in their incoming students. Today's undergraduates are more technologically savvy than ever before, with more than 78 percent having used the Internet for homework prior to entering college, more than 67 percent having used e-mail, and 80 percent acquiring a computer by the time they get to college. Undergraduate students report spending an average of twelve hours per week on the Internet (EDUCAUSE, 2003). In addition, today's students also appear to be older. About 43 percent of those enrolled in 1999–2000 reported that they were age twenty-four or over, and 82 percent of these older undergraduates were employed (Horn, Peter, & Rooney, 2002).

Many institutions are now developing courses that combine both fully online and face-to-face instruction. Faculty, students, and administrators are beginning to realize a number of advantages from these blended courses, and many see in them the potential of offering the best of both the physical and virtual instructional worlds. Courses that replace a portion of face-to-face instruction with asynchronous Web components increase flexibility while retaining both face-to-face and online interaction. Research investigating blended learning indicates the emergence of a number of trends. First, blended courses provide a powerful mechanism for meeting the educational needs of students. Because many students have job and family responsibilities, blended courses help provide the flexibility they require (McCray, 2000; Strambi & Bouvet, 2003; Wingard, 2004). Not surprisingly, many students have come to prefer blended courses over their face-to-face counterparts, and this is often displayed in high levels of student satisfaction with this mode of instruction (Dziuban, Hartman, & Moskal, 2004; Leh, 2002; Willett, 2002).

An additional benefit reported from blended courses is a higher level of interaction than commonly experienced in face-to-face courses (Dziuban, Hartman & Moskal, 2004; Waddoups & Howell, 2002; Wingard, 2004). The interaction tools available in most blended courses and course management systems, coupled with the asynchronous structure of such courses, combine to form a highly effective computer-mediated communication environment. They also facilitate access to material and experts that might not be otherwise available. The result is a learning environment where students can be actively engaged and potentially learn more than in a traditional on-campus classroom (Dziuban, Hartman, & Moskal, 2004). From an institutional standpoint, classroom space can be more efficiently used when a substantial portion of the course is offered in an online format. In theory, multiple courses can occupy the same classroom time slot, whereas in practice, universities and colleges are experimenting with how to leverage this effect to increase efficiency and reduce costs.

While the potential benefits are positive, the research is clear that for blended courses to be educationally effective, quality course design is critical (Dziuban, Hartman, & Moskal, 2004; King, 2002; Waddoups & Howell, 2002). Faculty must learn how to use Web resources effectively, including highly popular course management tools such as Blackboard or WebCT (Morgan, 2003). Perhaps more important are the pedagogical and instructional design components associated with how best to use online tools, including how to facilitate interaction in the course, what content or interactions are best delivered through the Web versus face-to-face, and how to motivate students to be actively involved in and take greater responsibility for their own learning. Faculty members are faced with significant challenges such as how to rethink the way they teach a class, and they often need access to instructional design support to guide them through this process. Having faculty and student support ready and available when things go wrong (and they will) is critical. Students and faculty need access to technical specialists who can provide them with information and guidance when difficulties or failures related to campus servers, course management systems, Internet service providers, or other technology elements occur (Strambi & Bouvet, 2003; Willett, 2002).

Blended Courses at the University of Central Florida

Figure 14.1 illustrates the initiative for the three Web modalities offered at the University of Central Florida (UCF): fully online (W), mixed mode (M), and Web enhanced (E) courses. Fully online courses and programs are predominantly determined at the college and department level. The E courses, which are face-to-face with added Web components, began when faculty became interested in using Web resources to enhance their classes. This E modality has become so prevalent that UCF has eliminated this designation since many face-to-face classes now are Web enhanced.

A blended (M) model was created in 1997 as an institutional response as a result of the finding that 75 percent of the students who enrolled in the first wave of fully online courses the previous year were also enrolled in face-to-face courses

FIGURE 14.1.   UCF INITIATIVE FOR ONLINE LEARNING MODALITY.

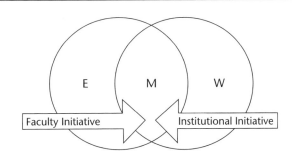

Source: Dziuban, Hartman, Moskal, Sorg, & Truman (2004).

(Dziuban, Hartman, Moskal, Sorg, & Truman, 2004). Blended courses were immediately popular with students, and enrollments increased from 125 in 1997 (eight blended courses) to more than 13,600 (508 blended courses) in academic year 2003–2004. The UCF approach replaces some classroom meeting time with online activity. A blended course typically holds one face-to-face class meeting per week, with the remaining course material and interaction being online; however, the model varies by faculty and discipline. For instance, "Exploring Wines of the World" is an elective in UCF's Rosen College of Hospitality Management. The nature of this course makes it an ideal fit for the blended model. The class originally met face-to-face for one hour and fifteen minutes every other week, with a laboratory wine tasting on alternate weeks.

Impact on Faculty and Students

Blended courses benefit the institution, the students, and the faculty in numerous ways. Institutional goals include more efficient use of classroom space, improved student retention, and enhanced student learning through increased interactivity and active student engagement (Dziuban et al., 2000; Hartman, Dziuban, & Moskal, 2000). If optimally scheduled, blended courses can reduce use of classroom time by 50 to 60 percent, thereby allowing two to three different course sections to be scheduled into a single weekly classroom slot.

Many students faced with work and family obligations are attracted to the flexibility of blended courses, and fully or partially online courses may be an important factor in determining whether they can complete a degree program. The millennial or Net generation students (Oblinger, 2003) have a natural affinity for the use of technology. They are familiar with the Internet, digital media, and the Web and see online courses as responding to their needs.

Faculty success in the online environment is one of the most critical factors in developing and sustaining an online learning initiative. It is an irony of the academy that few faculty members have ever studied learning theories, pedagogy, instructional strategies, curriculum development, assessment strategies, or curricular applications of instructional technology. As one UCF faculty member bluntly expressed it, "We do to them what was done to us." The culture of scholarship through which faculty teach, conduct research, publish, and seek tenure and promotion functions well within the academy. However, when applied to the development of instructional technology products, such as online courses, the results vary in quality, are not sustainable, and may find limited acceptance by other faculty (Hanley, 2001). Because the blended online course format at UCF is regarded as transformative, UCF faculty members are required to participate in an intensive faculty development program in order to teach a course in this modality.

Priorities for the development of blended courses are established by the respective college deans and chairpersons through consultations that occur once each academic term. Although faculty members responsible for the courses selected for blended learning development are identified by the respective colleges, it is expected that their participation in online learning will be completely voluntary.

Faculty Professional Development

The UCF faculty development program for blended learning is a simulation course titled "Interactive Distributed Learning for Technology Mediated Course Delivery" (IDL6543). The program is itself an authentic blended learning experience in which faculty members participate as "students," with instructional designers serving as the "instructors." IDL6543 is structured as a sixty-hour-plus, eight-week program: ten online asynchronous modules (thirty hours), nine classes (fifteen hours), six labs (seven and a half hours), and individual consultations with instructional designers for needs assessment and development (seven and a half hours). The program is designed and delivered by Course Development and Web services (CDWS) and supported by the Center for Distributed Learning (CDL).

The online modules provide faculty members with a situated learning experience from a student perspective, with subject matter covering asynchronous distributed learning, best practices, online interaction, assessment, group work, copyright, learner support, and course development processes. In-class activities include demonstrations, guest presenters (including experienced faculty, who are referred to as "Web vets"), cooperative learning activities, and group discussions. Lab sessions emphasize the development of specific skills related to online course maintenance and delivery. Homework consists of "assignments" relating to the development of materials for the courses the faculty will eventually teach online. Centralized faculty and course development support frees instructors from technical demands such as HTML programming, thus allowing them to concentrate fully on the design of their courses (Willis, 1994).

Before each session begins, an initial consultation is conducted with each faculty participant by an instructional designer to assess the faculty member's technical skills, the needs of the course he or she will be developing, and any special concerns or expectations the faculty member may have. As incentives, participating faculty members are provided with a one-course release or equivalent stipend and a new notebook computer equipped with wireless networking and a standard software load so that they can use it to complete their work. Consultations with an instructional designer occur on a regular basis to guide the faculty member through the learning process. The team experience of faculty working with an instructional designer for an extended period also helps develop the trust relationships necessary for faculty to accept the involvement of staff experts in the design and delivery of their courses; in effect, it builds confidence, shared knowledge, understanding of the role of instructional designers, and overall rapport.

The final session is the Faculty Showcase, where each instructor presents a module of the course he or she is redesigning to an audience consisting of fellow faculty, department chairs, deans, and CDWS staff, with an occasional visit by the university's provost or president. Although these presentations are brief, they clearly reveal the degree of transformation the faculty members have experienced. After faculty members have completed IDL6543, they continue to work with their assigned instructional designer to complete development of their initial course. When the online course is completed, instructional designers review it for quality before it is offered online.

During the first semester a new blended course is offered, the instructor has access to his or her instructional designer and production staff to resolve any last-minute problems or brush up on any skills needed to deliver the course. As faculty become more familiar with the tools and techniques necessary to develop online courses, they are encouraged to take greater responsibility for ongoing course maintenance activities. Many individuals initially choose the "full-service" option of having staff design, develop, and produce their courses, then later shift to a "self-service" model with increased personal responsibility.

The transformative nature of the UCF blended model results in a sense of continuous improvement in course design. For example, the design of the "Exploring Wines of the World" course was modified with the completion of a new hospitality management laboratory–classroom environment. This facility allowed the instructor to fulfill his initial plan to integrate the classroom and laboratory experiences fully. Both lecture and wine tasting could then occur simultaneously in a class so that students tasted a wine immediately after it was described, and discussion could occur. Online activities—exercises, quizzes, and modules—reinforced what was covered in class. The professor reports that this integration of activities will be enhanced in the future.

We find that this continuous incremental model of improvement is common in these blended courses as faculty become comfortable with the model and new and improved resources become available. Faculty find the flexibility of this modality allows them to use instructional resources and techniques they might not have had access to in a pure face-to-face or fully online modality. They are further encouraged by positive student perception of the course and improved student performance.

For many institutions, the initial engagement in online learning consisted of fully online courses and programs offered to distant students. With blended learning, the focus is on the institution's mainstream students, faculty, and academic programs. The differences in approach and impact can be significant. Internally directed initiatives require greater emphasis on systemic approaches, attendance to issues of campus and faculty culture, and increasing requirements for student business and academic support services to be accessible online.

Some Demographics for Blended Learning

The blended online course model has the potential to yield significant classroom space efficiencies. However, a review of blended course scheduling practices indicated this was not occurring as expected. While the university's scheduling guidelines enable sharing traditional Tuesday-Thursday and Monday-Wednesday-Friday time slots and alternate week (for example, every other Monday) offerings, some faculty have developed highly flexible instructional patterns using the blended model. Other instructors may have a preplanned but irregular on-again, off-again class meeting schedule, and some take advantage of real-time progress and learning assessment and develop their reduced seat-time strategies on a week-to-week basis throughout the term.

Scheduling personnel continually works toward a goal of having a high percentage of sections matched with other companion classes sharing the same room and block schedule time. The percentage of blended class sections that are matched and share classroom space and block schedule time slots grew from 24 percent in fall 2002 to 42 percent in fall 2004.

Outcomes for Blended Learning

A recent program sponsored by the EDUCAUSE National Learning Infrastructure Initiative (National Learning Infrastructure Initiative, 2003) on transformative assessment (TA) has led to new thinking on the manner in which we conceptualize and use data-based information regarding teaching and learning through technology. Considering evaluation in three phases (administrative, progressive, and transformative), the National Learning Infrastructure Initiative suggests that assessment is a fundamental component of higher education transformation. Simultaneously, the Sloan-C Consortium has developed a model for assessing quality education in asynchronous learning networks (Moore, 2002).

Two important elements of the Sloan pillar framework involve learning effectiveness and student satisfaction. Learning effectiveness concentrates on assessing whether technology-based instruction produces comparable or superior learning outcomes when compared to face-to-face environments. Student satisfaction considers how well learners adapt and thrive in technology-enhanced learning environments. In addition to asynchronous learning networks, these elements form an effective underpinning for evaluating blended learning. At the University of Central Florida, evaluation procedures encompass the two national initiatives, producing a protocol that is consistent with the blended learning metaphor—a mixture of face-to-face and online learning. (For more information on the blended learning impact evaluation at UCF conducted by the Research Initiative for Teaching Effectiveness, see *http://rite.ucf.edu.*)

Learning Effectiveness

At UCF, we use a declassification strategy to determine learning effectiveness with grades. By declassification, we mean reducing grades to a binary format that defines success in a course. Grade distributions vary widely across departments for reasons that reflect differences in instructional and assessment philosophies, as well as accepted academic norms. This causes difficulty comparing A's, B's, C's, and so on across departments in a way that reflects the impact of blended learning. The declassification approach attempts to mitigate these idiosyncratic differences by sacrificing some specificity to gain reliability. The process is straightforward: an A, B, or C grade is considered success, while any other grades—D, F, W, or I—are classified as nonsuccess. Obviously, the decision about where to define the cut-off point between success and nonsuccess is arbitrary. Another important variable in learning effectiveness is the withdrawal rate of students enrolled in blended courses compared to roughly comparable face-to-face and fully online courses.

Figure 14.2 shows the success rates for the spring 2003 semester for the three UCF colleges housing the majority of Web courses: Arts and Sciences (CAS), Health and Public Affairs (COHPA), and Education (COE). Success rates vary by college for all disciplines, but the trend is for blended courses to produce success rates equal to or higher than their face-to-face and fully online counterparts.

Figure 14.3 illustrates the college comparisons for withdrawal rates in the various modalities. As with success rates, withdrawal rates vary across the colleges, with the COE typically showing the lowest attrition. Overall, the withdrawal rates for blended courses are generally comparable to those in face-to-face sections.

FIGURE 14.2. SUCCESS RATES FOR FACE-TO-FACE, MIXED-MODE, AND FULLY ONLINE CLASSES (*N* = 18,284).

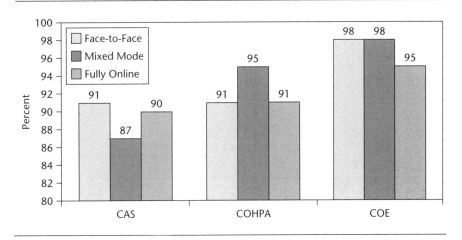

FIGURE 14.3. WITHDRAWAL RATES FOR FACE-TO-FACE, MIXED-MODE, AND FULLY ONLINE CLASSES (*N* = 18,284).

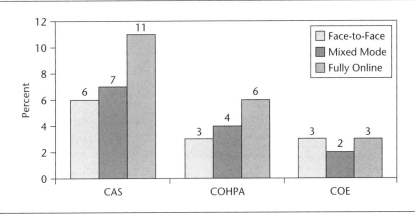

Student Satisfaction

Figure 14.4 summarizes the latest UCF blended learning student satisfaction survey (*N* = 473), and shows that approximately 86 percent of students were satisfied with their blended learning experiences.

FIGURE 14.4.   STUDENT SATISFACTION WITH BLENDED
LEARNING (*N* = 473).

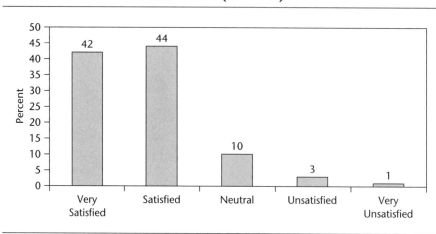

Blended Learning as a Transformative Construct in Higher Education

The blended environment serves as a prototype for universities of the future. Fully online initiatives are a phenomenon separate from the academy— essentially advocating deemphasis of traditional approaches and teaching strategies. However, the blended format coalesces Web-based and face-to-face instruction into an entirely new model that holds the potential to transform both teaching and learning.

Blended teaching and learning responds to what Oblinger (2003) and Wendover (2002) define as the new-generation learners (millennials). These students, born after 1980, have grown up with what other generations view as new technologies. They are connected (mostly to each other) and proficient in the use of communicative technology, often viewing what transpires in college classrooms as slow moving and uninteresting. Wendover (2002) describes a classroom scenario where four generations are present (matures, baby boomers, generation-Xers, and millennials). He suggests that matures' and boomers' preferred mode of communication is prolonged discussion. The generation-X students simply want to move on with it, while the millennials are quite content to sit and watch the goings on.

Our findings at UCF show that younger students are less satisfied with their online experience, with the millennials being the least satisfied of the generational groups. An important caution is that blended learning is not strictly an instructional phenomenon. All aspects of the university must be involved in a systemic way—colleges, departments, faculty, support services, and infrastructure—to enable student and faculty success in the online environment. When those elements are in place and functioning effectively, blended learning can produce satisfied and high-achieving students, professionally satisfied faculty, opportunities for innovative and responsive program design, more efficient and effective use of facilities, and improved relationships with the community. The blended learning model has the potential to transform. It can change online learning from something the institution does to something the institution is, and it can lead to fundamental changes in the way instructors teach and students learn, strategies for delivering services, and space needs and new resource use efficiencies. Blended learning, in the context of the academy, is a complex system that will inevitably have both positive and negative side effects. The task ahead of us is to better understand the dynamics of blended learning so that we can optimize its impact on our institutions, faculty, and students.

References

Allen, I. E., & Seaman, J. (2003). *Sizing the opportunity: The quality and extent of online education in the United States, 2002–2003*. Needham, MA: Sloan-C.

Ashby, C. M. (2002). *Distance education: Growth in distance education programs and implications for federal education policy*. Washington, DC: U.S. General Accounting Office.

Dziuban, C., Hartman, J., & Moskal, P. D. (2004, March 30). Blended learning. *ECAR Research Bulletin, 7*. Retrieved August 1, 2004, from http://www.educause.edu/ecar/.

Dziuban, C., Hartman, J., Moskal, P., Sorg, S., & Truman, B. (2004). Three ALN modalities: An institutional perspective. In J. Bourne & J. C. Moore (Eds.), *Elements of quality online education: Into the mainstream* (pp. 127–148). Needham, MA: Sloan Center for Online Education.

Dziuban, C. D., Moskal, P., Juge, F., Truman-Davis, B., Sorg, S. & Hartman, J. (2000). *Developing a web-based instructional program in a metropolitan university*. Unpublished manuscript, University of Central Florida.

EDUCAUSE. (2003). *The pocket guide to U.S. higher education*. Retrieved June 29, 2004, from http://www.educause.edu/ir/library/pdf/PUB2201.pdf.

Green, K. C. (2003). *Campus computing 2003*. Encino, CA: Campus Computing Project. Available online from *http://www.campuscomputing.net*.

Hanley, G. L. (2001). Designing and delivering instructional technology. In C. Barone & P. Hagner (Eds.), *Technology-enhanced teaching and learning* (pp. 57–64). San Francisco: Jossey-Bass.

Hartman, J. L., Dziuban, C. D., & Moskal, P. (2000). Faculty satisfaction in ALNs: A dependent or independent variable? In J. Bourne (Ed.), *Online education: Learning effectiveness and faculty satisfaction* (pp. 151–172). Nashville, TN: Center for Asynchronous Learning Networks.

Horn, L., Peter, K., & Rooney, K. (2002). *Profile of undergraduates in U.S. postsecondary institutions: 1999–2000.* Washington, DC: U.S. Government Printing Office.

King, K. P. (2002). Identifying success in online teacher education and professional development. *Internet and Higher Education, 5,* 231–246.

Leh, A. (2002). Action research on hybrid courses and their online communities. *Education Media International, 39*(1), 31–38.

McCray, G. E. (2000). The hybrid course: Merging on-line instruction and the traditional classroom. *Information Technology and Management, 1,* 307–327.

Moore, J. C. (2002). *Elements of quality: The Sloan-C framework.* Needham, MA: Sloan Center for OnLine Education.

Morgan, G. (2003). Faculty use of course management systems. *ECAR Research Bulletin, 2.* Retrieved August 1, 2004, from http://www.educause.edu/ir/library/pdf/ecar_so/ers/ers0302/.

National Learning Infrastructure Initiative. (2003). *Transformative assessment systems.* Retrieved June 28, 2004, from http://www.educause.edu/nlii/keythemes/transformative.asp.

Oblinger, D. (2003, July/August). Boomers, Gen-Xers, and Millennials: Understanding the new students. *Educause Review.* Available at http://www.educause.edu/pub/er/.

Strambi, A., & Bouvet, E. (2003). Flexibility and interaction at a distance: A mixed-mode environment for language learning. *Language Learning and Technology, 7*(3), 81–102.

U.S. Department of Education. (2003). *National Center for Education Statistics, Distance Education at Degree-Granting Postsecondary Institutions: 2000–2001.* Washington, DC: U.S. Department of Education.

Waddoups, G. L., & Howell, S. L. (2002). Bringing online learning to campus: The hybridization of teaching and learning at Brigham Young University. *International Review of Research in Open and Distance Learning, 2*(2). Retrieved August 1, 2004, from http://www.irrodl.org/content/v2.2/index.html.

Wendover, R. (2002). *From Ricky and Lucy to Beavis and Butthead: Managing the new workforce.* Aurora, CO: Center for Generational Studies.

Willett, H. G. (2002). Not one or the other but both: Hybrid course delivery using WebCT. *Electronic Library, 20*(5), 413–419.

Willis, B. (1994). Enhancing faculty effectiveness in distance education. In B. Willis (Ed.), *Distance education: strategies and tools (pp. 277–289).* Englewood Cliffs, NJ: Educational Technology Publications.

Wingard, R. G. (2004). Classroom teaching changes in web-enhanced courses: A multi-institutional study. *Educause Quarterly, 27*(1). Retrieved August 1, 2004, from http://www.educause.edu/pub/eq/eqm04/eqm0414.asp.

Charles Dziuban is director of the Research Initiative for Teaching Effectiveness at the University of Central Florida (UCF) where he has been a faculty member since 1970 teaching research design and statistics. He received his Ph.D. from the University of Wisconsin. Since 1996, he has directed the impact evaluation of UCF's distributed learning initiative, examining student and faculty outcomes as well as gauging the impact of online courses on the university. He has published in numerous journals and written several book chapters. He has received funding from several government and industrial agencies, including the National Science Foundation, the Ford Foundation, and the Centers for Disease Control. In 2000, he was named UCF's first ever Pegasus Professor for extraordinary research, teaching, and service.

Joel Hartman is vice provost for information technologies and resources at the University of Central Florida in Orlando. He has been an active author and presenter at industry conferences. He previously served as treasurer and 2003 chair of the EDUCAUSE Board and currently serves as chair of the EDUCAUSE National Learning Infrastructure Initiative Planning Committee. He also serves on the Florida Digital Divide Council, the Microsoft Higher Education Advisory Council, and the board of directors of Florida LambdaRail. He has served as information technology consultant to numerous public and private sector organizations. Hartman graduated from the University of Illinois, Urbana-Champaign, with bachelor's and master's degrees in journalism and communications, and received his doctorate from the University of Central Florida.

Frank Juge graduated from the LSU in New Orleans (now University of New Orleans) in 1962 with a B.S. in chemistry. He received his Ph.D. in physical organic chemistry from the University of Arkansas in 1967. In 1968 he joined the faculty of the University of Central Florida, rising from assistant professor of chemistry to professor. From 1988 until his retirement in 2004, he served as vice provost of academic affairs. Juge was instrumental in establishing UCF's Faculty Teaching and Learning Center, the Burnett Honors College, and the several offices that support and train faculty for distributed learning. He completed the faculty development program for online courses and after retirement rejoined the faculty as a professor in the Rosen College of Hospitality Management where he teaches two blended mode courses on wine education.

Patsy Moskal is the faculty research associate for the Research Initiative for Teaching Effectiveness at UCF, where she has been a faculty member since 1990. She received an Ed.D. from UCF, specializing in instructional technology and research methods, and holds B.S. and M.S. degrees in computer science. Since 1996, she has served as the liaison for faculty research of distributed learning at UCF. Moskal has publications in numerous journals and book chapters. She specializes in statistics, graphics, and applied data analysis. She has extensive experience in research methods, including survey development, interviewing, and conducting focus groups, and frequently serves as an evaluation consultant to universities,

school districts, industry, and government organizations.

Steven Sorg is assistant vice president and director of distributed learning at the University of Central Florida. In his twenty-six years at UCF, he has been a faculty member in the College of Education and has served as director of the Center of Education Research, interim chair of the Department of Instructional Programs, and distributed learning coordinator for the College of Education. Sorg has been principal investigator on over forty grants and has authored many publications, reports, and articles. He has served as the executive director of the Central Florida Consortium of Higher Education, a nonprofit corporation that includes seven community colleges and the UCF as member institutions. Sorg is a pioneer in teaching on the World Wide Web. He developed and taught the first fully World Wide Web-based courses offered at the University of Central Florida in the summer of 1996. He was named the first director of the Center for Distributed Learning in fall 1997.

CHAPTER FIFTEEN

INTEGRATED FIELD EXPERIENCES IN ONLINE TEACHER EDUCATION

A Natural Blend?

Thomas Reynolds, Cathleen Greiner

National University is a fast-growing private university headquartered in San Diego, California. It currently enrolls approximately twenty-six thousand students, of whom about half are enrolled in teacher education. In terms of teacher education, about 30 percent of the students take the majority of their classes online.

Candidates in National University's online teacher education program carry out field activities as part of every class they take while in the program. Although sending preservice teacher education candidates into schools or other parts of communities is not a new enterprise, how such activities answer to interests of blended learning in online contexts has received little attention as an area of study or analysis. While integrated field experiences in online teacher education classes would seem to be a natural blend for effective learning, they occur because of influences as diverse as institutional commitment, state standards for teacher education, and policies and perspectives of professional teacher education organizations and individual faculty rather than through specific application of strategies for building effective blended learning.

This chapter examines integrated field experiences in National University's online teacher education program. These experiences are first examined as a function of the institutional enterprise and the state and professional mandates that influence their enactment (the context). Then we explore the blended learning tenets and the instructional strategies and practices that encompass those ideals (the principles). Finally, we look at the conditions that mediate enactment of integrated field experiences as fully functional components of blended learning (the challenges).

Context

National University's dedication to online education stems in part from institutional commitments found in its core values of quality, access, relevance, accelerated pace, affordability, and community. When considering online education as an institutional enterprise, the key emphasis is access.

The university's mission statement supports making "lifelong learning opportunities accessible, challenging and relevant to a diverse population of adult learners [while facilitating] . . . educational access and academic excellence through . . . innovative delivery systems [that are] . . . responsive to technology . . . [and use] a diversity of instructional approaches." As a tuition-driven private nonprofit institution, National University's commitment to online education is also influenced by a correct reading of its adult students' learning needs and desires. The university currently offers nearly forty fully online programs across multiple disciplines (business administration, criminal justice, nursing, teaching credentials, forensic science) and has established a private entity, Spectrum Pacific Learning Company, to provide online development and support services. Accreditations from the Western Association of Schools and Colleges (WASC) and the California Commission on Teacher Credentialing endorse the online programmatic offerings while attesting to how institutional commitment and success in the online arena have been consistently developed and integrated. Figure 15.1 summarizes the rapid growth of online programs at National University over the past several years while providing an accounting of online growth from its inception in 1996.

Because of the growth in comprehensive online offerings by the university, Spectrum Pacific has also expanded its e-learning design and development activities to include a wider range of services to National University as well as to others interested in online development:

- E-learning consulting services
- E-learning training and workshops
- Content hosting and maintenance
- Content management
- 24/7 technical help desk services

Not surprisingly, since first offering courses online in 1996, there has been remarkable expansion in the National University student population choosing to

FIGURE 15.1.   WASC-APPROVED ONLINE PROGRAMS.

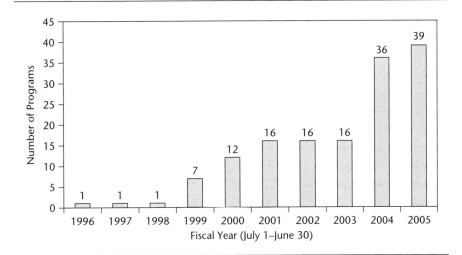

take a portion or all of a degree program online. As Table 15.1 indicates, there has been a dramatic growth in the number of students who have enrolled in online courses over the last four years. Online program enrollment has increased to nearly half of all students taking at least one course in their program online, and 12 percent of all students complete their entire program online.

The fact that the Department of Teacher Education at National University accounts for roughly 50 percent of these descriptive statistics attests to its prominence among California institutions that recommend candidates for teaching credentials. It also highlights the role of National University in the field of online teacher education. In addition, during the 2004 fiscal year, for the first time, more teacher education candidates enrolled as online students than on-site students. Institutional commitments, student preferences, and enrollment demographics all contribute to providing an important context in which to examine blended learning within National University's online teacher education program.

As with many other online educational programs, National University's teacher education program is offered to candidates without regard to the geographical location of the candidate. So it is feasible that in any online teacher education class at the university, candidates from various global locations are present, though the vast majority are from California. Therefore, classes within the teacher education program have no on-site meeting requirements, but they do include requirements for field activities that are carried out in schools within each candidate's geographical location. Integrated field experiences result in each candidate's

TABLE 15.1. STUDENTS ENROLLED IN ONLINE COURSES, 2000–2004.

Students in Online Classes	FY 2000		FY 2001		FY 2002		FY 2003		FY 2004	
	Count	Percentage of Total	Count	Percentage of Total	Count	Percentage of Total	Count	Percentage of Total	Count	Percentage of Total
Students enrolled in at least one class online	4,692	18%	7,684	29%	10,352	39%	10,070	37%	11,366	45%
Students enrolled in a majority of classes online	763	3%	1,321	5%	6,326	24%	4,852	18%	7,260	29%
Students enrolled in all classes online	332	1%	792	3%	2,494	9%	1,314	5%	3,067	12%
Total active students	25,436		26,419		26,955		26,359		25,704	

making at least two visits to K-12 classrooms in every online teacher education class. Further interpretation and expansion of Table 15.1 data reveal that there are easily five thousand candidates taking at least some of their classes online. Such enrollment tendencies mean that as a programmatic enterprise, teacher education candidates make roughly thirty thousand classrooms visits each year as part of their integrated field activities.

Although online classes are taught by individual faculty, the field experiences for each class are coordinated through a statewide field experience coordinator, as well as local field experience coordinators in each of the nine centers across California where National University teacher education programs are offered. Candidates living outside California are held to the same field service requirements as those living within California; however, the responsibility for coordinating and carrying out the field activities rests primarily with individual candidates along with support from online faculty and the statewide field services coordinator.

Like many other teacher education programs, preservice teacher candidates at National University study the foundations of education as well as various methodologies of teaching, and also perform student teaching. Field experiences are integrated in the National University teacher education program curriculum and are designed to be increasingly complex. Early field experiences may have candidates observe instruction, attend school functions, or interview teachers, whereas later field experiences may require individual tutoring, small group tutoring, lesson observation, analysis and modification, and, ultimately, large group instruction and student teaching.

For reasons of program consistency and integrity as well as accreditation, the field experience program requirements are applicable regardless of whether courses are taken online or on-site. As with nearly all content that migrates from on-site to online delivery, content within National University's teacher education online courses contains threaded discussions that replace other forms of classroom participation present in on-site courses. Despite the use on interactive threaded discussions, far more individual rather than collaborative learning and teaching takes place when content is delivered online. Also, some online curricular modifications place content into more manageable clusters or chunks than the on-site versions. In addition, in online courses, on-screen text is broken up into visual mixes, and instruction is continuously available through instructor contact and technical support rather than the more traditional on-site course delivery method. But in all courses, whether online or on-site, two of the eight required tasks for each course have candidates perform field experiences. In some instances, up to half of the tasks in a course require information or reflection on aspects of field experiences. Clearly field experiences hold an established place in program design at National University, occurring consistently throughout the program in increasing complexity.

Field experiences are designed to develop candidate competence as evidenced in the Teaching Performance Expectations (TPEs) from the California Commission on Teacher Credentialing. Divided into six domains, the thirteen TPEs establish arenas of teaching competencies while also serving as guideposts for program design and evaluation. To be recommended for a preliminary California teaching credential, candidates must demonstrate competence in domains A to F and the thirteen Teaching Performance Expectations (TPEs), as detailed below:

A. Making Subject Matter Comprehensible to Students
    1. Specific Pedagogical Skills for Subject Matter Instruction
B. Assessing Student Learning
    2. Monitoring Student Learning During Instruction
    3. Interpretation and Use of Assessments
C. Engaging and Supporting Students in Learning
    4. Making Content Accessible
    5. Student Engagement
    6. Developmentally Appropriate Teaching Practices
    7. Teaching English Language Learners
D. Planning Instruction and Designing Learning Experiences for Students
    8. Learning About Students
    9. Instructional Planning
E. Creating and Maintaining Effective Learning Environments for Student Learning
    10. Instructional Time
    11. Social Environment
F. Developing as a Professional Educator
    12. Professional, Legal, and Ethical Obligations
    13. Professional Growth

Articulations of teaching competence, like those in the TPEs, stem from coordinated efforts by state departments of education as well as professional societies concerned with teaching competency and the development of that competency. Organizations like the Interstate New Teacher Assessment and Support Consortium, the National Council for the Accreditation of Teacher Education, and the National Board for Professional Teaching Standards contribute to professional understanding of what constitutes competent teaching and how one develops and demonstrates that competence. Many such organizations endorse field activities as instrumental in a learning-to-teach system that unite policy, perspectives, and practices in the development of preliminary and professional teaching competence. Conceptual frameworks and course structures that integrate field activities and promote understanding of the TPEs provide candidates opportunities to develop and demonstrate competence in teaching through observing classroom situations, participating in these classrooms, and systematically reflecting on those experiences.

For example, as one of the two field experiences and one of the eight required activities for National University's teacher education course in educational psychology, candidates write a case study of a classroom observation where instructional approaches are used to address diverse learners, noting how instruction was adapted to meet individual needs as well as noting the specific California K-12 content standards the observed lesson met. This field activity is linked to TPEs regarding the development of pedagogical skills (TPE 1), making content accessible (TPE 4), developmentally appropriate teaching (TPE 6), and early knowledge about instructional planning (TPE 9), among others. The early placement of the educational psychology course in the candidate curriculum demonstrates the importance that this program places on observation of an in-service teacher, rather than activities that focus on candidate participation in instruction. In addition, it simultaneously signals an emphasis on analysis of the in-service teacher's instruction and curriculum rather than an analysis of lessons designed and taught by the candidate.

An example from a course that occurs later in National University's teacher education program has candidates, based on data collected from students in their field-activity classroom, write learner outcomes and developmentally appropriate and instructionally engaging educational activities to meet those outcomes. Later in the same course, candidates are asked, in collaboration with the teacher in their field activity classroom, to co-plan and co-teach a lesson, obtain the field activity classroom teacher's feedback, and then write a reflection on the effectiveness of the lesson design and implementation. The complexity and structure of these latter field activities, like those in the earlier example from the course in educational psychology, are designed to help candidates meet teaching performance requirements. This field activity is linked to the development of specific pedagogical skills (TPE 1), assessment of student learning (TPE 2 and TPE 3), making content accessible, engaging, and developmentally appropriate (TPE 4, TPE 5, and TPE 6), and assisting candidates in understanding students and planning for instruction (TPE 8 and TPE 9). Also clear is that the activities in the latter example are more complex and focus more on reflection and inquiry into teaching within the same essential mode of delivery—that of field experiences.

As evidenced in the examples as well as through discussion of National University and professional teacher education societies and standards, the context for blending field experiences into teacher education course content is highly influenced by institutional commitments as well as student learning preferences. Nevertheless, at the core, this blended learning context is supported by efforts of state education agencies and professional accreditation societies to systematically introduce meaningful experiences into learning-to-teach systems. How such activities relate to principles of blended learning, teacher knowledge, and teacher thinking, as well as thoughts on the complexity of online implementation, especially with regard to the offering of field experiences in online teacher education classes, is discussed in the following section.

Principles

Blended learning is an emerging field. Nonetheless, basic work on the identification of blended learning design features as well as articulation of specific strategies for building blended learning practices provide a useful basis for programmatic and instructional understanding. Those who have studied blended learning practices (Rossett, 2002) have established that blended learning is, at minimum, the use of more than one instructional methodology in an instructional context. Consequently, numerous combinations of instruction fall under the basic rubric of blended learning. For instance, the mixing of direct and group instruction, lecturing and coaching, self-paced instruction and simulations, and formal and informal instruction, as well as the blending of classroom instruction with online instruction and the blending of online instruction with, in the case of field activities, on-site instruction, all qualify as blended learning examples. At many institutions, the integration of blended learning practices has meant a progression from offering traditionally on-site classes with limited blended material, to the blending of online resources into on-site classes, and, finally, as with National University's teacher education program, the blending of on-site activities (field experiences) into online instruction. Given these blended learning possibilities, these are certainly unique and engaging times in teacher education.

Although most arguments in favor of blended learning resonate from the notion that multiple-method learners need blended models of instruction, best practices in any facet of education have always included those very notions through using a variety of delivery modes. As with other inquiries into instruction and learning, the examination of blended learning is informed by contributions from the fields of instructional design, curriculum and instruction, and learning psychology, among others. As indicated, National University's field experiences are requisite activities in the development of preservice teachers. Areas of particular interest include fields such as teacher knowledge and teacher thinking, which consists of knowledge of content, pedagogical content knowledge, and the knowledge of learners and learning. In addition, the field of instructional practices, which comprises planning for instruction, implementing instruction, and the assessment of learning, is of particular interest and importance.

Finally, as with other instructional development, blended learning programs benefit from specific guidance in planning, delivery, management, and evaluation. Blended e-learning, like integrated field experiences in online environments, is informed by perspectives found in Khan's global e-learning framework (2003). Khan argues that the following perspectives or factors are critical to online teaching and learning: (1) pedagogical, (2) technological, (3) interface design, (4) evaluation, (5) management, (6) resource support, (7) ethical, and (7) institutional. Ultimately, especially in the context of a tuition-based institution like National University, principled development of blended learning includes considerations of how to identify and allocate resources to achieve strategic purposes. Although blended learning, with regard to the integration of field activities into online classes, is guided by key principles from the fields of teacher education and instructional design, it is also an institutional enterprise, and therefore it is informed and mediated by institutional concerns such as resource support and management. So Khan's framework is a useful mechanism for better understanding the potential impediments to successful implementation of blended learning practices.

Challenges

Although endorsed as an integral component of the curriculum of preservice teacher preparation (Darling-Hammond & Cobb, 1996), field experiences have also come to be recognized as complex processes that are dependent on the collaboration between universities and schools (Knowles & Cole, 1996). And when instruction takes place online as opposed to on-site, there are clear challenges to maintaining collaboration and coordination between field experiences and the pedagogical purposes they serve in the preservice curriculum.

National University, like more and more institutions of higher education today, relies on services of adjunct faculty to deliver much of its instruction. This is clearly the case in teacher education classes containing field experiences. The merit of these adjunct instructors is not at issue, as many have advanced degrees—especially in the case of teacher education—as well as extensive experience teaching within K-12 classrooms. In fact, these instructors introduce needed perspectives into the lives of preservice teacher education candidates. Adjunct instructors teaching in public education also provide important employment linkages as well as linkages to classrooms needed to carry out field experiences. At the same time, the fact that many of these relationships are informal and not coordinated through the university is clearly troubling for the effective management of blended learning resources.

In addition, although National University employs a full-time faculty member as a statewide field services coordinator as well as full-time coordinators at each of its nine learning centers, the sheer volume of field-related activities (two per course per candidate), across thousands of candidates and hundreds of online instructors, clearly challenges the effective management as well as the academic integrity of how blended field experiences are implemented. As with many other teacher education programs, the field experience coordinators are primarily occupied with student teaching placements occurring at the end of the teacher education program. Such a focus, however, further detracts from efforts to coordinate and manage integrated field experiences.

National University's initial curriculum planning for blended field activities for online classes includes a comprehensive effort to enlist and certify individual teachers in the hundreds of school districts where the university's teacher education candidates carry out field activities. But current practices have adjunct teaching faculty assist in the identification and assignment of field experience sites, thereby holding a pivotal, yet largely unmanaged, position in how blended learning components are implemented. Clearly, the social as well as managerial infrastructure of this blended learning application could benefit from further support and development.

National University's implementation of integrated field experiences in online teacher education classes contains competent curriculum design, ongoing institutional commitment, and best instructional practices. Nevertheless, management and resource allocation as well as the institutional infrastructure are equally vital components for successful blending of field experiences into online teacher education. And as designers of e-learning environments attempt to blend a widening range of experiences into instructional contexts, the effective management and allocation of resources become more important implementation components. Whether considering internship experiences in business and industry or field activities for language learning, counseling, teaching, or other human services, the instructional viability of such experiences, especially when delivered in an online environment, is increasingly dependent on academically sound instructional models. Of course, these instructional models should be well managed and institutionally recognized and supported.

Conclusion

Integrated field experiences in online teacher education may seem an academically necessary and easily implemented natural blending for the collaborative roles that public and higher education play in the preparation and certification of teachers. What emerges from examination of National University's integrated field experiences in online teacher education is a set of complex circumstances that are interdependent. Such innovative field experiences require institutional commitments and instructional designs that support new forms of collaboration and extended notions of blended instruction. Providing well-prepared and effective teachers for its children is a challenge that every nation faces. The global expansion of e-learning resources provides both the opportunity and means to meet such challenges, but those applications of e-learning are clearly reliant on expanded forms of blended learning and new models of institutional support to accomplish those ends.

References

Darling-Hammond, L., & Cobb, V. L. (1996). The changing context of teacher education. In F. Murray (Ed.), *The teacher educator's handbook. Building a knowledge base for the preparation of teachers.* San Francisco: Jossey-Bass.

Khan, B. H. (2003, May/June). The global e-learning framework. *Technology Source.* Available at http://ts.mivu.org/default.asp?show=article&id=1019.

Knowles, J. G., & Cole, A. L. (1996). Developing practice through field experiences. In F. Murray (Ed.), *The teacher educator's handbook. Building a knowledge base for the preparation of teachers.* San Francisco: Jossey-Bass.

Rossett, A. (2002). *The ASTD E-learning handbook: Best practices, strategies, and case studies for an emerging field.* New York: McGraw-Hill.

Thomas Reynolds is associate professor and former chair of the Department of Teacher Education for National University in La Jolla, California. After earning his doctorate in curriculum and instruction at the University of Wisconsin-Madison, he developed performance and instructional software applications while working at the Wisconsin Center for Educational Research. During the 1990s, he served on the faculty at Texas A&M University, where he was awarded a Fulbright scholarship to lecture in Peru on Web-based education. Over the past ten years, Reynolds has developed, researched, and taught in blended learning contexts within his area of specialization in teacher education. His current work at National University centers on meeting performance and assessment teaching standards through online instruction.

Cathleen Greiner is provost and vice president of academic affairs for National University in La Jolla, California. She previously served as dean at the University of Idaho and associate dean at Chapman University in Orange, California. She earned her doctorate in higher education administration and public policy from Claremont Graduate University and holds an M.S. in education, educational policy, and management from University of Oregon and an M.A. in philosophical and systematic theology from the Jesuit School of Theology. Greiner is a member of the Association for the Study of Higher Education, the American Educational Research Association, and Pi Lambda Theta, the International Honor and Professional Association in Education.

PART FOUR

FOR-PROFIT AND ONLINE UNIVERSITY PERSPECTIVES

The for-profit university has received enormous attention recently. There is much controversy about the emergence of for-profit universities, especially those that address online environments. The chapters in Part Four are written by high-level executives of three well-known for-profit universities: the University of Phoenix, Capella University, and Jones International University. They make interesting predictions as to where blended learning can play a significant role in for-profit higher education enterprises.

Brian Lindquist, dean of the College of Graduate Business and Management and associate vice president of academic affairs for the University of Phoenix (UoP), discusses three modes of learning that UoP provides students: traditional face-to-face, completely online, and blended. All of the courses at the UoP last for five weeks. Blended courses come in two flavors in order to meet the needs of local and more distant students. For the local option, learners attend a four-hour face-to-face session for the first and fifth weeks of class, while the middle weeks are completely online. For the distance option, the learners attend a two-hour face-to-face session at the beginning and a two-hour face-to-face session at the end, with weeks 1 to 4 being online (the introductory session is intended to be directly after the ending session of the previous term's course so as to require only one trip). The UoP has seen an approximate doubling of its enrollments in the blended option each year since its inception in 2000; however, this option still accounts for only about 4 percent of enrollments. Competency requirements are the same for classes taught in each of the modalities. Nevertheless, it is felt that the online portions advantage student reflective thinking, while the face-to-face portions advantage student socialization and project presenting skills. In this chapter, Lindquist also discusses the efforts that UoP undertakes to train faculty in the requisite skills to facilitate online and traditional teaching.

Chapter Seventeen describes Capella University's approach to online and blended learning. Michael Offerman and Christopher Tassava note that Capella provides completely online learning opportunities for adult learners. Students enrolled in doctoral and some master's programs at Capella have residency requirements, which are the extent of the face-to-face blending that occurs at this university. The residency requirements for graduate students at Capella fill a largely social role in facilitating community, selecting a mentor, and understanding expectations. Capella takes the opposite approach to traditional universities. Instead of asking how online might supplement face-to-face instruction, they begin with the assumption that most learning can take place online, and face-to-face becomes a supplement to the online learning experience. In effect, this chapter calls into question assumptions that the traditional model or a blended model that still has roots in a traditional delivery of instruction model is more effective than a completely online model for the independent adult learners who tend to choose, and hence need, Capella University.

In Chapter Eighteen, Pamela S. Pease, former president of Jones International University (JIU), documents the birth and history of JIU and many of the decisions that helped this organization develop a completely virtual model of higher education. The virtual-only model of JIU is detailed and compared with models of other for-profit universities that blend face-to-face, site-based learning with online learning. Several issues and challenges faced by virtual-only institutions are discussed, such as quality versus cost, hybrid versus virtual, and nonprofit versus for-profit competition.

CHAPTER SIXTEEN

BLENDED LEARNING AT THE UNIVERSITY OF PHOENIX

Brian Lindquist

This chapter addresses the emergence of blended learning options at the University of Phoenix. Consider the fable of the three siblings of educational delivery. First born was "Classroom," on whom was lavished all kinds of curriculum development over many years of refinement. Then Higher Education gave birth to "Online," who received a new technology-laced wardrobe suitable for electronic delivery. But when the last sibling, "Blended Learning," came late in Higher Education's life, it had to stitch together the hand-me-downs of its two mature siblings, Classroom and Online, to tailor a format for effective learning. However, in the spirit of all fables that end happily, Blended Learning chose only the finest material from Classroom and Online to craft a wardrobe just right for its intended learners.

Global Perspectives

This section shares the details of two flavors of blended learning used by the University of Phoenix and the history behind the emergence of these models. In addition, the impact of the blended learning models on faculty roles and student enrollment trends is addressed.

Sources of the Blended Learning Model

At the University of Phoenix, "Classroom" was born in 1976, when a new learning model for working adults was introduced. Using the model today, learners meet with their faculty facilitators once a week and focus on one subject at a time, for five weeks (undergraduate courses) or six weeks (graduate courses). Between these classroom meetings, students meet as a learning team to accomplish projects related to the course objectives and to build their collaborative skills. Faculty facilitate learning in the classroom by drawing on the professional experiences of the learners, all of whom work full time when they enter the University of Phoenix.

In 1989 the University of Phoenix introduced "Online" to serve the needs of learners whose professional lives and travel schedules could not accommodate the weekly classroom and learning team meetings. The "classroom" is virtual, and learning is organized asynchronously. A lecture is posted to start the week's learning, and the faculty member engages the learners in threaded discussions. There is no place to hide in the back of this virtual classroom since everyone is required to participate several times each week. However, learners who may be reluctant to speak up in a face-to-face classroom have time to reflect on the discussion questions as well as the input of their colleagues before they make their own contributions. Separate newsgroups allow the learning teams to conduct their meetings and accomplish their learning objectives. Far from being an impersonal virtual space, online learners report that they get to know one another very well, as well as their faculty facilitator, in part because of the required participation as well as frequent interaction throughout the week. What continues to make these two delivery methods true siblings is that the course curriculum, learning objectives, and outcomes are virtually the same in each.

Both Classroom and Online at the University of Phoenix have matured quickly, with enrollments in each delivery mode exceeding 100,000 students by May 2004. As with many successful siblings, they have been encouraged to grow and flex their muscle without concern that the success of one would jeopardize the other. This constructive competition has revealed the relative strengths of each delivery system. Classroom offers synchronous learning for those who prefer face-to-face socialization and practice in oral presentation skills available only in a physical setting. Online offers asynchronous learning for those who prefer time to reflect before contributing to a discussion and whose schedules require more flexibility.

Some learners welcome the face-to-face interchange of a classroom environment that includes elements of socialization that they cannot find through online learning. However, they may live too far from a location where classroom delivery is offered. Although the University of Phoenix has physical classrooms in over one hundred locations, working adults in many rural or suburban areas cannot justify a multihour trip each way for the workshops required in classroom delivery. While learning completely online is one option, others would prefer to have some face-to-face time with their faculty member and their learner colleagues.

Blended Learning Models

In 2000 this clearly defined need gave birth to the third sibling, "Blended Learning," at the University of Phoenix, which has drawn on the strengths of two successful delivery systems, classroom and online. Two models are currently in use to organize the learning in this blended delivery. The first is the local model, which tends to attract learners within a reasonably close geographical perimeter who like the features of synchronous learning, at least some of the time, but whose travel schedules do not permit physical attendance weekly. These students meet in a classroom setting, called a workshop, for the first and last meetings of their course. The learning for the weeks in between is conducted online.

The advantage of the local model is that during the first four-hour workshop, the faculty facilitator can more easily frame the learning objectives and outcomes for each week of the course, assess the learners' preparation for the course, and quickly address concerns or issues. In addition, the faculty member has everyone together for the first meeting of the course to lay a solid foundation for the learning that will take place in subsequent weeks. The last workshop of the course also meets in the classroom. The curriculum in many courses suggests a project be completed by the learning team and presented in the last meeting of the course. When presented in the classroom, learners can demonstrate their oral communication and small-group presentation skills, and the faculty member can synthesize the learning in the course by comparing and contrasting the outcomes from each of the learning team's oral presentations.

The other blended learning model currently in use is the distance model; as the name suggests, it respects that many of the learners are more geographically dispersed. As in the local model, these learners meet in a classroom with their faculty facilitator twice during the course. The first meeting, an orientation to the course, lasts approximately two hours, and immediately follows the last meeting of the prior course, which was a classroom meeting. The advantage to this arrangement is that it respects the travel time for those who live far away from the classroom. By combining the last meeting of one course with the orientation to the new course, learners have to travel only once to a classroom for each course. The orientation meeting, however, does not count as one of the weeks of learning. Officially, the first week of learning is an online week, which commences the day after the orientation in the classroom. The last meeting is also in the classroom and offers all of the advantages of practicing oral presentation skills as in the local model.

The difference between the distance model and the local model is that in the distance model, no assignments are due when students first meet their instructor for the orientation in the classroom, since the distance model adds an online week to the schedule. The first assignment in the course is completed online. However, as in the local model, the first classroom meeting allows the instructor to frame the learning objectives and outcomes for each week of the course, as well as assess the learners' preparation for the course.

Other configurations of classroom and online learning are possible. In the examples above, both the local and distance models combine classroom and online learning in each course. However, the blend of these two deliveries can be combined throughout the program while maintaining delivery integrity within a course. For example, at the University of Phoenix's School of Advanced Studies, which offers the doctoral programs, most courses are delivered online, but the program requires three residencies, commencing each of the three years in the program. Each residency serves a different purpose. The first residency is a course in critical and creative thinking whose purpose is to develop the learner as a creative leader and problem solver and to begin the transformation process of questioning previous assumptions and conventional patterns of thinking. The second residency begins the formal development of the learner's doctoral project, and the third residency continues the process by assisting the learner in developing the approved doctoral proposal into the final submission of the doctoral project. By 2005, the first five days of the third residency will also include a collaborative case study, in which all learners who have completed the course work in the first two years of their program will work in teams to solve a series of problems by applying their course work to issues both within and outside their disciplines.

The outcomes from these residencies benefit from the face-to-face exchanges among learners and immediate feedback available from the faculty member. For example, in the course on creative thinking during the first residency, learners engage in brainstorming activities that build on each other's contributions. The collaborative case study will simulate a variety of problems that are introduced sequentially and timed before the next problem is added to the previous solution.

In fact, blended delivery of classroom and online delivery methods should be tailored to the needs of both the learner and the program's architecture. For example, suppose a program is designed around problem-based learning, in which the learner defines and solves broad problems over the course of three weeks per problem. It would make sense for the research on the problem to be conducted in an online learning environment, but for the learners to gather in a classroom to present and defend their solutions to the faculty member and their colleague learners. This face-to-face session would provide a realistic environment for learners to experience the real-time question-and-answer grilling that often accompanies a manager's presentation and defense of a proposed solution.

Roles of Faculty and Technology in Blended Learning

The coaching function of the faculty member is a consistent and essential thread that binds each of the delivery modes: classroom, online, and blended learning. The roles of questioner, facilitator of collegial learning, and moderator of discussions are essential for the faculty member, whether the week's learning is delivered in a classroom or online. This is the centerpiece of the teaching-learning model at the University of Phoenix. While the role of the faculty member in a classroom delivery is well established, the advent of online learning in general, with its technologically driven delivery and sophisticated learning assets, is sometimes viewed as a method to diminish the role of the faculty member, making learning a more individual, or isolated, activity. The University of Phoenix, however, has always viewed learning as a social experience, capitalizing on both the learner-faculty relationship as well as peer relationships. The university has approached the use of technology as an aid to the social dimension of learning to assist faculty and learners to achieve competencies, including collaborative learning.

The technology used at the University of Phoenix in its blended learning delivery is both simple and sophisticated. The online delivery portion of blended learning uses an online learning system, which is based on Outlook Express, and is convenient and easy to use. Its use of newsgroups and threaded discussions serves the purposes of allowing faculty to conduct discussions that involve all the learners, as well as allow learning teams to communicate and prepare their projects in a self-contained environment.

All three learning delivery systems at the University of Phoenix use a sophisticated portal to make the learning materials available to both students and faculty through a Web-based electronic campus. On a course-by-course basis, they access an electronic library of text materials; the syllabus for their course, which has been customized by their faculty member; simulations that support their course; the university electronic library, as well as a "reserve list" of library articles suggested for their course; guides to direct each week's learning; and a proprietary software that gives feedback on how to improve their writing, among many other services. The objective is to emulate how professionals access the information they need to do their jobs. That is, while most people still value a physical book for pleasure reading, professionals tend to search electronically for materials they require to solve their problems at work rather than consulting a textbook. The objective of this portal to learning materials is to develop this competency among learners to electronically access relevant materials, as they would in their professions, to achieve the learning objectives in the degree program.

TABLE 16.1.   BLENDED LEARNING ENROLLMENTS IN DEGREE PROGRAMS AT THE UNIVERSITY OF PHOENIX.

Date	Enrollment
May 2001	154
May 2002	1,433
May 2003	4,352
May 2004	8,449

Enrollment Trends and Staffing for Blended Learning

Since its inception in 2000, enrollments in blended learning have grown rapidly. Table 16.1 illustrates enrollments for May 2001 to 2004 (all campuses combined).

While the growth rate is significant over this time frame, as of May 2004, blended learning students still accounted for only about 4 percent of the learners at the University of Phoenix. Nevertheless, the growth to over eight thousand students selecting this delivery method has required significant preparation on the part of the over forty campuses that offer this option in a wide variety of programs that include business, information systems and technology, education, and health care. Each campus that offers its programs through blended learning dedicates a full-time faculty member to coordinate the delivery and ensure that the faculty have been certified by the University of Phoenix to teach in both the classroom and online delivery modes, both of which are used in blended learning (this training is described in greater detail later in the chapter). If growth in blended learning were evenly distributed among the campuses, the balance between demand and the capacity to meet it would be easier to accommodate. However, when growth in demand for blended learning is either unanticipated at one campus or outstrips the campus's ability to certify local faculty in the two component delivery methods, faculty from other geographically proximate campuses fly in to deliver the classroom workshops and conduct the rest of the week's learning online.

Local Designs

The University of Phoenix has faced several challenges in implementing its model of blended learning, in particular, the challenge of addressing faculty expectations and training to teach in a blended learning environment.

Faculty Training for Blended Learning

The pitfalls that could endanger blended learning are many if the faculty member is not prepared for the experience. At the University of Phoenix, learners are working adults whose needs and approaches to learning are different in key ways from younger, traditional-aged learners. For example, adult learners have more life experiences on which the faculty member can draw to achieve the learning objectives. It is important for the faculty member to understand how to address the needs of working adult learners and access the considerable pockets of knowledge that these learners already possess. Moreover, the faculty member needs to create and support an organized and collaborative learning environment. The risk is great that switching between classroom and online learning within a course could lead to chaos and a disorganized learning process. The faculty member needs to be able to understand the process and how blended learning serves different needs as well as to provide clear direction to the students. To ensure that the learning proceeds during the course, the faculty member must actively facilitate each online week, be prompt in responding to questions, and give constructive and timely feedback to assignments.

Earlier in this chapter, the role of the faculty member as the facilitator and coach in the learning process was established. While this essential function is similar in guiding learning in both classroom and online deliveries, the University of Phoenix does not expect that all new faculty members have the skills to deliver on the promise of this teaching-learning model. Prospective faculty members are assessed initially for their capacity to facilitate learning as well as their content knowledge, but before they enter the classroom, they must successfully complete a certification process. For blended learning, this certification is particularly important because the faculty member will need to guide learning in two modalities. To that end, faculty "go to class" themselves to learn the competencies and discover the tools available to both them and their students as they prepare for the learning process that blends classroom and online.

To prepare faculty for blended learning, the University of Phoenix guides them through a course that will certify them to teach. The course emulates the learning environment that faculty members will use to manage blended learning with their own students. The course, spread out over four weeks, delivers in detail the foundation of the teaching-learning model at the university. Topics include facilitating learning, collaborative learning, course management, assessment of student learning, faculty standards, and policies and procedures.

At the beginning of this chapter, a brief chronicle of the delivery systems the University of Phoenix offers identified first the classroom, then online, and finally blended delivery. For many years, the university has provided orientation to its new faculty, and over time this has evolved into separate certification processes for both classroom and online faculty. While the principles of facilitated learning and assessment are common to both, the certification training for online delivery places more emphasis on the online learning system, which online faculty must master before conducting courses in this delivery method. When blended learning was introduced a few years ago, it drew on faculty who were already seasoned facilitators. Some had taught only in the classroom delivery and needed to acquire the certification to teach online, while others were already certified in both classroom and online. More recently, blended learning has developed its own blended certification to prepare new faculty to qualify to teach in this delivery method.

The certification course introduces an overview of the University of Phoenix: its curriculum development process, its academic vision, faculty standards, and course newsgroups as the communication vehicle during online learning. To acclimatize prospective faculty members to the online learning system, the certification training provides them experiential lessons in attending an online class. They observe the structure of the online classroom and how assignments are posted as well as actively participate in newsgroups and discussion threads. After they are oriented to the online learning system, they begin to assume the role of facilitator of learning as they engage in their own learning in the types of content identified earlier: collaborative learning, grading, and feedback to students. This experience weaves their own learning about the University of Phoenix model with the delivery modalities that they will use during the classroom and online portions of the course.

In addition, the participants in the certification access their learning materials during the certification process in the same way that their students will in University of Phoenix courses. Their reading materials are available electronically on the learning materials portal, which includes multimedia exercises that allow them to demonstrate and apply concepts. The prospective faculty members see how the learning portal offers access to university-wide services, including the university library, assistance in improving writing skills, and proficiency assessments. This process increases the comfort level with these resources so that as faculty members, they can demonstrate their use to their own students.

The participants in the certification also engage in learning team projects to experience how their own students communicate as they deal with completing tasks as well as the collaborative process while working in an asynchronous environment. Such activities not only emulate how professionals actually accomplish group tasks, but prepare the prospective faculty members for how to manage segments of the learning that are independently accomplished by the learning team members. They must complete tasks on time, resolve issues that arise in the process, and accomplish this with little or no face-to-face contact. The faculty member needs skills to coach and guide them, particularly in a course early in the program.

Upon successfully completing the certification process, the faculty candidate is assigned a course to facilitate in blended learning delivery. As indicated above, the faculty candidate already has been introduced to the principles of the University of Phoenix teaching learning model and has practiced, under supervision, the behaviors that will lead to a successful learning experience for the students. But to ensure that the first course taught works well and for the faculty candidate to get additional feedback, a mentor is assigned to monitor the first course. The mentor has been trained to provide additional materials, as needed, to the faculty candidate and must give routine assessments as well as feedback.

Beyond this first teaching experience, the faculty member has several support systems to develop facilitation skills and seek best practices from facilitator colleagues. There are faculty development workshops, online learning system faculty lounges, peer reviews, and program chairs at each campus offering blended learning to offer assistance to the blended learning faculty.

Tailoring Competency Development in Blended Delivery

While the role of the faculty is essentially the same in both delivery modes, classroom and online, the tools available to the faculty member to accomplish the learning objectives vary somewhat in blended delivery but capitalize on the strengths of the other two. Classroom, by virtue of its face-to-face format, allows learners to practice presentation skills. The faculty member can give feedback on each presentation, and colleague learners can provide a broader reaction to the oral communication skills of the presenter. Since the last workshop in blended learning is conducted in class and typically includes oral presentations, learners build confidence in their speaking skills to small groups throughout the program.

Faculty also can use classroom activities that benefit from the synchronous nature of the workshop. For example, an exercise that requires learners to select from disparate materials to build something cooperatively to develop creative and collaborative skills is easier to implement in a classroom setting. During the online portion of the course, the faculty member posts discussion questions to stimulate conversation in support of a learning objective. If the question is of a reflective nature, the asynchronous learning environment allows learners to contribute as they are ready, over several days, and does not suffer from the compressed time requirements of a classroom.

The learning expectations for blended delivery do not appreciably differ from classroom and online expectations. Moreover, as in the case of selecting activities, blended learning capitalizes on the strengths of each. As illustrated above, building presentation skills is better done in the classroom, while reflective learning is better done asynchronously online. However, the learning outcomes that define the course are blind to the delivery method and hence are measured in the same way. Both the classroom and online components can accommodate a wide range of assessments, like problem sets, quizzes, papers, and debates. Given this range of learning assessments, many programs at the University of Phoenix require students to assemble a portfolio of their outcomes, which they align with the program competencies. All of these outcomes work equally well in classroom, online, or blended delivery.

Support Resources for Blended Delivery

The resources to support blended learning extend beyond those involved in faculty certification, and these are coordinated by a faculty development manager who is dedicated to blended learning. Each campus that offers blended learning has a program chair who monitors the development of certified blended learning faculty locally to ensure that the demand among students for the blended learning delivery option is aligned with the campus's capacity to offer it. Technical support personnel are dedicated to assist learners and faculty members who experience problems with the online learning system or with access to course materials. This technical support is available to all learners and faculty twenty-four hours a day, seven days a week. The technical support staff have been trained to handle questions and issues that will most likely be raised, and the types of questions asked are continually analyzed to refine not only the technical support but also how the curriculum and learning materials are delivered. This service is critical to the success of the blended learning delivery mode at the University of Phoenix.

Expectations of Faculty

To ensure the quality and timeliness of the learning process, the University of Phoenix has established expectations for the faculty, particularly to promote active learning in the online mode of the course. Questions posed directly by a learner to the faculty member should be answered within twenty-four hours. The faculty member should be actively engaged in discussions at least five out of the seven days during a week in which learning is conducted online. Such a practice suggests that the faculty member should not only log on to the discussion groups and observe the interactions among peer learners, but facilitate the learning by responding to the issues raised in the threaded discussions and offer additional probing questions to extend the learning.

This learning process becomes an excellent opportunity to develop critical thinking skills by challenging the assumptions, the logic of arguments, and the use of facts by learners as they make their case in responding to discussion questions posed by the instructor. The intended outcome is to develop the key competency among learners to substantiate arguments in a way that is logical and convincing. The faculty member promotes this skill in both the classroom and online portions of blended learning, but each modality offers a slight variation on the skill development. In classroom delivery, time for these debates and constructive arguments is more compressed, but nevertheless reflects the need to "think on your feet" when professionals are engaged in discussion during synchronous meetings. In online delivery, a more reflective environment for debate mirrors the asynchronous communication in which many professionals engage using e-mail. Both, however, require good critical thinking skills, which faculty members must encourage through their active participation in discussions, whether conducted in the classroom or online.

Research Opportunities

The outcomes of learners in blended learning, as well as those who complete their program exclusively in the two component delivery systems, classroom and online, provide a research opportunity to assess the comparative learning among the three deliveries of learning. As the populations of learners grow in each of the three delivery systems, other explanatory variables that identify these populations of learners and might influence their learning paths will emerge. The colleges in the university are preparing rubrics for key assignments, and in the future all students will submit their assignments electronically, to which the rubric will automatically attach. The faculty member will complete the rubric as part of the feedback to the student, and when the assignment is automatically returned to the student, both it and the graded rubric will simultaneously populate a database, which will identify the mode of delivery for the course. Such a process will enable the university to assess not only differences in outcome among the three delivery systems, but how specific competencies within the program are achieved among the three deliveries. From that research, the university can improve the curriculum to capitalize on the relative strengths of classroom and online as they are packaged into a more effective blended delivery. Just as in the fable that started this chapter, Blended Delivery is highly resourceful in drawing on the best material from the older siblings. Additional research should be able to further refine this process.

Conclusion

Blended delivery better emulates how professionals in the early twenty-first century conduct business. The norm today is to be proficient in face-to-face meetings but also to work asynchronously and electronically with other stakeholders to achieve the desired learning outcomes. Professionals must be precise in their communication in both synchronous, face-to-face environments and in e-mail communication and other asynchronous, electronic communication tools. They must be able to electronically access the materials they need, when they need them, to solve a problem. Seldom do professionals consult textbooks when they leave the formal learning environment, so it makes sense to develop the competencies to access information they need during their formal education. Blended learning is an ideal approach to capitalize on the relative strengths of classroom and online learning and to develop the communication and information acquisition skills needed for successful professionals.

Brian Lindquist is associate vice president for academic affairs and the dean of the College of Graduate Business and Management for the University of Phoenix. He has also served as the vice president and campus director of University of Phoenix campuses in New Mexico. He began his career as a corporate economist at Eastman Kodak and later the director of financial planning for the Graphic Imaging Systems Division at Kodak. Lindquist earned his Ph.D. in economics from Purdue University, his master's in economics from Purdue University, and his B.A. in international studies from Miami University.

CHAPTER SEVENTEEN

A DIFFERENT PERSPECTIVE ON BLENDED LEARNING

Asserting the Efficacy of Online Learning at Capella University

Michael Offerman, Christopher Tassava

Capella University offers a different perspective on blended learning, one grounded in its status as a regionally accredited adult-serving university that delivers most of its instruction online. The literature on blended learning seems slanted to a perspective that face-to-face learning is preferable to stand-alone online learning, and it is often asserted in the literature that online is best used as a supplement to face-to-face learning. In this view, online learning is viewed primarily as a way to effectively deliver information and concepts and to free up time in the face-to-face classroom for more substantive discussion. Certainly online delivery can be useful for this purpose. But Capella University questions the underlying rationale for this argument. Because we operate primarily online, we take an opposite perspective from that presented in much of the literature. Rather than asking when or how online might supplement face-to-face learning, we ask, "When is face-to-face interaction necessary in addition to online learning?" In effect, Capella's pedagogical philosophy and practices turn face-to-face instruction into a supplement to the primary activity of delivering learning online.

This difference in perspectives is fundamental to our approach to blended learning and our pedagogy. In delivering higher education to a nationwide audience of working adults, the use of face-to-face and even synchronous learning events potentially limits the student's participation. The fact that Capella delivers learning online and views face-to-face as supplemental challenges us to identify learning that can only happen face-to-face. We have concluded that most, if not all, learning can occur online. From this perspective, the use of face-to-face is valuable for social rather than pedagogical reasons. We use face-to-face in a blended delivery mode only for our graduate students and primarily in order to achieve social rather than pedagogical goals.

Perspectives from the Literature

A comprehensive understanding of blended learning, in all permutations from global perspectives to local designs, is still being developed by scholars, practitioners, and other experts in the academy, nonprofit organizations, and enterprises large and small. Over the remainder of this decade, a more robust body of theory and practice regarding blended learning will certainly evolve, in tandem with the continuing development of technologies (present and yet to be invented) that facilitate both computer-based and face-to-face learning.

Our review of the literature in academic and industry publications, from peer-reviewed articles in scholarly journals to human resource trade magazines, would indicate that online learning within a blended learning model is largely now a methodology to transmit information to employees and students rather than a means to achieve a meaningful change in basic pedagogy. The picture of blended learning that emerges from the literature is of a technique that organizations use to disseminate new information.

This kind of blended learning is usually based on the interaction between a person and a computer: the human absorbs information delivered via the computer monitor. The blended part of this process is the activity of a live faculty member in the face-to-face university classroom or a corporate trainer, who adds material that is not available in a digital or computerized form and engages the learner in discussion about the information. This approach is sometimes described as audio-over PowerPoint slide shows or similar presentation of information that is intended to free class time for discussion. Such a view of learning is fine if you start from the assumption that discussion must occur in a face-to-face classroom. However, Capella agrees with others that effective discussion can and does also occur in the online "courseroom" and that online discussion results in the effective acquisition by learners of the complex concepts and skills appropriate to higher education (Allen & Seaman, 2004). Furthermore, online discussion engages all learners in a process that of necessity is less faculty-centric and more appropriate for adult learners.

Blended Learning at Capella University

Capella seeks to address the specific needs of adult learners, who typically seek a high-quality learning experience above all but also often require highly flexible and convenient means to acquire new knowledge. Over the past decade or so, this has led many adults to choose online learning environments, which allow them to better balance the work, family, and community obligations that consume their time.

Since its founding in 1993, Capella University has expanded its degree offerings so that its five schools now offer a variety of higher education degrees, ranging from bachelor's to the doctorate (see Table 17.1). It is worth noting that during the first two to three years of the university's existence, courses were delivered in a directed study model that combined the British tutorial model with correspondence education methods (using postal mail and the telephone, not the Internet). Capella has always used a distance delivery model, and for most of our history that has been through online learning.

In all these areas except undergraduate studies, Capella has engaged in blended learning for more than a decade. From its inception, Capella has combined distance education methods with a limited number of face-to-face learning experiences. The latter take the form of residency requirements for learners such as those enrolled in the university's four doctoral programs and some of the master's programs, while the former are common to Capella learners in every degree level and in every school. All of Capella's learners complete the majority of their course work by Internet-based course delivery. In online courserooms, faculty instructors lead threaded discussions, which are predicated on thoughtful and dynamic interaction between learners. Individual courses are quite small, usually around fifteen to twenty learners, to facilitate vigorous and meaningful discussion and the mastery by learners of specific course-level competencies and program-level outcomes.

TABLE 17.1. DEGREE OFFERINGS AT CAPELLA UNIVERSITY.

School	B.S.	M.S.	M.B.A.	Ph.D.	Psy.D.
Business and Technology		X	X	X	
Human Services		X		X	
Psychology		X		X	X
Education		X		X	
Undergraduate Studies	X				

In this respect, Capella's fundamental perspective toward online learning is very different from the perspectives offered in the literature on blended learning. Some of the literature reveals a strong bias in favor of face-to-face instruction and relegates online learning to a supplemental and inferior role. This bias is true even for those scholars who advocate blended learning as a way to benefit from the unique strengths of online learning, such as the ability to deliver knowledge at a distance. Osguthorpe and Graham (2003), for instance, write that as "students share questions, insights, and perplexities they not only experience higher levels of mastery, but they open themselves to redefining and repositioning themselves in the world. . . . This is the ultimate purpose of a liberal education—to help individuals see themselves in a new light, to help them relate to others in new and more productive ways. . . . Purely distance delivery systems limit this kind of social contact, while blended environments enhance the possibilities" (p. 231). Osguthorpe and Graham continue by saying that face-to-face environments "bring learners together in an environment where they can question, experiment, and enjoy the energy and enthusiasm of group learning. This interaction occurs between learners as well as between learner and teacher" (p. 228).

The comments above reveal an assumption that face-to-face contact is somehow necessary to helping students redefine themselves and "see themselves in a new light." This assumption would not survive exposure to well-designed online courses. Faculty at conventional universities who are exposed to online courses, such as the Augsburg College faculty who teach in Capella University's online undergraduate programs, are frequently struck by the quantity and quality of the online interaction. In Capella's case, this is far from accidental: the university's mission to extend higher education to working adults means that Capella specifically designs courses that facilitate and emphasize both learner-to-learner and learner-to-faculty interaction.

Capella University faculty members work closely with instructional designers to develop all Capella courses. Faculty members with expertise in a particular subject perform the initial work of course formulation: identifying course goals and aligning them with broader program objectives, selecting appropriate course resources such as books and Web sites, writing requirements and assignments such as discussion questions, conceiving course content, and developing guides for grading learners. Instructional designers then join the faculty expert to ensure that the course adheres to the pedagogical principles used by Capella and by other higher education institutions, as well as to refine the course content and perform particular tasks such as Web page design. Key to our course design and development is a commitment to value the knowledge and experience of our adult learners. This is done by requiring them to share ideas and accomplishments with one another and create a highly interactive learning environment.

When a new course has been drafted, it is presented to department and faculty leadership for approval and subsequently revised, if necessary. On receiving this approval, school leadership assigns qualified instructors and formally opens the course for enrollment. Instructors, who are drawn from the full-time (core) and adjunct faculty, use the course schedule, discussion questions, assignments, and due dates to structure the course. With approximately six hundred online course sections offered each quarter, instructor adherence to the course schedule and resources is key to guaranteeing that learners enjoy consistency across all courses and instructors. Instructors can post new material such as questions or commentary to discussions, and they can always recommend changes to the course.

Many observers worry that students engaged in online education like Capella's will be overly focused on "book learning" and will miss the opportunity to acquire knowledge that can be learned only in other ways, from the nonverbal cues of fellow discussants in an undergraduate seminar to the professional comportment of a doctoral-level mentor. It is true that face-to-face communication involves verbal comments as well as nonverbal cues. But an example from beyond the academy calls into question the assumption that nonverbal cues are more important than thoughtful online interaction: in recent news reports, medical doctors and patients who regularly communicated by e-mail reported that their interchanges were superior to office visits because both parties had time to formulate their thoughts and thus more richly share ideas, questions, and answers (McKenzie, 2004). This begs the question of whether tacit or nonverbal communication is actually more important than effectively expressing ideas in writing.

Capella University courses put clear, concise written communication in the foreground. Discussion and assignment questions, posted by the instructor and germane to particular readings or other resources, require every learner to carefully formulate thoughts and clearly express them in writing. Such writing can then be posted online for other learners (and the instructor) to read and discuss. Certainly nonverbal cues will be missing from the posted writing, possibly detracting from the communication or even creating situations in which some learners (say, those who are already very comfortable with the written word) are overly empowered, while others (say, those for whom English is a second language or those for whom writing is a painful chore) are silenced.

Certainly the written word does allow the more forceful expression of the underlying ideas and eliminates many nonverbal complications that can otherwise impede expression or reception of those ideas. This may be why online learning typically draws in more women than men and disproportionately high numbers of racial/ethnic minority groups. And for these reasons, Capella expects to find that some students express an increasingly clear preference for online learning as it continues to evolve and expand. At the very least, Capella expects to see the range of higher education options expand to incorporate traditional and blended learning methods as well as entirely online methods. Face-to-face may make some learning easier, but that is different from face-to-face being essential for the learning to occur. Some students have style preferences that make face-to-face not only a preference but a requisite part of their learning. Online is not for everyone. But conversely, some students thrive in the online environment and even prefer it over face-to-face settings. Inevitably learners' preferences, institutions' comfort with any or all three forms of education, market forces, and other factors will lead learners to self-select a particular mode of learning or choose different modes at different times and for different purposes. This does not mean one medium is superior to the other or that either medium is merely a supplement to the other.

It seems important to state this outright because the bias of the existing literature on blended learning seems to be that online learning can offer only a few limited advantages, such as flexibility as to time and place and the ability to free physical classroom space. These limited advantages necessarily led university administrators and faculty, corporate human resource departments, and others to view online learning as a compromise that requires balancing against face-to-face or blended methods. Many theoreticians and practitioners are working to determine the right balance of methods or the kind of knowledge best conveyed online.

Capella too is interested in achieving the right balance, but, as indicated earlier, its administrators and faculty come at the question from a completely different angle. Because we serve adults who live and work all over the country, even minimal face-to-face requirements present our learners with a stiff challenge and one that, if not mitigated, might deter them from pursuing the education they desire. In response, Capella continuously challenges itself to understand and explain why a particular face-to-face requirement, including the mandated residency for doctoral and master's learners, is necessary for effective learning. Rather than begin with the assumption that face-to-face learning is best and then ask how online can supplement it, Capella asks, "When is face-to-face absolutely necessary in the first place? What kind of learning cannot be done online and must be done face-to-face?"

There may be some things that demand face-to-face interaction, but our experience tells us that little, if any, learning cannot be delivered online. This includes even the development of soft skills, such as acquiring professional values and engaging in a transformative re-visioning of oneself and the world. Capella holds that acquiring these skills is far more dependent on the quality of the instructor or mentor than on the milieu of the skill acquisition. For that reason, Capella ensures that every member of its faculty is well trained, comfortable, and skilled with online teaching. Faculty development activities, for instance, occur not only when new instructors are hired or when an online instructor moves up to become a doctoral thesis mentor, but throughout an instructor's career at Capella. All online instructors are continuously reviewed by their faculty chairs, who offer coaching and assistance in honing their skills for virtual instruction.

This concern with the quality of online instructors positively affects not only the quality of online, course-based interaction but also the activities that help build a sense of community among faculty, staff, and learners at Capella. Of course, universities relying primarily on online delivery cannot ignore the potential that this delivery format may create feelings of isolation in some learners. This serious concern is partially overcome through high-quality instruction and the design of engaging online courses. And, of course, Capella recognizes that online learning is not for everyone. Some students may be more comfortable in a face-to-face environment, and others may lack the motivation to succeed in a self-directed online course. Those who need the reassurance of face-to-face interaction find a way to attend that type of program, trading the convenience of online education for the structure or in-person community of traditional education.

Having said all this, Capella University uses face-to-face educational opportunities in the form of week-long residential colloquia as important supplements to online course work in all doctoral programs and many master's programs. Three such colloquia are required for doctoral students. Faculty and students gather at locations around the country, including Atlanta, Chicago, Orlando, Scottsdale, and the greater Washington, D.C., area. The week consists of classes, formation of cohorts that work together during the week, group and individual advising, and the provision of intensive support (writing, for example). Face-to-face instruction is provided, especially in experiential programs such as counseling, and learners find numerous opportunities to present and defend ideas with peers and faculty. In addition, there is instruction on research methodologies and writing for publication.

At the doctoral level it is clear that the colloquia serve to orient students to doctoral education and help them to complete their comprehensives and dissertations—in other words, less delivering discipline-specific content than building community and providing support to promote program completion. (These efforts resemble dissertation "camps" that have been described recently in the press.) The most important outcomes of the colloquia are the development of new relationships and networks that lead to mutual support among students, intense faculty advising and committee selection, and the creation of informal affinity groups, especially for minority students. These events are intense and exciting and very important to our work. But, again, we view them as supplemental to our basic online delivery mode.

Capella University retains its doctoral-level residency requirements less because they provide discipline-specific pedagogical opportunities (which are usually met through the programs' online courses) than because they provide extra-educational or social elements to the programs. Residencies are a powerful way for Capella learners, faculty, and staff to communicate with each other in less formal ways than online classroom interaction or telephone conversations. Faculty and staff learn a great deal from learners, and learners feel a greater sense of meaningful connection to their university. In addition, residencies offer a convenient "one-stop-shopping" opportunity for advanced doctoral students to seek out mentors and committee members.

Of course, learning does occur in these face-to-face residencies. Each event includes an array of workshops on matters as wide ranging as properly citing references and choosing a dissertation topic. Certainly learning is occurring in the social interactions with other students and faculty. Certainly the process of selecting a mentor and committee is important. But even these kinds of opportunities need not be done face-to-face, and, in fact, many are conducted online as well. Learners frequently use their online course experiences to identify faculty members they feel might serve well as a mentor or member of a dissertation committee.

There is no question that this model may be troubling to those with much at stake in the traditional face-to-face environment. There is great comfort for some in traditional classrooms, at least partly because the conventional classroom is literally and figuratively built to focus attention on the instructor, even when adult learning is the goal. The blended approach described in the literature only partially departs from this earlier model by mediating it with technology, thereby perpetuating this time-tested and comfortable role for the face-to-face classroom.

Nothing about online learning means that the "faculty-centricity" of traditional education will soon end. In fact, online courses can be as readily focused as face-to-face courses on the instructor. At Capella, administrators and faculty are striving to develop an educational model with active learning at the center. But it may be unsettling for some to imagine giving up the comfort of face-to-face components. Those who subscribe to the idea that face-to-face social contact is absolutely necessary for liberal education would be troubled by the idea that such learning can occur online.

As with any other innovation, blended learning mixes the new (computer-mediated delivery methods, for instance) with the old (an instructor-focused learning model). This mixture makes it difficult to separate the advantages of blended learning from those of traditional higher education. We wonder if blended learning, as described in the current literature, is taking advantage of the potential pedagogical opportunities presented by the computer-mediated portion of a blended approach. We are concerned that computer-mediated delivery may be relegated to merely presenting information in a different mode rather than getting at more fundamental pedagogical issues. Is blended learning important to the conventional, campus-based approach to education and corporate training? We believe that it is. Is blended learning intrinsically better than purely face-to-face education? No, but it is difficult to say when blended or online or face-to-face learning is superior to the alternatives. On the other hand, can online-only courses lead to effective learning? Adamantly, yes.

Capella's experience indicates that those concerned with higher education—as administrators, as faculty, or as students—should consider their ultimate goals, which can range from freeing classrooms to flexibly earning an advanced degree, and then choose the medium accordingly. Capella University is confident that these intelligent choices will lead us in time beyond the first generation of education, that of traditional face-to-face instruction, and beyond the second generation, which includes blended learning, to a completely new third generation in which the option of online-only instruction is accepted alongside face-to-face and blended models.

References

Allen, E., & Seaman, J. (2004). *Entering the mainstream: The quality and extent of online education in the United States, 2003 and 2004.* Retrieved March 1, 2005, from http://www.sloan-c.org/resources/entering_mainstream.pdf.

McKenzie, J. (2004, May 24). *Virtual visits.* ABCNEWS.com. Retrieved June 30, 2004, from http://abcnews.go.com/sections/WNT/MedicineCuttingEdge/email_doctor_visits_040524.html.

Osguthorpe, R. T., & Graham, C. R. (2003). Blended learning environments: Definitions and directions. *Quarterly Review of Distance Education, 4,* 227–233.

Michael Offerman has served as the president and chief executive officer of Capella University since June 2001. He is a frequent speaker at national conferences and brings to Capella University a wealth of experience in adult and distance learning. He has served on a number of national boards, including the American Council on Education, the University Continuing Education Association, and the National Technology Advisory Board. Offerman received a B.A. in history from the University of Iowa, an M.S. in higher education administration at the University of Wisconsin-Milwaukee, and a Ph.D. in educational policy studies at Northern Illinois University.

Christopher Tassava is a writer-editor in the Office of Assessment and Institutional Research and the Office of Faculty Communication and Engagement at Capella University. He works on accreditation and regulatory reports, outbound communication, and research projects related to the assessment of learning in higher education. He is especially interested in problems relating to building community among distance education students and faculty. Trained as a historian of the United States at Northwestern University, Tassava also teaches American history, specializing in business and technology. Tassava is currently researching the history of quality control, a topic that touches directly on the matters raised in this book. He can be reached at christopher.tassava@capella.edu.

CHAPTER EIGHTEEN

BLENDED LEARNING GOES TOTALLY VIRTUAL BY DESIGN

The Case of a For-Profit, Online University

Pamela S. Pease

Over the past decade, the growth and acceptance of for-profit universities in the United States has become a reality in higher education. I have been a pioneer in developing and leading the first U.S. online virtual, for-profit university to be regionally accredited. Such for-profit universities, notably, the University of Phoenix (UOP), Kaplan College, Jones International University (JIU), and Capella University, as well as the Sylvan Learning Systems, Corinthian Colleges, and Career Education network of colleges or universities, have transformed higher education into a viable business model. Many of these institutions have stock that is publicly traded on Wall Street, which continues to increase in value even while the U.S. economy remains tepid.

Corresponding with this explosion in for-profit institutions is the revolution in the electronic delivery of education that has been pioneered by many of these for-profit universities. The tension between profitability and the delivery of education has resulted in increased efficiency in the instructional models for delivering education. These models range over the entire spectrum, from site-based face-to-face to totally virtual. For many, the electronic delivery is often a means of increasing their reach to students worldwide. JIU is the first for-profit that was developed to deliver all of the content and instructional experience through the World Wide Web. Although the philosophy of how the instructional content is developed and delivered may differ across all of these institutions, there no longer is any doubt that many of these models differ substantially from traditional models of higher education.

From a global perspective, there has been a trend toward privatization of education. In Australia, Canada, and the United Kingdom, where the norm is for publicly supported university structures, the privatization of education has become more widespread as government funding has diminished while the demand has increased to serve the needs of an expanding student population. Many of the for-profit universities like Sylvan and UOP's Apollo Group from the United States have also developed international ventures by establishing on-site universities in Mexico, South America, and Spain.

Growth Factors for the For-Profit Universities

Looking back over the past decade, four primary reasons account for the growth of both for-profit and electronic education: (1) perceived value of American education around the world, (2) acceptance of online education delivery as mainstream, (3) changes in the global workforce needs for training and education, and (4) economic and social pressure on the traditional higher education system for serving adult learners.

Perception of American Education

America is the third largest exporter of education in the world, with the United Kingdom and Australia in the top two slots. Individuals around the world view American education as a valuable commodity. For this reason, foreign students are attracted to the United States in high numbers for postsecondary education. American-based business programs are considered particularly valuable by those outside the United States who are desirous of learning the key to American commerce. American for-profit institutions that deliver education through either site-based institutions located in other countries or electronically can piggy-back on this positive global perception by offering degrees that are in high demand and branding themselves as American based.

Online Education Becomes Mainstream

Several factors have contributed to the acceptance of online learning over the past ten years. The biggest factor has been the development and adoption of the electronic tools necessary for delivery of online learning. In the early 1990s, there were few Web-based learning management systems or platforms since there was little demand to foster more development of these systems and what existed was quite primitive. For example, JIU developed HTML Web pages for all its courses as well as a Web home page to support student services, and the interaction between students, faculty, and the university personnel through listservs rather than Web-based forums and asynchronous conferences. The development of content was quite expensive and time-consuming. As a result, it was typically only the most innovative faculty and students who were attracted to a totally online experience. Soon institutions such as the totally online ones developed their own learning platform to ensure that the content could be developed in a consistent and affordable manner.

By the late 1990s, as the use of online learning became adopted by most universities, the number of learning management systems commercially available grew, and all became easy for faculty and students to use. One of the critical events in shaping the acceptance of online learning was the accreditation by one of the major regional accreditation agencies in 1999 of a totally online institution of higher education: JIU. As more and more universities blended online learning into their site-based instruction, the delivery of content in this manner has become commonplace.

A Changing Workforce

The global nature of the modern workforce requires ongoing training and education. Coordination of education is a challenge for organizations located in different countries or states with different work schedules across many time zones. Online learning has demonstrated the ability to deliver content and instruction to any learner at any time by primarily employing the asynchronous nature of online learning. JIU, Capella, UOP, Kaplan College, and others have met this need by delivering courses in over fifty countries with students who access education according to their schedule.

Another example of how online learning has served the needs of a workforce is the United Nations Development Programme's Virtual Development Academy. Since inception of this program in 2001, JIU has been under contract to develop the Virtual Development Academy. This academy is designed to provide convenient access to ongoing training that is completely online to key leaders at the mid-range and top-level managers in more than 135 country offices.

Moreover, there are other issues that make it imperative to meet the educational needs of modern working adults using alternatives. No longer is it commonplace for today's workers to have the opportunity to take long periods of time away from their positions to attend a management program or institute. Time away from the job probably means losing that job. Time has become a commodity for most working adults since they have too little of it and feel pressure to balance personal and professional goals. Nevertheless, the reality is that individuals are expected to have five to seven careers over their working life, and such changes are tied to having the appropriate education. This situation creates challenges for adults who want to move forward with their careers, as most positions require more training and education. Online learning can provide a viable alternative for many of these individuals. This may be the reason that Australians have come to aptly call online learning "flexible learning."

Pressure on Higher Education

The demand for education is increasing to serve the needs of students worldwide. To meet these needs, there is room for many different types of institutions. For instance, for-profit institutions have largely served nontraditional working adults. Since the adult student represents well over 50 percent of the student population of higher education, it is little wonder that the flexibility offered by these institutions has resulted in a decade of growth.

The increase in demand comes at a time that traditional higher education has been hit by cutbacks in federal and state subsidies, which have resulted in hiring freezes and the elimination of programs. As a result of such budgetary restrictions and shortfalls, they are not readily equipped to serve the needs of increasingly nontraditional adult learners. Nevertheless, it is not a zero-sum game, as there are too few institutions to serve the needs of students, making room for all types of models of higher education.

Blended Learning Models for For-Profit Universities

In general, there is a wide range of instructional models employed by for-profit institutions. The models are often shaped by a hybrid model, blending face-to-face instruction through a site-based classroom with content that is offered electronically through the Internet. For the for-profits, the delivery of online instruction has created a boom for instructional design. As a business practice, these universities have committed financial and human resources to ensure that online delivery is as customer focused as site based. This has required implementing a model of design that would provide quality control of the content and the instructional experience.

TABLE 18.1. TYPOLOGY OF FOR-PROFIT INSTRUCTIONAL DELIVERY MODELS.

Type	Face-to-Face	Face-to-Face with Online	Totally Online (Asyn-chronous)	Online Using Real Time	Enrollment Growth Online	Online Design Model	Faculty
Virtual-only model (for example, JIU)	No	No	Yes	Sometimes	Moderate	Optimizes for the Web	Mostly part time
Resource-rich, opportunistic model (for example, UOP, Kaplan, Capella)	Yes	Yes	Yes	Sometimes	Aggressive	Modify for the Web	Balance of part and full time
Low-cost hybrid model (Career Education and Corinthian)	Yes	Yes	Yes	Infrequent	Aggressive	Replicate face-to-face	Balance of part and full time

A Typology of Delivery

Table 18.1 outlines the variety of delivery models using a sample of universities based in the United States. The delivery styles of these for-profit institutions may be collapsed into three categories of delivery: (1) the virtual-only model, (2) the resource-rich but opportunistic model, and (3) the low-cost hybrid model. The virtual-only model typically requires a dedicated instructional design staff to optimize educational content for Web delivery, and all financial resources are focused on the delivery of online instructional content and teaching. Student recruitment and marketing are totally focused on attracting students who want this model. The resource-rich model allows institutions to measure the effectiveness of a variety of instructional modalities beyond online delivery. With more extensive resources, such an institution can determine how to focus its resources by evaluating the most successful modality from an opportunistic, business perspective. For example, enrollment in UOP's online program has been growing at a faster rate than its site-based enrollments; hence, one would expect that the business would concentrate on expanding online.

The final category is the low-cost hybrid model. These include career and technical schools, which have largely built their business on site-based instruction. As online has not been their core business, they are containing costs by replicating the face-to-face content rather than optimizing content for Web-based delivery. This represents a typology of three instructional delivery models.

All of the models typically employ part-time faculty and do not retain faculty based on a traditional tenure and promotion system. However, part-time and full-time faculty members are still central to all of these models since they retain a faculty-led approach. This is the case even in the virtual-only model, which engages the learner through simulations and Web-based pages. In addition, all of the for-profits are concerned about delivering content that is applied. They are committed to blending theory with tangible practical examples and assignments that are relevant to a student's workplace.

Advantages of Instructional Options

The blended approach has served the for-profits well, as the site-based presence in a city, state, or country provides a vehicle for branding and marketing the university. Unlike a traditional university system, the newer for-profit universities are focused on marketing for student recruiting and branding their university experience. On an annual basis, these universities aggressively spend billions of dollars to increase their market share of students. It is little wonder that a large university such as the UOP with multiple campuses in nearly all the states across the United States has seen enrollment more than triple over the past two years. It has become the largest university in the United States. Moreover, the blended model offers the opportunity for adult learners to select a learning model that best serves their needs. UOP offers a hybrid model offering potential learners flexibility to choose either site based or online.

In the case of JIU, Capella, Kaplan Colleges, Sylvan Learning, and others, the number of offerings by for-profits has increased as public acceptance of on-line has grown. The demand for a virtual online delivery model is replacing the model of blending the instruction with face-to-face instruction. As noted below, JIU was a pioneer of this virtual model. It was the first for-profit institution whose business model was totally predicated on a virtual model.

Jones International University: A Virtual-Only Model

JIU was founded in 1993 as a private, total virtual university. The university's administrative headquarters are in Englewood, Colorado. There is little resemblance to a traditional campus or face-to-face classrooms at JIU. Even the staffing of approximately seventy-five full-time individuals is unique in that it is augmented by other core human resources from Jones companies, such as in the areas of technology, legal, and human resources. As is typical of the private for-profit model, JIU operations are more of a corporate business in which higher education is explicit in its core values and mission.

From the perspective of the consumer, JIU was actually launched in 1995 as an online university with one graduate program in business communication. In 1996, it added an undergraduate completion degree in business communication. With these two degree programs, in 1999 it became the first virtual university to receive the same accreditation status as the majority of educational institutions in the United States. Regional accreditation granted by the Higher Learning Commission, a Commission of the North Central Association of Colleges and Schools, is considered a critical event in the recent history of higher education. Importantly, regional accreditation provided tacit approval of the institution (and its students) for effectively delivering education totally online. As president and vice-president since JIU's inception in 1993, I have been the driving force for ushering this new university through accreditation and constructing an infrastructure to serve an international student population.

Throughout the 1990s, JIU developed its infrastructure and instructional delivery model. It has six degree areas with approximately twenty degree offerings, federal financial aid for students, and a viable degree student population with graduates. Federal financial aid is available to all accredited programs with the exception for those that provide more than 50 percent of their programs through online or telecommunications. In this case, an institution that would otherwise have access to federal financial student aid must seek a waiver from the U.S. Department of Education. This procedure required that JIU petition for a waiver for access to federal financial student aid, a process that took over a year.

Committing to the Technology-Based Model

From inception, JIU's mission has been to reach learners around the world by employing a technology-based learning model. Having had the luxury of spending two years to conduct market-research and to experiment with a variety of models, in early 1995, it concluded that using the Internet for delivery of the content would permit asynchronous delivery of content, which would overcome many of the time barriers reported by potential students and facilitate student and faculty interaction online. This was the model implemented to best meet the needs identified from potential adult learners.

Since there were stakeholders vested in other models, videotaped delivery of instruction that was highly produced and scripted with renowned experts serving as course content experts was one of the models considered. The high cost and complexity of this video-based model precluded it as a viable model. Also, there were internal political pressures to ensure that interaction be conducted over a proprietary e-mail system that the Jones companies had developed. However, this did not seem practical, as this e-mail system required sending via postal mail a diskette to each user around the world and required elaborate installation directions resulting in extensive customer service support.

In hindsight, JIU took a calculated risk on the Internet as an education delivery model. This was an innovative use of the Internet and required much consideration of how to deliver this virtual educational model effectively. Fortunately, that decision was followed by a wide-scale adoption of the Internet for education across all educational sectors.

An Iterative Development Model

Philosophically, the JIU model has been one of continuous improvement. Nevertheless, the elements as developed in 1995 are still in place. Three significant changes over the years are (1) the ease of developing content and delivering instruction using new electronic tools, (2) the decrease in costs for developing content from an average of $75,000 to $25,000 per course, and (3) moving from outsourcing the instructional and multimedia development to developing an internal instructional design staff.

The model contains the following core elements.

A Multitiered Faculty Structure. Four faculty bodies contribute to the development and governance of the degree programs. The Academic Program Board consists of experts in the specific degree areas to provide overall curriculum assessment of the program. There is a board for each program. The academic program chair provides administrative oversight for his or her specific program. This includes assigning faculty, reviewing content, identifying content expert faculty, and advising students. A content expert at JIU is an individual prominent in the academic field who is under contract to develop a specific JIU course. This person works primarily with the instructional design team and the academic chair and is guided by a JIU template for course development to ensure consistent and quality treatment of such instructional components as learning outcomes and assessment strategies. Finally, a teaching faculty is the teacher of record for a course. He or she is responsible for implementing the course as developed by the content expert and is responsible for facilitating and assessing student learning.

Course Media Mix. A JIU course includes the following mix: a course home page; multimedia simulations to facilitate learning of concepts using Flash or other programming tools; streaming audio and video; an asynchronous Web-based forum as well as a whiteboard for communication; the use of asynchronous or real-time tools for small-group interaction around specific class assignments; print or electronically delivered textbooks downloaded from an online bookstore; and occasionally a CD-ROM (such as a Spanish course). JIU's initial model included specific study guides designed to accompany each course. For the most part, these have been infused in a newly revised model of the online course Web pages, which was developed based on human usability testing. Another unique feature of JIU is that the course components are offered in both English and Spanish. Students in the Spanish programs must be able to have some level of reading proficiency in English, since many textbook publishers do not translate their materials from English to Spanish.

Delivery Tools. JIU has come a long way in adopting a learning management system used for course delivery. In 1995, the university developed separate HTML pages for each course, along with access to the JIU home page and a specific listserv to support student-faculty interaction. By 1997, JIU implemented its own learning management system (LMS). The LMS was first known as "e-education" and more recently as "Jones Standard Software." The creation of an internal LMS allowed the instructional design staff to review and manage the entire directory of courses and easily develop multiple sections of the course at any given time.

Instructional Model. JIU courses are offered beginning the first week of each month. This monthly "term" structure offers each three-credit course in eight weeks. All courses are instructor led and facilitated with a maximum enrollment of twenty-five students per course. However, enrollment in courses is unlimited, as any number of sections may be offered in a given term. Students typically enroll in an average of three and half classes a year, with some degree programs having an average of five courses per year taken. Students are expected to attend a formal online orientation.

Content Ownership. JIU believes that one of its assets is course content. It has always paid generous fees for course content experts. JIU retains ownership of all the content that is developed. Each content expert is paid a development fee plus a one-time copyright fee. This is a practice that has been in place since the inception of the university. The advantage for JIU is the ability to use the learning models and the courses for any purpose.

Research and Development. An important aspect of the model is the role of formal evaluation of course content and all aspects of the instructional experience. At the end of each course, students and faculty are asked to respond to a formal questionnaire. The extensive data that are collected for each course are analyzed by the specific course "term" and factored into the longitudinal analyses for the university. Feedback is used to improve the content, technology, support services, and teaching faculty. In addition, JIU scans the environment for new tools to increase the effectiveness of student interaction and learning. In fall 2003, it implemented a real-time Web-based language laboratory for its Spanish I course. This laboratory allows students to practice speaking Spanish with a live tutor and a group of students. Regardless of the logistics and departure from JIU's typical asynchronous model, it became obvious that students enjoyed the opportunity to have an oral practice lab and garner the support of other students. Another database software system has been implemented to manage both development costs and intellectual property resources. This is important as JIU owns all the copyright of content and intellectual property that is developed for the university. By design, all the multimedia components are developed to stand independently so that a library of electronic simulations, video and audio streaming, and Flash objects, for example, can be catalogued and reused as learning objects. In turn, this library of learning objects enables the multimedia team to focus on new applications.

A University Is More Than Course Content

Since JIU is a virtual university, the entire student experience is dependent on the development of virtual tools for student and faculty support. All current students may access the home page for general information and use their password to access myriad support services, including electronic advising, the course Web pages using the learning platform, grades, the electronic library, 24/7 technical support, and student services. The academic advisers and enrollment counselors are available by e-mail and telephone.

JIU faculty members have access to similar resources to those of students. All faculty members are certified through an online learning program in preparation for teaching at JIU. There are monthly electronic meetings for JIU faculty related to ongoing professional development and interaction.

Student Engagement Through Networking and Community Building

Students and faculty find that online learning promotes a type of intimacy in that people are much more accessible and interactive with one another. Because of this, JIU students develop communication networks and shared knowledge among themselves as they matriculate through classes. This communication was strengthened in 2003 when JIU began organizing student classes into a modified cohort model. An informal group of students is responsible for forming the formal JIU Student Association.

The annual graduation is conducted as a community building event. It is offered completely online, including the ceremony with the commencement speaker (such as recent graduations with the presidents of Mexico and Poland) and an electronic yearbook. This event is open to all students and to the public to celebrate graduation and interact with graduates online.

JIU Challenges for Development

While the cost for the development of courses decreased as JIU brought the instructional development function in-house, the cost of hiring top-notch content experts increased. JIU is now facing significant costs to maintain, update, and revise a huge inventory of course content. This is a challenge that all online universities with well-defined instructional design strategies will have to manage and plan for in order to preserve the integrity of the existing course product. If not adequately updated and revised, the academic product could be rendered less valuable as a commodity for any university but certainly for a for-profit entity.

Significant Issues and Questions

The hallmark of the JIU model is its attention to the role of quality design and instruction. The founding definition of quality includes:

- Institutional mission and purposes that incorporate quality standards
- Regional accreditation
- 24/7 technology support for students and faculty
- Customer-focused services for supporting students
- Commitment to course design for optimizing the content for the Web rather than replicating a face-to-face model
- Commitment to high standards for instructional content and teaching
- Continuous improvement of the model through evaluation and feedback

The sections below address important questions related to providing a quality education that JIU has had to grapple with.

Are There Common Standards and Measures for Quality?

Because there is still controversy around the role of business in education, the attention to quality is important for sustaining credibility and integrity for both virtual and other for-profit educational models. Quality assurance is an elusive concept for most organizations. In higher education, there are some espoused beliefs about quality but few core values around quality that are common across higher education. The struggle facing for-profit education is to avoid doing what it takes at any cost for profitability.

Everyone would be well served to develop a model of quality to measure, evaluate, and discriminate among a variety of new educational experiences. Even in the case of JIU or others with current models of quality, the concept can change depending on how the mission evolves, the marketplace pressures for student enrollment and cost containment, or changes in board or management leadership that influence the core organizational values.

Hybrid versus Virtual: What Works?

While it appears that increasingly students are attracted to a total virtual model, the hybrid model may have a greater advantage in branding, marketing, and recruiting students. While UOP's online program is growing at a rate faster than its site-based enrollment, its physical presence in major cities across the United States gives it instant brand recognition and credibility for students. Human beings are inherently comfortable with the familiar, whether it is a university or food product. The opportunity to see and participate in a physical environment may conceptually be important to students.

In turn, a total virtual institution such as JIU or Capella has begun to shift the paradigm of learning to a totally online model. The branding and marketing of this concept, which is not as tangible as the UOP model, has resulted in slow but steady student growth over the past five years. The jury is still out as to how soon or whether the totally virtual model will dominate in the marketplace.

What Role, If Any, Will Traditional Universities Have in Competing with the For-Profit Models of Blended Learning?

Many people involved in distance education believe that traditional universities will have to be transformed in order to compete with for-profit models. There is some truth that the painfully slow speed of change of traditional universities prevents most from being competitors in the short run. Today, many institutions have substantial commitment and a legacy in supporting their physical assets and infrastructure. However, there may be a few institutions that find a way of balancing their current business, while expanding their enrollments using an online model with the active support of some visionary leadership. Eventually well-recognized traditional universities will compete with for-profit institutions in marketing and online strategy.

Are There New Models of Instructional Design for Optimizing a Virtual Educational Experience?

With the growth in virtual applications of learning and training, there are numerous questions related to its impact on the training of new instructional design experts. At the very least, one would hope that the new perspective would focus on a variety of interactive strategies for student engagement and multimedia rather than computer-based instruction, which is often the background of many of the current designers.

Is There a Role for Blending Foreign Language into the Model of Blended Learning?

JIU has experimented with some success in delivering education in multiple languages. It seems that the Web offers unique opportunities to customize the language of instruction for a diverse student population; however, this feature has not been exploited.

Opportunities

At least two interesting opportunities on the horizon can offer insight into the future of evolving models of blended learning. The first relates to the role of the new generation of higher education learners, now in primary and secondary schools. Over the next five years, their comfort level and experience with technology for learning and communicating will likely become accepted as normal. Many of these students are already attending elementary school or high school online. There will be no great paradigm shift for these students to attend a virtual college. Perhaps they will seek a different experience by selecting a site-based college experience that might offer a hybrid model of face-to-face and online instruction.

Interestingly, the growth in virtual education offers the opportunity for cross-cultural partnership models to emerge. In theory, there are many opportunities to forge alliances for codevelopment and delivery of programs with any university in the world. These alliances offer a chance to develop new models of learning for both traditional and for-profit institutions.

Conclusion

Higher education is becoming a global business and, some contend, a highly competitive commodity. Educational issues of quality and consumer protection are important enough to be considered as part of the ongoing international World Trade Organization discussions. All the while, the for-profit sector in the United States continues to blossom and grow despite some allegations of unethical practices, lack of rigor of content, and other scandals. In fact, many of these American-based universities are partnering with international institutions to provide educational options for students. For example, Kaplan University recently partnered with Nottingham Kent University in Great Britain to serve students overseas, whereas others, such as UOP's Apollo Group and Sylvan Learning, have long recognized the importance of finding international university partners to serve the demand of the increasing global marketplace of learners.

Online learning, especially a hybrid or blended approach that facilitates some on-site presence, is one way to expand programs beyond country boundaries while still leveraging some of the infrastructure offered by traditional universities. Therefore, in general, both for-profit and nonprofit universities in the United States and around the rest of world are creating access to education by establishing online initiatives with learning options that enable either a site-based experience or a virtual experience. Even among the traditional-aged eighteen- to twenty-two-year-old campus-based students, the flexibility of coming to class virtually is becoming expected and desirable.

The challenges in the new flexible worldview of increasing education options are largely those that have plagued higher education for decades: quality assurance in the integrity of the content and the degree, as well as consumer awareness. Because of the Web, today's consumers are better informed than ever before of their educational options. Online learning is here to stay and is considered the fastest-growing segment of higher education. Learners may find that the content, the online instructional experience, the services, and support are more transparent for online for-profit universities and, as such, they are simultaneously considered competitive advantages. In the end, this transparency has translated into more accountability of the faculty and the institution for meeting the educational needs of learners.

Pamela S. Pease provides marketplace analysis of online education investments and regularly consults with Wall Street investors, accrediting agencies, and educational institutions. From 1997 to August 2004, she served as president of Jones International University (JIU) and was responsible for JIU's becoming the first totally online university to receive regional accreditation in the United States in 1999. She developed the virtual instructional model and JIU's infrastructure. Pease has received numerous awards for her accomplishments, including in 1999, the United States Distance Learning Association's Most Outstanding Achievement by an Individual in Higher Education. She serves as an active member of several boards and commissions and has written extensively on the application of technology in education.

PART FIVE

CASES OF BLENDED LEARNING IN HIGHER EDUCATION FROM AROUND THE WORLD

This handbook contains examples of blended learning from around the globe. In the eleven chapters of Part Five, specific case situations from twelve different countries: Japan, Korea, China, Malaysia, Singapore, Australia, Canada, the United States, Mexico, Israel, the United Kingdom, and South Africa, are highlighted. In addition to the specific examples of blended learning here, other parts of the handbook contain perspectives on blended learning from countries such as Jordan and Rwanda (Chapter Thirty-One), New Zealand (Chapter Twelve), and Wales (Chapter Thirteen). These cases show a rich variety of ways that blending can be implemented to address the learning needs of diverse environments and cultures around the world.

In Chapter Nineteen, Insung Jung and Katsuaki Suzuki focus on blended learning environments in a Japanese higher education context. They describe Japan's slow emergence into the distance learning realm and provide a framework for analyzing the types of blending prevalent in Japan: blending to support information dissemination, blending to support open interaction, blending to support knowledge creation, and blending to support efficient management. In all of these cases, the paradigm incorporates information and communication technology into a traditional face-to-face (F2F) context. Under knowledge creation, the use of distance experts as instructors is mentioned since it would not be practical to always bring experts into the F2F context. Explanations and cases describing the other areas are included. Blending is also discussed at a program level, with some F2F courses required and the rest allowed at a distance.

In Chapter Twenty, Okhwa Lee and Yeonwook Im share their perspectives on the growing popularity of blended learning in the Korean context. They begin with a history of the emergence of cyber-universities in Korea. From 2001 to 2004, seventeen cyber-universities in Korea were started, with fifteen having direct connections to traditional campus-based institutions. Despite the rapid growth in enrollments at the cyber-universities, the authors have collected interesting data that reveal a preference for learning experiences that combine aspects of F2F and online instruction over online instruction alone. Among the other findings reported, students in the cyber-universities spent less time studying for their courses each week, and yet 93 percent reported that the online format was more of a burden than the F2F format. Amazingly, one-third of the respondents reported that online learning was twice the burden. The chapter also discloses cyber-university data related to faculty workload, perceptions of academic achievement, and student satisfaction levels.

Ronghuai Huang and Yueliang Zhou address the emergence of blended learning in China in Chapter Twenty-One. They note that experiments with e-learning in China have not provided the expected results, in large part due to the Chinese culture of learning by rote, extensive instructor control, and student discomfort with self-regulated learning. In an attempt to move from such traditional instructional approaches and biases, they set out a model for creating blended learning instruction and present case summaries from two blended learning courses within Beijing Normal University. In the first course, Web-based resources and videoconferencing with remote experts are used to enrich the learning environment. In the second course, students meet in face-to-face lectures for seven out of eighteen weeks, while collaborative e-learning activities account for the remaining weeks.

In Chapter Twenty-Two, Abtar Kaur and Ansary Ahmed showcase a model of blended learning that is used by the recently established Open University Malaysia (OUM). In this model, learning experiences are offered through self-managed learning, F2F learning, and online (virtual classroom) learning. Self-managed learning (using print materials) is the dominant element in the model, accounting for approximately 70 percent of the expected forty hours of learning time per course credit. OUM learners also have the option of meeting in class with a tutor and other students five times in a fifteen-week semester. Increasingly, the self-managed and F2F components of the learning experience are being supported by online discussions and interactions with online digital learning objects. The chapter is summed up with ten major challenges for the OUM, including issues such as sustainability, pedagogical effectiveness, efficiency, and the democratization of education.

Chapter Twenty-Three, by Geraldine Lefoe and John G. Hedberg, provides examples of blending in two very different contexts: Wollongong, Australia, and Singapore. In the Wollongong case, the need for blending stemmed from the expansion of the university to satellite campuses where students were physically separated from core university facilities. The Singaporean case is an example of blending that was intended for the convenience of the learners as well as to bring in expert instructors who were separated by distance from the learners in Singapore (local students and tutors with expert instructors at a distance). The authors raise several important issues, including the movement toward student-centered approaches with blending; the changing roles and responsibilities of students, instructors, and support personnel; the need for better support for the online portion of learning; and the perceived increase in workloads for instructors and students.

In Chapter Twenty-Four, Ron D. Owston, Randy Garrison, and Kathryn Cook present a massive study of blended learning in eight courses across universities in Canada that were part of the Collaboration for Online Higher Education and Research network. In addition, they review basic data from a survey given to students in the eight courses. While instructors and students seemed generally satisfied with their blended experiences, some of the issues that were raised in this study included the link between interaction and level of satisfaction with the blended course, increased time required by students and instructors, and lack of support by peers and institutional policies. In addition, the authors raise issues related to the usability of online discussions in large enrollment courses, as well as the fact that students appreciated traditional course experiences such as F2F discussions.

Chapter Twenty-Five describes the progress being made in Mexico's educational system to use technological tools to support teaching and learning. Alejandro Acuña Limón highlights a history of educational technology use in Mexico, including satellite television and the recent emergence of Internet learning. Among the key programs described in this chapter is the Red Escolar program, which provides Web resources to K-12 schools across Mexico. Also detailed here are efforts to expand the Mexican Virtual University. Issues are discussed related to the choice and use of a learning management system as well as changing faculty and student roles in a blended environment.

Chapter Twenty-Six, by Paul A. Elsner, chancellor emeritus of Maricopa Community Colleges, discusses the history of blending in the Maricopa Community College system in the Phoenix, Arizona, area. It outlines a trend toward blending that seems to be driven by two factors: convenience and choice on the part of the student and the fact that it allows, and perhaps even encourages, more engaging pedagogical strategies. Five individuals from across the system are interviewed and provide their insights and perspectives into blended learning within the Maricopa system. One of many significant issues raised is the importance of socialization in the learning process.

The authors of Chapter Twenty-Seven share research data regarding the adoption and use of a learning management system (LMS) at Tel-Aviv University (TAU). Here, Rafi Nachmias, Judith Ram and David Mioduser, at TAU point to the steady increase in the number of faculty members using the university LMS as well as an even greater increase in the number of courses with a presence in the LMS. They share the results of an analysis of types of course content embedded in online courses at TAU and how frequently the content items were accessed by students. They found that much of the content placed in courses was accessed by only a small percentage of the students and provided several plausible explanations. They also investigated the extent to which asynchronous discussion tools were being used in courses and reported that an average of just 6 percent of courses used asynchronous discussion. In addition, they discovered that the average student participation in the courses that used online discussion to be four to six messages per student. This chapter shows that blending in university courses at TAU is on the rise but that there is still much progress to be made in the diffusion across instructors, students, and courses, as well as in the richness and depth of the pedagogical strategies used.

Chapter Twenty-Eight by Gilly Salmon and Naomi Lawless addresses an approach to blended learning in the United Kingdom's Open University Business School (OUBS). Since 2002, the OUBS has experimented with providing more flexible approaches to completing its management certificate program. These approaches include allowing students to do the program completely online or online with F2F tutoring sessions, as well as providing an online option to the traditional residential "management challenge" component of the program. Those who select the online option have been able to engage in group work and form social bonds with peers even though they are not meeting F2F. Salmon and Lawless also provide several basic guidelines for promoting self-managing groups in online environments. By allowing students the opportunity to choose a blend, the authors conclude that they are enhancing both the satisfaction and learning of their students.

Research presented in the final chapter of Part Five helped to analyze math education courses at the University of Pretoria, which has seen exploding growth of blended learning since 1999. In fact, Pretoria now has enrollments of over twenty thousand online students, the vast majority of whom are receiving blended learning experiences. Chapter Twenty-Nine, by Ansie Harding, Johann Engelbrecht, Karen Lazenby, and Irene le Roux, focuses on blended learning at the course level. An "anti-semester" course in calculus is available for students who have to repeat the course. This course takes a blended approach with predominantly online materials and group work. Students also have the option of attending a weekly lecture session. A detailed case study of the anti-semester course is provided. Importantly, a model is provided for analyzing the blendedness of mathematics courses. This model, which could be readily used at other colleges and universities, entails a radial with six dimensions. The top three dimensions deal with interaction, and the bottom three consider the course materials. The resulting radial or picture for a particular class allows one a quick assessment of the level of online versus F2F emphasis in these areas. Three brief examples and radials are provided.

CHAPTER NINETEEN

BLENDED LEARNING IN JAPAN AND ITS APPLICATION IN LIBERAL ARTS EDUCATION

Insung Jung, Katsuaki Suzuki

Blended learning is increasingly permeating and transforming schooling, university education, workplace, and corporate education worldwide. Japan is no exception to this development. This chapter focuses on the emerging practice of blended learning in Japan and discusses a variety of instructional approaches in blended learning in the context of a liberal arts college in Japan.

World Economy Not Leading E-Learning

According to the white paper from the Economist Intelligence Unit, Japan was ranked twenty-third in the 2003 e-learning readiness ranking (Economist Intelligent Unit & IBM, 2003). The rank was based not only on connectivity, but also the capability of delivering and consuming e-learning, content quality and pervasiveness of learning materials, and culture, including the number of institutions supporting e-learning. Among Asian countries, South Korea ranked fifth and Singapore sixth. For Japan, a world-leading economy, its twenty-third ranking out of sixty in e-learning readiness was certainly not as high as anyone had expected. At least three explanations seem possible for understanding this situation.

First, Japan, compared with other developed countries and emerging ones in Asia, was late in the development and implementation of a comprehensive national information and communication technology (ICT) strategic plan and the use of ICT in education. A comprehensive e-Japan Strategy (Prime Minister of Japan and His Cabinet, 2001) was initiated in January 2001 in pursuit of making Japan the world's most advanced IT nation within five years and connecting all its classrooms to the Internet by 2005. In contrast, the United States established a $200 million Technology Literacy Challenge Fund in 1997 to help every child in every school use technology to achieve high standards by the dawn of the twenty-first century. The major European countries—Germany, France, the United Kingdom, and Italy—all announced major programs for IT in education in the late 1990s. South Korea began to implement a more comprehensive national strategy, Cyber Korea 21, in 1999 to promote a vision of a cybernation, strengthen the IT industry and telecommunication services, and maximize the use of IT in various systems of the society, including education. Singapore began to implement the master plan for IT in education in 1997.

Another possible explanation for the late development of e-learning in Japan seems to be related to Japanese culture. Japan values synchronous modes of education and face-to-face interaction over asynchronous interaction more than other countries. The Japanese government used to allow only synchronous modes of interaction in distance education until 2001. In other words, until recently, distance education institutions in Japan could not offer their courses at a distance without adding face-to-face components or real-time interactions. Given the heavy uses of the asynchronous features of the Internet technology, e-learning could not easily proliferate in Japanese culture.

Finally, extensive use of mobile phones in personal communications and information search could have slowed the use of the desktop PC-based Internet in teaching and learning. As Tim Clark, who published the *Japan Internet Report*, pointed out, Japanese people in general are heavy users of Internet-enabled mobile telephones to send and receive e-mail, search for information, study simple languages, or play games. In this culture of using the Internet with mobile phones, "accomplishing quick errands" is more emphasized than studying (Clark, 2003).

But as the higher education market is becoming more competitive and new types of technologies challenge the way educational institutions teach, the Japanese government has begun to implement its e-Japan Strategy in various sectors of society, including education. In addition, the Advanced Learning Infrastructure Consortium was established in 2000 as Japan's center to promote e-learning.

Trends in Higher Education in Japan

Over the past few years, Japanese higher education institutions have become increasingly competitive in recruiting students. The student population of Japanese higher education has been declining since 1992, when there were more than 2 million attendants. In 2010, only 1.2 million students are expected to attend higher education institutions. Many colleges and universities in Japan have insufficient enrollment, and the academic abilities of the students they do have is low. Some worry they may have to shut down. Moreover, a new government policy changed the status of the national universities in Japan from public to private (they are now independent administrative corporations) in April 2004. This new policy requires all universities to be evaluated by external quality assurance agencies every six years for continuing governmental financial support.

At the same time, government regulations for higher education have been loosened. For example, the face-to-face schooling requirement in distance education was removed for graduate schools in 2001, so graduate degrees now can be obtained without attending any face-to-face classes, and fully online graduate programs can be offered to degree-seeking students. In addition, a maximum of 60 of 124 credit hours required for an undergraduate degree can be offered at a distance.

In this changing environment of Japanese higher education, e-learning has been adopted at several universities to attract more students by providing a better-quality education or to extend higher education to adult learners. The examples in this chapter illustrate how and why Japanese higher education institutions have blended e-learning with conventional modes of education.

Definitions and Development of Blended Learning in Japan

Blended learning combines various modes of teaching and learning. It can be a blend of face-to-face schooling with distance learning mode. It can also integrate e-learning components in face-to-face or conventional distance learning situations. In this definition, the Internet or network-enabled mobile phones can be used as either a supplementary or a main tool for instruction. A majority of blended learning cases in Japanese universities incorporate the Internet as a supplementary device in classroom instruction. Only a few use the Internet as a main delivery medium and provide online courses with face-to-face sessions as supplementary. The examples that follow illustrate the different modes of blended learning used in a Japanese context.

Old-Type Blended Example

The University of the Air (UoA) began to offer distance education to adult learners in Tokyo via terrestrial broadcast channels in 1985. It extended its service area to cover all regions of Japan in 1990 by establishing video-based learning centers and in 1998 by using Communication Satellite Broadcasting (University of the Air, n.d.).

Blended learning at UoA requires all students to take twenty credit hours of face-to-face classes, called "Schooling," during their course work. "Schooling" can take one of the following three forms: once-a-week schooling, weekend schooling, or an intensive schooling. For the twenty credit hours of face-to-face classes, regular classroom lectures are provided instead of broadcast lectures. UoA is a good example of broadly defined blended learning where face-to-face interaction is blended with conventional distance education. With the introduction of the Internet technology, this practice of blended learning begins to integrate online components in its conventional distance education system.

An Initiative for the Future

The WIDE Project was launched in 1988 by Keio University to establish a widely integrated distributed environment, a new environment based on operating systems and communications technology. In 1997, the Widely Integrated Distributed Environment (WIDE) project opened the WIDE School on the Internet (SOI), or the WIDE University, to provide a unique educational opportunity to students from all over the world (WIDE University, 1997). The WIDE University now has more than eight hundred hours of classes available through its archives. Each class consists of video lectures and class handouts to support learners' independent study. Bulletin boards are used for interaction, and an online report submission function is also available.

According to Jun Murai, known as the innovator of the WIDE project and referred to as "Mr. Internet of Japan," the way to improve the quality of conventional university education was to blend his online teaching environment called WIDE with his own face-to-face lectures.

Sharing a Learning Management System

A joint research team from the National Institute of Multimedia Education and the Interfaculty Initiative in Information Studies at the Graduate School of Interdisciplinary Information Studies at the University of Tokyo started a project called "iii online" in 2002. The "iii online" (Interfaculty Initiative in Information Studies, 2004) is an e-learning site with four graduate-level online courses, which also provides management functions such as online registration, report submission, upload and management of on-demand video and supporting materials, and asynchronous interactions using bulletin boards and e-mail. The iii online has also offered an open learning management system, exCampus, to the public. exCampus is known as an online tool to support blended learning. The iii online attracted more than forty-six thousand viewers, including students of the University of Tokyo and those in the general public interested in lectures from

Japan's most prestigious academic institution. In this example of blended learning, Internet technology was used as a main instructional tool.

More Toward Online Than Face-to-Face

Shinshu University created the Graduate School of Science and Technology on the Internet as the first case of a totally e-learning graduate program in Japan and accepted eighty-seven graduate students in 2002. It then started its online undergraduate program in 2004, targeting juniors who have completed sixty-four or more credit hours in other universities and now wish to earn an undergraduate degree by completing the remaining credit hours using the Internet. Twenty-two students were accepted to start their junior year at Shinshu University. Shinshu's undergraduate program is a blend of online and campus-based courses. An online course at Shinshu consists of lecture notes, a free bulletin board, and tests.

Blended Learning in a Liberal Arts College

Here, we discuss a case of blended learning adopted in a liberal arts college in Japan and analyze instructional approaches and strategies for integrating online technology into face-to-face instruction as supplementary.

A Liberal Arts Education

The International Christian University (ICU) is a small liberal arts college with a fifty-year history, consisting of about twenty-eight hundred undergraduate students and two hundred graduate students. Students represent forty different nationalities, including Japanese. It is a bilingual institute using both Japanese and English, and is composed of 158 full-time faculty, including 47 non-Japanese members (International Christian University, 2004). ICU has been recognized as one of the finest universities in Japan pursuing high-quality liberal arts education based on the ideals of democracy and Christianity. The following features seem to have stimulated some of ICU faculty to use online technologies to support their classroom teaching environments:

   • *Interdisciplinary General Education Program.* At the core of the liberal arts education available at ICU is the General Education program (GE). All ICU divisions are expected to offer interdisciplinary GE courses face-to-face in addition to the courses in their specialized fields of study. Many of the GE courses have an enrollment of over one hundred students.

• *Language programs.* ICU faculty can offer their courses in English or Japanese. Between 15 and 30 percent of ICU's courses are offered in English. To support the students, ICU offers two language programs: the Japanese Language Program (JLP) and the English Language Program (ELP). Each ELP or JLP course is conducted with a group of fewer than twenty students.

• *Interaction and internationality.* Emphasizing interaction and international-ity in teaching and learning, ICU has implemented a set of policies to support interactive teaching and learning and international collaborative activities. These policies include financial and administrative support for special lectures given by foreign scholars, fellowships for visiting scholars, support for student exchange programs, and support for a variety of international discussion forums.

• *Time constraints.* ICU adopted a trimester system. With three terms per year, students taking an average of fifteen credit units per term are fairly busy. Considering all the teaching and advising responsibilities, administrative and other social services, and personal research activities, ICU faculty members are also under a great deal of time pressure during the terms. For this reason, efficiency is valued at ICU.

Development of Blended Learning

As with many other universities in Japan, the Web has been used as a tool to pub-lish course syllabi at ICU. ICU Web syllabi can be retrieved only within the on-campus intranet. In addition to posted syllabi, a great number of ICU faculty members have used e-mail as a tool to collect assignments and communicate with students. However, using personal e-mail for these purposes has been noted as in-efficient. Consequently, after the introduction of WebCT, a commercially avail-able online learning management system, by one of the faculty members with the financial support from the university in 2000, several faculty have begun to adopt WebCT as an integral part of the teaching and learning process in their courses. Currently more than twenty courses are using WebCT.

Analysis of Instructional Approaches and Pedagogical Strategies

Most of the courses adopting WebCT at ICU follow a model in which online learning components are added to a traditional face-to-face environment in order to facilitate different types of instructional purposes. Four popular instructional approaches to blended learning have been identified. These approaches are shown in Figure 19.1.

FIGURE 19.1. A FRAMEWORK FOR ANALYSIS OF INSTRUCTIONAL APPROACHES TO BLENDED LEARNING.

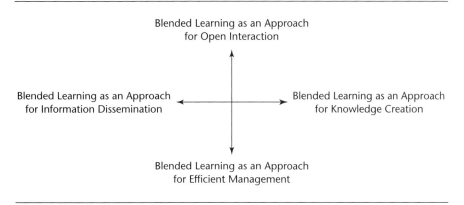

As seen in the examples of UoA, the WIDE project, and Shinshu University, many Japanese universities use online technology to disseminate lectures. A limited number of cases promote efficient class management and interactions by introducing online technology. At ICU, however, online technologies have been integrated into traditional classrooms to facilitate knowledge creation and support a variety of open interactions as well.

We now look at four dominant instructional approaches for a mix of online technology and face-to-face classes at ICU. These approaches are elaborated with a collection of pedagogical strategies indicated as effective by the instructors.

Blended Learning as an Instructional Approach for Open Interaction. This example uses blended learning to promote open interaction in a large GE course taught in English, where a majority of students are nonnative English-speaking students. With 147 students in a GE course on multicultural education, in-depth discussions on important or controversial issues could not be implemented during the face-to-face class sessions. The instructor decided to use the WebCT discussion board to stimulate in-depth discussions among students. The following major strategies are used:

- *Creating small-group debate teams.* The instructor created twelve debate rooms with one controversial issue in each room. Students were required to sign in to one of the rooms. For example, in room 1, students would debate on the issue of "whether foreign children should learn the main language quickly." Students would post their opinions with the following questions to guide their discussion: "What do you agree with or disagree with? Why? What evidence can you give? Look at the arguments on the other side." In addition, the instructor gave detailed explanations on each issue and directions for students to get involved in the debate.

• *Encouraging integration of classroom lectures in debate.* The instructor encouraged students to integrate what they learned in the classes and what they read in the class materials in their online discussions. Students whose primary language was not English seemed more comfortable participating in online debates and posting messages in English than participating in the face-to-face classroom discussions.

• *Assigning facilitator and "wrapper."* In each debate group, one facilitator and one "wrapper" were assigned. The role of the facilitator was to lead, monitor, and facilitate the debate, whereas that of the wrapper was to summarize the debate and post the summary note at the end of the discussion.

• *Integrating online activities in assessment.* This online debate lasted one week. Students were required to post at least one message a day. The number of messages posted and the quality of messages were evaluated by the instructor and included in the evaluation of student performance.

• *Reducing face-to-face classroom time.* During the online debate, no face-to-face classroom meeting was scheduled. The students were able to spend a whole week for the debate.

On average, each student posted about ten messages during the one-week discussion period. The instructor felt that the online discussion activity helped students apply face-to-face lectures in analyzing real-world problems and developing critical thinking on the given issues.

Blended Learning as an Instructional Approach for Knowledge Creation. This example uses blended learning to facilitate new knowledge development by promoting internationality in a small course. With five students in a graduate course on media education, international experts specializing in media education would be too expensive to invite to face-to-face classroom sessions to provide diverse perspectives on the use of media in education. The instructor instead invited three experts to the online classroom. This solution had a number of benefits:

• *Bringing internationality into the class.* To discuss a variety of ways of using different media in education and training, three experts with international experience in media education were invited to a one-week online discussion session and a one-hour online chat session. The three experts were from the United Kingdom, Korea, and Japan.

- *Combining asynchronous and synchronous online interactions.* The one-week asynchronous discussion focused on how different media were used in teacher education in different countries. Two experts, one from the United Kingdom and the other from Japan, participated in this online discussion. As a follow-up activity, the one-hour synchronous online chat was organized after the discussion. Two experts, one from Japan and the other from Korea, provided answers to students' questions and shared their own experiences during the chat.
- *Promoting anchored learning.* Before joining the discussion and the online chat, students were asked to read an article introducing various international applications in the use of media in education. One of the authors of the article was the invited expert for an online class activity. This reading was to provide anchored points for online discussions.
- *Integrating online activities in final assessment.* The number and quality of messages posted during the online discussion and the summary of the online chat were evaluated by the instructor and included in the final evaluation of student performance.
- *Reducing face-to-face classroom time.* During the one-week discussion, no face-to-face meeting was scheduled. Instead, the students were required to read the article before participating in the online discussion, post at least one message a day, and participate in the online chat.

Students' comments confirmed that these online activities succeeded in bringing internationality into the class and contributed to the development of new perspectives of the issues discussed. One student commented after the online discussion:

> I had a great time reading the comments and information about the usage of technology for education around the world. I want to make a great use of this rare opportunity for my paper. . . . (I have to write a twenty-page report about ICT usage in education for another course . . . [laugh].) Well, thank you very very much to all of you!! Thank you for so many postings and joining our online discussion. It was a great experience for me to share the opinions with the experts!! And also to our great facilitators!! Thank you!!

Blended Learning as an Instructional Approach for Information Distribution.
This example shows that blended learning can be used to distribute information efficiently. With fifteen students in a class, the instructor wanted the students to read all the articles before the class and check the related Web links. After the class, the students were asked to review PowerPoint materials and class handouts posted on the Web.

This approach had these components:

- *Posting articles to read before each class.* The instructor used WebCT to distribute article readings to the students. The articles were distributed one or two days before each class so that the students could read the materials, print them, and bring them to the class. Sometimes video materials and Web links also were provided.
- *Providing PowerPoint file and class handouts after each class.* The instructor used PowerPoint materials for each lesson. Other types of class handouts were also prepared and distributed during class hours. These materials were posted after each class was over. The instructor thought that the students might not pay attention to the lecture if they read the class materials beforehand.
- *Tracking students' viewing of the materials.* One of the features of WebCT is that an instructor can check log-in data. The instructor of this class wanted to make sure that his students checked the readings and class materials on the Web. He analyzed the access day of each student. For those who did not access the reading materials before the class, the instructor sent a private e-mail message.

For this instructor, WebCT was simply an additional teaching tool, like handouts, the chalkboard, and PowerPoint. The instructor felt that integrating Web technology in the class helped the students develop better ideas about the course by being able to read the materials before they came to class and also encouraged the instructor to become more structured.

Blended Learning as an Instructional Approach for Efficient Class Management.
This example uses blended learning to improve efficiency. In a course with sixty students, the instructor used WebCT to manage course assignments and provide individualized feedback more efficiently. The approach had the following features:

- *Submitting assignments electronically.* Students submitted all their assignments in the designated assignment boxes on WebCT. The instructor could easily check late submission since the WebCT system recorded the submission date and time of each student posting.
- *Providing feedback efficiently.* After receiving each assignment, the instructor provided feedback to each student with a grade. To provide feedback more efficiently, the instructor created a list of twelve kinds of feedback on common mistakes students would make. Each student was provided with one or more kinds of feedback from this list along with a short personalized message.

TABLE 19.1.   EXAMPLES OF PEDAGOGICAL STRATEGIES FOR BLENDED LEARNING.

Purposes of Blended Learning	Examples of Effective Strategies
Open interaction	• Creating small-group debate/discussion teams • Encouraging integration of classroom lectures and readings in debate and discussion • Assigning facilitator and wrapper • Integrating online activities in evaluation of student performance • Reducing classroom time during online activities
Knowledge creation	• Inviting external experts to online classroom • Combining asynchronous and synchronous online interactions • Promoting anchored learning by requiring students to preview materials for online discussion • Integrating online activities in evaluation of student performance • Reducing classroom time during online activities
Information distribution	• Posting articles to read before each class begins • Posting materials used during class to review afterward • Tracking students' viewing of articles and materials • Sending personal messages to students who do not check articles and materials
Efficient management	• Allowing electronic submission of assignments • Creating a list of standardized feedback • Combining standardized feedback with personal messages

By using WebCT, the instructor was able to handle assignment papers electronically (without hard copies) and quickly provide more individualized feedback to sixty students.

Table 19.1 summarizes some effective pedagogical strategies for blended learning at ICU to achieve different instructional purposes.

Conclusion

Blended learning in Japan in general, and at ICU in particular, takes many forms. Using a variety of blended learning cases and strategies in Japan, it is clear that blended learning is not only a matter of new possibilities but also brings with it new implications and challenges.

Adapting Instructional Designs for Blended Learning

With the emergence of e-learning and blended learning, the concept of instructional design is gaining public attention in Japan. While conventional instructional design models and strategies in general can be applied in blended delivery of instruction (Jung, 2003; Jung & Rha, 2000), specific strategies of instructional design still need to be developed and adapted for blended learning environments. For this purpose, continuous staff development programs that emphasize course design and interaction strategies for blended courses, and appropriate technical skills need to be integrated into a university system in order to improve the quality of blended learning.

Establishing an Integrated Support System for Blended Learning

In Japan, it is difficult to find a university that provides pedagogical and technical support services to its faculty for integrating online technologies in their courses. Our experience in blended learning tells us that an organized support system, including on-demand help, is necessary to encourage faculty and students to develop and strengthen their competencies in blended teaching and learning processes.

Establishing a Quality Assurance System of Blended Learning

There still exists strong doubt about the quality of e-learning and blended learning in Japanese universities. A university system for monitoring and evaluating the development and implementation of e-learning and blended learning will be required to ensure the quality of the educational services and provide accountability to the public (Jung, 2004a). In particular, continuous monitoring and feedback from students, which has not been popular in Japanese universities, will help identify problems in e-learning and blended learning and suggest possible solutions.

Improving the Cost-Effectiveness of Blended Learning

Most of the universities in Japan, as in almost any other country, have financial difficulties. Without proving or improving the cost-effectiveness of blended learning, it will remain difficult to secure funds necessary for integrating online technologies in conventional classroom teaching. Partnerships with business sectors can help reduce the investment costs of hardware systems (such as a computer networks), recruit high-quality students, and encourage advanced technical skills (Jung, 2004b).

Introducing Flexible University Policies

Most of those enrolled in Japanese universities are full-time students between ages eighteen and twenty-one. Classroom-based teaching and learning is a conventional mode of university education for those students. University policies and regulations have been developed based on this culture. However, recent changes in the legal status of universities and the introduction of online technologies in higher education are forcing Japanese universities to review and revise their policies and regulations. To attract part-time adult learners, flexible policies toward access, curriculum, methods, and learning processes have to be developed and institutionalized. Policies such as requirements for classroom attendance should be reviewed.

References

Clark, T. (2003, April). Message posted to Feature of hebig.com, archived at http://www.hebig.com/interviews/.

Economist Intelligent Unit & IBM. (2003). *The e-learning readiness rankings.* Retrieved June 30, 2004, from http://graphics.eiu.com/files/ad_pdfs/eReady_2003.pdf.

Interfaculty Initiative in Information Studies (2004). iii online. Retrieved June 30, 2004, from http://iiionline.iii.u-tokyo.ac.jp/index.php.

International Christian University. (2001). *FD handbook.* Tokyo: ICU Press.

International Christian University. (2004). *Bulletin of the College of Liberal Arts, 2004.* Tokyo: ICU Press.

Jung, I. S. (2003). Online education for adult learners in South Korea. *Educational Technology, 43*(3), 9–16.

Jung, I. S. (2004a, March 20–22). *Quality assurance and accreditation mechanisms of distance education (including e-learning) for higher education in the Asia Pacific region: five selected cases.* Paper presented at the UNESCO Workshop on Exporters and Importers of Cross-Border Higher Education, Beijing, China.

Jung, I. S. (2004b, March). *A comparative study on the cost-effectiveness of three approaches to ICT teacher training.* Paper presented at the International Council for Open and Distance Education 2004 International Conference, Hong Kong, China.

Jung, I. S., & Rha, I. (2000). Effectiveness and cost-effectiveness of online education: A review of literature. *Education Technology, 40*(5), 57–60.

Prime Minister of Japan and His Cabinet. (2001, January). *E-Japan strategy.* Retrieved June 30, 2004, from http://www.kantei.go.jp/foreign/it/network/0122full_e.html.

University of the Air (n.d.). *Chronology.* Retrieved June 30, 2004, from http://www.u-air.ac.jp/eng/index.html.

WIDE University. (1997). *SOI: School on the Internet.* Retrieved June 30, 2004, from http://www.soi.wide.ad.jp/aboutsoi/about-soi-e-2001f.

Insung Jung is on the faculty of the International Christian University (ICU) in Tokyo as a professor of education technology and communications. Before joining ICU in 2003, she served as the director of the E-Learning Center and associate professor at Ewha Women's University in Seoul. From 1992 through 2000, Jung was on the faculty of the Korea National Open University and has served as a consultant in distance learning to numerous national and international institutions, including Korean Ministries, United Nations Educational, Scientific and Cultural Organization (UNESCO), Asia-Pacific Economic Cooperation, and the World Bank. Since graduating from Indiana University in 1988, she has conducted extensive research in distance education and has numerous publications. She has also served as an editorial board member of several national and international journals.

Katsuaki Suzuki, who graduated from Florida State University majoring in instructional systems, is a professor of educational technology, Faculty of Software and Information Science, Iwate Prefectural University, Japan. His research interests include instructional design theories and models applied in various educational settings. Suzuki serves as a journal editor and member of the board of directors for educational technology–related associations and societies in Japan. He is one of the four honorary members of E-Learning Consortium Japan.

CHAPTER TWENTY

THE EMERGENCE OF THE CYBER-UNIVERSITY AND BLENDED LEARNING IN KOREA

Okhwa Lee, Yeonwook Im

With the rapid development of information and communication technologies (ICT) and the increasing demand for education, interests in the potential of e-learning have accelerated. Simply stated, e-learning uses ICT to supplement and enhance education across all sectors. After e-learning came blended learning, defined as a type of learning that includes the use of ICT and face-to-face instruction in varying degrees. Given the definition of blended learning, the majority of learning in higher education these days might be deemed blended learning. In fact, according to a study conducted in 2002 and 2003 (Allen & Seaman, 2003), one of the major findings is that both campus-based universities and online universities are focused on blended learning and the quality of e-learning.

The widespread growth of blended learning has found its way to Korea. According to a white paper published by the Ministry of Education and KERIS (Korea Education and Research Information System, 2003), blended learning was used in about 63 percent of university education courses in Korea in 2002 and 67 percent in 2003. According to statistics from June 2003, among the 204 universities in Korea, more than 50 percent of classrooms are now equipped with technology that might enhance the opportunities for technology use and blended learning (KERIS, 2003).

The extensive use of blended learning in Korea is due to the prevalence of Internet access and well-planned and well-supported infrastructure. In fact, Korea holds several world records in Internet usage and availability, including the highest broadband diffusion rate, the longest Internet access time, and the highest percentage of streaming media applications (World Economic Forum, 2004). Currently more than 65 percent of Internet users in Korea use audio-video streaming services. This pervasive Internet presence helps people become familiar with and take advantage of e-learning. At the same time, the Net generation in Korea seems to take for granted the ability to work and learn in cyberspace.

The trend to blended learning in Korea began in cyber-universities: those that offer courses online via cyberspace as a form of distance education. Courses in cyber-universities in Korea were exclusively online at first. Interestingly, they later began to offer face-to-face courses themselves or allowed students to take these courses in their affiliated campus-based universities. Some courses in cyber-universities incorporate both online and face-to-face elements in their design. Also, the learning community in cyber-universities uses both online and face-to-face modes. Students at cyber-universities meet regularly in formal study groups as well as casual social meetings. Given this history and sudden emergence of cyber-universities, the observations about cyber-universities in Korea in this chapter should clarify recent blended learning trends and practices.

The Cyber-University

As every country has its own educational environment, Korea is unique in its educational resources and demands on those resources. By the year 2002, the number of authorized entrants at Korean universities (723,683) exceeded the number of high school graduates (670,713). At the same time, there remains a high demand for quality higher education. Such trends and demands have caused a serious imbalance in student enrollments among universities. In fact, a severe disproportionality of entrants at Korean universities has caused competition and innovation within their respective educational services. Universities now recognize the need for educational reform that leads to student-oriented education and cost-effective management of an e-campus and e-learning. Part of this recognition stems from the fact that they have begun to reap enrollment gains from enabling students to work at their own pace at their own convenient time and place.

In 2001 Internet industries began to seek massive application of technology within higher education in response to the prevailing view that higher education was not as well equipped with IT as primary and secondary schools. In 2001 the Korean Ministry of Education (MOE) finished the first stage of support for ICT infrastructure in primary and secondary schools and was ready to begin supporting

Korean higher education with Internet infrastructure and applications. At that time, the Korean government encouraged universities to apply ICT in instruction and promoted the trial of the cyber-university within Korea. With strong political support from the government and a need for a new market for the booming IT industries in 1998, a consortium of universities and colleges for online learning opened in sixty-five universities and fourteen companies, which was the basis of the pilot project for a cyber-university in 1999 and 2000. The pilot cyber-university project was so popular that the MOE accepted more cyber-university applications than originally planned. Most of these trial cyber-universities were campus-based university consortiums located next to or within the traditional campus.

Due to the success of the pilot project, the government launched a new higher educational system, cyber-universities, in March 2001. A cyber-university is a unique instructional medium modeled after student admission policies used in the Open University. To date, these cyber-universities have drawn extensive attention from university administrators, the public, and the Korean media. The growth of the Korean cyber-university project from 2001 to 2004 is detailed in Table 20.1.

In 2001 the first nine cyber-universities, with thirty-nine study areas, were authorized by the Korean Ministry of Education and Human Resource Development. the actual enrollment rates in 2001 varied across the cyber-universities from roughly 89 percent of the authorized total (Kyung Hee Cyber-University) to a low of 38 percent, according to the educational statistics from the Ministry of Education and Human Resources Development (2004).

With the continued popularity and growth of cyber-universities, six more universities were authorized in 2002, which increased the number to fifteen, with seventy-nine study areas and 16,700 new entrants authorized; however, the actual enrollment rate varied greatly among the universities, from a high of nearly 90 percent at Seoul Cyber-University to a low of almost 10 percent (Ministry of Education, 2004).

In 2003, one more new cyber-university was authorized, bringing the total to sixteen cyber-universities and 149 study areas. Finally, in 2004, one more cyber-university was authorized, increasing the total to seventeen cyber-universities, including 2 two-year colleges and 15 four-year universities) with 23,700 students authorized and 162 study areas. While five universities received less than 20 percent of the students authorized, the total actual enrollment across these seventeen cyber-universities and colleges continued to climb to nearly 40,000.

Enrollment Rates

The total number of new entrants authorized has rapidly increased since the first year, but it is expected that in the short term, the number of new entrants

TABLE 20.1.   CYBER-UNIVERSITIES AND AUTHORIZED NUMBER OF NEW ENTRANTS PER YEAR, 2001–2004.

Name	2001	2002	2003	2004	Address
University name					
Kyung Hee Cyber-University	800	1,600	2,400	2,400	khcu.ac.kr
Sejong Cyber-University	500	1,300	1,300	1,600	cybersejong.ac.kr
Seoul Cyber-University	900	1,800	1,800	1,800	iscu.ac.kr
Seoul Digital University	800	1,600	2,400	2,400	sdu.ac.kr
Open Cyber-University	800	1,400	1,400	1,500	ocu.ac.kr
Korea Digital University	900	1,800	2,500	2,500	koreadu.ac.kr
Korea Cyber-University	900	1,650	1,650	2,000	kcu.ac.kr
Daegu Cyber-University	—	800	600	800	dcu.ac.kr
Wonkwang University	—	700	700	700	wdu.ac.kr
Hanyang Cyber-University	—	1,000	1,500	2,200	hanyangcyber.ac.kr
East West Cyber-University	—	400	600	400	ewcu.ac.kr
Hanseung Digital University	—	500	750	600	hsdu.ac.kr
Semin Digital University	—	—	600	800	usm.ac.kr
International Digital University	—	—	500	900	gdu.ac.kr
Cyber Foreign Language University	—	—	—	1,000	cufs.ac.kr
Subtotal	5,600	14,550	18,700	21,600	
Cyber-College name					
World Cyber-College	500	1,300	1,300	1,300	world.ac.kr
Semin Cyber-College	120	450	—	—	usm.ac.kr
Yeungjin Cyber-College	—	400	600	800	ycc.ac.kr
Subtotal	620	2,150	1,900	2,100	
New entrants authorized	6,200	16,700	20,600	23,700	New entrants
Actual enrollment	5,041	11,006	11,833	11,570	
Actual enrollment rate (%)	81.3	65.9	57.4	48.8	
Total of entrants authorized[a]	6,200	22,920	43,520	67,220	Total of entrants
Actual enrollment	5,041	16,874	28,707	39,450	
Actual enrollment rate (%)	81.3	73.6	66.0	58.7	

[a]The Ministry of Education and Human Resource Development (MOEHRD) authorizes the number of new entrants to the university (including cyber-universities), and then universities (including cyber-universities) can recruit new students for the number of new entrants authorized by MOEHRD for that year, plus any shortage from the previous year. As a result, the number of new students for a given year can be larger than the new entrants authorized by MOEHRD if the cyber-university failed to fill its new entrant allotment in the previous year (Korea Educational Development Institute, 2004).

authorized will stay around at levels similar to 2004. The statistics for 2004 are important because it was the first year that students across the four years of a university experience were enrolled. Up to 2003, the actual enrollment number of new entrants increased, but from 2004, a slightly lower new enrollment is evident. Nevertheless, total actual enrollment increased steadily (Table 20.1). It will be interesting to watch the actual enrollment rates of new students during the coming years to see whether the popularity of cyber-universities continues to grow.

The lower-than-expected or hoped-for enrollment rate is due at least in part to lower respect for cyber-universities as compared to traditional campus-based universities in Korea. In addition, traditional universities have attempted to expand their e-learning courses so that many potential cyber-university students can have their needs met at campus-based universities.

Types of Cyber-University

The seventeen cyber-universities, all private, are classified into three types: (1) cyber-university linked to an existing campus-based university institution (eleven cyber-universities), (2) cyber-university consisting of a campus-based university consortium (four cyber-universities), and (3) cyber-university without affiliations with any other universities (two cyber-universities) (KERIS, 2003).

The first type of cyber-university, based in an existing campus setting or institution, has some immediate name recognition and infrastructure to build from. The brand name provides an identity for the cyber-university. Cyber-universities typically can use the resources of the campus-based university, such as support from the professors, digital libraries, and research facilities. For example, Hanyang Cyber-University and Kyung Hee Cyber-University borrowed the identity of a campus-based university for the cyber-university since both universities are known for their strong campus-based programs. In fact, Hanyang University allows students to take classes at the Hanyang Cyber-University and vice versa. Although cyber-university students are allowed to take courses from the campus-based university, most are unable to due to time and location constraints. While some cyber-universities have attracted students using the brand name of the traditional campus, cyber-universities that are not on prestigious campuses tend not to attract students as readily.

The second type of cyber-university is based on a university consortium. Such cyber-universities have the privilege of having access to students from all participating universities even though they are not students of the cyber-university. Cyber-universities of this type have their own enrollment. Among the four cyber-universities of this type now in Korea, Seoul Digital University, a consortium of twenty-one universities and led by Donga University, is quite successful and offers the greatest variety of areas of study (eight areas with fifteen subareas). Korea Digital University, which is based on a consortium of six universities led by Korea University, is a successful example, as indicated by its relatively high enrollment rates when compared to authorized enrollments (over 80 percent).

Seoul Cyber-University and Hanseung Digital University are examples of the third type of cyber-university, which does not rely on a specific university affiliation or consortium. Interestingly, Seoul Cyber-University now offers campus education, which is somewhat unique among the Korean cyber-universities, though some cyber-universities (those with traditional university affiliations) offer off-line education. In effect, this third type of cyber-university has started to venture into blended learning.

Demographics

Recent reports from the Korean government reveal that the largest percentage of freshmen at a typical cyber-university were between thirty and thirty-nine years old. The second largest group was in their late twenties (21 percent). In addition, 17 percent were in their early twenties and 18 percent in their forties (KERIS, 2003). This report confirms that, as expected, the typical student in a Korean cyber-university is older than the average freshman in traditional universities. Such data indicate that cyber-universities seem to be meeting the needs of lifelong education.

Cyber-Korean students primarily have a high school degree or equivalent (nearly 87 percent in 2003). The remaining ones are two-year college graduates (4 percent), four-year university graduates (4 percent), high school diploma certificate examination holders (4 percent), and graduate degrees (1 percent). Some students are enrolled for a second university degree.

Rates of enrollment of female students were 35 percent in 2001, 38 percent in 2002, 38 percent in 2003, and 42 percent in 2004. In traditional universities, the female student population is almost 39 percent (MOE, 2004). These rates are similar to those in the United States, where females in college slightly outnumber the male population (Oblinger, 2002).

In terms of job status, 86 percent of cyber-university students in 2003 were employed and viewed this as a chance for a degree as well as useful for job retention. Nearly three out of four cyber-university students live in or near the Seoul area (KERIS, 2003).

Study Areas

Program area offerings within cyber-universities continue to increase. For instance, 39 program areas in 2001, 79 in 2002, 149 in 2003, and 162 in 2004 were offered. While many programs were replicated, the growth of program areas and study disciplines reveals how cyber-universities try to satisfy students with more refined areas of study. The study disciplines include business management (23 percent),

IT (22 percent), and many others, including nongovernmental organizations, social welfare, theology, foreign languages, and oriental humanities.

The areas of study offered by cyber-universities are crucial for student recruitment. To succeed, cyber-universities should have their own identity, not just mimic the campus-based universities in cyberspace. In response, many have different curricula and services because they have different students with distinct needs. Consequently, administrators at cyber-universities must pay special attention to the needs of the marketplace to make decisions about what academic programs they might support and what programs might lose resources.

Trends of Online Learning

In order to understand how online learning is perceived by those in the cyber-university system, surveys and interviews were conducted in May and June 2001 with 630 faculty and 219 staff, and May and June 2004 with 401 students, all who had some online instructional experience. The 2001 study was conducted to find out how students, academic faculty, and staff perceive online learning. Key aspects of this study that were replicated in 2004 focused on student weekly working hours, work load, levels of satisfaction, academic achievement, and difficulties of e-learning.

Weekly Study Hours per Course

Students were asked how many hours per week they spent studying for each e-learning course. In 2001, including online classroom hours, students spent on average 3.4 hours a week studying (see Figure 20.1). Interestingly, the largest percentage of students, 38 percent, spent 2 to 4 hours studying an online course each week. An additional 32 percent spent fewer than 2 working hours per course per week. In total, then, more than 70 percent of cyber-university students studied fewer than 4 hours per week in each course.

In the 2004 study, excluding any online classroom time, nearly 40 percent of cyberstudents spent just 1 to 2 hours studying for each course each week, and another 30 percent spent less than 1 hour per course per week. It thus appeared that they were studying even less per week than the previous sample from the first year of the program in 2001.

Although they may have been studying less than their 2001 counterparts, the 2004 online class students studied slightly less than or about the same number of hours as face-to-face students (You, 2004). And while the data from 2001 showed that students with more online learning classes tended to spend more hours

FIGURE 20.1. HOURS PER WEEK STUDIED PER COURSE, ONLINE STUDENTS, 2001.

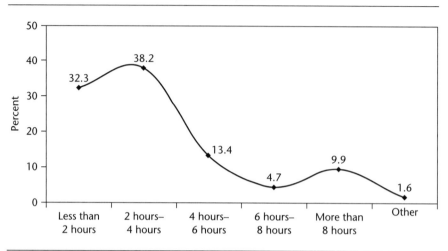

studying, this was not replicated in the 2004 study. The 2004 findings are also somewhat in contrast to those from Oblinger (2002) in the United States, which claimed that online students (cyber-university students) tended to spend more time studying because they were more motivated and eager to do self-directed learning.

Workload

In 2001, students and faculty were asked how their cyberclasses compared with face-to-face classes in terms of effort. In general, students (81 percent) and academic faculty (93 percent) reported more burden with cyberclasses compared with that of face-to-face classes. Nevertheless, additional stress was more frequent among online faculty (45 percent felt it was twice the burden) than among online students (34 percent felt it was twice the burden). In contrast, in the 2004 study, more than 40 percent of the students felt that the workload of their cybercourses was similar to face-to-face courses. Still, nearly 30 percent felt overworked with online learning, which is somewhat ironic since our research indicates that they tended to study slightly less than students in face-to-face settings. Given these findings, there seems to be a high need for more faculty and student guidance and support in online courses.

Level of Satisfaction

When students were asked whether they were satisfied with their online learning class experience compared with face-to-face classes, over half of the 2001 students (57 percent) were satisfied. However, in the 2004 study, just 32 percent of students were equally satisfied. In addition, 35 percent of students were slightly less satisfied, and just one in four students were slightly more satisfied.

As shown in Figure 20.2, cyberstudents in 2004 were slightly less satisfied with their online learning experiences than cyberstudents in 2001. When they were asked about the level of satisfaction for online learning contents and instructional

FIGURE 20.2.   COMPARISON OF SATISFACTION LEVEL
WITH E-LEARNING.

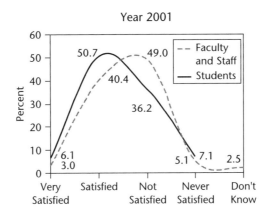

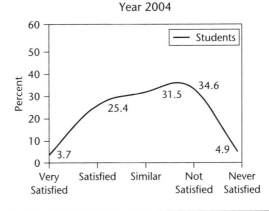

strategies, they also were less satisfied with the instructional methods or strategies employed online. Again, it is interesting that students showed less satisfaction with e-learning in 2004. Apparently Korean students are displaying higher expectations for their online learning courses as they gain more experience with this educational delivery method.

The data from 2001 were analyzed again according to instructional media. We found that students' satisfaction was the highest when the main instructional format was blended learning, such as face-to-face instruction with online supplements (68 percent) or online courses with face-to-face supplements (59 percent). Student satisfaction with fully online courses was lower but still positive at 55 percent. Similarly, the 2004 study also showed that students prefer blended learning (face-to-face with online learning support, 42 percent; online learning with face-to-face support, 32 percent).

Perception of Academic Achievement

The survey asked how different faculty members perceived students' academic performance compared to face-to-face courses. Overall, faculty members in 2001 responded that the academic achievement for e-learning would be lower than that of face-to-face courses. Specifically, while about one in four thought it would be the same as face-to-face and another one in four thought it would be better, the remaining 50 percent thought it would be lower. Students in 2001 also reported that they would have better levels of academic achievement in face-to-face classes than in online classes.

A similar trend regarding student perceptions of their value of their learning occurred in the 2004 study (this study did not deal with faculty). In this study, 42 percent of students reported they would expect lower achievement, 34 percent expected similar achievement, and 13 percent higher achievement. Interestingly, in the 2004 data, female students were more critical about cyberlearning than male students. The reason that female students were more skeptical about academic achievement needs to be investigated because female students are often known to be more active in online discussions (Gadio, 2001; Im & Lee, 2003).

Difficulties in Online Learning

In the 2001 study, students claimed that there were many online learning difficulties. Among the more salient were problems in receiving help for instructional or administrative questions, too heavy a workload, lack of course-related information, and Internet inaccessibility. Some of the other issues included boring instructional content, a lack of interactivity with instructors, and too frequent evaluation. In the 2004 study, cyberstudents were more concerned with boring instructional content, inadequate management of the learning process, the slow speed of the Internet, inadequate cyberinstructional pedagogy, and minimal feedback from the instructor. In addition, some voiced concerns about inadequate evaluation, inadequate amount of content, high difficulty level of the course content, and little chance for peer communication and interaction. Interestingly, when comparing the results of the two surveys, the students showed different priorities over just a three-year span. For instance, the 2004 students were much more aware of the importance of content and instructional processes than administrative support and technical problems that were salient issues in 2001.

Discussion and Conclusions

Although e-learning is becoming a common medium for instruction in Korean higher education, there still are many areas where growth is possible, though the expansion of cyberlearning may hinge on meeting key student and instructor needs. Based on the analysis of student and faculty member perceptions of online learning and cyber-universities in Korea, there are several important implications and suggestions that are valid for both fully online learning and blended learning.

First, blended learning will likely continue to grow rapidly in Korea during the coming decade. In fact, in our surveys, blended learning was suggested to be the preferred instructional format by both cyber-university students and instructors. Clearly, online learning has not yet met the satisfaction level that faculty and students desire. Faculty members continue to seem anxious about student academic achievement since the delivery of instruction is physically separated, so the degree of students' learning depends more on individual students than on imparting knowledge in face-to-face instruction. The perception of lower academic achievement in Korea is consistent with the Sloan Consortium research (Allen & Seaman, 2003) in the United States, which reported that chief academic officers in higher education perceive that the quality and outcomes of online learning are currently inferior to those of face-to-face. However, these same individuals predicted the quality of online learning would equal or surpass face-to-face instruction in the next few years. Recent research by Bonk and Kim (2004) on college faculty and administrators related to the future of e-learning replicated the Sloan findings related to expectations that both e-learning content quality and student outcomes would surpass face-to-face environments in the next few years.

Interestingly, as students acquire more experience with online learning, they spend less time studying and are slightly less satisfied. Once again, such results suggest that online learning should be blended with face-to-face instruction.

Second, in terms of the preferred delivery format of course content, cyber-university students wanted Web-streamed content, while students from off-line universities preferred Web-based materials and resources. Online students in particular wanted to see their own professor in the online video. In essence, they wish to have the feeling of presence in a real classroom. When cyber-university facilities were being designed, there were debates in Korea about which system was more suitable for e-learning: rely primarily on Web-based content (such as lecture notes, PowerPoint slides, and Web resources) or video-based lectures (a "talking head" instructor delivering lectures with PowerPoint notes via video streaming). Although each type of content delivery method has its own advantages and potential uses, when both methods deliver the same information, campus-based students prefer Web-based content since the Web can deliver information in a flexible and condensed way. In contrast, students from cyber-universities want video lectures for their online classes (Lee, Kwak, & Cho, 2004). For cyber-university administrators, the cost for Web content delivery is a serious matter. Currently, video-based lectures in Korea cost about $7,000 per course, compared with $35,000 per course for the typical development of Web-based course contents, and students have shown a similar level of achievement (personal communication with the dean of Kyunghee Cyber-University, February 2004). Of course, most classes now use both formats in different degrees, often supported by various supplemental materials such as printed books. Another factor that administrators must keep in mind is the reusability of these content resources, so while the reusability of Web-based contents may be higher, video streaming contents tend to be used for areas with low reusability such as IT. Fortunately, in Korea, the infrastructure exists for live online video-streamed lectures, thereby enabling cyber-universities to use whatever format they need.

Third, a new definition of instructors may be needed. When the content developer and the teacher for the video streaming are different (which is often the case), the teacher on the video should be a person with authority in that content area. In vocational education, content developers and teachers are usually not identical. Authorities are invited to provide content, and those instructional packages sell through educational institutions. When expert-generated content is used, a new role for instructors is required. Having the authority on the video is one way of enhancing the quality of the class, especially when online learners have low expectations or unfavorable attitudes regarding the quality of online contents.

Fourth, professional development for instructional strategies and blended learning content development is needed. As shown in the research reviewed here, many cyberprofessors feel overwhelmed and not happy about the quality of their e-learning classes. Particularly when new roles for instructors are required and materials are boring or there is inefficient pedagogy (as the cyberstudents claimed in our survey research), faculty should want to learn about content development and instructional strategies for online learning. In response, most major Korean universities have begun building and operating centers for teaching and learning, which include a focus on supporting e-learning pedagogy.

Fifth, instructor success stories should be recognized and rewarded. In our research, faculty and staff typically felt a much greater burden than students. One reason for the high stress may come from their perception of the wide exposure of the e-learning medium. Faculty members tend to try to provide additional and better content for online classes than in their face-to-face classes since online content is reusable and possibly open to public view. But instructional activities are equally important, and online success stories learned during professional development can be a model for them. Providing instructional environments for blended learning can also help faculty become aware of alternative pedagogy for online learning (cybergogy).

Sixth, students need guidance and support for the use of blended learning given that they spend fewer study hours, feel significant stress or burden, and their satisfaction level of the online learning is low.

The emergence of the cyber-university has brought significant change to the Korean higher education system in just a short amount of time. One immediate impact was to initiate online learning in higher education including campus-based universities. The experience of cyber-universities points to the new educational mode of blended learning. Students at cyber-universities seem to appreciate the visual appearance of instructors as in streaming video and the opportunity to take face-to-face courses as well as meet face-to-face with their peers. Studies of the psychological and social factors that are attributable to the need for blended learning are necessary as well as those that explore the benefits of blended learning as a mode of education. It will be interesting to watch trends in fully online learning as well as blended learning in Korea and around the world during the next few years.

References

Allen, I. E., & Seaman, J. (2003). *Seizing the opportunity: The quality and extent of online education in the U.S., 2002 and 2003*. Sloan Consortium. Retrieved August 29, 2004, from http://www.sloan-c.org/resources/sizing_opportunity.pdf.

Bonk, C. J., & Kim, K. J. (2004, August). Future of e-learning in higher education and training environments. In *Proceedings of the 20th Annual Conference on Distance Teaching and Learning*. Madison, WI.

Gadio, C. M. (2001). Exploring the gender impact of the world links program: Summary of the findings of an independent study conducted in four African countries. *World Links*. Retrieved July, 30, 2004, from http://www.world-links.org/english/assets/gender_study_summary.pdf.

Im, Y., & Lee, O. (2003, Winter). Pedagogical implications of online discussions for preservice teacher training. *Journal of Research on Technology in Education, 36*(2), 155–170.

Korea Education and Research Information System. (2003). *Adapting education to the information age: A white paper 2003.* Seoul: Korea Education and Research Information System.

Korea Educational Development Institute. (2004). *Educational statistics: Seoul, Korea.* Retrieved July 18, 2005, from http://cesi.kedi.re.kr/jcgi-bin/index.jsp.

Lee, O., Kwak, D., & Cho, D. (2004). *Direction for e-learning at the Central Officers Training Institute in Korea.* Unpublished report, Central Officers Training Institute, Seoul.

Ministry of Education. (2004). *Educational statistics.* Seoul: Ministry of Education and Human Resources Development, Korea Educational Development Institute. Retrieved September 28, 2004, from http://univ.kedi.re.kr/index.jsp.

Oblinger, D. (2002, August). *E-Learning: Evolution or extinction.* Paper presented at the 18th annual Distance Teaching and Learning Conference, University of Wisconsin-Madison, Madison.

World Economic Forum. (2004). *The global information and technology report 2003–2004.* New York: Oxford University Press. Retrieved October 1, 2004, from http://www.weforum.org/site/homepublic.nsf/Content/Global+Competitiveness+Programme percent5CGlobal+Information+Technology+Report.

You, Y. (2004). *Freshmen college students' life.* Hanyang: Center for Teaching and Learning, Hanyang University.

Okhwa Lee is a professor of computer education at Chungbuk National University in Korea. She received the B.S. from Ewha Women's University in Korea and master's and Ph.D. from the University of Wisconsin. She was a research fellow at Korea Educational Development Institute and Korea Advanced Institute of Science and Technology, where she participated in the development of educational policies and dissemination of computer education for primary and secondary school levels in Korea. Lee's work includes e-learning for tertiary level as well as gifted education, vocational education, and informal education. She has authored nine books (the most recent one on the use of instructional materials for computers in 2005) and about fifty articles. She has been active on the boards of various ministries and international organizations.

Yeonwook Im, an assistant professor in the department of educational technology at Hanyang Cyber-University, received a doctoral degree from the University of Pittsburgh. Her doctoral thesis was titled, "A Study of Spatial Ability and Window Presentation Styles in Web-Based Instruction." Her research interests include online education and instructional design. A recent example of her work, "Pedagogical Implications of Online Discussions for Preservice Teacher Training," appeared in the *Journal of Research on Technology in Education* (2003). Ongoing research projects include "An Empirical Study of the Association Between Dropouts and Learner Variables in E-Learning," supported by the Korea Research Foundation.

CHAPTER TWENTY-ONE

DESIGNING BLENDED LEARNING FOCUSED ON KNOWLEDGE CATEGORY AND LEARNING ACTIVITIES

Case Studies from Beijing Normal University

Ronghuai Huang, Yueliang Zhou

With the fast-growing economy and changing society in China, there has been large-scale development of both regular higher education and distance education in recent years. But we also have to face the challenges of inferior schools, lack of teachers, and lack of understanding about instructional theory and methods. Following world trends, many universities and colleges in China have carried out numerous experiments with e-learning but have not achieved the expected results.

This chapter puts forward a module of curriculum design based on blended learning while summarizing our research and practice in this area during the past several years, which aims at integrating the advantages of traditional instruction and e-learning as well as overcoming their disadvantages. The module, which considers the learner, the learning objectives, the design of learning resources and activities, the delivery methods, and associated assessment techniques, has demonstrated its viability in designing blended learning. In the end, this chapter gives two practical cases that use this blended learning model: one related to curriculum resource development and the other to the instructional implementation of curriculum.

Needs of Blended Learning

Since 1998, four universities in China have been engaged in network education experiments under the approval of Ministry of Education (MOE). In expanding these efforts, at the end of 2003, sixty-four additional universities established their own special School of Network Education (SNE). An SNE mainly uses e-learning instead of delivering instruction via correspondence or broadcasting (Huang, Zhang, & Dong, 2003). The sixty-eight SNEs have approximately 2 million registered students and 13,540 teachers distributed in about 2,790 learning centers. Interestingly, many SNEs once recruited full-time students and issued the same diplomas as their counterparts in ordinary universities. This situation resulted in censure from the MOE. Thus, according to official views, e-learning cannot be used as a substitute for classroom teaching. As a result, the SNEs are now limited to continuing and adult education.

Actually, there are very few instructional institutes that use only e-learning for instruction. Although some schools claim that they use e-learning as their main teaching method, most university learning centers undertake many methods in traditional instruction, such as the use of tutorships. Moreover, many other instructional institutions within China offer e-learning in combination with traditional distance education. So an enormous framework of blended learning has been set up in various certificate education and in-service training programs in China.

In traditional universities and colleges, many external factors help people realize the value of blended learning, thereby facilitating its effectiveness and wide use in teaching practices. First, university and college enrollments in China have jumped quickly: the number of students increased at a rate of over 20 percent annually between 1999 and 2002. In 2000, college and universities enrollments increased by one-third or more (see Table 21.1). These sharp increases put a strain on educational resources and highlighted the dearth of classrooms and experienced teachers. These resource constraints forced many universities and colleges to expand beyond traditional classroom instructional methods. Second, due to the SARS epidemic in China, especially in Beijing in the first half of 2003, personal movement and communication were badly interrupted; even normal face-to-face communication was considered dangerous. Therefore, when normal classroom instruction was halted, the idea of e-learning became popular since it could achieve similar objectives without face-to-face communication. During the SARS epidemic, over one-third of the students of Beijing Normal University (BNU) left Beijing; the percentage was higher at other universities. During this period, most universities tried to tutor their students through correspondence and e-learning.

As a result of these events and trends, the introduction of the concept and method of blended learning was a natural start for the application of e-learning in regular university instruction. Not only do more people understand the value of blended learning in university environments, but they also now understand that it offers a way to continue instructional activities when emergencies or disasters interfere with regular instruction. Therefore, we expect that blended learning will continue to develop

TABLE 21.1.   NUMBER OF COLLEGE STUDENTS IN CHINA, 1998–2003.

Year	Number of College Students (million)	Percentage of Annual Increase
1998	3.409	7.4
1999	4.134	21.27
2000	5.561	34.52
2001	7.191	29.31
2002	9.034	25.63
2003	11.736	16.6

Source: Based on statistics from the National Statistics Bureau, excluding graduate students. Available at http://www/stats.govc.cn/tjsj/ndsj/index.htm.

in universities and colleges in China over the next few years. But one problem is that the institutions and staff involved in network education as well as traditional universities lack the appropriate knowledge for developing correspondence methods of instruction and also the organization to take full advantage of blended learning. Four factors are important to the quality of education when using blended learning methods: (1) the curriculum, (2) organization of learning activities, (3) learning support, and (4) instructional evaluation (Huang, Zhang, & Dong, 2003). How to deal effectively with those four issues is one of this chapter's focuses.

There are various ways of delivering instruction, from traditional classroom instruction to the complete implementation of e-learning. And there are many different forms of blended learning, most of which combine e-learning and regular classroom learning. There is tremendous diversity in the instructional organization and implementation of blended learning, which makes its design extremely difficult. Clearly, blended learning cannot be regarded simply as a type of technology-intensive activity that replaces the functions of classroom instruction. Instead, those effectively incorporating blended learning must think about how it might enhance, extend, or transform the classroom learning experience, not simply replace it.

Challenges Faced in Implementing Blended Learning

This section addresses three challenges to implementing blended learning: designing the curriculum, designing and using online resources, and changing the strategies students use to learn.

How to Design the Curriculum of Blended Learning

Blended learning adjusts to the essential learning methods and overall learning environment, but teachers lack the necessary theoretical preparation and experimental experience to take full advantage of these changes. In fact, the main challenge in blended learning is that most instructors in higher education do not know enough about effective instructional activities based on blended learning. In China, for example, instructional activities in a traditional university are not well suited to students who prefer self-paced and self-regulated learning.

The urgent issue of carrying out blended learning is to put forward a series of curriculum design methods and ideas concerning blended learning that teachers can easily use. The module promoted in this chapter is intended to help teachers design blended learning.

How to Design and Use Online Resources

The styles and organizing methods of learning resources in blended learning, the second factor important to the quality of blended learning, involve many types of media and instructional designs unlike the resources of e-learning, which are more independent and stable. Blended learning resources need to be integrated with learning activities (especially in normal classrooms) and embedded into online curriculum resources. Therefore, the flexibility of blended learning not only provides more choices for knowledge delivery and skill development, but it simultaneously makes resource development more difficult. The design of blended learning resources should be considered within the overall design of the curriculum in order to adjust to the vast new resources and activities of e-learning and classroom learning.

Changes in Student Learning Strategies

The third challenge of quality blended learning relates to getting students to adopt or use learning strategies that are different from what they are used to in the traditional didactic, lecture-based classroom. College students in China have been receiving classroom instruction training using typical drill-and-practice models, forcing them to overrely on the requirements and demands of teachers (Robinson, 1999). Using the Learning and Study Skills Inventory (LASSI) (Weinstein & Palmer, 2002), we surveyed students' learning strategies at BNU. As in other universities, the level of students' learning and study strategies was not high. In fact, American student scores exceeded those obtained by Chinese students, especially on motivation and attitudes (Huang & Zhou, 2003). These findings begin to explain why, in technology-rich environments, Chinese students are often slow to take advantage of Web-based learning methods and often fail to develop the learning skills that match this instructional approach (Zhou & Zhang, 2001).

Moreover, blended learning requires that students change learning environments frequently, which may cause confusion regarding the learning objectives and make students unable to select and use proper cognitive activities. Such confusion will eventually make it difficult for students to form a stable and effective learning approach or strategy. In regular instructional situations, students' learning activities can be adjusted with the help of their teachers' external control and advice. But in blended learning, there is more reliance on student metacognition and self-directed learning, exactly the type of skill base that is often lacking among most Chinese students (Huang & Zhou, 2003). Hence, teachers and instructional designers must consider how to promote students' self-regulated learning capability in the process of instructional design.

In blended learning, the representation, delivery, and transaction of knowledge are altered somewhat, so it is important to consider the theoretical framework and instructional implementation of blended learning in universities and colleges. Many of the problems that Chinese universities encounter with blended learning likely exist in other parts of the world. In addition, these problems are closely related to one another.

Designing Blended Learning

In China, any new educational delivery approach or method needs to be easy to follow for instructors and not be too different from their usual way of doing things. This is especially true when implementing blended learning since it is still new to our teaching staff and students. The three key challenges can also cause students to get confused or lost. In the next section, we put forward instructional design procedures suitable to the requirements of blended learning.

From the perspective of pedagogy, teaching and learning in a blended learning environment can be highly unstable and fluctuating. Consequently, the organization and instructional methods of each curriculum program, course, or module are different. Indeed, blended learning does not yet have a specific instructional design plan or framework that can be used for all curricula.

Theoretical Considerations for Design

Many well-known models of instructional design usually correspond to classroom instructional settings, which fail to meet the requirements of blended learning. We regard blended learning as the integration of e-learning and classroom learning. As a result, there is a pressing need to consider many instructional design questions and issues, such as those related to time distribution, the design of online as well as classroom activities, the relationship between resources and different learning modes, and the balance point of e-learning and classroom learning. Clearly, with all these factors to consider, as well as the recent emergence of this approach, blended learning needs a theoretical framework or model to support it.

In his instructional design approach, *The Conditions of Learning and Theory of Instruction*, Gagné (1999) promotes the idea of "providing different instruction for different learning outcomes" (p. 302). In effect, there should be a close relationship between learners' internal mental processes and external instructional activities. Combining this idea with Anderson's idea of knowledge categories, Chinese scholars Shao and Pi and others put forward the idea of "knowledge category and objective-oriented instruction" and set up the "instructional process module of pan-knowledge" (Pi, 1998), which provides a sound basis for designing instructional activities and events suitable for e-learning and classroom learning. They argue that a teacher should design different learning and teaching activities for different types of knowledge and set out practical methods to design learning and teaching activities.

In order to confirm the relation between learning activities and types of knowledge, we use Bloom's taxonomy of educational objectives as revised by Anderson and Krathwohl (2001). Using this taxonomy, we can determine what type of delivery method is suitable to the content: online or classroom learning. The technique should be employed according to one's knowledge of the advantages as well as the disadvantages of e-learning and ordinary classroom learning. We believe that attempts to list such activities and methods will be highly similar to the second-generation instructional design (ID2) proposed by Merrill and his colleagues (Merrill, Li, & Jones, 1990). According to ID2, learning results from a given organized and elaborated cognitive structure, and different learning outcomes require different types of mental models. However, the learner's construction of a mental model is facilitated by instruction that explicitly organizes and elaborates the knowledge being taught during the instruction. The difference is that Merrill and his colleagues' instructional design environment was based on multimedia environments, whereas we are concerned with network environments.

As a knowledge construction process with learner intention and self-consciousness, learning activities need the support of reflection and self-regulated learning (Jonassen & Land, 2000). Blended learning requires that students have the consciousness and capability for self-regulated learning. As Zimmerman (2002) points out, the basic components of self-regulated learning are planning, monitoring, and reflection. The learning activities listed in Table 21.2 are in accordance with traits of self-regulated learning and embedded in various Web-based activities. Integrating the metacognitive knowledge with the other types of knowledge will help foster the successful implementation of blended learning.

TABLE 21.2. BIDIMENSIONAL TAXONOMY OF EDUCATIONAL OBJECTIVES AND ACTIVITY DESIGN.

Knowledge Dimension	Cognitive Process Dimension					
	1. Remember	2. Understand	3. Apply	4. Analyze	5. Evaluate	6. Create
A. Factual knowledge		Tests; Search on Internet				
B. Conceptual knowledge		Concept maps	Online tests			
C. Procedural knowledge	Reading (textbooks and online hypertexts)	Discussion; Communication; Concept mappings; Online collaboration	Practice; Resolve well-structured problems	Case studies	Reflection	Resolve ill-structured problems
D. Meta-cognitive knowledge		Communication; Brainstorming	Making up learning strategy	Activity record study	Reflection	

Design Procedures for Blended Learning

Blended learning should be designed carefully. The procedures shown in Figure 21.1 are intended to clarify how to design blended learning. The procedures have three main stages: (1) preanalysis, (2) activity and resource design, and (3) instructional assessment. Of course, instructional implementation is the ultimate objective of any instructional design model or viewpoint, including those related to blended learning.

Preanalysis. In order to ascertain whether blended learning could be used, several observations and analyses need to be conducted. These analyses mainly consist of three factors: (1) regular assessment of learners' prior knowledge, learning styles, and strategies; (2) content analysis of the curriculum according to the criteria of Table 21.2; and (3) environmental features analysis. Here, the learning activities and organizing methods should be clearly spelled out and defined, thereby enabling the creation of an initial analysis report.

Activity and Resource Design. This stage consists of three substages (see Figure 21.1). A detailed design report in the second stage should be emphasized; it is the basic document for blended learning and focuses on teachers' instructional methods for organizing course events and activities and also the basic principles

FIGURE 21.1.   DESIGN PROCEDURES FOR BLENDED LEARNING.

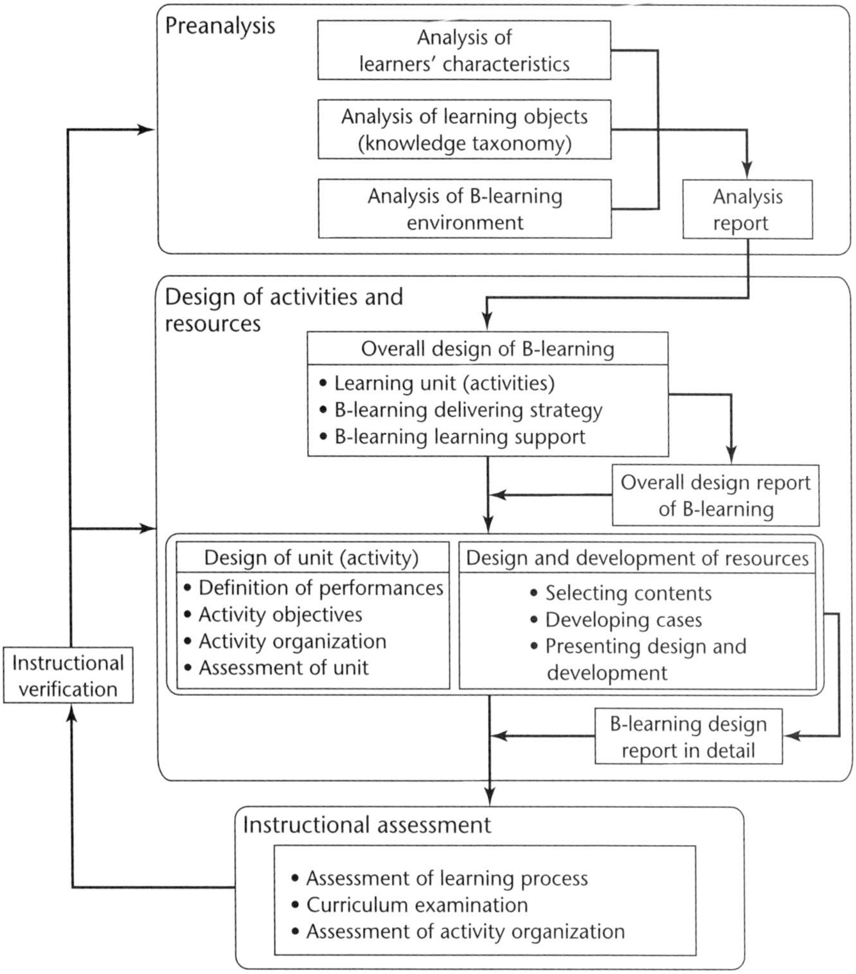

Note: B-learning = blended learning.

for curriculum assessment. The most important difference from ordinary instructional design is that it focuses on which activities and resources fit the e-learning context and which fit the typical classroom context.

Instructional Assessment Design. The assessment design depends on the activity objectives, performance definitions, and the general environment of blended learning. It chiefly uses the assessment of the learning process (for example, using e-portfolios), the examination of curriculum knowledge (for example, online tests), and the organization of learning activities.

Case One: "Introduction to Educational Technology," an Online Course

"Introduction to Educational Technology" is a course in the master's degree program in education for English teachers in the SNE within BNU. It is a typical blended learning curriculum, but uniquely developed through the cooperation of Chinese and British colleagues as funded by the two governments. The project started in May 2003, and was completed in May 2005.

Preanalysis

"Introduction to Educational Technology" is designed for in-service teachers to take from home. Not only is e-learning a suitable way for them to get credit hours, but this course exemplifies the integration of theory and practice since these teachers are learning much subtle and tacit knowledge about how to deliver course information and learning activities using the Internet. Given the lack of teacher knowledge or experience in this area and the need for modeling and sharing ideas, an appropriate amount of face-to-face instruction is needed in this case.

The course consists of seven relatively independent modules: (1) overview of educational technology, (2) integration of information technology into the curriculum, (3) instructional media, (4) instructional resources, (5) instructional design, (6) Web-based learning methods, and (7) a conclusion of the curriculum with an emphasis on teachers' professional development. The curriculum aims to foster teachers' capability of using educational technology effectively to achieve better results of classroom instruction and promote teachers' professional development and reflection.

The curriculum implementation and main learning activities will be put into a Web-based platform. The basic learning modes include case studies, discussion of key themes, and group learning. The group learning is crucial since it will help learners share their experiences and feelings, develop skills for analyzing and solving problems, and make better decisions about strategies for using technology and fostering better instructional design. Learners can constantly improve their understanding in course concepts using discussion and communication, thereby equipping them with a better understanding of theory and method and how to put them into practice.

Learners of the curriculum come from K-12 schools. They need to take a 144-hour course over eighteen weeks while they are still teaching in their respective schools.

Activity and Resource Design

This course uses a Web-based curriculum. Since the curriculum uses blended learning methods, it embeds a plethora of resources and activities. The actual curriculum involves all kinds of resources that are organized according to the activities reflected in Table 21.2. As such, this organizational framework provides the basis for the overall design of the curriculum. At the start of the course, a lead-in activity introduces the course content, learning objectives, learning methods, assessment methods, and even the appropriate navigational methods.

A typical unit example is shown in Table 21.3. This example is the basic frame of activities and resource design for the unit on instructional design. It is obvious that the curriculum needs the support of a powerful blended learning support system, so that different types of roles or activities can enhance student interaction and meet the stated learning outcomes. Most activities listed in Table 21.3 will be performed using a learning management system. But at the end of every

TABLE 21.3. BASIC DESIGN FRAMEWORK OF THE INSTRUCTIONAL DESIGN MODULE.

Learning Objectives	Students' Activities	Resources	Teachers' Activities
1. To understand the basic concepts of instructional design. 2. To get familiar with the process of instructional design	Mostly reading	Articles, video (lectures given by experts, recommended Web sites	Answering questions online, videoconferencing
3. To design instructional case of the learners' own subjects	Reading, problem solution (practice and implementation of instructional design), discussion and communication (the process of submission and the record of reflection)	Articles, cases (video and articles)	Tracking the design and implementation process of cases, offer advice and feedback, face-to-face discussion
4. To master the assessment methods for instructional design cases	Discussion and communication (analyze cases in groups), case analyses (submission of group reports)	Case studies (video), article cases (description of lesson plans)	

activity, a face-to-face session will be held. Thus, the tutors can see their students' authentic progress and discuss the content and procedures with them.

In the design process, the curriculum refers to the requirements of curriculum content design and the learning management system (LMS) as detailed in the Sharable Content Object Reference Model (SCORM) developed at the Advanced Distributed Learning Lab (2004).

Assessment Design

The evaluation of the curriculum uses formative assessment in exploring specific records of learning process including learner e-portfolios and computer log data.

Case Two: "Multimedia Technology," On-Campus Curriculum

This case relates to an instructional reform program at BNU, "Multimedia Technology," a required course for junior undergraduate students majoring in computer science. One of us was involved in creating this course as part of a master's program in the early 1990s.

Preanalysis

"Multimedia Technology" was built on a practical curriculum with many concepts concerning broad fields and fast-emerging technologies. Therefore, the curriculum not only stresses basic concepts and theories but also targets students' learning skills and metacognitive strategies. The aims are to enable students to learn actively and obtain new multimedia technology skills and experiences as well as to develop an understanding of the basic principles of multimedia. The curriculum includes various types of knowledge and different levels of learning activities.

This eighteen-week course typically has about 120 junior undergraduate students, one lecturer, and two tutors. These students have already taken other computer courses. As a result, they have enough knowledge and skill preparation for learning multimedia technology. However, they still lack a personal understanding of relevant learning strategies and self-regulated learning (Huang & Zhou, 2003). They are also accustomed to face-to-face lectures in traditional classrooms instead of cooperative learning and complex curriculum-projects.

In response, the major group collaboration project was guided regularly by tutors through a network learning environment, WebCL (Web-based Cooperative

Learning System), which was developed at BNU. Except for the textbooks, we also developed most of the other relevant e-learning resources and provided reference Web sites and bibliographies. (WebCL is a management platform based on cooperative learning developed by the Research Center of Knowledge Engineering, BNU. It provides a learning space for each group, including discussion areas, resource management, online chat, group work, online testing, and various tools for communication and exchanges.)

Activity Design

The course uses task-driven group learning to organize activity units in a blended learning format, including seven weeks of classroom instruction and eleven weeks of e-learning. There are four main types of activities: the lead-in activity, classroom lecture activity, e-learning activity, and curriculum-level project-based learning (PBL) activity.

A lead-in activity uses face-to-face instruction such as a typical classroom lecture activity. Afterward, the tutor and students kept in contact with each other through the WebCL. In general, their online correspondence has dealt with the learning method and fundamental knowledge. The e-learning activity includes online discussion, case studies, online debates, online testing, and individual concept mapping. The course has two key PBL activities, designing a multimedia player and developing an XML-based Web site, which are completed by collaborative groups during off-line class time. All activities were generated according to the principles detailed above and assigned to either the face-to-face or e-learning delivery methods. The instructional process of the curriculum and organization of the basic activity units are shown in Figure 21.2.

Learning activities at both the unit and curriculum levels contain objectives, definition of performance, and organization and evaluation. The students can check their own learning process records as well as that of their groups on WebCL at any time, and evaluate their learning through reflection. Using this system, the chief lecturer and tutors can communicate with the students individually and in groups through bulletin board systems, e-mail, and instant messaging. In addition, instructors can obtain instant assessment and feedback regarding the performances of each student and each group.

Evaluation

At the end of this curriculum, we interviewed a few group leaders and their members to learn how they viewed blended learning. In general, the students thought that the blended learning activities offered them a full range of learning

FIGURE 21.2. SEQUENCE OF ACTIVITIES
IN "MULTIMEDIA TECHNOLOGY."

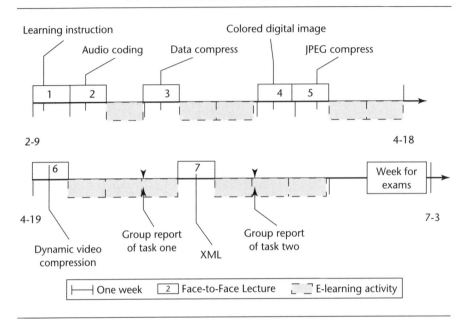

opportunities and resources that better matched reality. Most students were favorable toward combining network-based and classroom instructional techniques. In addition, they felt that with help from their tutors regarding how to collaborate online, they can learn how to communicate and collaborate with others to complete learning tasks more effectively. These interviews indicated that the online learning resources provided by the platform helped push highly motivated students to expand their knowledge and dig deeper in an area. The formative assessment of student e-portfolios helped reduce the all-too-common goal of simply learning for exams, so students could truly devote themselves to learning. This was an important finding, especially for Chinese students, who tend to overly focus on scoring high on exams and final grades.

Conclusions

Blended learning is having a significant impact on learning in higher education settings in China. It has not only changed traditional instructional approaches but also reduced the pressure brought about by the lack of instructional equipment and experienced teachers. However, blended learning is not a new instructional method in China. In fact, with the growth of Chinese universities and social needs brought on by the SARS epidemic, it has existed for three years. But from a systemic view of blended learning design, there is a new and highly unique significance from an encompassing model or design procedure for blended learning because it has many new challenges as well as opportunities.

The two cases in the chapter reflect the conditions of blended learning in China. The procedures are also feasible and can suit different kinds of blended-learning courses. To determine learner adaptations to blended learning, we interviewed students after they finished the "Multimedia Technology" course. They perceived that the activities in the course changed the typical flat instructional method of higher education and gave them more resources and personal choices. They also claimed that the WebCL tool played an important role in their learning process because it provided an effective way to cooperate and communicate. Such results imply that it is vital to select an appropriate learning management system for blended learning. Nevertheless, students are not accustomed to learning without their teacher at their side, causing them to spend more time attempting to understand given contents than in traditional classes. Given these findings, there is a pressing need to explore more effective interactive avenues between online tutors and students.

As we close this chapter, we would like to point out that e-portfolios can play special roles in blended learning settings. First, they can motivate students and help them to shake off their rooted notions of learning for the test. This change has special meaning in the Chinese educational system, which is rooted in teachers' telling and students' responding on exams. Second, e-portfolios might eventually be charged with the role of individual knowledge management so that they can serve as a basis for students to monitor, manage, and reflect on their performance (Zimmerman, 2002). We find this approach is more beneficial to the two PBL activities of our "Multimedia Technology" course. While these activities may need greater emphasis on self-regulated learning, e-portfolios can facilitate movement in that direction. We think the use of e-portfolios is necessary in blended learning, which we believe is superior to other learning approaches in higher education.

References

Advanced Distributed Learning. (2004). *Sharable Content Object Reference Model.* Available http://www.adlnet.org/.

Anderson, W., & Krathwohl, D. R. (Eds.). (2001). *A taxonomy for learning, teaching, and assessing: A revision of Bloom's educational objectives.* White Plains, NY: Longman.

Gagné, R. M. (1999). *The conditions of learning and theory of instruction* (4th ed.). Shanghai: East China Normal University Press.

Huang, R. H., Zhang, J. B., & Dong, Y. (2003). On the four key parts of Web-based instructional course. *Chinese E-Education, 192*(1), 61–64, *193*(2), 66–68.

Huang, R. H., Zhang, Y., & Zhang, J. B. (2003). On-line learning activities design for college students based on learning strategies—instruction case of the course "Multimedia Technology." *Research of E-Education, 124*(8), 25–29.

Huang, R. H., & Zhou, Y. L. (2003). Analysis on distance learning characteristics. *Chinese E-Education, 194*(3), 75–79, *195*(4), 69–71.

Jonassen, D. H., & Land S. M. (Eds.). (2000). *Theoretical foundations of learning environments.* Mahwah, NJ: Erlbaum.

Merrill, M. D., Li, Z., & Jones, M. K. (1991). Second generation instructional design (ID2). *Educational Technology, 30*(2), 7–14.

Pi, L. S. (Ed.). (1998). *Knowledge category and objective instruction: Theory and practice.* Shanghai: East China Normal University Press.

Robinson, B. (1999). Asian learners, Western models: Discontinuities and issues for distance educators (L. S. Li, trans.). *China Distance Education, 2,* 17–19.

Weinstein, C. E., & Palmer, D. R. (2002). *Users manual for those administering the Learning and Study Strategies Inventory* (2nd ed.). Retrieved May 24, 2003, from http://www.hhpublishing.com/_assessments /LASSI/index.html.

Zhou, Y. L., & Zhang, J. P. (2001). Internet-based learning traits and instructional design. In *Proceedings of the IEEE International Conference on Systems, Man and Cybernetics* (Vol. 1, pp. 459–463). Piscataway, NJ: IEEE.

Zimmerman, B. J. (2002). Becoming a self-regulated learner: An overview. *Theory into Practice, 41*(2), 64–71.

Ronghuai Huang is dean of the School of Educational Technology Beijing Normal University (BNU), and director of the Research Center of Knowledge Engineering, as well as head of the Lab of e-Learning, BNU. His research mainly focuses on educational technology, networked education, and information security, as well as knowledge science and engineering.

Yueliang Zhou is an associate professor of education technology, College of Education, Zhejiang Normal University. He is also a doctoral candidate at the School of Information Science, Beijing Normal University. His research mainly focuses on virtual learning environments and virtual learning communities (VLC), VLC and cognitive strategy, and instructional design.

CHAPTER TWENTY-TWO

OPEN DISTANCE PEDAGOGY

Developing a Learning Mix for the Open University Malaysia

Abtar Kaur, Ansary Ahmed

Blended learning can be viewed as learning that combines several learning modes with the view of optimizing resources and maximizing learning. Although it is not a new concept, many organizations are innovatively combining new forms of electronic delivery with nonelectronic delivery modes.

Recent literature reviews show that one's focus or perspective on blended learning will depend on the technological resources available. Still, most authors contend that blended learning simply combines online and face-to-face learning methods (Bersin and Associates, 2003; Garrison, Kanuka, & Hawes, 2003). In addition, blended learning is used to describe learning that mixes various event-based activities, including face-to-face classrooms, live e-learning, and self-managed and self-paced learning (Open University Malaysia, 2001; Valiathan, 2002). Within these broad categories, various other microblends might evolve. For example, at Open University Malaysia, a learner might prefer to read a standard textbook rather than the specially designed print module, attend three out of the five recommended face-to-face meetings, and be an active participant in online discussion forums.

This issue of having various mixes within the blends is growing. For example, Rossett, Douglis, and Frazee (2003) view blended learning as a variation of the following combinations of approaches: coaching by a supervisor; participation in an online class; breakfast with colleagues; reading on the beach; reference to a manual; collegial relationships; and participation in seminars, workshops, and online communities. While their description primarily relates to corporate training environments, the forms and types of blended learning in higher education are also proliferating. In higher education, a blended learning course might combine synchronous and asynchronous technologies, videoconferencing with online meetings, face-to-face orientation sessions with online modules, and online field experiences or internship reflections with live class meetings.

Research on Blended Learning

Preliminary research results show that learners in institutions that have identified the purposes of different blends tend to benefit more in terms of increased employee productivity, increased program completion rates, and improved interaction and satisfaction.

Increased Employee Productivity

A study by Thomson Corporation (2004) found that a combination of e-learning or online instruction, simulations, texts, mentor and instructor support, and live classroom-based training has the power to increase employee productivity significantly. The second phase of this study sought to identify essential instructional components of successful blended learning. Three types of blended learning solutions—instructor-led training, text-based programs, and scenario-based exercises—were compared with e-learning. The first group, instructor-led training, received scenario-based exercises. A second group, text-based programs, received scenario-based exercises that had access to text objects. A third group, scenario-based exercises, incorporated e-learning. In addition, a fourth group was given a standard e-learning course. The control group (the fifth group) was established to benchmark performance and did not receive any training. The results confirmed that a defined blended learning solution heightens overall on-the-job performance in terms of accuracy and speed compared to the performance achieved by e-learning alone. When compared with the e-learning group (fourth group), the blended learning groups (first group, second group, and third group) were 27 to 32 percent more accurate in task performance and performed the tasks 41 to 51 percent faster.

Increased Program Completion Rates

Singh and Reed (2001) conducted research at Stanford University on the mechanisms by which blended learning might be better than both traditional methods and individual forms of e-learning for motivated gifted youths. Studies provided evidence that a blended learning strategy improves learning outcomes by providing a better match between how a learner wants to learn and the learning program offered.

Singh and Reed stressed that in order for blended learning to be successful, the right ingredients for a blended program are needed. In particular, those coordinating the blended program must know or specify the target audience, content, program costs, and overall infrastructure components. When it was discovered that only about 50 percent of their highly motivated gifted youths would complete their programs, it was determined that there was a mismatch between the student's desired learning styles and the program's delivery format. The introduction of live e-learning using synchronous interaction with Centra (a software program) resulted in improved student completion rates of up to 94 percent.

Improved Interaction and Satisfaction

A study at Harvard Business School (HBS) indicated that student interaction and satisfaction improved when e-learning options were added to traditional forms of learning (DeLacey & Leonard, 2002). It was found that blending tradition with technology may be HBS's best approach for continuous renewal to develop its core capabilities around learning. HBS had integrated face-to-face classroom meetings with new approaches such as taking learning out of the classroom by including simulations, video cases, multimedia cases, computerized exercises, and polls. According to students from the Program for Global Leadership, the strengths of this approach included being able to share their learning and enter into debates with an entire online group. They also noted that online discussion provided a great learning experience. In fact, many of them wanted to keep their document and file-sharing systems online for their future projects, either academic or job related.

Research by Bersin and Associates (2003) focused on corporate blended learning programs. The principal goal of this research was to provide detailed information about real-world implementation and strategies that work. Listed below are some of their major findings.

Reason for Program Failure

From interviews with dozens of blended learning program managers, Bersin and Associates found that the biggest reason for program failure was not the content but program management. Rather than focusing on the types of media elements to blend to enhance learning, most institutions were merely managing media elements such as finding and retrieving better graphics, video clips, or animations. Technology was emphasized over the learning process or overall effectiveness.

Blended learning need not cost millions of dollars. When properly thought out, it involves selecting a dominant mode of electronic learning or media (for example, using the Web) and surrounding it with human interactive content.

An Overview of Blended and E-Learning in Malaysia

In most organizations in Malaysia, some form of blended learning is the preferred choice; however, e-learning is becoming increasingly important. A survey of e-learning initiatives, with sections on blended learning, was conducted among twenty-six organizations, including higher learning institutions, government agencies, and public libraries (Abtar, 2003). From the survey, it was found that 79 percent of these organizations used blended learning, followed by 17 percent face-to-face and 4 percent online only.

Of the twenty-six organizations that provided feedback, seventeen indicated that they had an existing strategy or policy for their e-learning approach that included some mention of off-line support due to technology challenges. The challenges were seen as threefold: (1) building sustainable Internet facilities, (2) finding or developing powerful content, and (3) managing the interactions into a knowledge database to be tapped by others in the learning environment.

Other research findings included reasons for not implementing e-learning. The barriers to e-learning implementation included e-learning course materials that were not efficiently administered in their respective organizations (23 percent), inadequate training opportunities for staff and users (15 percent), lack of organizational strategies for e-learning (15 percent), and expensive or no budget available (15 percent). Furthermore, most employees were adequately satisfied with their current face-to-face training system (12 percent).

In terms of implementing e-learning, 50 percent of the organizations surveyed planned to implement online training or e-learning programs in the next one to three years, 30 percent within a year, 10 percent within three to five years, and an additional 10 percent indicated that they had no plans. Most of the organizations in the survey agreed that online training or e-learning programs will be the dominant method of learning in the future.

Most of the organizations were in the implementation stage of their online training or e-learning development. Nine considered their e-learning activities as centralized, four were departmentally based, and three relied on individual efforts. At the operational level, learners and lower-level staff had high acceptance level for e-learning compared to top or senior management and academic or middle management staff.

In sum, although Malaysian organizations recognize that e-learning has many benefits, they are not ready to implement it in its entirety. Perhaps the key is blended learning, that is, selecting the right combination of technologies, content, activities, and learning modalities that will bring equal and satisfying returns to both the organization and the learners.

Open University Malaysia's Blended Learning Model

As an extremely young and fast-growing university, the Open University Malaysia (OUM) was established on August 10, 2000, as the seventh private university in Malaysia and started operations in August 2001. The OUM thrives on a vision "to be leader and innovator in open learning" and leverages the quality, prestige, and capabilities of its owners—a consortium of eleven Malaysian public universities. Within just three years, OUM has established itself as the first open and distance learning (ODL) higher education provider in the country. As of September 2004, it had an enrollment of close to twenty-five thousand students.

The OUM provides learners the freedom to choose where, when, and what they want to learn and how they want to go through their study programs. Due to the unique capabilities of OUM learners, such as their diverse educational and working knowledge backgrounds, access to the nearest learning center, the availability of learning time, and the accessibility to the Internet, the OUM offers flexible blended learning using three main methods: self-managed learning, face-to-face learning, and online learning (Figure 22.1). Within these three main or macromodes exist many other microapproaches. For example, in the second option of face-to-face learning, a student may opt for a formal classroom meeting of five times a semester or alternatively select a personalized study option wherein the learner formally meets the tutor twice a semester. In the following section are a few examples of the microblends within the blended pedagogy:

- A learner in the remote areas of Sabah and Sarawak in East Malaysia may depend entirely on the specially designed print module and attend three out of the five assigned face-to-face classes.
- A learner in the towns of Sabah and Sarawak in East Malaysia may use the specially designed print module as a guide, use textbooks and online digital resources as core study materials for self-managed learning, attend all five face-to-face classes, meet with peers for small-group discussions, and actively participate in online discussion forums.
- A learner in Kuala Lumpur City in West Malaysia may depend entirely on online resources (such as digital books, journal articles, and related links) and online discussions but also attend classes two out of five times, mainly to sit for the tests.

FIGURE 22.1. OPEN UNIVERSITY MALAYSIA'S BLENDED LEARNING MODEL.

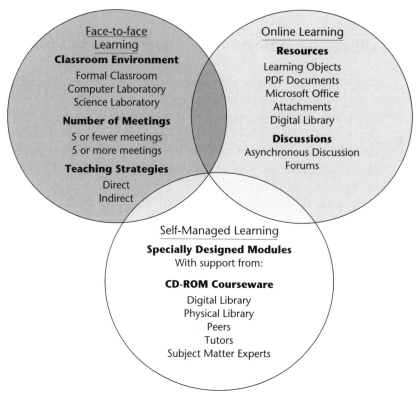

- A learner in Kuala Lumpur studying computer science might attend all five laboratory classes, use the print module as a guide, rely entirely on online resources, and meet up with the tutor on a personal arrangement.

Self-managed learning (SML) is the most important of the three methods. In fact, on average, about 70 percent of the expected forty hours of student learning time per credit is taken up with this method. Self-managed learning at the OUM is essentially based on specially constructed print-based modules supported by other forms of learning resources (CD-ROM courseware) and digital content from the OUM's digital library. At the OUM, print is the foundation of blended learning and the basis from which all other delivery systems evolve.

The modules developed at the OUM undergo a rigorous content and instructional development process, whereby it takes approximately six to eight months to produce one learning module of about two hundred pages. In the design of the module, sound pedagogical classroom-like techniques are incorporated, among which include: "think," "your idea," "activity," "take a break," and "practice exercises." The OUM takes the whole process of module design and development as something pivotal so that learners are better able to manage their own learning. We believe in the adage: "When something can be read without effort, great effort has gone into its writing."

To further support SML processes, all new learners are required to take "Learning Skills for Open Distance Learners," a three-credit-hour course that covers learning-to-learn skills, information and communication technologies (ICT) skills, and information skills. The course has had considerable success in helping learners manage their time and overcome problems of adjusting to ODL methods of learning. To date, close to five thousand students have taken the course. According to a OUM student counselor, "The number of students seeing me about coping with learning at OUM has reduced substantially after they started taking the Learning Skills for Open Distance Learners course."

Variations of self-managed learning occur depending on learner characteristics, content area, resourcefulness of the tutor and learner, the overall quality of the module, availability of learner time, and accessibility to other learning resources. In initially charting the blended learning approach, we envisaged that a learner should put in an average of two hours of self-study time per day so that they are ready for the two-hour face-to-face meeting (every two weeks) and a minimum of one and a half hours of online time weekly. Within this proposed SML time frame, other factors, such as learner resourcefulness and pivotal support on a personal basis, are key variables for SML success.

Face-to-Face Learning

Face-to-face learning brings OUM learners to a socialization stage. Adult learners at the OUM demand that their face-to-face classroom interactions be as personally gratifying as possible. Therefore, the role played by our pool of sixteen hundred part-time tutors is extremely important. Consequently, we greatly emphasize tutor effectiveness and competence.

In face-to-face interactions, OUM learners are given the option of attending classes five times in a normal fifteen-week semester, with each meeting lasting for two hours per course or subject. During the meeting, tutors are advised to conduct a mini-lesson for about twenty to thirty minutes in an area that is challenging. The rest of the time is used to conduct discussion on the given tutorial question and address student concerns. The teaching strategies employed are a mix of minilectures, discussions, exercises, hands-on activities, and presentations. Although students are required to meet five times a semester for two hours, the face-to-face methods may be blended; thus, the meeting can occur two to eight times and last anywhere from one hour to four hours, depending on the need to conduct laboratory work. The appropriate blends depend on the number and variety of students, the total classroom climate (structure, interactions, and resources), tutor experience, and learner as well as tutor readiness.

Where tutor readiness is concerned, tutor recruitment, selection, and training are given high priority. Toward this end, the ODL Pedagogy Center has been established to investigate all issues pertaining to tutor effectiveness. The pedagogy center has the support of close to forty lead tutors who were selected based on their performance in the OUM. Together, tutors are constantly trained, monitored, advised, and counseled so that they are giving their best to students. Thus far, evaluations on tutor effectiveness from 4,903 students related to 193 of the 672 tutors for the May 2004 semester among others show that more than 90 percent of OUM tutors were eager to support learners in their learning processes, well prepared for all tutorials, competent in the subject, and pivotal in helping learners understand the content area (ODL Pedagogy Center, 2004).

Online Learning

At the OUM, online learning is another method for reaching and supporting learners by providing the best possible method of harnessing the Internet and related technologies to create an effective and efficient learning support system that complements self-managed learning and face-to-face classroom interactions. The online or virtual classroom consists of all elements found in an actual classroom. In addition, two key instructional perspectives and practices are expected to evolve: (1) learner-centered learning and (2) resource-centered learning. In learner-centered learning, the focus is on learner engagement in active and interactive learning. In active learning, the learner may take a pretest to determine his or her level of understanding of a particular chapter in the module, or enhance his or her knowledge by trying out the digital learning objects; both of these are individual or self-paced activities. In interactive learning, the learner may engage in an asynchronous discussion forum to contribute ideas related to a particular topic of interest with the intent of achieving the following results: elevated content understanding, improved cognitive ability or higher-order thinking, and enhanced collaborative and cooperative learning skills. In fact, OUM learners receive up to 5 percent of their final grade on the level of their participation in online discussions.

In learner-centered learning, the role of the online tutor is important. The OUM notes that the online tutor is to provide "learning support by stimulating discussions to enhance learners' collaborative, content and thinking skills, support learners in increasing ownership of learning and enable flexible, lifelong learning" (Open University Malaysia, 2004, p. 14). Since the virtual classroom is an extension of the actual classroom where face-to-face learning occurs, we expect online tutors to play an equally effective role. As aptly noted by Salmon and Giles (1997), high-quality online tutoring is really no different from excellence in other forms of teaching. Excellent online instruction, like its face-to-face counterpart, requires instructor enthusiasm, continued involvement, intellectual engagement of students, perceptions of problems in understanding, continued insight, and the ability to model an understanding of subject matter. In effect, online instruction must be highly interactive and collaborative.

In resource-centered learning, the online learner can get access to at least 40,000 titles of digital books; 150 titles of online dictionaries, encyclopedias, handbooks, and thesauruses; close to 11,000 journal articles; and about 1,000 journal titles. Apart from that, digitized versions of print modules and specially designed digital content, and other tutor-created content (such as PowerPoint slides, Word documents, and Excel sheets and files) are available. These resources are highly important, as OUM learners are distributed and such immediate access to learning resources will aid them in obtaining the right mix for maximizing their learning time.

To support the OUM's online endeavors, a learning management system, myLMS (see Figure 22.2), has been built, and successfully used by close to 80 percent of our students.

FIGURE 22.2. myLMS ENTRY Page.

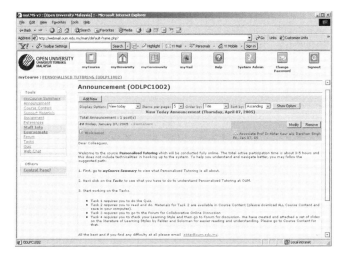

Note: For more information on myLMS, visit the OUM Web site at www.oum.edu.my.

Blended Learning Challenges at Open University Malaysia

Despite the OUM's ideals of providing a blended learning environment suited to working adults, there are many challenges that we face and continue to address.

Democratization of Education

While the OUM is championing democratization of education, the use of technology will inevitably lead to some form of exclusivity. However, at the OUM, our philosophy is that no learner will be excluded since a variety of media will be used. Thus, we have a delicate task of ensuring that learners are constantly supported so that the digital gap is minimized. The concept of lifelong learning indicates that learning, unlearning, and relearning with regard to technology are perpetuated. In order to narrow the digital divide, the OUM is in discussions with several telecommunications companies, computer and software manufacturers, and financial institutions to provide our students with attractive and affordable computer packages bundled with the right software and relatively cheap broadband access.

Optimization of Resources

There are variations to the resources available at our respective learning centers. Hence, the optimization of these resources is critical to ensure that all OUM learners receive the best learning support so that media can be effectively used based on their characteristics and potential effectiveness. The challenge is in identifying the appropriate resources and using them to benefit OUM learners. Of course, in some remote areas, the best resources are the teacher, the board, and the book. In the light of the fact that total tutor effectiveness is a factor beyond the OUM's control, identifying some basic resources such as videotapes and audiotapes may be a good alternative to online learning.

Efficiency

Learners demand efficiency in the different methods offered. More crucial is the fact that they hold on to the 24/7 concept of learning and expect quick responses and rapid feedback. Tutors, for their part, are not totally committed to the OUM since they are typically recruited on a part-time basis. Thus, we have a difficult and sometimes thorny situation of unequal commitments, which becomes an enormous task to tackle. The appointment of lead tutors from the best of the tutors has helped to increase commitment as well as strengthen the OUM's tutor support system. In addition, the university will be introducing scholarship awards for tutors to further their studies at the OUM. It is hoped that these measures will increase the tutors' level of commitment.

Pedagogical Effectiveness

As much as we try to be rigorous in our choice of tutors for enhanced pedagogy, maintaining individual effectiveness can be an arduous task as tutors carry forward their old mental schemata of teaching and learning. Constant improvement of the tutor training materials as well as close supervision and coaching of the tutors in the performance of their duties is helping to alleviate this problem.

Suitability of Blended Approach

The issue of whether the three methods of learning (self-managed learning, face-to-face learning, and online learning) are a suitable and effective mix is an ongoing challenge. We are continually challenging ourselves as to the combinations that will maximize student learning. For example, we have started to explore on-the-job coaching, mentoring, and modeling in place of face-to-face meetings. At the OUM, we are constantly studying the educational environment, including our selection of ODL providers, in order to find the most effective mix.

Effectiveness of Blended Approach

How effectively are the different learning methods and options capitalized on by both learners and tutors? For example, in self-managed learning, are students sufficiently skilled and competent to maximize the learning impact of the modules, CD-ROM courseware, and associated digital library collections? Is learning effectiveness improved when they consult tutors and peers? Are tutors effectively supporting learners as envisioned by OUM? How might these tutors and peers be trained to provide more effective consulting? To address these challenges, periodic surveys are carried out to obtain feedback from learners, tutors, and administrators on the effectiveness of our primary methods. This constant attention to the mix of options ensures that students are getting the best possible pedagogy.

Implementation Issues

What may retard the effective implementation of the blended pedagogy? For example, online learning processes may encounter problems because of connectivity issues, a student's inability to purchase a computer, and tutors who are not proficient in providing adequate and appropriate online support.

Sustainability

Can we sustain all the blended pedagogy? Will increasing numbers of students enrolled in OUM programs mean we may have to switch to different and more innovative blends, specifically where face-to-face learning is concerned? This is an important issue for the OUM. In fact, we are finding that as the number of students increases exponentially—as we have experienced at the OUM during the past three years—the infrastructure and infostructure constraints and barriers have to be addressed. We are reaching maximum capacity at many of our associated learning centers. As an alternative, the OUM will introduce more opportunities for personalized (self-paced or individualized) learning.

Flexibility to Change

Will students buy into new ideas and strategies used by the OUM? Will the institution make forthcoming changes seamless? Adults are extremely sensitive to constant changes, which could be detrimental to their studies. The OUM has continually been fine-tuning its blended pedagogy. Each time we have introduced change, we took great pains to explain to the students the reasons. This open and transparent dialogue has made it easier to introduce changes.

Courseware Development

Despite the availability of sufficient print, Internet links, and digital library resources, the OUM still faces several significant challenges in courseware development. Effective courseware is crucial for subjects that are not readily understood because the content involves abstract or complex concepts that often can be made understandable only with graphics, animation, and video. Developing interactive and effective courseware requires the skills of good instructional design and content expertise.

Future Plans

Despite the challenges, OUM's future plans are in high gear as the student body is set to increase and will soon include students from other countries. We have started plans to incorporate mobile technology in a more rigorous manner as our initial studies show that more learners have mobile phones than Internet lines. We are also looking into the possibility of offering more personalized learning with such technologies. In terms of hands-on learning, we are planning to develop virtual laboratories for engineering and science-related courses. Video streaming is another option that has recently been implemented and been well received. As technology becomes more seamless in certain sections of the country, we are preparing a more advanced version of blended and collaborative online learning.

Conclusion

Blended learning is and will be the main form of pedagogical orientation for the Open University Malaysia. Currently, print-based materials form the main resources for self-managed learning. We foresee that digital resources will play a more prominent role in the future of the OUM. In particular, the availability of cheaper mobile ICT infrastructure will be a key contributing factor for this transition. Such orientations and changes toward Web-based learning will not significantly affect the current emphasis of having self-managed learning form the core pedagogical blend at the OUM as it caters well for our working adult learners. However, we foresee the virtual classroom becoming a more significant component than actual classroom interactions. The contributing factors to this shift to online learning will be continuing technological advancements (including better Internet connectivity), more acceptance for this type of learning among Malaysians, and better-trained online tutors. In sum, the blended pedagogy of self-managed learning, face-to-face learning, and online learning will be maintained, but changes will occur in the importance of each method in creating the right mix for our students.

References

Abtar, K. (2003, October). *E-learning initiatives in Malaysia*. Paper presented at E-Learning Symposium, Kuala Lumpur.

Bersin and Associates. (2003, May). *Blended learning: What works?* Retrieved August 14, 2004, from http://www.e-learningguru.com/wpapers/blended_bersin.doc.

DeLacey, B. J., & Leonard, D. A. (2002). Case study on technology and distance in education at the Harvard Business School. *Educational Technology and Society 5*(2). Retrieved August 14, 2004, from http://ifets.ieee.org/periodical/vol_2_2002/delacey.html.

Garrison, R., Kanuka, H., & Hawes, D. (2004). Blended learning in a research university. *Learning Commons: Communities of Inquiry*. University of Calgary, Retrieved August 14, 2004, from http://www.commons.ucalgary.ca/documents/BlendedLearning_1.pdf.

ODL Pedagogy Center. (2004, August 24). *Tutor monitoring report for Tutorial 2 and Tutorial 4*. Report presented at the 55th Dean's Meeting, Open University Malaysia, Kuala Lumpur.

Open University Malaysia. (2001). *OUM learner's guide to open and distance learning*. Kuala Lumpur.

Open University Malaysia. (2004). *September tutor training manual*. Kuala Lumpur.

Rossett, A., Douglis, F., & Frazee, R.V. (2003, June 30). Strategies for building blended learning. *Learning Circuits*. Retrieved August 14, 2004, from http://www.learningcircuits.org/2003/jul2003/rossett.htm.

Salmon, G., & Giles, K. (1997). *Moderating online*. Paper presented at Online Educa Berlin. Retrieved August 14, 2004, from http://www.atimod.com/presentations/MOD.html.

Singh, H., & Reed, C. (2001). *A white paper: Achieving success with blended learning.* Centra Software. Retrieved August 14, 2004, from http://www.centra.com/download/whitepapers/blendedlearning.pdf.

Thomson Corporation (2004, February 24). *Thomson job impact study confirms blended learning yields up to 163 percent increase in on-the-job performance.* Santa Clara, CA: Learning Solutions Alliance. Retrieved August 14, 2004, from http://www.learningsolutions.com/right_page/Best_Practices/blended.html.

Valiathan, P. (2002, August). Blended learning models. *Learning Circuits.* Retrieved August 14, 2004, from http://www.learningcircuits.org/2002/aug2002/valiathan.html.

Abtar Kaur has twenty-two years of teaching and instructional design experience at various levels of learning. Her expertise is in instructional technology, having received her M.S. in instructional design and Ph.D. in Web-based learning. Currently, Kaur is heading the Open and Distance Learning Pedagogy Centre, Open University Malaysia, where she oversees a group in enhancing teaching and learning in actual and virtual classrooms. Abtar is a Fulbright recipient and has served on the following advisory committees: Program Committee of ED-MEDIA, Online Educa Berlin, and EISTA Conference. She has presented widely in international conferences as an invited speaker, and her most recent writing and research are related to e-learning. To date, two papers on learning objects that she co-wrote and presented had been given Best Paper Awards by EISTA and Sloan-C.

Ansary Ahmed graduated with a bachelor of science in microbiology from the University of Liverpool and received his Ph.D. in molecular biology from the University of Manchester. He started his career as a tutor and received a full professorship in 1998. At the University of Malaya, he held the following posts: head of the Department of Genetics, deputy dean of the faculty of science, and dean of the Institute of Postgraduate Studies and Research. At the national level, he was a member of National Bio-technology Group, National Coordinator for Molecular Biology Cooperative Centre, and head of the Pharmaceutical Secretariat for the Malaysian Industry Government Group for High Technology. Currently, he serves as a senior consultant for the same organizations. He left the University of Malaya and joined the Open University of Malaysia as its senior vice president in April 2002.

CHAPTER TWENTY-THREE

BLENDING ON AND OFF CAMPUS

A Tale of Two Cities

Geraldine Lefoe, John G. Hedberg

From an examination of two universities in different cities, this chapter discusses the ideas that they have emphasized in blended learning and the lessons that can be drawn for others moving into the field and seeking to form a successful implementation.

The past decade has seen unprecedented change in higher education throughout the world. Predictions of wholesale moves to totally online degrees, greeted initially with enthusiasm and by some with total skepticism, have proved elusive. The recent closure of the U.K. eUniversities Worldwide (UKeU) follows earlier failures of such schemes in the United States, where the low numbers of enrolled students indicate that this is not always what the majority of students seek for their university education. When reporting on the closure of the UKeU, the funding body noted that universities now favored a blended approach "involving a mixture of IT, traditional, work-based and distance learning to meet the diverse needs of students" (Higher Education Funding Council for England, 2004). While some distance education universities and their partners have achieved moderate success in the area, many campus-based universities, especially in Australia, have taken a more conservative approach, opting to increase student numbers through the expansion of their structures through the creation of international partnerships.

Many higher education institutions have been bombarded with change efforts, driven by the new market economy that found universities competing for funds in a changed resource environment (Adams, 2002). Universities looked beyond their walls for ways to increase funds and became more entrepreneurial in their outlook through the inclusion of full fee-paying international students and more vocationally oriented postgraduate courses to raise revenue (Gallagher, 2000). They looked offshore, forming relationships with other institutions to provide a university education in partnership or establishing their own offshore campuses.

Universities worldwide were finding it difficult to meet the challenge of decreased funding from government sources with requirements to improve access to education and the quality of the educational experience, pressures, and agendas supported by government reports (National Board of Employment Education and Training, 1996). While attempting to reduce costs created a challenge for universities, many believed this could be met by improving teaching and learning, especially with information and communication technologies (Yetton & Associates, 1997).

However, the history of technological innovation in higher education (Hedberg & McNamara, 2002) demonstrates that technological solutions do not always address pedagogical needs of learners and teachers. The educational technology literature supports the view that pedagogy, not technology, should determine how it is best used (Collis & Moonen, 2001; Laurillard, 2002). As the use of technology matures in the learning environment in higher education, a more pragmatic approach is being demonstrated. Universities are combining the best features of distance and face-to-face learning environments to produce blended learning environments supported by the use of technology.

An effective blended learning environment takes a learning design approach that looks at the learning goals and aligns them with teaching and learning activities and assessments, thereby ensuring the integration and appropriate use of technology (Boud & Prosser, 2002). This integration can also be reflected in the wider university through, for example, the provision of student portals where students can manage and interact with all administrative areas, including subject choice, timetable changes, and personal information management (Cornford & Pollock, 2003).

This chapter examines two examples of blended learning implementation in two vastly different universities. One is a regional university in Australia; the other is one of the three state-funded universities in Singapore.

Background to Each Context

The Australian university adopted a blended approach to meet the requirements of institutional change that resulted in a radical change to the nature of the student body. The composition changed from a largely local body of students, attending the local campus and coming straight from high school, to one that included a diverse range of students, in a number of locations, and a significant increase in the percentage of mature-age and international students. We provide an overview of the strategic changes this university made to pedagogy and an example of implementation of a new degree developed specifically for students located at a satellite campus and access centers. From this case study, we identify aspects of blended learning that support and challenge improvements for student learning.

In contrast, the Singapore institution adopted the technologies as part of a major government initiative to quickly develop the technical expertise of its teachers and students. The employment of information and communication technologies in blended ways was seen as a mechanism by which the university would be able to participate in global alliances and demonstrate levels of sophistication in modern teaching approaches. From these contexts, we develop some broader ideas that are still proving elusive as the institution attempts to change its teaching strategies and create greater invention and challenge in the curriculum. We use the Singapore institution by way of a contrasting and matching comparison as we explore the blended learning context.

Government imperatives to increase access to higher education for rural and remote students in Australia provided a large pool of money for the development of satellite campuses and access centers. Many universities took advantage of this opportunity with the resultant expansion to multicampus institutions. The use of technology combined with a desire for increased flexibility for students, saw a blended approach to teaching and learning underpin many of the developments, combining strategies from distance and traditional education with many of the latest technological developments. Several studies, in fact, documented the challenges in establishing these new learning environments (Chalmers, 1999; Taylor, 1999).

In Singapore, it was a series of government initiatives that challenged the whole of the educational sector over two separate five-year master plans to review their approaches to teaching and learning and employ the technologies in more creative and engaging ways. Thus, the emphasis was on the modernization of educational practice, some improvement to the learning experience for the student often taught in large classes, and the use of the most modern tools to familiarize a technically oriented workforce.

Blended Learning in Wollongong

The University of Wollongong is a regional university in southeastern Australia with approximately twenty thousand students. It includes the main campus in Wollongong, a campus in Dubai in the United Arab Emirates, a satellite campus about one hour from Wollongong, and four access centers for students (up to four hours' drive from the main campus). The university received substantial government funding to establish the satellite campus and centers to promote access to education for students in remote and regional areas. Blended learning involved a number of early adopters in the mid-1990s, but by 2000, the impetus for change was driven by the needs of the Australian and overseas students studying away from the main campus.

At the University of Wollongong, approximately 35 percent are international students, with two-thirds of this group studying on the Wollongong campus and the rest studying in their homeland through partner universities or at the Dubai campus. Only 50 percent of students are studying full time. A large portion are mature-age students, often balancing work, home, and study. Finally, with only 25 percent of all students under age twenty-one, there is a much smaller cohort who have just completed secondary school. Many of the school leaver cohort are also working part time to support themselves while at the university. As a result, such individuals require flexibility but still want an on-campus experience and opportunity to work with and meet other students and their lecturers.

A single model of blended learning would not meet the needs of the different student groups, and consequently a variety of models are in use. They may vary from a traditional one-hour lecture, two-hour tutorial with supplementary resources provided through a Web-based learning management system (LMS) for students on campus to subjects where the majority of communication and collaboration occurs online with only occasional face-to-face meetings with tutors. Other subjects rely on Web-based streaming audio of lectures supplemented by resources accessed through the LMS but supported by weekly face-to-face tutorials with a local tutor. Many of the overseas cohorts see a different blended model, whereby they meet regularly with a local tutor to work on identified learning tasks designed by the Wollongong lecturer and then come together for a block teaching session of a few days once during the semester to meet with the lecturer.

A recent case study at University of Wollongong provides an example of how subjects are tailored to meet the needs of the students (Lefoe, 2003). The bachelor of arts in community and environment was a new degree program developed specifically for the satellite campus and access centers. The program was designed to be flexible in terms of time and place. This involved a blended approach that combined reduced face-to-face teaching with both synchronous and asynchronous interaction, often mediated by technology, to produce an environment for learning that is student centered. Because the locations were geographically distributed, the teaching and learning activities were dispersed across a number of settings, including the centers, the library, the main campus, and the student's home; across time; and through a variety of technologies, including print, videoconferencing, and online tools.

The core subjects in the arts degree were not designed to use traditional lecture delivery methods for transmitting information to students. They used a student-centered approach, requiring students to take responsibility for learning the content through reading material themselves, watching a video, or engaging in activities during the tutorial and then making their own connections with the concepts discussed or presented in the tutorials or practicals. Students were required to prepare for the tutorials in some subjects by reading the lecture notes or content modules before attending the tutorial, so that they could participate in the tutorial activities and discussions.

There were seven subjects offered in 2000 through the bachelor of arts, which included five required subjects and two elective subjects. The perceptions of academic staff and students on the first year of implementation of four subjects were assessed through focus groups, semistructured interviews with staff and students, and subject surveys.

There were a variety of teaching and learning strategies in the first year. Tutorial or practical support was provided locally through tutors, while course design and coordination occurred at the Wollongong campus. A number of common themes emerged in the perceptions of the benefits of teaching and learning in a blended learning context. The supportive areas identified included:

- The opportunity for students and tutors to participate in higher education in their local community
- The commitment of the local tutors and the benefit of the small tutorial classes to student learning
- The student-centered subject designs, which included workbooks or study guides containing learning objectives, content, learning activities, and assessment tasks

Six common themes were identified in the perceptions expressed by those interviewed regarding the constraints of teaching and learning in a blended learning context:

- Teaching and learning strategies chosen were not always the most appropriate.
- Emerging roles were different from those experienced on campus.
- Improved communication was required between the main campus and the centers.
- A need to develop new skills and understandings related to the changed learning environment.
- Workloads were perceived as high by students and staff.
- The role of technology was new and unfamiliar.

Singaporean Blended Learning Contrasts

Singapore is a nation-state of approximately 4 million people. The major resource is seen as the people, and indeed the educational systems and aspirations seem to be overarching issues in daily life. Access to schools and universities is highly competitive, and the demand far outstrips the places available. The undergraduate programs are largely populated by students who have come directly from school; only in the postgraduate courses do mature-age students predominate. However, the strong tradition for many polytechnic diploma students to study offshore to gain their degrees has created increased interest in enrolling some of these students in the undergraduate programs. These students are also slightly older and often more prepared to study in blended learning contexts.

Overall, the tertiary system is highly evolved, with a strong emphasis on business, technical, manufacturing, and the new information economies. Unlike situations in larger countries, blended learning for most Singaporean students is a convenience to decouple time and space rather than a necessity for access. However, travel, while not costly, is time-consuming.

While blended strategies are used in on-campus courses, largely they have been supplementary rather than key to addressing core pedagogy. The challenges of campus extension have largely not been present. However, while students have attitudes with varying degrees of ambivalence toward the blending of approaches, some notable initiatives in terms of strategic benefits about the nature of blending have been adopted. Blended approaches have been used to support international linkages and establish specialized niches for a high level of technical skill. Alliances have been developed with prestigious international institutions to leverage off postgraduate specializations with particular relevance to a planned and controlled economy. Once such alliance has been with Massachusetts Institute of Technology to teach a special master's program in engineering. Here, the technological connection was maintained with video recording and conferencing to expertise in North America, with local tutors providing face-to-face support. Interestingly, the program also supports and attracts students from other Southeast Asian countries to study in Singapore. Thus, this linkage is seen as a less expensive alternative to living overseas and with the benefits of accessing cutting-edge ideas. This approach to learning also supports the government's initiative to become an educational hub.

Another unique point of departure is the use of blended approaches that focus more on matching the technology's affordances and the learning task. Choosing learning tasks, which cannot be undertaken without a blended approach, is not just a convenience but a necessity. One such initiative is the development of students' creative skills as they can be applied to the design and programming of computer games. Rather then simply playing these games, students integrate skills sets that have practical commercial potential.

Learning from the Tale of Two Cities

While the two contexts we are describing are very different, there are some common elements that can provide some guidance in selecting and designing blended learning contexts.

Student-Centered Teaching and Learning Strategies Build on Blended Contexts

Delivering and accessing a blended program requires new ways of thinking about teaching and learning. In the Wollongong case, the project team had determined that traditional teaching paradigms used at the main campus would not meet the needs of students and academic staff in the distributed context. This meant that the courses had to include appropriate learning outcomes, teaching and learning strategies, content provision, assessment strategies, and learning resources, as identified in models of teaching and learning in higher education (Biggs, 1999; Laurillard, 2002; Ramsden, 1992). Such courses typically include an activity-focused study guide, which incorporates more than just content or lecture notes by providing scaffolding for student learning. They also require strategies that engage students by encouraging them to make the links between theory and practice and provide feedback on students' learning performance. The Wollongong course developers devoted significant time and energy to reconceptualizing teaching and learning activities, so that the students could make and use their own professional role contexts as the basis for their understandings. A curriculum focus on interdisciplinarity also emphasizes the need for students to draw links and comparisons beyond narrow subject domains. Blended approaches are ideal for presenting illustrations from different areas, and online components can support access to a wide diversity of resources, which can be integrated by students as part of their assessable tasks. In the Singapore context, this approach is also used; however, the focus on international business issues and linkages with the large economies of China, India, and the United States requires the compilation and explication of multicultural resources.

At Wollongong, there is also a corollary: new course coordinators and other members of the faculty were not involved in the initial design process and did not have the same opportunity to develop the new conceptions required to move from a teacher-centered approach to a student-centered approach. This resulted in some course implementation that differed from the original design and caused concern for students. Students and tutors perceive the courses that support student-centered approaches to learning as more appropriate in a blended context.

Establish Clear Roles and Responsibilities

A dominant theme from the perceptions of students, tutors, and course coordinators is the need for clarity of the roles they play in a distributed learning context. This affects the level of responsibility they assume for aspects of teaching and learning. In the Wollongong case, students indicated some uncertainty about their roles, a common problem for first-year university students (Pargetter, McInnis, James, Evans, & Dobson, 1998). In a student-centered learning environment, students need to understand their own role and that of their instructor, since this may differ considerably from their previous experience if they have participated only in teacher-centered instruction, such as at high school. If students are to take responsibility for their learning, they need to have a clear idea of what this entails. From both cases, the more mature students are often more comfortable with this expectation.

New roles are also required in the distributed learning context. Course coordinators, for instance, saw their role as administrative; however, the distributed context meant that they needed to take more responsibility for communication with the tutors and students and also had a more proactive student adviser role. In the Wollongong context, one coordinator felt his responsibility ended with the preparation of the resources, and in another, the coordinator taught the same subject to 180 students on campus. In both cases, they responded to questions from the tutors but had little contact with the students. As roles emerge, it is important to recognize the need for supportive understanding of the changes required and to acknowledge the changes through policy documents, to suggest new forms of communication, and to clarify roles through clear statements of expectations and responsibilities.

Ensure Communication Matches the Type of Blending

In the evaluation of the Wollongong experience, communication was identified as the third concern for students and tutors. Collaboration between the course coordinators and tutors across the distributed sites may have prevented some specific problems. Such problems included an inconsistency with implementation and marking of an assessment in one course, and the perception of the coordinator in another course that students were not capable of the work, yet they achieved better grades than the main campus cohort in the final results. Regular meetings during the semester would have helped to address these problems. For example, given the distance, they could have used teleconferencing, chat, or video-conferencing if people were available at the same time, or they may have used an asynchronous discussion forum or e-mail to address concerns and share strategies. The divergence between design and teaching expectations has not been as critical when the one teacher is responsible for both.

In one instance, while student-student and student-tutor interaction was high because of the small numbers, interaction between the course coordinators and the students was low and often just to solve specific problems. The research on student-faculty interaction points to the importance for student learning of this kind of interaction (Pascarella & Terenzini, 1998). The students and the tutors in one course responded positively to a videoconference the coordinator held after complaints of too little interaction during the semester. Regular face-to-face meetings or videoconferencing two or three times during the session can improve relationships and address concerns for many students. This indicates the possibility of finding ways to communicate between the groups that harness the affordances of the technology when face-to-face meetings are not possible, thereby helping to remove feelings of isolation from activities and people at the main campus (Collis, 1998; Kuh & Hu, 2001).

Develop Supporting Academic Skills and Understandings

While support is provided for students though the library, student support, and information technology services, finding ways to encourage students to access this support needs further attention. Even when skill development support was provided during orientation, some students require support beyond the initial orientation for the development of new academic and technical skills, especially when they are in their first year (Taylor & Blaik, 2002). Students often require skill development for technical and information literacy and for tertiary literacy skills development. They need effective just-in-time support, but to make use of this support, they need knowledge of the support that is available and flexible access to it (Choy, McNickle, & Clayton, 2002). Incorporating skill development such as computer and essay-writing skills within core courses could improve the overall outcomes for students.

Support and encouragement is required for tutors and academic staff to engage with their changed roles and responsibilities to develop basic student skills, and this needs to be enhanced by changes in the institutional recognition, reward, and incentive systems (Anderson, Johnson, & Saha, 2002; University of Queensland, 2002). Interestingly in the Singapore context, this has always been a component of the staff role, since for many students, English is a second or third language, so most programs include specific writing and communication components.

For the tutors, such changes might include recognition of the additional workload in this role through financial rewards for extra hours resulting from the blended model and provision of office space and access to resources. Tutors also need to be included in the culture of the faculty through acknowledgment of their skills and expertise. For this to occur, it will require the establishment of effective policies on the working conditions and roles of tutors.

For the course coordinators, there will be changes in workload allocations, which take into account the changed nature of the work (Coaldrake & Stedman, 1999; McInnis, 2000) and policy changes, which reflect the changed role of the course coordinator in a blended learning context. Such actions will require changes to the institutional rewards and incentives systems that truly value teaching as much as research, especially in the promotions system.

Expect Higher Workloads with Blended Learning

At Wollongong, students, tutors, and course coordinators identified increased workloads in the blended learning context. Some students perceived the workload as high and measured their workload as related to the amount of time they spent on campus or in an access center. The reduction of face-to-face time meant increased responsibility for students to work outside the class. Not surprisingly, such an expectation needed to be made clearer to students. In two courses, students specifically commented on the high workload. For one course, this was due to misunderstanding of the requirements of the assessment task in one center, and, in another course, this was due to the separation between the lecture material and the practical classes. A tutor expressed concern that students saw the independent work they were required to do as additional to their load rather than as part of the student role in this environment.

Research on student workload points to the importance of balancing workload for students. Some studies report that students will adopt a surface approach to learning when they identify workload as high (Kember & Leung, 1998; Ramsden, 1992). Niklova and Collis (1998) point out that in a student-centered learning environment, students are expected to be more independent and require "self-initiative, self-motivation, and self-control" (p. 60). They caution that increased flexibility for the learner correlates with greater workloads for the teacher as academic staff move to "consultant, collaborator, and facilitator" (p. 60).

Choose Appropriate Technologies for the Learning Tasks

Technology plays a critical role in the delivery of blended courses that use communication technologies to carry the key information and interactions, such as videoconferencing, audiotapes and videotapes, e-mail, and aspects of a LMS. The use of technology requires the development of new skills for students, tutors, and lecturers. The participants often report concerns about inappropriate use of technology, such as videotaped lectures and online lecture notes; the need to learn computer literacy skills; technical difficulties with equipment, including the videoconferencing facility, computers, and printers; and the difficulties of relying on critically time- and place-dependent media like videoconferencing, which invariably requires technical support to be available.

Students support the use of technology when they feel it enhances the learning experience. For example when interactive Web-based content was provided in one course, and, in another, where videoconference was used for tutorials, students felt positive about the experience once they overcame their initial concerns about the technology-mediated environment. In the brief Singapore example, when the curriculum and pedagogy is built around the inherent technology affordances, the match and relevance are quite clear to both students and staff.

Conclusion

While quality, access, and cost are identified as major issues for higher education in the future, sustainability of new developments in an era of increased workload and the lack of downtime is becoming a major contention for academic staff. The notion of blended learning, combining the best features of traditional and distance education with appropriate use of the affordances of technology, may serve the sector well, allowing a better balance between teaching and research but still providing the quality and flexibility that students and faculty expect of a university. However, the critical factor will be juggling the pedagogical options so that the reduction in face-to-face contact hours and an increase in asynchronous interactions do not become opportunities to expand the working events of faculty to fill the remaining time. Time needs to be provided for knowledge generation and planning activities, not just the servicing of students' immediate learning needs. Getting the right mix in the blended learning context will be the challenge for the future.

References

Adams, D. (2002). The unintended consequences of deregulation: Australian higher education in the marketplace. In P. Trowler (Ed.), *Higher education policy and institutional change: Intentions and outcomes in turbulent environments* (pp. 108–125). Buckingham: Society for Research in Higher Education and Open University Press.

Anderson, D., Johnson, R., & Saha, L. (2002). *Changes in academic work: Implications for universities of the changing age, distribution and work roles of academic staff.* Canberra: Department of Education, Science and Technology.

Biggs, J. (1999). *Teaching for quality learning at university: What the student does.* Buckingham: Society for Research in Higher Education and Open University Press.

Boud, D., & Prosser, M. (2002). Appraising new technologies for learning: A framework for development. *Educational Media International, 39*(3/4), 237–245.

Chalmers, D. (1999). A strategic university-wide initiative to introduce programs of study using flexible delivery methods. *Interactive Learning Environments, 7*(2–3), 249–268.

Choy, S., McNickle, C., & Clayton, B. (2002). *Learner expectations and experiences: An examination of student views of support in online learning.* Leabrook, South Australia: National Council for Vocational Education Research.

Coaldrake, P., & Stedman, L. (1999). *Academic work in the twenty-first century. Changing roles and policies.* Canberra: Department of Education, Training and Youth Affairs. Retrieved September 28, 2000, from http://www.deet.gov.au/highered/occpaper/99H/academic.pdf.

Collis, B. (1998). New didactics for university instruction: How and why? *Computers and Education, 31,* 373–393.

Collis, B., & Moonen, J. (2001). *Flexible learning in a digital world: Experiences and expectations.* London: Kogan Page.

Cornford, J., & Pollock, N. (2003). *Putting the university online: Information, technology and organizational change.* Buckingham: Society for Research in Higher Education and Open University Press.

Gallagher, M. (2000, September). *The emergence of entrepreneurial public universities in Australia.* Paper presented at the Institutional Management in Higher Education General Conference of the Organization for Economic Cooperation and Development, Paris.

Hedberg, J., & McNamara, S. (2002). Innovation and reinvention: A brief review of educational technology in Australia. *Educational Media International, 39*(2), 111–121.

Higher Education Funding Council for England. (2004, February 27). *HEFCE to discuss restructuring of e-universities venture: Background statement.* Retrieved July 22, 2004, from http://www.hefce.ac.uk/News/HEFCE/2004/euni/further.asp.

Kember, D., & Leung, D.Y.P. (1998). Influences upon students' perceptions of workload. *Educational Psychology, 18*(3), 293–307.

Kuh, G. D., & Hu, S. (2001). The effects of student-faculty interaction in the 1990s. *Review of Higher Education, 24*(3), 309–332.

Laurillard, D. (2002). *Rethinking university teaching: A conversational framework for the effective use of learning technologies.* London: Routledge Falmer.

Lefoe, G. (2003). *Characteristics of a supportive context for distributed learning: A case study of the implementation of a new degree.* Unpublished doctoral dissertation, University of Wollongong.

McInnis, C. (2000). *The work roles of academics in Australian universities.* Canberra: Australian Government Publishing Service. Retrieved May 25, 2001, from http://www.dest.gov.au/archive/highered/eippubs/eip00_5/fullcopy.pdf.

National Board of Employment Education and Training. (1996). *Equality, diversity and excellence: Advancing the national framework for higher education equity.* Canberra: Australian Government Publishing Service.

Niklova, I., & Collis, B. (1998). Flexible learning and the design of instruction. *British Journal of Educational Technology, 29*(1), 59–72.

Pargetter, R., McInnis, C., James, R., Evans, M., & Dobson, I. (1998). *Transition from secondary to tertiary: A performance study.* Canberra: Australian Government Publishing Service.

Pascarella, E. T., & Terenzini, P. T. (1998). Studying college students in the 21st century: Meeting new challenges. *Review of Higher Education, 21*(2), 151–165.

Ramsden, P. (1992). *Learning to teach in higher education.* New York: Routledge.

Taylor, P. G. (1999). *Making sense of academic life: Academics, universities, and change.* Philadelphia: Open University Press.

Taylor, P. G., & Blaik, J. (2002). *What have we learned? The Logan Campus 1998–2001.* Unpublished report. Brisbane: Griffith Institute of Higher Education.

University of Queensland. (2002). *Training, managing and supporting sessional teaching staff.* Retrieved February 28, 2003, from http://www.tedi.uq.edu.au/sessionalteaching/home_frameset.html.

Yetton, P., & Associates. (1997). *Managing the introduction of technology in the delivery and administration of Higher Education.* Canberra: Australian Government Publishing Service. Retrieved June 1, 1998 from http://www.detya.gov.au/highered/eippubs/eip97_3.

 Geraldine Lefoe is a lecturer in the Centre for Educational Development and Interactive Resources at the University of Wollongong, Australia. She coordinates the academic staff development program and collaborates with faculty on pedagogically driven integration of technology in course development. Her research interests include new models for staff development in higher education and designs for blended learning environments. She is an executive member of the Australasian Society for Computers in Learning in Tertiary Education (ASCILITE) and coordinates the ASCILITE Community Mentoring Program.

 John G. Hedberg is Millennium Innovations Chair of ICT and Education at Macquarie University in Sydney, Australia, and is director of the Macquarie ICT Innovations Centre. He was previously professor of learning sciences and technologies at Nanyang Technological University, Singapore. He has previously worked with Geraldine Lefoe on several projects at the University of Wollongong. His most recent book is *Evaluating Interactive Learning Systems,* coauthored with Thomas Reeves.

CHAPTER TWENTY-FOUR

BLENDED LEARNING AT CANADIAN UNIVERSITIES

Issues and Practices

Ronald D. Owston, D. Randy Garrison, Kathryn Cook

There is a growing recognition and belief that the quality of higher education cannot be ensured by continuing with the current models of instructional design and delivery. Extrapolating from current practices reveals a downward spiral of compromised quality due to larger classes and less interaction (Pocklington & Tupper, 2002). To compound this, university higher education faculty and administrators have resisted innovation and change in terms of adopting new methods and technologies that, ironically, they have been instrumental in creating. Moreover, arguments about preserving the ideals of higher education as well as limited resources have fallaciously been used to resist change. Preserving the values of higher education and limited resources, however, are the very reasons that we need to reconceptualize the teaching and learning transaction. Without doubt, the redesign approach with the most promise to maintain and enhance the ideals of higher education in a resource-restricted context is blended learning.

Canadian universities realize that they are vulnerable to global competition for the best faculty and students. A group of eight research intensive universities from across Canada, known as COHERE (Collaboration for Online Higher Education and Research), have recognized that communication and information technologies are a serious catalyst for change and the solution to the challenges facing them in order to be innovative and competitive. The COHERE institutions have begun to focus on blended learning and have taken the lead to understand the policy and practical implications of this approach and to promote its application. The theoretical and case study research reported here reveals the progress and challenges faced by most Canadian universities.

Blended Learning Rationale

On the surface, blended learning is an intuitively obvious design approach that combines the appropriate capabilities of both face-to-face and online learning to meet the particular needs of a course or program of studies. Educationally, blended learning has the potential to integrate immediate, spontaneous, and rich verbal communication with reflective, rigorous, and precise written communication, as well as visually rich media and simulations. Such capabilities help meet the disciplinary demands and needs of learners in particular disciplinary contexts. Most important, the designation of a blended learning approach is reserved here for those (re)designs that are more than add-ons or enhancements of traditional face-to-face classroom experiences. They will eventually represent significant redesigns where faculty consider disciplinary and student needs from a fresh perspective of communication technology as an enabler. Inevitably this means traditional class contact hours must be rethought and restructured with the integration of meaningful online access to information and reflective discourse.

We can attribute the great potential for blended learning in Canadian universities to the transformative potential of blended learning to support the traditional ideals and values of a higher education learning experience. Universities are defined by their research as well as their inquiry approaches to teaching and learning. These approaches have been described in terms of the ideal community of inquiry comprising open and sustained discourse dedicated to developing competencies such as critical and creative thinking, written and verbal communication skills, and interpretive and evaluation abilities. However, this higher learning experience is seriously compromised with the persistent reliance on the lecture. The existing situation, in fact, is being made worse by increasing demands and expectations resulting from societal transformations and innovation of information and communication technologies.

Interaction is the key element and quality standard of a quality learning experience in higher education. Sustained interaction between and among faculty and students leading to knowledge construction and validation will require an opportunity to share and test ideas in a secure environment and with a manageable number of students. Communication and Internet technology is not only capable of supporting and enhancing this engagement, but has the capacity to extend the learning experience to critically consider the technology itself and critically access and assess the virtually limitless information at one's fingertips.

If Canadian universities are to remain relevant and competitive, they must embrace the reality that communication and information technologies are both the catalyst and solution to many of the quality and resource challenges they face.

While enhancing the quality of the learning experience must always be at the forefront for Canadian universities, this does not mean that costs can or will simply continue rising. Without technological innovation and redesign, there is a zero-sum game between quality and cost. Blended learning has the very real potential of avoiding the false choice of having to decide between effectiveness and efficiency. The reason is that blended learning represents and necessitates a fundamental redesign of a course or program. It provides an opportunity to abandon flawed approaches to teaching and learning, gives faculty the chance to play a more effective role, and demands less of classroom and laboratory facilities. There is considerable support for the cost-effectiveness of blended learning (Heterick & Twigg, 2003) and emerging evidence of improved student achievement (see Research Initiative for Teaching Effectiveness, 2004). Not only are there higher completion rates, but both faculty and students gain considerable convenience. However, notwithstanding these early successes, considering the contextual contingencies and complexities of implementing blended learning course redesigns, there is much to be learned institutionally, pedagogically, and technologically to advance blended learning in the Canadian context.

Pedagogically, an important contingency in designing blended learning is that inquiry approaches vary across disciplines. Differences in the nature and structure of knowledge across disciplines require specific thinking processes and skills. For example, the social sciences tend to be more inductive in terms of making sense of ill-defined knowledge, while the sciences tend to be more deductive in finding solutions to well-defined problems within accepted theories and laws (Donald, 2002). The flexibility of blended learning in being able to address the varying design needs is both a strength and challenge.

Blended learning in the Canadian university context will initially have its greatest impact on increasing effectiveness and efficiency with first-year high-enrollment and high-demand courses. The reason is that large lectures are not very effective at facilitating a quality (higher levels of learning) experience. Moreover, first-year high-enrollment courses are often offered in multiple sections, which reduces efficiency. There are also high-demand courses that faculty cannot effectively offer in a large lecture format, and where blended approaches could expand enrollment. Considering that large enrollment courses are the foundation for more advanced courses, they are not particularly cost-effective in ensuring students are well prepared for advanced courses requiring deep understanding and critical thinking skills. Finally, because of generally recognized deficiencies of high-enrollment and -demand courses, there is a real opportunity to implement and innovate with blended approaches to learning.

Another challenge is at the strategic and institutional level. Some of these challenges relate to policy, planning, resource, scheduling, and support issues (Garrison & Kanuka, 2004). Considering the decentralized nature of most large universities, institutional policy is essential to communicate priorities and provide the incentives, recognition, and rewards necessary to initiate and sustain action. An essential component of policy is to develop concrete operational plans that define specific goals and responsibilities. Financial, human, and technical resources must also be provided, although this can be modest, with a recommended gradual implementation plan. One major barrier for blended learning in many large universities is resistance to breaking with the traditional scheduling format, and this is a prime example of the need for operational plans that enable educators to move forward. Finally, faculty will need sustained support to reconceptualize how they approach and redesign their courses.

Blended Learning Practices at COHERE Universities

To increase our understanding of the policy and practical implications of blended learning, we conducted case studies of how blended learning is being implemented by instructors at COHERE member institutions (For full details on the study, readers are referred to http://www.yorku.ca/irlt/pubs.html/.) With the help of contact persons at each of the eight COHERE universities, we selected one blended learning course at each institution to study from a list of two to three courses nominated by the contacts. The criteria for nominating a course were that (1) online learning replaces some face-to-face time or classroom activities and (2) the instructor was willing to participate voluntarily. We made our final selection of the course to study from each institution by attempting to get a variety of academic disciplines represented in the national sample. We then interviewed all eight instructors and asked them to invite their students to complete an anonymous on-line survey. The survey consisted of fourteen Likert items, six background questions, and four open-ended questions. Table 24.1 lists the pseudonyms used for each university, a brief description of each blended learning course, the number of survey responses, the number of students enrolled, and the student response rates for the online survey.

How Instructors Blended Their Courses

The blended learning class studied at Albatross U is a third-year nutrition course with content at an advanced science level. The course consisted of traditional lectures twice a week and a one-hour tutorial; classroom time did not change

TABLE 24.1. CASE STUDY DESCRIPTIONS AND SURVEY RESPONSE RATES.

University	Course Description	Number of Responses	Number of Students Enrolled	Approximate Survey Response Rate
Eagle	First-year foundations of computers	169	239	70%
Nuthatch	Third-year gender studies	15	16	94
Heron	First-year chemistry	320	1,764	18
Redwing	First-year communications and teamwork	55	380	14
Albatross	Third-year nutrition	26	120	21
Yellowlegs	Third-year social work practicum	10	18	55
Kingfisher	Third-year communications in organizations	128	159	66
Oriole	Fourth-year plant biology	18	18	100
Total		741	2,714	27

compared to a traditional format. Online weekly group discussions were worth only 5 percent of the students' final grades; however, both students and the instructor valued the online interaction. In addition, the instructor said that online participation helped students "get it" and that they seemed "more excited to come to class" because of prior exposure to the issues in the online discussions.

The introduction to computers course at Eagle U is a large-enrollment first-year university course that the instructor developed as a fully online course but has now converted to a blended format. Students can attend the weekly lectures in person, participate in the lecture real time over the Web using the collaborative software application HorizonLive, or watch the recorded lectures online for a limited time. Students can choose to take the course fully online, but the option to attend face-to-face lectures or talk to the instructor during office hours was also available to them.

The instructor said the face-to-face contact was necessary for some first-year university students who need more direction, and that was the reason for changing the course from fully online to a blended format. The instructor also said that the blended format improved "my capacity to deal with a lot more students . . . in a way that I get to know them well." In addition to their support and satisfaction with the discussion tool, students benefited because "the archived lectures help by allowing students to refer back to the lecture if they do not understand a concept." As another student wrote, being able to listen to the lecture more than once "is such an important point for the international student." Finally, this instructor was technically very skilled, and students enjoyed being "exposed to cool things." In addition, students appreciated that the blended format helped them "by applying their understanding of the technology."

The blended learning course in the Heron U case study was a large-enrollment first-year chemistry course. Students at Heron U could optionally attend face-to-face lectures in a five-hundred-seat hall and listen to e-lectures online. The e-lectures consisted of audio narration by the instructor and static screens with text and graphic formulas; the instructor recorded the e-lectures in a studio. Some of the lab assignments and all exams required face-to-face attendance by students. The instructor believed "that the justification for that [blended learning] was it would make scheduling a little easier." In other words, students' timetables had more flexibility if attendance at the lecture was not required. Although the instructor believed that the e-lectures "were just as effective as the [face-to-face] lecture," the instructor was dissatisfied that the administration would offer only the blended version as an option. The instructor observed that "the university did not want to face the fact of, perhaps, parents saying, 'I didn't send my kid to university so that they could sit in front of the computer. They should be in front of a real lecturer.'" In addition, the instructor said, "in some ways I feel it [e-lectures] would probably be even more effective because the student actually is the participant."

The purpose of the Kingfisher U course was to familiarize third-year students with the main concepts, viewpoints, and research findings in the field of organizational communication. This large-enrollment course consisted of streamed audio and video lectures with accompanying slides using Mediasite Live. There were no face-to-face lectures, but there were mandatory tutorials one hour per week conducted by teaching assistants. The weekly online lecture was available for a limited time. One of the benefits for the instructor with the blended format was that it was "a focusing technique for me." The instructor explained, "My lecturing now is much more coherent; that is, it is a one-hour piece. It's canned; it has to make sense." In addition, the instructor said, "I think it offers some choices to me professionally, but also to the department." However, the instructor recognized that teaching a course without being there—by using prerecorded lectures—was potentially controversial.

The U Nuthatch course was an upper-level class in contemporary feminist theories offered to about sixteen students. The instructor omitted one face-to-face lecture as compensation for student participation in online discussions, which accounted for 20 percent of their grade. The idea behind the online responses was to promote dialogue, but students had the option of submitting a response privately to the instructor if the subject was too personal. Although this course was mostly face-to-face, the students and instructor supported the online components very much. Most students valued the online discussions, and the instructor believed that the blended approach "raised the bar, and was good pedagogy." The only notable limitation for these students was their access to and familiarity with computers. However, the advantage of increased student interaction, students' improved computer skills, and more freedom for both students and the teacher justified the use of technology.

The Oriole U senior-level course examined current molecular techniques used to study plant development physiology. Students earned 50 percent of their course grade by completing a thesis proposal that they posted online. Groups of two to three students worked together on the thesis proposal, and each student commented on the other groups' proposals within the Angel course management system. The instructor reported many benefits with the blended format, and said, "It's absolutely the most satisfying teaching I do." However, both the instructor and the students indicated that the blended format took more time; for example, all but one student agreed with the statement on the online survey that this course required more time and effort. The instructor also acknowledged that answering the students' critiques "took me ages." In spite of the extra work, the thesis proposal and critique was a "thinking assignment" according to the instructor, where students were "learning how to critique," and they were "very proud of how well they can do that."

The course at Redwing U introduced first-year university students to foundational studies in teamwork and communications; the course has been in the blended format since its inception about five years ago. Face-to-face classes alternated weekly with online conferencing, so the mix was half online and half face-to-face course activities. The instructor interviewed enjoyed the "flexibility of the blended learning model," and said, "I absolutely love this course. . . . I feel like I'm always learning from students that are coming in." Recent institutional changes, as well as only just offering the course to students in a variety of different programs, may have had an impact on the range of responses from students. For example, technology students in previous years knew how to build a Web site before taking this course, but "now we have students coming in that are transferring to other programs that the only Internet experience that they've had is searching the Web or using e-mail, and they have no idea how to set up a Web site." Thus, the instructors were coming to grips with changes in students' backgrounds and the varying level of integration with other courses in the students' programs.

A social work practicum seminar was the focus of Yellowlegs, the eighth university in our study. Students from three remote areas participated in both face-to-face and online discussions related to their field practice experiences in social work. Participation in the class discussions accounted for 40 percent of the course grade with 20 percent face-to-face and 20 percent online interaction. The course was thirty-six hours in total, with twelve hours devoted to online interaction and twenty-four hours to face-to-face activities. The main purpose for using blended learning in this case was to enable students to interact with their peers at a distance, where previously they could interact with peers only in their own practicum locations. This blended learning course combined the advantages of distance learning for remote students with the benefits of reflection in asynchronous discussions for students who are beginning practitioners in social work, adding to the depth of interaction and range of experiences for students in this class. This case study was a particularly good marriage between face-to-face and online components and is well suited to the social work discipline, according to the instructor.

Technology Used in Courses

Five of the universities used WebCT to support the e-learning components of their blended learning courses. One university used Blackboard, another used Angel, and one developed an in-house course management system (CMS). Both Angel and Blackboard are competitive with WebCT, and all three are commercial products. Thus, all eight universities had some type of CMS. In addition, three instructors developed animated learning objects, and another instructor had online video demonstrations of the assignments. Two instructors used traditional Web sites to house course outlines, syllabi, assignments, and other course materials and resources, in addition to the CMS. These instructors did this partly because they developed their Web sites before the university adopted a CMS, but also because the CMS did not provide the functionality they wanted. One technically skilled instructor used server log files to track attendance and participation, as well as to script birthday announcements posted daily on the course home page. Finally, all but one instructor posted course documents and resources online, although the technology used ranged from static document files to streamed high-end audio and video presentations. The instructor who did not post any course documents online believed that it was simpler and safer for students to have that information in a printed source.

Eighty percent of all students disagreed that technology interfered with their learning, and this survey question had the least variation among the Canadian universities in this study. In addition, 77 percent of all students agreed that their course made excellent use of Web resources. Again, there was no statistically significant difference on this question among the eight universities, despite the wide variation in technologies used by instructors. Although there were a few open-ended comments by individual students about bandwidth, downtime, or incompatibilities, these comments made up less than 6 percent of coded statements written by students. In general, technological problems did not trouble students very much, and no type of technology emerged as burdensome to students.

Online Pedagogy

Online discussions were a primary part of the e-learning components for five of the blended learning courses. Most instructors awarded 20 percent of the course grades for online discussion activities; however, one instructor awarded only 5 percent for online discussions. Five percent was probably not sufficient, and 42 percent of these students wrote that the online discussions were too much work for a small amount of credit. In addition, one instructor did not grade the online discussions, but participation in them was a component of a team presentation grade worth 30 percent. In addition to the use of online discussions, one university had online labs and online quizzes (17.5 percent of course work), and another had online thesis proposals worth 50 percent of the students' course grade. Only one instructor did not award any grades for online activities; nevertheless, the lectures for that course were available only online (no face-to-face lecture).

Encouraging higher-order thinking skills among students was a pedagogical goal mentioned by six of the instructors. Both students and instructors saw the online components as a means to encouraging critical thinking. Flexibility and freedom were also important goals for both students and teachers. Students were especially happy with the ability to schedule course work when it was convenient for them, and in the case of courses with online lectures, students liked being able to "fast-forward or rewind" the instructor. In addition, although there was wide variation in the elements that were blended, nearly 70 percent of all students agreed that the balance between face-to-face and e-learning components was about right. There were no statistically significant differences across universities on the survey item asking this question. Moreover, students appreciated the traditional values (such as face-to-face discussions) that the blended format supported. One student wrote, "I could work out the problems online, but if I had trouble there was always the face-to-face contact that could enhance my understanding."

Five instructors said that the online component of their course enabled them to get to know their students better than in a traditional face-to-face class, and they saw this as a major benefit of blended learning. In addition, all eight instructors enjoyed the blended format and said they would teach in that format again.

Instructors mentioned other benefits of blended learning, such as being able to track students' progress more closely, having the opportunity to be creative, and a perception that students were learning more.

Instructor Challenges

The challenges facing the instructors were often dependent on the size of the class. Two instructors of large-enrollment lecture courses believed there was no realistic way to incorporate online discussions, yet another instructor of a large-enrollment first-year course did this quite successfully. A slight majority (55 percent) of all students agreed on the survey that it was easier to relate to other students' viewpoints than in a traditional class. However, there were strong statistically significant differences ($p = .000$) in means across universities to the survey question that asked students if online interaction with other students contributed to their understanding of course materials. Interestingly, removing the two large-enrollment courses with the least amount of online student-student interaction from the ANOVA calculations reversed the results and produced no significant differences among the means ($p = .980$). Approximately 72 percent of students in these remaining six universities agreed that online interaction with other students contributed to their understanding.

According to our survey, students who did not regularly see their professors (at Kingfisher and Heron, for example) and students whose instructors took a less active role in online discussions (at Yellowlegs and Redwing, for example) were significantly less likely to agree that the amount of online interaction with their instructor was appropriate. In other words, students were attentive to the amount and quality of interaction with their instructors as well as with their peers. Finally, the correlation coefficients between survey items about students' general satisfaction with their course and the amount of online and face-to-face interaction with other students were significant at the .01 level. Thus, the amount and quality of interaction among students and with their instructors, whether online or face-to-face, was a statistically significant factor in students' overall satisfaction with their courses.

Finally, 57 percent of all students agreed that the blended learning format required more time and effort than traditional on-campus courses. However, there were statistically significant differences among the eight university means; for example, only 10 percent of students at Yellowlegs agreed the course took more time and effort, but 94 percent of students at Oriole agreed with this statement. All instructors said the blended learning format took more time and effort on their part, but none objected to the extra work or indicated they would abandon the blended learning model.

Policy and Support

All of the instructors had access to some type of technical or teaching support at their university for their blended learning courses. However, five of the instructors observed that their peers were not supporting their efforts with blended learning; for example, when describing a technical problem, one instructor said, "It's disheartening, and my colleagues who can't get motivated to do things [with blended learning] just look at me and say, 'See!' " Even students wrote that their blended learning course "receives hardly any attention or funding from the university." Only three of the instructors were able to get some funding or release time to develop their blended learning courses. Such findings highlight the need for universities to continue to develop support policies.

Conclusions

Instructors blended their courses to put together a more flexible, efficient, accessible, and varied learning experience for their students. However, student satisfaction seems highly dependent on the level of interaction with instructors and other students. This is consistent with previous research (Swan, 2001). It strongly suggests that online interaction should be a core issue when designing blended learning courses, not only for student satisfaction but because both instructors and students saw online discussion as a means to encourage critical thinking and contribute to their understanding. This might also partially explain why some students viewed blended learning as requiring more time and effort. Finally, the success of online discussion in one large-enrollment class suggests that student interaction can enhance large-enrollment classes with proper design.

From an institutional perspective, it is essential that there be clear policy, direction, and support of blended learning if the positive benefits are to be realized. In addition, there must be incentives, such as release time, as well as recognition and rewards for creating innovative blended learning course designs. In other words, university administrators need to recognize this work as a scholarly activity. More specifically, administrators need to create an institutional action plan with the explicit and sustained commitment of senior administration. The plan should ramp up the redesign process by targeting a select few courses that will ensure success and provide the best exemplars and prototypes. Formal systematic and sustained design support is also a necessity. It is essential to study and evaluate progress and outcomes to not only improve the design but provide the information that will keep senior administration committed. A steering group of representatives across the institution may be essential to get buy-in and feedback in order to learn and adjust.

Blended learning offers a thoughtful redesign of courses consistent with the traditional values of a university, such as engaging in interaction and discourse, as well as a means to address quality and diminishing resource issues. In the context of the challenges facing universities from a funding, expectation, and technological perspective, there is a pressing need for change and leadership to reposition Canadian universities to remain competitive globally. Scholars must direct inquiry to teaching and learning as much as to research. The efforts reported here represent an exploration of new approaches and technologies to enhance the quality of the learning experience in Canadian universities. Such a thoughtful response will also be a sign of the creative and bold leadership that is required to meet the educational challenges of a society in transformation.

References

Donald, J. G. (2002). *Learning to think: Disciplinary perspectives.* San Francisco: Jossey-Bass.

Garrison, D. R., & Kanuka, H. (2004). Blended learning: Uncovering its transformative potential in higher education. *Internet and Higher Education, 7*(2), 95–105.

Heterick, B., & Twigg, C. (2003, February). *The learning marketspace.* Retrieved December 5, 2003, from http://www.center.rpi.edu/LForum/LM/Feb03.html.

Pocklington, T., & Tupper, A. (2002). *No place to learn: Why universities aren't working.* Vancouver: UBC Press.

Research Initiative for Teaching Effectiveness. (2004). *Distributed learning impact evaluation.* Retrieved June 30, 2004, from http://pegasus.cc.ucf.edu/~rite/impactevaluation.htm.

Swan, K. (2001). Virtual interaction: Design factors affecting student satisfaction and perceived learning in asynchronous online courses. *Distance Education, 22*(2), 306–331.

Ronald D. Owston is professor of education and founding director of the Institute for Research on Learning Technologies at York University in Toronto, Canada. He has spoken at numerous national and international conferences, and published in a variety of fields, including technology in education, program evaluation, and teacher development. Currently, he is an external evaluator for the Teacher eLearning Blended Learning Project in Mathematics and Science sponsored by the Learning Partnership in Toronto and evaluator for online modules being developed by Health Canada for health care professionals. He is also methodology theme leader in the SAGE project, based at Simon Fraser University, that is researching the educational applications of games and simulations.

D. Randy Garrison is the director of the Learning Commons and a full professor in the Faculty of Education at the University of Calgary. He served as dean, Faculty of Extension, at the University of Alberta from 1996 to 2001. Garrison has published extensively on teaching and learning in higher, adult, and distance education contexts. He has published five books and over one hundred refereed articles and papers. He recently coauthored a book, *E-Learning in the Twenty-First Century,* where he identifies the unique properties and provides a framework for the core elements of online learning. His current research interests focus on supporting and facilitating critical reflection and discourse in an online educational environment, particularly blended learning designs.

Kathryn Cook is a tenured full-time faculty member at Georgian College in Barrie, Ontario, Canada. Since completing a Ph.D. in education, she has been a research associate at York University's Institute for Research on Learning Technologies. She was an early adopter of Internet technologies and the first at Georgian College to teach an online course in 1995. She is currently involved in evaluating online modules developed by Health Canada for public health care professionals across Canada. Past research projects include evaluating a public health information system for Health Canada, determining the Web presence of faculty-authored Web sites, and studying student use of e-resources in a large-enrollment undergraduate course.

CHAPTER TWENTY-FIVE

TECNOLÓGICO DE MONTERREY IN MÉXICO

Where Technology Extends the Classroom

Alejandro Acuña Limón

This chapter presents the main uses of technology in the formal education system in Mexico and focuses on the Instituto Tecnológico y de Estudios Superiores de Monterrey (ITESM) and its model of technology use.

Brief History of the Intensive Use of Technologies in Formal Education in Mexico

The first efforts to use technology in the Mexican classrooms date to the 1960s in the Faculty of Medicine of the University National Autonomous Mexico, where surgery was transmitted live using closed-circuit television. However, the real pioneer in using technology to improve formal education in Mexico was the Telesecundaria, which uses a model that combines distance education with traditional education. The classes begin with a fifteen-minute television program that presents a lesson and continues with thirty-five minutes of work in class with aid of a professor and printed materials. For more than three decades, the Telesecundaria has responded to the educational needs of Mexico's rural communities, where it was not feasible to implement traditional secondary schools (levels 7 to 9) due to the small student population and difficulty in attracting instructors.

The Telesecundaria has experienced substantial growth since its creation in 1968. After educational reform was implemented in 1993 and satellite broadcasts were introduced, its coverage increased considerably. In fact, it has grown from 304 schools and approximately 512,700 students in 1993, to 817,200 in 1998, to 890,400 in 1999. In 1968, when it began to function, there were only 304 schools in the Telesecundaria program. Ten years later, there were 7,289 schools in the system and by 1998, there were 13,054 schools and 38,698 instructors. Current registrations in the Telesecundaria account for 16.6 percent of all registrations in grades 7 to 9 in Mexico. Traditional general schools account for 53.6 percent of the registrations, technical schools account for 28.5 percent, and the schools for in-service training the remaining 1.3 percent. It is anticipated that Telesecundaria will have nearly 1.1 million students in 2004.

As the success of the Telesecundaria and support for educational television programs grew, the Mexican government created EDUSAT (Satellite Educational System) to provide educational programming via satellite television. With more than thirty-three receptors in an equal number of schools and libraries, EDUSAT is now the major system of educational television of Latin America. With six channels broadcasting 360 hours of programming per week, there is a wealth of formal and informal educational content broadcast, from basic education to graduate-level distance programs.

Growth of the Internet in Mexico

Tecnológico de Monterrey and the Autonomous National University of Mexico (UNAM) were the first educational institutions in Mexico to use the Internet during the 1980s. Since that time, many other educational institutions in Mexico have used the Internet to support their educational programs. In fact, many private and public universities in Mexico now use the Internet as exclusive support of information and promotion.

The ITESM has continued to be a well-respected pioneer in the use of the Internet for education. For instance, it was the first institution in Mexico to use Lotus Notes and LearningSpace for classroom delivery in the early 1990s (Acuña, 1995).

According to statistics presented by the INEGI (National Institute of Statistics, Geography and Informatics; see http://www.inegi.gob.mx) in México, the number of Internet users has grown tremendously since 2000. In 2000, there were around 5 million users; just two years later, there were more than 10 million. Since then, this number has continued to grow exponentially. The sudden increase of those with Internet access in Mexico could be due in part to the diverse uses that it is given. Common uses in Mexico include e-mail (4.2 million), consultation or investigation on the Web (4.2 million), online chatting (2.8 million), various educational uses (2.3 million), entertainment (2.1 million), software (308,829), and videoconferencing (245,036), among many others (Instituto Nacional de estadística, Geografía e Informática, 2004). This increase in access and use of the Internet in Mexico sets the stage for the success of the K-12 Red Escolar program and the ITESM Virtual University described in the following sections.

La Red Escolar: Internet Tools for Children

In 1997 the Latin-American Institute for Educational Communication (Instituto Latinoamericano de Comunicación Educativa, ILCE) initiated the Red Escolar project, which provides Web resources for K-12 schools. In the initial phase of this project, five networks were installed across 140 schools. From 1999 to 2001, 223 educators used this school network. During the past few years, the use of this project has exploded. At present, Red Escolar receives an average of more than 417,000 daily visits, with more than 180,000 students involved in collaborative projects and more than 8,000 teachers participating in the training. In addition, more than 15,000 educators now connect to Red Escolar, with more than 185,000 computers. The content of Red Escolar has been focused primarily on the second and third grades and then the other levels of K-12 education.

The main purpose of Red Escolar is to offer the same educational opportunities to all Mexican students. This program helps bring materials to improve teaching and learning to each school and each center for teachers. With the support of information and communication technologies (ICT), it promotes the exchange of educational proposals and didactic resources, while fostering student and school success experiences.

Children in the early grades benefit tremendously from this program. For example, they use computers to carry out simple activities with CDs, read online texts, and become familiar with children's stories through the Internet. Recognizing that Red Escolar benefits the entire educational community, strategies have been established so that the population knows the products and can develop collaborative projects.

The main objective of Red Escolar is to support formal basic education and elevate the quality of the teaching–learning process. It can be used from different pedagogical perspectives (for example, constructivist, humanist, and cognitivist), offering students educational models that encourage them to be become builders, mediators, and investigators of knowledge. Those coordinating this project consider students active beings, with their own individual characteristics and interests, who benefit from independent study as well as multiple social and individual interactions. The projects and courses of Red Escolar propose diverse activities, such as documentary investigations using online technology, CD-ROMs, and videos. The teacher can divide the students into teams that rotate roles so that each student can participate in some phase of the project. This program proposes, over the next few years, to introduce computers with multimedia, connected to the Internet and with an extensive range of educational content to all public secondary and primary schools of Mexico.

Fifteen Years of Teaching with Technology in ITESM

The third project of educational significance and with wide success using technology in Mexico is the creation of the Virtual University within the Instituto Tecnológico y de Estudios Superiores de Monterrey (ITESM) in 1989. In taking advantage of the satellite systems and the Internet, the Virtual University has graduated more than forty-eight hundred students at the master's and doctoral levels on thirty-three campuses and in thirty-four national and international headquarters. In addition, it has contributed to the formal education of more than 200,000 professionals in Mexico, Latin America, and other parts of the world. Currently, the Virtual University supports professional careers with courses given by specialists through Internet and satellite broadcasts. Since the fall of 2003, it has placed in motion a postgraduate course program series that is entirely online in the areas of education, administration, sciences, and engineering, as well as the areas of political science and public administration.

Parallel to the development of the Virtual University, since 1995 the Technological of Monterrey has had a program of intensive use of technology supporting classes with the use of a learning management system (LMS). The use of technology such as LMS is in accordance with its mission statement for the year 2005. The model is based on the use of a LMS such as LearningSpace, WebCT, and Blackboard with the support of different didactic and interactive techniques, including problem-based learning, cooperative and collaborative learning, and project-oriented learning.

In addition to the LMS, the technological elements of the blended learning model of the Institute of Monterrey include the Internet, e-mail, digital libraries, and simulations. The digital library, accessible over the Internet, gives all students access to valuable resources even if they are physically distant from those resources. In addition, e-mail permits instructors and students separated by time and place to communicate with each other. Electronic discussion group tools and virtual team spaces enable virtual collaborative work and have made possible the Mastery in Educational Technology program of the Virtual University, which integrates undergraduate and graduate students from all over the globe.

Educational software packages including simulations are also available on the network to support teaching and learning. Among the electronic applications that can promote learning are flight simulators (Promodel, Intopia), virtual laboratories (Labview, Matlab, Applet), word processors (Word, Works), calculation tools (Excel, Lotus Notes), presentation applications (PowerPoint, Flash), design applications (Autocad, 3dstudioPhothoshop), and others that professors incorporate in their online courses.

Learning Management Systems to Support a Blended Approach

The use of interactive technology tools can help configure a course or program according to the educational models specified or delivery methods required. In the ITESM, technology is employed to offer two different types of courses: fully online courses and blended courses in which asynchronous tools are used to support face-to-face activities. In the past five years, a blended model has become a requirement in the ITESM. The use of the computer on the part of the professor and students as a work tool is now a requirement for all courses that apply the current educational model of the ITESM.

The tendency in the institute is to promote network-based learning, which is composed of diverse interactive and collaborative technologies that provide compact and agile administration of the didactic process as well as rich and engaging learning experiences. This system of tools employed by the ITSEM is housed within a technological platform; the first platform we used at the institute was LearningSpace. While such a tool brings the advantages of standardization across an extensive and dispersed system, there are also distinct disadvantages, such as being tied to a single product or educational vendor.

The LearningSpace, which was based on Lotus Notes, was one of the first LMSs available. Another competing LMS that is being used in our system is Blackboard. The basic functions of these platforms are very similar, although Blackboard has a more centralized infrastructure to support online learning. Understanding the differences between LearningSpace and Blackboard can be useful for professors or instructional designers who desire to pass information from the LearningSpace platform to that of Blackboard. In fact, this migration of courses from one platform to another is among the key trends within the institute. Table 25.1 contains some of the strengths and limitations that we have identified of the two LMS options.

As with any other online learning implementation, there are specific needs that arise from professors and students within these online environments

TABLE 25.1. STRENGTHS AND LIMITATIONS OF LEARNINGSPACE AND BLACKBOARD.

	Strengths	Limitations
LearningSpace	• The databases are interconnected and permit students to easily switch between them. • Students can work online or off-line, thereby allowing more flexible use. • The operation of the tool is distributed and centralized. • The content is portable and highly accessible.	• One is supposed to work off-line with a replica of the system and then synchronize the two systems periodically. Sometimes the synchronization of information fails to work properly. • It is a complex tool that requires training for its use. • It is not very feasible to use the platform through Web. • The administration of course accounts is complex. • A strong investment in infrastructure is required.
Blackboard	• It uses the Web to allow one to design a course that uses electronic resources. • It is compatible with international standards related to the development of online content. • It allows both synchronous and asynchronous communication. • It has a simple interface, which does not require much training. • It provides a work space that gives users access to all the courses in which they are registered using a unique account.	• Working with this tool requires being connected to the Internet. • The areas of information are not highly interconnected, which reduces speed of access and overall navigation capabilities. • The simplicity of the tool also means that it may not be as powerful as more complex online tools and management systems.

(Marín, 2002). In response, the online learning resources and overall support and infrastructure within the ITESM are evolving based on the internal requests of the institute and the work of the professors and their students. Currently, the desired infrastructure is more similar to what is offered in Blackboard than LearningSpace. From an administrative perspective, a few of our goals for implementation of this system are:

- To store the knowledge that professors generate in the process of establishing the blended educational model
- To fortify the process of evaluation by offering students the opportunity to know their learning growth, while providing the professor with ways to monitor and assess individual student progress
- To handle international standards of learning objects by using the knowledge base of other educational companies
- To offer greater integration and better control of course content
- To deliver specific courses to the students with virtual spaces that enable both synchronous and asynchronous interaction

The use of technology in the institution is now oriented toward centralizing and unifying the administrative processes, the television communications infrastructure, and computational services while simultaneously reducing the costs of operation. To achieve all of this, we are attempting to define uniform and efficient processes across all the campuses, develop an information system tailored to our needs, create a single center of computation that gives service to the entire system, and install excellent systems of telecommunications and computational networks.

Student and Faculty Roles in Blended Learning

The experience of generating blended learning through the use of virtual spaces offers enormous potential in Mexico, including significant educational benefits for students as well as professors and for improving the educational process itself.

The educational model used by the Tecnologico de Monterrey involves an active blended learning approach that is centered on the student. Participating in a course in this network requires that the student be continuously involved in relevant and meaningful activities. We also believe that student learning requires social interaction, collaboration, and reflection by learners. As evidence of this social and cognitive commitment, the online activities we employ include actively contributing to and engaging in online discussion, responding to companions, making valid arguments, and coherently sharing ideas in writing. To participate in such a manner fosters cognitive depth while fostering shared knowledge and a sense of community among the students. These activities help students order their thoughts and improve their written communications skills. At the same time, it requires that students competently process, monitor, filter, and evaluate information.

Blended learning offers educational opportunities for students that are not typically available through traditional face-to-face instruction alone. In an environment of online or networked learning, there is more equality as all students participate when they desire and wherever they are located. The fact that the learning content and associated activities are available all the time and from any geographical location with an Internet connection permits students to reflect more on their ideas as well as the ideas of their peers and to engage in learning according to their own rhythm or preferences. Such systems of learning stand in sharp contrast to those that assume, incorrectly, that all students advance at the same time and with the same antecedents.

Blended learning can change the relationship between professors and students. In fact, it can break typical learning hierarchies, forcing the professor or course expert to be more of a facilitator in the process of learning than an authority figure. In our blended learning approach, the professor defines the objectives of a course, suggests texts and other materials of study, gives instructions and guidelines, fosters collaborative teams, and supervises continuously what occurs.

Conclusion

There is a wealth of technological innovation in Mexico, in both formal and informal settings. As the number of Internet users in Mexico has increased during the past few years, the Internet has played an increasing role across the entire spectrum of the Mexican educational system. For instance, with the innovative and expanding use of resources in the Red Escolar program, the integration of the Internet in K-12 education is having a significant impact on young learners in Mexico. Such students will soon enter higher education with expectations for similar engaging and personalized learning opportunities. At the same time, the evolving educational model of the ITESM is highlighting the success of blended learning approaches in Mexican higher education.

When successful, authentic communities of learning are formed in blended environments. The enormous possibilities of communication technology combined with the opportunities brought by endless seas of online information offer personal enrichment as well as innovation within a group. The communication that flows is an intellectual stimulus and source of personal satisfaction for all participants. In the virtual community, members share interests, knowledge, and ideas and begin to self-reflect. We have found that both professors and students declare that interaction and learning are more frequent, deeper, and more personal than in a traditional course. So onward we happily push into this age of blended learning.

References

Acuña, A. (1995). *Nuevos medios, Viejos Aprendizajes: Las nuevas tecnologpias en la educación*. Mexico City: Universidad Iberoamericana.

Instituto Nacional de estadística, Geografia e Informática. (2004). *Usuarios de internet por países seleccionados, 1998–2003*. Retrieved September 23, 2004, from http://www.inegi.gob.mx/est/contenidos/espanol/rutinas/ept.asp?t=tinf142&c=4870.

Instituto Tecnológico y de Estudios Superiores de Monterrey. (1995–2004). Mission. Retrieved September 23, 2004, from http://www.itesm.mx/.

Marín, M. (2002). *El modelo educativo del Tecnologico de Monterrey*. Monterrey, Nuevo León: Instituto Tecnologico de Estudios Superiores de Monterrey.

Alejandro Acuña Limón is the director of the Virtual University Instituto Tecnológico y de Estudios Superiores de Monterrey for the Mexico City campus. He was previously the director of the Center for Studies in Communication and Educational Technologies. He received a master's degree in communications from the Universidad Iberoamericana and a Ph.D. in instructional media and technology from the University of Connecticut. He has published in international journals and has been the keynote speaker at an international conference on distance education.

CHAPTER TWENTY-SIX

FROM ANALOG TO WEBLOG

The Community College Evolution Toward Blended Learning

Paul A. Elsner

In something like what we would call the beginning, before the Internet spawned true interactivity, community colleges had explored distance education. Certain community college districts were prolific producers of distance course content, including the Dallas Community College District in Texas and the Coast Community College District in Costa Mesa, California. There were cooperatives and consortia that produced and rented commercial-quality courseware to community colleges, usually in thirteen to fifteen half-hour segments. Many universities used similar courseware through public broadcast media; these include media outlets like PBS and local commercial television stations that provided high production support and quality technical systems for educational programming. The University of Maryland, the University of Nebraska, and others had a strong role in the production of telecourses for distance education.

The Maricopa Community College District (MCCD), which serves the greater Phoenix, Arizona, area, was an early pioneer in large-scale commitment to distance education. Rio Salado College, a designated flagship college in the Maricopa system, was granted full authority by its governing board to use distance education; in its founding year of 1978, this involved telecourses, radio courses, and correspondence courses. Rio Salado has over twenty-five thousand unduplicated enrollments in what they still call distance education. Mesa Community College, the largest of the Maricopa colleges, offers over one hundred sections of online courses enrolling about thirty-eight hundred students.

Blended Learning: Simple Socialization

Naturally, Web-based courses were not part of the early architecture of telecourses, so blended learning required the arranging of personal face-to-face discussion or symposia sessions that were sometimes embedded in the course schedule. Most early distance education pioneers quickly discovered that students still desired some face-to-face interaction—with other students as well as the instructor. Dropout rates were often very high and still are, although Rio Salado College boasts an impressive 85 percent retention rate; even modern, interactive Web-based courses retain, in too many cases, less than 50 percent of their enrollees.

I often evaluated proposals for courses funded by the Corporation for Public Broadcasting and the Annenberg Foundation. It was disconcerting to seldom find a telecourse proposal that came in under $1 million for production. The costs of producing thirteen commercial-quality half-hour segments to fit the semester format scared many away from establishing production centers. Luckily, the Dallas County Community College District and the Coast Community College District, with public educational channel KOCE, laid out huge expenditures to achieve production capacity. Others followed, such as Miami-Dade Community College and Maricopa, but both districts became sobered by the prospect of such high production costs. Thus, many community colleges rented courseware from the Coast Community College District, the Dallas County Community College District, PBS, and other university providers and consortia.

These experiences shaped a number of significant factors that affect distance education today, such as the emphasis many of us put on course facilitation, which constituted a simpler but more effective learning support. Many discovered that technology does not stand alone very well; although the course segments were often of high production quality, learning support was critical to telecourse success. Such support included everything from staffing call centers to delivering tape cassettes to homes. In addition, supporting printware was essential. Often the planning processes that went into a successful telecourse far exceeded the preparation we might have found in traditional lecture courses.

Even while designing and implementing adequate learning support, distance education was often attacked for its lack of rigor and general quality by the traditionalists of the academy. Blended learning was virtually nonexistent at this point, save for the attempt to increase opportunities for face-to-face discussion in teaching along with the technology. While there has always been a need for this hybrid, it has been difficult for faculty to arrange meetings with students, many of whom are adult learners burdened with jobs and inflexible work hours. Socialization does not eclipse technology, but students seek it anyway. Ron Bleed expressed this need in his article, "A Hybrid Campus for the New Millennium" (2001, p. 19): "When we stop for a moment and think about higher education experiences, what we generally remember most often are those moments we connected with the faculty or students." Our problem has been our failure to blend these good social experiences with good technology. Bleed goes on to say:

> I find it interesting to walk around the Maricopa Community College District campuses to see the impact of technology on the students. I recently visited Phoenix College at 7:30 A.M. I went into the new Library Computer Commons area, and it was nearly full! There were not many students at other places on campus. A day later I went over to Mesa Community College at four o'clock in the afternoon, and the new Elsner Computer Commons Library was bursting with students and activity. If you visited any of the computer labs at our colleges and had some kind of Geiger counter to measure student energy, you would discover that the greatest student activity and energy is now occurring in computer labs [p. 19].

Bleed emphasized blended socialization in describing St. Petersburg Junior Colleges, where they have created "a hard drive cafe, a multi-function, specialized facility centered within an academic office and classroom building. Included in this facility are a one-hundred-station open computer lab, deli lounges both inside and outside, a tutoring center, a career counseling center, and a testing center—all in one facility where food, counseling, testing and tutoring are all intermixed" (2001, p. 22).

Crude Forms of Blended Learning

Early distance education also got caught up in a swirl of enthusiasm for network systems that attempted to integrate voice, video, and printware. At Maricopa, we can recall using a device that enthralled us: an NEC (Nippon Electronic Company) product called CODEX. With an eye-camera on its top, it swiveled to catch live pictures of several students in a classroom. Network facilitators or instructors at the head-in studio could tune the video and sound, conducting a fairly socialized classroom discussion with his or her lecture, using preproduced material as additional course content. This system worked; however, it took less than a year to jam up all of the channels with courses. An energetic music instructor at one college commandeered and dominated most of the channels, prohibiting other faculty from this somewhat socialized and blended technology.

The above MCCD videoconferencing network was established in this brief heroic history—a cutting-edge socialized technology that became a fading flower within a couple of years. Nevertheless, we often boasted during this short period that Maricopa was one of the first higher education institutions to fully integrate voice, video, and print on a network.

Following this early development, some colleges pioneered and developed point-to-point interactive technology. Kirkwood Community College in Cedar Rapids, Iowa, was successful here, linking several rural community college sites through such a network. Its investment was considerable and facilitated course delivery and interaction with students spread across a large rural region.

In Arizona, Northern Arizona University invested in an analog telecourse system, mainly serving community colleges in rural Arizona. It still operates, but has lost much of its early luster that many policy leaders and legislators often praised. Just when these systems were reaching their peak, the ubiquitous Internet and its Web-based services recast these simple blended technologies with interactive Web-based courses that allowed a richer mix of pedagogy and content.

The Shift to Web-Based Blended Methodology

Each year, the MCCD supports a series of services through a group called Ocotillo. The Maricopa Center for Learning and Instruction (MCLI), a division of educational services, hosts an Ocotillo Visioning Forum. In January 2001, a forum, "Designing the Hybrid Campus," attempted to define hybrid courses. The MCLI offered this definition:

> For many years the discussion on online technology for learning has been seen as an either/or—we looked at it as "traditional" or "F2F" (Face to Face) versus complete online distance learning. In fact, what we know and see being used at Maricopa is that the bulk of instructional technology integration is somewhere in the grey middle ground, a mixing of online technology use and F2F, and what in the latest edu-jargon is called "hybrid courses" [MCLI, 2004, p. 1].

I prefer the definition Roger Yohe offers in an unpublished paper, "Experiencing the Best of Both Worlds by Teaching a Hybrid Course." Yohe is one of Maricopa's gifted teachers and the Ocotillo Chair at Estrella Mountain Community College. Yohe feels this definition describes the hybrid courses at Maricopa:

> Hybrid courses make significant use of the Web technology to facilitate access to class materials and support communication between faculty and students, among students, and between students and resources. A key characteristic of a

hybrid course is that the communication hub of a course has shifted from the physical classroom to the Web. Hybrid courses are a blend of face-to-face and online learning experiences with heavy reliance on Web technology and tools [Yohe, 2002, p. 1].

Yohe feels that when faculty choose hybrid courses, they are able to discover the structure best suited to them and their students, allowing a compromise of preferences about how best to learn. Other reasons Yohe likes his hybrid course experiences are listed as follows:

1. I really was getting tired of hearing myself talk so much.
2. My redesigned hybrid courses enhanced student interaction.

At Estrella Mountain Community College, faculty believe that the course format is more varied, student performance increased, and student engagement was more stable. Yohe quotes Ron Freeman, a humanities faculty member: "The approaches and tools available in creating my hybrid course provided something I knew was possible and [hybrid] let me do it" (Yohe, 2002, p. 2). Instructors can use interactive media, shift classroom arrangements and formats, pass along the motivation, and, surprisingly, experience higher student energy. For the faculty, this approach seemed less restricted by a single text of lecture-centered syllabi. Some colleges, according to Yohe, permit and even encourage online learning but do not give appropriate attention to the support required to help faculty. Designing hybrids is a collaborative activity; without cooperation and systemwide sharing, such efforts can be a gigantic struggle.

At Maricopa, support often comes from the Centers for Teaching and Learning (CTL)—innovation centers with varied versions of learning and support for faculty and for students teamed with faculty. Naomi Story says that the Mesa Community College CTL strives to take a nondoctrinaire approach to technology. They will view "interesting failures" as worthy, value-added experiments. Story believes and supports this practice; it is a good mantra for the entire system. The MCLI, centered at the district with the experienced arm of its long-standing Ocotillo Project, allows workshops, visioning processes, research and development, best practice symposia, and comprehensive Web services for faculty and staff. Alan Levine, a talented technology advocate and thoughtful transformist, presides over several data and best practice informative systems. He also summons shared vision communities that focus on effective teaching and learning. Blended and hybrid methodologies have been at the center of many symposia, workshops, and larger Ocotillo successes.

Roger concludes his paper with both admonitions and thoughtful considerations:

> As with any new program at a college, the early adopters were ready to go. All of the details for our new hybrid program were not in place, and our motto was (and still is), "Don't punish the pioneers." Early adopters are risk takers—they need support and colleagues to confide in when clarifications are needed.
>
> Three major "lessons" learned from developing a hybrid redesign program are clear:
>
> 1. The process of faculty developing a hybrid course leads to instructional improvement in their face-to-face traditional classes.
> 2. Faculty who receive instruction design support in redesigning courses report more satisfaction in their teaching and better student learning and retention. We must provide the same level of support to faculty with creating hybrid courses as we do with fully online courses.
> 3. A rich collaborative environment amongst the faculty developing hybrid courses emerges within and across disciplines [Yohe, 2002, p. 3].

The three lessons learned are more than sufficient to justify hybrid course experimentation. But what actually occurs in hybrid courses?

Instructor Variation

In hybrid or blended courses, the course content, facilitation, and mix of methodologies vary widely. The following examples from Mesa Community College faculty and staff reflect varied approaches.

Rick Effland: Social Science, Anthropology

Rick Effland teaches anthropology and has also taught both Culture and English in China, an experience that enormously influenced his views on hybrid courses. As a long-standing innovator at Mesa Community College and in various leadership capacities in the Maricopa Community College District, he believes that language cannot be taught unless we put it into individual, cultural, and spiritual context. He accepts the common definitions of the terms *hybrid* and *blended*, but believes the variations of what learning events or combinations go into hybrid courses are infinite. Effland finds comfort in the three-legged model shown in Figure 26.1.

He reasons that time is a constant factor; the structure of most courses, credits, semesters, and entire schedules is experienced in time. However, in blended courses,

FIGURE 26.1.   RICK EFFLAND'S VISUAL MODEL OF HYBRID OR BLENDED COURSES.

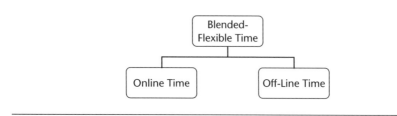

"students were conditioned to time, perhaps more so." Effland adds that we are harnessed to a structure for learning that has less and less relationship to time.

According to Effland, the first thing to be done in creating blended courses is to deconstruct time. To achieve this, he began offering "Open Fridays," a classroom-style forum where students voice their questions or concerns that had accumulated over the week. "Open Fridays were the connective times, but I initiated the connection—the students didn't." However, Effland says he soon doubled his work time for more connection with students: "I break away from time by redefining my relationship to it. As soon as I went to an Open Friday, I was able to escape the time schedule constraint."

Effland even set up collaborative chatrooms for cooperative learning projects, but the students would still turn in their presentations as individuals, not collaborators. "The Open Fridays may have allowed me to serve three or four times more students through this blended arrangement from online courses, but I felt I was doing twice the amount of work. So I achieved a blended course, but I created twice my teaching load," says Effland:

> After looking at my allocation of time, I had not thought of looking at all the hours, whether they were lecture or online. I discovered that I could use them for facilitation, guidance of learning [and] content expertise on my part at the right learning moment and any variation of pedagogy and method I wished to implement.
>
> This epiphany came suddenly. Among the three time modes of the triangle, I could use all three in any combinations I wished. I discovered that the more I mixed these time models, the less constricted I was by old inductive models; seat-time structure became less of a burden. I dumped off seat-time and found that by introducing learning objects on the Open Fridays, I could give concept building so students could exchange, chat [room]] explore, try out interpretations of single learning objects.

An example Effland described was the learning object of the concept of God-King, ubiquitous in anthropological and archaeological content. Understanding how the deification of leaders assisted control and consolidated power and divine authority, students could link the concept of divine right of kings. "They grasped this concept better than if I delivered their learning as I might do online or through print distribution or even lecturing," adds Effland.

Open Fridays became enriching learning events. Effland believes that in the last third of his courses, students began taking control of their own learning. Transmitting content by the instructor gives way to facilitation of learning. Students are guided rather than taught, according to Effland: "As the students tie their concepts together through dialogue, collaborative papers, and the suggested Internet links, we find blended learning puts us all in the position of learners, including me." He continues, "The next stage of growth is that I have all of the hours of the assigned credit to use for such facilitation. I can go back to straight online, back to open facilitation, back to leading students to their own collaborations, and I even can go back to the occasional but less frequently used lecture. I am liberated."

In Effland's case, another feature of blended courses is that students will blog from concept formation, suddenly linking together two or three concepts. Once the students have their "aha!" moment, the blogging commences. This capturing of synthesis and integration of concepts is a very exciting process to watch; Effland and other instructors say it would not be possible in a lecture or a fully online course. "Hybrid or blended courses deliver what we have always only idealized and dreamed about as student learning behavior," concludes Effland.

Shelley Rodrigo: English Department, Instructional Design, Innovator, and Blended Course Advocate

Like most other instructors teaching blended courses, Shelley Rodrigo describes herself as on an exploratory journey. Our definition of blended courses differs as we become more immersed into the process of both redesigning and teaching these courses. "I am now more prepared to offer a visual schema," states Rodrigo. "Before, we sort of jumped in, not knowing or realizing what activities were merging, separating themselves out, or even expiring in a blended course."

Rodrigo offered this way of looking at the distinct elements of her blended courses: "They may not help others, but they are the way that allows me to conceptualize courses." According to her, hybrid courses are technologically mediated; technology is ancillary; there is seat-time (not face-to-face; possibly fully online); and there is no (or very little) face-to-face time.

Rodrigo likes to design courses using the whole spectrum of possibilities. Most instructors think "online" means exclusively Web based. Unfortunately, this concept has betrayed good pedagogy. Instructors have flocked to online course assignments, but have also abandoned online efforts for several good reasons, such as "exhaustive preparation of work," or "I miss the faces, even the little socialization we had." Many never considered a blended option in the beginning, because it was not in our early mental models of online course delivery. "You were online or not," adds Rodrigo.

Rodrigo uses the entire spectrum, feeling that the combinations are not set in stone; rather, the elements shift and change to match learners' needs and evolve with her aim as an instructor. It can also be changed depending on the content as well. For example, if the instructor is teaching political science, C-Span links to congressional debate may enrich one syllabus, while a chemistry lab experiment may be hugely technologically mediated. "You cannot always tell—or prescribe a simple option," says Rodrigo. Blended learning exudes variation. Rodrigo thrives on the designing process, so blended learning fills her needs better. She is also a highly conceptual thinker.

Early experimenters jumped in too quickly perhaps, according to Rodrigo. "Teachers went online and felt 'this is it.'" Rodrigo emphasizes that there is a delicate balance between technology and a sensitivity to what is really working. "I have tried to start with having students come to think about what he or she can do to learn more about this subject." Relying on the online protocol between instructor and student does not facilitate learning: "I want the student to think, go to a chatroom with other students; go to a link on the subject; wait for a discussion or class meeting; design my own learning activities with a collaborative group or with friends."

Rodrigo believes that the ultimate hallmark of a successful blended class learner is self-direction through the navigational tools and resources. "This self-direction may not occur until late in the course," Rodrigo emphasizes. This is not unlike Rick Effland's observation that students take control of their learning in the last third of a blended course.

Rodrigo was not hesitant to look out on the horizon, naming some of the issues policy leaders and faculty must confront:

- There will be more and more hybrid courses because students want more face-to-face, but on their own terms (matching work life, family obligations, etc.)
- Much better administrative support, e.g., more reassigned time for course planning and rewarding experimentation, even if it falls short.
- Much more technology support for students and faculty. Students don't acquire sufficient memory resources or are limited by various bandwidths at home.

- Making students aware that the courses they have selected are blended courses. Students need to know this, as they may expect to be either online or in a lecture classroom.
- The majority of classes in the future will be hybrid. This trend can and probably will eclipse institutional technological preparations and support.
- Access to technology must be improved for faculty as well as for students (personal computers are still prohibitively expensive for many).
- Inadequate support for adjunct faculty as community colleges and universities rely on the use of part-time faculty.
- Course hour and calendar issues; we need to deconstruct credit from the clock hour.
- More emphasis on learning objects and movements toward certification.
- Confronting the possible reality that what is not hybridized may not be around any longer.

Richard Felnagle: Author, Long-Standing Media and Online Advocate

Richard Felnagle emphasizes that the classroom still supports closer interaction for many students. Although he feels that blended approaches are the trend of the future, students who have become reliant on lecture-style teaching will feel some disorientation without the classroom contact.

Felnagle maintains there are a number of students who prefer cyberdominated delivery. They enjoy it, thrive on it, and have no burning need to attempt the blended experience. Other students desire contact, welcoming the blended modules' collaborative experience in a class. Having said that traditional classroom instruction is preferred by many students, the reality seems to indicate that good interaction reaches only a few in a lecture mode. Most students stay passive, so traditional courses reach fewer students, and engagement is not constant.

Hybrid approaches encourage more individual interaction and engagement. According to Felnagle, "This is the reverse of many students' perceptions of cybercourses, which carry the perception that online courses are impersonal, detached from the instruction. From an instructor's point of view, not only is there more contact via blended methodology, it is much more work and time consuming—just from e-mail alone." Like other teachers with whom we have talked, e-mail is read every four to five hours just to keep up with student needs—contact not characteristic of lecture classes.

Felnagle believes that the future is blended courses and that the conventional semester should be discontinued. "Five weeks would be better . . . we don't need to keep students in 15–16 week patterns just to use a traditional calendar," he stressed.

Other improvements Felnagle envisions would be to better prepare help desks to manage learning assistance and student problems. According to Felnagle, faculty carry this burden almost entirely because they are more learning based and centralized: "Many students turn back to us when help desks fail to help, even with ordinary problems."

Felnagle also feels that colleges and their students must confront the variability of equipment that students own; many of the cheaper PCs do not carry the capacity for document searches and the downloading that is required. Mesa Community College's technology offers many public ports and student workstations, but students must question the suitability of their own equipment. Some have weak Internet service providers; others have state-of-the-art connections. Some improvement has occurred through building-to-building wireless, but the students without significant financial resources are not as well positioned for online commerce, for which faculty increasingly assume students are prepared.

Since Felnagle's background is in media production and communications, he predicts "video streaming, more digital media content, and more varied and richer links" as future trends. Both faculty and students have to be technologically prepared and supported for this blended learning approach.

Donna Gaudet: Chief Instructional Designer, Center for Teaching and Learning, Mesa Community College

Donna Gaudet supports the faculty who experiment with and implement blended learning. According to her, methodology is derived by the availability of time and of technology. As an instructional designer, Gaudet predictably emphasizes one feature: design. She also presupposes that faculty should be allowed exploration within a safety zone. Urging faculty to try an activity that would be manageable, she insists that "baby steps are okay!"

Gaudet believes that Mesa Community College has several "go-go" online instructors who were early innovators. She now sees them returning to face-to-face interaction protocols, "de-cybering" their approaches to find a comfortable blended mode of teaching.

Blended courses make the perfect transition for faculty development. Having faculty work with the blended course vision legitimizes the role of the instructional designer. "We are now really needed. More than any previous time, we may be more valued than ever as a supporting agent to faculty. This is a good era we are entering," adds Gaudet.

To support blended learning, Gaudet emphasizes that we work from the instructional objectives. The learning objective drives the mini-intercessions that support the online delivery that makes blended course development so exciting. Gaudet adds that hybrid is the ideal, with heavy emphasis on design. "This is sort of 'designer's heaven,'" adds Gaudet.

When asked what is needed at the CTL to support her work, Gaudet suggests two areas:

- Faculty bring an important reality to the CTL. The faculty should have more internships here, more fellow-type arrangements. When the experimental classes and labs are filled with faculty, it creates a new buzz and energy.
- We need to do more online learning and dissemination from the CTL, better Web resources, links, and simple help. We do that well in interactive sessions, but the CTL hopes to step up online services for those who need blended online help in their courses.

Naomi Story: Director of the Center for Teaching and Learning, Mesa Community College

Naomi Story has a long history of supportive learning. She directs the CTL and is a tenured faculty member. Her training and professional preparation is in instructional design.

When asked about the CTL's philosophy on blended learning, she listed several characteristics that are integral to the mission of the center. She acknowledges that the CTL cannot be all things to all people; instead, Story sees two roles for the CTL to support the development of blended learning.

The first area involves extended discussion and learning about the blended learning movement. The center provides ways to explore issues like the redefinition of time, frequency of contact, breaking down content, and establishing an intermittent formula. To facilitate this exploration, the CTL provides experimental classrooms. The goal is simple: test it, evaluate it, and tweak it as blended methodology components. "We try to reward interesting failures as well as triumphs," says Story. She maintains that there is not just one formula for blended learning. Like Gaudet, she believes the combinations of blended approaches are infinite.

The CTL's main philosophical approach has been nondoctrinaire; it advocates outside-the-box thinking, but it may not always involve technology. When it comes to blended learning, where so many faculty members are experimenting and adapting, the CTL supports "proof of concept." Story believes this encourages her and her impressive team to avoid template solutions:

> Inventing our own way may be the reason we foster greater faculty engagement. We try to deemphasize template solutions. What works for the learner

and the faculty should govern the nature of the blend. . . . The faculty for years have examined elegant off-the-shelf commercial products, but often learn that they can't use them. We think their exploration, their design, their engagement—with a variety of options for blended learning—has caused blended learning to become the movement that it is. We could not have done that as an organizational development or staff development intervention alone.

When asked what an ideal situation for the CTL would be, both Story and Gaudet said they can always use more time and money. Both were clear: blended learning is best based on design, not templates. Even elegant computer-based instructional programs like Plato and Ticket never achieved the wide participation and engagement that blended learning has accomplished.

Story, like Gaudet, would opt for a fellows' program at the CTL: with more faculty, mentors, and experimenters, enriching our energy and aligning our innovation with realities only faculty can bring.

Final Note

We have been on a trajectory of technology adaptation. We evolved from distance education alone to our current environment: an open and exciting blend of online and off-line learning. It has all been innovative and valuable, but blended learning heralds a new age of deeper and wider engagement of more teachers and learners. The progression from analog to Weblog is a continuing story.

References

Bleed, R. (2001, January–February). A hybrid campus for the new millennium. *Educause Review, 36*(1).

Maricopa Center for Learning and Instruction. (2004). *Hybrid courses.* Retrieved September 23, 2004, from http://www.mcli.dist.maricopa.edu/ocotillo/hybrids/index.php.

Yohe, R. (2002). *Experiencing the best of both worlds by teaching a hybrid course.* Unpublished manuscript. Mesa, AZ: Maricopa Community Colleges.

Paul A. Elsner served as chancellor of the Maricopa Community College District in Arizona from 1977 until 1999. He received his doctorate from Stanford University and graduated from Harvard's Institute for Educational Management. Throughout his career as professor and administrator, Elsner served in various capacities for organizations such as Educational Testing Service, American Association of Community Colleges, American Council on International Intercultural Education, League for Innovation, and Campus Compact. The *Chronicle of Higher Education* and *Change Magazine* named him one of the most influential college leaders of our time. His publications include articles, books, and even a morality play on the future of higher education. His current efforts to advance the cause of education have led him to speaking engagements on six continents. In his retirement, he is founder and president of the Sedona Conferences and Conversations, Paul Elsner and Associates, and Los Vientos—organizations dedicated to worldwide education.

CHAPTER TWENTY-SEVEN

VIRTUAL TAU

The Study of a Campuswide Implementation of Blended Learning in Tel-Aviv University

Rafi Nachmias, Judith Ram, David Mioduser

The use of the Internet as an instructional tool in higher education is rapidly increasing. In the past decade, implementation of the new technologies in higher education has generated a rich variety of teaching configurations, from fully online courses to blended learning (American Federation of Teachers, 2001; Bonk, 2001; Bonk, Cummings, Hara, Fischler, & Lee, 2000; Collis & Moonen, 2001; Harasim, Hiltz, Teles, & Turoff, 1995; Mason, 2000; Mioduser & Nachmias, 2002). These developments challenge the 2,500-year-old Socratic, face-to-face instructional mode, currently implemented in most college and universities around the globe. However, alongside the enthusiasm and creativity typical to this process, essential questions regarding the learning quality and effectiveness of online courses emerge (American Federation of Teachers, 2000; Guri-Rosenblit, 2001; Phipps & Merisotis, 1999). In order to examine these issues, a comprehensive research study is currently being conducted to investigate the blended learning taking place in Tel-Aviv University's (TAU) academic courses. In this chapter, we briefly present the rationale of blended learning at TAU, along with excerpts of empirical data on some of the issues related to its implementation.

Background and Rationale of Virtual TAU

TAU is one of the largest research-oriented universities in Israel. Located in the center of the country, it serves some twenty-seven thousand students. These students are enrolled in about six thousand courses annually, which are taught by twenty-five hundred instructors in almost every academic discipline. The Virtual TAU project (http//:virtual.tau.ac.il) was launched in the 2000–2001 academic year in response to a government initiative to advance the implementation of learning technologies in the Israeli higher education system. The project aimed to initiate and stimulate a process by which more faculty members will gradually use the Internet to enrich prevailing learning processes and make instruction more efficient and flexible. The Web shell used by Virtual TAU is Highlearn, a multilingual (including Hebrew) Internet course management system developed by Britannica Knowledge Systems. Highlearn is similar to other Web-supported course systems (such as Blackboard and WebCT). It allows easy creation of an information base for course content and didactic activities and supplies synchronous and asynchronous communication tools for the students and the instructor. In addition, it provides tools that assist the instructor in administrating the course, such as course schedulers, test builders, and address books.

One of the fundamental principles of the project is that the instructors, most of them TAU faculty members, maintain full responsibility for their course Web sites. Their views of the objectives, syllabus, and instructional methods lead to the development and the implementation of the course. No predesigned pedagogical solution is imposed; rather, each instructor acts according to his or her own pedagogical approach. Most of Virtual TAU's support center activities are aimed at empowering the instructors, helping them in the realization of their pedagogical vision.

One major objective of the research project is to evaluate the learning potential embedded in typical Web-supported courses and examine the conditions needed to realize this potential. The research framework of Virtual TAU (VT) consists of three levels of research and analysis. First is the *macrolevel*, which focuses on the assimilation process of the Internet into the campus instruction from the institutional point of view. Second is the *mezzolevel*, which focuses on the characteristics of teaching and learning processes emerging in Web-supported courses. Finally, there is the *microlevel*, which is concerned with the characteristics and consequences of the actual use of Web features in the teaching and learning of specific courses. A detailed description of the research framework can be found in Nachmias (2002).

In this chapter, we address four major issues relating to the macro- and the mezzolevels derived from different studies over a period of four years (2000–2004): (1) the diffusion process of Web-supported instruction in TAU, (2) the pedagogical configuration of course Web sites developed and used by instructors, (3) the use of course content by students, and (4) the use of asynchronous learning processes in blended learning courses.

Diffusion of Web-Supported Academic Instruction

The major question addressed in this section relates to how the diffusion process of Web-supported instruction in TAU developed over time. To examine this process for the academic years 2000–2004, we rely on the number of courses developed and used by faculty and students within VT.

Figure 27.1 shows the increase in the number of courses and lecturers using VT during the four years. The number of courses has grown about eight times from its number in the first year, up to almost three thousand courses. This represents nearly 50 percent of the courses offered at TAU. At the same time, the number of lecturers using VT increased rapidly to over a thousand, which represents about 40 percent of the lecturers in Tel-Aviv University.

In the first year of the implementation, each lecturer taught one or two courses using VT (an average of 1.5 courses per lecturer). In the fourth year, this ratio almost doubled to an average of 2.71 courses per lecturer. Such data indicate that lecturers who began implementing VT in one of their courses adopted its use in other courses as well. Consequently the number of students who use VT increased as well. In the year 2003–2004, about twenty thousand out of twenty-seven thousand students were registered in the system. During 2004, about 1.5 million user sessions were recorded and about 4 million content items were viewed.

FIGURE 27.1.   INCREASE IN THE NUMBER OF COURSES AND LECTURERS INVOLVED IN VIRTUAL TAU, 2000–2004.

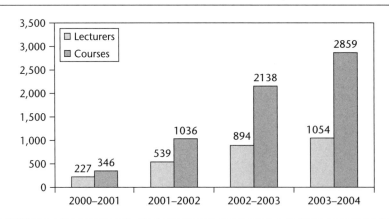

The data indicate that by all parameters (as defined by Rogers, 1995), the diffusion of the Internet use for instruction at TAU was extremely rapid and beyond any expectation. The original attempt to build an initial phase of implementation based on the gradual creation of course Web sites, as well as the allocation of limited budget and technical and pedagogical support, proved to be highly naive. In a very short time, the demands by lecturers and academic units far surpassed the initial prospects.

Several factors might have contributed to the rapid development of VT. First and foremost, it seems that the very concept of blended learning and the tools for facilitating its implementation satisfied real instructional and pedagogical needs for both faculty and students. Being already aware of the role of information and communication technologies (ICT) for learning and working at the personal level, it took our faculty members little time to foresee the potential of these tools for the creation of sound pedagogical solutions aimed to enhance their instruction.

Institutional policy was another influential factor. VT was conceived as a campuswide project. All interested lecturers were given the opportunity to receive technical and pedagogical training and support in the use of the online learning tools and associated integration into their courses.

Finally, the efforts of the efficient and knowledgeable support center staff, and the relative user-friendliness of the various components of the system, undoubtedly contributed to accelerate the adoption rate of VT among lecturers and students.

In summary, timely educational policy, pedagogical and technical solutions based on real needs, and proper infrastructure and support contributed to the impressive diffusion process of Virtual TAU.

Pedagogical Configuration of Course Web Sites

A main objective in our studies was to assess the course Web sites' pedagogical configuration as conceived and used by the instructors. For this purpose, a random sample of 109 course Web sites (from about 2000 courses in the academic year 2002–2003) was selected. The courses pertained to the faculties: Art, Humanities, Medicine, Engineering, Social Sciences, Life Sciences, Education, Exact Sciences, Law, and Management. These Web sites were analyzed using a course Web site characterization scheme comprising 116 variables in four main dimensions: (1) content, (2) educational activity, (3) learning management, and (4) instructional environment (a detailed description of this tool can be found in Shemla and Nachmias, 2004).

The analysis of the configuration of the 109 Web sites is described in Tables 27.1 and 27.2; 821 learning activities were found (an average of about

TABLE 27.1.   FREQUENCY OF LEARNING ACTIVITY TYPES IN 109 COURSE WEB SITES (*N* = 821 ITEMS).

Learning Activity Type	Sum of Items	Percentage from All Items
Exercise/assignment	264	32.16
Simulation	215	26.19
Online exercises with feedback	169	20.58
Survey	28	3.41
Discussion group on articles	26	3.17
Reading assignment	17	2.07
Experiments with virtual lab	13	1.58
General forum	10	1.22
Other	79	9.62

TABLE 27.2.   FREQUENCY OF CONTENT TYPE IN 109 COURSE WEB SITES (*N* = 3,131 ITEMS).

Learning Activity Type	Sum of Items	Percentage from All Items
Content items	1,168	37.30
Lecturer presentations	410	13.09
Exercise solutions	312	9.96
Article, book chapter	260	8.30
Sample tests	208	6.64
Lesson or lab preparation	134	4.28
Assignment instruction	93	2.97
Syllabus	91	2.91
Students' work	87	2.78
Technical help	75	2.40
Other	293	9.36

8 per Web site). Table 27.1 indicates that over 80 percent of the learning activities were assignments, exercises (including online), and simulations. Very few group activities, and, in particular, asynchronous-tool-based activities, were implemented.

In the course Web sites examined, over thirty-three hundred content items were included. The average number of items presented in each site was 28, ranging from 2 to 118 items for each Web site. For most courses (88 courses, comprising 75 percent of the courses in the study), up to 35 items were in existence. Only in one course were over 100 items presented. There were no differences in the number of content items presented in Web sites of Exact Sciences faculties and Social Sciences and Humanities faculties. Likewise, there were no significant differences between undergraduate and graduate courses. There was a positive correlation between the number of students in a course and the number of content items presented in the Web site ($R = 0.21$; $p < 0.05$). A close look at the content items by type shows that the most frequent categories (about 60 percent of the items examined) refer simply to plain information (for example, readings, lecturers' presentations, and content). However, only about 25 percent of the items concerned task-related information (for example, assignments, lab preparation, and tests). Unfortunately, even in this world of learner-centered instruction and the power of the Web to exploit it, there were very few courses that took advantage of student-generated items.

In a study published in 2000 aiming to characterize the pedagogical profile of educational Web sites, we defined the situation then as

> one step ahead for the technology, two steps back for the pedagogy. One can depict that way the usual loops affecting educators' assimilation of new technologies for the last decades. . . . As experienced educators we hold substantial models regarding the varied facets of our practice (e.g., how to build a lesson plan, to assess a learner's performance or behavior, to develop a learning unit). These models are usually tied to the (technological) resources at hand, and they affect each other mutually. It seems reasonable to assume that when facing the assimilation of a new technology we use these models as input to the process. The result is usually a transition period during which the known models are replicated by means of the new technology [Mioduser, Nachmias, Oren, & Lahav, 2000, pp. 73–74].

Academic instruction is by its very nature more conservative than instruction in other educational settings, such as school-level or informal education. Academic instruction has long been based on lecturing and individual reading and the structuring of scientific content to be delivered according to the epistemological model of the textbook. The fortunate (but perhaps not incidental) conjunction of new theories of learning and instruction, and new technologies facilitating the development of novel pedagogical solutions, implies a challenge for educators in general, and for academic instruction in particular. However, it appears that a transition time is unavoidable. Our observations of the evolving character of the blended courses at TAU show clearly that different lecturers adopt the innovation at different rates and that many configurations in the pedagogical continuum can and do coexist. This continuum of blended courses ranges from digital mirrors of the traditional courses at one end, to exciting examples of original pedagogical solutions at the other end. While many lecturers are still in the transition phase, the seeds of new models of blended learning are already there.

Use of Content Included in the Course Web Sites

The third issue addressed in our studies is the extent to which content items in the course Web sites were actually viewed by the students. To examine this question, 117 courses in the academic year 2001–2002 were investigated using the automatically recorded computer logs (see Nachmias & Segev, 2003, for more details). This automatic recording includes textual and numerical identification of content items, date and time in which the item was viewed, and the ID of the student accessing it. A content item is defined as a unit of information uploaded into the course's Web site (for example, presentations, lesson summaries, and exercises). Content items may vary in their format (documents, pdf's, and presentations, for example) as well as in their size. In this system, students can access only the learning materials of the courses in which they are registered. "Viewing a content item" is referred to each time a student clicks on a link to a content item and opens it. Our analysis is based on the assumption that "viewing a content item" meant that the student read it. The information accumulated in the computer log comprised the database used for the study.

Figure 27.2 presents the distribution of the percentage of content items viewed by students in 117 courses. In the 117 course Web sites examined, 3,301 content items were presented. The average number of items presented in each site was 28, ranging between 2 to 118 items for each Web site.

Examining the individual differences in content use among students, one of the central findings of this study was that only 62 percent of the students viewed at least one content item, whereas 38 percent of the students listed in the courses did not view even a single item. However, there was a large variance among students with regard to the number of items viewed. Most students viewed only a small number of the available items, whereas few students viewed all of them. Figure 27.2 presents the distribution of the percentage of content items viewed by students. About 50 percent of the students accessed no more than one-tenth of the items available, using only a small part of the information presented in the courses' Web sites. Only 18 percent of the students accessed more than half of the content items, and less than 4 percent accessed all content items presented on the courses' Web sites. Students viewing at least one content item viewed on average 38 percent of the items available.

An examination of differences in use by discipline shows that students in the Social Sciences and Humanities faculties viewed a significantly larger number of items compared to students in the Exact Sciences faculties. In addition, graduate students viewed a significantly larger number of items than undergraduates did. The study also revealed that the rate of students who did not use the items at

FIGURE 27.2.   DISTRIBUTION OF PERCENTAGE OF CONTENT ITEMS VIEWED BY STUDENTS.

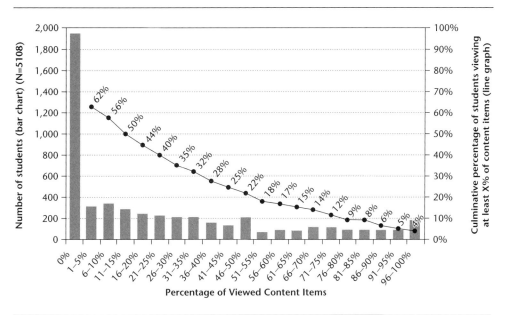

Note: N = 3,167 in 117 courses.

all was significantly higher among undergraduate than graduate students. This rate was higher among Social Sciences and Humanities students compared with Exact Sciences students.

Different conclusions can be drawn from these data. First, it appears that in most courses, the effort invested by many lecturers to include large amounts of digital materials in their Web sites was not fully rewarded (by reasonable content-consumption levels). It appears that many instructors made their course development decisions focusing more on intrinsic or content-based considerations and less on actual implementation considerations (for example, students' capability to access and read all content items in the course or actual allocation of time for reading assignments along the instruction). However, a contrasting conclusion may be based on the concept that the content items component of the Web sites is an ever-growing repository of content resources, which can be reconfigured according to changing objectives and student needs in each teaching cycle. In such a model, there is not necessarily an exact correspondence between a given item and a specific class, but a more flexible perception of content base to be used by different students at different stages according to their needs and objectives; in other words, under this model, it is unrealistic to expect all items to be retrieved or all students to access each and every item.

When we consider the interplay between the lecturers' motivations and conceptions for developing content and the students' needs and goals for consuming it, an evolving process during which different models emerge and are tested in each teaching cycle of the blended course.

Implementation and Use of Asynchronous Forums

A fourth issue addressed in our studies relates to the extent to which instructors implement asynchronous forums in their blended courses and the associated level of student participation in such activities. To deal with these questions, all courses during the academic years 2000–2001 to 2003–2004 were examined (over fifty-nine hundred courses). Table 27.3 presents the data on forum implementation and use over these years. On the one hand, the data show a gradual increase in the number of courses in which asynchronous activities were implemented. It seems that progressively more lecturers become aware of the potential contribution of the communication tools for teaching. On the other hand, the actual proportion of courses implementing communication tools, such as discussion forums relative to the total number of blended courses, is still discouraging: about 4 to 6 percent in the last couple of years.

From the students' perspective, the data show a slight increase over time in the total number of messages posted in the course forums and in the average number of messages per course as well. The average number of messages per student per course (about four to six) remained unexpectedly low over the years.

TABLE 27.3.   ASYNCHRONOUS DISCUSSION FORUMS IMPLEMENTATION AND PARTICIPATION OVER TIME.

Academic Year	2000–2001	2001–2002	2002–2003	2003–2004
Number of courses with active forums	34	40	74	163
Percentage of all courses	10%	4%	4%	6%
Number of messages	4,704	4,531	9,830	23,400
Average of messages per course (SD)	138 (176)	112 (222)	133 (192)	144 (150)
Average number of messages per student (S.D.)	5 (5)	4 (5)	6 (10)	4 (4)

A strong claim favoring the adoption of new ICT for educational purposes stresses the potential embedded in the communication tools for empowering teaching and learning processes (Hara, Bonk, & Angeli, 2000; Nachmias, Mioduser, Oren, & Ram, 2000; Oren, Mioduser, & Nachmias, 2002). Despite this claim, the slow pace of actual adoption of communication-based activities in the courses indicates that a reexamination of needs, goals, and procedures in the development of blended instruction is required. It appears that the lecturers are neither aware of the educational potential of these tools nor trained in their implementation for teaching. For both teachers and students, the integration of technology-mediated communication into their teaching or learning implies first and foremost a change in the way they perceive the transactions involved in their shared academic experience. Such transactions might include those that are not tied to a predetermined space or time slot; that may be configured in formats other than the common one-to-many lecture-dominant structure; that may follow varied interaction models typical of different human transactional situations (a trial, a design group, a contest, or a distributed production team, for example); or that represent the distribution of functions and allocation of control and leadership roles other than that characterizing the classic teacher-student interrelationship. It appears that the required change in perception takes place gradually with the attempts to devise communication-based activities. It is by this process that more innovative and complex models progressively evolve and enrich the repertoire of learning opportunities.

Conclusion

This chapter briefly surveyed four aspects of a campuswide implementation project aimed at integrating the Internet into the academic instruction at Tel-Aviv University. This initiative is being accompanied by comprehensive research and evaluation, focusing on multiple aspects at the macro-, mezzo-, and microlevels.

From our continuous examination of the progress of the project, two main preliminary and apparently contrasting conclusions can be drawn. The first is related to the impressive pace at which the implementation of the Internet in the academic instruction has grown at TAU. Beyond any expectation, many lecturers adopted the technology over a very short time, triggering the diffusion of blended learning all over the campus and at all academic levels.

The contrasting conclusion relates to the still limited pedagogical range of the implemented activities. From the pedagogical point of view, most instructors conceive the use of course Web sites in their most basic form: as content provider rather than communication facilitator (asynchronous forums were included as teaching mode only in about 4 to 10 percent of courses in the past three years). Only about 5 percent have developed novel pedagogies in which the Web has added value, such as hyperlinked information and Web-supported collaborative work. However, some instructors (5 to 10 percent) do experiment and add novel pedagogical features to their Web sites in new cycles of their courses' implementation.

We can conclude that blended learning at TAU remains in a transitional phase characterized by the implementation of traditional pedagogical solutions by means of the new technologies. For greater transformation of teaching and learning to occur, most lecturers need appropriate support to make the conceptual shift toward the generation of more sound technology-based learning activities.

A salient feature of the majority of the courses developed over the years is that these were conceived as blended courses in varied degrees. Thus, an increasingly rich continuum of course models has evolved. On the one end, the Web site serves as a repository of varied content and administrative information resources. On the other, the Web site represents a complete pedagogical component complementing the campus-based face-to-face activities in a virtual way. However, total flexibility (Collis & Moonen, 2001) in learning time and space was hardly achieved. Only one or two lecturers created fully online courses, and very few gave up their actual meeting in the class. In the vast majority of the courses, all Web activities were additional to the classes, in some cases increasing the workload of the students and the instructors as well.

These issues were usually related to the implementation process of blended learning at TAU. Our research agenda for the near future includes the study of issues in several areas, such as the cost-effectiveness of blended learning, evaluation of different types and models of blended courses, development of appropriate methodological tools for the analysis of large amounts of logged data, and consolidation of new pedagogical models fostering the mindful formation of the academic staff.

Aware that we are only at the first stages of a long and complex implementation process, we do believe that blended learning has the potential to evolve into a paradigm shift in the organization and pedagogies of academic instruction.

References

American Federation of Teachers. (2000, May). *Distance education: Guidelines for good practice.* Retrieved September 27, 2004, from www.aft.org/higher_ed/downloadable/distance.pdf.

American Federation of Teachers. (2001, May). *A virtual revolution: Trends in the expansion of distance education.* Retrieved September 27, 2004, from www.aft.org/higher_ed/downloadable/VirtualRevolution.pdf.

Bonk, C. J. (2001). *Online teaching in an online world.* Bloomington, IN: CourseShare.com. Retrieved September 22, 2004, from http://PublicationShare.com.

Bonk, C. J., Cummings, J. A., Hara, N., Fischler, R., & Lee, S. M. (2000). A ten level Web integration continuum for higher education. In B. Abbey (Ed.), *Instructional and cognitive impacts of Web-based education* (pp. 56–77). Hershey, PA: Idea Group.

Collis, B., & Moonen, J. (2001). *Flexible learning in a digital world: Experiences and expectations.* London: Kogan Page.

Guri-Rosenblit, S. (2001). The tower of Babel syndrome in the discourse on information technologies in higher education. *Global E-Journal of Open, Flexible and Distance Education, 1*(1), 28–38.

Hara, N., Bonk, C. J., & Angeli, C. (2000). Content analysis of online discussion in an applied educational psychology course. *Instructional Science, 28,* 115–152.

Harasim, L., Hiltz, S. R., Teles, L., & Turoff, L. (1995). *Learning networks.* Cambridge, MA: MIT Press.

Mason, R. (2000). From distance education to online education. *Internet and Higher Education, 3*(1–2), 63–74.

Mioduser, D., & Nachmias, R. (2002). WWW in education. In H. Adelsberger, B. Collis, & M. Pawlowski (Eds.), *Handbook on information technologies for education and training* (pp. 23–63). New York: Springer.

Mioduser, D., Nachmias, R., Oren, A., & Lahav, O. (2000). Web-based learning environments (WBLE)—current technological and pedagogical state. *Journal of Research on Computing in Education, 33*(1), 55–76.

Nachmias, R. (2002). A research framework for the study of a campus-wide Web-based academic instruction project. *Internet and Higher Education, 5,* 213–229.

Nachmias, R., Mioduser, D., Oren, A., & Ram, J. (2000). Web-supported emergent-collaboration in higher education courses. *Educational Technology and Society, 3*(3), 94–104.

Nachmias, R., & Segev, L. (2003). Students' use of content in Web-supported academic courses. *Internet and Higher Education, 6,* 145–157.

Oren, A., Mioduser, D., & Nachmias, R. (2002). The development of social climate in virtual learning discussion group. *International Review of Research in Open and Distance Learning, 3*(1), 1–19.

Phipps, R., & Merisotis, J. (1999). *What's the difference? A review of contemporary research on the effectiveness of distance learning in higher education.* Washington, DC: Institute for Higher Education Policy. Retrieved September 22, 2004, from http://www.ihep.com/Pubs/PDF/Difference.pdf.

Rogers, E. (1995). *Diffusion of innovations* (4th ed.). New York: Free Press.

Shemla, A., & Nachmias, R. (2004). *Current state of Web-supported courses in higher education.* Paper presented at the Ed-media World Conference on Educational Multimedia, Hypermedia and Telecommunications, Lugano, Switzerland.

Rafi Nachmias is a professor of science education in Tel-Aviv University's School of Education. He is currently heading the Science and Technology Education Center, the Exact Sciences Education, and the Virtual TAU project in Tel-Aviv University. His major research areas are Web-based learning, innovative pedagogical school practices using information and communication technologies, and mathematics and science education.

Judith Ram has been the director of the Virtual TAU project that integrates advanced learning technologies into academic instruction at Tel-Aviv University since 2000. Heading a department for many years in the Center for Educational Technology, she gained considerable experience with integrating computers in the school system. She holds a master's of educational research and evaluation.

David Mioduser is a professor of education in Tel-Aviv University's School of Education. He is currently heading the graduate program of Information and Communication in Education. His major research areas are learning with information and communication technologies, and technology education.

CHAPTER TWENTY-EIGHT

MANAGEMENT EDUCATION FOR THE TWENTY-FIRST CENTURY

Gilly Salmon, Naomi Lawless

In many senses, the U.K. Open University (OU) was founded on the idea of blended learning long before the phrase came into common use. The combination of the latest technology and a high level of knowledgeable and skilled human support and intervention is just as relevant today as in the OU's foundation years of the 1970s. In this chapter, we focus on two major areas of development within blended learning: offering group skills development in the online environment and the change in the role of tutors.

The Open University's Approach to Blended Learning

The OU was founded in 1969 as a single-mode distance teaching university, offering a wide range of undergraduate degrees, master's degrees, and professional qualifications. The university is state funded and fully accredited in the United Kingdom. It maintains exceptionally high quality and is recognized as the premier open university in the world, on which many others are modeled.

The learning support system still operates on the "industrial model." Phase One consists of developing high-quality and paced learning materials, originally through print and broadcast. Over the years, more new learning technologies such as CD-ROMs and Web sites have been included. The second phase is the delivery of group tutoring, feedback on individual assignments, and support by part-time tutors. Clearly, students' working together for knowledge sharing forms a critical part of the learning. Tutors have gradually learned to run their classes and groups in the online environments as well as face to face. Currently, around 220,000 students study with the OU, most with some online element to their programs. Programs operate throughout the United Kingdom and mainland East and West Europe.

Business Schools and Learning Innovations

Business schools, since their inception, have sought to explore the nature of flexibility in learning and have rejected some of the traditional lecture-style pedagogies, which rely on the teacher as expert. Hence, the introduction of online *ought* to be a blessing within business schools. However, the transition from dependent-on-authority pedagogies to one where students take more responsibility for their own learning includes difficulty in their expectations and satisfaction, especially in relationships with teaching staff (Felder & Brent, 1996). Costello, Brunner, and Hasty (2002) show that management students have difficulty with participative, cooperative, and collaborative learning and its responsibilities. However, on reflection at the end of the experience, many recognize the associated empowerment, new skill development, and benefits of persevering with self-directed learning.

Managers studying and working need a high level of flexibility to acquire, practice, and apply new concepts and skills. Successful and effective management education needs to go beyond the idea of traditional distance learning and embrace the much wider range of understandings required in the complex networked organizations of the twenty-first century. Business schools are under tremendous pressures to maintain relevance and authenticity in their programs, including their mode and approach of learning, as well as content (Hamlin, Griffy-Brown, & Goodrich, 2003; Reisel & Watson, 2003). Currently, all business schools face challenge from in-house corporate universities and work-related training.

Mass Management Education

The Open University Business School (OUBS) rapidly grew during the 1980s and now offers a range of programs leading to professional qualifications, as well as bachelor's and master's degrees. It uses collaborative online work extensively in its courses with more than thirty thousand students per year in over thirty countries. Collaboration online is increasingly a requisite of organizations sponsoring students with the OUBS.

The Professional Certificate in Management Program is a recognized professional qualification based on all-around managerial competence, with open entry. Students do not need prior qualifications or tests in order to take part. It is truly open in the best traditions of open distance learning. It is available in two variants: as a general program for managers in any industry or sector or tailored to the needs of managers from the public and nonprofit sectors.

The main program involves a year of self-directed distance learning with tutor support and can be taken with either total online support (tutorials and other support online) or face-to-face tutorials and an element of online tutor support. It has been offered in various forms since the late 1980s, always attracting thousands of students each year, mainly in the United Kingdom, Western Europe, and Eastern Europe. In addition to study in English, the program is offered in six European languages, through partners, but all supported directly by the course team at the Open University's Center at Milton Keynes in the United Kingdom, including the transfer of quality procedures and recruitment, monitoring, and supervision of teaching and assessment.

The learning paradigms for the Certificate in Management are those of constructive, collaborative learning through undertaking consensual activities in groups and reflection on action (Schön, 1987). A blend of printed and online materials and resources framed within the OU's established and supported open learning method is offered. In addition, each student is allocated a personal tutor who communicates electronically. In terms of assessment, most assignments require all students to work in problem-based learning groups online. Assessment of students is through assignments and examinations.

Students have a wide variety of choices, including a mix of online and offline tutorial support. There is also a compulsory element of the certificate program where students either attend the group skills-based "Management Challenge" over a residential weekend or cover the equivalent ground online and asynchronously over eighteen days. "The Challenge" consists of a series of personal creativity and team-building exercises followed by a consultancy-based team case study, with a focus on problem solving in a complex scenario and clearly presenting ideas for action. Regardless of the mix or the mode and whether they mingle face-to-face or online, all students are expected to achieve the same learning outcomes and high standards of achievement, assessed through assignments and examinations.

There is a success rate of around 80 percent completion and pass for all versions of the program from the five thousand or so enrollments annually. Successful completion of the program results in the award of a Certificate in Management and leads completers to the Professional Diploma in Management and the M.B.A. Alternatively, credit can be used toward undergraduate degrees.

In addition, many managers study individual modules for professional development purposes.

At the end of 2001, an internal university survey of students provided by the Institute of Educational Technology at the OU showed that the overall satisfaction with the program is very high, with a slight edge to the version deploying online collaboration (Table 28.1).

All Open University courses are subject to scrutiny by a peer assessor. The Certificate in Management, despite its huge scale and complexity, consistently is much valued. For example, the following is an extract from the External Examiner's Report in January 2004: "Tutoring, as shown by monitoring, continues to be of a very high standard and the course materials, structure and content appropriate. The assessment strategy continues most appropriate and the balance between elements excellent."

Rethinking Approaches for the Twenty-First Century

In autumn 2002, we undertook a study of the need for flexible approaches in the OUBS Certificate in Management program. In order to address improvements in the slight variations in the responses to differing mixes and to continue to position the program better for the twenty-first-century manager, a random sample of five hundred students was conducted with usable results from nearly two hundred. The results showed that flexibility in studying for both personal and vocational development was of critical importance to our students, along with flexible pace and a choice of study methods. In addition, there was evidence that students felt there was variable quality in tutoring. Some acknowledged truly outstanding tutors that they had, while others were less so, especially in the online environment. As we engaged in reviewing and revamping the program, we focused on tutors and study options.

We also addressed issues of problem-based learning (PBL) in and through the online environment. The Certificate in Management has always used authentic tasks and assignments for teaching and assessment. However, with the revision of the pedagogy, we adopted a more explicit approach to problem-based assessment in both assignments and exams (Jonassen, 2002). PBL encourages open-minded, reflective, critical, and active learning and reflects that nature of knowledge as complex and changing since problems are always part of a problem situation or what is problematic about a situation. PBL tries to close the gap between theory and practice. We think that the use of the term *problem* suggests notions of problem identification, deconstruction, seeking and using knowledge and experience, understanding, thinking, choosing a strategy, acting, and then critically

TABLE 28.1.   CERTIFICATE IN MANAGEMENT STUDENT SATISFACTION RATINGS.

	Number of Students Responding	Very or Fairly Satisfied That Course Met Expectations	Very or Fairly Helpful in Increasing Management Knowledge and Competencies	Very or Fairly Satisfied with Overall Quality and Support from Tutor	Plan to Continue Studying to Diploma or M.B.A.`	Recommend Course to Other Managers
Full online version of program	131	94.7%	96.9%	81.8%	73.6%	94.7%
Version with face-to-face tutorials	276	91.6	95.6	76.4	73.3	93.1

evaluating (reflecting on) the action and strategy. This includes metacognitive knowing about knowing, which does not determine how a person uses a strategy but whether he or she will use it in other situations.

We chose to create a range of online activities, which we call e-tivities. E-tivities acknowledge the importance in Web-based education of offering access to information *and* communicating with others, not merely one or the other, within a structured and viable framework (Gallagher, 2003). E-tivities require the design of an authentic task that can foster engagement with a small spark of content, individual response, an example from one's own experience, and a collaborative discussion or product (Salmon, 2002). Although authentic tasks had previously been offered in face-to-face tutorials, using the online environment in this explicit way was introduced in 2004. Tutors are trained to facilitate these approaches.

Choices for Certificate in Management Students

Many of the OUBS courses contain a residential element. This is an opportunity for students who have been studying remotely to meet and interact with their peers, learning with and through others. Our students are usually already working as managers in some type of workplace setting. It is our intention to help them relate course theory to their own workplace through reflection on action (Schön, 1983, 1987), while also enabling them to become self-directed learners.

The format of the residential school is designed to promote the advantages of peer collaboration (Vygotsky, 1979) where students work in self-directed groups, rather than listen to lectures or have someone teach content to them. Although students espouse their enthusiasm for working in face-to-face groups, they often find it dissatisfying (Bruffee, 1999). Some scholars argue that this dissatisfaction may be directly related to their lack of teamwork and group processing skills (Dirk & Smith, 2004). For this reason, the main theme of the Certificate in Management residential school (the Management Challenge) is that of teamwork, with reflection directed at process issues more than the results of activities.

As part of its open access policy, the OUBS needs to ensure that there is an equivalent experience available to students who cannot attend the residential Management Challenge, whether they have been studying the online-only version or not. In addition, we planned to use the online version of the Management Challenge to expose managers to the key business skill of working in remote groups. The equivalent course for the certificate residential school is an online learning experience, the "Online Management Challenge" (OMC). Most students prefer the residential option, but a significant percentage opt for the online experience. Of the students studying the main course online, 78 percent go on to study the OMC, making their studies completely online; the rest blend their studies through attending the residential Management Challenge. Conversely, there is an element of students (one-third of those taking the OMC) who have thus far attended face-to-face tutorials but opt for the online experience, again choosing to blend their learning.

Such experiences show a real need for offering a blended learning approach to suit student needs. The main reasons given for opting for the online experience are those of wanting flexibility and not being able to attend the schools that offer the needed courses. Students work in groups of around ten with a tutor to facilitate the learning and answer queries; the main learning material is provided either in their course books or on the dedicated Web site. Each year, around 350 students take part in the OMC, which runs four times during that period.

The OMC has to have equal teaching and learning hours to the residential school, so it is only twenty-one hours long. It cannot be spread over too long a time period as it runs concurrently with the course, which can lead to a conflict with other course work demands; these dual commitments can make it difficult for students to prioritize their time. In the early days of the OMC, this resulted in a loss of motivation and a tail-off in activity during the last few days. For this reason, the original twenty-one-day OMC was compressed to eighteen days, ensuring that it covered only two weekends, a key drop-off time for activities, while maintaining the same learning content and outcomes.

Students are given introductory activities in order to start to get to know their tutor and other group members. These social icebreakers are followed by more complex group activities aimed at getting them to practice using management theory as well as learn about working in online teams. The format is such that the tutor introduces the activity, the students break into subgroups to work in their own conference area to complete the activity, and then the tutor and group of ten students meet again in their group conference area, where the tutor facilitates a discussion of their findings and their reflection on what has been learned about management theory and work environments.

Completing such a rigorous and important program in less than three weeks is expecting a lot from people who have not met each other before, especially given the demands that they perform and learn together. For this reason, we are researching the factors that can aid the success of a group working together online. The intent is to identify actions that can be taken to speed up the time taken for the group to begin performing and learning.

Having already carried out group work in their tutorials or as part of their course work online, the majority of the students taking the OMC (80 percent) expect to learn in groups; however, they are fairly evenly split as to whether they prefer to learn in a group or on their own (52 percent prefer group learning and 48 percent self-directed study). Although some researchers relate that students find that online "consensus decision-making and the production of a common product [are] much less satisfying" than when this occurs face-to-face (Dirk & Smith, 2004), on the whole, many OMC students value the experience. The following comment by an OMC student in March 2004 reflects students' general satisfaction with this program: "Everyone in the group [felt] motivated by the experience and the support of all involved made it not only educational but fun."

One of the advantages of having the course spread over a few days and using text for communication is that this enhances more reflective interaction, a keystone of the OUBS approach to learning. However, the students are aware of a number of difficulties that they feel they would not encounter face-to-face, such as planning and coordinating activities under tight time lines (Kitchen & McDougall, 1999). The time pressures arise because of the delays inherent in asynchronous conversation. Students may concentrate on the task and avoid discussion and constructive criticism (Kitchen & McDougall, 1999), so it is important for the tutor to maintain a role that encourages individual and group reflection. The individual student reflection is aided by the learning diary students are encouraged to keep, where they note and reflect on activities on a daily basis, referring back to it when it is time for group discussion.

One of the key differences when compared to the residential school is the lack of social presence experienced online (Walther, 1992). While some scholars caution that this can significantly retard the development of group relationships (Walther, 1992; Yoo & Alavi, 2001), we find that by the end of the eighteen days in the OMC, some students prove to be extremely loyal and supportive of each other. The key to developing group cohesion is the development of trust (Lawless, 2004). Like Haywood (1998), we have found that a sense of trust in online environments can be established fairly quickly if students feel that they can predict the behavior of others and that there is a commitment to the team.

Students on the OMC recognize the importance of team commitment. Of the thirty-one students asked whether they felt that the "online group's success depends on members wanting the group to succeed," 16 percent felt that this was important and 84 percent felt that this was very important (no one felt that it was quite important or not important). Furthermore, these students reported that they had experienced team commitment during the OMC, with 39 percent feeling that their group members had wanted the group to succeed quite a lot and 61 percent very much indeed (Lawless, 2003).

The Role of the Tutor Online

Although the groups are self-managing, there is also an opportunity for their tutor to facilitate the group-forming process. We offer specific advice to tutors to assist with the formation of self-managing student groups based on our research on the OMC:

E-moderating large groups can be time consuming and participants benefit from becoming self-managing. The basic process includes:

- Divide larger groups into smaller work teams. Give them ample time to complete an e-tivity and then report back to the larger group.
- Where necessary, offer clarification about the task, the timescale, and the form of presentation.
- Leave the group to get on with the task, only intervening if they fail to post their contribution to the plenary on time.
- Start a discussion on the results of the plenary contributions but do not dominate it. Summarize the discussion or ask an experienced participant to do this.

However there are some specific actions shown in Table 28.2 for the moderator to take that will help groups to self-manage online.

TABLE 28.2.   MODERATOR ACTIONS FOR PROMOTING SELF-MANAGING GROUPS.

1. Ask individuals to confirm when they have joined in.	A simple joining activity in the thread will leave a trace to indicate that participants arrived. A cross-check against a list of participants will reveal who is late. Designate a participant from each work team to follow up less visible contributors.
2. State the purpose of the task.	The task will motivate the participants. Offer clarification, if necessary, but allow opportunities for flexible interpretations.
3. Describe how groups will be formed.	An element of self-selection helps to maintain interest, but ensure that the method is simply described and incapable of being misunderstood.
4. Set up a thread for each group, and let the group know where to locate the thread.	Otherwise they will ask you!
5. Describe the form and type of content that the group should produce and where they should post it.	Aim to be prescriptive without being too restrictive. Indicate the main issues that must be addressed.
6. Set out the plenary process in the plenary thread.	This can be part of your welcoming message.
7. Ask the participants to review both content (their main focus) and the process.	Include setting up the group, the degree to which they found the task motivating, how they collaborated, and their approach to feeding back as part of the learning points—so it becomes natural and normal to reflect on, not just their outputs but how they worked together.

Authentic Blend for Tutor Development

As we built newly mixed opportunities for our students, we realized that we must use a blended approach for our tutors' professional development. In addition, since they are more used to the inclusion of face-to-face tutorials in the blend, there is a need to enhance their experience and skills of working online. Work by Hodgkinson (2000) identifies barriers to universities' becoming learning organizations due to cultural problems, a lack of teamwork and sharing ethos, imposition of programs and ideas rather than emergence, and no roll-out of knowledge gained through tutors' own learning. We wished to avoid falling into such a trap. We recognized that tutors need considerable support in their change of approach (Arbaugh & Steizer, 2003; Jonassen, 2002; Salmon, 2004; Walker, 2002). In addition, we wanted to ensure that the OU's spirit of openness and support transferred successfully to the increased use of online work in the distance mix.

Our tutors need to develop the ability to "recognize communication styles and learning patterns from other cultures" (Simons, 2002, p. 126). Knight's summary (2002) of the move toward online facilitation is instructive: "It is ironic that what some take to be dehumanising technology may actually need tutors in order to be more empathetic and considerate" (p. 12.).

The latest version of the Certificate in Management, which started in May 2004, focuses especially on solving real-world management problems through its online student groups, which it calls Webgroups. As a rehearsal for supporting their students, the tutors work through a two-week, five-hour online staff development program instead of the usual face-to-face one-day briefing. The course development team offers a Webcast, a dedicated Web site, and also a set of e-tivities and discussion forums on the OU's collaborative online environment, FirstClass. Specially trained tutor-peers act as e-convenors for the forums and e-tivities, all of whom (willingly) went through the online briefing first.

The e-tivities focus on the use of management concepts and application in practice. Here, critically important online skills are emphasized, such as encouraging participation and achievement (especially from reluctant busy managers), weaving together contributions, and adding value through summaries. The nature of online time management and the different rhythms of e-learning spark a great deal of interest. The discussion topics are wide ranging but always focus on the key management skills that certificate students will need and involve much dialogue between remote tutors and the central course development team.

Sixty OUBS tutors took part in the Certificate in Management program between January and April and another fifty in August and September 2004, working together in groups of ten to twelve. Nearly all successfully completed the program, developed their personal development plans, and received their

Certificates of Participation. The main comment from tutors is that they are very happy to have made space to "have a go" for themselves. They feel an increased confidence in their abilities and empathy with their students. They recognize that much of the knowledge and skill they already have can be used, but that the online environment puts new and rather different demands on everyone taking part. In particular, they mention the nature of online time and "communicating without the usual signals." One of the experienced tutors wrote, "I now realize how daunting, confusing and 'loud' the online environment can be." Another said, "This is a fantastic reality check for me. . . . I really need to focus on what matters to promote a great online experience for managers . . . and forget what doesn't. I believe I've started to distinguish between the two."

The feedback questionnaires and their personal development plans demonstrated that all participants felt they had developed skills of direct use in working with their students, including how to entice full participation online, be inclusive, encourage independent learning, enable successful student interaction and groups, use sparks of information to promote dialogue and knowledge sharing, and use archiving, weaving, and summarizing. This program will be rolled out to further cohorts of tutors. Costs are tiny compared with bringing tutors together for a face-to-face briefing.

Overall, the development has proved effective, efficient, acceptable, and coherent. Such "attendance" and acceptability are almost impossible to achieve when asking tutors to drive or fly to a physical meeting. One online staff development participant wrote: "I have learnt a great deal about myself and my continuing development needs. It was really valuable being able to network like this with such a stimulating and professional group. It has transformed my approach to working online with my management students—I'm sure for the better!"

Conclusions

By addressing the blend of online and more traditional approaches to learning within the supported open learning paradigm of the OU, we can enhance student choice, satisfaction, and, most important, learning. We have demonstrated the potential of encouraging wider student participation through offering alternative learning experiences, such as online equivalents of some components of courses. This has been achieved through improved understanding of online practice for self-managed groups and through the provision of targeted tutor training. These two aspects, along with exploration of online assessment, will be the focus of our attention over the next two years.

At the OU Business School, we ensure that a range of blends is available in order to maximize flexibility. An essential part of the blend is carrying the choices through the human development of staff along with the readdressing of pedagogical approaches and technologies. Without the associated staff development, the success of the blend cannot be assumed. In this way, management education arrives not in one shape but many good shapes, for the huge challenges of educating managers in networked organizations of the twenty-first century.

References

Arbaugh, J. B., & Steizer, L. (2003). Learning and teaching management on the Web: What do we know? In C. Wankel & R. DeFillippi (Eds.), *Educating managers with tomorrow's technologies* (pp. 17–51). Greenwich, CT: Information Age Publishing.

Bruffee, K. A. (1999). *Collaborative learning: Higher education, interdependence, and the authority of knowledge* (2nd ed.) Baltimore, MD: Johns Hopkins University Press.

Costello, M. L., Brunner, P. W., & Hasty, K. (2002, July). Preparing students for the empowered workplace: The risks and rewards in a management classroom. *Active Learning in Higher Education, 3*(2), 117–127

Dirk, J. M., & Smith, R. O. (2004). Thinking out of a bowl of spaghetti: Learning to learn in online collaborative groups. In T. S. Roberts (Ed.), *Online collaborative learning: Theory and practice* (pp. 132–159). London: Information Science Publishing.

Felder, R. M., & Brent, R. (1996). Navigating the bumpy road to student centered-instruction. *College Teaching, 44,* 43–47.

Gallagher, J. (2003). The place and space model of distributed learning: Enriching the corporate e-learning model. In C. Wankel & R. DeFillippi (Eds.), *Educating managers with tomorrow's technologies.* Greenwich: Information Age Publishing.

Hamlin, M. D., Griffy-Brown, C., & Goodrich, J. (2003). From vision to reality: A model for bringing real world technology to the management education classroom. In C. Wankel & R. DeFillippi (Eds.), *Educating managers with tomorrow's technologies.* Greenwich, CT: Information Age Publishing.

Haywood, M. (1998). *Managing virtual teams: Practical techniques for high technology project managers.* Norwood, MA: Artech House.

Hodgkinson, M. (2000). Managerial perceptions of barriers to becoming a "learning organization." *Learning Organization, 7*(3), 156.

Jonassen, D. H. (2002). Learning to solve problems online distance education and distributed learning. In C. Vrasidas & G. V. Glass (Eds.), *Current perspectives in applied information technologies: Distance education and distributed learning.* Greenwich, CT: Information Age Publishing.

Kitchen, D., & McDougall, D. (1999). Collaborative learning on the Internet. *Journal of Educational Technology Systems, 27*(3), 245–258.

Knight, P. T. (2002*). Being a teacher in higher education.* Buckingham: SRHE and Open University Press

Lawless, N. J. (2003, December). *Leadership and team roles for online learning.* Paper presented at Online Educa Conference, Berlin, Germany.

Lawless, N. J. (2004, November). *Managing student expectations in order to fast-track online group learning.* Paper presented at European Conference on E-Learning (ECEL), Paris, France.

Reisel, W. D., & Watson, E. F. (2003). Global management education: The case of ERP enabled business school programs. In C. Wankel & R. DeFillippi (Eds.), *Educating managers with tomorrow's technologies* (pp. 191–209). Greenwich, CT: Information Age Publishing.

Salmon, G. (2002). *E-tivities: The key to active online learning.* London: Taylor and Francis.

Salmon, G. (2004). *E-moderating: The key to teaching and learning online* (2nd ed). London: Taylor and Francis.

Schön, D. A. (1983). *The reflective practitioner.* New York: Basic Books.

Schön, D. A. (1987). *Educating the reflective practitioner.* San Francisco: Jossey-Bass.

Simons, G. F. (2002). *Eurodiversity.* Burlington, MA: Butterworth-Heinemann.

Vygotsky, L. S. (1979*). Mind in society.* Cambridge, MA: Harvard University Press.

Walker, R. (2002). Is there anyone there? Distance education ands distributed learning. In C. Vrasidas & G. V. Glass. (Eds.), *Current perspectives in applied information technologies: Distance education and distributed learning.* Greenwich, CT: Information Age Publishing.

Walther, J. B. (1992). Interpersonal effects in computer-mediated interaction. *Communication Research, 19*(1), 52–90.

Yoo, Y., & Alavi, M. (2001). Media and group cohesion: Relative influences on social presence, task participation, and group consensus, *MIS Quarterly, 25*(3), 371–390.

Gilly Salmon is professor of e-learning and learning technologies at the University of Leicester in the United Kingdom, where her research and practice focus on the change opportunities associated with the "e-world." Previously she was at the Open University Business School, where her interests were in the role of the online teacher and tutor in large-scale open and distance learning systems. She is the author of e-moderating and e-tivities and director of All Things in Moderation Ltd., a global online training company.

Naomi Lawless has a background in engineering, business management, and management consultancy and training. She has an M.B.A. from London Business School and an M.Sc. in information technology and learning from Lancaster University. She currently works as a lecturer at the Open University Business School, where she is also studying part-time for a Ph.D. in the success factors in online group learning.

CHAPTER TWENTY-NINE

BLENDED LEARNING IN UNDERGRADUATE MATHEMATICS AT THE UNIVERSITY OF PRETORIA

Ansie Harding, Johann Engelbrecht, Karen Lazenby, Irene le Roux

The University of Pretoria (UP) is one of the largest residential universities in South Africa. The academic offerings are organized into nine faculties: Engineering, Information Technology and the Built Environment; Law; Education; Humanities; Economic and Management Sciences; Health Sciences; Veterinary Science; Natural and Agricultural Sciences; and Theology. The university offers 1,235 programs, including 302 undergraduate and 933 postgraduate programs to approximately sixty thousand students. Of these, about sixteen thousand students are traditional paper-based distance education students.

The University of Pretoria is committed to delivering education of a superior quality. As has happened around the globe, changes in the teaching and learning environment over the past few years, together with developments in the field of information and communication technology (ICT), have transformed the educational environment at the University of Pretoria. The traditional model of contact education has been significantly expanded, and new learning environments have been created using innovative, flexible educational opportunities (Boon, 2003).

The Department of Telematic Learning and Education Innovation (TLEI) was founded in 1998 with the task to lead, facilitate, and actively participate in actions aimed at educational innovation, with a focus on establishing flexible learning environments. To support such an approach, the TLEI Department, together with a team representing core support departments and lecturers, spearheaded the creation of an integrated virtual campus.

Following an in-depth comparative study that was conducted in collaboration with two other universities, the course management system WebCT was selected and implemented. Student services were Web enabled and wrapped around WebCT to provide students, faculty, and administrators a seamless and secure Web interface to access information, perform transactions, and engage in learning activities. By the end of 1999, 12,700 students used Student Online Services and close to 1,600 students were enrolled in WebCT-supported courses (Lazenby, 1999). Currently more than 27,000 students use Student Online Services and more than 26,000 students have access to Web-supported courses. A portal (Lecturers Online) was also developed for lecturers. Since 1998 the growth in the use of the Web environment has been exponential, as indicated in Figure 29.1.

Top management at the University of Pretoria supports the promotion of ICTs in teaching and learning. Strategic targets have been approved: to have 50 percent of undergraduate modules and all postgraduate programs supported by appropriate information and communication technology. The reaction to the target setting has been varied. The Faculty of Engineering, Information Technology, and the Built Environment reacted positively by preempting the due date and aiming to have all their undergraduate modules on the Web by the end of 2004. Other faculties did not react as positively in general, although there are champions in all the faculties. This is reflected in the number of modules per faculty department that are currently available on the Web (see Table 29.1).

FIGURE 29.1.   WEBCT MODULES AT THE UNIVERSITY OF PRETORIA BY YEAR.

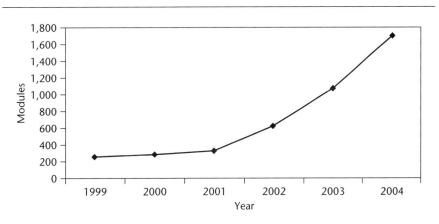

TABLE 29.1. NUMBER OF WEBCT MODULES CREATED BY FACULTY DEPARTMENTS.

Faculty	Number of WebCT Modules
Dentistry	7
Veterinary Sciences	8
Law	15
Education	50
Humanities	122
Natural and Agricultural Science	133
Theology	199
Health Sciences	219
Economic Management Sciences	331
Engineering, Information Technology, and the Built Environment	393
Other (short courses, for example)	289
Total	1,751

A key factor in the successful adoption of Web-supported learning at the University of Pretoria is the support offered to lecturers by the Department of TLEI. Instructional designers are available to design and develop modules in WebCT or in combinations of ICTs. Together with the department's education consultants and faculty, instructional designers determine the most appropriate combination of instructional methodologies to be used within the flexible learning environment. The team is experienced in developing different types of multimedia, including tutorials, simulations, case studies, and collections of visually rich resources. Several campuswide projects are currently in development, including vitally important e-portfolio and electronic assessment systems.

TLEI also provides training to academic staff to facilitate student success in the online learning environment. The training focuses on how to effectively use WebCT (technology training) as well as the pedagogy of teaching online. Lecturers may choose to attend only basic training to facilitate their courses, or they can choose to follow the advanced designer training in order to take full control of the development and maintenance of their online courses.

At the university, the Web is widely used in combination with contact sessions; in effect, blended learning is the norm. The teaching model naturally varies to accommodate student needs and program requirements. Various new programs at the postgraduate level have been designed with the possibilities of the Web in mind. Examples of highly successful programs, with good learning facilitation and student participation, are the master's degree in early childhood intervention (Alant, Dada, Fresen, & Marx, 2002) and the master's of philosophy in wildlife management. Our experience has been that new programs provide the possibility to design appropriate teaching and learning strategies for the Web from the start, whereas the adaptation of existing face-to-face activities to the Web environment is usually more challenging.

One of the concerns regarding ongoing innovation is that the higher education sector in South Africa has been restructured. The new funding formula has had a detrimental effect on the University of Pretoria, in particular, which may affect the availability of resources to support and fund educational innovation in the future.

In the sections that follow, we use an undergraduate mathematics course as an example of how the Web can be integrated into the teaching model. We reflect on this model through the all-encompassing lens that blended learning provides.

Online Teaching and Learning in Undergraduate Mathematics

In mathematics, the century-long practice of chalk-and-talk teaching has been resilient and resistant to change until recently. Mathematics is a conceptual subject, and common opinion is that face-to-face contact with demonstrated exposition is necessary for conveying these concepts. The technology revolution experiences during the past two decades of the previous century offered the first real challenge to this tradition. Resistance tentatively began to crumble as the advantages of a more visual and experimental approach, with increased ease of calculations, became widely apparent. Traditionally presented mathematics was reformed to incorporate the use of technology for a more hands-on and visual approach (Hughes-Hallett et al., 1994). This revised approach was initially received with varying degrees of enthusiasm but gradually infiltrated almost every aspect of mathematics. In so doing, the first step to a more blended approach was taken, in this case, blending educational technology (such as CDs, computer-assisted instruction software, hypermedia, and multimedia) into the traditional approach. Having barely adapted to change brought about by this onslaught, the second wave of change, the Internet, emerged to offer even more hands-on, exploratory learning opportunities for mathematics education.

Again change came slowly, and mathematics courses have certainly not been at the pioneering front of Internet course development. This slow pace of acceptance and curriculum change can perhaps be blamed on the strong role of tradition in teaching mathematics. At the same time, it might be more accurately pinned on the problems surrounding symbol presentation in HTML, the language commonly used for Internet presentation. Yet mathematics could not withstand the onslaught of opportunity made possible by the Internet either. In fact, in recent years, mathematics courses on the Internet are no longer a rarity, whether these are fully or partially Web based. Well-designed mathematics material on the Web offers a multitude of visual facilities and exploratory opportunities, often animated for enhanced effect. Bookbinder (2000) argues, "Enhancing the mathematics curriculum with Web-based technology takes time and effort, but the effort is well worth it" (p. 8).

The mathematics teaching fraternity has taken notice of the Internet, but in many cases fear of the unknown and skepticism still manifests itself in a reluctance to venture into virtual worlds in what was a highly traditionally taught subject matter area. Concerns on how much of material should go on the Web, how to get students to work regularly, and whether it is possible to learn mathematics outside the chalk-and-talk paradigm are common. Web-based courses have by no means replaced traditionally presented courses and possibly never will, but the Internet has had a definite impact on mathematics teaching. There is no single answer to the question as to how one should harness the Internet in mathematics, but, as noted below, it may simply be a matter of blending. We describe one particular case at the University of Pretoria where blended learning in mathematics has been implemented for the past four years.

Historical Background

When, at the beginning of 2000, teachers at the Mathematics Department took the first steps toward designing a calculus course on the Web, a wise decision was made to run the course for a trial semester in parallel with the conventional lecturer-driven course, giving online access to all the mainline calculus first-year students (all one thousand of them). Calculus is the bread-and-butter mathematics course taken by all first-year mathematics students. There were definite hiccups to sort out, and this period of grace was invaluable (Engelbrecht & Harding, 2001a). It gave us the necessary experience and confidence to run a blended calculus course in the follow-up semester, mainly Web based but with paper and face-to-face components.

The blended calculus course has a specific target market. Students typically enroll for their first calculus course at the start of the first semester. If successful, they continue with a follow-up course. If not, they can repeat the same course in the second semester with the benefit of not having to skip a semester. This course is then called an *anti-semester course*. The majority of students enter the anti-semester course as repeaters and are reluctant to attend class, since, from their perspective, they have heard it all before. Given that situation, it seemed obvious that all anti-semester courses should go on the Web. It was an obvious and relatively easy decision to use WebCT to supplement this course since it was the platform implemented at the University of Pretoria and had excellent support.

Since 2000, we have continued offering anti-semester courses in calculus topics using the blended calculus teaching-learning model described later in this section. This model has been adapted somewhat and is in the process of undergoing a major revamp to enrich the course. Most courses in the department (more than twenty to date) have a WebCT Web site with various degrees of blending. On the lower end of the scale are Web sites that serve only as notice boards, with other courses making increasing use of one or more of the many WebCT tools. The model described is on the upper end of the scale.

Course Structure

This section provides details about how we structured our approach to the mathematics course.

Didactic Approach. There are few detailed examples of mathematics courses conducted over the Web with the continuous guidance and support from the lecturers. As noted by Crowe and Zand (2000) in an extensive survey of existing Internet activities and resources in undergraduate mathematics teaching, "The balance of costs at present is heavily geared towards production of material, rather than maintaining it and supporting its presentation to students" (p. 147). Engelbrecht and Harding (2004, 2005a) report on the full spectrum of undergraduate mathematics courses taught online.

Since we firmly believe that most of our students are not academically mature enough to follow a course that does not structure their learning in some way, we decided to develop a course that falls within the slender category of courses conducted over the Web with continuous guidance and support from the lecturers. For example, our approach uses the textbook for the actual subject content through which the students are guided on a day-by-day basis.

Running the Course. The dynamical day-by-day running of the course is done through the Calendar facility or diary, the entry point for the course. Here, we list the study unit of the day, linked to the Study Guide (supplying detailed learning objectives and references to the applicable section in the textbook) and the corresponding short Lecture Notes (supplying a shorter version of what one would normally do in a live class but still acting as facilitator between the Study Guide and the textbook). A number of practice problems are also listed daily. Announcements and administrative issues complete the daily communication.

Assessment. We also follow a blended approach for course assessment, employing both online and paper components. The weekly quiz is an online activity completed individually by students on the Web with rapid feedback. Although there is no security check, quiz marks do contribute to the semester aggregate, and students soon get to use it as a formative tool and as a fair judge of their progress. The assignments and projects component is a paper activity in which students hand in four hard copy assignments and one project during the semester, completed in groups. Assignments mainly consist of problems selected from the textbook. In contrast, projects consist of application problems requiring the use of mathematical software such as Matlab or Maple.

For the two semester tests as well as the final examination, online and paper assessment are blended. Each of these assessment activities consists of an online section (for which the QUIZ facility of WebCT is used) as well as a paper section, carrying equal weight. The online section is done in a computer lab under supervision, posing no security risk.

Blending assessment modes uses the best of two worlds. Paper questions assess skills such as formulation, exposition, sketching, and the logical development of mathematical thought. Online questions are particularly suited to testing conceptual understanding and visualization. Setting online questions is challenging and also refreshing because it requires the lecturer to think differently. From the lecturer's side, there is the added benefit of reduced grading and the additional diagnostic features of the online assessment. We are convinced of the possibility of setting questions of a high standard on the Web (Engelbrecht & Harding, 2003, 2004).

Other Components and Activities in the Course. Our experience is that when following a blended approach within an online environment, a premium should be placed on cooperative learning. For this reason, we let the class (normally about 150 students) divide themselves into groups of two to four members each. Group activities then include assignments and projects (Engelbrecht & Harding, 2002). On submitting the finished tasks, students have to make a small declaration that all group members contributed (more or less) equally.

Communication also follows the blended approach. Most communication happens online (via WebCT's Discussion Forum and the E-Mail facility) with face-to-face office consultation possible but not the rule. A face-to-face hour-long live weekly meeting provides an opportunity for questions and an extra example or two. Attendance is voluntary.

On the technical side, for material containing mathematical symbols, we use Scientific Workplace (a front end for LATEX, the software tool generally used for typing mathematics) and publish this in pdf format (Hutchinson, 1999).

Feedback and Performance

The most significant feedback result, obtained from student questionnaires, was that in the trial run leading up to the first semester of full implementation (when the Web was optional), only 6 percent of students indicated that they preferred the Web course to a more traditional classroom-based model. However, by the end of the first presentation of the Web-based course, this figure increased to an impressive 58 percent. Perhaps students are stuck in the traditional classroom paradigm mentality, but when they are forced to experience a different way of learning, they find that not only can they cope with it, the majority of students actually prefer it (Engelbrecht & Harding, 2001b).

On the importance of the different activities, students rated the assignments highest, with the projects a close second. Somewhat surprisingly, the live weekly meetings were only moderately successful and were not particularly well attended. This may be because most of the students were repeating the course and did not feel a need to attend a scheduled event a second time.

The pass rates of the Web-presented courses from 2000 to 2003 were consistently higher than those of the preceding four years of live classroom instruction. The average pass rate over the period 2000–2003, when the course was presented over the Web, was nearly 78 percent. Over the period 1996–1999, when the course was still presented face-to-face, the average pass rate was just 64 percent. A contributing factor for this phenomenon could be that students performed particularly well in the online assignments because they can consult and work in groups.

The percentage of student distinctions in the blended version of the courses, however, was somewhat lower than in previous years. The average rate for the four years prior to 2000 was higher than the average percentage for the four years of teaching over the Web: 4.8 percent compared to 3.1 percent. An explanation could be that it is not easy to master the finer points of a conceptual subject such as mathematics when direct interaction and modeling from an instructor are limited.

A concern often expressed by those who are unfamiliar with Web courses is that the lecturer will be flooded by e-mail enquiries. Our experience does not support this at all. In the example course (group of about 150 students), over a fifteen-week period we received 300 messages in the Discussion Forum and 150 via e-mail, on average about 5 messages per day. It required no more of our time than a typical face-to-face group of students. In addition, we had the benefit of answering all these postings first thing in the morning.

Scope of Blended Learning in Mathematics

Having described one particular model of blended learning in mathematics, we now widen our horizons to look at the scope of blended learning in mathematics as practiced worldwide. We develop a structure to visualize the extent of blending in mathematics courses. (For a more detailed survey and classification of existing Web sites in undergraduate mathematics, see Engelbrecht & Harding, 2005a, 2005b.)

We focus on mathematics courses that have Web-based presentation as at least one of its components. The Web component could be an add-on to a mainly lecture-based course, or it could be the main component of the course with little or no face-to-face contact. The latter includes courses that run within a virtual learning environment such as WebCT or within a created and customized structure that facilitates content conveyance, communication, assessment, and other online components.

Taking reconnaissance of existing examples of blended learning is not an easy task. Part of the difficulty is the large number of available online courses worldwide. A second, and more problematic, issue is that many universities have strict security measures on their academic Web sites, reserving access for registered students. As a result, external access is often impossible.

When comparing two blended courses, one should realize that both might be lacking in certain, not necessarily the same, aspects and exceed again in other aspects. In an attempt to visualize at one glance what the scope and extent of blending is and to indicate the associated strengths and weaknesses, a radar chart is proposed (see Figure 29.2). Six radials are identified in this chart, each with a question to quantify a measure.

Dynamics and Access: What Is the Frequency of Access Necessary for Success in the Course?

    1—Once per term

    2—Once per month

    3—Once per week

FIGURE 29.2.   RADAR CHART FOR THE UNIVERSITY OF PRETORIA COURSES.

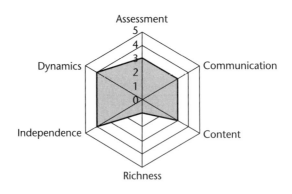

4—Two to three times a week

5—Daily

Assessment: How Much of the Assessment Is Done Online?

1—Little

2—Almost half of it

3—More than half of it

4—Most of it

5—All of it

Communication: How Much of the Communication Happens Online?

1—Little

2—Almost half of it

3—More than half of it

4—Most of it

5—All of it

Content: How Much of the Course Content Is Available Online?

1 each for book, course information, course administration, lecture notes, and study objectives, with a maximum score of 5

Richness: How Many Enriching Components Does the Online Part of the Course Have?

1 each for a computer algebra system, graphics, Java applets, slide presentations, video clips, and sound clips; in effect, more than text communication, with a maximum score of 5 components

Independence: How Independent Is Success in the Course from Face-to-Face Contact?

1—Fully contact lecture and tutorial driven; Web site an add-on

2—Contact lectures but Web-based tutorials or assessment

3—Limited regular contact

4—Sporadic contact

5—No face-to-face contact

The area of the radial diagram gives an indication of the extent of Internet use. The larger the area, the bigger the Internet component, and the smaller the area, the bigger the face-to-face component. A convex shape, partially filling the chart area, points to a well-blended course.

The first three radials—dynamics, assessment, and communication—could be grouped under a heading *interaction*. In the radial diagram, they are to the top. A top-heavy radial diagram indicates more interaction over the Web. The second three radials—content, richness, and independence—could be grouped under the heading *material*. Radial diagrams of courses with content provided on the Web will therefore be heavier toward the bottom.

As an illustration of this model, we look at several examples. It may be mentioned that in doing the grading for the examples below, the rating was done on what was available from the Web site and approved by the course designers. The three examples illustrate various degrees of blending.

Calculus Course

The calculus course (University of Pretoria) described in the previous section serves as our first case study. The course representation on a radar chart appears in Figure 29.2.

Although this course does not have any formal lectures, it does not run fully online. Students need to access the Web site at least two or three times per week since more than half of the assessment is done online. However, communication happens mostly online but also during contact sessions. Success in the course is dependent on sporadic face-to-face contact. As can be seen from the radar chart, this course lacks richness and could be supplemented by additional multimedia material.

NetMath Project

The second example is the NetMath project of the University of Illinois Urbana-Champaign, which offers various online courses conducted via Mathematica notebooks and assisted by a NetMath support team. NetMath grew out of the Calculus&Mathematica project of the University of Illinois Urbana-Champaign. This course made use of the computer algebra package Mathematica and originally was supported by conventional lectures. Due to student feedback, the lectures were eventually dropped, and the course became an on-campus distance learning course. As a result of extensive interest from other institutions, the NetMath consortium now consists of the University of Illinois Urbana-Champaign, Ohio State University, the University of Pittsburgh, the University of Iowa, and Harvard University. The courses are also used at a number of other universities in the United States.

FIGURE 29.3. RADAR CHART FOR THE NETMATH COURSES.

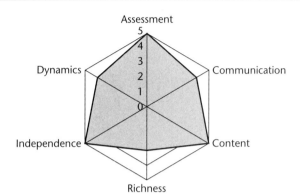

NetMath is a distance education program with communication between student and the NetMath team using e-mail, telephone, and online discussions. Students need to submit a weekly report to NetMath on their progress and problems. Content delivery is with Mathematica notebooks, and cooperative learning is encouraged. Students have a degree of electronic support: courseware and assignments are placed on the course Web site, and a human mentor is available for help by telephone or e-mail. Assignment problems are submitted online and marked by the NetMath team.

As indicated, this program has attracted great interest and has grown to include differential equations, linear algebra, and probability theory. The radar chart representation appears in Figure 29.3. The chart shows that this course is conducted almost exclusively online and addresses both the content and interaction radials but is slightly lacking in richness.

Notice Board

The third case explored here is a "notice board" site that mainly contains administrative information such as syllabi, announcements, handouts, reference to homework problems, and past papers. This is a popular way of starting out on the Web, and many courses have grown from this humble beginning. The example we offer here is "Introduction to Calculus Fall 2003" at Stony Brook University in New York, a lecture-based course with a supplemental Web site. Figure 29.4 gives the radar diagram for this course. In this case, the radar chart clearly shows limited blending. As indicated earlier, such courses are fairly common in mathematics

FIGURE 29.4.   RADAR CHART FOR STONY BROOK COURSES.

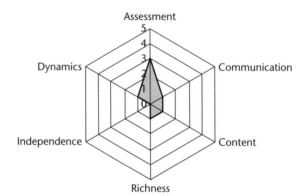

education. In fact, at the University of Pretoria, we now have a number of courses that fall into this category of a Web-supported course. Of course, a Web-supported course is fast becoming the minimum requirement for all courses.

Other aspects related to this radar chart presentation are described by Engelbrecht and Harding (2005a, 2005b).

Conclusion

The radar presentation in this chapter presents a first attempt to visualize blended courses in undergraduate mathematics. Although the environment is fluid, the structures presented should be robust enough to accommodate unforeseen changes and expansions. In addition, they could be employed in other subject areas. This visual representation could also be used as a positioning or comparison system for teachers designing their first Web course or others wanting to evaluate the degree of blending of an existing course for comparison or possible expansion purposes.

With the sudden emergence of online learning, and, in particular, blended learning, online instructors are in dire need of frameworks and guides such as this to be a check on course quality, efficiency, and professional reflection. At the University of Pretoria, this situation is especially acute, with tens of thousands of students learning in blended learning formats, with mathematics education being one of the key areas leading this growth.

There is no doubt that the use of the Web has enhanced the quality, flexibility, and accessibility of university courses. Further growth of blended learning environments will depend on continued funding and support from top management.

References

Alant, E., Dada, S., Fresen, J., & Marx, A. S. (2002). A formative evaluation of the master's degree in early childhood intervention: Feedback on the S.A.I.D.E. recommendations. *Open Learning Through Distance Education, 8*(3), 6–7.

Bookbinder, J. (2000, May). *Enhancing the mathematics curriculum with Web-based technology.* Hangzhou, China: International Congress on Mathematical Education.

Boon, J. A. (2003). *2002 in review.* Pretoria: University of Pretoria.

Calculus&Mathematica, University of Illinois at Urbana Champaign. Retrieved August 19, 2004, from http://www-cm.math.uiuc.edu/.

Crowe, D., & Zand, H. (2000). Computers and undergraduate mathematics 3: Internet resources. *Computers and Education, 35,* 123–147.

Engelbrecht, J., & Harding, A. (2001a). WWW mathematics at the University of Pretoria: The trial run. *South African Journal of Science, 97*(9/10), 368–370.

Engelbrecht, J., & Harding, A. (2001b). Internet calculus: An option? *Quaestiones Mathematicae* (Suppl. 1), 183–191.

Engelbrecht, J., & Harding, A. (2002, July). Cooperative learning as a tool for enhancing a Web-based Calculus course. In *Proceedings of the ICTM2,* Crete.

Engelbrecht, J., & Harding A. (2003). Online assessment in mathematics: Multiple assessment formats. *New Zealand Journal of Mathematics, 32*(Suppl.), 57–66, 2003.

Engelbrecht, J., & Harding A. (2004). Combining online and paper assessment in a Web-based course in undergraduate mathematics. *Journal of Computers in Mathematics and Science Teaching, 23*(3), 217–231.

Engelbrecht, J., & Harding, A. (2005a). Teaching undergraduate mathematics on the Internet 1: Technologies and taxonomy. *Educational Studies in Mathematics, 58*(2), 235–252.

Engelbrecht, J. & Harding, A. (2005b). Teaching undergraduate mathematics on the Internet 2: Attributes and possibilities. *Educational Studies in Mathematics, 58*(2), 253–276.

Hughes-Hallett, D., Gleason, A. M., Flath, D. E., Gordon, S. P., Lomen, D. O., Lovelock, D., McCallum, W. G., Osgood, B. G., Pasquale, A., Tecosky-Feldman, J. B., Thrash, J. B., Thrash, K. R., Tucker, W. T., & Quinney, D. (1994). *Calculus.* New York: Wiley.

Hutchinson, I. (1999). *Approaches to WWW mathematics documents.* Retrieved April 6, 2004, from http://hutchinson.belmont.ma.us/tth/webmath.html#tthFtNtAAB.

Lazenby, K. (1999). Using WebCT at the University of Pretoria, South Africa. *International Journal of Educational Telecommunications, 5*(4), 293–307.

Ansie Harding is a senior lecturer in the Department of Mathematics and Applied Mathematics at the University of Pretoria. Her field of interest is mathematics education and especially the use of technology in teaching undergraduate mathematics, on which she and her research partner, Johann Engelbrecht, have published extensively. They are particularly interested in harnessing the Web for educational purposes.

Johann Engelbrecht, professor of mathematics at the University of Pretoria, is cofounder of the South African Mathematics Education Reform Network and the 1998 recipient of the Claude Harris Leon Championship in Mathematics Teaching Award in South Africa. He has been involved in developing undergraduate mathematics courses on the Internet for the past five years. With his research colleague, Ansie Harding, he has published extensively on the topic and is a regular speaker at conferences on mathematics education. In 2001, Harding and Engelbrecht received the University of Pretoria's Laureates award for distinction in teaching innovation.

Karen Lazenby has extensive knowledge and eight years' experience of e-learning and organizational innovation in higher education. Her career includes being a lecturer, head of academic staff development, instructional designer, and manager of institutional research. After establishing the virtual campus of the University of Pretoria in 1999, she was appointed deputy director of telematic learning and education innovation. In 2001 she was seconded to establish a one-stop multimedia contact center for students and other clients of the university. She is currently the director of client service and is responsible for student recruitment and student services. Lazenby has presented more than a dozen papers at international conferences and has published several articles in the field of technology and educational innovation.

Irene le Roux's extensive experience in the e-learning environment started in 1991 with the successful development and implementation of the computer-based testing facility at the University of Pretoria. She presented the M.Ed. module on computer-based testing and developed various multimedia products, including the award-winning "Music in South Africa." She was appointed deputy director in the Department of Telematic Learning and Education Innovation in 2003. Her recent responsibilities include the strategic management of the e-learning environment at the university. She has published various articles and presented papers and workshops both nationally and internationally, some by invitation.

PART SIX

MULTINATIONAL BLENDED LEARNING PERSPECTIVES

As new learning technologies and online programs, courses, and resources emerge in education, there are concerns about the reach of these educational innovations to needy learners around the world. The chapters in Part Six discuss a few innovative programs and approaches developed by Cisco Systems and the World Bank. Among the many lessons learned from these programs as they are extended around the planet are the lack of required technological infrastructure and teacher training. As innovative blended learning programs are delivered, they must address a plethora of implementation complexities, such as those relating to different cultures, languages, time zones, and educational systems. In addition to specific program initiatives, there is a need for thoughtful governmental policies related to blended learning.

In Chapter Thirty, Jane Massy sets out an informed critique of current progress in the integration of information and communication technologies (ICT) into Europe's education and training systems. She provides a narrative of the development and progress of the European Union's policies related to e-learning. Many important issues are raised that challenge prevailing assumptions about adoption levels, the perceived value of self-managed learning, formal versus informal learning, and the impact of ICT use on the social divide.

In Chapter Thirty-One, Michelle Selinger provides a personal journey from her academic post in the United Kingdom to becoming a key education adviser at Cisco in Europe, Africa, and the Middle East. Selinger describes her involvement in three major blended learning initiatives: Rwanda teacher training, the Cisco Networking Academy (CNA), and the Jordanian e-maths curriculum. The Rwandan initiative involved the use of the Internet, satellite TV, and face-to-face training. The CNA incorporated e-learning materials and online testing mediated by teaching from local tutors and instructors. The Jordanian e-maths curriculum was built on the CNA model in developing a technology-rich math curriculum used by local teachers. From this experience, Selinger reflects on the important role of the teacher in mediating learning experiences to make e-learning content culturally and pedagogically relevant to the learners. Based on her experience, the most successful e-learning was blended learning, since it usually involved personal contact with a tutor or instructor.

In Chapter Thirty-Two, Sheila Jagannathan from the World Bank Institute provides a global perspective on the context of e-learning in developing countries. She addresses issues such as the digital divide and the ability to absorb and adapt locally relevant information from a global knowledge base made available through ICT. She then articulates various types of e-learning supported by the World Bank, ranging from formal learning to informal learning. The majority of courses intended for use by clients of the World Bank in developing countries use video-conferencing for face-to-face interactions blended with print, CD-ROM materials, and Web-based modules. A two-by-two matrix contrasting blended learning with largely Web-based learning on one axis and facilitated courses versus independent study on the other axis provides a useful framework for several sample cases that are presented in this chapter.

CHAPTER THIRTY

THE INTEGRATION OF LEARNING TECHNOLOGIES INTO EUROPE'S EDUCATION AND TRAINING SYSTEMS

Jane Massy

Europe's future economy and society are being formed in the classrooms of today. Students need to be both well educated in their chosen field and digitally literate if they are to take part effectively in tomorrow's knowledge society. E-learning, the integration of advanced information and communication technologies (ICT) into education systems, achieves both aims. Europe also needs to make learning a lifelong endeavor, with people of all ages continuously developing their skills. Here too e-learning can make a significant contribution, with both workers and organizations transforming the way they learn, interact, and work. Moreover, e-learning can promote social integration and inclusion, opening access to learning for people with special needs and those living in difficult circumstances, such as marginalized groups, migrants, and single parents (European Commission, Information Society, n.d.).

This chapter examines the development of e-learning across Europe and proposes that the construct of blended learning, as a trend in its own right, is largely an artificial one in the European context. As the quotation above indicates, e-learning is perceived as "the integration of advanced information and communication technologies (ICT) into the education system." In other words, it is generally conceptualized in Europe as the integration of technologies within education and training systems, not as something separate. While the term *blended* is used in this chapter interchangeably with the term *integration*, the latter term is more likely to be used in Europe.

For readers outside Europe, it is important to understand the context in which learning technologies are being integrated. There are different systems of education within Europe, especially in further and higher education and training; the history of major policy developments relating to learning technologies is included to aid readers in understanding the current status of blended learning in Europe.

In addition to exploring the development of learning technologies across Europe, this chapter discusses the ambiguity attached to policies and practices that aim to leverage learning technologies as an instrument in education and training reform yet recognize that in the short term, blended learning in general is characterized by rather limited and unexceptional ICT use within the education and training systems as they exist today.

Current Status

Technologies are slowly being blended within existing education and training systems. In spite of early hopes that there would be rapid change and reform of education and training systems enabled by technology, the truth is that this has not occurred. Instead, these systems are changing very gradually. Integration usually occurs as teachers, trainers, and users gain competence using particular applications. In most cases, these are standard everyday ICT applications: spreadsheets, e-mail, word processing, PowerPoint, and texts or pictures from the Internet. In general, this is simply exchanging old technologies for new: PowerPoint instead of the blackboard, word processing for pen and paper.

The expansion of infrastructure and the acquisition or building of virtual learning environments has fueled questions about the relevant technology applications to support and enhance the learning process. Nevertheless, real innovation through blended learning is still rare. The most innovative applications in Europe tend to be among advocates of a constructivist approach to learning who have high levels of ICT skills, often in higher and adult education.

Advanced approaches to blended learning encourage collaboration and require different social interactions among learners and between learners and their teachers or trainers. For example, medical technicians or biotechnicians might be offered opportunities to simulate experiments both in and away from a training experience or workshop. And voice recognition technologies can be used to practice pronunciation in language learning. There is strong emphasis on adopting technologies to support those at risk of exclusion. For example, ICTs are employed to assist and engage those needing to improve literacy by enabling them to construct their own learning resources within interactive media-rich environments. However, such cases remain peripheral to mainstream education and training and are often developed as pilots with dedicated funding rather than as part of sustainable mainstream change.

Education and Training Systems

Each country in the European Union has its own unique formal education and training system linked to its cultural, social, and economic development. Some have very strong links between training (especially vocational training) and their employment systems, where labor market mechanisms demonstrate interdependencies between training, qualifications, and job mobility. Others operate more flexible approaches, where job mobility is freer and less embedded in formal occupational profiles and qualifications. Some more rigid systems (such as in Germany) are becoming more flexible, and at the same time, systems known to be more liberal, such as in the United Kingdom, are moving toward establishing stronger links between qualifications, skills, and job occupations.

All European countries recognize that learning is for life and are trying to encourage, support, and leverage opportunities for citizens to learn, as well as to recognize learning that takes place outside the formal systems. This attention to non-formal and informal learning is currently emerging and is an area of growing interest in relation to the adoption of learning technologies.

For over a decade, there has been much public consideration and agreement that in order to assist Europeans in their active participation in social and economic life, education and training systems need to be reformed. European education and training systems need to be more flexible, relevant to the learning needs all citizens, and supportive of changing needs of society.

Self-Learning

Most Europeans have access to free and, to most eyes, high-quality education, including vocational training and higher education. Vocational training systems in countries in northern Europe, in particular, have traditionally provided excellent workplace training and development.

With some few exceptions, self-learning (usually as ODL—open and distance learning) has been attractive to a small minority in European countries. In most instances, successful ODL programs have offered courses that earn formal qualifications. For instance, the United Kingdom's Open University mainly offers undergraduate and postgraduate degree programs. Traditionally these courses and programs have always been blended with on-site workshops, residential weekends, and telephone support even when relying on print and video media broadcasts. There is no evidence that the blending of new technologies has increased the number of self-learners except for growth in those learning ICT skills for qualifications such as the European Computer Driving Licence.

The majority of adults in Europe do not expect to undertake self-managed learning, especially if there is no evidence that this improves their opportunities for employment and promotion. For most, learning remains something that is done either in a formal learning environment or, if for work, during the employer's time and as part of a system of occupational competence development. In addition, in many countries, occupational training is approved and promoted on a sectoral basis, specific to the occupation and job level.

There is increasing emphasis on continuing workplace training, but the expectation and practice is that the setting in which this occurs is provided by the employer and takes place in dedicated work time. There have been cases, in some companies, for example, where a learning management system has been installed with access to libraries of learning courses for voluntary learning. However, reports reveal that these courses have very little take-up. Self-learning, undertaken as part of an individual's career decision making, applies to only an extremely small minority.

Some newer sectors, such as mobile telecommunications, have larger numbers of self-learners. Reasons for this difference may be because the occupational learning requirements for these industries have not been available in mainstream systems. Until fairly recently, the skills required for jobs within the sector (telecommunications technicians, network engineers, software developers) have been evolving, and so qualification pathways have remained uncertain. Therefore, being qualified at the right level for a particular occupation has often been unclear. In response, individuals have, in effect, often designed their own jobs as the IT industry has matured. As highly expert users of technology, those working in the IT sector are often more willing to experiment with their training delivery methods. Typically, those in this field need flexible access to training and education and fast, unorthodox ways to learn. However, while important and growing, employment in the ICT sector represents only a very small percentage of European jobs.

The importance of equality and social cohesion in European education and training systems cannot be sufficiently emphasized. Many Europeans express concern that technologies may increase the social divide. In fact, the concept of e-learning as a self-learning activity undertaken by individuals or what some refer to as "pure e-learning" is often perceived as a model that favors a minority of already highly educated and advantaged individuals.

eEurope

In March 2000, what has become known as the Lisbon Strategy for eEurope was launched. This stated that by 2010, "Europe shall become the most competitive and dynamic knowledge-based economy in the world, capable of sustainable economic growth with more and better jobs and greater social cohesion" (European Commission, 2000).

In this context, the role of education and training has taken on a new importance, while technologies to support fundamental changes in education and training are given significant prominence. Given the importance attached by policymakers to the role of learning in developing competitiveness and social cohesion, the conclusions of the Lisbon Strategy stimulated a process of enhanced cooperation in education and training. A year later at Barcelona, concrete objectives for education and training were established, focusing on quality, access, and opening up European education and training to the wider world (European Commission, 2003a).

The nexus of these two policy initiatives was expressed by the commission president in 2002: "Education, training and research are the key to economic renewal. . . . We need an integrated strategy for education and research based on networking and mobility giving priority to the technologies of the future" (Prodi, 2002).

Education and Training and Technology Policies

In 2002, in the context of the Lisbon Strategy and the eEurope action plan, there was a leap forward in policy. ICTs were presented as a key driver in achieving the economic and social aims of the eEurope strategy. The dominant concerns were social cohesion (an overriding political concern in Europe since the end of World War II) and improving European competitiveness. In this context, there is explicit concern for the personal needs and circumstances of the learner and ensuring access and flexibility to meet the needs of all citizens.

The member states took the view that coordinated structural investment was needed with initiatives to encourage take up and adoption. A new e-learning initiative (2002–2004), later formalized into the E-Learning Program (2004–2006) (European Commission, 2003b), was intended to "coordinate (European) Community actions concerned with e-learning mobilizing the educational and cultural communities, as well as the economic and social players in Europe" (European Commission, 2001).

From Distance to Blended Learning

Research proposals relating to learning technologies have been awarded R&D funding in Europe for nearly fifteen years, from the Second (1987–1991) Research and Technical Development (RTD) Framework Program to the current Sixth Framework Program (Information Society, Research Program, n.d.). By the mid-1990s, technologies to support formal education and training systems were also being piloted through mainstream education and training programs, such as the Socrates and Leonardo da Vinci programs (European Commission, n.d.a; European Commission, "The Socrates Programs," n.d.b).

What is quite noticeable is the changing terms used in these reports, which reflect the evolving understanding of factors that need to be considered when applying new technologies in the established world of practices, structures, and systems of education and training. Until about 1994, terminology reflected the expectation that ICT technologies to support learning were largely about overcoming distance and providing accessibility to those to a large extent outside mainstream systems.

In the past decade, however, the dominant view has been that technologies should be integrated (blended) with the existing systems. More important perhaps, from a policy perspective, that integration will support reform of those systems. By the mid-1990s, there was a clear conceptual shift. Earlier reports and documentation called for research proposals relating to technologies for "flexible and distance learning," but by the Fourth Framework, the terms *telematics for education and training* and *educational multimedia* were used. By the Fifth Framework program, the term *e-learning* appears and then all but disappears in the Sixth Framework, where the phrase *technology-enhanced learning* is used.

E-Learning for Some or All?

These R&D programs focused on the development of technologies for the future. Even in the Second Framework Program, there was a hint that these new technologies were for more than just open and distance learners. Following the work of the Educational Multimedia Task Force in 1996, there was an initiative to bring together programs that were funding socioeconomic research, R&D in emerging technologies, and pilot initiatives in mainstream education and training (Bélisle et al., 2001).

The aim of this initiative was to bring full life cycle focus to integrating learning technologies in education and training organizations and the workplace. This coordinated exercise was not repeated, but its raison d'être was maintained in future policy. At its simplest, it recognized that approaching learning technology research and pilot and experimental activity as a set of separate technological, pedagogical, and organizational components was ineffective as a means to drive the development of new methodologies and applications, as well as their adoption and evaluation.

Of significance in the Educational Multimedia Task Force report, the idea that technologies will be a means to reform education and training systems becomes central to expectations for their future use. This shifts the expectations for ICT technologies away from solely serving the current and future needs of those outside the mainstream systems and brings their use right into the heart of the evolution (and, some hope, revolution) of the formal education and training world. From this time onward, e-learning increasingly is seen as fulfilling a major change role in Europe's knowledge and skills agenda as well as disrupting institutional structures and practices.

The Fourth Framework Program (1994–1998) arguably represents the high point of R&D investment in education and training technologies within Europe. By the Fifth Framework Information Society Technologies (IST) Program (1998–2002), while 10 percent of proposals were for education and training research, the area received only 5 percent of available funding. This reduction in funding may indicate growing disappointment with a policy based on a belief that financing research into innovative technologies would generate products and services that would be taken up and, in doing so, help to drive the reform process. It also represents a shift in the interests of policymakers, with those responsible for education and training policy taking over from those running R&D programs and pushing forward the agenda. In effect, implementation efforts were given priority over basic development. It was at this time that the E-Learning Initiative was born.

The E-Learning Initiative (2002–2004)

Within the eEurope strategy, this initiative set clear targets to support, through structural investment, greater adoption of ICTs within European education and training systems. These targets included benchmarking across countries, ratios of computers to children in schools, raising the speed of ICT networks for higher education and research institutes, and the massive task of training and retraining teachers and trainers. Viviane Reding, former European commissioner for education and culture, said, "The Member States of the European Union have decided to work together to harmonise their policies in the field of educational technology and share their experience. E-Learning aims to support and coordinate their efforts and to accelerate the adaptation of education and training systems in Europe" (European Commission, Education and Training, n.d.)

The initiative was operationalized through the E-Learning Action Plan, 2002–2004. It undertook studies, supported working groups, commissioned an e-learning portal, supported cooperation across the European Commission and related agencies, consulted with political actors, and funded relevant projects through a call for proposals process. It has been followed by the E-Learning Program, which is now the main European policy instrument focused on the integration (that is, blending) of technologies into European education and training systems.

E-Learning Program (2004–2006)

A European definition of e-learning is encapsulated by the tag line to the e-learning program used on the European Commission's Web site: "A program for the effective integration of Information and Communication Technologies (ICT) in education and training systems in Europe (2004–2006)" (European Commission, Education and Training, E-Learning Program, n.d.). Here, the idea of using technologies to reform European education and training systems is no longer merely hinted at but addressed directly.

The E-Learning Program is a further step toward realizing the vision of technology serving lifelong learning. It focuses on a set of actions in high-priority areas, chosen for their strategic relevance to the modernization of Europe's education and training systems (European Commission, Education and Training, n.d.)

The E-Learning Program has four action lines:

- Promoting digital literacy
- European virtual campuses
- E-twinning of schools (that is, using communications technologies to connect two schools that want to carry out a number of structured activities to know about and learn from one another) in Europe and promotion of teacher training
- Transversal actions for the promotion of e-learning in Europe

These action lines address some of the institutional and social issues requiring change if technologies are to be blended into mainstream systems. For example, behind the idea of a European virtual campus is the aspiration for students to be able to accumulate credits from multiple institutions across Europe. These credits might be earned from online courses as well as on-site programs, with local and remote support being provided from different institutions, encouraging not just physical but virtual mobility within Europe. The existence of online technology might enable widening access to education and training as well as flexible course selection blended with traditional on-site attendance. The challenge here is not related to technology but rather overcoming the institutional and legal barriers as universities move toward a fully operational European credit transfer system (European Commission, European Credit Transfer System, n.d.).

The action line of e-twinning of schools in Europe and promotion of teacher training also has a strong mobility dimension. Aimed at encouraging young people to increase their networks and understanding of one another across Europe, it seeks proposals to expand student exchange and collaborative learning by blending ICTs into classroom and social learning activities.

Some Reflections

The E-Learning Initiative and Program can be seen as an initiative undertaken by the political leadership of Europe to align their investments in ICTs for education and training alongside the broader eEurope and e-learning strategies. Investment and application of technologies should help to drive Europe's economic and social agenda. As documented here, there are efforts to make technologies available and provide policy support for their use in education and training. Such efforts are perceived positively across Europe. After all, if the future is about technology, then everyone must have access to ICT applications and be able to use them effectively.

At another level, the E-Learning Initiative, and more so the E-Learning Program, reinforces earlier sentiments concerning the need to reform education and training systems and to use learning technologies as a key means of reform. Earlier vocalization from many in the education and training sector that the systems in Europe did not need reform are now much more muted than in the mid-1990s. Some have continued to argue against the dominance of an instrumentalist approach to education, disliking the fact that the economic rather than social value of education is in the ascendant. Technology deployment is associated with the instrumentalist approach in spite of the many funded research and action pilot initiatives that have focused on specific social aims (for example, the application of technologies to overcome exclusion, disabilities, or the digital divide).

The technology push from policymakers and market players is still resisted (or ignored) by many associated with education and training in Europe. E-learning policies are often viewed as being driven as much by concerns for efficiency as for interest in quality and the social function of education. Other concerns suggest that the attempt to speed up the pace of integration of technologies into educational and training systems fails to recognize the stark reality of the capacity of the systems to absorb the changes. Many suppliers would prefer to see blended learning evolve organically rather than using public funds to push technology into a market that simply is not ready. There are huge amounts of investment, public and private, that have created infrastructures, tools, content, and services that are clearly not being used at anything like the level at which they are supplied.

Politics, Policies, and Change

It is interesting to see how policymakers have taken up the idea that technologies will be a tool to help solve major social and economic dilemmas in Europe. These initiatives imply a frustration with the slow pace of change and reform in education and training systems. In addition, they point to the need to evolve and develop new systems to support lifelong learning and the social inclusion agenda, especially in an enlarged Europe with serious potential labor shortages resulting from the aging population. The answer has been to push various emerging technologies into education and training systems in the hope that absorption of some of them will effect the desired changes. Sadly, not only are the expected changes not occurring (at least not at the pace hoped for), but the absorption rates of the technologies are significantly less than expected.

Among players in the education and training systems, the position has moved over a decade from one of generalized resistance and antipathy to technology to one of passive acceptance but relatively little active experimentation to see where the technologies can really effect change and drive reform on the ground. The primary policy dilemma therefore is how to simultaneously push open the envelope of education and training possibilities while recognizing the reality of slow, incremental change.

Ambitious policies continue to be developed; however, recent evidence suggests that political leaders are concerned with negative press related to high-profile failures (such as the United Kingdom's e-University venture). Clearly, they are worried that technology investment is not achieving the desired educational improvements and changes. Adding to this mounting tension and state of caution, there are concerns about the replacement and upgrading of equipment and sustainability of services. Coinciding with this growing concern, the market for e-learning-related products and services in corporate and workplace training markets remains at best slow, but generally stagnant.

The reality is that adoption or blending of new learning technologies is occurring extremely slowly and is typically not at a very advanced level. It is more about "stretching the mold" (Collis & van der Wende, 2002) of existing practices and approaches than any education and training revolution. A tiny number of institutions, the best known being the University of Twente, have taken the opportunity to make real changes in practice, However, in most educational institutions, what mostly occurs is the use of tools such as PowerPoint and the inclusion of Web sites into reading and reference lists. Virtual learning environments such as Blackboard and WebCT have gained a foothold, and there are many home-grown environments across European higher education, including some open source systems. However, actual use remains limited to a minority of academic institutions and individuals within them. Few take advantage of the communications opportunities offered, with the exception of posting information for discussion on the occasional bulletin board, uploading of a document to read, or noting the URL of a particular Web site.

While there has been huge investment in teacher training, the actual blending of technologies by teachers into educational practice in schools remains disappointingly low. Some educational suppliers believe that with two-thirds of European teachers over the age of forty, the tipping point will happen only with generational change.

In workplace learning, there has not been the same level of investment in e-learning content libraries in European companies as in the United States, in part, because of the factors influencing the relatively low levels of self-learning activity. In Europe, technologies are being increasingly blended with other training and learning activities, typically to provide course-related information for example, timetabling or assessment requirements or course preparation and follow-up. Trainers are learning to use e-learning technologies; but as with higher education, the evidence suggests they are used primarily as vehicles for information delivery rather than to support work-related problem solving or develop new knowledge and skills in a constructivistic or collaborative approach. There remain many huge hurdles in getting senior and line management to see learning as an ongoing activity where technologies can provide continuous learning. Generally the perception persists that learning is an activity that occurs at a specific time and place, and resources (in terms of both budgets and time) are allocated accordingly. Blending technology therefore is viewed positively only if it is perceived as reducing the time spent at a learning event, and not necessarily to improve the quality of training or use technology to link learning to task application and performance improvement.

Using Public Instruments

One problem with this public policy intervention is the fragmented and time-bound nature of any policy initiatives with limited large-scale or long-running activities that can be fully tested for change impact and value. An unusual large-scale and ongoing initiative is EUN Schoolnet (see http://www.eun.org/portal/index-en.cfm), but it is always the case that there is a constant national pull as each country deals with own issues and asserts its own way of doing things.

These public policy initiatives have revealed some of the major barriers (legal, institutional, cultural) that are preventing greater integration. Dealing with these complex and interdependent factors is part of a long-term change process. These changes are high on the policy agenda. In fact, the attempts to blend technology in mainstream learning systems have helped to throw the spotlight on what really needs changing if technology is to serve education, training, and business performance needs.

Conclusion

Almost all learning supported with technology in Europe could be described as blended learning. This embrace of blended learning is currently being pushed along with ambitious public polices at both member state and European levels. The goals of these blended learning initiatives and programs have provided both a future direction as well as a set of challenging objectives for those in education and training to achieve. If the desired reform and change occurs in the European education and training systems, then a decade from now, we may find that the very term *blended learning* has disappeared from our vocabulary with the seamless integration of technology into lifelong learning, whether in full-time or part-time education, in the workplace, at home, or in our communities.

References

Bélisle, C., Rawlings, A., & van Seventer, C. (2001, May). *The Educational Multimedia Task Force 1995–2001: Integrated research effort on multimedia in education and training.* Retrieved July 2, 2004, from http://www.proacte.com/downloads/emtf.doc.

Collis, B., & van der Wende, M. (2002). *Models of technology and change in higher education. An international comparative survey on the current and future use of ICT in higher education.* Twente: Center for Higher Education Policy Studies, University of Twente, The Netherlands.

European Commission. (2000, March). *The EU heads of state or government in the Lisbon European Council.* Retrieved July 2, 2004, from http://europa.eu.int/information_society/policy/index_en.htm.

European Commission. (2001, March 28). *The E-Learning Action Plan communication from the Commission to the Council and the European Parliament.* Brussels. Retrieved July 14, 2004, from http://www.europa.eu.int/eur- lex/en/com/cnc/2001/com2001_ 0172en01.pdf.,

European Commission. (2003a). *Detailed work programme on the follow-up of the objectives of education and training systems in Europe.* Retrieved July 14, 2004, from http://europa.eu.int/comm/education/doc/official/keydoc/2002/progobj_en.pdf.

European Commission. (2003b, November 27). *A Programme for the Effective Integration of Information and Communication Technologies (ICT) in Education and Training Systems in Europe (2004–2006).* Retrieved July 13, 2005, http://elearningeuropa.info/doc.php?lng=1&id=4552&doclng=1.

European Commission. Education and Training. (n.d.). E-learning Program Webpage Retrieved July 2, 2004, from http://europa.eu.int/comm/ed.cation/programmes/elearning/programme_en.html.

European Commission. European Credit Transfer System. (n.d.). *European Commission Education and Training.* Retrieved July 14, 2004, from http://europa.eu.int/comm/education/programmes/socrates/ects_en.html.

European Commission. Information Society. (n.d.a). *E-learning pages.* Retrieved July 2, 2004, from http://europa.eu.int/information_society/eeurope/2005/all_about/elearning/index_en.htm.

European Commission. (n.d.b). *The Leonardo da Vinci Program.* Retrieved July 14, 2004, from http://europa.eu.int/comm/education/programmes/leonardo/leonardo_en.html.

European Commission. (n.d.c). *The Socrates Programs.* Retrieved July 14, 2004, from http://europa.eu.int/comm/education/programmes/socrates/socrates_en.html.

Information Society, Research Program. (N.d.). Technology enhanced learning webpages managed on behalf of the European Commission by Cordis. Retrieved July 2, 2004, from http://www.cordis.lu/ist/directorate_e/telearn/index.htm.

Prodi, R. (2002, January). *Address to the European Parliament.* Retrieved July 2, 2004, from http://europa.eu.int/comm/education/programmes/elearning/index_en.html.

Jane Massy is a researcher, consultant, and evaluator in professional education and workplace training and performance based in Cambridge, U.K. Specializing in learning technologies, she has worked as an evaluator for the European Commission for over a decade. Her client base includes large firms, educational bodies, and public institutions in economic and social development. She publishes and speaks widely on European developments, including public policy. Her publications include "European eLearning Market Report 2002" (Bizmedia www.elearningage.co.uk) and a study of the supply side of eLearning across Europe (co-authored with Knud-Erik Hamann, Danish Technological Institute.

CHAPTER THIRTY-ONE

DEVELOPING AN UNDERSTANDING OF BLENDED LEARNING

A Personal Journey Across Africa and the Middle East

Michelle Selinger

The past four years have been the most formative of my life. I have a teaching background first as a secondary mathematics and economics teacher, then as a teacher educator working in distance education at the U.K. Open University, and then in a traditional university setting at the University of Warwick, where I also directed a research center for new technologies in education. At both institutions, I pioneered blended learning situations, through which I came to an understanding of how online communities could enhance and support learning. I discovered different needs dependent on the location of students and their proximity to tutors and peers (Selinger, 1998).

In this chapter, I document three further learning experiences that have developed my understanding of blended learning and the factors that can ensure successful implementation. I start by describing a plan to implement a blended learning solution in Rwanda, where the infrastructure is only just now being installed. Next, I describe the insights I gained from evaluating the Cisco Networking Academy Program in eleven countries. Finally, I discuss the development of a blended learning solution to teach mathematics in grades 1 to 12 in Jordan. In each situation, the extent of the blend of traditional instruction with e-learning comes from the availability of technology, which is relatively scarce in Rwanda and Jordan; from the focus on either the teacher (Rwanda and Jordan) or the student (the Cisco Networking Academy Program); and from the nature of the course being studied (practical or theoretical). In each context, pedagogical models and cultural norms all have a part to play.

Technology for Teacher Training in Rwanda

This story begins in May 2000, when I was still training teachers and undertaking research in information and communication technologies (ICT) and education at the University of Warwick. At that time, I was invited by Cisco to move away from my closeted existence as a British academic and forgo my upcoming study leave to exploit my experience of using technology as a teacher, a teacher trainer, and a researcher to help solve the crisis in education in sub-Saharan Africa. This is not as pompous as perhaps it sounds. Prime Minster Tony Blair had asked Cisco Systems CEO John Chambers to support one of his millennium initiatives, which was to find a way to use technology to train teachers in developing countries, with a focus on sub-Saharan Africa. In effect, this initiative directly addressed one possible solution to meeting the Education for All agenda set in Jomtiem, Thailand, in 1999, by the World Economic Forum.

I felt inadequate to cope with this daunting task, but I was delighted to have been asked and agreed to take up the challenge. I then set about researching everything I could about sub-Saharan Africa. The post was to be based in the U.K. Department for International Development (DFID). I spent the first two weeks based at DFID simply listening. I was new to development, although it had been a topic that had fascinated me when I studied in my undergraduate degree in economics many years earlier. The team, which became known as Imfundo: Partnership for IT in Education, was composed of people with a diverse range of experiences. We were led by Blair's economic adviser, Owen Bader, who had worked in sub-Sahara Africa while at the Treasury. In addition, there was a project officer from the Foreign and Commonwealth Office, a project assistant in training at the DFID, plus two other secondees from industry—one from Marconi with wireless technology expertise and the other an ex-teacher from Virgin One Account who had business development experience. We were briefed and advised by a range of consultants who had worked in the field for many years, although few were experienced with using technology to enhance education in a developing country.

The next eight months involved meetings and workshops with stakeholders in Rwanda, Gambia, and South Africa. The extent of poverty and lack of technology infrastructure, particularly in Rwanda, but also in parts of Gambia and South Africa, opened my eyes in a way that only firsthand experience can. The same bandwidth requirements for Internet-based solutions implemented in the North, and, most notably, in the United States, Scandinavia, and the United Kingdom, were totally out of the question. The University of Butare in Rwanda, for example, had a 256 MB downlink and 128 MB uplink for the whole university via a satellite system known as a V-Sat, certainly not enough to support any intensive e-learning program. To make matters worse, dial-up connections were not possible since extremely few people we worked with had telephone land lines. And if they did have a telephone, the cost of Internet connectivity was more than twenty times the cost in the United Kingdom in real terms, which was unafford-able to most of the population.

Many developing and least developed countries have large numbers of un-trained and poorly qualified teachers. Rwanda is one of these. After the war in 1994, the shortfall of teachers in Rwanda was addressed by the recruitment of un-qualified teachers, 70 percent of whom had no more than secondary education themselves; a few had not even completed that. An emergency short training pro-gram of five days on teaching methodologies had been mounted, but this mea-sure was less than sufficient for teachers to gain the appropriate skills. However, it was all that could be done at a time when the priority was to rehabilitate and refurbish schools so that children could return to school with sufficient teachers to teach them. Teachers could not be taken out of school in large numbers for the extensive training that was needed.

In reality, this should have been, at the very least, a three-year, full-time train-ing program and equivalent to a preservice program in both subject knowledge and pedagogy. However, removing teachers from the classroom for this length of time was and still is unworkable in Rwanda. Teacher training institutions in that country have neither the physical capacity nor the human resources to train such large numbers. It seemed that distance education was the only feasible alternative, whereby teachers would receive valuable training while still teach-ing. The benefits would be to keep them in classrooms while undergoing train-ing so school attendance targets could be maintained. In addition, it would allow teachers to put new ideas into practice, thereby directly integrating theory and practice.

In Rwanda, the possibility of a blended learning solution linking teachers elec-tronically with the Kigali Institute of Education had also been explored. This solution would not necessarily be available directly to students but would support the tutors who were to be placed in each regional center and recruited from the current teaching force. However, these teachers would not be specialists in all sub-jects. Furthermore, as the distance learning materials would teach subject knowl-edge as well as pedagogy, it was anticipated that there would be questions from teachers that tutors would not be able to answer. At the very least, e-mail could provide a valuable resource for the tutor to relay questions to experts in the Kigali

Institute of Education. (I believe that even simple e-mail capability has not yet been established.)

In terms of curriculum materials, support was enlisted from those involved in curriculum development in the Shoma project based in South Africa since the cultural relevance was much closer to the Rwandan situation than similar programs from the North. Shoma had produced a mathematics education package for primary and secondary teachers funded by the satellite and media company, MultiChoice. It was a blended learning program based on a three-stage model that made use of a mix of satellite broadcast TV with interactive Internet-based materials to train teachers. The teachers were released to attend Shoma sessions at a local teachers' center for a half-day a week. On average, they spent one-third of their time watching and discussing a satellite broadcast video, one-third working on related interactive Internet-based materials cached locally that had been streamed overnight via satellite to the center, and the final third was a planning session for their classes the following week. It was envisaged that a version of Shoma could be developed for Rwanda with the Kigali Institute of Education to supplement the distance learning materials being developed by consultants funded by the World Bank.

From Academic to Industry Education Adviser at Cisco

My second assignment ended before the program in Rwanda could be initiated fully. However, the ideas and development plans were handed over to an incoming team. My learning during that time was immense; not only did I come to understand satellite and wireless technology better, but it also started me on a journey that later was to show me that a solution in one country imposed on another can be problematic and irrelevant if the culture and pedagogical models of the recipient country are not taken into account. Technology imposition can also be a threat and can often be an inappropriate solution (Selinger & Gibson, 2004). Soon I realized that to implement technologically based learning solutions, all three considerations—technology, pedagogy, and culture—needed to be taken into account when working with developing countries or, indeed, emerging and developed countries. Blended learning appears, however, to be a model in which the opportunities for customization occur with local teachers making the adaptations (Selinger, 2004b).

The next stage of my journey was to leave academia entirely to pursue a career as an education adviser in the IT industry. This was a whole new world with a completely new language and culture to which I had to make personal adaptations. There were times when the thought of being a secondary mathematics teacher again, teaching the worst group I had ever taught on a wet Friday afternoon, seemed like heaven. However, that sentiment was only fleeting, and the opportunity to be at the cutting edge of technology while continuing to undertake research was enticing and stimulating.

I found myself positioned as an "e-learning expert" when really my background in e-learning had mainly been in the use of online communities, particularly with beginning teachers at the U.K. Open University (Selinger, 1997, 1998), and, more recently, in the use of e-learning materials in a blended learning environment with teachers in training while at the University of Warwick. In actuality, both experiences had little to do with the type of corporate e-learning that Cisco was engaged in. Nevertheless, I began to draw many parallels between e-learning in industry and e-learning in academia. It was interesting to come to understand how industry developed e-learning and how a company like Cisco used a system where a common application was piloted and then deployed across the company rather than each business unit using its own preferred applications. The approach at Cisco was unlike academia, where it seemed that every faculty member who was engaging in e-learning was using a different system— although in more recent years, this has begun to change as universities have licensed large virtual learning environments and managed learning environments (MLE), such as Blackboard and WebCT, which are then deployed across the entire campus and replace proprietary systems.

Blended Learning Instead of E-Learning

What intrigued me at Cisco was the fact that not all learning was e-learning; it was actually blended learning. Increasingly, learners were offered choices about how they were to learn. Many courses were offered as Web-based training or instructor-led training or with a blend of learning offerings so that learners could choose the mode that met their learning preference or work styles. Support communities were set up so that Frequently Asked Questions could be developed and each application used for productivity or for learning had a set of troubleshooting instructions as well as a 24/7 help desk facility. All possible new applications were piloted with a small group before being deployed across a theater or across the whole company. Each business function then selected the tools and applications that were most appropriate for its training needs. The range of tools used and available for use for e-learning—virtual classroom, IP telephony, video on demand, IP television broadcasts, simulations, and virtual lab facilities—was also impressive; I had never seen many of them used in an educational setting.

Increasing awareness of the functions and features of these tools combined with an understanding of how e-learning could in fact be a set of Web-based instructional materials with virtual community support, or the downloading of a video-on-demand plus some discussions with colleagues or experts face-to-face, or perhaps some Web-based training with hands-on practical labs, led me to think about some of the educational uses these tools could be put to. I then started developing ideas and strategies for education customers as well as talking about the e-learning practices at Cisco with more confidence.

Evaluation of a Blended Learning Program

The team I am currently assigned to is the Cisco Networking Academy Program group. The program comprises a suite of Web-based content designed to teach aspects of the Internet and a range of other related skills in educational and other nonprofit settings through a public-private partnership arrangement (Cisco, 2004). Cisco provides the necessary Web-based materials free of charge, the MLE, and assessment and instructor support, and the institution provides the computers and teaching facilities, the lab kit (purchased at a substantial discount from Cisco), and the instructors to teach the course.

The courses are instructor led, in face-to-face settings, using the e-learning materials, and have a strong, practical hands-on element. Therefore, the courses represent a truly blended learning program where instructors teach students face-to-face, and students read the Web-based curriculum before or after an introduction or explanation from their instructor, take quizzes online and off-line, and are assessed on both practical skills and theoretical knowledge and understanding through Web-based, electronically scored tests.

The system has a managed learning environment, which includes both student and instructor communities. Instructors are increasingly given ideas for teaching as well as opportunities and resources to share their best practices. In addition, good practice guides are provided. This environment supports a blended learning model wherein the role of the instructor is held in high regard and is increasingly recognized on a global level. As evidence of just how global it is, the academy program is now taught in 154 countries and has around half a million students worldwide, making it probably the largest blended learning program in the world.

In late 2001 and early 2002, my manager asked me to visit a range of academies within the theater (that is, across Europe, the Middle East, and Africa, also known as EMEA) to examine and report on the development of the Cisco Networking Academy program in these areas. We wanted to take stock of the deployment of the academy program to date and explore the underlying issues influencing successful implementation, particularly those relating to culture, pedagogy, and Internet access within the different countries in the region. At that time, the academy program was taught in 147 countries worldwide, and 65 percent of those countries fell within the EMEA region. Countries within EMEA have extremely diverse cultures and cover the whole spectrum of economic development, from the most developed to the least developed. As a result, this evaluation provided a broad perspective of the academy program's acceptance over a range of economic, cultural, and pedagogical environments.

Data were gathered through a Web-based questionnaire available across EMEA in four languages. In addition, interviews were conducted with students and instructors in Cisco Networking Academies in eleven countries within the region in order to gather more detailed profiles of students and instructors and to add a qualitative research focus. In terms of demographic data, students tended to have an older profile than in the United States, and instructors came from a wide range of backgrounds, often with industry experience and little teaching experience. This was particularly true for the one hundred or so instructors interviewed.

Pedagogical practices were examined in each of the countries visited, as was the subsequent impact on how the curriculum was taught. Several cultural differences were revealed, most notably in Scandinavia, where the responsibility for learning is given to students, and their teachers do not expect to have to repeat what they have taught. In these countries, students are taught from an early age that it is up to them to revisit a concept and be sure they have understood it. This is in sharp contrast to the philosophy of the Cisco Networking Academy program, developed in the United States, where the pedagogical model at the time of the evaluation was to summarize for students what had been taught, explain what was to be taught, and after teaching it, sum up what they should have learned. In both Sweden and Denmark, this model was seen as too repetitive, and they often told the students that they could leave out the summaries if they so chose. (See Selinger, 2004a, for more discussion on these and other cultural issues and findings.) Overall, there were few significant differences between countries in the teaching approaches used; however, the cost and speed of access to the Internet, reflecting the current state of technological developments in each country, and reactions to the online curriculum, varied tremendously.

The report (Selinger, 2002, pp. 2–3) concluded:

> To ensure that the Academy program continues to succeed as it grows it is essential that instructors are made fully aware that they are the most important element to its success. It is their role to make the Academy program culturally and pedagogically relevant for their students. . . . Instructors have to ensure that students are prepared for work in their own country and will also need to make any adaptations to the presentation of the curriculum to ensure that students are comfortable in their normal learning environment. In this regard, recommendations regarding developments in instructor training are made

suggesting that more time is spent on developing a range of teaching strategies for both labs and theory. Decision makers within the institutions where Academies are based need to be made fully aware of the time instructors need for preparation for their Academy program training, and the time needed subsequently to ensure the effective management of their Academy.

The Importance of Adapting to Cultural Needs

The evaluation work left little doubt that awareness of or attention to cultural and pedagogical norms has an impact on the success of a blended learning program. As we move toward globalized education, fueled by the increasing availability of the Internet and new tools to support content development and collaboration between students wherever they are, blended learning will become increasingly important, as shown by the experiences of the Cisco Networking Academy program. Locally based tutors will become increasingly important as mediators between content and students.

The academy program is based on the development of vocational skills, which are international and where little cultural adaptation needs to be made to ensure that the content is relevant. Nevertheless, some situational adaptations will need to be made. The evaluation work served to highlight my awareness that both content and presentation have to be of relevance to the culture of the students; it cannot be assumed to be the same in any two countries. This proved to be a useful realization for my subsequent involvement in the Jordan Education Initiative.

Developing Jordanian Teachers Through Blended Learning

The latest blended learning program I have been involved in is the development of e-curricula for the Jordan Education Initiative (JEI; www.wef.org/jei). The JEI has enabled me to bring together my experience as a mathematics teacher, a mathematics educator, and a researcher on both the impact of technology in education and the role of the teacher in any learning environment.

The JEI represents a unique opportunity to improve the lives of Jordanian citizens. Jordan was selected during an Extraordinary Meeting of the World Economic Forum in early 2003 because of the country's vision for the future of its education. Among Jordan's immediate priorities was the desire to build a knowledge-based economy and help its citizens become entrepreneurs and participate in the ICT industry. It has already taken steps in that direction through its E-Readiness for the Knowledge Economy project.

One hundred "Discovery Schools" have been selected to pilot the initiative in Jordan. They will serve as a test-bed of how ICT can enable new systems to be used and benefit schools and their students. Although focused on the advancement of learning in Jordan, the plan also provides the opportunity for the sustained development of the local IT industry through infrastructure expansion and various e-content development activities.

One aspect of JEI is the development of a set of e-curricula for which Cisco agreed to sponsor the first of these: the Maths e-Curriculum. This was an opportunity for me to come full circle from my background as a mathematics teacher and teacher-educator and to harness all the new skills I had developed over recent years. The objective of the Maths e-Curriculum project is to develop and deploy in grades K-12 interactive, Web-based, multimedia-rich mathematics materials in both Arabic and English. The Maths e-Curriculum is based on research from some of the best mathematics education practices worldwide and is premised on a modern pedagogical approach applying constructivist, collaborative learning aimed at high levels of mathematical knowledge, skills, and motivation. In particular, it seeks to strengthen students' skills in applying mathematics across a broad range of other subjects and situations, recognizing that such skills will be critical to Jordan's future in the knowledge economy.

The Maths e-Curriculum content supports and develops teachers as well as students through high-quality lesson plans, rich interactive media, and sophisticated electronic assessment and feedback. It is used by teachers in their daily lessons with students in the classroom (with the aid of portable computers and a data projector), in exercises carried out by students in groups in the classroom (with the aid of a few computers in the classroom), and also in periodic self-learning (with the aid of one-to-one computers in existing computer labs in the schools). It has been developed by various players including Jordanian mathematics teachers and supervisors; Rubicon, a Jordanian software company; Cisco; and Cisco Learning Institute. The project consists of three elements:

- Teacher professional development
- Teacher presentation resources for classroom projection and whole class teaching
- Student activities

Teachers are encouraged to engage in professional development shortly before the lessons they have to teach. In such training, their own subject matter knowledge is tested and strengthened. In addition, their misconceptions are highlighted, and sound pedagogical practices are discussed. This means that teachers do not need to spend time away from the classroom in professional development courses. Instead, they undertake relevant and timely professional development online when needed. Some of the media items used to teach subject matter knowledge to teachers are the same ones used for the students as either e-learning items or whole-class resources. By engaging teachers in their own learning using the media they will later use with students, their understanding of the benefits is personalized, and they are more likely to use the media in their teaching.

Once teachers have completed the requisite professional development, they are shown a scope of work for the subject they are to teach. Teachers are presented with a series of lesson plans linked to media items, together with a set of suggestions of how they might engage a class or a group of students in a way that will encourage students to collaborate, discuss, and engage in the mathematical activity. Suggestions are also made for follow-up work either at or away from the computer; this might include teacher-mediated group work around a computer, self-learning activities for consolidation and practice in the maths lab, practical mathematics, or some other form of practice. The instructional elements are media rich and sometimes designed to encourage mathematical activities away from the computer.

Issues of cultural relevance have been at least partly addressed by having the media and the lesson plans designed by Jordanians. Rubicon, the media development company, is a growing Jordanian firm based in Amman. To add to this relevance, the Ministry of Education has released around thirty teachers from their teaching to work in the Rubicon offices for twelve months, and their salaries are paid by Rubicon, through the funding that they have received to develop the program. These individuals receive pedagogical support from people like me and other educators working for the Cisco Learning Institute.

Through development of the e-curriculum, it is hoped that the consequent longer-term benefit is a contribution to Jordan's economic development by equipping Jordanian students with a higher level of mathematics knowledge and skills, as well as an ability to apply knowledge as needed in a knowledge economy. The plan is for the curriculum to be made available to other countries and in a format whereby it can be fairly easily customized for the curriculum and culture of other countries.

Blending Can Remove the Technology Dissonance in E-Learning

All the evidence from the three initiatives I have worked on—the Rwanda teacher training initiative, the evaluation of the Cisco Networking Academy Program, and the Jordan Maths e-Curriculum—has led me to believe that however many educational resources are made available on the Web and however much animation and simulation is employed in whatever new and engaging ways, students still need support and scaffolding for their learning. I have learned that when people work together, whatever the resources and the level of detail, the classroom situation provides a focal point to channel students' thinking and help them focus on the subject they are studying. The classroom provides direction and rigor, and the teacher acts as the orchestrator of learning. The teacher directs the activities, helps students overcome hurdles, picks them up when they stumble, and encourages and helps them to develop the skills of collaboration and cooperation with others, as well as many valued critical thinking and problem-solving skills.

How a course is blended is dependent on a number of factors, several of them described in this chapter. In areas where teachers are lacking in skills, a blended learning solution can be designed for them as learners. A blended learning model might also be used directly in their own classroom to scaffold their mastery of new teaching skills, as in the Maths e-Curriculum in Jordan. If we are to develop blended learning solutions that are truly effective, then we have to consider the audience for the content. Is it for teachers or for students? Do the Web-based resources and approaches taken meet cultural norms and pedagogical practices? Is there the necessary Internet access readily available and at an affordable rate? Do users know how to make the most effective uses of it?

Clearly, the globalization of learning has significant repercussions on learners. E-learning materials based on widely differing pedagogical models can now be created for and rapidly distributed to students in different cultures. However, the imposition of many of these technology solutions may be inappropriate or perhaps may need modification by local instructors, as demonstrated in the context of the Cisco Networking Academy Program. Ian Gibson and I have termed this "technology disssonance" (Selinger & Gibson, 2004).

In effect, what most people are calling e-learning is in actuality blended learning. Without teachers to act as cultural and pedagogical mediators, e-learning will not be successful. In any course, there needs to be a face-to-face component with local facilitation. Without blended learning, it may be difficult to overcome technology dissonance in e-learning materials. Sometimes this blended learning will occur when local instructors make global e-learning materials relevant and use localized methods for teaching that material. At other times, the oral culture, common to developing countries, will also necessitate a blended learning approach whereby e-learning materials are made available to learners who are used to a storytelling teaching environment. And so ends this story—for now.

References

Cisco. (2004). *Academy connection.* San Jose: Cisco. Retrieved August 9, 2004, from cisco.neta-cad.net/public/index.html.

Selinger, M. (1997). Learning to teach at a distance: Exploring the roles of electronic communication. In D. Passey & B. Samways (Eds.), *Information technology: Supporting change through teacher education.* New York: Chapman Hall.

Selinger, M. (1998). Forming a critical community through telematics. *Computers in Education, 30*(1/2), 23–30.

Selinger, M. (2002). *The Cisco Networking Academy program evaluation in Europe, the Middle East and Africa: Executive summary.* London: Cisco. Retrieved August 9, 2004, from www.cisco.com/edu/emea/docs/exec_summary.doc.

Selinger, M. (2004a). Cultural and pedagogical implications of a global elearning programme. *Cambridge Journal of Education, 34*(2), 213–229.

Selinger, M. (2004b). The role of local instructors in making global elearning programmes culturally and pedagogically relevant. In A. Brown & N. Davis (Eds.), *World Yearbook 2004 Digital technologies, communities and education.* London: Kogan Page.

Selinger, M., & Gibson, I. (2004, June). Cultural relevance and technology use: Ensuring the transformational power of learning technologies in culturally defined learning eEnvironments. In *Proceedings of EdMedia 2004 Conference.* Lugano, Switzerland.

Michelle Selinger is an education strategist, corporate responsibility at Cisco Systems. She draws on her academic experience from the U.K. Open University and the University of Warwick to research and disseminate effective solutions for e-learning in all aspects of education and training. She works at the interface of academia and industry to help organizations develop their e-learning strategies and competences. Her expertise in the field of e-learning is wide ranging, from professional development of teachers in all sectors of to the development of skill sets for teachers and trainers in vocational education using e-learning materials in a blended learning environment. She is a member of the Advisory Group of the European Commission's eEurope 2005 Action Plan.

CHAPTER THIRTY-TWO

BLENDED E-LEARNING IN THE CONTEXT OF INTERNATIONAL DEVELOPMENT

Global Perspectives, Local Design of e-Courses

Sheila Jagannathan

The economic development paradigm has undergone some fairly significant changes during the past two decades. The earlier paradigm for developing countries centered around how best investments in social and physical infrastructure could be accompanied by capacity building. For the latter to take place, technical assistance was mainly in the form of advisory services from internationally renowned subject matter experts (or gurus). These persons advised developing country counterparts through face-to-face consultations, extension work, and voluminous reports aimed at transferring relevant knowledge. (Some exceptional individuals who led these knowledge transfers were Norman Borlaug, Sir Arthur Lewis, and Gunnar Myrdal.)

At a country level, few comprehensive knowledge transfers have taken place. The best examples of knowledge transfers have been Korea and Singapore, both of which dramatically increased per capita incomes between 1960 and 1990. Both countries accomplished this largely by acquiring and systematically using global knowledge for national economic development and poverty eradication. However, partial transfers of knowledge have taken place in several other countries, including Brazil, Mexico, China, South Africa, and India. In these countries, localized centers of excellence in knowledge transfer have not yet led to widespread diffusion of knowledge and associated poverty eradication (Millet, 2003). (For the latter to take place, one needs the universalization of primary and secondary education so that all citizens are able to access these high-quality learning institutions.)

The Information and Communication Technologies Revolution

In addition to massive economic transformation, the focus of education and knowledge transfer in these countries has changed during the past two decades, from knowledge transfer from the gurus to a much more varied transfer using technologies such as computer, CD-ROMs, Web sites, voice, and video communications. This shift has been made possible by the enormous advances in capturing knowledge with various digital technology innovations. These changes have placed knowledge at the hands of any individual anywhere in the world who has access to technology and the skills to use it. In effect, such an individual has at his or her fingertips all the information that he or she needs access to at a given point of time.

This revolution in information and communication technology (ICT) has changed the way technical assistance is being viewed by the development community. The focus has now shifted to exploring how electronic infrastructure development can be used to build cost-effective knowledge for institutional capacity. Clearly, this process works well when a country's key stakeholders have the capacity to apply global knowledge on best policies and practices to their individual country, including both regional and local contexts. It is simultaneously important that there is a commitment to the needed infrastructure and high-level governmental strategic planning and support for emerging information and communication technologies.

Many assume that the growth of ICT infrastructure is the key driver to bring about effective global knowledge transfer. The argument advanced is that a country's development strategy could get enormous traction by applying just-in-time learning that incorporates in-country experiences with the global knowledge available through the use of digital technology. The new paradigm envisages a multidimensional knowledge-sharing and learning focus, in which debates, discussions, knowledge syntheses, and applications of ideas to a local context are emphasized. (Local refers to a national, regional, or purely local context. With an enhanced ICT infrastructure, learning could more effectively move from one level to another.)

In this idealized world, all the stakeholders, regardless of whether they are senior public officials, businesspersons, nongovernmental organizations, students, journalists, farmers, or service providers, become the learners, who are able to access, debate, and absorb relevant knowledge from the enormous quantity of information available from the Internet, digital knowledge bases, CD-ROMs, and other sources. Knowledge transfer no longer is the preserve of the gurus alone, but a dynamic process involving all key stakeholders as a gigantic, multilaterally linked learning community.

The challenge for learning design in this context is how to develop a quality learning experience that maintains an appropriate balance between the global and the local aspects. In addition, in the developing country environment, there are two other significant prerequisites before knowledge captured through digital technology can be shared in the local community. These prerequisites relate to:

- Creating the local context by distilling locally relevant knowledge from the global information base and ensuring that the cultural context is adequately preserved
- Diffusing and using that knowledge efficiently and equitably

The Track Record

The ideal is for the local learning community to cull out global knowledge on best practices in a subject, adapt these to the country context through a vigorous process of discussions and debates, and thereby secure productivity gains and income generation. ICT developments provide the vehicles to make this happen.

The practice is still far from ideal. ICT developments have moved at different speeds in the industrialized and developing countries, leading analysts to describe a growing digital divide between the rich and poor countries. Content design has also not moved rapidly enough to facilitate stakeholders at various capability levels being transformed into a community of learners. If this does not happen fast enough, the knowledge divide would grow as well.

Analysts also point out that ICT developments are growing at a faster rate in many developing countries compared to industrialized ones, albeit from a smaller base (Figure 32.1). For example, the growth rates of mobile telephone and Internet usage in many developing countries of Asia and South America are much greater than in the more advanced countries. (Levels of development are usually classified into three categories. High income represents the United States, Japan, Western Europe, and some other resource-rich countries. Middle income represents countries with a per capita annual income of over $865, and low income countries are those with a per capita annual income of less than $865.) This

FIGURE 32.1.   AVERAGE ANNUAL GROWTH OF INTERNET
USERS/CAPITA, BY LEVEL OF DEVELOPMENT.

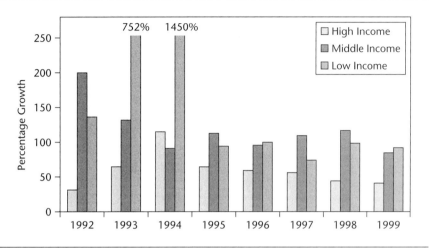

Source: Fink and Kenny (2003).

FIGURE 32.2.   INTERNET USERS/GDP, BY LEVELS
OF DEVELOPMENT.

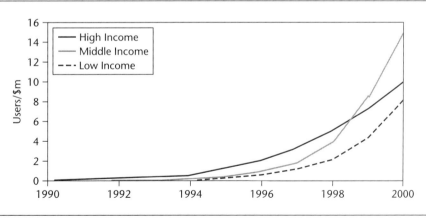

Source: Fink and Kenny (2003).

explosion in mobile phone and Internet use, as well as private investments in digital technologies, has created employment and income opportunities for a significant section of university graduates in several countries (Figure 32.2). The digital divide exists, but it is perhaps shrinking.

The Challenge: Bridging the Knowledge Divide

Recent research by two World Bank economists (Fink & Kenny, 2003) suggests that the problem is more than just the digital divide between rich and poor countries; the real challenge lies in bridging the knowledge divide: "Internet usage, which grew by around 50% per year in high-income countries in the late 1990s, compared with 100% per year in low and middle-income countries. The rich are ahead, but the poor are catching up fast" (Canyon or mirage? 2004).

More fundamentally, Fink and Kenny (2003) caution that gains from digital leapfrogging are limited if productivity benefits do not materialize (due to lower adoption levels) or if the adoption of ICTs is restricted to an affluent minority. For example, even if all developing countries are wired to the world's best knowledge resources with the Internet, not much would change because the institutional capacity and individual capability to learn and apply the knowledge would remain key educational constraints. In effect, wiring and other technological infrastructure, while vitally important, cannot alone change educational institutions and organizations.

To sum up, what is evident is the following:

- The knowledge divide is pervasive and can be bridged only by effective development of country-specific learning strategies.
- This knowledge divide needs to be addressed through (1) improved access to ICT, (2) lowered costs of access, and (3) relevant content that is of good instructional quality.
- From the learner's point of view, the key challenges include the capability and capacity to adapt and absorb locally relevant information from the vast knowledge available through ICT.
- The knowledge divide is likely to get wider as creation and diffusion of global knowledge accelerate through lowered costs of ICT, unless effective learning and knowledge-sharing strategies are implemented.

Blended Learning in Developing Country Environments

I have suggested that that the knowledge divide widens if the learning environment does not encourage localized applications of global knowledge or provide adequate incentives for participation by the widest cross-section of learners. The social, linguistic, and cultural contexts are often extremely important to factor into the learning strategy, especially when delivered at a distance. For example, the "geek" language or chatroom humor used in the United States could be considered inappropriate in many other cultures.

Furthermore, the learning context is typically complicated by inequitable access to technology. Computer penetration in developing countries, for example, is substantially lower than in industrialized countries; telephone lines are still limited to a minority of affluent residents. Frequent power outages, atmospheric pollution, and a lack of air-conditioning lengthen the downtime of computer equipment, while simultaneously aggravating access problems of users.

Finally, the learner's preparedness for the course varies widely not only between countries but even within regions of the same country. An insurance executive in a sub-Saharan African country, for example, faces a different set of regulatory issues compared to his or her counterpart in Mexico or Thailand. The same holds true within large countries: learner preparedness in the province of São Paolo, Brazil (where human development indicators are as high as in Western Europe), will be substantially higher when compared to the Amazonas province (where the same indicators are comparable to some of the poorest developing countries).

Tailoring the learning environment to the learners' specific context becomes a key element of learning design. A response has been to use distance learning technologies to connect development practitioners with the relevant global and local experts to create blended experiences that combine real-time, group learning, and knowledge sharing (for example, by videoconferencing and local facilitation) with self-paced learning (for example, by computers and the Internet). The actual design of blended e-learning could take many forms, depending on the objectives of the program and the audience it is targeted toward. The blended learning design will also hinge on learner access to and familiarity with technology as well as the local context of the learning environment.

Table 32.1 summarizes some models of e-learning. The two rows represent modules of e-courses that are either part of a blended activity or are fully Web based. The two columns represent the format of instruction, either as facilitated or as independent study. *Facilitated* means that the course has a definite beginning and ending date and is actively managed by virtual instructors and local experts to guide the learning process. In the case of independent self-study, learners can

TABLE 32.1.   MODELS OF E-LEARNING.

	Facilitated Course	Independent Study
Part of a blended learning activity	A	B
Largely Web based	C	D

begin and end the course at any time that suits them and work primarily on their own. The four boxes (A to D) are described through illustrations from the World Bank Institute's courses.

Categories A and C in Table 32.1 deal with facilitated learning models. An example of category A is the "Key Labor Markets Issues in Africa" blended course, which is extensively facilitated at both the local and global levels. The course was offered over an eight-week period to up to four Anglophone African country sites. Participants met each week for a two-hour videoconference. In between the weekly videoconference sessions, participants undertook two to four hours of independent study (browsing the Internet, engaging in self-paced e-learning, and reading print materials). In addition, each week, local facilitators provided several hours of face-to-face support to discuss local cases, culture, and adaptations. For participants who did not have access to the Internet, multimedia rooms of the distance learning centers were made available.

This was a blended course offering, which combined real-time interaction using videoconferencing and local facilitation with self-paced explorations and various other forms of online learning. E-learning was used at the beginning of the course (for example, for reading background materials and getting familiar with the course), during the course (for example, between videoconference sessions for questions, discussions, and self-paced activities), and after the course (for example, to build a community of practitioners while they work on their action plans with feedback and review from both their peers and experts).

An example of category C is "Health Outcomes and the Poor," a fully Web-based course delivered entirely over the Internet and extensively facilitated by virtual experts and mentors. Targeted toward those who write or evaluate special programs aimed at reducing poverty, the course offers a unique opportunity for action learning. Here, participants do not leave their job to come to the course but rather incorporate the course in their daily work. This course was offered over a six-week period and covered six modules that introduced key concepts, recommended readings, interactive exercises, and self-tests. These activities were augmented by weekly e-discussions that were moderated by virtual facilitators, who provided an opportunity for participants to ask questions and share documents that they were working on for peer review. The use of facilitated asynchronous discussion was a very effective way to keep participants on track and motivated while they participated in the virtual learning experience. Online discussions were also extremely useful because there was time to reflect on and evaluate contributions on a real-time basis, resulting in higher-quality dialogues.

Categories B and D deal with independent study or self-paced learning models with minimal facilitation in the sense that the learner is expected to learn on his or her own. However, if the learner has questions, resource persons are available to provide support. Examples of each are provided below.

An example of category B in the World Bank is the Trust Fund Learning Accreditation Program. All staff members are required to clear this program before they are allowed to manage funds for project preparation and technical assistance. The course is entirely self-paced in that a person can start and end the course at his or her convenience, working through the various modules at his or her own pace, and finally taking the accreditation examination. The model works well in situations where, as in the accreditation course, passing the examination is mandatory. Clearly, if the learner motivation level is low or Internet access is difficult for participants, this model may not work.

An example of category D within the World Bank is when participants are sent learning materials through CD-ROMs and Web pages, which they review at their own convenience and pace. There is no specific learning strategy recommended; instead, learners are expected to develop their own pedagogical approaches, with knowledge sharing validated through seminars and workshops. It is important to point out that every thematic group within the World Bank organizes an annual knowledge-sharing event (such as "Water Week," "Energy Week," "Poverty Week," and "Poverty Reduction and Economic Management Week") in which sector specialists participate with the goal of updating their specialized knowledge. Preparing for these events is through independent study, for which learning materials are provided.

In the context of the World Bank's client learning agenda, in situations where peer learning and knowledge sharing are key outcomes, facilitated e-learning appears much more effective in motivating learners and sustaining their interest. However, the self-paced learning model works well when there is a clear-cut incentive for the learner to update his or her skills.

Trends in Learning Design

Figure 32.3 illustrates different forms of e-learning currently being practiced in the World Bank group. They range from structured time-bound activities that usually require the support of virtual facilitators to highly informal learning and knowledge sharing that require only self-initiative on the part of the learner. Self-paced learning modules are used largely for bank staff, as part of their professional development.

FIGURE 32.3.   TYPES OF E-LEARNING.

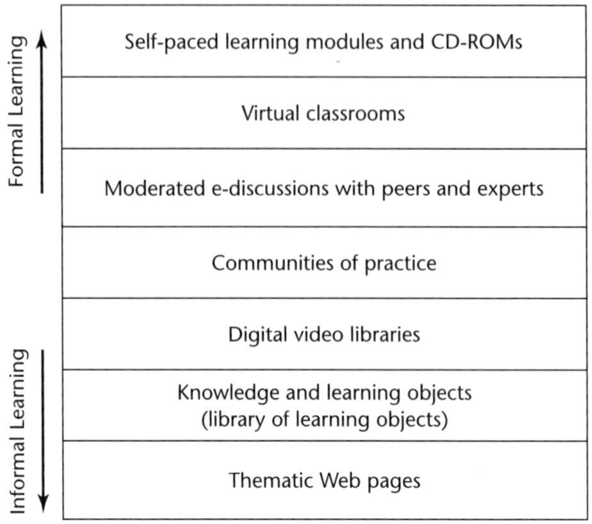

In the vast majority of courses targeting clients in developing countries, the blending of face-to-face time through interactive videoconferencing with print, CD-ROMs, and Web-based modules is used. These courses are designed to handle common ICT access constraints of countries at different levels of development. Overall, ICT advances are increasingly salient in World Bank learning events, while print and traditional face-to-face classrooms still play an important role.

Figure 32.4 illustrates a typical blended learning course, incorporating the ideas discussed above. For example, a five-day face-to-face course could be redesigned for distance delivery to several sites as a blended learning activity that comprises eight weekly sessions covering many of the following elements:

- Two-hour videoconference sessions
- One hour of participation in e-discussions
- Two-hour locally facilitated face-to-face sessions
- Two to four hours of self-paced, independent work (using CDs, Internet, or print)

Among the goals of such a redesigned course would be maintaining a high degree of interactivity and dialogue.

FIGURE 32.4.   EXAMPLE OF BLENDED LEARNING.

Session 1	Session 2	Session 3	Session 4
Background readings and intros	Small-group discussion	Apply model to real case	Self-paced work to reinforce learning
Print or Web	Facilitation/ online	Print, face-to-face, or e-discussions	Web, CD-ROM, print

Via Videoconferencing

Topic 1	Topic 2	Topic 3	Topic 4
Introduce analytical model	Comment on group work, new concepts	Groups present, instructor clarifies and summarizes	Links from self-paced to analytical model

Session 5	Session 6	Session 7	Session 8
Read second case, apply model and send analysis via e-mail	In country groups, discuss policy implications	Self-paced resources on best practice of policy framework. Begin formulating their own country focus	Work in groups to complete policy framework and submit for evaluation
Print or Web Local face-to-face or electronic	Local facilitation and post to discussion forums	Print or Web Face-to-face discussion	Web, CD-ROM, taped videos and print

Via Videoconferencing

Topic 5	Topic 6	Topic 7	Topic 8
Discussion and lecture to introduce policy issues	Continue presentation on policy debate	Questions, debate, and explanations	Group presentations and summary

The Global Distance Learning Network Experience with Blended Learning

The World Bank, through the World Bank Institute and Global Distance Learning Network (GDLN) programs, has been at the forefront of piloting new models aimed at capacity enhancement in developing countries through knowledge and learning programs. Since 2000, it has supported the growth of a GDLN of over sixty-two centers worldwide, all of which are engaged in capacity enhancement. These centers are mostly owned and operated by independent partner institutions. The objectives of GDLN are to improve the development impact by using distance learning methods and connect development decision makers to a global knowledge exchange.

The blended learning experience of GDLN uses an integrated mix of distance learning technologies in order to connect policy and decision makers in a cost-effective manner. This began with the use of videoconferencing, which can be used to simulate a face-to-face experience, and with good instructional design, to provide a forum for immediate dialogue, interaction, knowledge exchange, and feedback despite the distance (Foley, 2003). It is also cost-effective since a number of learners at different sites can participate together. For example, many courses are simulcast to four or five countries with thirty participants in each site. With the dramatic decline in archiving costs, a library of videotapes can also be made available for playback to interested learners after the videoconference session is actually over. In fact, the bank's B-SPAN program provides access to Webcasts of World Bank seminars, lectures, conferences, interviews, and other knowledge-sharing events. Such Webcasts feature many of the world's leading policymakers, experts, and practitioners in all major developmental fields who discuss the latest events, experiences, and trends in their fields.

The availability of the multimedia rooms in the Global Distance Learning Centers (GDLCs) with access to computers and the Internet provides an opportunity to extend the length of the two-hour videoconferencing experience (see Figure 32.5). This type of distance learning infrastructure enhances the overall learning experience in a cost-effective way by deepening and widening the interactions, and permitting dialogue on a continuous basis, thereby creating and

FIGURE 32.5. TYPICAL INFRASTRUCTURE OF A GLOBAL DISTANCE LEARNING NETWORK CENTER.

1. Videoconference Room
   - 30 seats
   - Video screen—256K connection
   - Data screen—for slides and file sharing
   - Teaching desk
2. Multimedia Room
   - 30 PCs
   - Connection to Internet
3. Connectivity: Satellite, fiber, ISDN

nurturing a community of practitioners. For example, the Internet is now being used before the course to allow participants to introduce themselves, state their expectations, and access relevant learning resources. In addition, between weekly videoconferencing sessions within the course, participants can ask questions about the topics being discussed and continue the dialogue with their peers and experts. Finally, after the course session, participants can obtain feedback on their course-related projects and continue networking with each other.

The blended learning of the GDLN is an educational experience created cost-effectively using a mix of distance learning technologies including videoconferencing and Internet and supported by print, CD-ROM, and video. Such learning experiences in most cases also include local face-to-face sessions, where the key interlocutor is the local facilitator, who ensures that the local context and cultural sensitivities are fully reflected in the learning experience.

In effect, a learning community emerges from the global distance learning experience. Participants meet colleagues whom they would not have met otherwise. More fundamental, they share knowledge of best practices as well as concerns and hesitations and secure feedback from their global colleagues. The flexibility and diverse capabilities of the various media, especially the Internet, promote this knowledge sharing and exchange of experiences that enhance the capacity of the development community.

There are constraints on those global collaborations since a reasonably intensive graphic, Web page, or shared document that takes a few seconds to load in the United States on a high-bandwidth line may take five to ten minutes to load in Tanzania or Cambodia (assuming one does not get disconnected during the process). Since Internet time is expensive in developing countries, technology is minimized and creative options that rely on low-bandwidth design are explored. Such low-bandwidth alternatives include e-mail-based listservs (which is more prevalent than Internet-based technology in poorer countries), opportunities to work offline (in terms of readings and compiling discussion posts to read offline, for example), and distributing high-bandwidth items such as multimedia, video, and audio clips using CD-ROM. The disparity in access to technology in the developing world is mitigated in the near term through blended learning models that use public facilities like GDLN multimedia rooms and the World Bank's public information centers.

LESSONS LEARNED

Overall, blended e-learning activities have taken the best from different media to connect a wider community of development practitioners across national and regional boundaries for just-in-time learning and knowledge exchange. Resource persons are provided as "guides on the side" at relatively lower costs compared to conventional learning methods. In addition, the flexibility offered by blending various technologies allows content to be distilled from various sources while simultaneously facilitating team-based learning with a high degree of interactivity and peer-to-peer knowledge sharing. By bringing learning directly to the practitioner's work environment, blended learning activities offer unique opportunities for action learning, whereby learners can immediately apply knowledge and information on the job. This process enables decision makers at both the policy and project levels to share knowledge and ideas on global best practices and interact virtually with peers from across the world. In addition, by reducing travel time and costs for both instructors and participants, blended learning becomes much more cost-effective when compared to the conventional technical assistance programs of the past decades.

Despite the cost-benefits of blended learning there continue to be several key challenges in making blended e-learning work in developing countries. Five major challenges are summarized below:

• *Difficulties in accessing technology for e-learning.* In many developing countries, access to technology is uneven, and innovative solutions need to be developed for e-learning to be effective. To address this problem, technologies that are widely used in developed countries can be creatively adapted to improve access and lower costs for learners. For example, in Malawi, as part of the bank-assisted Population Family Planning project, messages initially broadcast on the radio were put on audiocassettes. Community-based distributors working for the project played these on their cassette recorders to listener groups formed at the village level, which met on specific days. Feedback from these groups was also recorded and fed back into the radio messages, packaged on CD-ROMs and even the Web.

• *E-learning design costs.* Designing interactive e-learning components is a multidisciplinary effort requiring a team of subject matter experts, instructional designers, graphic and Web designers, and multimedia programmers and editors. As a result, it also requires different skill profiles compared to traditional course design, and thereby increases costs. The costs of maintaining quality of design and content have some common elements that could be shared across countries.

• *Creating mechanisms for sharing and scaling up.* The world community needs to identify commonalities in strategies, policies, and principles related to e-learning so as to come up with international standards that promote shareability and scalability of e-learning assets. Such standards need to be able to support cultural and linguistic diversity as well as inclusiveness (particularly for the disabled as well as the elderly). There is also a need to use a modular design approach so that learning objects can be designed once and repurposed for many stakeholders, regions, and learning formats.

• *Reducing learner dropout.* In e-learning, the dropout rate is often high. These risks are mitigated on the supply side through virtual and local facilitators' playing a critical role in managing and supporting the learning experience. However, the roles of the facilitators and learners change in an e-learning environment. As a result, there needs to be well-planned training related to how to teach and learn online as well as training on the use of technology. Proper learner supports to scaffold the learning experience in terms of pedagogy, logistics, and technology therefore become critical. On the demand side, sustaining and motivating learners should target student selection, content relevance, maintaining appropriate levels of instruction, language backgrounds, familiarity with technology, adequate learner support, and, above all, access to the enabling environment (including time to learn).

• *Improving measurement of impacts.* Measuring impacts is key to understanding whether the investments in blended e-learning have led to adequate returns. To measure the impact of blended learning initiatives in developing countries, one needs to develop collaborative evaluation processes for e-learning programs that have been undertaken by both donor and academic institutions interested in economic development.

Conclusion

Blended e-learning courses for developing countries have been successful in improving the quality of the learning experience. Through this, institutional capacity has been built on a range of development issues. These experiences enhance the effectiveness of investment programs and create a greater sense of ownership among country-level stakeholders. For example, over the past few years, leading developing country policymakers and academic institutions have become active partners in the teaching, learning, and knowledge-sharing process. Continued exchange of ideas and experiences among learning designers from developed and developing countries could perhaps help bridge the knowledge gap in the near future.

References

Canyon or mirage? A new paper questions the notion of a worsening digital divide between rich and poor. (2004, January 22). *Economist.* Retrieved November 6, 2004, from http://economist.com/printedition/displayStory.cfm?Story_ID=2367710.

Fink, C., & Kenny, C. (2003). W(h)ither the digital divide? *Info: Journal of Policy, Regulation and Strategy for Telecommunications, 5*(6), 15–24.

Foley, M. (2003). The global development learning network: A World Bank initiative in distance learning for development. In M. G. Moore & B. Anderson (Eds.), *Handbook of distance education* (pp. 829–843). Mahwah, NJ: Erlbaum.

Millet, K., (2003, December). *The knowledge divide and its implications.* Washington, DC: World Bank Institute.

World Bank. (2004). *World development report.* Washington, DC: World Bank.

Sheila Jagannathan is an education specialist at the World Bank Institute. She brings a blend of experience in technology and education, with over twenty years of experience in both private and public sectors, designing and managing distance learning programs and knowledge products in the United States, India, Philippines, Vietnam, and Singapore. Her focus is on e-learning, including Web, computer, and CD-ROM, as well as learning management systems, portals, and learning e-communities.

PART SEVEN

WORKPLACE, ON-DEMAND, AND AUTHENTIC LEARNING

The blending of technology is linking colleges and universities with corporate and other authentic learning settings. To begin to understand what is occurring or possible as well as increasingly required in the area of workplace learning, the chapters in Part Seven detail emerging trends in workplace, work flow, and on-demand learning. Several of these chapters discuss how learning in the workplace can offer opportunities for mentoring and apprenticeship that are not possible in more formal academic settings. The authors suggest that the results of these trends toward learning authenticity will be learners who have more control over their own learning and are more satisfied with it.

Chapter Thirty-Three by Betty Collis from the Netherlands discusses two major challenges that many global companies face. The first stems from the rapid growth of knowledge within a company, and the second is the direct result of personnel changes as an older workforce is replaced by a younger, more global workforce. These challenges are being met by blending aspects of both classroom (formal) learning and workplace (informal) learning. Technology is used to mediate much of the learning that occurs. About half of the sixty-five courses created using this model still have classroom components, while the other half do not. For example, in the case provided in this chapter, learners are mentored to complete projects in the local workplace by managers and peers as well as at a distance through the use of Web-based tools. Materials that once formed the center of classroom training environments are also available electronically for guidance in each step of the process.

Chapter Thirty-Four by Harvey Singh shares a vision of the past, present, and future of blended learning. Singh paints a picture of how blended learning environments have become increasingly sophisticated in addressing learning challenges. He argues that blended learning will increasingly support real-time work flow learning. In a real-time work flow environment, learning and work are seamlessly integrated and supported with knowledge and performance tools. To make his point, Singh highlights several differences between the current paradigm of blended learning and the real-time work flow learning paradigm. Components of a real-time work flow learning architecture are outlined, and an example is provided.

In Chapter Thirty-Five by Nancy DeViney and Nancy J. Lewis, the focus is on the change in training at IBM toward a more embedded approach, where learning is built into the work flow. In this context, perceived corporate needs such as improved transfer of learning, accelerated deployment of best practices, and enhanced learner-worker interactions are discussed. Also described is IBM's new Edvisor online tool, which functions as an "e-coach" to learners. The Edvisor system is an intelligent agent that provides the learner with guidance in creating a personalized learning path through online learning modules in preparation for a face-to-face training experience. The guided online learning component of the training reduces the required amount of face-to-face workshop time and transforms what was originally a single classroom event into a learning process more embedded throughout the day-to-day work.

Chapter Thirty-Six by Ron Oliver, Jan Herrington, and Thomas C. Reeves focuses on the use of blended learning approaches to support authentic learning activities. Ten research-supported characteristics of authentic learning activities are outlined and coupled with opportunities for blended learning. Two illustrative cases are presented that use blended learning to support authentic learning activities. The first case is a research methods course that combines a Web-based virtual learning environment with face-to-face collaborative sessions for scaffolded learning and community building. The second is a course for realtors, to be taken in a workplace setting. Many of the authentic activities take place in a virtual reality environment supported by face-to-face discussions and interactions with peers and mentors.

CHAPTER THIRTY-THREE

PUTTING BLENDED LEARNING TO WORK

Betty Collis

This chapter describes a type of course for professionals in a multinational organization that blends formal and informal learning. The portions of courses carried out in the workplace are not e-learning but rather are based on work-based activities that involve the supervisor and others with relevant experience as learning partners. A Web-based course management system is used to support all aspects of the course, including studying of conceptual material, communication, collaboration, and submission and reuse of contributions from the participants. There may or may not be a face-to-face portion of the course, but there is always considerable interaction between participants, with subject matter experts, with the course facilitator, and with workplace colleagues. The goals of this kind of blended learning are to capture and build on experience within the company and to integrate work and learning while retaining the strengths of a course with a competent leader. This sort of blended learning is seen in close to one hundred course events within the Learning and Leadership Development (LLD) unit of Shell International Exploration and Production, B.V. (Shell EP).

Global Perspectives

Two particular issues face many multinational companies, particularly those that operate in technical or production domains. The first relates to keeping employees up to date with rapidly changing developments in the field and within the company. Even if a new course can be developed quickly, employees cannot get to the course fast enough to meet the company's need. The second is the change in the demographics of the workforce and marketplace as companies operate more and more globally. As highly experienced senior staff near retirement or move to another company, those who replace them often represent a wide range of regional, cultural, and professional backgrounds. In this context, key issues are that there is scant opportunity for experienced senior employees to work in face-to-face mentoring and coaching roles in order to pass on their knowledge, and members of the same company, the senior employees who are leaving and the junior employees who will be moving into their places, are likely to live in different parts of the world, making face-to-face interaction among them not feasible.

Dealing with Rapidly Changing Developments

With regard to the problem of keeping up to date with rapid developments, forms of e-learning are often seen as a solution. Employees can stay at the workplace and learn "just in time" with access to an appropriate selection of learning objects. Because of the time lag in designing and developing an entire course, the use of a learning management system (LMS) combined with a learning content management system (LCMS) is often seen as a way to build a repository of relatively small learning objects, index them with appropriate metatags, save them within the LCMS, and call up different combinations of the small objects with a learner profiling tool in the LMS. One assumption of this approach is that building the smaller objects will require less time than designing and building a course as a whole. However, for the approach to work, many different components must be in place.

Collis and Strijker (2004) have analyzed six stages in the life cycle of learning objects (obtaining, labeling, offering, selecting, using, and maintaining) and documented many human and technical issues in each stage. In the case of rapidly emerging knowledge, particularly knowledge that is sensitive to the company involved, the initial step of obtaining even small learning modules fast enough is a serious challenge. Professional developers are needed to create modules that are interoperable and compliant to the standards needed for learning object management in an LCMS and LMS. These developers will not be the in-house experts who are creating the new knowledge within the company and are the main source of fast-breaking developments for their colleagues. Bringing the experts together with the software developers in order to create accurate but also engaging content resources can take considerable time.

For this reason, most large organizations maintain various knowledge-sharing activities, such as global communities of practice supported by forum software and best-practices databases (Allee, 1997). These knowledge-sharing resources typically are not seen as part of courses offered by a learning department but rather are associated with human resource or knowledge management units. Learning through these resources represents best practices within the company, shared often by those involved in creating the new knowledge, and shared at the speed of typing the reports into one of the knowledge-sharing systems. This form of informal sharing stimulated by knowledge management units leads to informal learning that is typically not associated with courses or repositories of learning objects managed by an LCMS.

Dealing with Changing Demographics in the Workforce

The second major problem facing multinational companies is that of changing demographics within their own workforce and customer base. The knowledge sharing that occurs within the informally organized knowledge environments in the company can provide some of the cross-fertilization needed for passing on the tacit knowledge of experienced persons in the company regardless of geographical location. However, not all persons are regular contributors to such communities of practice. Adding to the problem is the lack of support for the sorts of coaching and mentoring that are necessary for learning from persons with experience. Cultural differences among senior employees and new professionals also can be barriers to informal electronically mediated personal interactions.

Blending Formal and Informal Learning in Courses with Work-Based Activities

A response to these two sets of problems—rapidly changing in-house knowledge and barriers to knowledge sharing and learning from the experiences of others in the company—can be addressed by a new form of course experience that combines the strengths of both formal and informal learning and is facilitated by technology through courses that focus on work-based activities, carried out as part of the participant's job. Courses oriented around work-based activities may or may not include classroom components but will include different types of learning activities (with a focus on work-based problems), different types of learning resources (with a focus on reuse of experience from within the company), different times and places for learning activities (with a focus on activities being carried out in the workplace), and different ways that people work and network together (with a focus on collaboration in the process of doing work-based activities). The key to this learning approach is authentic work-based activities, the sharing of experiences related to these activities, and guidance by experienced facilitators (course instructor and workplace coaches and other learning partners) using a Web-based learning support platform (Collis & Margaryan, 2003).

In this context, authentic work-based activities are learning activities that are anchored in workplace practice and are focused on developing the participants' ability to solve problems in their everyday professional job roles (Merrill, 2002). Knowledge and skills that learners acquire while carrying out the work-based activities are acquired in the situation and context in which they will be used rather than in an abstract way. In contrast to well-defined textbook problems, work-based problems are complex and ill defined and need to be solved in social settings, involving others for team working, and with coaching and scaffolding by an expert (Fox, 2002; Reeves, Herrington, & Oliver, 2002). Within this form of learning, not only are work-based activities emphasized but also the submissions by the participants of different types of reports and reflections based on those activities become important additions to the learning resources of the course. Such activities help make cognitive and problem-solving processes explicit and serve as a basis for reflection and feedback. Furthermore, follow-up activities can build on these submissions and be structured to involve contacts and interactions with others in the company, regardless of location. Externally developed content objects are still available, but are seen as resources for the activities, not as the initial drivers of the activities. Selected learner submissions are reused as valuable content objects for others. Just as learning from experience is shared within the informal communities of practice, learning is also shared and reused within the courses.

This type of blended learning is currently operating in practice in one of the business units of a multinational oil company, growing in extent since 2001 from several pilot courses to approximately one hundred different course events in 2004, with continual requests for help in redesign coming from the instructors in the remaining courses as well as in other units of the overall company.

Putting Blended Learning to Work in Shell EP

Shell EP business activities include exploring, assessing, and producing hydrocarbon reserves. The Exploration and Production business has interests in exploration and production ventures in over forty countries and employs over twenty-five thousand people. The technical professionals in Shell EP are predominantly university graduates who represent the areas of wells engineering, field engineering, production engineering, petroleum engineering, and geoscience disciplines. Two major problems facing the company are the rapidly changing developments in oil production technology, and the "big crew change" that is occurring as senior technical professionals, typically from the United Kingdom, the Netherlands, and the United States, are retiring and being replaced by new professionals from the

Middle East, Malaysia, Nigeria, and other non-Western countries. To deal with these two key problems, the form of blended learning focused on courses with work-based activities has been evolving since 2001. A collaboration with educational technologists and researchers from the University of Twente supports the evolution.

Blended Courses with Work-Based Activities

As part of this research collaboration, an instructional design method, the Shell Blended Learning Development Path, based on research and best practices in using technology to support activity-based learning, has been developed and validated. A suite of innovative tools has been built to guide each course team through the process of course redesign (Bianco, Collis, Cooke, & Margaryan, 2002). The key steps in the design and delivery process are:

1. Begin each course with an identified business need or competence gap; then restate that need or gap into terms that indicate measurable performance in the workplace.

2. Design the course around a multistep work-based activity, not around sequences of content. Content serves as a resource for the work-based task, not as the driver.

3. Lead each participant and his or her supervisor to the completion of a learning agreement for the course in which they jointly identify a workplace problem or opportunity related to the overall course topic. Express this in terms of the individual's competence development by indicating the sorts of performance that should be demonstrated during and by the end of the course. Guide the participant and supervisor toward the selection of a locally relevant problem that is manageable within the course period and relates to the general business need that has motivated the course. This is to ensure enough parallelism among the different work-based activities that will be occurring so that peer interaction can occur during the course even though participants each have their own specific work-based situations.

4. Design, according to research-based, best practice guidelines, a Web-based learning support environment to serve as the common electronic work space, the environment for collaborative learning and discussion, and for submissions from the participants, all under the leadership of a skilled instructor.

5. Build in (1) peer interaction, (2) use of the Shell Global Networks (the software environments that support informal knowledge sharing within communities of practice throughout the company), (3) contacts with experts outside the course, (4) reuse of submissions from previous participants, and (5) carefully crafted

interactions with the supervisor throughout the course into the instructions for the activities. Retain records of all interactions, submissions, feedback, and assessment in the Web environment.

6. Integrate evaluation from different perspectives (participant, supervisor, instructor, course design, and technology-design experts) into every course. Use the evaluation not only for course improvement but for cross-course analyses and impact measurement.

7. Coach the supervisors and instructors in how to plan for and manage this new type of course, including building on teachable moments that arise from participant submissions.

8. Reuse selected participant submissions as resources for the next cycles of the same course or other courses, thereby increasing the local relevance of the course materials (Collis & Strijker, 2004).

Over one hundred different course events, involving approximately sixty-five fully redesigned courses, have occurred at Shell EP since 2001 following this model. As the process is also evolving, not every course event demonstrates each of the eight steps but the general orientation can be seen. Approximately half of the courses blend work-based activities with a classroom component, while the other half of the courses take place only in the workplace, with no classroom component. Satisfaction with the courses is high, and the general response from all involved is that the shift toward work-based activities has made the courses more relevant as well as increasing the learning that has occurred (Collis, Margaryan, & Kennedy, 2004).

Categories of Work-Based Activities at Shell EP

Various analyses of the work-based activities in the Shell EP courses with work-based activities have occurred, carried out by the LLD Research Team (see Collis et al., 2004; Margaryan, Collis, & Cooke, 2003; Margaryan, 2004). Analyses of work-based activities in these courses shows that they can be grouped into the following generic categories:

• Orientation
• Collecting information from the workplace
• Product development
• Sharing and reflecting
• Comparing and contrasting
• Self-analysis
• Reflections

Orientation. Orientation activities include the learner's signing a learning agreement with his or her line supervisor, getting acquainted with the ground rules for the course (expectations in terms of participation in discussions, regularity of checking out the course site, and completion requirements, for example), and reflecting on his or her own knowledge gaps and learning needs and expectations from the course in terms of addressing those needs. It also includes posting information related to his or her background and work experience as well as personal details to help learners get to know each other.

Collecting Information from the Workplace. Activities in this category begin with a problem related to the subject matter of the course and involve steps for finding information about that problem in the participant's own workplace. Examples of these types of activities include participants' finding pertinent equipment (for example, valves, joints, hardware) in their own environment, similar to a scavenger hunt. The activities could involve conversations with subject matter experts, enabling dialogues on use, maintenance, and repairs, thereby establishing a link between new content and real-world applications. From a broader Shell EP perspective, the activities may encourage interaction with a discipline community using the Global Networks. By integrating these informal knowledge-sharing channels within a formal course environment, learning is expanded beyond the boundaries of the course, and learners are stimulated to make use of various existing company resources (people and technology) to solve their particular problems. Once the report on the results of the activity is submitted to the course Web environment, follow-up activities can occur. These activities often include the participants' comparing and contrasting their problems and solutions or giving feedback to each other's submissions. Figure 33.1 shows a portion of the Web environment supporting a course in this category.

Product Development. The third category of work-based activities appearing in Shell EP courses relates to developing a product that can be directly used in the workplace. The products can range from the development of an online bidding project for the workplace to the development of technical models or inventories or personal leadership development plans. The work (and hence the learning) here can get quite complex and engaging, as these are often multistep activities following a systematic procedural framework (assess-plan-design-develop-implement-evaluate). After each step, reports summarizing the results in that step are submitted to the course Web environment, and the course instructor and the other participants can give feedback on those submissions. This category of activities sometimes involves a midcourse checkpoint with the participant's supervisor to discuss participant learning progress and performance. Figure 33.2 shows a portion of the Web environment supporting this sort of course.

FIGURE 33.1.   WEB-BASED COURSE ROSTER IN WHICH CONCEPTS ARE INTRODUCED, ACTIVITIES BASED DIRECTLY ON STUDY MATERIALS ARE PRESENTED, AND A WORKPLACE APPLICATION OCCURS.

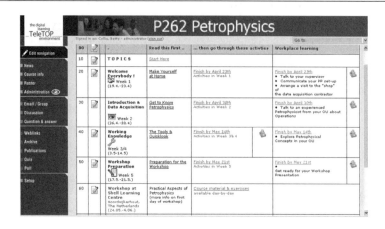

FIGURE 33.2.   WEB ROSTER SHOWING HOW EACH CONCEPTUAL STEP OF A PROCESS IS ACCOMPANIED BY SUBMISSIONS IN WHICH THAT STEP IS ACTUALLY CARRIED OUT IN THE WORKPLACE.

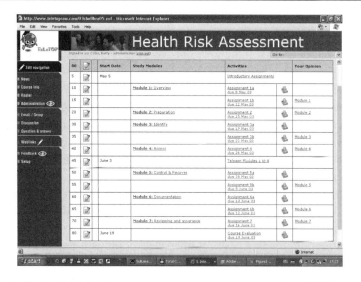

Sharing and Reflecting. This category of activities relates to sharing experiences on a given topic, by posting reflective reports in the course environment. This is followed up by synchronous and asynchronous group discussions of the submitted issues in the discussion areas of the web environment. The course instructor participates and monitors these discussions, and gives feedback or guidance when needed.

Comparing and Contrasting. These activities involve comparing and contrasting each other's submissions, comparing course content with the real situation in the learner's own workplace, or comparing the learner's own experiences and ideas on the subject matter of the course with company standards.

Self-Analysis. In this category of activities, participants are guided through a multistep process of self-analysis and reflection activities to identify their own knowledge and skill gaps and development needs.

Reflections. Although this is also part of many of the other categories of activities, the final type of activity, reflection, is emphasized here as a separate category since it is often used as the final course activity. Reflective tasks might ask learners to reflect on what they learned and recognize key applications in their workplace. Many times the final activity of the class is to check with their supervisor on the learning agreement and determine how closely their learning experience has met or exceeded expectations and defined business challenges.

More Traditional Learning Activities

In addition to the work-based activities, more traditional learning activities also occur in the workplace portions of the Shell EP LLD courses. These include activities such as studying the conceptual material related to the subject matter of the course available in the course Web site. Calculation exercises, quizzes, case studies, and working with simulation software are also familiar types of activities carried on outside a classroom setting with the support of the course Web environment. Case studies and simulations are used in courses where, because of time, manageability, or safety constraints, it is not possible to use real workplace situations or tasks as the main project of the course. However, such courses often use some of the above-described work-based types of activities to accompany the use of the simulation and make the learning as relevant to work as possible.

In Shell EP LLD courses built on the work-based model, many of the activity types are used in combination. In the next section, a specific example of a course redesigned using the work-based approach will be discussed to illustrate this sort of combination.

Example Course: Health Risk Assessment

This course is focused on health risk assessment and incorporates a number of the types of work-based activities described in the previous section. The interface of a portion of its Web environment was shown in Figure 33.2. Health risk assessment (HRA) is a complex and critical process in Shell EP. Health risks for employees associated with potentially dangerous tasks such as drilling or handling chemicals must be regularly monitored and prevented. In addition, health risks associated with Shell processes for the local environments must be managed at all times with great care to prevent environmental disasters. HRA is a carefully documented process in Shell EP. Hundreds of Shell professionals worldwide must be trained each year to take responsibility for the assessment process in their workplaces. The person carrying out the assessment never works in isolation, but must lead a team that includes the drilling foreman and superintendent, technicians, company physicians and physiotherapists, workplace team leaders, plant managers, security advisers, and general asset managers.

The course typically used to take place in a one-week classroom setting, but there were difficulties in participants' not being able to travel to the classroom sessions or in the instructors' being able to travel to individual regional sites. Also, the classroom sessions did not provide the opportunity to carry out a health risk assessment as it actually happens in the workplace and get guidance and feedback from an expert or peer collaborators helping one another during this process. The need to access fast-breaking information about the risks in new drilling or chemical-handling processes could not be met with a face-to-face course that sometimes had a waiting list of many months. A decision was made to redesign the course so that the activities could be carried out in participants' individual workplaces. The participants would take responsibility for carrying out a health risk assessment in their own workplaces as the main activity of the course.

The result of the redesign process is a course that involves a number of work-based activities that progressively build on each other to take the learner through an actual HRA process. Such activities naturally include HRA preparation, including the identification of a competent HRA team to coach and assist the learner with the work-based assignments during the course; planning; and getting permission from the manager of the assessment team to perform an HRA. Other course activities include the identification and rating of HRA hazards, assessment of health risks to the business, application of identified hazard and exposure ratings, effective documentation for the HRA results, and reviewing the HRA and assurance process. For each step, participants are coached by experienced persons in their own workplaces but also in other locations within the company over the Web environment. Also, for each step, participants submit their working documents into the Web environment, study each others' submissions, and provide feedback and support for each other. Although they never meet face-to-face, considerable knowledge sharing occurs. The study resources that had previously formed the base of the face-to-face course are electronically available using the Web environment, to serve as conceptual guidance for each step of the HRA process.

The course has run eleven times in this blended learning format, with evaluation results from the participants consistently high (Collis & Margaryan, 2003). Some of the participants reported that they had already moved on to new job roles as a result of their increased competence or were entrusted with new projects of high business impact, in either their own operating unit or other parts of the organization, as a result of the course even before it was completed. As one participant noted, "I worked virtually with HRA teams in Shell Egypt sister companies and now am supervising their HRA processes." Overall, the results of the evaluations show that the work-based activities in this course resulted in increased competence, application of learning, and sharing of knowledge in the workplace and globally, as well as significant workplace impact. However, there is a need to continue to improve some aspects of the course, such as interaction among the participants, which could be more strongly integrated into course activities, and ensuring that the participants are given enough time and resources to carry out course activities such as studying resource materials, preparing reflections and analyses of other participants' work, and interacting with other participants to share experiences. While the participants have not complained about these aspects in the HRA course, both are important issues being studied in all Shell EP courses in order to improve the impact of the courses.

Key Issues

The Shell EP example indicates some of the key issues and challenges in redesigning courses to this new form of blend. Many types of changes must occur, particularly in the expectations of all involved with regard to what constitutes a "course." Work-based activities by their very nature are more difficult to manage in terms of time expectations, compared with a preset number of days for a classroom-only course. The new expectations for the workplace supervisor will meet with resistance because they will be seen as new work unless the supervisors are carefully supported by the course instructor team (Bianco & Collis, 2004). The work-based activities must be directly relevant and valuable in the workplace. In a shift from content delivery to activity management, instructors must learn new roles. The Web technology used must be simple, flexible, and easy to access, yet make sharing and communicating as transparent as possible. An integrated approach to implementation and course design is needed to manage these complex interrelated requirements. All of these aspects are being tackled simultaneously at Shell EP. And for company support, the approach to blended learning must reflect corporate strategy and needs, which also is the case at Shell EP.

References

Allee, V. (1997). *The knowledge evolution: Expanding organizational intelligence.* London: Butterworth-Heinemann.

Bianco, M., & Collis, B. (2004). Tools and strategies for engaging the supervisor in technology-supported work-based learning. In T. M. Egan, M. L. Morris, & V. Inbakumar (Eds.), *Proceedings of the AHRD Conference 2004* (pp. 505–512). Bowling Green, OH: Academy of Human Resource Development.

Bianco, M., Collis, B., Cooke, A., & Margaryan, A. (2002). Instructor support for new learning approaches involving technology. *Staff and Educational Development International, 6*(2), 129–148.

Collis, B., & Margaryan, A. (2003, September 9). *Work-based activities and the technologies that support them: A bridge between formal and informal learning in the corporate context.* Presentation at the conference LearnIT: Information and Communication Technologies and the Transformation of Learning Practices, Gothenburg, Sweden.

Collis, B., Margaryan, A., & Kennedy. M. W. (2004, October 11). *Blending formal and informal learning offers new competence development opportunities.* Paper presented at the 11th, Abu Dhabi, United Arab Emirates.

Collis, B., & Strijker, A. (2004). Technology and human issues in reusing learning objects. *Journal of Interactive Media in Education* [Special Issue], *9*(1). Retrieved August 1, 2004, from http://www-jime.open.ac.uk/2004/JIME-2004-EduSemWeb.pdf.

Fox, S. (2002). Studying networked learning: Some implications from socially situated learning theory and actor network theory. In C. Steeples & C. Jones (Eds.), *Networked learning: Perspectives and issues* (pp. 77–92). London: Springer-Verlag.

Margaryan, A. (2004, April 8). *Course scan results.* Presentation to the Knowledge, Innovation and Design Leadership Team, Shell EP LLD, Rijswijk, the Netherlands.

Margaryan, A., Collis, B., & Cooke, A. (2003). Activity-based blended learning. *Human Resources Development International, 7*(2), 265–274.

Merrill, D. (2002). First principles of instruction. *Educational Technology Research and Development, 50*(3), 43–59.

Reeves, T. C., Herrington, J., & Oliver, R. (2002). *Authentic activities and online learning.* Retrieved August 1, 2004, from http://elrond.scam.ecu.edu.au/oliver/2002/Reeves.pdf.

Betty Collis is head of the Technology for Strategy, Learning and Change research team in the Faculty of Behavioural Sciences at the University of Twente, the Netherlands. As leader of a five-year collaborative research project with the Learning and Leadership Development Organization of Shell International Exploration and Production (Shell EP LLD), she is also head of the research team for Shell EP LLD. In both roles, she studies changes in organizations related to their use (or nonuse) of technologies. She also focuses on new pedagogies for corporate learning that stress knowledge sharing and the blending of formal and informal learning. In addition, she has led many design and development projects relating to software tools, systems, and resources for learning support.

CHAPTER THIRTY-FOUR

BLENDING LEARNING AND WORK

Real-Time Work Flow Learning

Harvey Singh

Today, organizations are having a tough time coping with the unfulfilled promise of e-learning. Why has e-learning lost favor among those who once thought it was the one-step solution to all their training and knowledge transfer needs?

One mistake that organizations made was to deliver too much e-learning. Companies dumped hundreds or even thousands of courses into a portal or learning management system (LMS) and expected learners to swim and find relevant courses. Learners did not know which of the thousand courses was best for them and how to extract specific information from the courses in order to fulfill job- or task-specific requirements. This left learners without the context in which to make effective decisions. They also wasted time trying to choose the right course and were frustrated; even if they found the right course, they could not apply this learning effectively at their workplace.

First-Generation Learning Systems

First-generation learning systems (learning management systems and learning content management systems) provide a static library or catalogue of courses. These systems use the Internet to deliver traditional educational products and services such as textbooks, articles, and training courses in the form of e-learning courses. Some of the courses are more sophisticated and incorporate a high degree of interactivity by using animation, streaming video, simulations, and games. The first-generation learning approach delivers anytime, anyplace learning and provides numerous online content libraries to a large audience at an attractive cost.

While organizations using these first-generation learning systems and courses save cost and time, they do not achieve the objective of increasing productivity and fulfilling the real training and job performance needs of employees, partners, and customers. These systems suffer from lack of engagement, lack of motivation, lack of time, and, most important, lack of tangible and immediate value or relevance. These learning systems simply attempt to compile subject matter expertise into a large, linear, and predominantly page turner course format. Even the addition of media rarely improves the applicability of the course and the transfer of knowledge and skill to a workplace context. First-generation learning fails to recognize the essential link between theory and practice—between learning and its direct application in the job environment.

As first-generation e-learning evolved, attempts were made to shift the control from the instructor to the learner and make learning self-paced and personalized with pretests to determine skill gaps and provide links to specific learning units or learning objects targeted toward the identified gaps. However, these early learning systems followed a courseware-centric learning approach and failed to provide a job context in the learning process. These early learning systems had a number of limitations:

• Content remains a silo or a separate repository. This requires the learner to log on to a separate Web site and search for courses that may not be relevant to the task at hand.

• Often learners do not recall what they learned during classroom training or virtual online experiences in order to apply that knowledge or skill during the performance of the job or tasks. Moreover, at the time of need, learners fail to find relevant information from the huge library of courses and modules.

• Considering the fast-paced and complex job environment in today's economy, learners lack the time or motivation to complete long online courses. Therefore, the completion rate of e-learning courses remains low, undermining the effectiveness and intent of those courses.

• E-learning systems do not have an automated mechanism to verify or monitor the actual job performance of the learner or knowledge worker. This places serious constraints on course designers who wish to design courses relevant to the work scenario of the learners and managers who wish to provide remediation or mentoring in order to ensure expert performance.

Recognizing these limitations of the early e-learning systems, organizations began to experiment with blended learning. This approach aimed to improve learner engagement, optimize learners' performance, and reduce delivery costs by combining self-paced (for example, Web-based tutorials) and collaborative (for example, mentoring by a live instructor) learning models. The objective of blended learning is to provide knowledge workers with practical tools and insights that lead to improved job performance. To achieve this, blended learning models need to evolve to a higher level of maturity.

Evolution of Blended Learning

The practice of blending more than one delivery mode of instruction is not new. Initially the blended learning approach was used to supplement classroom learning with activities such as discussions or collaboration. However, blended learning is not just about mixing and matching various delivery modes. To be successful, blended leaning needs to focus on combining the right delivery technologies to match the individual learning objectives and transfer the appropriate knowledge and skills to the learner at the right time.

The ultimate success and effectiveness of learning lies in blending work with learning. Learning is optimum when work and learning are simultaneous—a situation where learning is embedded in business processes such as hiring, sales, product design, and development. In this paradigm, work becomes a source of content that can be captured and organized as small granular chunks of content, or "knowledge nuggets." In the context of the learners' workplace needs, these knowledge nuggets are shared, accessed on demand, or pushed at the moment of need.

As delivery modes and choices of technologies have expanded dramatically over the past few years, blended learning has continued to evolve. We will look at the stages of evolution of blended learning in the corporate training industry (see Figure 34.1).

Initial Stages of Blending

Traditionally, blended learning involved a simplistic blend of physical classroom training and supporting materials such as student handbooks or self-paced printed workbooks. Many times the instructor-led classroom lectures also involved hands-on labs, workshops, and field trips.

FIGURE 34.1.   PAST, PRESENT, AND FUTURE
OF BLENDED LEARNING.

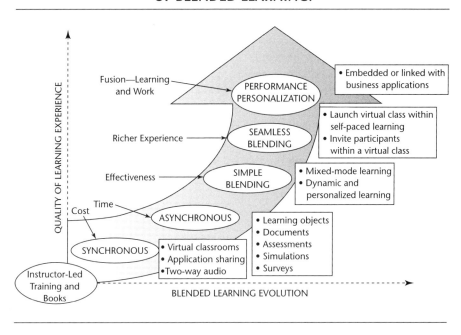

Synchronous Learning

As the practice of blended learning evolved, virtual classrooms were added to the mix involving communication and collaboration between instructors and learners in live capacity. This involved e-meetings, Web seminars, and instant messaging. This kind of training ensured cost savings through elimination of travel and related expenses while preserving the benefit of live human interactions and mentoring.

Asynchronous Learning

Unlike the physical classroom training that is typically instructor paced, asynchronous learning is learner paced. It brings flexibility of time, enabling students to learn at their own pace and revisit learning activities as many times as they want. Web-based training modules, computer-based training modules, assessments, tests, online learning communities, and discussion forums are the typical asynchronous learning modes.

Simple Blending of Different Delivery Modes

A simple blended learning program is a combination of synchronous or asynchronous learning and face-to-face instructor-led learning. Often this means that learners have a combination of self-paced and collaborative learning experiences spanning different learning styles. In this approach, learners ask questions and receive feedback from instructors or experts. Blending asynchronous learning with synchronous, live learning and physical face-to-face learning addresses diverse learning needs and styles (some learners require more mentoring and instructor support than others). This type of blended learning allows learners to gain an understanding of concepts at their own time and pace and refine their understanding through the help of a human mentor or guide. Furthermore, practice activities, simulations, and assessments may be included to this mix to enhance the learning experience.

Seamless Blending

This is an advanced form of blended learning experience that leverages integrated learning and content management and virtual classroom systems. This form of blended learning allows learners to move between self-paced learning and collaborative learning technologies through a seamless or unified interface. For example, an instructor or a learner may expand the self-paced learning experience by inviting others and sharing the learning activity or presentation. Learners can brainstorm ideas and mark up the presentation content through an engaging discussion. Similarly, a collaborative experience may be recorded, broken down into parts, and rearranged for future learning experiences.

Performance and Personalization

The next evolution of blended learning is blending learning with work. Here, learning activities need to be embedded within business processes and tasks in the form of performance support. The performance support guides or mentors the learner and provides supporting materials to perform the task in an optimal fashion. The knowledge worker can seamlessly move between training, simulation, performance support (access to information and knowledge while performing job tasks), to direct work space environments. Furthermore, the access to information can be refined or personalized by pushing very specific pieces of information based on the skill level of the performer.

Real-Time Work Flow Learning: Blending Learning and Work

The industry has learned a critical lesson: you cannot move all your training to e-learning or distance education in the form of a large library of monolithic lectures or courses. In fact, even the classroom, physical or virtual, may not be the best place to learn. The knowledge gained in the classroom is typically lost before it can be applied in a job setting.

Earlier it was assumed that any e-learning system could instantly solve a company's training and knowledge transfer needs. Many did not even consider knowledge worker skill profiles and the job tasks and work flows as part of the system. Without addressing the issues of transfer of learning to the workplace and the job and task environment, e-learning will continue to pose barriers to deeper penetration within organizations.

Real-time work flow learning aims to remove these barriers and bridge the learning and transfer gaps that the first-generation e-learning systems were unable to address. To narrow the gap between knowledge and its application, organizations need to continuously capture and organize every bit of information from their customers and their working environment. Furthermore, next-generation systems are needed to help organizations analyze and synthesize the essential knowledge needed to ensure expert performance, optimal and error-free execution of tasks, and, most important, create the next best-selling product or service. In effect, organizations need to see learning as part of work, not as an activity separate from work. The real-time work flow learning is most critical in knowledge-intensive and process-oriented business functions such as supply chain management, sales force automation, inventory management, facilities management, point of care, law enforcement, and scientific research and development.

Can learning transform itself by aligning, linking, and embedding itself into business applications, work flows, and the overall work context? To facilitate this transformation, there has to be a paradigm shift in the way we think about learning and human performance improvement. This shift will not occur dramatically or in isolation; it will augment, complement, coexist, and, in some cases, transform the current first-generation learning systems over an evolutionary time period. Next, we look at this paradigm shift involving real-time work flow learning.

From Content Focus to Context Focus

First-generation learning and content management systems focus on capturing, managing, and distributing content. Content is king! Regardless of the job context, large reservoirs of knowledge and information are created for employees or customers.

In real-time work flow learning, content is relevant only within a context. For example, while repairing a complex digital telephone switch, step-by-step instructions are pushed at the moment of need to a field technician to replace the faulty chip.

From Just-in-Time to Real-Time Learning (Pull versus Push)

"Just-in-time" means finding information when needed—that is, "pull" what you need. This requires the learner to first know about the information resource or best practice available in the knowledge base and then spend time finding and retrieving it. Similarly, in a classroom learning situation, the learner needs to remember large amounts of information to be used later.

Real-time learning is more proactive. It "pushes" the right information in the right context, at the right time, and in the right format. Real-time learning pinpoints the exact type of information needed and automatically delivers that information to a learner.

From Courseware to Performanceware

In real-time work flow–based learning, common stand-alone learning content models are transformed into context-driven, task-sensitive, and performance support models. Examples of such real-world learning include guided tasks, procedures, step-by-step instructions, job aids, and referenceware. The most common use of real-time work flow learning can be seen in Microsoft Office. For instance, in Microsoft Excel, the Office Assistant pops up when it senses users trying to use specific features of Excel application. The Office Assistant offers help in the form of tips, suggestions, or step-by-step instructions to perform a desired task.

In the past, e-learning standards initiatives such as SCORM (Sharable Content Object Reference Model) focused on defining the notion of interoperable and reusable learning objects that usually mapped to modular course objects. Standards need to evolve to be extended to include the notion of performance objects (task-based organization of information to support effective performance) that can be delivered within the context of job tasks.

From Learning and Course Management to Business Work Flows

Business work flows and processes are the delivery platforms for learning and performance support in a real-time work flow learning environment. Real-time work flow learning links performance objects with automated business work flows. For example, a loan calculator and a dialogue box containing a set of questions for the client automatically pop up within a loan processing application to assist the agent in working through the loan application. This is a major shift from the earlier learning management systems and knowledge management systems that created catalogues of passive knowledge and vast libraries of information for the learner.

From Instructional Design to Performance-Based Design

Content compilation has undergone a shift in design approach, from instructional and content design to task-based performance design that maps information and knowledge nuggets to the job, tasks, or activities.

In real-time work flow learning, information is organized into task-based decision structures that support information and knowledge nuggets at each step. Learners or job performers can easily understand and use these nuggets while performing on the job.

From Desktop or Web Browser to Highly Distributed Mobile Delivery Environments

Today, information can be accessed on the Web browser and other client applications on desktop computers, tablets, laptops, and other mobile devices such as cell phones and personal digital assistants (PDAs). Suppose a person wants to buy a ring tone on his cell phone but is unable to process the payment. The cell phone prompts him with relevant information to help him make the payment. This is an example of real-time work flow learning that presents context-specific content. Unlike a desktop computer, a mobile device interface can work flexibly into multiple job task environments (for example, field based, manufacturing, retail, and clinical).

This shift also includes new forms of interactivity such as keyboardless (small or nonexistent keyboard) interfaces, pen-based handwriting recognition systems, and voice recognition information systems.

Building a Real-Time Work Flow Learning Architecture

Real-time work flow learning environments share a certain similarity to the first-generation leaning systems; for example, both contain features and options for user management, registration, content management, course catalogues, and metatagged information models. However, in order to blend learning with work, a real-time work flow learning architecture needs to provide seamless integration of rich content and interactive performance support with the computer-supported job-task environments. Now we look at the components of real-time work flow learning architecture.

Portals and Web Parts

Portals provide a front-end access point for job tasks and integrated learning activities. The "Web parts" or sections within the portal environment allow information from different sources to be aggregated and organized for easy access to support different day-to-day processes and job roles. Portals support role-based views where information is organized around specific job functions. A portal is also a delivery mechanism for real-time alerts and notifications.

A single integrated portal that links learning and work tasks can become a doorway to business processes and associated learning. Learners will not need to switch the context or log on to multiple applications. Portals may also foster continuous learning and knowledge communities or communities of practice by providing a sense of identity (for example, team logos), learning rituals (for example, online chats), learning membership, a shared space for learner collaboration, and a place to promote accomplishments.

Internet and Mobility

Real-time work flow learning uses a distributed and heterogeneous architecture including Web, mobile, and wireless technologies such as PDA, tablets, and hybrid phones to deliver and collect relevant information in the right context at the right time and in the right form. Powerful and flexible mobile computing models provide seamless access to information and knowledge within the work environment: office, manufacturing, retail floor, or field based. Alternate interfaces such as pen-based digital ink, handwriting recognition, and voice-based information lookup provide the convenience to access, navigate, and manipulate the learning and knowledge content more easily within the work context.

Granular Knowledge Nuggets

Granular knowledge nuggets are small, reusable, and stand-alone pieces of information that can be reused in multiple contexts. These nuggets are pieces of dynamic content just right for the context. Each nugget has a single learning objective linked to a specific job task or skill.

Examples of granular knowledge nuggets include step-by-step instructions, calculators, job aids, look-up tables, hints, tips, and advice. For instance, in an assembly line of an automobile manufacturing unit, the workers can see a screen in their workplace that provides step-by-step instructions and tips. Such information helps them move the assembly line without delays and errors.

Knowledge Repository

Content management refers to the process of handling information in the knowledge repository. It refers to the process of capturing, storing, sorting, codifying, indexing, integrating, updating, and protecting any or all knowledge nuggets in the knowledge repository. Different kinds of knowledge nuggets may be stored in the repository. They may range from performance support, job aids, and data lists through tips, suggestions, and instructions.

Collaboration

Synchronous and asynchronous collaboration tools such as chatrooms and discussion threads can be linked and invoked within business applications to provide real-time, context-specific learning. For example, in an e-learning scenario, the mentor of the discussion board acts as a collaborator to provide relevant information to the learner. Collaboration tools are especially useful to impart soft skill training. Not every form of knowledge can be converted into a structured learning format. Also, a lot of knowledge resides in the head of subject matter experts and cannot be captured as knowledge nuggets. Therefore, collaboration tools and technologies enable real-time knowledge creation and problem solving. For example, a sales rep may collaborate in real time with a product manager at the corporate office while addressing detailed inquiries from a client and may later refer to the notes captured during the online meeting to learn more about client requirements.

Work Flow Automation and Knowledge Linking

Work flow–based learning is characterized by task and performance support embedded within business processes, work flows, or enterprise software applications involving real-time collaboration with people and computer systems. Human work flow management and automation systems ensure coordination of tasks (for example, insurance claim processing and approvals) between multiple knowledge workers and learners in real time.

As work progresses, work flow automation facilitates the assignment of tasks and pushes the appropriate performance support, knowledge support, and mentoring needed based on the knowledge worker's skill level. Knowledge nuggets can be linked dynamically to work flow nodes (where each node represents a specific unit of work or task within a work flow) to push learning, performance support, and other media. Each work flow node provides an opportunity for short, granular bursts of learning and performance support. When a task is assigned or a knowledge worker receives an alert related to the task status on his or her dashboard or portal, the associated learning and performance support content automatically appears next to the task listing or alert.

Human and Automated Virtual Mentoring

Real-time work flow learning may also include mentoring support where the knowledge worker can either connect with a human mentor directly from the task–work flow interface (for example, using an instant messaging function) or an automated (nonhuman or virtual) mentor for help or consultation. The automated mentor captures relevant information in various formats such as slides, narratives, images, videos, tips, and instructions. When needed, the learner can pull this information, or the mentor can push this information to the learner.

Presence Awareness

Presence awareness enables knowledge workers to be aware of the presence of other colleagues or subject matter experts. This feeling of presence of others who can assist as needed is a powerful motivational tool for knowledge workers or learners. Presence awareness and instant messaging provide powerful tools to create collaborative spaces where knowledge workers can meet, collaborate, chat, or discuss within the context of business applications and work flows. For example, marketing and product engineering managers may collaborate with instant messaging tools within document management and product design applications.

Simulations

Simulations situate the learner in the environment that imitates reality or takes the learner closer to the task. The more effectively the simulation imitates reality, the better are the chances of applying the learning on the real job. Well-designed instructional simulations offer both right and wrong paths to arrive at the results and allow learners to make mistakes and get feedback. In the e-learning scenario, simulations offer a safe environment to practice and test learners' ability to perform the requisite tasks.

Simulations may also be used as performance support. For example, an aircraft maintenance technician may call a simulation object (a three-dimensional model to understand the relationship between an engine part and its connecting parts) on a tablet computer while repairing an engine.

Business Process and Performance Monitoring

Automated business process monitoring tools track the processes (for example, status, time taken, task assignments, and completed tasks) in real time. Furthermore, tasks within the business processes and performance of workers may also be tracked to prevent potential errors and provide additional information for remediation. Performance monitoring tools can assist in improving workforce skills, competencies, and the quality of performance support.

Such tools or systems also facilitate the monitoring and measurement of performance, delivery of personalized content, and management and routing of tasks. There are also automation tools to identify productivity bottlenecks. Combined with business process management systems, these tools assess the exact nature of the bottleneck and push the precise knowledge nuggets needed to offset performance problems.

Constant Knowledge Capture and Feedback

Traditional e-learning systems are typically designed as a one-way flow of information or instructional content. However, in real-time work flow learning, knowledge workers can provide feedback or capture best practices on the fly and link them to the business work flows. The information collected from the field can be reviewed by other experts. Then best practices and corrections to the existing knowledge can be collated and distributed back to everyone concerned in real time to create a closed-loop or continuous learning process.

Real-Time Notification, Aggregation, and Decision Support

Traditional online or Web-based learning systems track course completion and test score status; in contrast, real-time work flow learning tracks job and task performance, accuracy, consistency, and skill gaps.

Executive dashboards provide administrators and managers a cockpit view into the business process and overall business operation. Dashboards aggregate multiple data points into consolidated summary views and visual charts that highlight key performance indicators and pinpoint performance gaps that need immediate attention.

Integration Between Learning and Enterprise Applications Through Web Services

Web services help software applications communicate with each other over the Internet. A Web service is a collection of functions packaged as a single entity and published to the network for use by other applications. Web services are building blocks for creating open distributed systems and are essential to integrate business process work flow systems with performance support and learning systems.

Web services streamline business processes by allowing software applications to be delivered over the Internet and run on different types of computers, from large servers to mobile handheld devices. Web services technology allows applications to be integrated in real time so that data or information can be exchanged between the applications.

For example, an automated work flow–based application can call a knowledge nugget stored in a content repository, or data from a business application (for example, a spreadsheet) can be passed to a real-time collaboration or mentoring application. Web services are the essential underlying technology for facilitating real-time work flow learning environments.

Integrated, Interoperable, and Reusable Content Framework

Real-time work flow learning is supported by an integrated, interoperable, and reusable content object framework in which knowledge nuggets may be used within training applications, simulations, and on-the-job performance support. Furthermore, the knowledge nuggets (in the form of data, information, or performance support) can be used with business processes, work flows, and work spaces or portals.

Real-Time Work Flow–Based Learning Example

The following example describes real-time work flow -based learning in action. It highlights a sophisticated form of blended learning in which learning, performance support, and the job- or task-based work space environment integrate together to deliver context-based knowledge to support and augment a job or task at hand.

Field customer service technicians in the telecommunications industry work in a challenging and knowledge-intensive environment in which they need to support multiple requests or customer problems, including maintenance, repair, part replacement, and installation of complex equipment. In order to perform these complex tasks, they need on-demand access to procedures, manuals, schematics, learning, and technical data.

Although these technicians are trained and go through certification, they need access to a complex set of information in a highly mobile and fast-paced work environment. Long sequences of e-learning courses do not provide an adequate model to support day-to-day field technician knowledge needs.

Real-time work flow–based learning is embedded in the field technician's work space portal in which the tasks are assigned and presented along with the package of documents, performance objects (procedures and step-by-step instructions), and other reference information required to perform the tasks (see Figure 34.2). The field technician can download the task information along with supporting materials onto a mobile device so that the information can be pulled up during the performance of the tasks (see Figure 34.3). The technician can pass on queries or information from the field to the corporate office through an automated work flow process. The technician can also connect with other peers or experts by

FIGURE 34.2.   A PORTAL TO SUPPORT THE REAL-TIME WORK FLOW OF A FIELD TECHNICIAN.

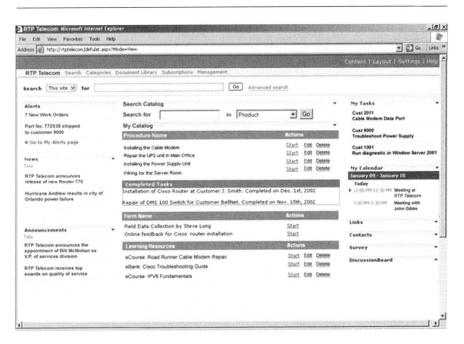

FIGURE 34.3. A MOBILE DEVICE USED TO SUPPORT THE PERFORMANCE NEEDS OF A TECHNICIAN IN THE FIELD.

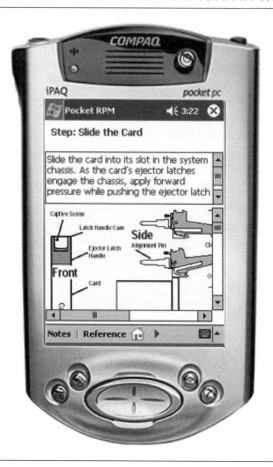

conferencing to get live mentoring to perform a nonroutine task. Field technicians can also access e-learning modules, technical manuals, equipment parts, and technical data in a Web and mobile environment.

The task and work flow status is tracked in real time along with the time and path taken to perform the tasks. Aggregated data are presented using management dashboards and portals for performance analysis, rapid decisions, and remediation (to correct bottlenecks, prioritize task, plan resources and skills, and manage training needs).

Benefits of Real-Time Work Flow–Based Learning

Real-time work flow–based learning offers many benefits:

- The organization obtains expert performance from each knowledge worker. The knowledge worker has access to performance support about what to do and how to perform the task.
- Learners or performers obtain tangible value from the combination of business processes and learning as opposed to learning being separate from the real work.
- Organizations gain substantially from the reduction in overall training time and time away from work for learning activities. They can reduce the initial time spent on learning (for example, training of new employees) because most of the knowledge can be delivered through an on-demand model.
- Real-time learning ensures a significant reduction of errors because information needed to perform the job is pushed automatically during task execution. This eliminates the scope for information loss that may occur when learning and execution happen separately. In effect, the skills obtained by the learner are better transferred to the real world when they are learned in the real world.
- Business processes are built into the architecture that supports Web services–based dynamic linking with knowledge and performance objects. This linking of learning to job performance ensures that learning is automatically aligned with the actual business operation (such goals have been wishful thinking on the part of traditional training and first-generation e-learning systems).
- The executive dashboard provides managers and administrators with a cockpit view of the business operation in the form of aggregated performance views, graphical charts, and other analysis to support real-time decision making and remediation.
- The feedback captured during the performance of a task may be used to influence future training, practice, and performance support.
- Real-time work flow–based learning ensures business process optimization and cost-effective business operations.

Conclusion

While first-generation e-learning was successful in reducing the cost of information and instructional content delivery, the resulting virtualized classroom or courseware model remains ineffective to meet the requirements of an increasingly challenging business environment.

Blended learning addresses many of the shortcomings of traditional physical classroom or pure e-learning courseware models by combining self-paced, collaborative, and human mentoring approaches, which lead to higher learning completion rates. However, blended learning must continue to evolve to blend learning directly with work or job tasks in a convergence of learning space and work space.

The paradigm of blending learning with the work paradigm proposes to transform e-learning from a silo repository or catalogue of courses and classes to a world where learning is tightly integrated and interwoven with business processes and mission-critical jobs and tasks. Real-time work flow learning is the next-generation learning that delivers real-time communication, collaboration, and knowledge transfer within the context of business processes or work flows to engender optimal individual, team, and organizational performance and productivity.

Real-time work flow–based learning not only provides on-demand access to very specific and relevant information and knowledge transfer to ensure expert performance, but also aims to bring much-sought-after alignment between learning and work and business processes. The evaluation of effectiveness and return on investment of such learning is not an afterthought but is automatically linked and tracked in real time.

Harvey Singh is a pioneer in the field of e-learning, human performance technology, and knowledge management. He is the founder and CEO of Instancy, a real-time learning and business intelligence solutions company. Prior to Instancy, he cofounded MindLever, which merged with Centra Software in 2001. He has served in a board and advisory capacity to the Department of Defense's Advanced Distributed Learning and IMS initiatives and was nominated as e-learning executive of the year in 2001. MindLever received the Intrepid Company of the Year award in 2001 from the North Carolina Center for Entrepreneurial Development. In 1993, Singh cofounded Empower, an advanced multimedia, simulation, and learning product design company. He has graduate degrees in computer science and education technology from Stanford University and a bachelor's degree in computer science from North Carolina State University.

CHAPTER THIRTY-FIVE

ON-DEMAND LEARNING

How Work-Embedded Learning Is Expanding Enterprise Performance

Nancy DeViney, Nancy J. Lewis

Over the past thirty years, IBM employee Louise Andres has evolved from trainee to a company executive as IBM has changed from a product- to a services-driven organization. For both Andres and IBM, employee training played a critical role in their growth.

When Andres first joined IBM, she spent a full year in a sales training program learning to do her job. She participated in four in-person classes that often lasted weeks, shadowed several IBM sales representatives, learned about IBM products and services, studied a prescribed workbook and class curriculum, and was tested on all of the above as she learned the ropes. Today Andres is a delivery and risk management executive for small and medium business, where her continuing professional training has evolved into a daily activity embedded into her work.

Andres is among the more than 300,000 employees at IBM who spend a combined 17 million hours each year (about 55 hours per employee) in training. Approximately 47 percent of IBM learning is now conducted online anywhere, anytime, allowing employees, who are often off-site at client locations, to stay focused on work-related activity. Andres describes the transformation: "When I started at IBM, learning was an event that happened every now and then for an extended period of time. Today, it's a continuous process that I can access anytime, wherever and whenever I need it."

Andres's tenure and career success at IBM exemplifies a link the company has identified between learning and employee retention, finding that 79 percent of new employees, when given meaningful learning and developmental opportunities, are less likely to leave the company in their first three years. Studies such as these have led to a significant investment in learning initiatives at IBM: about $750 million annually.

Andres and many of her peers, including this chapter's authors, are a product of an organization committed to learning. IBM's learning commitment can be traced back to 1915, only four years after it was incorporated. Approximately ninety years ago, a separate and distinct IBM education organization was established to train and develop employees. One year later, IBM's education program was formally started to instruct employees on the use of the company's product line.

This learning legacy carried the company through the 1990s, when it underwent a massive transformation from a hardware-driven to a services-driven organization, a change that required rebuilding and reskilling most of the employee base. Learning played, and continues to play, a critical role in helping to align employees around new business models in order to capture business opportunities in the marketplace.

This ongoing commitment to succeed by harnessing the power of learning to develop its employees has enabled IBM to maintain the highest learning standards in the business world. Today IBM's own commitment to learning and leadership in the marketplace as a services organization places the company in a unique position. We can take lessons learned from our own programs and apply them to generate real return on investment for our clients.

The guiding principle of IBM's learning initiatives is the requirement to align our learning models to meet the changing needs of the marketplace and our employees. At IBM, we believe there is a pressing need for a learning model to incorporate fundamentally the crucial, on-the-job aspect of how people learn. We have designed a new patent-pending model for learning that incorporates learning intervention within the workplace itself—to extend learning beyond formal curricula by embedding learning into work flow. In this chapter, we examine the powerful market forces that are changing learning paradigms by:

- Empowering learners to shape their learning experiences rather than passively receive it
- Driving innovation and business growth by shaping individual, team, and organizational learning
- Embedding learning in process work flows, increasing learning while doing
- Using technology to deliver personalized, easily accessible, role-enabling and collaborative learning

Today's training and development has undeniable strengths and has served organizations well in the past. But its development and delivery methods are often a poor fit for tomorrow's needs and tomorrow's pace. A growing discontinuity exists between what business has become and what training has remained. To close this gap, future learning solutions must address three issues that confound current practices:

1. We must amplify the transfer of skill and knowledge. The impact of common training practices is shockingly small. According to many studies, little of the investment in training pays off in transfer to the job. We must find new ways to boost productivity through learning by linking skills, knowledge, and performance to powerful new techniques for learning transfer.

2. We must accelerate the deployment of best practices in the workplace. As organizations become more nimble in their response to market needs and customer issues, the shelf-life of best practices has shrunk significantly. However, a typical corporate training initiative takes a year to develop, pilot, refine, and roll out to employees. This lag almost guarantees that training will be dated before it is delivered. Tomorrow's training function must use advanced communications and collaboration technologies to develop, package, and deliver best practices at the moment of need, not the moment when training development is completed.

3. We must facilitate and enhance learning interactions among workers within the workplace. Traditional corporate training removes workers from the work and builds skills within the artificial context of the case study, simulation, Web site, or classroom. At times this distance from the workplace is beneficial. But when facing workplace change, 70 percent of respondents in a Capital Works survey sought more coworker interaction, not more classes. Because change lies at the heart of the knowledge-driven economy, we must enable more effective learning interaction opportunities among employees within their workplace experiences.

To meet these three challenges, today's learning must be realigned and enhanced using solid learning theory and proven collaboration techniques and technologies. With purposeful design and deployment, the old and new can be combined into a powerful learning solution for the future.

The Ever-Changing Global Marketplace

In 2004 the following statement was issued regarding the changing needs being felt in the United States workforce: "Today's economy is an innovation economy. Two-thirds of America's economic growth in the 1990s resulted from the introduction of new technologies—and 60% of the new jobs of the 21st century require post-secondary education held by only one-third of America's workforce. We need to close the skills gap in America. Not enough workers are being trained quickly enough to take advantage of many of the new jobs that are being created" (White House, Office of the Press Secretary, 2004).

In the United States, the demand for skilled jobs increased from 40 percent in 1950 to 85 percent in 2000 (Goman, 2004). And consider that by the year 2010, the average ten year old will have access to more computational power than existed on the planet in 2001 (Harris, 2002). By 2010, the codified information base of the world is expected to double every eleven hours (Bontis, 1999). Examining this phenomenon, the American Society of Training and Development has concluded that new knowledge is growing at a rate much faster than our ability to learn it. In 2010, we will all have a skills gap *all the time*, and that skills gap will be a ubiquitous characteristic of life (Levy, 2004).

Equally alarming is the workforce gap that will be left this decade as the working-age population undergoes a substantial shift toward a greater number of older workers and a relative scarcity of new entrants in the labor force (Purcell, 2002). The void will create a significant gating factor for growth across most industry sectors in the U.S. economy.

These demographic forces are creating additional challenges for organizations grappling with the implementation of talent supply chains that enable increased productivity, transformation, and innovation. In order to survive and thrive in an increasingly service-led and knowledge-driven economy, individuals and organizations must continually acquire and apply new skills and develop new ways of leveraging information and knowledge. Organizations that can provide opportunities for ongoing learning and growth will naturally attract and retain the most capable and competent workers, a trend many top-level executives are noting.

IBM recently conducted a survey of over 450 CEOs worldwide. The results told us that chief executives know they need to build new internal capabilities and skills while enabling their leaders to be change agents. They recognize the paramount importance of aligning learning initiatives to address market challenges. And finally, they see organizational responsiveness in meeting customer needs as critical to driving growth.

Yet, ironically, while skill development becomes more important, the demands of the work environment leave employees with limited time for formalized learning. In today's market economy, individuals operate with a high level of business urgency and very little time to attend a class. There is such a consistent and rapid churn of the skills and knowledge required to maintain job performance that learning can no longer be provided as a set of events. In the light of this environment, organizations must provide employees with the right type of learning opportunities—that is, employees must have the information they need when and where they need it.

Indeed, on-demand organizations require on-demand thinking and behavior at every level. In the future, employees must be better equipped for the unexpected as the on-demand enterprise develops a perpetual state of readiness for a changing market environment.

Defining Embedded Learning

In many ways, embedded learning is based on the premise that the closer a person is to needing to know something to do his or her job, the more motivated this person is to learn. If organizations can make critical learning available at that moment of need, they create an inherent teachable moment, the ideal time to leverage learning without having to remove the learner from work.

To maximize the effectiveness of the teachable moment, we can use technology to make the right information available at the right time, thereby transparently embedding learning into our work. The paradigm then evolves from "learn, then do," to "learn while doing." Content is delivered within the context of a person's role, interests, and current activity, creating dynamic, personalized, role-based "workplaces" that include access to both formal and task-relevant learning. Research has shown that aligning learning and performance contexts results in a 10 to 55 percent improvement in learning absorption (Tahlheimer, 2003).

In an on-demand learning environment, access to work-embedded learning, advice, and performance support is as central to learning as the traditional classroom event was in past generations. The on-demand experience is based on the recognition that new approaches to instructional design and technology offer the opportunity to integrate learning with work in order to enhance performance in a dynamic, interactive, and measurable way.

This is a very different way of thinking about learning for most organizations. Today, most learning is designed to deliver a consistent, uniform experience and is frequently based on an instructor-student relationship. The curriculum is typically structured and prescribed by the institution. The role of the instructor is often to convey information. The role of the student is to receive and apply this information.

In an embedded learning environment, that paradigm is turned upside down as learners become increasingly empowered to shape when, where, and how they learn. Organizations will continue to define learning paths, assess value, and reward outcomes in support of overall organizational objectives. However, learners will have greater flexibility as to how they achieve those objectives and consequently affect business results. Even in the future, structured curriculums will not go away. However, the formal education experience will focus more on observation and reflection in applying new concepts being taught rather than being just a means to transfer information.

Moreover, technology and new delivery options will enable just-in-time access to information within the context of the individual's role, task being performed, and amount of time available. This type of embedded learning delivery will have a profound impact on productivity and enable two-way information sharing. Learners will become both producers and consumers of information. As they access embedded learning, they will also be expected to interact with colleagues with the latest insights from real-world market experiences. This way, others within the enterprise can benefit from and leverage that understanding, enabling a culture of organizational learning.

At IBM, we are in the process of implementing embedded learning through our enterprisewide intranet. Our goal is to give learners a single, consistent interface, tailored by function and job role, to access content, applications, business processes, and people. This embedded learning environment will enable individuals to learn what they need to know to perform their jobs. Looking forward, we also believe that advances in technologies will enable learning to become more embedded into our lives, not just our jobs.

Expanding Learning Beyond the Individual

As Peter Senge, chairperson of the Society for Organizational Learning, has said, "Organizations learn only through individuals who learn. Individual learning does not guarantee organizational learning. But without it, no organizational learning occurs" (Senge, 1990, p. 139).

In the on-demand enterprise, value is created by groups of individuals who can rapidly address (and ultimately anticipate) customers' needs in real time. Emerging information technologies enable the flow of information between multiple points without centralized control, which makes possible rich exchanges without the need for formal structures. Such nonlinear dynamics are beginning to challenge the traditional, ordered frameworks of every organization, as well as empowering individuals to work and think more autonomously.

Management best practices today involve the use of cross-functional teams, dynamically formed around specific projects and customer requirements. Breakthroughs such as expertise locators, instant messaging, and community tools can be applied to support teaming across boundaries of time, space, and geography. If an organization creates a safe environment where learners can share what they have learned, learning will also facilitate feedback into the organization, enabling a culture where the learner contributes to institutional knowledge.

Moreover, the embedded learning design that incorporates dynamic access to relevant experts and teams provides a freer-flowing dialogue between more experienced coworkers and junior team members. Enabling participation in shared (collaborative) problem solving between the novice and the more experienced worker further facilitates individual, team, and organizational capability growth and helps contextualize content. Local experts add a layer of understanding that converts the generic to the specific (Cross, 2003).

The development of and provision of access to experts is the lifeblood of the on-demand enterprise. In this information-rich ecosystem, people become nodes in a network that is aware of who they are, what they are capable of doing, and, perhaps most important, what they are keenly interested in doing. IBM's work-embedded learning solutions leverage the network to tap into those resource nodes to address a surfaced need within another part of the network and will be able to successfully conduct business within a culture that fosters learning and growth.

Furthermore, in the context of rapid change, it is primarily workers (not systems or processes) who have to change to lift productivity by becoming more skilled and flexible (Watkins & Marsick, 1993). Changes in work practice are as certain as the need to be able to adapt to them in order to sustain currency in practice. Experts available in the workforce provide the enterprise with the confidence to respond to change (Cross, 2003).

As most senior leaders know, the linkage between strategy and execution will not occur without everyone understanding the strategy. Equally important is the education and collaboration with the extended enterprise, including customers, partners, and suppliers. Accelerating learning opportunities will help suppliers better understand an organization and how they can help address its requirements. Similarly, business partnerships are built on trust, awareness, and appreciation of each other's unique capabilities. Learning methods can also be applied to marketing and customer support programs to deepen client relationships by increasing their understanding of products and services.

As embedded learning extends across the enterprise within work flow processes and the teams that do that work, organizations will then be in a better position to integrate horizontally outside the company as well. Learning will serve as a key enabler of this integration process, becoming the binding factor of extended enterprise community.

IBM's E-Coach: The Next Generation of Personalized Learning

"Learning is at the core of our business. But it's a complex endeavor and requires that we bring learning opportunities to employees in a meaningful way, relating them to the individual in the context of who they are and their role in the organization. And that is what Edvisor does. It allows IBMers to received personalized guidance around the learning that is most valuable to them," said IBM's chief learning officer, Ted Hoff.

At IBM, employees have access to a patent-pending online learning tool known as Edvisor, which acts as an expert e-coach. Consistent with IBM's vision to embed learning into everyday work flow, Edvisor offers its employees a personal development guide that recommends a customized development path. It helps IBM managers shape their individual learning experience to fit their job roles, professional goals, and organizational priorities.

Using Edvisor, an IBM employee can create a prescriptive learning plan based on an individual and unique user expertise profile that can be customized by geography, business unit, or managerial level. In addition, Edvisor is an intelligent agent able to administer and understand the feedback given on 360-degree assessments on leadership competencies, managerial styles, and climate to intelligently work with each individual manager on a personalized development plan. Edvisor's three tracks help employees find best practice content immediately, helps guide them through a blended learning initiative, and can advise and guide them through a longer-term development plan.

This e-coach is the latest addition to IBM's award-winning Role of the Manager@IBM program, a broad-reaching, comprehensive training program designed to help managers focus on improving those leadership competencies most critical in helping them achieve their individual and team business goals. Through this program, managers acquire additional leadership expertise to lead remote and mobile teams effectively and create an environment that encourages continual innovation and creativity.

By engaging Edvisor as part of Role of the Manager@IBM program, managers take advantage of creating a personalized learning path, built especially for them to prepare for the face-to-face learning lab component of the program. Edvisor's guidance is based on that individual's functional role in the organization and the assessment feedback received on 360-degree assessments. Edvisor guides managers through this prelearning to ensure that all fundamentals and individual learning are mastered, thereby ensuring that precious face-to-face time is used to work on higher-order learning and team-based objectives. Thus, learning is transformed from the traditional single classroom event into a continuous, personalized process.

To encourage a learner to complete courses and master the necessary skills identified by his job function, Edvisor sends reminders to complete all learning activities. It tracks the learner's progress in the learning plan and helps each one manage the time needed to complete specific learning modules. Also, as a coach would, Edvisor tests an employee's understanding of a course or a skill by conducting mastery tests. All of these components of Edvisor help IBM learners prepare for the courses they will face in the Role of the Manager@IBM Learning Labs.

Over twenty-four months, thirty-two thousand managers and executives in seventy countries participated in Role of the Manager@IBM. In addition, Edvisor was used by 73 percent of these participants, and 95 percent felt it was relevant for preparation for the courses. The average amount of time spent on mastering Edvisor-led learning modules was three and a half hours, thereby reducing the amount of workshop time needed to meet this initiatives learning objectives.

Conclusion

Much of the learning that happens in the workplace today occurs outside the formal education context. Rather than simply labeling this kind of learning as informal and leaving it to chance, it is our perspective that it would be much more advantageous to analyze how learning happens within a given work flow and role and then define learning solutions that are tuned to accelerating and enhancing it.

Just as enterprises have had to evolve as a result of dynamic market economies, so too must the training function. Critical to navigating this change successfully is to understand the difference between learning and training in the on-demand era. Training functions must begin to realize that the path to strategic leverage within the firm hinges on the cultivation of a collaborative learning culture across the enterprise. Successful learning functions must stretch beyond the realm of formal training to focus on enabling productivity through more informed workplace learning approaches. Creating an enterprise that truly has the capacity to learn so that it can quickly adapt to the speed and complexity we will need in building ever-growing new market-valued skills is the new challenge that we are being asked to undertake as learning professionals. IBM is creating new learning approaches that allow us to shift the emphasis from bringing the worker to the learning to bringing the learning to the work, an exciting new era of learning that promises to leverage the collective expertise of employees, teams, and organizations throughout its enterprise.

References

Billett, S. R. (2001). *Learning in the workplace: Strategies for effective practice.* Sydney: Allen & Unwin.

Bontis, N. (1999). Managing organizational knowledge by harnessing intellectual capital. *International Journal of Technology Management, 18*(5–8), 433–462.

Cross, J. (2003). *Informal learning-The other 80%.* Internet Time Group. Retrieved November 15, 2004, from http://www.internettime.com/Learning/The%20Other%2080%25.htm.

Geus, A. D. (2001). E-learning as a strategic corporate asset. *DM Review Magazine.* Retrieved November 15, 2004, from http://www.dmreview.com/article_sub.cfm?articleId=4403.

Goman, C. K. (2004). The forces of change. *Link and Learn eNewsletter.* Retrieved November 15, 2004, from http://www.linkageinc.com/company/news_events/link_learn_enewsletter/archive/2004/05_04_forces_change_goman.aspx.

Harris, J. (2002). *The learning paradox: Gaining success in a world of change.* Oxford: Capstone Publishing.

Levy, J. (2004). The future of learning technology. *Chief Learning Officer Magazine.* Retrieved November 15, 2004, from http://www.clomedia.com/content/templates/clo_feature.asp?articleid=548&zoneid=30.

Purcell, P. J. (2002). *Older workers: Employment and retirement trends.* Washington DC: Library of Congress.

Senge, P. M. (1990). *The fifth discipline: The art and practice of the learning organization.* New York: Random House.

Tahlheimer, W. (2003). Percentage improvements likely when key learning factors are utilized. *Work-Learning Research.* Retrieved November 15, 2004, from http://www.work-learning.com/white_papers/percent_improvement/Percentage_Improvements_pdf4.pdf.

Watkins, K., & Marsick, V. (1993). *Sculpting the learning organization.* San Francisco: Jossey-Bass.

White House. Office of the Press Secretary (2004, April 5). *Better training for better jobs.* Retrieved July 13, 2005, from http://www.whitehouse.gov/news/releases/2004/04/20040405-7.html on.

Nancy DeViney is general manager for IBM Learning Solutions, where she leads a global team responsible for advancing IBM's learning portfolio and expertise, spanning consulting, integration, outsourcing, content design and development, software, hardware, and research. DeViney brings more than twenty-nine years of experience at IBM to her current role. Previously, she was general manager of IBM Learning Services, where she was responsible for IBM's information technology product training and education services businesses. Prior to that, she was vice president of sales operations and channels marketing for IBM Global Services, Americas. Earlier, she managed various U.S. sales operations responsibilities for IBM's outsourcing, consulting, and systems integration business. DeViney is cochairwoman of the IBM Americas Women's Leadership Council and is a speaker at key training and customer-focused conferences.

Nancy J. Lewis is vice president, IBM On Demand Learning, with responsibility for IBM's leadership in learning design and development, learning systems, collaborative learning, and expertise. Her organization is focused on learning innovation and the effectiveness of IBM's top strategic learning initiatives. A regular speaker at industry conferences on learning best practices, Lewis has been selected to serve on the American Society of Training and Development Certification Institute board of directors; is a member of the Conference Board's Council on Learning, Development and Organizational Performance; and serves on *Training Magazine*'s editorial advisory board.

CHAPTER THIRTY-SIX

CREATING AUTHENTIC LEARNING ENVIRONMENTS THROUGH BLENDED LEARNING APPROACHES

Ron Oliver, Jan Herrington, Thomas C. Reeves

There is growing use of authentic forms of activities as contexts for learning within many courses and programs across all sectors of education. Influenced by constructivist philosophy and new learning technologies, there is increasing interest among higher education faculty in authentic activities as a basis for learning (Bennett, Harper & Hedberg, 2001; Challis, 2002). Whereas traditionally, activities have primarily served as vehicles for the practice of discrete skills or processes taught in courses using such instructional methods as lectures and readings, an alternative approach being employed by innovative instructors is to build a whole course of study around a large-scale authentic activity. The use of a large-scale activity enables the learning to be undertaken within a meaningful context and provides meaning and purpose to the activities of the learners.

Creating effective learning settings that employ authentic activities requires a high degree of creativity and organization on the part of the teacher as well as the instructional designer, and often it is very hard to provide the necessary supports and scaffolds learners need. Contemporary research has identified that blended learning approaches provide many opportunities for the delivery of such courses. Blended learning enables the courses to be delivered in ways that provide flexibility for both the learners and the teachers in terms of resources, supports, and scaffolds.

Authentic Activities in Learning Environments

Learner activities have always had a firm place within instructional settings. Activities form the basis of learner engagement and are often used to lead learners to practice and apply what has been demonstrated by teachers or read from course materials (Brophy & Alleman, 1991; Lockwood, 1992). In a teacher-centered mode of teaching and learning, activities are often used after material has been presented to learners as a means of consolidating and revisiting the content.

In recent years, the integration of constructivist learning theory and problem-based and case-based learning strategies with immersive scenarios and virtual role playing, have taken the activities that students complete to the heart of the design of the curriculum. Unfortunately, few instructors have ever experienced this type of learning environment themselves, and, thus, they are unable to design and implement these types of authentic activities in their own courses. Our previous research has identified a number of courses that model best practice in the use of authentic activities as contexts for learning.

The design of learning settings that use authentic activities as anchoring tasks can be a difficult process for instructors whose previous experience has been with more conventional teacher-centered settings. As part of our research, we have identified characteristics that we see as essential elements to the design of truly authentic activities. In fact, we have used these to help designers in their course development processes.

Authenticity in Learning Environments

While some researchers will question if it is possible to design truly authentic learning experiences, others are less worried with the esoteric nature of this question. The fact that the learning is occurring in a classroom or in a learning space that is removed from the workplace or such other interpretations of reality is of concern to some writers (Petraglia, 1998a, 1998b). But Barab, Squire, and Dueber (2000) argue that authenticity occurs "not in the learner, the task, or the environment, but in the dynamic interactions among these various components . . . authenticity is manifest in the flow itself, and is not an objective feature of any one component in isolation" (p. 38).

There is increasing evidence that in order to fully engage with an authentic task or problem-based scenario, students need to engage with a process that is called the *suspension of disbelief* (Herrington, Oliver, & Reeves, 2003; Kantor, Waddington, & Osgood, 2000). The suspension of disbelief is that which members of audiences do when they become absorbed in movies with fantasy or fictional elements. When disbelief is truly suspended, the audience accepts as real conditions and states situations or circumstances that they might otherwise consider false and unrealistic. In scenario-based learning environments, where conditions, characters, circumstances, and parameters are drawn to simulate a real-life context for learning, a similar suspension of disbelief is required. For some students, there appears to be some misapprehension about the approach, because it is so different from the more academic approaches with which they are familiar. Many students initially perceive authentic environments to be nonacademic, nonrigorous, time wasting, and unnecessary to efficient learning. It is often only when the suspension of disbelief occurs that these students see the complexity and the value of the learning environment.

In our research, we have identified the critical characteristics of authentic activities that are needed to support learners' suspension of disbelief and their acceptance of the activity as real. The characteristics have been based on a wide literature review of recent research and theory. In reflecting on the characteristics of activities described by researchers, ten broad design characteristics of authentic activities have been identified (cf. Herrington, Reeves, Oliver, & Woo, 2004):

- *Authentic activities have real-world relevance.* Activities match as nearly as possible the real-world tasks of professionals in practice rather than decontextualized or classroom-based tasks (Brown, Collins, & Duguid, 1989; Cognition and Technology Group at Vanderbilt, 1990a; Jonassen, 1991; Lebow & Wager, 1994; Oliver & Omari, 1999; Resnick, 1987; Winn, 1993).
- *Authentic activities are ill defined, requiring students to define the tasks and subtasks needed to complete the activity.* Problems inherent in the activities are ill defined and open to multiple interpretations rather than easily solved by the application of existing algorithms. In such situations, learners must identify their own unique tasks and subtasks in order to complete the major task (Bransford, Vye, Kinzer, & Risko, 1990; Brown et al., 1989; Cognition and Technology Group at Vanderbilt, 1990a; Lebow & Wager, 1994).
- *Authentic activities comprise complex tasks to be investigated by students over a sustained period of time.* Activities are completed in days, weeks, and months rather than minutes or hours. They require significant investment of time and intellectual resources (Bransford, Vye, et al., 1990; Cognition and Technology Group at Vanderbilt, 1990b; Jonassen, 1991; Lebow & Wager, 1994).
- *Authentic activities provide opportunities for students to examine the task from different perspectives, using a variety of resources.* The task affords learners the opportunity to examine the problem from a variety of theoretical and practical perspectives, rather than allowing a single perspective that learners must imitate to be successful. The

use of a variety of resources rather than a limited number of preselected references requires students to distinguish relevant from irrelevant information (Bransford, Vye, et al., 1990; Cognition and Technology Group at Vanderbilt, 1990b; Young, 1993).

• *Authentic activities provide the opportunity to collaborate.* Collaboration is integral to the task, within the course and the real world. It provides opportunities that are not available to an individual learner (Gordon, 1998; Lebow & Wager, 1994; Young, 1993).

• *Authentic activities provide the opportunity to reflect.* Activities need to enable learners to make choices and reflect on their learning both individually and socially (Gordon, 1998; Myers, 1993; Young, 1993).

• *Authentic activities can be integrated and applied across different subject areas and lead beyond domain-specific outcomes.* Activities encourage interdisciplinary perspectives and enable students to play diverse roles, thus building robust expertise rather than knowledge limited to a single well-defined field or domain (Bransford, Sherwood, Hasselbring, Kinzer, & Williams, 1990; Bransford, Vye, et al., 1990; Jonassen, 1991).

• *Authentic activities are seamlessly integrated with assessment.* Assessment of activities is seamlessly integrated with the major task in a manner that reflects real-world assessment rather than separate artificial assessment removed from the nature of the task (Herrington & Herrington, 1998; Reeves & Okey, 1996).

• *Authentic activities create polished products valuable in their own right rather than as preparation for something else.* Activities culminate in the creation of a whole product rather than an exercise or substep in preparation for something else (Barab et al., 2000; Duchastel, 1997; Gordon, 1998).

• *Authentic activities allow competing solutions and diversity of outcomes.* Activities allow a range and diversity of outcomes open to multiple solutions of an original nature, rather than a single correct response obtained by the application of rules and procedures (Bottge & Hasselbring, 1993; Bransford, Sherwood, et al., 1990; Bransford, Vye, et al., 1990; Duchastel, 1997).

Authenticity and Blended Learning

Blended learning appears to offer strong supports for instructors looking to create learning settings based on authentic tasks. Blended learning approaches provide instructors with many affordances and opportunities for creating engaging and supportive settings. Other chapters in this book have provided lengthy and detailed descriptions of blended learning settings, so we will not duplicate this discussion in this chapter. It is the capability of blended learning to draw the

FIGURE 36.1.   A CONTINUUM DESCRIBING BLENDED LEARNING.

Face-to-Face Communications	Technology-Mediated Communications
For example, classroom settings, workplace learning, mentoring	For example, online bulletin boards, asynchronous communications, e-mail

maximum benefit from the technology affordances while retaining the best features of face-to-face teaching that makes it ideal for supporting authentic activities within larger learning designs.

The key element underpinning a blended learning environment is the scope and nature of the communication channels provided to support learners. The blend often depends on the level of face-to-face communication that can be provided for students. In most settings, there can be unlimited scope for technology-mediated communication but far more restrictive amounts of face-to-face communication. Writers often use a continuum to illustrate blended learning with the alternative forms of communications as the extremes and the blend comprising a planned mix (see Figure 36.1). Interestingly, there is still a degree of uncertainty in the discussion concerning the precise nature of communication. There are, for example, ways to simulate face-to-face communications through videoconferencing and other interactive forms of technology. In such settings, the forms of interaction can be very close to what occurs when participants are in the same room despite their real distance.

The notion of blended learning describes environments where there are deliberate levels of both face-to-face and technology-mediated communication. The exact amount of these forms of communication can be chosen to suit the situation at hand.

McArthur (2001) argues that in any blended learning setting, one should take account not only of the technology use but also the blended learning strategy. The forms of strategies guiding the use of blended learning have potentially large impacts on the learning achieved. Franks (2002) describes a four-stage model for instructors implementing a blended learning approach that moves from (1) an initial mode that simply provides administrative information on a course, (2) through a communications element, (3) leading to materials delivery, and, finally, (4) a more engineered and deliberate use of technology for particular learning needs. Any attempt to use blended learning to support authentic activities would clearly represent an activity at the extended stage of this implementation cycle.

When one examines learning environments based on authentic activities and the forms of communication that can be used to support them, it becomes readily apparent that blended learning provides strong opportunities for such learning designs. Table 36.1 lists the essential elements of authentic learning settings and indicates where these elements are supported through blended learning examples. It shows how blended learning designs can be employed to support and implement the majority of the characteristics of authentic activity in units and courses. In fact, it is really only in the case of design characteristics associated with the selection and description of the authentic tasks themselves where blended learning cannot be planned as a key factor in the delivery of effective learning environments that are based around authentic tasks.

Blended Learning Courses with Authentic Activities

It is possible to illustrate how blended learning approaches can support the delivery of courses based on authentic learning tasks by describing several case studies of such courses and identifying the opportunities for blended learning in their delivery. An ideal course to demonstrate how successfully blended learning approaches can support authentic activities is the course "Research Methods," being delivered at Edith Cowan University (Angus & Gray, 2002). This master's-level course challenges students to learn both quantitative and qualitative research methods within the context of evaluating the impact of a school closure on a small rural community. Students are supported in the task by a Web-based virtual learning environment (see Figure 36.2) and through face-to-face classes attended at strategic points within the course. The use of the face-to-face sessions helps students to form networks and connections that assist in their collaborative work throughout the course.

The authenticity of the course is provided through the virtual setting and the role that the students undertake. The technology provides access to a multitude of resources that have been prepared to assist them in their actions. The technology provides a means for communication and collaboration as students work in groups to explore the situation and seek solutions. The blended approach sees the teacher playing a pivotal role in supporting the learners, encouraging and motivating their participation, and dealing with issues and problems as they arise. For many of the students, working in a computer-mediated fashion alone is discomforting and unproductive. For others, the opportunity to work at their own pace and with minimal teacher intervention is quite powerful. Both forms of

TABLE 36.1. CHARACTERISTICS OF AUTHENTIC ACTIVITY, SHOWING OPPORTUNITIES FOR BLENDED LEARNING.

Number	Characteristic of Authentic Activity	Blended Learning
1.	Have real-world relevance	Online communication can be used to connect learners with the workplace and cases beyond the classroom. ICTs can be used to provide access to real-life data from online sources.
2.	Are ill defined, requiring students to define the tasks and subtasks needed to complete the activity	Forms of face-to-face teaching can be used to provide scaffolds and supports for the planning and strategic thinking required for task solutions.
3.	Comprise complex tasks to be investigated by students over a sustained period of time	This characteristic is more a function of the way the authentic tasks are designed than the way they are implemented.
4.	Provide the opportunity for students to examine the task from different perspectives, using a variety of resources	Online communication and face-to-face opportunities can be used to connect learners with external players and supports.
5.	Provide the opportunity to collaborate	Online communication opportunities and face-to-face settings can be employed to facilitate and support group-based activities and teamwork.
6.	Provide the opportunity to reflect and involve students' beliefs and values	Reflection can be supported and encouraged through face-to-face activities and online communication tools such as personal diaries and Weblogs.
7.	Can be integrated and applied across different subject areas and lead beyond domain-specific outcomes	The integration of activities across discipline areas can be supported by online communication and information access.
8.	Are seamlessly integrated with assessment	This characteristic is more a function of the way the authentic tasks are designed than the way they are implemented.
9.	Create polished products valuable in their own right rather than as preparation for something else	This characteristic is more a function of the way the authentic tasks are designed than the way they are implemented.
10.	Allow competing solutions and diversity of outcome	This characteristic is more a function of the way the authentic tasks are designed than the way they are implemented.

FIGURE 36.2.   RESEARCH LABORATORY FROM THE "RESEARCH METHODS" COURSE.

learning support, technology and instructor driven, are within the spirit of the authentic learning setting, but each supports the preferred learning styles of different students. In fact, the blended approach sees the teacher playing a pivotal role in face-to-face as well as distant communications and involvement.

When the nature of the learning design and its intended delivery modes are investigated, it is possible to identify the precise way in which blended learning is able to support students' participation in the authentic learning activities. Table 36.2 demonstrates how blended learning is able to support the achievement of a number of the critical characteristics required to maintain the highest degree of authenticity in the activities of this course.

While this course could conceivably be delivered in a fully online mode with no blended learning, there are many reasons that a blended approach can be a far more effective setting for the students. For example, in many online learning courses, the lack of a face-to-face component creates difficulties for the students and teacher in relation to the form of learning community that results. A number of studies into the factors that influence the development of sense of community among learners are pointing to the benefits and advantages of approaches where some form of face-to-face communication is provided as a means to

TABLE 36.2. FORMS OF BLENDED LEARNING USED TO SUPPORT STUDENTS' COMPLETION OF AUTHENTIC TASKS.

Number	Characteristic of Authentic Activity	Blended Learning
1.	Have real-world relevance	Students use e-mail and discussion to connect with people in the workplace and explore cases beyond the classroom.
2.	Are ill defined, requiring students to define the tasks and subtasks needed to complete the activity	Face-to-face teaching is used to contextualize the authentic tasks and provide learners with supports and guidance in the task solutions.
4.	Provide the opportunity for students to examine the task from different perspectives, using a variety of resources	Discussion boards, e-mail, and face-to-face sessions are used to enable learners to gain access to a multitude of viewpoints and meet different stakeholders.
5.	Provide the opportunity to collaborate	Face-to-face sessions are used to form groups and establish learning communities. Discussion boards, e-mail, and online tools are used to support group-based activities and teamwork.
6.	Provide the opportunity to reflect and involve students' beliefs and values	Students use discussion boards to share reflective experiences and consider multiple perspectives.

establish norms and processes prior to the students' undertaking independent and distant activities mediated by the technology alone (Brook & Oliver, 2003).

Workplace Learning

Another example of an authentic learning setting where a blended learning environment promotes and supports the learning outcomes is a unit developed as one of the National Flexible Learning Toolboxes within Australia. The virtual realty course provides a set of online learning materials for students studying for a Certificate IV in Property, a qualification for realtors in Australia (see Figure 36.3).

The learning design within this course is based on authentic activities. The principal learning setting for this course is intended to be online learning, although the environment is supported by face-to-face teaching in a number of ways. When students are learning to value properties, they are given a role as property valuers. They are given the task of valuing a virtual property, and the online course provides a large number of supports and resources to assist them in this process. Part of the learning setting involves a number of elements of blended learning.

FIGURE 36.3.   LEARNER ACTIVITY FROM THE VIRTUAL REALTY ONLINE COURSE.

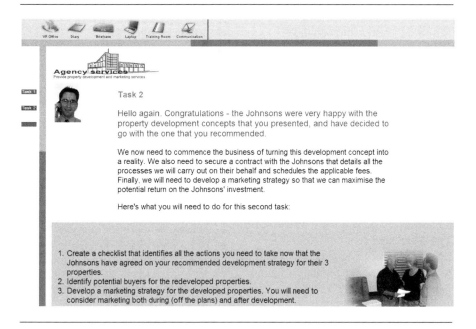

Students are typically enrolled in face-to-face classes where a teacher provides many of the supports they need. They learn to work in groups and to share ideas and resources. As part of their task solution, they use technology to find information and to share and discuss ideas. The students spend considerable time working in the online setting to complete the tasks and have a variety of face-to-face sessions to support this activity. The face-to-face teaching enables the teacher to provide immediate feedback to students in relation to their plan development and problem-solving strategies and processes, activities for which there is little written help within the course materials. In an extension from the previous example, students are also exposed to workplace activities that see them communicating with supervisors and mentors in the workplace as part of the task completion. This activity also enables them to practice and demonstrate their learning to workplace assessors.

Table 36.3 provides a summary of how the authentic learning activity is aided by the various elements of the blended learning approach used in this course. It shows the blended learning approach contributing to maintaining the relevance

TABLE 36.3. CHARACTERISTICS OF AUTHENTIC ACTIVITY, SHOWING OPPORTUNITIES FOR BLENDED LEARNING.

Number	Characteristic of Authentic Activity	Blended Learning
1.	Have real-world relevance	E-mail and Web forms are used to enable learners to communicate with mentors and workplace assessors.
2.	Are ill defined, requiring students to define the tasks and subtasks needed to complete the activity	Face-to-face teaching supports students in understanding their role and the associated activities in the planning and task solution.
4.	Provide the opportunity for students to examine the task from different perspectives, using a variety of resources	Discussion boards, e-mail, and face-to-face experiences provide opportunities for gaining multiple perspectives on the tasks.
5.	Provide the opportunity to collaborate	Classroom settings supported by Web-based communication provide support to group-based activities and teamwork.
6.	Provide the opportunity to reflect and involve students' beliefs and values	Differing solutions are used to provide opportunities for students to compare their work with others and to reflect on the steps taken and solutions achieved.

of the task through the connections to the workplace and workplace mentors, problem support, and various forms of assistance for the learners in their group work and reflective practices.

Conclusion

The use of authentic activities as a context for learning provides many opportunities for both instructors and students. But the opportunities come at a cost. Learners are often required to engage in a raft of unfamiliar activities and to take ownership of what is a complex and difficult learning experience. The use of blended learning provides a number of supports for this form of teaching and learning, in both the affordances it offers for using real-life problems and the supports it provides for the learners and their interactions. Strong support for students in their immersion into student-centered learning environments is crucial. This support is particularly important when the students are required to take ownership of the problem and where they can feel isolated and distant from the rest of the learning community.

Well-designed blended learning settings can provide the forms of teacher support and peer scaffolding that many students will need to more effectively engage in student-centered and problem-based tasks. Blended learning also provides the forms of assistance learners need to overcome any initial difficulties and uncertainty. This chapter has described distinct ways in which blended learning provides many supports for authentic activities. It also argues for the use of blended learning in any form of learning design seeking to create opportunities for learners to be immersed in complex and student-centered tasks. Our work suggests a strong need for researchers to continue to explore this form of learning design and investigate design strategies that will guide instructors and designers in the appropriate forms of blended learning they choose to employ.

References

Angus, M. & Gray, J. (2002). *Description of a situated learning approach in a research methods postgraduate subject.* Retrieved July 1, 2004, from http://www.learningdesigns.uow.edu.au/exemplars/info/LD13/index.html.

Barab, S. A., Squire, K. D., & Dueber, W. (2000). A co-evolutionary model for supporting the emergence of authenticity. *Educational Technology Research and Development, 48*(2), 37–62.

Bennett, S., Harper, B., & Hedberg, J. (2001). Designing real-life cases to support authentic design activities. In G. Kennedy, M. Keppell, C. McNaught, & T. Petrovic (Eds.), *Meeting at the crossroads: Proceedings of the 18th Annual Conference of the Australian Society for Computers in Learning in Tertiary Education* (pp. 73–81). Melbourne: University of Melbourne.

Bottge, B. A., & Hasselbring, T. S. (1993). Taking word problems off the page. *Educational Leadership, 50*(7), 36–38.

Bransford, J. D., Sherwood, R. D., Hasselbring, T. S., Kinzer, C. K., & Williams, S. M. (1990). Anchored instruction: Why we need it and how technology can help. In D. Nix & R. Spiro (Eds.), *Cognition, education and multimedia: Exploring ideas in high technology* (pp. 115–141). Mahwah, NJ: Erlbaum.

Bransford, J. D., Vye, N., Kinzer, C., & Risko, V. (1990). Teaching thinking and content knowledge: Toward an integrated approach. In B. F. Jones & L. Idol (Eds.), *Dimensions of thinking and cognitive instruction* (pp. 381–413). Mahwah, NJ: Erlbaum.

Brook, C., & Oliver, R. (2003). Online learning communities: Investigating a design framework. *Australian Journal of Educational Technology, 19*(2), 139–160.

Brophy, J., & Alleman, J. (1991). Activities as instructional tools: A framework for analysis and evaluation. *Educational Researcher, 20*(4), 9–23.

Brown, J. S., Collins, A., & Duguid, P. (1989). Situated cognition and the culture of learning. *Educational Researcher, 18*(1), 32–42.

Challis, D. (2002). Integrating the conceptual and practice worlds: A case study from architecture. In A. Goody, J. Herrington, & M. Northcote (Eds.), *Quality conversations: Research and development in higher education* (Vol. 25, pp. 106–113). Jamison, A.C.T.: Higher Education Research and Development Society of Australia.

Cognition and Technology Group at Vanderbilt. (1990a). Anchored instruction and its relationship to situated cognition. *Educational Researcher, 19*(6), 2–10.

Cognition and Technology Group at Vanderbilt. (1990b). Technology and the design of generative learning environments. *Educational Technology, 31*(5), 34–40.

Duchastel, P. C. (1997). A Web-based model for university instruction. *Journal of Educational Technology Systems, 25*(3), 221–228.

Franks, P. (2002). Blended learning: What is it? How does it impact student retention and performance? *World Conference on E-Learning in Corporate, Government, Health, and Higher Education, 2002*(1), 1477–1480. Available at http://dl.aace.org/9593.

Gordon, R. (1998). Balancing real-world problems with real-world results. *Phi Delta Kappan, 79,* 390–393.

Herrington, J., & Herrington, A. (1998). Authentic assessment and multimedia: How university students respond to a model of authentic assessment. *Higher Education Research and Development, 17*(3), 305–322.

Herrington, J., Oliver, R., & Reeves, T. C. (2003). Patterns of engagement in authentic online learning environments. *Australian Journal of Educational Technology, 19*(1), 59–71.

Herrington, J., Reeves, T. Oliver, R., & Woo, Y. (2004). Designing authentic activities in Web-based courses. *Journal of Computing and Higher Education, 16*(1), 3–29.

Jonassen, D. (1991). Evaluating constructivistic learning. *Educational Technology, 31*(9), 28–33.

Kantor, R. J., Waddington, T., & Osgood, R. E. (2000). Fostering the suspension of disbelief: The role of authenticity in goal-based scenarios. *Interactive Learning Environments, 8*(3), 211–227.

Lebow, D., & Wager, W. W. (1994). Authentic activity as a model for appropriate learning activity: Implications for emerging instructional technologies. *Canadian Journal of Educational Communication, 23*(3), 231–244.

Lockwood, F. (1992). *Activities in self-instructional texts.* London: Kogan Page.

McArthur, J. (2001, September 19). *Blended learning: a multiple training strategy* [Video Webcast]. Available at http://www.connectlive.com/events/opm/.

Myers, S. (1993). A trial for Dmitri Karamazov. *Educational Leadership, 50*(7), 71–72.

Oliver, R., & Omari, A. (1999). Using online technologies to support problem based learning: Learners' responses and perceptions. *Australian Journal of Educational Technology, 15,* 158–179.

Petraglia, J. (1998a). The real world on a short leash: The (mis)application of constructivism to the design of educational technology. *Educational Technology Research and Development, 46*(3), 53–65.

Petraglia, J. (1998b). *Reality by design: The rhetoric and technology of authenticity in education.* Mahwah, NJ: Erlbaum.

Reeves, T. C., & Okey, J. R. (1996). Alternative assessment for constructivist learning environments. In B. G. Wilson (Ed.), *Constructivist learning environments: Case studies in instructional design* (pp. 191–202). Upper Saddle River, NJ: Educational Technology Publications.

Resnick, L. (1987). Learning in school and out. *Educational Researcher, 16*(9), 13–20.

Winn, W. (1993). Instructional design and situated learning: Paradox or partnership. *Educational Technology, 33*(3), 16–21.

Young, M. F. (1993). Instructional design for situated learning. *Educational Technology Research and Development, 41*(1), 43–58.

Ron Oliver is the professor of interactive multimedia in the Faculty of Communications and Creative Industries at Edith Cowan University in Australia. He has a background in multimedia and learning technologies and leads a research team at ECU in these fields. He has extensive experience in the design, development, implementation, and evaluation of technology-mediated and online learning materials.

Jan Herrington is associate professor in information technology in education at the University of Wollongong in Australia. She is a member of the Research Centre for Interactive Learning Environments at the university. Recent research and development interests have focused on the design of effective Web-based learning environments for higher education, instructional design, and the use of authentic contexts and problem-based scenarios as a central focus for Web-based delivery of courses.

Thomas C. Reeves is a professor of instructional technology at the University of Georgia, where he teaches program evaluation, multimedia design, and research courses. He has developed and evaluated numerous interactive multimedia programs for both education and training. He has been an invited speaker around the world. In 1995, he was selected as one of the "Top 100" people in multimedia by *Multimedia Producer* magazine, and from 1997 to 2000 he edited the *Journal of Interactive Learning Research*. In 2003, he was the first recipient of the AACE Fellowship Award from the Association for the Advancement of Computing in Education.

PART EIGHT

FUTURE TRENDS IN BLENDED LEARNING

This final part of the *Handbook of Blended Learning* contains three exciting chapters on future directions of blended learning. Here, emerging technologies are showcased: simulations, mobile technologies, augmented reality, and reusable content objects. Without a doubt, dozens of emerging technologies will dramatically expand blended learning options and opportunities. As online learning technologies continue to evolve and bandwidth increases while becoming more affordable, a handbook of blended learning a decade from now (assuming handbooks still exist) will have chapters vastly different from those presented in this book. Of course, the pedagogies and instructional frameworks that are ultimately selected in conjunction with these technology tools will determine the overall learning results.

Chapter Thirty-Seven by Robert A. Wisher, of the Advanced Distributed Learning Initiative within the Department of Defense, provides interesting insights into a wide range of blended learning environments that are emerging in the U.S. military. Wisher addresses the use of intelligent tutoring systems, simulations, and the use of electronic collaborative learning tools in the context of individual training. In the area of training collectives or groups of individuals, this chapter provides examples of distributed simulations as well as Live-Virtual-Constructive simulations: large-scale operations that involve the interaction between forces operating in live fire ranges with forces using virtual simulators and constructive simulations to help combine the parts together in a way that the participant cannot tell the difference between them. This chapter also addresses the Advanced Distributed Learning vision and the importance of standards such as the Sharable Content Object Reference Model (SCORM) for facilitating the interoperability and use of learning objects.

Chapter Thirty-Eight by Jamie Reaves Kirkley and Sonny E. Kirkley introduces the concept of mixed-reality training that blends elements of real-world and virtual reality training experiences. Three types of mixed reality are introduced with examples: (1) augmented vision (adding visual information into the learners' context), (2) augmented reality (overlays virtual information onto the real world), and (3) augmented virtuality (places some real objects in a mostly virtual world). In addition to providing two example cases, the authors introduce a model of problem-based learning (called problem-based embedded training) for use in mixed reality training environments.

In the last chapter, Curtis J. Bonk, Kyong-Jee Kim, and Tingting Zeng recap many aspects of this handbook, while also pushing ahead with new data and predictions related to blended learning. They begin by sharing the results of two studies conducted on the future of online teaching and learning—one in higher education and one in corporate training. The data show a perceived shift over the next decade toward the use of blended approaches in both higher education and workplace environments. Results are also presented regarding survey respondent perceptions of what pedagogical techniques and technologies will be most widely used within e-learning. Importantly, similar data are shared from the perspective of corporate managers and higher education instructors, instructional designers, and administrators. To conclude this chapter, Bonk and Kim provide an insightful list of ten major trends and predictions for the future direction of blended learning.

CHAPTER THIRTY-SEVEN

BLENDED LEARNING IN MILITARY TRAINING

Robert A. Wisher

The U.S. Department of Defense (DoD) represents a massive training and education enterprise. Beyond instruction for the 1.4 million active-duty personnel, training and educational services are provided to 870,000 ready reservists, more than 750,000 civilian personnel, and 110,000 military dependents in K-12 schooling. Each year approximately $17 billion is spent to train and educate service members, with thousands of courses for hundreds of specialized occupational areas. These courses are taught at training centers, military academies, staff colleges, armories, reserve centers, and training ranges around the world.

The DoD uses nearly every instructional delivery method imaginable. Examples are conventional classroom instruction, correspondence courses, graphic training aids, videotapes, audio teletraining, CDs, intelligent tutoring systems, satellite delivery of distance learning classes, online instruction, simulators, training that is embedded in equipment, hands-on laboratories, and field training. Additional resources are allocated to unit-level training, field exercises, distributed simulations, and immense training exercises engaging tens of thousands of learners in multifaceted, interconnected physical and virtual learning environments. Clearly, military training blends many forms of instruction.

Note: The views expressed are those of the author and do not necessarily reflect the views or policies of the U.S. Department of Defense.

The core competency of the military involves violence and the credible threat of violence—to safeguard, coerce, deter, or defeat others in support of national interests. Military training must prepare individuals to enter into harm's way and perform physically and mentally demanding tasks at the highest possible levels of proficiency (Fletcher & Chatelier, 2000).

With modern challenges of unconventional threats as well as the integration of information systems for netcentric operations, it is not surprising that the DoD is undergoing a transformation in the way it trains. The global war on terrorism challenges training to prepare the force to learn, improvise, and adapt to constantly changing threats and do so in a more integrated manner across the military services as well with intergovernmental, interagency, and multinational partners (Department of Defense, 2004).

Along with its research investments in future weapons and other systems, the military sponsors substantial research and development in forward-looking learning and job-aiding technologies. These include intelligent tutors, distributed simulations, learning objects, content repositories, embedded training, and multiplayer online games, to name just a few. It is worthwhile to note that technologies developed by the military can find their way into public and commercial use; a relevant example of technology transfer is the transition of the restricted ARPAnet to the ubiquitous Internet.

Explaining how learning environments are blended across the military requires some background. Readers are probably more familiar with learning in educational settings or industry, so the pathways of military training need framing. A brief description of how training requirements are established is followed by a description of how military training is structured. Examples of blending various methods of instructional delivery are illustrated with real examples, beginning with individuals' learning specialized skills and ending with large-scale, multinational training exercises for masses of units. Note that the focus here is on training to enhance skills for staffs and other military units rather than professional military education, although there are plenty of examples of the latter. The orientation is to the U.S. military, though many nations follow a similar pattern.

Creating Training Requirements

The national military strategy responds to the National Security Strategy of the United States, which is issued annually by the president (White House, 2004). The military strategy imposes security requirements to five regional combatant commands. The commands span every corner of the globe with the exception of Antarctica, which by treaty prohibits any military measures. The Pacific

Command, headquartered in Hawaii, for instance, is responsible for military operations in the forty-one-nation Pacific Rim region. The commands issue what are termed joint mission essential tasks. Subordinate commands respond with their more detailed mission essential tasks. It is the job of the military services to train their units to perform these tasks. Readiness is the key.

The essential tasks are based on an analysis of a military unit's mission: what it is expected to do. Such tasks are considered absolutely necessary, indispensable, and critical to the success of a mission. An example of a mission-essential task is "conduct river crossing operations." Commanders establish supporting conditions for each task, such as whether a bridge is to be constructed in a jungle or a desert terrain. The resulting training objective—a set of conditions and standards that relate to a task—provides a clear statement of expected training performance.

How does the military training enterprise respond to these requirements? It is accomplished through multiple levels of training, from individuals to large units. The learning environments for individuals are partitioned into categories, preparing them for assignments in operational units. At this point, individual tasks are executed in a specific context in a unit while collective skills are developed.

Overview of Military Training

Military training involves the preparation of both individuals and collectives, such as crews, teams, and units. The six categories of individual training listed in Table 37.1 represent formal institutional environments. Individuals continue to refresh and sustain skills long after the schoolhouse. Individual training is intended to provide service members the skills and knowledge that will qualify them to perform effectively as members of military units.

The metric "training load" specifies the number of student-years in formal institutional training and education during a one-year period, so a training load of 1 is equivalent to a full-time, year-round student, attending class for five hours per day, five days per week, fifty-two weeks per year. On this basis, the military training load computes to approximately 184,000 (Department of Defense, 2002). Stated differently, on any given day, 184,000 service members are in class.

Blended Learning in Individual Training

There are few opportunities for blended models of learning in recruit training. Instilling discipline, indoctrination into the rigors of military life, and a regiment of physical conditioning are offered in a face-to-face manner by drill instructors. America's Army, a popular single and multiplayer online game sponsored by the army, offers a preview of recruit training. It is not part of recruit training, but

TABLE 37.1. INSTITUTIONAL TRAINING CATEGORIES AND LOADS IN THE U.S. MILITARY.

Recruit training: 38,000	Provides introductory physical conditioning and military training to indoctrinate and acclimate enlisted entrants to military life.
Specialized skill training: 99,100	Provides personnel with initial job qualification skills and new or higher levels of skill in military specialties to meet specific job requirements
One-station unit training: 9,600	An army training program that meets the objectives of both recruit training and specialized skill training through a single course
Officer acquisition training: 19,300	Provides education and training that leads to commissioning in one of the services; also known as precommissioning training
Flight training: 5,500	Provides initial flying skills needed by pilots, navigators, and naval flight officers
Professional development education: 12,900	Includes educational courses conducted at service schools or at civilian institutions to broaden the outlook and knowledge of personnel or to impart knowledge in advanced academic disciplines

research reported by the Army Research Institute has demonstrated a positive learning effect among delayed-entry recruits (Belanich, Sibley, & Orvis, 2004). Specifically, the findings demonstrated that game participants recalled procedures better than facts, while graphic images and spoken text were recalled more accurately than printed text.

A different picture for blended learning emerges with the largest institutional category: specialized skill training at the individual level. Numerous examples of combining technology with classroom and hands-on laboratories are available, but space limits the description to two examples.

A Blending with Intelligent Tutoring Systems. An instructional technology that has matured in recent years is intelligent tutoring. Intelligent tutoring systems have evolved from an arcane art of knowledge engineering to development methods and delivery options that are becoming more commonplace. Fundamental to an intelligent tutor is a body of domain knowledge encoded as an expert system of rules (Farr & Psotka, 1992). This expertise is accessible to the student during a learning exercise under the control of an instructional strategy governed by production rules, Bayesian networks, or other computational schemes representing expert knowledge. The goal is to have the student construct a mental representation of the domain knowledge—the expert's facts, rules, and procedures—for later application.

One example is the blending of an intelligent tutoring system within an advanced course in field artillery. The eighteen-week course employs the instructional methods of lectures on theory, doctrine, and tactics with peer discussions and reading assignments. A culminating activity is the integration of what was learned into a four-hour practice lab, called a sand table exercise. This exercise requires small groups working collaboratively to demonstrate their knowledge with operational planning. Limitations of the conventional sand table, such as small group versus individual instruction, led to the development of an intelligent tutor for this one learning activity.

The conventional sand table is a low-fidelity training device: an actual table of sand with molded terrain features and rocket assets, such as loaders and vehicles, depicted by miniature objects. It is used to evaluate reconnaissance, selection, and occupation of position strategies. During the exercise, students review an operations order, evaluate a terrain, and strategically decide where to place firing points, ammunition hiding areas, and so forth within a terrain model.

The virtual sand table is the intelligent tutoring counterpart for conducting the same training but on an individual basis. It is essentially a simulation game, where a student's actions are evaluated against a set of expectations governed by a set of rules. Although an actual sand table may appear useful, an individual cannot truly benefit unless there is a trained expert present to critique the process through regular and informative feedback. In reality, an insufficient number of instructors are available to critique students during the exercise. An intelligent tutor offers a remedy.

The tutoring component is designed to simulate an instructor coaching a student at a conventional sand table. The focus is the evaluation of the student's selected positions and routes. The basis for the coaching is a three-step process: a situation assessment of the map area, diagnosis and evaluation of the student's decisions, and generation of feedback (coaching) to the student. As the student places assets for occupation of position, a simulation component calculates the line of sight, mobility, and trajectories for the rockets in real time. The results from the simulation are displayed and sent to the intelligent tutor component for evaluation. Coaching templates can consequently be triggered. An example of a coaching experience is displayed in Figure 37.1.

In an evaluation of the effectiveness of the intelligent tutor to the conventional sand table, an effect size of 1.05 standard deviation units for the intelligent tutor was reported, based on a sample of 209 for the conventional sand table and 105 for the intelligent tutor (Wisher, Abrahmson, & Dees, 2001). This translates to a 35 percentile increase in learning above the mean performance of the

FIGURE 37.1.   COACHING THE STUDENT DURING MAP RECONNAISSANCE.

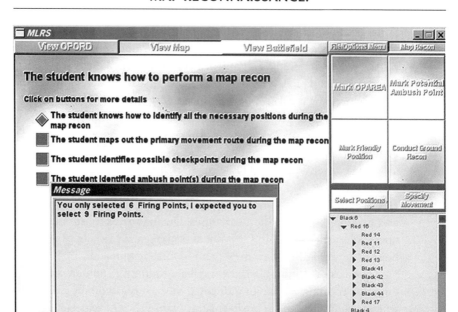

Note: The diamond icon identifies the subtask causing the message.

conventional group. The effect size reported is in line with those reported in other studies of intelligent tutors in the military and higher education, which is about 1.0 (Woolf & Regian, 2000).

A Blending with Collaborative Learning Tools. A second example of blending concerns a career course for armor officers who belong to the Army National Guard or Army Reserve. This course used a blend of three instructional phases: (1) an asynchronous training phase delivered over the Internet, (2) a synchronous Web-based phase in a collaborative, virtual environment, and (3) a two-week face-to-face resident training. In the asynchronous phase, students learned basic concepts with feedback from both the learning management systems and the instructor. The second phase consisted of seventy hours of synchronous instruction in a Web-based, virtual environment. The third phase was face-to-face instruction in which the students engaged in realistic classroom and field exercises for two full weeks. Part of the formula for the blending was based on the number of training days available per year, which is one weekend a month and two full-time weeks.

Of interest is a study on the interactions during the synchronous phase (Orvis, Wisher, Bonk, & Olson, 2002). Here, small groups of students "convened" in a virtual operations center, a visual rendition of an actual tactical operations center. Students connected from different geographical locations, generally their homes. Training sessions lasted between four and eight hours on two consecutive weekend days. The collaboration tools available were group as well as private chat, shared whiteboard, shared book shelf, shared-text application, and three-dimensional terrain tools. The students' learning environment involved solving problems collectively concerning military operations and generated work products, such as a mission analysis.

More than sixty-five hundred acts of text chat were recorded during the synchronous training sessions. Results indicated shifting patterns of interaction over the six-month period; technology concerns gradually diminished, while on-task discussion peaked in the middle months, and social interactions were higher at the start and end of the training, just prior to the face-to-face resident phase. Overall, student chats were categorized as on task 55 percent, social 30 percent, or technology related 15 percent. Examples of chats and focus group data indicated that there was an emphasis on fostering student problem solving within the online course.

Blended Learning in Collective Training

Collective training, also referred to as unit training, concerns the development of skills needed to accomplish a unit's mission essential tasks: its wartime objectives. It is a primary contributor to readiness, along with equipment, supplies, and personnel availability. (Readiness is a peacetime measure of how well the force is prepared to conduct its missions.) A parallel to face-to-face classroom instruction concerns training on ranges and in operational areas. These are physical zones set aside specifically for testing weapon systems and training units of all sizes. Some examples are ground maneuver areas, drop zones, torpedo alleys, and live-fire ranges. Excluding airspace, sea surface, and underwater training areas, there are approximately 440 range complexes covering nearly 30 million acres in the United States.

Unit training frequently entails activities that pose risk to the safety and well-being of participants. During the 1988 to 1991 period, for example, 752 active-duty personnel died while engaging in peacetime training. About 64 percent of these were due to aviation mishaps. For this and other reasons, simulators and simulations are being blended more and more into collective training.

Ranges and Simulations. Military ranges and operating areas are enablers of unit performance. However, encroachment pressures such as private housing developments adjacent to ranges, restrictions imposed by environmental regulations, and growing competition for airspace and the electronic frequency spectrum are impeding the ability to train in realistic environments. An area of blended learning being exploited concerns distributed simulations. Simulations are simply abstractions of the real world. When distributed, individuals and crews can synchronize to activities in other simulators or even to concurrent activities that are occurring on an instrumented training range. All activities are sensed, timed, and linked through advanced technologies.

How is this accomplished? A key technology is high-level architecture (HLA), a standard for constructing distributed simulations. It was approved as an open standard through the Institute of Electrical and Electronics Engineers (IEEE Standard 1516) in 2000. It is intended to facilitate interoperation between a wide range of simulation types and to promote the reusability of simulation software. HLA encompasses virtual, constructive, and live simulations. A group of simulations interoperating under HLA is called a *federation*.

Distributed Simulations. Distributed simulations seek to create a highly realistic, widely distributed, seamless environment for training and mission rehearsal. The goal is to resolve actions within a setting that integrates terrain, ocean, atmosphere, and dynamic environmental effects. Command behaviors are credibly simulated along with information from sensors and interfaces to command-and-control systems. Manned simulators as well as live, instrumented systems can be federated as needed.

This technology is a blend of three technical areas: (1) synthetic environments, representing areas within the real world; (2) synthetic forces, which are computer-generated entities operating in synthetic environments programmed to employ the tactics and techniques of friendly and opposing forces; and (3) networking, that is, communications technology linking human and synthetic forces in shared synthetic environments. The objective is to faithfully represent the spectrum of conflicts in conducting operations.

The networking of simulators for training started in the 1980s with funding from the Defense Advanced Research Projects Agency. One advancement in blended learning is distributed mission training. In the air force, for example, these systems have full-domed visuals, interconnected simulators, and a networked training center that incorporates live feeds from other simulators hundreds of miles away. They provide realistic training to pilots and air crews through precise time-space-position information with convincing weapon engagement simulations. The benefits are tremendous because pilots are now able to train with multiple aircraft platforms on the same mission scenario. Recent advances now allow simulators to be linked to actual weapons platforms, providing increased fidelity to the virtual training experience.

Blended Learning in Large-Scale Exercises. A related model of blended learning is emerging for integrating the training during large exercises. The model is known as live-virtual-constructive (L-V-C) simulations. The model reflects an ambitious effort to link simultaneously the activities that occur on instrumented, live fire ranges with virtual activities in widely dispersed simulators. These activities are linked to computer models that construct outcomes based on intricate mathematical models of how a unit is expected to perform under a given set of circumstances. Work is underway to develop a global, multinational network of live forces, learner-in-the-loop virtual simulators, and constructive simulations to provide a robust training and mission rehearsal environment.

The L-V-C environment allows troops to train together even if they are not physically located in the same area. In the past, large numbers of forces needed to be moved at great expense. An air force pilot can now target a blip on the screen representing someone sitting in a simulator located far away. Training and targeting can be based on real-time outcomes from virtual simulators and probabilities from constructive simulations rather than live targets.

An example of this blended learning environment was a combined joint task force exercise dubbed Operation Blinding Storm conducted in June 2004. Nearly thirty thousand U.S., British, Canadian, and coalition forces from seven other nations participated in this major L-V-C exercise intended to prepare troops for multinational operations. Tasks such as "conduct amphibious assault and raid operations" were executed through a networking of seventeen military units (live), six simulators (virtual), and twenty-one simulations (constructive). As depicted in Figure 37.2, mine warfare operations were conducted at range complexes in North Carolina, as seen through a Sea Dragon helicopter simulator in Florida, while a command group at sea monitored the activities of a live assault group landing on the North Carolina beach that had just been cleared through the simulation.

The idea is to meld live, virtual, and constructive forces on the battleground so that a player-learner cannot tell the difference between one and the other. Based on a global network, the concept is eventually to conduct an exercise with the capacity to integrate players from around the world. For example, people training in Korea could potentially be tied into a network that will include forces on the East Coast of the United States and in Europe. The Joint National Training Capability initiative is pursuing this goal.

FIGURE 37.2. DEPICTION OF A LIVE-VIRTUAL-CONSTRUCTIVE LEARNING EXERCISE.

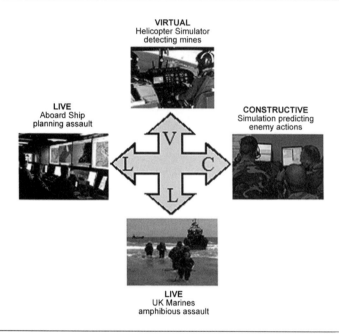

Source: Photo of simulator courtesy CAE.

Future Programs

The extraordinary change in the strategic environment demands a similar transformation in how the military prepares for new missions. Emphasis must shift from deliberate planning against a known capability to adaptive planning for an opposition whose tactics and techniques are uncertain. A shift from large hierarchies to smaller, distributed forces trained to adapt to uncertain scenarios is underway.

A set of instructional technologies under development that can enable such a transformation comes under the general term *advanced distributed learning* (ADL). The blend here is across a variety of existing technologies made possible through interoperability standards for online instruction. Also tied in is a Web services model that communicates across learning environments through a common architecture (Blackmon & Rehak, 2003). The blend can also be across content areas, allowing the learner to combine a selection of learning exercises from a variety of authors, vendors, and sources into one seamless, adaptive learning experience.

The Advanced Distributed Learning Vision

The ADL Initiative originated in 1997 through the President's Office of Science and Technology Policy (Wisher & Fletcher, 2004). An executive order gave the DoD a leadership role within the federal government. ADL is based on three main components: (1) a global information infrastructure, with registered repositories populated by reusable instructional objects; (2) a server, which discovers, locates, and then assembles instructional objects into education, training, and performance-aiding materials tailored to user needs; and (3) devices that serve as personal learning associates on which the materials are presented.

This material will be tailored to the needs, capabilities, intentions, and learning state of each individual or group. Much of the work of the server is expected to be accomplished by middleware in the form of learning management systems. Within ADL, this implies a server-based environment in which the intelligence for controlling the delivery of learning content resides with the learning management system.

Learning Objects and Learning Management Systems. To date, most ADL effort has been devoted to the specification of reusable, sharable instructional objects. ADL development envisions the creation of learning libraries or repositories where learning objects may be accumulated and catalogued for broad distribution and use. Such repositories will provide the basis for a new instructional object economy that rewards content creators for developing high-quality learning objects and assembling them into adaptive learning experiences.

The key function of a learning management system in this context is to manage content objects, so that it should be possible for a learning management system to launch content that is authored by using tools from different vendors and to exchange data with that content. The function of launching content has largely been solved with the Sharable Content Object Reference Model (SCORM). This model constitutes an important first step toward releasing learning content objects from local implementations (Dodds & Thropp, 2004). It is intended to provide specifications that enable content objects to be easily shared across multiple learning delivery environments. Indeed, one reason for its creation was an earlier frustration with a multitude of proprietary systems and learning content designs that were barriers to broader use of technology for military training (Government Accounting Office, 2003).

Sharable Content Object Reference Model. The current version of SCORM is realizing worldwide adoption among hundreds of vendors and other developers. A successful reference model must support full articulation of guidelines that can be implemented in the production of content objects. Much of the work needed to create the reference model is accomplished in a collaborative manner involving industry, academia, and governmental agencies, and on a global scale. One function of the ADL leadership in this process is to organize, encourage, orchestrate, and document their development efforts.

In terms of common repositories of content, ADL is examining the Handle System (Corporation for National Research Initiatives, 2004) as a comprehensive system for assigning, managing, and resolving persistent identifiers, known as "handles," for digital objects (content objects) and other resources on the Internet. The Handle System consists of a unique and persistent identifier for a resource and its owning organization, a protocol for resolving its location, and a reference implementation of the protocol so that a resource can always be found. The Handle System has the backing of the International Digital Object Identifier Foundation, which provides a framework for managing intellectual content, such as electronic journal articles, images, and instructional objects (International Digital Object Identifier Foundation, 2003).

ADL envisions a blended environment where learners are engaged with interconnected learning activities, such as moving from a multiplayer online instructional game to a sequence of learning objects relevant to a game strategy and perhaps then to an intelligent tutor and then back to the online game.

Closing Comments

An examination of the military training reveals blending of instructional technologies not found in other learning environments. The blended environments address individual and unit skills. The extent to which the military employs technology for training and its sheer complexity is not always apparent to others. A day on the exhibit floor of a large military training technology conference, such as the Interservice/Industry Training Simulation and Education Conference, can be an awesome experience.

There is no preestablished formula for a model of blended learning. Media selection models provide recommendations, but time, facilities, and instructor availability are critical factors. The need to reduce travel costs is another. Safety, environmental factors, and the call for readiness clearly play a role. Military research on education and training attends to the many excellent ideas emerging on learning environments created in academia or practiced by industry. An examination of practices and trends in the military can be of similar value. This chapter serves to make others aware of the innovations from military research and experimentation in designing next-generation learning environments. Through technology transfer, learners everywhere may ultimately benefit.

References

Belanich, J., Sibley, D. E., & Orvis, K. L. (2004). *Instructional characteristics and motivational features of a PC-based game.* Alexandria, VA: U.S. Army Research Institute for the Behavioral and Social Sciences.

Blackmon, W. H., & Rehak, D. R. (2003). *Customized learning: A Web services approach.* Pittsburgh, PA: Carnegie Mellon University: Learning Systems Architecture Lab. Retrieved August 20, 2004, from http://www.lsal.cmu.edu/lsal/expertise/papers/conference/edmedia2003/customized20030625.html.

Corporation for National Research Initiatives. (2004, February 9). *Corporation for National Research Initiatives, "The Handle System."* Retrieved August 12, 2004, from http://www.handle.net/introduction.html.

Department of Defense. (2002). *Military manpower training report.* Washington, DC: Pentagon, Office of the Deputy Under Secretary of Defense (Readiness).

Department of Defense. (2004, June 9). *Department of Defense training transformation implementation plan.* Washington, DC: Pentagon, Office of the Under Secretary for Personnel and Readiness.

Dodds, P., & Thropp, S. (2004, February 9). *Sharable Content Object Reference Model, SCORM 2004 overview.* Retrieved August 12, 2004, from http://www.adlnet.org/index.cfm?fuseaction=rcdetails&libid=648.

Farr, M. J., & Psotka, J. (Eds.). (1992). *Intelligent instruction by computer: Theory and practice.* Washington, DC: Taylor & Francis.

Fletcher, J. D., & Chatelier, P. R. (2000). Military training. In S. Tobias & J. D. Fletcher (Eds.), *Training and retraining: A handbook for business, industry, government, and the military* (pp. 267–288). New York: Macmillan.

Government Accounting Office. (2003). *Military transformation: Progress and challenges for DoD's advanced distributed leaning programs.* Washington, DC: Government Accounting Office.

International Digital Object Identifier Foundation. (2003). *The Digital Object Identifier System.* Retrieved August 12, 2004, from www.doi.org.

Orvis, K. L., Wisher, R. A., Bonk, C. J., & Olson, T. M. (2002). Communication patterns during synchronous Web-based military training in problem solving. *Computers in Human Behavior, 18,* 783–795.

White House. (2004). *The national security strategy of the United States of America.* Washington, DC: White House. Retrieved July 13, 2005, from http://www.whitehouse.gov/nsc/nss.html.

Wisher, R. A., Abramson, L. J., & Dees, J. J. (2001). The effectiveness of an intelligent tutoring system for rocket training. In *Proceedings of the IEEE International Conference on Advanced Learning Technology.* Madison, WI.

Wisher, R. A., & Fletcher, J. D. (2004). The case for advanced distributed learning. *Information and Security: An International Journal, 14,* 17–25.

Woolf, B. P., & Regian, J. W. (2000). Knowledge-based training systems and the engineering of instruction. In S. Tobias & J. Fletcher (Eds.), *Training and retraining: A handbook for business, industry, government, and the military* (pp. 339–356). New York: Macmillan.

Robert A. Wisher is director of the Advanced Distributed Learning (ADL) Initiative within the Office of the Secretary of Defense. He has oversight of the three ADL Co-Laboratories and serves as the U.S. delegate and chairman of the NATO Working Group on Training and Education. Previously, he served as a research psychologist at the Army Research Institute in Alexandria, Virginia. Throughout his career, he has specialized in research on the effectiveness of instructional technologies. He received a B.S. in mathematics from Purdue University and a Ph.D. in cognitive psychology from the University of California, San Diego. He was a visiting scholar at the Center for Research on Learning and Technology at Indiana University. Among his recent awards are the U.S. Distance Learning Association Most Outstanding Individual Achievement Award.

CHAPTER THIRTY-EIGHT

EXPANDING THE BOUNDARIES OF BLENDED LEARNING

Transforming Learning with Mixed and Virtual Reality Technologies

Jamie Reaves Kirkley, Sonny E. Kirkley

Blended learning has been discussed primarily in the light of using currently available learning approaches and technologies, particularly with a focus on how online learning can be integrated with face-to-face learning. However, as new technologies emerge and training becomes increasingly just-in-time and embedded within specific situations and equipment that people use, instructional designers will be challenged to blend learning in ways that expand beyond our current understandings. This chapter addresses how an emerging class of technologies, mixed and virtual reality, can be blended with current technologies and approaches to create highly innovative and authentic learning opportunities.

Expanding Boundaries of Learning

As stated by Oliver, Herrington, and Reeves (Chapter Thirty-Six, this volume), constructivist learning theory has challenged instructional designers to create learning environments that are more authentic, complex, and geared to support performance-based learning. The hope is that by capitalizing on the elements of increased authenticity, complexity, and real-world performance, we can support learners in developing greater domain expertise, problem solving, and transfer of learning. To do this, we must provide increased immersion into the community of practice, as well as an enculturation into its way of seeing, interpreting, and acting. New technologies can potentially provide access to and make visible how experts view, interpret, and act. However, new technologies alone cannot meet the need; instructional designers must design innovative learning environments using appropriate learning methodologies that can support learners with complex problem solving and development of greater expertise.

To meet the need for creating learning environments that provide greater complexity and authenticity, instructional methodologies such as problem-based learning (PBL) (Barrows, 1992; Kirkley et al., 2003; Woods, 1992) and case-based reasoning (CBR) (Riesbeck & Schank, 1989) have been increasingly used as design frameworks in a wide variety of fields, including business, engineering, military, and medicine. Both focus on facilitating processes of student inquiry and real-world cases or problems as an impetus for learning, thus providing greater complexity in the learning environment. Learning occurs through the complex interactions among learners' existing knowledge, the social context, and the problem to be solved (Duffy & Cunningham, 1996). By centering the learning situation in real-world problems, we have the opportunity to acculturate the learner into the processes, practices, and language of a specific domain (Reiser, 2002).

In order to blend learning effectively, we need to better understand how to use learning methodologies such as PBL and CBR, strategies such as discussion and role playing, and various technologies such as face-to-face and online learning in order to make learning effective. However, as new technologies emerge, instructional designers must expand their notion of blended learning and constantly assess and reassess how to use methodologies, strategies, and technologies in order to create highly innovative learning environments. Thus, we can assume blended learning will become exponentially more complex as we are challenged to determine how to best design and develop a learning environment using specific methodologies, learning strategies, and technologies. This applies to all parties with an interest in the learning environment: instructional designers who must create the instructional content and environment and keep it up-to-date over the life cycle of use; trainers and instructors who must facilitate the learning; learners who must learn how to learn with these new capabilities; and administrators who must decide what technologies to support and how to pay for their implementation within budget constraints.

A secondary challenge lies with determining how to move a learner seamlessly through the overall process in a way that effectively supports learning. This challenge relates to creating appropriate processes and scaffolding that can support learners within learning environments that are cognitively and technologically complex (Hedberg, 2002). This requires special focus on designing effective scaffolding supports that are embedded within these learning environments. Kirkley et al. (2003) define *embedded scaffolds* as systematically designed elements of support that are integrated directly within the learning environment. These are based on a performance support metaphor where the goal is to provide just-in-time, adaptive scaffolding using resources, learning tools and software, pedagogy, content, or the environment.

In order to address these challenges, our team has been researching and designing training environments for military, corporate, and educational contexts that use mixed and virtual reality technologies. In this chapter, we present two examples of blended learning environments where different training goals, contexts, strategies, and technologies have been used within specific design frameworks to create innovative training environments. The goal is not only to provide examples of emerging technologies available for blended learning environments but to provide design models of how to combine and use different technologies with specific methodologies and design frameworks.

Applications of Mixed and Virtual Reality to Support Training and Performance

Mixed and virtual reality technologies hold much promise for providing authentic and complex learning environments through realistic simulations, visualization of data, and new forms of collaboration and community building. Due to space limitations, we will not report on the effectiveness of virtual reality (such as video games) for training and learning, which has been reported elsewhere. Instead, our focus is primarily on the use of mixed reality technologies, which are likely new to most people. Taken together, mixed and virtual reality technologies provide unique opportunities to support a range of learning goals.

Mixed reality provides the ability to enhance reality. These technologies often involve merging real and virtual worlds in which virtual objects are superimposed on real ones or real objects are used as part of a primarily virtual reality world. As illustrated in Figure 38.1, there is a continuum of types of mixed and virtual reality. On the far left is the real world. On the far right, we find virtual environments in which learners are completely immersed in a virtual world using one or more senses (for example, sight or sound). Mixed reality blends both real and virtual worlds. *Augmented vision* provides information relevant to a learner's context (for example, location, task, skill level). In this example, a technician sees a job aid while working on the vehicle. *Augmented reality* overlays virtual information onto the real world so that people perceive that information as part of the world. In this example, a novice ship navigator sees a virtual highway on the water. *Augmented virtuality* takes a mostly virtual world that is enhanced with some real objects. In this example, virtual building models are intermixed with models of real buildings to analyze architectural designs.

FIGURE 38.1.   REALITY-VIRTUALITY TRAINING CONTINUUM.

Source: The continuum is adapted from Milgram, Takemura, Utsumi, & Kishino (1994) by adding in the augmented vision category in order to illustrate a fuller range of learning approaches with these technologies.

Mixed reality systems come in a variety of forms, from stationary systems where the person is relatively immobile but is able to visualize data in useful ways (for example, looking through mounted video binoculars in a museum to see the skin on a dinosaur skeleton) to mobile systems in which wearable computers are used and the display is worn on the head (as when an automotive repair technician looks at a real car engine and sees relevant parts labeled to perform a procedure). For a general overview of the field, two surveys of augmented reality provide an excellent overview (Azuma, 1997; Azuma et al., 2001).

The field of mixed reality began to show the promise of viable applications in the 1990s. Specifically, augmented reality was used for applications to support maintenance and repair, as well as medical applications. The Boeing Company used augmented reality to support maintenance and assembly for aircraft wiring harnesses (Caudell & Mizell, 1992). Feiner and his colleagues at Columbia University developed KARMA (knowledge augmented reality for maintenance assistance), a test-bed system for automating the design of systems for maintenance and repair tasks. The Columbia group also developed a system termed "architectural anatomy" that enabled a user to "see through" walls and view wiring and other types of infrastructure (Feiner, 1992; Feiner, Webster, Krueger, MacIntyre, & Keller, 1995). Within medicine, augmented reality has been used to support surgeons by overlaying medical information, such as ultrasound images, directly onto the body to guide the doctor in performing a biopsy (Bajura, Fuchs, & Ohbuchi, 1992).

More recently, in a move toward highly mobile environments, Feiner and colleagues (Feiner, MacIntyre, Hollerer, & Webster, 1997; Hollerer, Feiner, Terauchi, Rashid, & Hallaway, 1999) have described prototype wearable systems to be used for travel, history, recreation, and touring. Their tour guide application provides information about a university campus (names of buildings, Web information about academic departments) through head-worn displays as well as palm-sized computers.

Building on the work at Columbia University, the Naval Research Lab has developed the Battlefield Augmented Reality System (BARS). Figure 38.2 illustrates how augmented reality simulations can be used for training. In this example, we see virtual minefields on the ground, a virtual rock, and information on the screen (for example, location). The BARS system provides situational awareness to soldiers by overlaying important information such as routes on the ground, outlining buildings, and identifying the location of enemy soldiers (Gabbard et al., 2002). In related work, the U.S. Army has been investigating how to use augmented reality simulations for training. The Mobile Augmented Reality Contextual Embedded Training and EPSS (MARCETE) project enables three-dimensional computer-generated characters and events to be displayed in the real world. Basically, the soldiers can participate in video-game-like experiences using the real world as the playing board (Kirkley, Borland, et al., in press).

FIGURE 38.2.   MARCETE CONCEPTUAL TRAINING EXAMPLE.

FIGURE 38.3. MAGICBOOK.

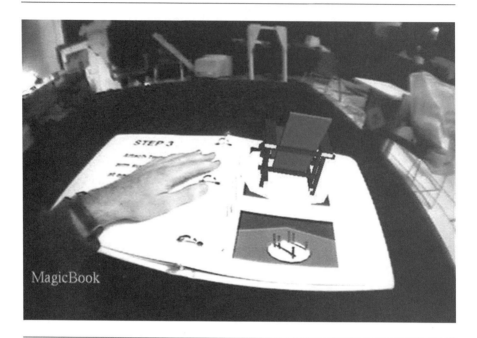

The MagicBook project at the University of Washington Human Interface Technology (HIT) Lab (Billinghurst, Kato, & Poupyrev, 2001) seeks to blend mixed and virtual reality. It consists of a video see-through augmented reality system (shown in Figure 38.3) that is used to view a book or other document with embedded symbols. When the system recognizes the symbol, it displays a three-dimensional model such as a building in that location. The person using the system can choose to zoom into a scene and is at that point in a virtual reality scene (for example, walking around inside the building).

The blending of these two technologies offers many possibilities for training and learning environments. However, there are technical challenges that still exist with implementing and using these technologies.

Challenges of Using Mixed Reality for Training

Although mixed and virtual reality technologies offer much promise for creating innovative learning environments, there are still many technical challenges with regard to obtaining accurate and precise tracking systems (for example, determining exactly where someone is looking), high-quality visual display outputs, and computer processing power. While these technical issues will be addressed with new technological advancements, it is even more critical that we develop models of training using these technologies. While the technologies themselves offer much promise for innovating learning and performance, the design of the training methods, processes, and tools is critical to ensuring that these promises of developing expertise, problem-solving skills, and transfer are realized.

Much of the literature on mixed reality training focuses either on providing examples of training environments or addressing technological or hardware issues (Nakajima & Itho, 2003; Schwald & de Laval, 2003). There have also been some studies focused on comparing the use of augmented reality for training versus more traditional techniques (Boud, Haniff, Baber, & Steiner, 1999; Ong & Nee, 2004). In general, research supports that on procedural and performance-based tasks, overall performance improves and error is reduced when using augmented reality as compared to other modes of interacting with content. For instance, Tang, Owen, Biocca, and Mou (2004) found that on procedural tasks, error was reduced by 82 percent when using augmented reality when comparing paper instructions, instructions on a computer LCD, instructions on a head-worn display (augmented vision), and augmented reality. In addition, the subjects' perception of task load, that is, how hard something is to do, was reduced with augmented reality. One caveat is that only minimal research has been conducted in this area, so we need to understand what is working better, in what conditions, and for what kinds of learning.

Yet as these new technologies expand the possibilities of training approaches, the field of instructional design and development must provide methodologies, processes, and models that meet the needs of these new training environments. Currently, existing instructional methodologies do not adequately address how to design and deliver blended learning using mixed and virtual reality or how to move seamlessly among these different modalities in the instructional environment. This requires envisioning design models that are flexible, adaptive, and based on innovative methods as well as technologies.

As new technologies continue to drive performance and training needs, they will also continue to push training methodologies to use more innovative training development and implementation techniques. Iterative cycles of development as well as early input from experts, trainers, and trainees will increase the quality and effectiveness of training designs and development. Reigeluth (1996) has stated that new models of instructional design will rely more heavily on input from user-designers. This requires not only developing new methods of training but also using innovative development processes such as rapid prototyping (Tripp & Bichelmeyer, 1990) and participatory design (Schuler & Namioka, 1993) to meet the needs of supporting learners in achieving complex performance goals. In the following section, we describe two blending learning environments that have been designed using mixed and virtual reality technologies.

Designing Blended Learning Environments Using Mixed and Virtual Reality

Mixed and virtual reality can be used in a variety of ways within a learning context. In this section, we describe a few of the ways in which these tools can support standard learning activities in the context of two case studies.

Using Augmented Vision to Provide Training and Performance Support Assembly and Maintenance

While one of the common criticisms of training is that it is often divorced from the situations and ways in which it is used, mixed reality offers the opportunity to provide information, resources, and performance support in the place and context in which it is needed: on the job. On the flip side, the workplace can now be brought into the training environment by using augmented reality-based simulations of the workplace as a context for training.

Using current technologies (Figure 38.4), an automotive service technician or assembly worker could engage in learning activities (see Table 38.1) in which they learn how to perform procedural tasks.

Table 38.1 provides examples of various instructional activities where mixed and virtual reality technologies can be used.

Problem-Based Embedded Training

Within the military, there is an push toward the development of authentic and situational training due to new training readiness goals set by the U.S. Department of Defense (Bonk & Wisher, 2000; Harris, 2002), along with emerging technological advances. Military training is moving to be more soldier-centric, just-in-time, and embedded within the equipment that soldiers use. Embedded training uses built-in or add-on training and support components (hardware and software), such as computer-based tutorials and simulations, in effect, the equipment that soldiers use during operational and training modes (Morrison & Orlansky, 1997).

The U.S. Army's Future Force Warrior (FFW) (Figure 38.5) and Future Combat Systems (FCS) will transform the way soldiers fight and are trained (U.S. Army Natick Soldier Center, 2003). Within the first increment, a family of manned

FIGURE 38.4. A SEE-THROUGH DISPLAY TO ACCESS JOB AIDS WHILE PERFORMING A REPAIR TASK.

TABLE 38.1. INSTRUCTIONAL ACTIVITIES FOR A MIXED REALITY EXAMPLE.

Instructional Activity	Mixed Reality Example
Classroom lecture to introduce concepts	Instructor uses virtual reality simulation to illustrate how a procedure is performed.
Practice	Students use head-worn displays to access instructions that guide them through learning the procedure; students work on problems normally reserved for experts, thus accelerating their performance gains.
Online collaboration and chat forum	Students on their home computers simultaneously view a virtual reality model and problem-solve solutions; students can try procedures, while others observe and problem-solve; a learning management system monitors their activities and can automatically pause the simulation and offer remedial training on the task before they continue.
Job aid	Students return to their job and use the head-worn displays to access job aids based on their skill level; the system can monitor their activities and present relevant information based on current tasks, allowing them to work hands free and not waste time looking for the help they need.

FIGURE 38.5.   PROTOTYPE FUTURE FORCE WARRIOR SOLDIER UNIFORMS WITH THE CAPABILITY TO DELIVER MIXED AND VIRTUAL REALITY.

systems will provide tomorrow's soldiers with high battlefield mobility and unprecedented organic reconnaissance and surveillance capabilities. These systems require radically innovative training solutions that can prepare soldiers to meet new military training readiness goals. Both FFW and FCS systems will require the development of embedded training and performance support systems during the systems acquisition process, and mixed and virtual reality technologies will play a vital role in these approaches. In fact, without these training technologies, FFW and FCS cannot be deployed and used effectively due to the increased complexity of decision making required in using these systems effectively.

Unfortunately, blended learning approaches that take full advantage of mixed and virtual reality technologies have not been developed for these programs. Much of the embedded training as currently described provides simple access to reference materials or the ability to pull up a simulation and practice. However, these approaches seem to lack the benefit that a blended learning approach could bring, including greater authenticity and the development of more robust knowledge. As part of an effort to help people think about the different modes that could be employed in an embedded blended learning capability for FFW, we have developed a matrix of technologies and modes of training support (Table 38.2).

For the past two years, Information in Place, with support from the U.S. Army Research Institute, has been developing and prototyping an instructional methodology and training support package for embedded training using mixed and virtual reality technologies (Kirkley, Kirkley et al., in press). As part of this initiative, PBL was adapted to develop a training methodology, problem-based embedded training (PBET). The PBET instructional model was designed to include four main components of the learning process:

- The *mission* is the problem and stimulus for learning.
- The *action plan* phase is a set of instructional events in which soldiers practice specific skills, rehearse aspects of mission execution, explore resource materials related to the mission, discuss solutions with colleagues and commanders, and perform other activities as needed.
- The *implementation* phase is when the soldiers participate in an authentic simulation where skills can be integrated and tested. This can be in a virtual reality environment or a field exercise.
- The *after-action review* phase is when soldiers, trainers, and commanders evaluate performance.

In Figure 38.6, the process is generally linear but may be iterative depending on training goals and trainee needs.

Using the PBET methodology as a guide, an instructional designer will develop a comprehensive training support package. Within this package, there is a training module with a range of learning activities, scaffolding elements to support learners at various stages of the process, and guidelines for trainers and instructors.

Using current and next-generation technologies, the FFW soldier would engage in learning activities (see Table 38.3) in which they learn how to perform multiple war fighting tasks (for example, learning to use small unmanned robotic systems to perform reconnaissance). Table 38.3 contains an example of how mixed reality technologies could be used for PBET types of training events.

TABLE 38.2. TYPES OF BLENDED TRAINING CAPABILITIES THAT CAN BE USED WITH DIFFERENT EMBEDDED TRAINING TECHNOLOGIES IN THE FUTURE FORCE WARRIOR.

	Handheld Computers or Head-Worn Displays	Audio (Stereo and Three-Dimensional Spatial Sound)	Augmented Reality (Three-Dimensional or Coregistered with Environment)
Reference			
Simple reference materials	Text reference materials	Audio version of text reference materials	Overlay or coregister labels of parts or components onto real equipment
Advanced reference materials	Multimedia examples of how to troubleshoot a problem	Audio "narration" of how to perform a task	Show computer-generated unmanned system performing task to illustrate capabilities (for example, maneuverability)
Job aid			
Generalized job aid	Provides list of key steps in general procedure	Provides audio list of key steps in general procedure	Overlay or coregister list of generic tasks step-by-step onto real equipment
Context-specific job aid	Provides specific list of key steps related to current task or learner profile	Provides audio list of key steps related to current task or learner profile	Overlay/co-register specific steps for performing tasks based on learners' skill level
Coaching			
Virtual	Virtual coach provides information and tips on tasks and performance	Virtual coach whispers in ear	Virtual coach walks trainee through performing tasks, adjusting amount of information based on performance
Live trainer or expert	Trainer remotely monitors and sends information as needed	Remote trainer provides audio feedback during training	Remote expert mentor "gestures" and highlights item of interest at training site using augmented reality technologies
Interactive simulations and games	Use virtual reality simulation of how to treat injured team member	Rehearse identifying the location of enemy entities by listening to audio cues	Provide augmented reality simulation of injured person overlaying virtual injury onto a real person
Simulation			
Training game	Play three-dimensional game to rehearse key mission components	Provide computer-generated audio and sound effects during live field training exercise	Engage fully interactive computer-generated entities (friendly and enemy forces) in Military Operations in Urban Terrain (MOUT) site during field training exercise

FIGURE 38.6. PBET INSTRUCTIONAL MODEL.

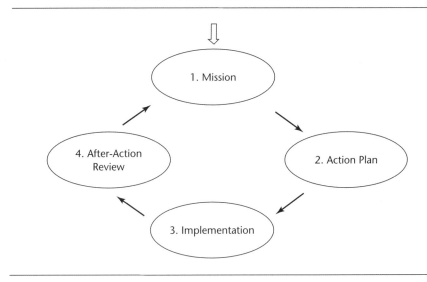

TABLE 38.3. INSTRUCTIONAL ACTIVITIES FOR A MIXED REALITY EXAMPLE.

Instructional Activity	Mixed Reality Example
Mission	Face-to-face, the commander (trainer) introduces the soldiers to the mission and uses an augmented virtuality model of the city (see Figure 38.1 for an example)
Action plan	Soldiers practice maneuvering virtual robots using augmented reality models of the real robots outside the barracks; in the vehicle on the way to training site, individuals practice using robots in virtual reality simulation on tablet-sized computer; they access reference materials from the online library; the commander instructs all the soldiers in the various vehicles to link up live, and they conduct a mission rehearsal in virtual reality
Implementation	Soldiers arrive at the location, dismount the vehicle, and begin the field exercise; the soldiers enter the training site consisting of three real buildings and ten virtual buildings simulating a small town; a soldier maneuvering a real robot through a building accidentally damages it and pulls up a job aid on how to perform the necessary repair
After-action review	Commander and soldiers gather in the middle of the training site and review performance; virtual reality views on their tablet size PC screens enable them to replay actions in a recreation of the training and from different points of view; in the vehicles heading back to base, the soldiers repeat aspects of the field exercise, practicing tasks they performed low in

Next Steps and Technological Evolution

The case studies are just two examples of how technologies can be used to support instructional and assessment events. As we move into the future with the advancement of both technologies as well as the design of learning environments, we will need to continue research and development efforts in order to identify appropriate uses and best practices.

Mixed and virtual realities will be an integral part of future learning environments across industries, in educational settings, and in the military. In order for these systems to be effective at improving learning and strengthening performance, the stakeholders in the learning process must be educated about the possibilities and trade-offs for effectively implementing them. As part of this decade-long effort, several research and development activities must continue to advance.

Mixed and virtual reality learning methodologies must be developed and tested to determine the most effective ways to blend these technologies into the overall learning environment. While some research has been conducted on performance improvement (for example, speed and error reduction), little validated research has been focused on what aspects are most beneficial for learning or on how to generalize findings into methodologies that can be applied in other settings. For example, using these technologies to increase domain knowledge, problem solving, and transfer is particularly important if we are to realize important gains potentially offered by these new types of learning environments.

Authoring tools, instructional design guidelines, and instructor guidelines must be developed that will ensure effective learning occurs using these technologies in a blended learning environment. We are developing what we believe to be the first system like this for the U.S. Army Research Institute for the Behavioral and Social Sciences (Kirkley, Borland, et al., in press).

Mixed and virtual reality technologies must continue to mature in a way that is beneficial for learning. Much of the research in the field is focused on how to make the technology work or be usable. Learning scientists must begin to push the technologists for features that matter to learning. The industry as a whole must begin to explore the return on investment of these technologies.

Implementing and integrating these three research tracks effectively will not be an easy task and will not happen overnight. Our challenge is to look toward future possibilities as an inspirational guide, while we implement this new kind of blended learning environment in the best way we can, given current knowledge and technologies.

References

Azuma, R. T. (1997). A survey of augmented reality. *Presence: Teleoperators and Virtual Environments, 6*(4), 355–385.

Azuma, R., Baillot, Y., Behringer, R., Feiner, S., Julier, S., & MacIntyre, B. (2001). Recent advances in augmented reality. *IEEE Computer Graphics and Applications, 21*(6), 34–47.

Bajura, M., Fuchs, H., & Ohbuchi, R. (1992). Merging virtual objects with the real world: Seeing ultrasound imagery within the patient. *Computer Graphics, 26*(2), 203–210.

Barrows, H. S. (1992). *The tutorial process.* Springfield: Southern Illinois School of Medicine.

Billinghurst, M., Kato, H., & Poupyrev, I. (2001). The MagicBook: Moving seamlessly between reality and virtuality. *Computer Graphics and Applications, 21*(3), 2–4.

Bonk, C. J., & Wisher, R. A. (2000). *Applying collaborative and e-learning tools to military distance learning: A research framework* (Tech. Rep. No. 1107). Alexandria, VA: U.S. Army Research Institute for the Behavioral and Social Sciences. Available at http://php.indiana.edu/~cjbonk/Dist.Learn%20(Wisher).

Boud, A. C., Haniff, D. J., Baber, C., & Steiner, S. J. (1999). Virtual reality and augmented reality as a training tool for assembly tasks. In *Proceedings of International Conference on Information Visualization 1999* (pp. 32–36). Los Alamitos, CA: IEEE Computer Society.

Caudell, T., & Mizell, D. (1992). Augmented reality: An application of heads-up display technology to manual manufacturing processes. In *Proceedings of Hawaii International Conference on System Sciences* (Vol. 2, pp. 659–669). Los Angeles: IEEE Computer Society.

Duffy, T. M., & Cunningham, D. J. (1996). Constructivism: Implications for the design and delivery of instruction. In D. Jonassen (Ed.), *Handbook of research for educational communications and technology* (pp. 170–198). New York: Macmillan.

Feiner, S. (1992, May). *Annotating the real world with knowledge based graphics on a see-through head mounted display.* Paper presented at the Graphics Interface '92, Palo Alto, CA.

Feiner, S., MacIntyre, B., Hollerer, T., & Webster, T. (1997). A touring machine: Prototyping 3D mobile augmented reality systems for exploring the urban environment. *Personal Technology, 1*(4), 208–217.

Feiner, S., Webster, A., Krueger, T., MacIntyre, B., & Keller, E. (1995). Architectural anatomy. *Presence, 4*(3), 318–325.

Gabbard, J. L., Swan, J. E., Hix, D., Lanzagorta, M., Livingston, M., Brown, D., & Julier, S. (2002, January). *Usability engineering: Domain analysis activities for augmented reality systems.* Paper presented at the SPIE 2002, Electronic Imaging Conference, San Jose, CA.

Harris, P. (2002). How the U.S. military is reinventing learning. *Learning Circuits.* Available at http://www.learningcircuits.org/2002/nov2002/harris.html.

Hedberg, J. (2002). Ensuring high quality thinking and scaffolding learning in an online world. In *Proceedings of ACSILITE 2002.* Retrieved October 10, 2003, from http://216.239.37.104/search?q=cache:vp6znmjh1ssJ:www.unitec.ac.nz/ascilite/proceedings/papers/166.pdf.

Hollerer, T., Feiner, S., Terauchi, T., Rashid, G., & Hallaway, D. (1999). Exploring MARS: Developing indoor and outdoor user interfaces to a mobile augmented reality system. *Computers and Graphics, 23*(6), 779–785.

Kirkley, J. R., Kirkley, S. E., Lindsay, N., Myers, T. M., & Barclay, M. (2003). Embedded training for designing mixed reality based military training systems. In *Proceedings of the Interservice/Industry Training, Simulation and Education Conference (I/ITSEC) 2003*, Orlando, FL.

Kirkley, J., Kirkley, S., Myers, T., Borland, C., Swan, M., Sherwood, D., & Singer, M. (in press). *Embedded Training for Objective Force Warrior: Using problem-based embedded training (PBET) to support mixed and virtual reality simulations* (Tech. Rep.). Orlando, FL: U.S. Army Research Institute for the Behavioral and Social Sciences.

Kirkley, J. R., Kirkley, S. E., Myers, T. E., Swan, M. B., Sherwood, D., & Singer, M. (2004). Developing an embedded scaffolding framework to support problem-based embedded training (PBET) using mixed and virtual reality simulations. In *Proceedings of the Interservice/Industry Training, Simulation and Education Conference* (I/ITSEC), Orlando, FL.

Kirkley, S.E., Borland, S.C., Pendleton, W., and Myers, T. M. (in press). *MARCETE: Mobile augmented reality contextual embedded training and EPSS: A Research project investigating the creation of a mobile augmented reality simulation and training system for the army's future force soldier system* (Tech. Rep.). Orlando, FL: U.S. Army Research, Development and Engineering Command Simulation and Training Technology Center.

Milgram, P., Takemura, H., Utsumi, A., & Kishino, F. (1994). Augmented reality: A class of displays on the reality-virtuality continuum. *SPIE, 2351,* 34.

Morrison, J., & Orlansky, J. (1997). *The utility of embedded training.* Alexandria, VA: Institute for Defense Analyses.

Nakajima, C., & Itho, N. (2003, September). *A support system for maintenance training by augmented reality.* Paper presented at the 12th International Conference on Image Analysis and Processing. Mantova, Italy.

Ong, S. K., & Nee, A.Y.C. (2004). *Virtual and augmented reality applications in manufacturing.* Berlin: Springer-Verlag.

Reigeluth, C. M. (1996, May-June). A new paradigm for ISD? *Educational Technology, 36*(3), 13–20.

Reiser, B. J. (2002). Why scaffolding should sometimes make tasks more difficult for learners. In *Proceedings of Computer Support for Collaborative Learning (CSCL) 2002* (pp. 255–264). Boulder, CO.

Riesbeck, C., & Schank, R. (1989). *Inside case-based reasoning.* Mahwah: NJ: Erlbaum.

Schuler, D., & Namioka, A. (Eds.). (1993). *Participatory design: Principles and practices.* Mahwah, NJ: Erlbaum.

Schwald, B., & de Laval, B. (2003). An augmented reality system for training and assistance to maintenance in the industrial context. *Journal of WSCG'2003, 11*(3), 425–432.

Tang, A., Owen, C., Biocca, F., & Mou, W. (2004). Performance evaluation of augmented reality for directed assembly. In A. Nee & S. Ong (Eds.), *Virtual and augmented reality applications in manufacturing.* Heidelberg: Springer-Verlag.

Tripp, S., & Bichelmeyer, B. (1990). Rapid prototyping: An alternative instructional design strategy. *Educational Technology Research and Development, 38*(1), 31–44.

U.S. Army Natick Soldier Center. (2003). *Objective Force Warrior.* Retrieved May 23, 2003, from http://www.natick.army.mil/soldier/WSIT/.

Woods, D. R. (1992). Ideas about curriculum. *Chemical Engineering Education, 26*(1), 34–37.

Jamie Reaves Kirkley is a research scientist and senior learning designer for Information in Place. She specializes in the research and development of technology-based training environments, such as distributed problem-based learning. She has been instrumental in the development of a methodology to support embedded training using mixed reality technologies and scaffolding techniques to support problem-based training and performance support. Previously, she co-led the development of the federally funded Learning to Teach with Technology Studio, a collaborative effort of several universities, the Public Broadcasting System, and IMS Global Learning Consortium. She is coeditor of *Learner-Centered Practice in Distance Learning: Cases from Higher Education* (2004). She is also a doctoral candidate at Indiana University in Instructional Systems Technology and Language Education.

Sonny E. Kirkley is chief executive officer and a research scientist at Information in Place. He is an adjunct professor in the School of Informatics at Indiana University (IU) and holds a Ph.D. in Instructional Systems Technology. For over a decade, he has developed mobile and Internet-based learning environments. He has published and presented in the fields of augmented and mixed reality technologies, embedded training, problem-based learning, human-computer interaction, and new technologies for learning. He is cofounder of the WorldBoard Forum, a group researching mobile augmented reality. Before starting Information in Place, he was a cofounder of WisdomTools, which develops scenario-based e-learning, and served as assistant director of R&D at the IU Center for Excellence in Education.

CHAPTER THIRTY-NINE

FUTURE DIRECTIONS OF BLENDED LEARNING IN HIGHER EDUCATION AND WORKPLACE LEARNING SETTINGS

Curtis J. Bonk, Kyong-Jee Kim, Tingting Zeng

As is clear from reading this book, blended learning is more than fashionable; it is the training and educational delivery method of choice. Blended learning is dominating news in higher education, corporate America, and governmental training settings. It is now a standard part of the education and training lexicon. Organizations and institutions of learning must now account for blended learning in all its various disguises. Blended learning is seen in the linkages between instructors, learners, and classrooms located in two or more states, provinces, regions, countries, or continents. Blended learning occurs in those exciting opportunities where students debate and discuss scholarly ideas in an asynchronous forum and then bring in the authors for a synchronous chat or videoconference. Blended learning happens when some course meetings or training events are conducted virtually rather than face-to-face. Such classes or training experiences can blend students located at various remote regions or perhaps instructors collaboratively teaching a class at two or more locations. Blended learning might simply supplement course readings and activities with online articles, simulations, events, and other resources. Indeed, the forms and functions of blended learning, as detailed throughout this book, are simultaneously mind-boggling and inspiring.

Perhaps that is the take-away from this book: blended learning surrounds us. In this handbook, there are societal and governmental needs for blended approaches such as when the SARS crisis forced entire cities and countries to consider how learners and workers might best acquire access to knowledge without physical contact.

It might fill an education or training need in countries facing political turmoil, corruption, or poverty. There are also blended learning initiatives created by institutional or governmental policies that seek to individualize learning opportunities, such as seen in the chapters from Korea (Lee and Im, Chapter Twenty, this volume) and Malaysia (Kaur and Ahmed, Chapter Twenty-Two, this volume).

In addition to societal needs for blended learning, there are institutional and organizational ones. For instance, there are blends that dramatically reduce the travel time required for learning, such as those discussed by Lewis and Orton (Chapter Five, this volume) concerning management training at IBM. And there are blends that simply push out corporate-developed materials and resources to instructors located around the globe, as in the Cisco Networking Academy (see Chapter Nine, this volume, by Alan Dennis and his colleagues). At the same time, there are naturally occurring blended events, as seen in the field experience components of the teacher education program at National University. National University's live field experiences blend with online courses in teacher education to help the largest teacher education program in the United States expand its enrollments and activities throughout California and beyond (Reynolds and Greiner, Chapter Fifteen, this volume).

The promises (and, we hope, the benefits) of blended learning are extensive: increased learning, a reduction in the need for brick and mortar, engagement, collaboration, success, ownership, and higher-quality learning. Further research and innovation in the blended learning arena will help sort out the key contributions, benefits, and impact areas.

During the coming decade, crucial decisions related to blended learning will continue to face all of us. Accelerating growth in blended learning has been documented in this book at Microsoft, IBM, the University of Pretoria, the University of Glamorgan, Beijing Normal University, National University in California, and the Open University of Malaysia. In fact, each of the organizations and institutions featured in this handbook has had to wrestle with new strategic directions, agendas, and visions brought about by the blending of learning opportunities. In addition to strategic planning, many have entered into unique online learning partnerships (see, for instance, the chapters by Ziob and Mosher, Chapter Seven; Selinger, Chapter Thirty-One; Pease Chapter Eighteen; Jagannathan, Chapter Thirty-One; and Lee and Im, Chapter Twenty).

Studies on the Future of Online Teaching and Learning

In response to these trends and issues, instructors and administrators in postsecondary institutions in North America (primarily) were surveyed to explore the current status and future directions of online education in higher education settings.

We then conducted a second survey of those involved in e-learning in corporate training environments. Brief descriptions of our survey procedures and some of the key findings from those surveys are presented below. Then we provide our own predictions of the future of blended learning.

The higher education survey targeted college instructors who are members of MERLOT, a higher education association of more than fourteen thousand college professors, instructional designers, and administrators who share and peer-evaluate their Web resources and materials (note that less than a year later, MERLOT has more than twenty-six thousand members and over twelve thousand contributed materials). Also surveyed were approximately two thousand members of the World Lecture Hall (WLH) and five hundred to six hundred members of the Western Cooperative for Educational Telecommunications (WCET). The first author had previously surveyed MERLOT and WLH members on the state of online learning (Bonk, 2001). This follow-up survey took place in SurveyShare, a Web-based survey tool, from late November 2003 to early January 2004.

The higher education survey consisted of forty-two questions primarily related to the future of online learning in higher education. Out of more than twelve thousand survey requests, there were 562 completed surveys. Unlike the previous higher education study, which was dominated by males (Bonk, 2001), in this study, more than 53 percent of the respondents were females, a sign that perhaps females have growing interest and experience in online teaching environments. In addition, 65 percent of the respondents in the higher education survey were professors or lecturers, while another 28 percent were administrators or technical support personnel. The rest were in educational consulting or other areas. Half of these respondents came from public colleges (26 percent of which were comprehensive universities—those with a significant amount of research activity and a wide range of programs at the undergraduate and graduate levels) and another 17 percent were from private colleges (only 5 percent of which were comprehensive universities). In addition, 23 percent worked in community colleges and 3 percent in online institutions.

A second survey was conducted of training professionals (for example, chief learning officers, training managers, trainers and instructors, and e-learning developers) on the current status and future trends of e-learning in workplace learning settings. These survey participants belonged to various types of organizations in the United States, including government, business, and nonprofit organizations. This forty-nine-item survey was completed by 239 individuals who were part of an e-learning conference distribution list.

Extensive demographic information was collected. For instance, in terms of e-learning backgrounds, most respondents were optimistic about the field of e-learning, possessed considerable knowledge in the field, and were involved in e-learning strategic decision making within their respective organizations. In contrast to the higher education survey, 67 percent of the respondents to the corporate training survey were males. The respondents were employed in organizations of various sizes; for instance, 25 percent worked in organizations employing fewer than one hundred people. In terms of the respondent's job function, about 20 percent were executives (CEO, chief technology officer, or president) and about 22 percent were at the management level (e-learning manager, human resource manager, or training manager). In addition, 15 percent of the respondents were instructional designers, performance technologists, or trainers or instructors, while the balance were in some type of administrative support positions.

Future Growth of Blended Learning

Respondents of the higher education survey, a majority of whom had experience using Web technologies in their teaching, not surprisingly, indicated that they were using blended learning in their teaching. In fact, 93 percent of the respondents were already using blended learning in some way (see Figure 39.1). However, the use of blended learning was still modest for most of these individuals. More specifically, more than six in ten participants were using blended learning for 20 percent or less of their campus courses.

What about future projections of blended learning? A quick scan of Figure 39.1 clearly shows that respondents expected a dramatic rise in their use of blended learning approaches in the coming years. For instance, 40 percent predicted that 21 to 40 percent of their courses would be blended by the year 2006, and another 37 percent expected this to be higher than 40 percent. And by 2013, more than seven in ten respondents anticipated that they would offer more than 40 percent of their courses in a blended format. Such findings indicate that blended learning is proliferating across college and university campuses, and this trend will increase.

Blended learning is now a prevalent delivery method in workplace learning settings as well. The majority of our respondents from the corporate world were already using blended learning in some format. Such findings correspond with those from a recent survey by The eLearning Guild (2003). In fact, 86 percent of our workplace participants were currently implementing blended learning. However, as was seen in the higher education survey, a majority of respondent organizations (58 percent) were using blended learning only in 20 percent or less of their courses (see Figure 39.2). The corporate survey respondents also projected a considerable increase in their use of blended learning approaches in coming years. More specifically, more than four in ten respondents predicted that 21 to

FIGURE 39.1.   EXPECTED FUTURE GROWTH OF BLENDED LEARNING IN HIGHER EDUCATION SETTINGS.

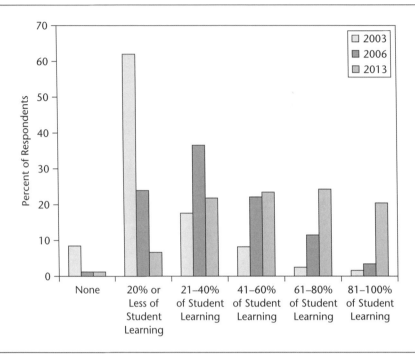

Note: The question asked was, "What percentage of student learning in your college, university, or organization is blended (i.e., courses having online as well as face-to-face components) today and how might this change in 3 years and in a decade?"

40 percent of the courses offered in their organization would be blended by 2007, and another 32 percent indicated that it would be more than 40 percent. And by 2013 this latter number nearly doubles, with roughly 60 percent of the respondents anticipating that they would offer 40 percent or more of their courses in a blended format.

Such findings indicate that blended learning is a permanent trend rather than a passing fad in both higher education and workplace learning settings. Given this significant adoption of blended learning in both higher education and corporate training settings, it is vital to create strategic plans and directions for it. When asked, 60 percent of the corporate survey respondents indicated that they had a strategic plan for e-learning; however, only slightly more than half of those indicated that their plan was working effectively, and even fewer (37 percent) calculated the return on investment from e-learning courses, programs, and other initiatives.

**FIGURE 39.2.   EXPECTED FUTURE GROWTH OF BLENDED LEARN-
ING IN WORKPLACE LEARNING SETTINGS.**

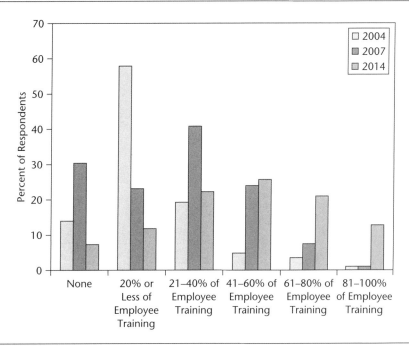

Note: The question asked was, "What percentage of employee training in organization is blended (i.e., courses having online as well as face-to-face components) today and how might this change in 3 years and in a decade?"

Pedagogical Techniques in E-Learning

In addition to such general blended learning trends, there is a need to focus on the pedagogy and technology that will be used in these blended environments. Although course management systems have increased rapidly in use in higher education settings and are likely the foundation for the rapid increase in online learning enrollments during the past decade, some researchers argue that course management systems are simply ways to "manage" learners (by emphasizing administrative tasks) rather than a means to promote rich, interactive learning experiences (Bonk, Wisher, & Lee, 2003; Stephenson, 2001). Despite these primitive e-learning tools and systems, a variety of pedagogical techniques can be embedded within e-learning, and those techniques could have serious implications for the design and implementation of blended learning.

TABLE 39.1.   FUTURE PREDICTIONS OF MOST WIDELY USED PEDAGOGICAL TECHNIQUES FOR E-LEARNING IN HIGHER EDUCATION SETTINGS.

Response Options	Number of Respondents	Response Ratio (%)
1 Group problem-solving and collaborative tasks	356	65.4
2 Problem-based learning	316	58.1
3 Discussion	237	43.6
4 Case-based strategies	228	41.2
5 Simulations or role play	198	36.4
6 Student-generated content	190	34.9
7 Coaching or mentoring	162	29.8
8 Guided learning	155	28.5
9 Exploratory or discovery	147	27.0
10 Lecturing or teacher-directed activities	60	11.0
11 Modeling of the solution process	49	9.0
12 Socratic questioning	47	8.6
Total	544	

Our higher education survey found that online collaboration, case learning, and problem-based learning were the preferred instructional methods during the coming decade for online instructors in colleges and universities. When asked to select four pedagogical techniques that would be used most widely online during the next few years from a list of twelve instructional methods, over 65 percent selected group problem-solving and collaborative tasks, while 58 percent chose problem-based learning. In contrast, only about one in ten thought they might use lectures, modeling, or Socratic instruction (see Table 39.1). In addition, most respondents saw the potential of the Web in the coming years as a tool for virtual teaming or collaboration, critical thinking, and enhanced student engagement instead of as an opportunity for student idea generation and expression of creativity.

Although the list of pedagogical techniques given in our corporate survey was slightly different and had one more item, similar responses were received in the corporate training survey. As shown in Table 39.2, the survey respondents predicted that authentic cases and scenario learning would be the most widely used method in the coming decade (63 percent), followed by simulations or gaming (50 percent), virtual team collaboration (47 percent), problem-based learning (42 percent), and coaching or mentoring (39 percent). Once again, few expected wide use of teacher-centered or didactic activities (for example, lecturing, Socratic questioning) when training employees in coming years. However, modeling was selected by twice as

TABLE 39.2. FUTURE PREDICTIONS OF MOST WIDELY USED PEDAGOGICAL TECHNIQUES FOR E-LEARNING IN WORKPLACE LEARNING SETTINGS.

Response Options	Number of Respondents	Response Ratio (%)
1 Authentic cases and scenario learning	145	63.0
2 Simulations or gaming	115	50.0
3 Virtual team collaboration	107	46.5
4 Problem-based learning	97	42.2
5 Coaching or mentoring	90	39.1
6 Guided learning	86	37.4
7 Self-paced learning	79	34.4
8 Exploration or discovery	45	19.6
9 Modeling of the solution process	44	19.1
10 Discussion	41	17.8
11 Debates and role play	36	15.7
12 Lecturing or instructor-directed activities	31	13.5
13 Socratic questioning	5	2.2
Total	230	

many respondents as in the higher education survey. In addition to modeling, simulations and gaming, as is emphasized in the military training chapter by Wisher (Chapter Thirty-Seven, this volume), were also a more popular technique in the corporate training survey than in the higher education one.

In both cases, the methods of choice seemed to center on active learning, problem solving, authentic learning, and collaboration. In fact, when asked what learning styles or preferences e-learning courses address today and might target a decade from now, the answers from both the higher education and the corporate respondents revealed an upcoming surge in hands-on learning activities as opposed to additional auditory, visual, or reflective ones. In fact, hands-on learning was deemed the weakest area today in online higher education courses, but during the coming decade, it is anticipated to become the most salient aspect of e-learning courses in both formal higher education settings as well as corporate training ones.

Emerging Technologies

The technologies that can be used in blended learning environments today will only increase in the coming years. Therefore, an understanding of emerging technologies that will have an impact on the delivery of e-learning will help in predicting promising technologies for blended learning.

Those participating in the higher education study were asked to choose one technology that would have the most impact on the delivery of online education during the next few years. Out of fourteen technologies listed, the respondents predicted that reusable content objects would have the most significant impact, followed by wireless technologies, peer-to-peer collaboration tools, digital libraries, simulations and games, assistive technologies, and digital portfolios (see Figure 39.3). These findings underscore the importance of sharing content in online teaching and learning (see Wisher, Chapter Thirty-Seven, this volume). In contrast, less than 5 percent of the respondents predicted that e-books, intelligent agents, tablet PCs, virtual worlds, language support, or wearable technologies would have a significant impact on the delivery of online learning in higher education settings. Of course, given the discussion in Chapter Thirty-Eight by Kirkley and Kirkley, those involved in online learning within higher education may be in for a surprise in the area of wearable and augmented reality technology. Perhaps these areas are simply too new or perhaps college instructors are overwhelmed with the technology choices they already have.

FIGURE 39.3. EMERGING TECHNOLOGIES FOR E-LEARNING THAT WILL HAVE THE GREATEST IMPACT ON THE DELIVERY OF E-LEARNING IN HIGHER EDUCATION DURING THE NEXT FEW YEARS.

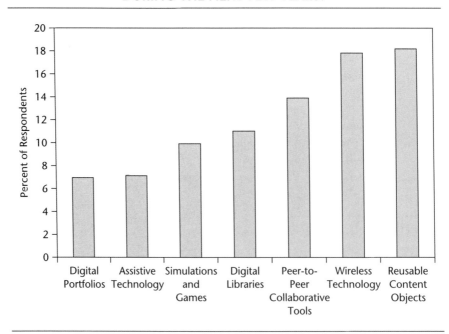

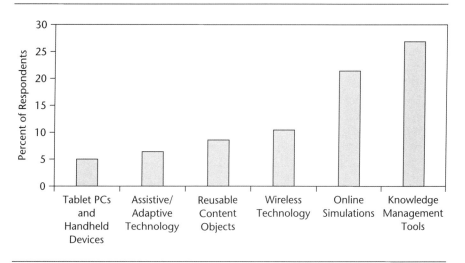

FIGURE 39.4. EMERGING TECHNOLOGIES FOR E-LEARNING THAT WILL HAVE THE GREATEST IMPACT ON THE DELIVERY OF E-LEARNING IN WORKPLACE LEARNING SETTINGS DURING THE NEXT FEW YEARS.

The corporate survey respondents were also asked to choose a technology that would have the greatest impact on the delivery of e-learning in their organization in coming years. The respondents predicted that knowledge management tools would have the most significant impact, followed by online simulations, wireless technologies, reusable content objects, adaptive technologies, tablet PCs, and handheld devices (see Figure 39.4). In contrast, less than 5 percent of the respondents thought that digital libraries, e-books, intelligent agents, Weblogs or Web diaries, and massive multiplayer online gaming would have a significant impact on the delivery of e-learning during the next few years.

Across these findings, it is clear that learning environments are changing, especially blended ones. They are changing in terms of student needs, technological opportunities, and pedagogical preferences. We now elaborate on ten key trends in which blended learning will play a significant role in workplace and higher education learning environments during the coming decade.

Future Trends in Blended Learning

Today blended learning primarily functions as a replacement for or extension of face-to-face environments. For instance, it might be used to foster learning communities (see Hanson and Clem, Chapter Ten, this volume), extend training events, offer follow-up resources in a community of practice, access guest experts, provide timely mentoring or coaching, present online lab or simulation activities, and deliver prework or supplemental course materials. While such uses may be unique and engaging, they are not exactly novel. As online environments push into their second decade of extensive use in higher education and corporate training, the forms and formats of blended learning will be extended as well. We predict ten trends linked to this expansion, which are summarized in Table 39.3.

TABLE 39.3.   TRENDS AND PREDICTIONS RELATED TO BLENDED LEARNING.

1. Mobile blended learning	Increasing use of mobile and handheld devices will create rich and exciting new avenues for blended learning
2. Greater visualization, individualization, and hands-on learning	Blended learning environments will increasingly become individualized, in particular, emphasizing visual and hands-on activities.
3. Self-determined blended learning	Blended learning will foster greater student responsibility for learning. Decisions about the type and format of blended learning will be made by students instead of instructors or instructional designers. Learners will be designing their own programs and degrees.
4. Increased connectedness, community, and collaboration	Blended learning will open new avenues for collaboration, community building, and global connectedness. It will be used as a tool for global understanding and appreciation.
5. Increased authenticity and on-demand learning	Blended learning will focus on authenticity and real-world experiences to supplement, extend, enhance, and replace formal learning. As this occurs, blended learning will fuel advancements in the creation and use of online case learning, scenarios, simulations and role play, and problem-based learning.
6. Linking work and learning	As blended learning proliferates, the lines between workplace learning and formal learning will increasingly blur. Higher education degrees will have credits from the workplace and even credit for work performed.
7. Changed calendaring	The calendar system or time scheduling of learning will be less appropriate and predefinable.
8. Blended learning course designations	Courses and programs will be increasingly designated as blended learning paths or options.
9. Changed instructor roles	The role of an instructor or trainer in a blended environment will shift to one of mentor, coach, and counselor.
10. The emergence of blended learning specialists	There will emerge specialist teaching certificates, degree programs, and resources or portals related to blended learning courses and programs.

Trend 1: Mobile Blended Learning

It is not too difficult to predict that blended learning will increasingly involve hand-held devices, especially cell phones, where one can call up the learning that is needed or demanded (see in this volume, Wagner, Chapter Four; DeViney and Lewis, Chapter Thirty-Five; and Kirkley and Kirkley, Chapter Thirty-Eight). With the increasing use of mobile and wireless technologies, the time and the place for learning, working, and socializing will blur even more. It is possible that such technologies will also be able to make learning more easily accessible for a wider range of individuals, thereby creating greater opportunities for lifelong learning (Ahonen, 2003; Keegan, 2002).

Trend 2: Greater Visualization, Individualization, and Hands-on Learning

As part of this added mobility, learning will be increasingly individualized, visual, and hands-on. This prediction is backed up in part by our survey data, which revealed that online learning will soon support a greater range of learning styles and individual differences in learning. For instance, blended environments will bring pictures, charts, graphs, animations, simulations, and video clips that the learner can call up and manipulate. The blending of delivery mechanisms, instructional approaches, technologies, and learning situations will evolve to support learning that is individualized yet collaborative and interactive (see Wagner, Chapter Four, this volume), timely and directed toward a specific need yet part of a lifelong learning journey, and complex and yet ubiquitous and seamlessly integrated into the learning landscape. As Wenger and Ferguson (Chapter Six, this volume) point out, there is a need to consider and appreciate the learning ecology for studying, practicing, teaching, and coaching that e-learning presents.

Trend 3: Self-Determined Blended Learning

As the options for blended learning proliferate, blended learning will increasingly address individual needs while becoming a highly complex decision-making process. A key result of this trend will be that the percentage of one's program that is blended as well as the forms of blended learning employed will increasingly fall to the learner. It is not just the complexity and individuality of learning that will fuel this trend, but greater use of exploratory and self-paced learning will demand that the learners self-regulate their own learning. When learners take more responsibility for their own learning, there will emerge entirely new possibilities to promote and monitor or research self-determined learning (Deci & Ryan, 1985). For instance, researchers might ask whether such self-determined learners choose courses based primarily on convenience, access, and flexibility, or decide on those that offer rich pedagogy fostering learner engagement, collaboration, and interaction. As the need for the blending of learning becomes a decision primarily made by learners, they will assume greater control over the choice and labeling of their courses and degree programs. Complicating such decisions in the coming decade, adult learning environments will have multiple modes of delivery—fully online, blended, face-to-face, and others—depending on learner needs. Already the University of Illinois at Springfield is retooling all of its face-to-face courses and programs for parallel online versions (Carnevale, 2004). Options such as these will proliferate in the coming decades.

Trend 4: Increased Connectedness, Community, and Collaboration

In addition to greater individualization, blended learning will foster increased connectedness, collaboration, and global awareness. Among its many strengths, blended learning connects people, activities, and events. It will soon be a key tool for building shared cultural understanding on a global basis. Instead of, or in addition to, huge investments in military arsenals, government officials should be building online communities and learning practices in which knowledge, ideas, and learning products are exchanged and valued. If there is a need for an expert opinion or knowledgeable guest to evaluate or respond to student work, one can be called up on demand. If you need an online simulation, you might find one in a site like MERLOT and provide the appropriate linkages for students. If you want to incorporate peer evaluation or exchanges of student work in a class or program, you might apply at the appropriate student exchange or mentoring sites. No longer are classes one-dimensional. With the blending of learning, there are now intraplanetary cafés, cross-cultural projects, and global work teams that push the envelope of learning (Bonk, Hara, Dennen, Malikowski, & Supplee, 2001) while expanding the need for shared knowledge, communities of practice, and collaborative learning (Bonk & Cunningham, 1998). With shared knowledge comes greater opportunity to negotiate meaning and form communities of learning (Bonk, Wisher, & Nigrelli, 2004).

Trend 5: Increased Authenticity and On-Demand Learning

As DeViney and Lewis (Chapter Thirty-Five, this volume) make apparent, on-demand learning is a requirement of a global workforce with fast-changing expectations and job requirements. Authentic and hands-on learning is needed when demanded. In partial response to this trend, Oliver, Herrington, and Reeves (Chapter Thirty-Six, this volume) indicate that increased authenticity during blended learning will occur through real-world scenarios and cases. In effect, the Web will be called on to provide access to timely information that can help solve case problems as well as situate problems in real-life events and places. As this occurs, blended learning will add fuel to the trend toward online case learning, scenario learning, simulations and role play, and problem-based learning. As alluded to by Hanson and Clem (Chapter Ten, this volume), it is the pedagogy employed and the learning results that ultimately matter, not the form of the technology actually employed.

Trend 6: Linking Work and Learning

As these pedagogical innovations are deployed (as discussed in trend #5), the differences between workplace training and formalized learning environments will continue to shrink. This graying of the lines between training and formalized learning will be caused by blended learning as much as it will cause new avenues for it. In business, for instance, it will be common for students to be embedded or situated in a company or other type of work setting and then report back daily or weekly through Webcams, asynchronous discussions, desktop videoconferencing, instant messaging, and wearable computing devices such as those detailed in Chapter Thirty-Eight by Kirkley and Kirkley (Botelho, 2004). In addition, degrees one may obtain will increasingly take place in the workplace, both in terms of credits received and credit for work performed.

Trend 7: Changed Calendaring

The expansion of learning avenues will begin to reform notions of when learning occurs. As a result of this trend, learners will be less tied to traditional calendars for learning. Such movements from normal semester constraints and calendars will occur in part for learners to take advantage of unique learning blends when they become available and in part for them to complete courses, degrees, and learning experiences when their schedules permit. Given the multiple versions of learning that will be available, there will fewer prescriptions for learning. As learning time is less predefined, instructors and trainers as well as instructional designers and administrators will have to deal with increased ambiguity when designing distance learning courses and programs. Learning will occur when the learner feels the need and has the time, not when the institution or organization has prearranged it. For instance, grabbing a learning object when walking on to a plane or bus will become a common and widely accepted activity by the end of the decade.

Trend 8: Blended Learning Course Designations

Courses with reduced classroom meetings or seat time will grow as universities and corporations find that blended learning not only reduces brick-and-mortar needs but simultaneously can increase learning outcomes. Courses may be designated as traditional, reduced seat time, or fully online. For instance, Chuck Dziuban and his colleagues (Chapter Fourteen, this volume) note that the University of Central Florida was among the first to give courses a special designation for reduced seat time. This begs many questions, however, including whether blended courses and associated degree programs will be more respected and accepted than either traditional or fully online ones. And will this differ according to the type and amount of the blend? For instance, courses that have one-third of their course meetings online might become more respected in the near term than those that meet live only once or twice. Naturally, what a "live" meeting is will continue to change and evolve as synchronous conferencing or virtual classroom tools become more cost-effective, stable, and widely accepted.

Trend 9: Changed Instructor Roles

The role of the instructor or trainer will continue to shift and change in these rich online learning environments. Blended learning highlights the need for instructional skills in multiple teaching and learning environments. Instead of reducing the importance of the instructor, access to an instructor is more essential. In effect, as blended learning nurtures greater choices and learning opportunities, various instructional skills will become more prominent, including coaching, mentoring, and counseling. Such skills are increasingly vital as learners seek someone to turn to for support and guidance in their various learning quests (see trend 3).

Trend 10: The Emergence of Blended Learning Specialists

Blended learning is typically more complicated and multifaceted than either fully online or face-to-face learning. For example, blended learning instructors must know when to shift gears and add new tasks or resources and when to let the learners wander off and explore their own interests. Within the next few years, there will be specialist certificates and perhaps even master's degrees for blended learning instructors. Such instructors will be sought out since they will have skills for both traditional classroom instruction and virtual environments. Coinciding with such trends will be portals or Web sites to support the sharing of best practices among blended learning instructors as well as freelance instructor exchange portals for sharing and receiving interesting job opportunities (Bonk, 2001).

Final Reflections

This book is about expanding the options for adult learners around the planet. With blended learning, adults can stay in the workplace while grooming themselves for new positions or simply updating their skills. And in many programs, they can decide to go back to school without ever showing up on campus. Without a doubt, adult learners will continue to have more exciting learning options and avenues in the coming decades. Most of the adult learning opportunities outlined in this handbook would not have been possible or even conceivable ten or twenty years ago. The authors of this book have pushed the envelope of the possible in adult learning. They are succeeding in making life a lifelong blended learning event.

References

Ahonen, M. (2003). *Accessibility challenges with mobile lifelong learning tools and related collaboration.* Retrieved November, 5, 2004, from http://www.idi.ntnu.no/~divitini/umocec2003/Final/Ahonen.pdf.

Bonk, C. J. (2001). *Online teaching in an online world.* Bloomington, IN: CourseShare.com. Retrieved October 20, 2004, from http://www.publicationshare.com/docs/faculty_survey_report.pdf.

Bonk, C. J., & Cunningham, D. J. (1998). Searching for learner-centered, constructivist, and sociocultural components of collaborative educational learning tools. In C. J. Bonk & K. S. King (Eds.), *Electronic collaborators: Learner-centered technologies for literacy, apprenticeship, and discourse* (pp. 25–50). Mahwah, NJ: Erlbaum.

Bonk, C. J., Hara, H., Dennen, V., Malikowski, S., & Supplee, L. (2000). We're in TITLE to dream: Envisioning a community of practice: "The Intraplanetary Teacher Learning Exchange." *CyberPsychology and Behavior, 3*(1), 25–39.

Bonk, C. J., Wisher, R. A., & Lee, J.-Y. (2003). Moderating learner-centered e-learning: Problems and solutions, benefits and implications. In T. S. Roberts (Ed.), *Online collaborative learning: Theory and practice* (pp. 54–85). Hershey, PA: Idea Group Publishing.

Bonk, C. J., Wisher, R. A., & Nigrelli, M. L. (2004). Learning communities, communities of practice: Principles, technologies, and examples. In K. Littleton, D. Miell, & D. Faulkner (Eds.), *Learning to collaborate, collaborating to learn* (pp. 199–219). Happauge, NY: NOVA Science.

Botelho, G. (2004, August 13). Online schools clicking with students. *CNN.com.* Retrieved October 31, 2004, from http://www.cnn.com/2004/EDUCATION/08/13/b2s.elearning/.

Carnevale, D. (2004, April 16). *U of Illinois at Springfield want to "mirror" all classroom programs online.* Retrieved November 6, 2004, from http://chronicle.com/prm/weekly/v50/i32/32a03201.htm.

Deci, E. L., & Ryan, R. M. (1985). *Intrinsic motivation and self-determination in human behavior.* New York: Plenum.

The eLearning Guild. (2003). *The blended learning best practices survey.* Retrieved September, 10, 2004, from http://www.eLearningGuild.com.

Keegan, D. (2002). *The future of learning: From elearning to mlearning.* Hagen, Germany: Fern University Institute for Research into Distance Education.

Stephenson, J. (2001). Learner-managed learning—an emerging pedagogy for learning online. In J. Stephenson (Ed.), *Teaching and learning online: Pedagogies for new technologies* (pp. 219–224). London: Kogan Page.

Curtis J. Bonk, a former corporate controller and CPA, is now professor of educational psychology as well as instructional systems technology at Indiana University (IU). Bonk is also a senior research fellow with the Advanced Distributed Learning Lab within the Department of Defense. He received numerous teaching and mentoring awards from IU as well as the CyberStar Award from the Indiana Information Technology Association, Most Outstanding Achievement Award from the U.S. Distance Learning Association, and Most Innovative Teaching in a Distance Education Program from the State of Indiana. Bonk publishes widely and is a popular conference keynote speaker and workshop presenter. He is president of CourseShare and SurveyShare.

Kyong-Jee Kim is a doctoral candidate in instructional systems technology (IST) at Indiana University, Bloomington. She also received her master's in IST from Indiana University. Since 1996 she has worked as an instructional designer for several corporations and educational institutions in the Asia-Pacific region, including Korea, and in the United States. Her research interests include pedagogy, motivation, and evaluation for e-learning. She is conducting research on designing and evaluating e-learning in higher education and professional development settings.

Tingting Zeng is an e-learning application analyst who specializes in developing e-learning solutions for the corporate sector in the United Kingdom, the United States, and China. She is an e-business management M.Sc. graduate from the University of Warwick, with a physics background and practical experiences in performance improvement and knowledge transfer projects. She is an active member of Birmingham e-business club. Her research interests include technology transfer and knowledge sharing; performance improvement and change management; and the development, use, and management of information and communication technologies and systems and their implication for work and organization. She has produced reports addressing e-learning standards, blended learning trends, Web conferencing innovations, course management system comparisons, and virtual learning environment delivery and implementation.

Name Index

Subject Index

A

Access: to higher education, 156–157, 327; increased with blended learning systems, 9; Internet, 281–282, 352–353, 446–448; to K-12 education, 166; wireless, 42

Accreditation: of online teacher education program, 210, 213; of total online university, 247, 251; World Bank course for, of staff members, 451

Achievement: academic, in online vs. face-to-face courses, 121–122, 290; student, framework for understanding factors affecting, 131–132

Activity-level blending, 11

Advanced distributed learning (ADL), 528–530

Advanced Distributed Learning Lab, 306

Advanced Learning Infrastructure Consortium (Japan), 268

American Federation of Teachers, 374

American Society for Training and Development, 3

America's Army, 521–522

Angel, 345

ARIADNE European Knowledge Pool, 43

Assessment: blended approach to, at University of Pretoria, 405–406, 409; of instructional design, in China, 303–304; of learners in Cisco Networking Academy, 129–130; Microsoft Learning tool for, of organizations, 95–97. *See also* Evaluation

Asynchronicity: in corporate training industry, 93, 477; discussion encouraged by, 173, 174; synchronicity vs., 35, 122

Attrition rates: for blended vs. face-to-face courses, 202–203; high, with e-learning, 188; lower, with blended learning, 312–313

Augmented reality, 535, 536–537

Augmented virtuality, 535

Augmented vision, 535

Australia, authentic learning course for realtors in, 510–512. *See also* University of Wollongong (Australia)

Authentic learning activities, 460, 502–513; blended learning approach to, 505–507, 508, 512–513; as central to designing learning experiences, 503; characteristics of, 504–505; examples of, with blending, 507, 509–512; increasing use of, 502, 562–563; suspension of disbelief needed for, 503–504

Autonomous National University of Mexico (UNAM), 352

Avaya, 58–59, 106–118; Customer Relationship Management (CRM) Portal of, 108–109; ESSba curriculum of, 112–118; knowledge management at, 107; shift from product to customer focus at, 106–107; Solutions Knowledge (ASK) Center of, 109–112